A SIMPLIFIED DICTIONARY

A SIMPLIFIED DICTIONARY

COMPILED BY
C. W. AIRNE, M.A.

EDITED BY
OSWALD HARLAND, M.A.

SCHOFIELD & SIMS LTD.
HUDDERSFIELD

0 7217 0121 3 (without Exercises)
0 7217 0122 1 (with Exercises)
First Printed 1958
Fourteenth Impression 1969
Revised and Reprinted 1970
Reprinted (Twice) 1971
Reprinted 1972
Reprinted 1973
Reprinted (Twice) 1974
Reprinted (Twice) 1975
Reprinted 1977
Reprinted 1978
Reprinted 1979
Reprinted 1981
Reprinted 1982
Reprinted 1984

Printed in Great Britain by
Butler & Tanner Ltd., Frome and London

PREFACE

In the systematic education of children some form of dictionary is a necessity, intended not merely for casual reference but also for constant use in what may be termed dictionary drill.

Properly used, a dictionary will clarify for us the meanings of known words, so that they may be used boldly and intelligently. The emphasis, therefore, is on clarity and simplicity of definition.

This dictionary, which includes a vocabulary of over 18000 words, introduces us to words hitherto beyond the range of our vocabulary—words not in daily colloquial use but encountered on the printed page, over the radio or TV., or in formal discourse at church, in school or in the lecture-room.

It opens up new fields of knowledge by its inclusion of terms used in science, technology, and the arts, and it fulfils the final duty of bringing precision of thought into speech, writing and reading.

Since this is a Simplified Dictionary, intended for children from nine to twelve or thirteen years of age, it would be obviously futile to include the whole vocabulary of English, for this undergoes subtle changes from year to year, and equally futile to go into details of pronunciation and etymology, for there is a place in the English-speaking world for Regional Standard English, and etymology is a complex and specialized branch of learning.

However, it must include and define such words as the child may hear in intelligent conversation, such words also as he may encounter in books, magazines and newspapers, and such as may be used by teachers or examiners to test his ability to distinguish meanings and express his own thoughts. It should, moreover, include the most commonly-used general and specific terms used in modern science, technology and the various arts, for all these have a vivid interest for the young of this generation.

In this Dictionary, therefore, the following principles have been observed:

(1) Words, set in alphabetical order, are defined simply yet very briefly, often using synonyms, or near-synonyms, with which the child may be unfamiliar and which will extend the range of his vocabulary.
(2) Old-fashioned spellings are discarded and obsolete words omitted.
(3) Plurals and feminine forms are given when they vary from the norm.
(4) Derived words are included literally as an aid to spelling.
(5) Words which may be used as nouns, verbs or adjectives are defined in their grammatical variants.

(6) Words of negative import are given a positive meaning.

(7) Words often confused because of similarity in sound are carefully distinguished.

(8) Where it is necessary to distinguish between two pronunciations of the same word, this is done.

(9) Where a word has an interesting origin in fable, legend or history, the child is referred to Appendix A.

(10) Abbreviations are explained in Appendix B, without an overloading of scholastic, governmental and service contractions and initials.

The final shape and content of this Junior Dictionary have been the product of long experience in the teaching of English, and the bringing to bear of common sense.

ABBREVIATIONS USED IN THIS DICTIONARY

abbrev.	abbreviation	*pl.*	plural
adj.	adjective	*prep.*	preposition
adv.	adverb	*pron.*	pronoun
conj.	conjunction	*sing.*	singular
fem.	feminine	*v.*	verb
inter.	interjection	*nn.*	Each word is a noun
n.	noun	*adjs. advs.,*	Each word is an adjec-
		etc.	tive, adverb, etc.

Pronunciation (abbreviation pron.)

The meanings of many words spelt alike can be made known in speech only by pronouncing one syllable with a stronger emphasis or stress than another.

In this Dictionary such a word has its stressed syllable printed in small capitals, and it is separated from its unstressed syllable by a hyphen (-). Also, where necessary, the word is respelt in letters combined to convey sounds familiar to a child.

Examples.

    object (*n.* pron. OB-ject) an aim: purpose. His OB-ject was to be head of his class.

    object (*v.* pron. ob-JECT) to disapprove: protest. He did not ob-JECT to my plan.

    record (*v.* pron. re-KORD) to write down. John's duty was to re-KORD the score made by each batsman.

    record (*n.* pron. REK-ord) a written account. John kept a REK-ord of important events in a small book.

Alternative ways of spelling are shown in brackets, as in **abridg(e)ment**.

APPENDIX A

(page 264)

WORDS WITH AN ORIGIN IN FABLE, LEGEND OR HISTORY

APPENDIX B

(page 268)

ABBREVIATIONS

A SIMPLIFIED DICTIONARY

A

aback (*adv.*) backwards. TAKEN ABACK means surprised.

abandon (*v.*) to leave; to forsake. ABANDON (*n.*) lack of restraint.

abase (*v.*) to lower; to humble.

abash (*v.*) to make one feel shy or ashamed.

abate (*v.*) to lessen; to become quieter.

abattoir (*n.*) a public slaughterhouse.

abbess (*n.*) the lady head of a nunnery.

abbey (*n.*) a church; once part of a monastery.

abbot (*n.*) the head of an abbey.

abbreviate (*v.*) to cut short. ABBREVIATION (*n.*).

abdicate (*v.*) to give up a throne or high position ABDICATION (*n.*).

abdomen (*n.*) the stomach, bowels, etc.

abduct (*v.*) to carry off by force.

abduction (*n.*) a kidnapping. ABDUCTOR (*n.*).

abet (*v.*) to help a wrongdoer. ABETTOR (*n.*).

abhor (*v.*) to turn from with disgust. ABHORRENCE (*n.*).

abide (*v.*) to stay; to dwell.

abiding (*adj.*) lasting; changeless.

ability (*n.*) skill or power to do things. (*pl.* ABILITIES).

abject (*adj.*) unhappy-looking; downhearted.

abjure (*v.*) to deny; to give up.

able (*adj.*) clever; talented.

abnormal (*adj.*) unusual; strange.

abode (*n.*) a home or dwelling.

abolish (*v.*) to do away with; to end.

abolition (*n.*) a destruction; finish.

abominable (*adj.*) unpleasant; loathsome.

aborigines (*n. pl.*) a country's original inhabitants.

abound (*v.*) to be plentiful; to teem.

abrasion (*n.*) an injury made by rubbing or scraping.

abreast (*adv.*) 1. side by side. 2. up-to-date.

abridge (*v.*) to lessen; to reduce.

abridg(e)ment (*n.*) a shortened account.

abroad (*adv.*) far away; overseas.

abrupt (*adj.*) very sudden; unexpected. ABRUPTLY (*adv.*).

abscess (*n.*) an inflamed boil or ulcer.

abscond (*v.*) to flee secretly or hurriedly. ABSCONDER (*n.*).

absence (*n.*) non-attendance; a lack.

absent (*adj. pron.* AB-sent) not present; away. ABSENT (*v. pron.* ab-SENT) to keep away; to stay away.

absolute (*adj.*) complete; perfect.

absolution (*n.*) forgiveness; pardon.

absolve (*v.*) 1. to set free from a promise or duty. 2. to pardon sin or wrongdoing.

absorb (*v.*) 1. to soak up. 2. to be interested in. ABSORPTION (*n.*).

abstain (*v.*) to avoid doing; to forbear. ABSTENTION (*n.*).

abstinence (*n.*) temperance.

abstract (*v. pron.* ab-STRACT) to take away. ABSTRACT (*n. pron.* AB-stract) a short account, a summary. ABSTRACT (*adj.*) shadowy; vague; unreal.

abstruse (*adj.*) hard to understand.

absurd (*adj.*) ridiculous; senseless. ABSURDITY (*n.*).

abundance (*n.*) an overflow; plenty.

abundant (*adj.*) plentiful.

abuse (*n. pron.* ab-USE) 1. a wrong use. 2. insulting language. ABUSE (*v. pron.* ab-UZE) to misuse; to harm.

abusive (*adj.*) insulting; offensive.

abut (*v.*) to lean or rest upon.

abysmal (*adj.*) bottomless; very deep.

abyss (*n.*) a deep gorge or pit.

acacia (*n.*) a kind of tree or shrub with feathery leaves.

academy (*n.*) a college; school.

accede (*v.*) 1. to come to the throne. 2. to agree to.

accelerate (*v.*) to increase speed.

acceleration (*n.*) an increase in speed. ACCELERATOR (*n.*).

accent (*n.*) 1. stress; emphasis. 2. a manner of pronunciation.

accentuate (*v.*) to stress or emphasize.

accept (*v.*) to take as a gift. ACCEPTABLE (*adj.*). ACCEPTANCE (*n.*).

access (*n.*) the way in.

accessible (*adj.*) within reach.

accession (*n.*) a coming to the throne or other high office.

accessory (*n.*) a helper. (*pl.* ACCESSORIES). ACCESSORY (*adj.*) additional.

accident (*n.*) a mishap; an unexpected happening.

accidental (*adj.*) unintended; happening by chance.

acclaim (*v.*) to applaud; to hail.

acclamation (*n.*) shouts of welcome; applause.

acclimatize (*v.*) to become settled or used to.

accommodate (*v.*) 1. to fit in with. 2. to provide for or lodge.

accommodating (*adj.*) helpful; obliging.

accommodation (*n.*) 1. a lodging place. 2. a service.

accompaniment (*n.*) music played to help a chief performer.

accompanist (*n.*) a helper; one who plays for a singer.

accompany (*v.*) 1. to help with music. 2. to go with; to be a companion.

accomplice (*n.*) one who helps another in wrongdoing.

accomplish (*v.*) to finish; to complete.

accomplished (*adj.*) gifted; talented.

accomplishment (*n.*) a thing done well.

accord (*v.*) to be in agreement or harmony. ACCORD (*n.*) agreement; friendship.

accordion (*n.*) a musical hand-instrument worked by keys and a bellows.

accost (*v.*) to go up to someone and begin a conversation.

account (*n.*) 1. a statement of money received and spent. 2. a tradesman's bill. 3. a story or description. ACCOUNT (*v.*) to explain; to give a reason for.

accountant (*n.*) a keeper or examiner of accounts.

accrue (*v.*) to increase gradually, like the interest on money.

accumulate (*v.*) to gather more and more; to pile up.

accumulation (*n.*) a heap, which has grown up by degrees.

accumulator (*n.*) a container for storing electricity.

accuracy (*n.*) exactness; precision.

accurate (*adj.*) right; exact.

accusation (*n.*) a charge or statement fixing the blame.

accuse (*v.*) to blame. ACCUSER (*n.*).

accustom (*v.*) to grow used to a thing.

ace (*n.*) 1. the one-spot of cards and dominoes. 2. a first-class airman.

acetylene (*n.*) a gas which burns with a bright, white light.

ache (*n.*) 1. a lasting pain. 2. a longing; yearning. ACHE (*v.*) 1. to continue giving pain. 2. to yearn.

achieve (*v.*) to succeed in doing; to attain.

achievement (*n.*) an exploit; a success.

acid (*adj.*) sour; bitter. ACID (*n.*) a bitter-tasting chemical. ACID TEST (*n.*) the hardest test.

acidity (*n.*) sourness; bitterness.

acknowledge (*v.*) to admit the truth or the receipt of something.

acknowledg(e)ment (*n.*) 1. an admission. 2. a receipt.

acme (*n.*) the highest point; perfection.

acorn (*n.*) the fruit of the oak-tree.

acoustic (*adj.*) concerned with hearing or sound.

acoustics (*n.*) the study of sound. ACOUSTICAL (*adj.*).

acquaint (*v.*) 1. to tell someone. 2. to learn something about.

acquaintance (*n.*) 1. a person one knows. 2. one's knowledge about something.

acquiesce (*v.*) to agree to.

acquiescence (*n.*) agreement; consent.

acquire (*v.*) to earn; to obtain.

acquisition (*n.*) anything earned; a prize.

acquisitiveness (*n.*) greed. ACQUISITIVE (*adj.*).

acquit (*v.*) to declare a person innocent; to do work well or ill.

acquittal (*n.*) a discharge or release from guilt or debt.

acre (*n.*) an Imperial measure of land; an area (4840 yd²).

acreage (*n.*) the number of acres; the area of land.

acrid (*adj.*) very bitter; irritating.

acrimonious (*adj.*) 1. harsh. 2. bad-tempered; ill-natured.

acrimony (*n.*) 1. severity. 2. ill-nature.

acrobat (*n.*) a gymnast; trapeze artiste. ACROBATIC (*adj.*).

act (*v.*) 1. to do. 2. to perform on a stage. 3. to pretend. ACT (*n.*) 1. a deed. 2. a law made by Parliament. 3. a section of a stage play.

action (*n.*) 1. a style of movement. 2. a law case. 3. a battle. 4. a thing done.

active (*adj.*) 1. lively; busy. 2. still working.

activity (*n.*) 1. an occupation. 2. alertness; quickness. (*pl.* ACTIVITIES).

actor (*n.*) a player on stage, screen, or radio. (*fem.*. ACTRESS).

actual (*adj.*) real; existing. ACTUALLY (*adv.*).

actuality (*n.*) a reality; fact. (*pl.* ACTUALITIES).

actuary (*n.*) an expert calculator; an accountant.

actuate (*v.*) to make something work; to set in motion.

acumen (*n.*) common sense; shrewdness.

acute (*adj.*) sharp; quick-witted. ACUTENESS (*n.*). ACUTELY (*adv.*).

acute angle (*n.*) one less than a right angle.

adage (*n.*) a proverb; an old, wise saying.

adamant (*adj.*) hard; stubborn. ADAMANT (*n.*) the hardest of substances.

adapt (*v.*) to fit in; to use in the best way.

adaptation (*n.*) the thing or method used when the best is not at hand.

add (*v.*) 1. to count up. 2. to join one thing to another.

adder (*n.*) a small, poisonous snake.

addition (*n.*) 1. the process of counting. 2. a thing joined on to another. ADDITIONAL (*adj.*).

addle (*v.*) to muddle; to confuse. ADDLED (*adj.*).

address (*v.*) 1. to speak or write to. 2. to make a speech. ADDRESS (*n.*) 1. a speech. 2. one's residence or place of business. 3. one's manner or behaviour. 4. skill; readiness.

adenoids (*n. pl.*) a nose ailment which affects speech and breathing.

adept (*n.*) an expert. ADEPT (*adj.*) skilful.

adequate (*adj.*) enough; sufficient. ADEQUACY (*n.*).

adhere (*v.*) 1. to stick to. 2. to be loya to.

adherence (*n.*) loyalty; attachment.

adherent (*n.*) a supporter; an ally.

adhesion (*n.*) unity; devotion.

adhesive (*adj.*) sticky. ADHESIVE (*n.*) a sticky substance.

adieu (*inter.*) good-bye. (God be with you.) ADIEU (*n.*) a farewell.

adjacent (*adj.*) next to or near by.

adjective (*n.*) a word which describes a thing. ADJECTIVAL (*adj.*).

adjourn (*v.*) to put off; to postpone. ADJOURNMENT (*n.*).

adjudicate (*v.*) to judge. ADJUDICATION; ADJUDICATOR (*nn.*).

adjust (*v.*) to put in order; to make right. ADJUSTMENT (*n.*).

administer (*v.*) 1. to manage. 2. to carry out the law. 3. to give.

administration (*n.*) 1. the ways or methods used to manage affairs. 2. the government.

admirable (*adj.*) excellent; most satisfactory. ADMIRABLY (*adv.*).

admire (*v.*) to be pleased with. ADMIRATION (*n.*).

admission (*n.*) 1. an entering in. 2. a confession.

admit (*v.*) 1. to allow to enter. 2. to acknowledge. 3. to confess.

admonish (*v.*) to correct; to warn. ADMONITION (*n.*).

ado (*n.*) bustle; fuss.

adolescence (*n.*) the period of youth.

adolescent (*n.*) a youth; maiden. ADOLESCENT (*adj.*) growing up; youthful.

adopt (*v.*) to take another's child as one's own; to choose. ADOPTION (*n.*). ADOPTIVE (*adj.*).

adorable (*adj.*) admirable; worthy. ADORABLY (*adv.*).

adore (*v.*) to reverence. ADORATION (*n.*).

adorn (*v.*) to decorate; to enhance. ADORNMENT (*n.*).

adrift (*adj.*) 1. floating without control. 2. unsettled.

adroit (*adj.*) skilful; clever. ADROITNESS (*n.*). ADROITLY (*adv.*).

adulation (*n.*) flattery. ADULATORY (*adj.*).

adult (*adj.*) grown up; responsible. ADULT (*n.*) a man; woman.

advance (*v.*) 1. to go forward. 2. to increase the price. 3. to lend money. ADVANCE (*n.*) 1. progress. 2. a loan. 3. an increase in price.

advancement (*n.*) 1. promotion. 2. progress.

advantage (*n.*) 1. ability or knowledge that places one above or before others. 2. a profit; benefit. TO TAKE ADVANTAGE means to act unfairly.

advantageous (*adj.*) profitable; beneficial.

advent (*n.*) a coming; an arrival.

adventure (*n.*) an exciting event; a new experience. ADVENTURE (*v.*) to dare; to do something new.

adventurous (*adj.*) ready to dare; venturesome.

adverb (*n.*) a word which tells more about a verb, adjective, or other adverb. ADVERBIAL (*adj.*).

adversary (*n.*) an enemy; opponent. (*pl.* ADVERSARIES).

adverse (*adj.*) against one; unfavourable. ADVERSELY (*adv.*).

adversity (*n.*) hardship; distress. (*pl.* ADVERSITIES).

advertise (*v.*) to make public or well known.

advertisement (*n.*) a public notice, or one in a newspaper. ADVERTISER (*n.*).

advice (*n.*) counsel; opinion.

advisable (*adj.*) sensible; prudent. ADVISABILITY (*n.*).

advise (*v.*) to offer one's best opinion; to counsel. ADVISER (*n.*).

advocate (*v.*) to speak in favour of; to support. ADVOCATE (*n.*) 1. one who favours; recommends. 2. a lawyer; barrister.

aerial (*n.*) a wire which sends or receives wireless messages. AERIAL (*adj.*) 1. thin, like air. 2. imaginary.

aerobatics (*n. pl.*) looping, rolling and spinning exercises by an aeroplane in the air.

aerodrome (*n.*) an aeroplane station; an airport.

aeroplane (*n.*) a flying machine.

afar (*adv.*) far away; from far; remote.

affability (*n.*) friendliness.

affable (*adj.*) kindly; friendly.

affair (*n.*) a matter; business of any kind.

affect (*v.*) to pretend. AFFECTATION (*n.*).

affected (*adj.*) not natural; pretended.

affection (*n.*) love; fondness. AFFECTIONATE (*adj.*).

affinity (*n.*) 1. relationship; kinship. 2. an attraction.

affirm (*v.*) to state that a thing is true; to vouch for.

affirmation (*n.*) a truthful declaration.

afflict (*v.*) to hurt; to distress. AFFLICTION (*n.*).

affluence (*n.*) wealth.

affluent (*adj.*) wealthy. AFFLUENT (*n.*) a tributary.

afford (*v.*) 1. to be able to buy or act without loss or injury. 2. to spare. 3. to supply or furnish.

affray (*n.*) a fight; disturbance.

affront (*v.*) to offend. AFFRONT (*n.*) an insult.

afloat (*adv.*) at sea; on board ship.

afoot (*adv.*) 1. on one's own feet. 2. happening; taking place.

afraid (*adj.*) frightened; alarmed.

aft (*adv.*) toward, or at, the stern or back part of a ship.

aftermath (*n.*) the result; consequence.

afternoon (*n.*) the time of day from noon to evening.

afterwards (*adv.*) later.

again (*adv.*) once more; another time.

against (*prep.*) opposite to; facing.

agate (*n.*) a hard precious stone.

age (*n.*) 1. the length of time a person or animal has lived. 2. the time when a person becomes an adult. 3. a particular period in history, e.g., the Stone Age. AGE (*v.*) to grow old.

agency (*n.*) 1. the office of an agent. 2. the means by which a thing is done.

agent (*n.*) one who acts for another; a representative.

aggravate (*v.*) to make worse; to annoy. AGGRAVATION; AGGRAVATOR (*nn.*).

aggression (*n.*) an attack. AGGRESSOR (*n*).

aggressive (*adj.*) quarrelsome.

aghast (*adj.*) dumbfounded; horrified.

agile (*adj.*) nimble; active. AGILITY (*n.*). AGILELY (*adv.*).

agitate (*v.*) to shake; to stir. AGITATION; AGITATOR (*nn.*).

aglow (*adj.*) very warm; healthy.

agog (*adj.*) eager; excited.

agony (*n.*) great pain; anguish. AGONIZING (*adj.*).

agree (*v.*) to be alike; to give consent. AGREEMENT (*n.*).

agreeable (*adj.*) 1. pleasing; delightful. 2. willing.

agriculture (*n.*) farming; cultivation. AGRICULTURAL (*adj.*).

aground (*adv.*) fast in the ground in shallow water; stranded; beached.

ague (*n.*) a fever marked by shivering.

ahead (*adv.*) on in front; in advance.

aid (*v.*) to help. AID (*n.*) help; relief.

ail (*v.*) to be unwell; to suffer. AILING (*adj.*).

ailment (*n.*) a malady; an illness.

aim (*v.*) to point at. AIM (*n.*) an intention; a purpose.

aimless (*adj.*) purposeless; haphazard.

air (*n.*) 1. the atmosphere. 2. a tune. AIR (*v.*) to dry; to warm.

airborne (*adj.*) carried by the wind; flying.

aircraft (*n.*) a flying machine; an aeroplane.

airless (*adj.*) badly ventilated; stuffy.

airport (*n.*) a station for passenger aircraft.

aisle (*n.*) a walk or passage in a church.

ajar (*adj.*) slightly open.

akin (*adj.*) related to; like.

alabaster (*n.*) white limestone.

alacrity (*n.*) quickness; readiness.

alarm (*v.*) 1. to warn of danger. 2. to startle. ALARM (*n.*) 1. a sudden warning. 2. fear.

albatross (*n.*) a gigantic seabird.

album (*n.*) a book containing a collection of pictures or specimens.

alcohol (*n.*) spirit formed in wine, beer, etc. ALCOHOLIC (*adj.*).

alcove (*n.*) an arched wall-recess.

alderman (*n.*) a city or town councillor next in rank to mayor.

ale (*n.*) light-coloured beer.

alert (*adj.*) watchful; vigilant. ALERTNESS (*n.*).

alias (*n.*) a name other than that generally used. (*pl.* ALIASES). ALIAS (*adv.*) otherwise.

alibi (*n.*) person's plea that he was not where he was thought to be at a stated time.

alien (*n.*) a foreigner. ALIEN (*adj.*) foreign.

alienate (*v.*) to spoil a friendship; to estrange.

alight (*v.*) to dismount; to get down. ALIGHT (*adj.*) lighted; on fire.

align (*v.*) to place in a straight line. ALIGNMENT (*n.*).

alike (*adj.*) resembling; similar. ALIKE (*adv.*) in the same way, manner or form.

alive (*adj.*) 1. having life. 2. aware of; alert. 3. filled with living beings.

alkali (*n.*) a substance which makes a salt.

all (*adj.*) the whole quantity, time, extent, etc. ALL (*adv.*) wholly; completely. ALL (*n.*) everyone; everything.

allay (*v.*) to soothe; to ease.

allegation (*n.*) an unproved statement; a charge.

allege (*v.*) to state; to declare.

allegiance (*n.*) loyalty.

allegory (*n.*) a story with more than one meaning. (*pl.* ALLEGORIES). ALLEGORICAL (*adj.*).

alleviate (*v.*) to relieve; to lessen. ALLEVIATION (*n.*).

alley (*n.*) a narrow passage.

alliance (*n.*) a union of allies or friends.

alligator (*n.*) a crocodile-like reptile.

allocate (*v.*) to share out; to distribute.

allocation (*n.*) a fair share; ration.

allot (*v.*) to give or grant a share. ALLOTMENT (*n.*).

allow (*v.*) 1. to let; to permit. 2. to grant a payment. ALLOWANCE (*n.*). ALLOWABLE (*adj.*).

alloy (*n.*) a mixture of metals.

allude (*v.*) to mention; to refer to.

allure (*v.*) to tempt; to ensnare. ALLUREMENT (*n.*).

alluring (*adj.*) attractive.

alluvium (*n.*) soil left by a flood. ALLUVIAL (*adj.*).

ally (*n.*) a friend; partner. (*pl.* ALLIES). ALLY (*v.*) to unite with.

almighty (*adj.*) all-powerful; omnipotent.

almond (*n.*) a nut grown from the almond-fruit tree.

almost (*adv.*) very nearly; well nigh.

alms (*n. sing.*) money or gifts to help the poor. ALMONER (*n.*).

aloft (*adv.*) above; overhead.

alone (*adj.*) single; solitary. ALONE (*adv.*) by itself; separately.

aloof (*adv.*) 1. at a distance. 2. unfriendly. ALOOFNESS (*n.*).

aloud (*adv.*) with a loud voice or noise; audibly.

alphabet (*n.*) the letters of a language arranged in order; the A.B.C. ALPHABETICAL (*adj.*).

also (*adv.*) in addition; besides.

altar (*n.*) the communion table in a church.

alter (*v.*) to change. ALTERATION (*n.*). ALTERABLE (*adj.*).

altercation (*n.*) a dispute; quarrel.

alternate (*adj.*) every other one; every second one. ALTERNATE (*v.*) to happen in order, first one, then another.

alternative (*n.*) one or the other of two things.

although (*conj.*) though; otherwise; supposing.

altitude (*n.*) the height.

altogether (*adv.*) entirely; wholly.

altruism (*n.*) regard for others. ALTRUIST (*n.*).

altruistic (*adj.*) unselfish; philanthropic.

aluminium (*n.*) a very light, whitish metal.

always (*adv.*) at all times; continually.

amalgamate (*v.*) to join; to combine. AMALGAMATION (*n.*).

amass (*v.*) to collect; to heap up.

amateur (*n.*) one who does things for pleasure, not money.

amaze (*v.*) to astonish; to astound. AMAZEMENT (*n.*).

amazon (*n.*) a brave, fearless woman. See appendix.

ambassador (*n.*) a state's representative in a foreign state. (*fem.* AMBASSADRESS).

amber (*n.*) fossil resin, a hard, yellow substance. AMBER (*adj.*) yellow.

ambiguity (*n.*) an uncertainty in meaning, because words used have a double meaning.

ambiguous (*adj.*) uncertain; doubtful.

ambition (*n.*) a determination to win success. AMBITIOUS (*adj.*).

amble (*v.*) to stroll; to saunter. AMBLE (*n.*) an easy pace. AMBLING (*adj.*).

ambulance (*n.*) a van for conveying the sick or injured.

ambush (*v.*) to hide; to lie in wait. AMBUSH (*n.*) a surprise attack from a hiding place.

amen (*n.* or *inter.*) so be it.

amend (*v.*) to improve; to set right. AMENDMENT (*n.*).

amends (*n. pl.*) a repayment for injury.

amenity (*n.*) something that gives pleasure or makes life easier. (*pl.* AMENITIES).

amethyst (*n.*) a violet-coloured gem.

amiable (*adj.*) friendly. AMIABILITY (*n.*). AMIABLY (*adv.*).

amid, amidst (*prep.*) in the middle of; in the course of.

amiss (*adv.*) in a faulty way; wrongly. AMISS (*adj.*) wrong.

ammonia (*n.*) gas with a pungent smell which brings tears to the eyes.

among, amongst (*prep.*) mixed with; making part of; amidst.

amity (*n.*) friendship; harmony.

ammunition (*n.*) bombs, explosives for firearms, etc.

amount (*n.*) the quantity, value or sum. AMOUNT (*v.*) to add up to; to total.

amp (*n.* abbrev. of AMPERE) unit of electrical current. See appendix.

amphibian (*n.*) an animal able to live both on land and in water. AMPHIBIOUS (*adj.*).

ample (*adj.*) enough; sufficient. AMPLY (*adv.*).

amplify (*v.*) to make larger or louder; to magnify.

amputate (*v.*) to cut off. AMPUTATION (*n.*).

amuse (*v.*) to please; to cause laughter. AMUSEMENT (*n.*). AMUSING (*adj.*).

anæsthetic (*n.*) a drug which causes loss of feeling.

anagram (*n.*) a word formed from the letters of another word.

analyse (*v.*) to find what a substance is made of.

anarchy (*n.*) lawlessness. ANARCHIST (*n.*). ANARCHIC (*adj.*).

anatomy (*n.*) the study of the human body. ANATOMIST (*n.*). ANATOMICAL (*adj.*).

ancestor (*n.*) a forefather; forbear. ANCESTRAL (*adj.*).

ancestry (*n.*) lineage; descent; series of ancestors.

anchor (*n.*) a heavy metal hook which grips the sea-bed and holds a ship at its moorings. ANCHOR (*v.*) to secure a ship with an anchor; to cast anchor. TO WEIGH ANCHOR means to haul up the anchor.

anchorage (*n.*) a place suitable for ships to anchor; a roadstead.

ancient (*adj.*) very old; in times long past.

and (*conj.*) also; together with. A word used to join words, classes or sentences.

anecdote (*n.*) a little story.

anemone (*n.*) a woodland flower, also called wind-flower.

aneroid (*n.*) a kind of barometer.

angel (*n.*) a heavenly messenger or guardian. ANGELIC (*adj.*).

anger (*n.*) displeasure; rage. ANGER (*v.*) to vex; to provoke.

angle (*n.*) a corner; elbow-bend. ANGLE (*v.*) to fish.

angler (*n.*) a fisherman.

angry (*adj.*) vexed; annoyed. ANGRILY (*adv.*).

anguish (*n.*) 1. unbearable pain. 2. great distress.

angular (*adj.*) having corners or angles.

animal (*n.*) a living being. ANIMAL (*adj.*) concerning animals.

animate (*v.*) to make alive; to rouse. ANIMATION (*n.*).

animosity (*n.*) ill-will; dislike. (*pl.* ANIMOSITIES).

ankle (*n.*) the joint between foot and leg.

annals (*n. pl.*) yearly records. ANNALIST (*n.*).

annex (*v.*) 1. to take; to possess. 2. to add on; to attach. ANNEX(E) (*n.*) a part added to a building.

annexation (*n.*) act of taking over territory and adding it to a country.

annihilate (*v.*) to destroy utterly. ANNIHILATION (*n.*).

anniversary (*n.*) the date of a yearly celebration. (*pl.* ANNIVERSARIES).

announce (*v.*) to make known. ANNOUNCEMENT (*n.*).

announcer (*n.*) one who broadcasts news and other items.

annoy (*v.*) to vex; to tease. ANNOYANCE (*n.*).

annual (*adj.*) happening yearly. ANNUAL (*n.*) a plant that lives only for one year; a book published yearly. ANNUALLY (*adv.*).

annul (*v.*) to cancel; to cross out.

anodyne (*n.*) a drug which eases pain.

anoint (*v.*) to rub with oil or ointment.

anon (*adv.*) soon; shortly.

anonymous (*adj.*) nameless; not known. ANONYMITY (*n.*).

another (*adj.*) not the same; different. ANOTHER (*pron.*) anyone else; one more.

answer (*v.*) to reply. ANSWER (*n.*) a reply.

answerable (*adj.*) responsible to for some duty, money, etc.

ant (*n.*) a small, busy insect.

antagonist (*n.*) an opponent; a competitor. ANTAGONISTIC (*adj.*).

antarctic (*n.*) the south polar region. ANTARCTIC (*adj.*) concerning the south polar region.

antelope (*n.*) African animal resembling a deer.

anthem (*n.*) a song of praise.

anthology (*n.*) a collection of short, choice poems, usually gems from the works of different poets.

anthracite (*n.*) a smokeless coal.

antibiotics (*n.*) drugs that kill disease-germs.

anticipate (*v.*) to use in advance; to forestall.

anticipation (*n.*) a looking forward to; an expectation.

antics (*n. pl.*) amusing or silly actions.

anticyclone (*n.*) widespread air conditions bringing dry weather.

antidote (*n.*) a cure, usually for poison.

antipathy (*n.*) a dislike; distaste.

antipodes (*n.*) the opposite ends of the earth.

antiquarian (*n.*) one who studies ancient things.

antique (*adj.*) extremely old. ANTIQUE (*n.*) anything very old.

antiquity (*n.*) ancient times.

antiseptic (*n.*) a germ-killer.

antler (*n.*) a branch of a stag's horn.

anvil (*n.*) a smith's iron block.

anxiety (*n.*) worry; disquiet.

anxious (*adj.*) troubled; worried.

any (*pron. and adj.*) one out of many; some; whichever you please.

apace (*adv.*) swiftly; quickly.

apart (*adv.*) aside; separately; independently.

apartment (*n.*) a single room. APARTMENTS (*n. pl.*) lodgings.

apathy (*n.*) unconcern; indifference. APATHETIC (*adj.*).

ape (*n.*) a tailless monkey. APE (*v.*) to mimic.

aperture (*n.*) a hole; gap.
apex (*n.*) the tip; peak.
apiary (*n.*) a bee-farm.
apiculture (*n.*) bee-keeping.
aplomb (*n.*) coolness; self-confidence.
apologize (*v.*) to express sorrow for a fault **APOLOGY** (*n.*). **APOLOGETIC** (*adj.*).
apostle (*n.*) a messenger; missionary.
apostrophe (*n.*) the sign (') used to denote (1) the omission of a letter or letters (don't, for do not, or 'tis, for it is), or (2) possession (the boy's cap).
appal (*v.*) to shock; to frighten. **APPALLING** (*adj.*).
apparatus (*n.*) instruments or tools needed for work.
apparel (*n.*) clothing; dress.
apparent (*adj.*) easily seen or understood; plain; clear.
apparition (*n.*) a vision; spirit.
appeal (*v.*) to beg; to entreat. **APPEAL** (*n.*) 1. an earnest request. 2. request for a trial to be reconsidered by a higher court.
appear (*v.*) 1. to come into sight. 2. to seem. **APPEARANCE** (*n.*).
appease (*v.*) to soothe; to mollify. **APPEASEMENT** (*n.*).
append (*v.*) to add in writing.
appendage (*n.*) an addition; a supplement.
appendicitis (*n.*) inflammation of the appendix.
appendix (*n.*) 1. an internal organ. 2. information added at the end of a book. (*pl.* APPENDICES).
appetite (*n.*) a desire for food. **APPETIZING** (*adj.*).
applaud (*v.*) to praise by handclapping. **APPLAUSE** (*n.*).
apple (*n.*) the fruit of the apple-tree.
appliance (*n.*) anything needed to do work.
applicant (*n.*) one who asks for or seeks.
application (*n.*) 1. a request. 2. attention to work; perseverance.
apply (*v.*) 1. to ask for. 2. to attend to; to persevere.
appoint (*v.*) 1. to place in a post or job. 2. to arrange a meeting. **APPOINTMENT** (*n.*).
appreciable (*adj.*) enough to notice or value.

appreciate (*v.*) 1. to think well of; to esteem. 2. to grow in value.
apprehend (*v.*) 1. to fear. 2. to understand. 3. to arrest. **APPREHENSION** (*n.*).
apprehensive (*adj.*) nervous; afraid.
apprentice (*n.*) one learning a trade.
apprenticeship (*n.*) the years spent in training.
approach (*v.*) to come nearer. **APPROACH** (*n.*) the way leading to a place.
approbation (*n.*) praise; approval.
appropriate (*adj.*) suitable; proper. **APPROPRIATE** (*v.*) to take; to seize. **APPROPRIATION** (*n.*).
approve (*v.*) to be pleased with; to accept. **APPROVAL** (*n.*).
approximate (*adj.*) very near; nearly correct.
approximation (*n.*) a nearly correct result.
apricot (*n.*) an orange-coloured, plum-like fruit.
April (*n.*) fourth month of the year.
apron (*n.*) 1. a garment worn to protect the clothes. 2. the concrete platform before an aircraft hangar.
apt (*adj.*) 1. suitable. 2. sharp; clever. **APTNESS** (*n.*).
aptitude (*n.*) an ability; inclination.
aquarium (*n.*) a tank for live fish.
aquatic (*adj.*) living in or taking place in water.
aqueduct (*n.*) a bridge built to carry water.
arable (*adj.*) land fit for tillage or ploughing.
arbitrary (*adj.*) self-willed; despotic. **ARBITRARILY** (*adv.*).
arbitrate (*v.*) to settle a dispute not concerned with law. **ARBITRATION**; **ARBITRATOR** (*nn.*).
arbour (*n.*) a bower; shady retreat.
arc (*n.*) 1. a curve; rainbow. 2. a powerful electric lamp.
arcade (*n.*) an arched passage.
arch (*n.*) a curved structure upholding weight. (*pl.* ARCHES). **ARCH** (*adj.*) playful; roguish.
archbishop (*n.*) a chief bishop.
archer (*n.*) a bowman.
archery (*n.*) shooting with bow and arrows.
archipelago (*n.*) a group of islands. (*pl.* ARCHIPELAGOES).

architect (*n.*) one who plans buildings. ARCHITECTURAL (*adj.*).

architecture (*n.*) the science or art of building.

archives (*n. pl.*) public records. ARCHIVIST (*n.*).

arctic (*n.*) the north polar region. ARCTIC (*adj.*) north-polar.

ardent (*adj.*) eager; keen.

ardour (*n.*) keenness; zeal.

arduous (*adj.*) difficult.

area (*n.*) 1. the extent of a surface. 2. a region; tract.

arena (*n.*) a circus-ring; place for a performance.

argue (*v.*) to discuss; to debate. ARGUMENT (*n.*). ARGUMENTATIVE (*adj.*).

arid (*adj.*) dry; parched. ARIDITY (*n.*).

aright (*adv.*) rightly.

arise (*v.*) to get or come up; to rise.

aristocracy (*n.*) the nobility.

aristocrat (*n.*) a noble; peer. ARISTOCRATIC (*adj.*).

ark (*n.*) a box; chest. THE ARK (*n.*) Noah's vessel.

arm (*n.*) 1. an upper limb. 2. an inlet of the sea. ARM (*v.*) to equip with weapons; arms.

armada (*n.*) a fleet or warships. THE ARMADA (*n.*) the strong fleet sent by Philip II of Spain to attack England, 1588.

armistice (*n.*) a truce; an agreement to stop fighting for a time.

armour (*n.*) protective covering for the body.

armoury (*n.*) a storage-place for arms; an arsenal.

arms (*n. pl.*) weapons; firearms.

army (*n.*) a large body of trained soldiers. (*pl.* ARMIES).

aroma (*n.*) a sweet smell; fragrance. AROMATIC (*adj.*).

arouse (*v.*) to rouse; to awaken.

arrange (*v.*) 1. to put in proper order. 2. to make plans. ARRANGEMENT (*n.*).

arrant (*adj.*) complete; thorough.

array (*v.*) 1. to display. 2. to dress. ARRAY (*n.*).

arrears (*n. pl.*) anything overdue or behindhand.

arrest (*v.*) 1. to stop. 2. to take prisoner. ARREST (*n.*).

arresting (*adj.*) attracting attention; interesting.

arrive (*v.*) to come to; to reach a destination. ARRIVAL (*n.*).

arrogant (*adj.*) haughty; overbearing. ARROGANCE (*n.*).

arrow (*n.*) a straight, barbed shaft shot from a bow.

arsenal (*n.*) an arms factory; a weapon store.

arson (*n.*) the crime of setting property on fire purposely.

art (*n.*) skill, especially in painting, music, etc.

arterial (*adj.*) chief; main.

artery (*n.*) a bloodvessel carrying blood from the heart. (*pl.* ARTERIES).

artful (*adj.*) cunning, sly.

artfulness (*n.*) craftiness.

artichoke (*n.*) a vegetable bearing eatable flowers.

article (*n.*) 1. a single thing. 2. an account in a newspaper.

articulate (*v.*) 1. to speak clearly. 2. to put together. ARTICULATION (*n.*).

artificer (*n.*) a skilled craftsman; engineer.

artificial (*adj.*) not natural; manufactured.

artillery (*n.*) guns; cannon.

artisan (*n.*) a craftsman; skilled workman.

artist (*n.*) one skilled in any art. ARTISTIC (*adj.*).

artistry (*n.*) artistic ability.

artless (*adj.*) 1. unskilful; clumsy. 2. innocent, unaffected.

artlessness (*n.*) simplicity; innocence.

as (*adv.*) like; similar to. AS (*conj.*) since. AS (*pron.*) that; who; which.

asbestos (*n.*) a mineral, fireproof fabric.

ascend (*v.*) to climb up; to rise. ASCENSION (*n.*).

ascendancy (*n.*) the control; mastery.

ascent (*n.*) 1. an upward movement. 2. a slope.

ascertain (*v.*) to find out; to make sure.

ascribe (*v.*) to give up; to refer to.

asdic (*n.*) apparatus used to locate a submerged submarine or wreck.

ash (*n.*) 1. a silvery-grey tree. 2. the powdery remains left after burning.

ashamed (*adj.*) feeling disgraced.

ashen (*adj.*) pale; wan.

ashore (*adv.*) 1. on shore. 2. aground; stranded.

aside (*adv.*) to, or at, one side; away.
ASIDE (*n.*) words spoken to a person (especially in a play) which others are supposed not to hear.

asinine (*adj.*) foolish.

ask (*v.*) to inquire; to request.

askance (*adv.*) sideways; with distrust or suspicion.

asp (*n.*) a small poisonous serpent.

asparagus (*n.*) an eatable garden plant.

aspect (*n.*) 1. a view; outlook. 2. one's appearance; bearing.

aspen (*n.*) a tree having quivering leaves.

asperity (*n.*) harshness; severity.

asphalt (*n.*) a kind of pitch used for road-making.

aspirant (*n.*) one who tries hard.

aspirate (*n.*) the letter H.

aspire (*v.*) to desire; to long for. ASPIRATION (*n.*).

ass (*n.*) a donkey.

assail (*v.*) to strike; to attack. ASSAILANT (*n.*).

assassin (*n.*) a treacherous murderer. ASSASSINATION (*n.*).

assault (*n.*) a sudden attack. ASSAULT (*v.*) to attack.

assemble (*v.*) to gather or meet together.

assembly (*n.*) 1. a council; parliament. 2. a gathering of people.

assent (*v.*) to agree to; to consent. ASSENT (*n.*) a consent; sanction.

assert (*v.*) to say; to state. ASSERTION (*n.*).

assertive (*adj.*) decided; insistent.

assess (*v.*) to fix the value of. ASSESSOR (*n.*).

assessment (*n.*) an estimate of value.

asset (*n.*) a possession worth something.

assiduous (*adj.*) industrious; busy. ASSIDUITY (*n.*).

assimilate (*v.*) to take in; to digest. ASSIMILATION (*n.*).

assist (*v.*) to help. ASSISTANCE; ASSISTANT (*nn.*).

assize (*n.*) a court of justice.

associate (*v.*) to join in with. ASSOCIATE (*n.*) a companion.

association (*n.*) a society; company.

assortment (*n.*) a mixture of different kinds; a variety.

assume (*v.*) to suppose; to pretend.

assuming (*adj.*) bold; proud.

assumption (*n.*) 1. a guess; supposition. 2. forwardness.

assurance (*n.*) 1. certainty; confidence. 2. a form of life insurance.

assured (*adj.*) certain.

aster (*n.*) a star-shaped flower.

asterisk (*n.*) a small, star-shaped mark.

asthma (*n.*) a disease making breathing difficult.

asthmatic (*n.*) one suffering from asthma. ASTHMATICAL (*adj.*).

astir (*adv.*) out of bed; in motion.

astonish (*v.*) to surprise. ASTONISHMENT (*n.*).

astound (*v.*) to amaze; to shock. ASTOUNDING (*adj.*).

astray (*adv.*) lost; wandering.

astrology (*n.*) fortune-telling by the position of the stars. ASTROLOGER (*n.*).

astronaut (*n.*) one who travels in space (U.S.A.).

astronomy (*n.*) the scientific study of heavenly bodies. ASTRONOMER (*n.*). ASTRONOMICAL (*adj.*).

astute (*adj.*) wise; shrewd. ASTUTENESS (*n.*).

asunder (*adv.*) 1. taken apart; in pieces. 2. separated by distance.

asylum (*n.*) 1. a shelter; refuge. 2. a home for the care or cure of the deaf, dumb, or mentally afflicted.

at (*prep.*) a word expressing (1) exact, or vague position, as at noon, at home, or (2) motion towards, as, arrive at, snatch at.

ate (*v.*) past tense of verb to eat.

athlete (*n.*) one active in sports.

athletic (*adj.*) 1. well built. 2. fond of games.

athletics (*n. pl.*) outdoor games and sports.

athwart (*adv.*) across; from side to side.

atlas (*n.*) a book of maps. (*pl.* ATLASES). See appendix.

atmosphere (*n.*) the air surrounding the earth. ATMOSPHERIC (*adj.*).

atom (*n.*) smallest particle of an element. ATOMIC (*adj.*).

atone (*v.*) to right a wrong; to make amends. ATONEMENT (*n.*).

atrocious (*adj.*) very bad; wicked.

atrocity (*n.*) an extremely cruel or wicked deed.

attach (*v.*) 1. to fasten to. 2. to be fond of. ATTACHMENT (*n.*).

attack (*v.*) to begin to fight ; to assault. ATTACK (*n.*) a battle; an onslaught. ATTACKER (*n.*).

attain (*v.*) to reach; to gain. ATTAINMENT (*n.*).

attempt (*v.*) to try. ATTEMPT (*n.*) a trial; an endeavour.

attend (*v.*) 1. to be present. 2. to give heed. ATTENDANCE (*n.*) presence.

attendant (*n.*) a servant; waiter.

attention (*n.*) heedfulness; regard.

attentive (*adj.*) mindful; heedful.

attest (*v.*) to witness; to certify.

attic (*n.*) a loft; garret.

attire (*v.*) to clothe. ATTIRE (*n.*) dress.

attitude (*n.*) the way one stands, thinks or acts.

attorney (*n.*) a lawyer.

attract (*v.*) to draw towards. ATTRACTION (*n.*).

attractive (*adj.*) pleasing.

auburn (*adj.*) golden-brown.

auction (*n.*) a sale in which goods are sold to one who bids or offers the highest price.

auctioneer (*n.*) one who sells by auction.

audacity (*n.*) boldness; courage. AUDACIOUS (*adj.*).

audible (*adj.*) loud enough to hear. AUDIBLY (*adv.*).

audience (*n.*) 1. a group of listeners. 2. an interview.

audit (*v.*) to examine accounts. AUDIT (*n.*) an examination of accounts. AUDITOR (*n.*).

audition (*n.*) hearing given to a singer, speaker or actor as a test.

auditorium (*n.*) an assembly place for an audience; a theatre.

auger (*n.*) a boring tool.

aught (*adv. & n.*) anything.

augment (*v.*) to increase; to enlarge.

augury (*n.*) a sign; token.

August (*n.*) the eighth month. AUGUST (*adj.*) noble; stately. See appendix, AUGUSTUS.

aunt (*n.*) 1. father's or mother's sister. 2. uncle's wife.

aural (*adj.*) concerned with the ear and hearing.

aurora (*n.*) a display of coloured lights in the northern night sky.

auspicious (*adj.*) promising; favourable.

austere (*adj.*) 1. stern; severe. 2. simple; plain. AUSTERITY (*n.*).

authentic (*adj.*) genuine; true. AUTHENTICITY (*n.*).

author (*n.*) 1. a creator; inventor. 2. a writer of books or plays. (*fem.* AUTHORESS).

authority (*n.*) 1. legal power; right. 2. body of persons exercising legal powers.

authorize (*v.*) to give legal power to; to empower.

auto- means self.

autobiography (*n.*) the writer's own life story.

autocrat (*n.*) a ruler whose own will is law.

autocratic (*adj.*) self-willed; domineering.

autograph (*n.*) a person's name written by that person.

automatic (*adj.*) self-acting.

automatically (*adv.*) machine-like; mechanically.

automaton (*n.*) a mechanical figure; a robot.

automobile (*n.*) a motor-car.

autumn (*n.*) year's third or harvesting season. AUTUMNAL (*adj.*).

auxiliary (*n.*) a helper. (*pl.* AUXILIARIES). AUXILIARY (*adj.*) giving extra help.

avail (*v.*) to assist.

available (*adj.*) near; handy.

avalanche (*n.*) a down-rushing mass of snow.

avarice (*n.*) greed, especially for money.

avaricious (*adj.*) greedy; covetous.

avenge (*v.*) to return evil for evil; to get one's own back. AVENGER (*n.*).

avenue (*n.*) a tree-bordered road.

aver (*v.*) to say with certainty.

average (*adj.*) ordinary; everyday.

averse (*adj.*) unwilling.

aversion (*n.*) a dislike; distaste.

avert (*v.*) to avoid; to ward off.

aviary (*n.*) a bird-house.

aviation (*n.*) the art of flying.

aviator (*n.*) an airman; air pilot.

avid (*adj.*) over-eager; greedy.

avidity (*n.*) eagerness; greediness.

avoid (*v.*) to keep away from; to shun. AVOIDANCE (*n.*). AVOIDABLE (*adj.*).

avow (*v.*) to admit; to acknowledge. AVOWAL (*n.*).

await (*v.*) to wait for.
awake (*v.*) to rouse from sleep. AWAKE (*adj.*) not asleep; alert. AWAKENING (*n.*).
award (*v.*) to give a prize or penalty. AWARD (*n.*).
aware (*adj.*) knowing about; watchful. AWARENESS (*n.*).
awe (*n.*) a feeling of respect or fear. AWE (*v.*) to fill with reverence. AWESOME (*adj.*) causing awe.
awful (*adj.*) terrible; dreadful.
awhile (*adv.*) for a short time.
awkward (*adj.*) 1. clumsy. 2. inconvenient. AWKWARDNESS (*n.*).
awl (*n.*) a small boring tool.
awning (*n.*) a canvas cover giving shade from the sun.
awry (*adv.*) twisted; crookedly.
axe (*n.*) a sharp-edged chopping tool.
axiom (*n.*) a statement needing no proof.
axis (*n.*) a central line, diameter or altitude.
axle (*n.*) a bar or rod on which a wheel turns.
aye (*adv.*) always; for ever.
azure (*adj.*) sky-blue. AZURE (*n.*) the sky.

B

babble (*n.*) 1. baby-talk. 2. the sound of running water. BABBLE (*v.*) 1. to prattle; to murmur. BABBLER (*n.*).
babel (*n.*) a noisy confusion.
baboon (*n.*) a long-faced ape.
baby (*n.*) a very young child. (*pl.* BABIES).
babyhood (*n.*) infancy. BABYISH (*adj.*).
bachelor (*n.*) an unmarried man.
bacillus (*n.*) a germ; microbe. (*pl.* BACILLI).
back (*n.*) the hinder part of anything. BACK (*v.*) to go backwards; to bet on; to support.
backbite (*v.*) to speak against one absent. BACKBITER (*n.*).
backbone (*n.*) 1. the spine. 2. courage; determination.
backgammon (*n.*) indoor game for two, played on a board with dice.
backhanded (*adj.*) unfair.
backhander (*n.*) a foul blow.

backslide (*v.*) to slip back into bad ways. BACKSLIDER (*n.*).
backward (*adj.*) 1. slow; shy. 2. behindhand.
backwash (*n.*) water thrown back by a moving ship.
bacon (*n.*) pig's flesh salted and cured.
bacteria (*n.*) disease germs; microbes. (*sing.* BACTERIUM).
bad (*adj.*) 1. wicked. 2. decayed. BADNESS (*n.*).
badge (*n.*) a special button worn as member of a society; a token.
badger (*n.*) a burrowing, wild animal. BADGER (*v.*) to bother; to tease.
badinage (*n.*) playful chatter; banter.
badminton (*n.*) game with shuttlecocks, played like tennis.
baffle (*v.*) to puzzle; to bewilder. BAFFLING (*adj.*).
bag (*n.*) a pouch or container made of paper, fabric, etc., and having an open top. BAG (*v.*) 1. to put in a bag. 2. to swell; to bulge. 3. to droop; to hang in folds.
bagatelle (*n.*) 1. an indoor game. 2. a trifle.
baggage (*n.*) 1. luggage; all belongings required by a traveller or party. 2. a merry, thoughtless girl.
bagpipe (*n.*) Highland wind-instrument having bag and pipes.
bail (*n.*) 1. to pay money to secure the release of an accused person, which sum is forfeited if he fails to appear for his trial. 2. to ladle water out of a boat (see BALE OUT). BAIL (*n.*) 1. the sum paid to secure the release of a prisoner pending his trial. 2. small bar placed on top of the stumps in cricket.
bailie (*n.*) magistrate in Scottish towns.
bailiff (*n.*) 1. a law-officer. 2. a farm-manager; steward.
bairn (*n.*) a child.
bait (*v.*) to torment. BAIT (*n.*) a temptation; lure.
baize (*n*) coarse, woollen cloth.
bake (*v.*) to cook hard by heat.
baker (*n.*) a breadmaker.
bakery (*n.*) a bakehouse. (*pl.* BAKERIES).
balance (*v.*) 1. to keep steady; upright. 2. to make things equal. BALANCE (*n.*) 1. scales. 2. steadiness; stability.

balcony (*n.*) platform projecting from a window or wall.

bald (*adj.*) 1. hairless. 2. plain. BALDNESS (*n.*).

balderdash (*n.*) nonsense.

baldly (*adv.*) straightforwardly; without restraint.

bale (*n.*) a large bundle.

baleen (*n.*) whalebone.

baleful (*adj.*) woeful; injurious.

bale out (*v.*) 1. to throw water out of a boat. 2. to jump from an aircraft in flight.

balk, baulk (*v.*) 1. to hinder; to thwart. 2. to stop suddenly in one's course, BALK (*n.*) a rafter; beam of timber.

ball (*n.*) 1. any round or spherical body. hollow or solid. 2. an assembly for dancing.

ballad (*n.*) a simple song.

ballast (*n.*) a steadying weight.

ballet (*n.*) performance wholly dancing, gesture and music.

balloon (*n.*) 1. a large airtight envelope which, when filled with gas lighter than air, rises skywards. 2. anything which, when inflated, rises in the air. BALLOON (*v.*) 1. to ascend in a balloon. 2. to swell out like a balloon.

ballot (*n.*) a system of secret voting. BALLOT (*v.*) to vote.

balm (*n.*) soothing ointment.

balmy (*adj.*) gentle; pleasant; fragrant. BALMINESS (*n.*).

bamboo (*n.*) giant, wood-like grasses.

bamboozle (*v.*) to hoax; to cheat. BAMBOOZLER (*n.*).

ban (*v.*) to forbid; to prohibit. BAN (*n.*) a prohibition.

banana (*n.*) a yellow, finger-shaped fruit.

bandage (*n.*) a strip of cloth or swathe, used in dressing an injury. BANDAGE (*v.*) to bind with a bandage.

bandit (*n.*) a brigand; robber. BANDITRY (*n.*).

bane (*n.*) a poison; a cause of injury. BANEFUL (*adj.*).

bang (*v.*) to strike noisily; to thump. BANG (*n.*) a loud thump.

bangle (*n.*) a bracelet.

banish (*v.*) to send away; to exile. BANISHMENT (*n.*).

banjo (*n.*) a stringed musical instrument.

bank (*n.*) 1. an institution which receives and pays out money on behalf of its customers. 2. the sides of a river or lake. 3. a shallow place in river or sea. 4. an earthen mound, ridge or barrier. BANK (*v.*) 1. to place money in a bank. 2. to raise an earthen mound or barrier. 3. to cover a fire with fine coal. 4. to put an aircraft at an angle in turning to avoid side-slip.

bankrupt (*n.*) one legally declared unable to pay his debts.

bankruptcy (*n.*) a legal insolvency, or inability to pay all debts.

banner (*n.*) a flag; ensign.

banns (*n. pl.*) announcement in church of intended marriage.

banquet (*n.*) a feast. BANQUET (*v.*) to feast.

banshee (*n.*) a wailing fairy.

banter (*n.*) chaff; fun. BANTER (*v.*) to tease.

banyan (*n.*) Indian fig-tree.

baptism (*n.*) a christening; naming.

baptize (*v.*) to christen and name. BAPTISMAL (*adj.*).

bar (*n.*) 1. a rigid rod. 2. any obstruction. 3. counter where drinks are sold. BAR (*v.*) 1. to hold back with bars. 2. to stop; to obstruct.

barb (*n.*) a V-shaped point. BARB (*v.*) to provide with barbs.

barbarian (*n.*) a savage; brute.

barbaric (*adj.*) uncivilized; savage.

barbarity (*n.*) inhumanity.

barber (*n.*) a man's hairdresser.

barbican (*n.*) a castle gateway.

bard (*n.*) a poet; singer. BARDIC (*adj.*).

bare (*adj.*) 1. naked. 2. empty. BARENESS (*n.*).

barefaced (*adj.*) impudent.

bargain (*v.*) to haggle. BARGAIN (*n.*) goods bought for less than their true worth. BARGAINER (*n.*).

barge (*n.*) a flat-bottomed canal boat. BARGEE (*n.*).

baritone (*n.*) a deep-toned voice.

bark (*n.*) 1. voice of dog or fox. 2. outer coat of trees. BARK (*v.*) 1. to give voice. 2. to speak sharply. 3. to knock one's shin, elbow, etc.

barley (*n.*) a grain; cereal.

barn (*n.*) a farmer's grain-store.

barnacle (*n.*) a small, tightly-gripping shellfish.

barometer (*n.*) an instrument which measures air pressure. BAROMETRICAL (*adj.*).

baron (*n.*) title of a noble of the lowest rank, that next below a viscount. (*fem.* BARONESS).

barque (*n.*) a three-masted sailing ship.

barracks (*n. pl.*) a building in which soldiers live.

barrage (*n.*) 1. a river dam. 2. a continued hail of gunfire.

barrel (*n.*) 1. a cask. 2. the steel tube of a gun.

barren (*adj.*) 1. fruitless. 2. bare.

barricade (*n.*) a block of stones or earth across the road; a low, wall-like fortification. BARRICADE (*v.*) to build a barrier.

barrier (*n.*) anything which compels one to stop; a fence; wall.

barrister (*n.*) a lawyer who may plead in any court.

barrow (*n.*) 1. a small handcart. 2. an ancient burial-mound.

barter (*n.*) the exchange of goods for other goods. BARTER (*v.*) to exchange goods.

base (*n.*) the bottom; foundation. BASE (*adj.*) low; vile.

baseball (*n.*) a ball-game like rounders and played nine on a side. Popular in the United States.

basement (*n.*) the floor below ground-level.

bashful (*adj.*) shy. BASHFULNESS (*n.*).

basin (*n.*) 1. a bowl. 2. a harbour. 3. the land drained by a river.

basis (*n.*) 1. a foundation. 2. the chief ingredient. (*pl.* BASES).

bask (*v.*) to lie in the warmth; to sun oneself.

basket (*n.*) open-topped, carrier-container with handle, and made of twigs, rushes or grasses.

bass (*n.*) 1. a perch-like fish. 2. a deep-toned voice.

bassoon (*n.*) a long, deep-toned, wood-wind instrument.

baste (*v.*) 1. to grease roasting meat. 2. to beat soundly.

bastion (*n.*) a strong corner-tower; a defence.

bat (*n.*) 1. a club for striking a ball, as in cricket. 2. a night-flying, mouse-like mammal. BAT (*v.*) to strike with a bat. BATSMAN (*n.*).

batch (*n.*) a single set or group. (*pl.* BATCHES).

bath (*n.*) 1. a large tub or vessel in which to bathe. 2. a large indoor or open-air tank for public bathing, swimming, or water-sports.

bathe (*v.*) 1. to bath. 2. to go swimming. BATHING (*n.*).

baton (*n.*) 1. a short stick used by a choral or orchestral conductor. 2. a short truncheon carried by a field-marshal or policeman.

battalion (*n.*) a division of a regiment of soldiers.

batten (*n.*) a strong bar of wood. BATTEN (*v.*) 1. to strengthen with battens. 2. to fatten. 3. to live in luxury.

batter (*v.*) to strike again and again. BATTER (*n.*) cake materials beaten up with liquid.

battery (*n.*) 1. a group of big guns. 2. an apparatus for making electricity. 3. a beating; attack. (*pl.* BATTERIES).

battle (*v.*) to struggle with; to fight. BATTLE (*n.*) a mass fight; combat.

battledore (*n.*) a light bat for striking a shuttlecock.

battleship (*n.*) a strongly-armed warship.

bawl (*v.*) to yell loudly. BAWL (*n.*) a loud cry; a continued yelling.

bay (*n.*) 1. an evergreen shrub. 2. an inlet of the sea. 3. a wall recess. 4. the long, low bark of hounds. BAY (*adj.*) reddish-brown. BAY (*v.*) to make a hound's cry.

bayonet (*n.*) a sword-like weapon fixed on a rifle's end. BAYONET (*v.*) to strike with a bayonet.

bazaar (*n.*) 1. an Eastern market-place or shopping-centre. 2. a sale of work to raise money for a charity.

be (*v.*) 1. to have life or being. 2. to become.

beach (*n.*) the seashore; sands. BEACH (*v.*) to run a ship ashore.

beacon (*n.*) a warning signal light or fire; a lighthouse.

bead (*n.*) a small, pierced ball or pellet.

beady (*adj.*) small and bright.

beak (*n.*) 1. a bird's bill. 2. a bill-like projection.

beaker (*n.*) a large, straight-sided vessel or cup.

beam (*n.*) 1. a ray or pencil of light. 2. a long piece of timber. 3. a bright, smiling look. 4. a radio signal used to direct aircraft. BEAM (*v.*) to give light; to shine.

beaming (*adj.*) bright; smiling.

bean (*n.*) plant with a long pod containing eatable seeds.

bear (*n.*) 1. a large, flat-footed, furry animal. 2. a grumbler. BEAR (*v.*) 1. to carry; to sustain. 2. to endure suffering.

bearable (*adj.*) endurable.

beard (*n.*) the hair grown on cheeks and chin. BEARD (*v.*) to defy.

bear-garden (*n.*) a noisy, rowdy place.

bearing (*n.*) 1. one's behaviour; manner. 2. a direction; an aim. 3. the supports of a moving piece of machinery. BEARING (*adj.*) enduring patiently.

beast (*n.*) 1. a four-footed animal. 2. a brutal person. BEASTLY (*adj.*).

beastliness (*n.*) nasty habits or behaviour.

beat (*v.*) 1. to strike. 2. to defeat. 3. to throb. BEAT (*n.*) 1. a stroke; throb. 2. a policeman's round.

beaten (*adj.*) 1. defeated. 2. hammered into shape.

beating (*n.*) a defeat.

beautiful (*adj.*) lovely; pleasing.

beautify (*v.*) to adorn; to make lovely.

beauty (*n.*) a person or thing pleasing to the eye; loveliness.

beaver (*n.*) a furry animal that lives both in water and on land.

becalm (*v.*) to still; to keep still for lack of wind.

beck (*n.*) a little stream.

beckon (*v.*) to invite with a nod or wave.

become (*v.*) 1. to begin to be. 2. to suit; to grace.

becoming (*adj.*) seemly; fitting.

bedlam (*n.*) a scene of uproar; confusion.

bee (*n.*) a winged, honey-making insect.

beech (*n.*) a nut-bearing, hardwood tree.

beef (*n.*) meat from ox, bull or cow.

beefeater (*n.*) a yeoman of the guard.

beefy (*adj.*) fleshy; overheavy.

beehive (*n.*) the bees' home and store.

bee-line (*n.*) a straight line; the shortest way.

beer (*n.*) a drink brewed from barley, hops and malt; ale.

beet (*n.*) a vegetable with sweet, fleshy root.

beetle (*n.*) insect with horny wing-covers. BEETLE (*v.*) to overhang; to jut out. BEETLING (*adj.*).

befall (*v.*) to happen to; to occur.

befit (*v.*) to fit; to suit.

befitting (*adj.*) suitable.

before (*prep.*) in front of; earlier in time. BEFORE (*adv.*) in front; preceding; already BEFORE (*conj.*) sooner than.

beforehand (*adv.*) in advance; in readiness.

befriend (*v.*) to be a friend to; to help.

beg (*v.*) 1. to beseech; to implore. 2. to ask for help or food.

beggar (*n.*) one who begs.

beggarliness (*n.*) 1. shabbiness. 2. meanness.

beggarly (*adj.*) slight; trifling.

beggary (*v.*) utter poverty.

begin (*v.*) to start; to commence.

beginner (*n.*) a learner; novice.

beginning (*n.*) a start; origin.

begrudge (*v.*) 1. to give regretfully. 2. to envy another's success.

beguile (*v.*) 1. to tempt. 2. to idle the time away.

behave (*v.*) to act properly.

behaviour (*n.*) conduct, good or bad.

behest (*n.*) an order; a command.

behindhand (*adv.*) backward; late.

behold (*v.*) to look at; to see.

beholden (*adj.*) obliged to; indebted to.

beholder (*n.*) a looker-on; an observer.

beige (*n.*) material of undyed wool. BEIGE (*adj.*) natural colour; undyed.

bel (*n.*) a unit measure of the loudness of sound.

belabour (*v.*) to beat severely; to thrash.

belated (*adj.*) late-coming; delayed.

belay (*v.*) to fasten; to secure.

beleaguer (*v.*) to surround; to besiege.

belfry (*n.*) a bell-tower. (*pl.* BELFRIES).

belie (*v.*) to give a wrong idea, or false impression.

belief (*n.*) faith; confidence.

believable (*adj.*) can be believed; accepted.

believe (*v.*) to trust; to accept.

believer (*n.*) one who places trust or confidence in another, and especially in God.

belittle (*v.*) to think lightly of.

bellow (*v.*) to roar. BELLOW (*n.*) a bull-like roar.

bellows (*n. pl.*) a bag for blowing air into a fire or organ.

belong (*v.*) to be one's property; to be the business or concern of; to be part of.

belongings (*n. pl.*) all a person's goods or properties.

beloved (*adj.*) much-loved; dear. BELOVED (*n.*) a loved one.

belt (*n.*) 1. a band; girdle. 2. a zone. BELTED (*adj.*).

bemoan (*v.*) to sorrow over; to lament. BEMOANING (*n.*).

bench (*n.*) 1. a seat. 2. a work table. 3. a group, as bench of bishops.

bend (*v.*) 1. to curve. 2. to submit. 3. to subdue. BEND (*n.*) a curve, angle, or turning, especially in a road.

beneath (*prep.*) under; lower in rank, dignity, etc. BENEATH (*adv.*) below; in a lower place.

benediction (*n.*) a blessing.

benedictory (*adj.*) well-wishing; comforting.

benefaction (*n.*) a goodwill gift.

benefactor (*n.*) a doer of good.

beneficence (*n.*) kindness; goodness.

beneficent (*adj.*) kind; generous.

beneficial (*adj.*) helpful; wholesome.

benefit (*n.*) a gain; an advantage. BENEFIT (*v.*) to do good.

benevolence (*n.*) kindness; generosity.

benevolent (*adj.*) kind; charitable.

benign (*adj.*) mild; gentle.

bent (*adj.*) curved. BENT (*n.*) a liking for; an inclination.

bequeath (*v.*) to leave by will; to devise.

bequest (*n.*) anything left by will; a legacy.

bereave (*v.*) to leave sorrowful; mournful.

bereavement (*n.*) a loss causing sorrow; loss caused by the death of friends.

beret (*n.*) a flat, peakless woollen cap, fitting close to the head.

berry (*n.*) any small, stoneless fruit. (*pl.* BERRIES).

berth (*n.*) 1. a ship's place at a wharf.

2. a sleeping-bunk. 3. a situation; post.

beseech (*v.*) to ask earnestly.

beset (*v.*) to attack or surround; to hem in on all sides.

beside (*prep.*) by the side of; next to.

besides (*adv.*) moreover; in addition. BESIDES (*prep.*) over and above; in addition to.

besiege (*v.*) to surround; to hem in.

besom (*n.*) a kind of broom.

bestial (*adj.*) brutish.

bestir (*v.*) to rouse; to awaken.

bestow (*v.*) to grant; to place in safety.

bet (*n.*) a stake or wager. BET (*v.*) to stake; to wager.

betray (*v.*) to help the enemy. BETRAYER (*n.*).

betrayal (*n.*) disloyalty; treachery.

betroth (*v.*) to promise to marry.

betrothal (*n.*) an engagement to marry. BETROTHED (*n.*).

betterment (*n.*) improvement.

between (*prep.*) 1. in the space separating two persons or things. 2. shared by two or more.

bevel (*n.*) a sloping edge. BEVEL (*v.*) to slope; to incline.

beverage (*n.*) a refreshing drink.

bevy (*n.*) a group; flock.

bewail (*v.*) to sorrow; to mourn.

beware (*v.*) to be mindful of danger.

bewilder (*v.*) to puzzle. BEWILDERED (*adj.*).

bewilderment (*n.*) puzzlement.

bewitch (*v.*) to charm; to delight. BEWITCHING (*adj.*).

beyond (*prep.*) on the farther side of; out of reach. BEYOND (*adv.*) yonder; at a distance.

bias (*v.*) to lean to one side. BIAS (*n.*) a leaning to one side. BIASED (*adj.*).

Bible (*n.*) the Holy Scriptures of the Christian Church.

biblical (*adj.*) scriptural.

bicentenary (*n.*) the 200th anniversary

biceps (*n. pl.*) muscles allowing one to bend arms and legs.

bicker (*v.*) to quarrel. BICKERING (*n.*).

bicycle (*n.*) a two-wheeled riding machine. BICYCLIST (*n.*).

bid (*v.*) to invite; to offer a price. BID (*n.*) price offered.

bidder (*n.*) one who offers a price.

bide (*v.*) 1. to wait for; to endure. 2. to inhabit (in poetry or dialect).

biennial (*adj.*) occurring every two years.

big (*adj.*) large; great. BIGNESS (*n.*).

bigot (*n.*) an obstinate person; a fanatic. BIGOTED (*adj.*). BIGOTRY (*n.*).

bilberry (*n.*) a tiny, blue fruit. (*pl.* BILBERRIES).

bill (*n.*) 1. a proposed law. 2. an account of money owing. 3. a bird's beak. BILL (*v.*) to announce; to advertise.

billet (*n.*) 1. a soldier's lodging. 2. a stick; faggot.

billhook (*n.*) a narrow chopper with a curved end.

billiards (*n.*) an indoor table-game.

billion (*n.*) one million millions.

billow (*n.*) a great wave of the sea.

bin (*n.*) a storage can; box; tub.

binary (*adj.*) with 2 (not 10) as the base of a number system.

bind (*v.*) 1. to fasten with a band or cord. 2. to promise faithfully.

binding (*n.*) an outside cover. BINDING (*adj.*) fastening; firm.

bingo (*n.*) a game of chance based on numbered squares.

binnacle (*n.*) a box for a ship's compass.

binoculars (*n. pl.*) field-glasses.

biographer (*n.*) the writer of a life-story. BIOGRAPHICAL (*adj.*).

biography (*n.*) the written life-story of a person. (*pl.* BIOGRAPHIES).

biologist (*n.*) a student of biology.

biology (*n.*) the study of living things. BIOLOGICAL (*adj.*).

biped (*n.*) a two-footed animal.

biplane (*n.*) an aeroplane having two pairs of wings.

birch (*n.*) 1. a forest tree. 2. a rod; cane. BIRCH (*v.*) to flog with a cane.

birching (*n.*) a whipping.

bird (*n.*) animal with feathers and wings.

biscuit (*n.*) a thin, crisp, hard-baked cake.

bisect (*v.*) to cut into two equal parts. BISECTION (*n.*).

bisector (*n.*) a middle line.

bishop (*n.*) 1. a clergyman of high rank. 2. a chesspiece. BISHOPRIC (*n.*).

bison (*n.*) the wild ox.

bit (*n.*) 1. a morsel. 2. a boring tool. 3. part of a bridle.

bite (*v.*) 1. to cut or nip with the teeth 2. to sting. 3. to take bait. BITE (*n.*)

1. the piece bitten off. 2. a wound made by biting.

biting (*adj.*) cold; bleak. BITER (*n.*).

bitingly (*adv.*) hurtfully.

bitter (*adj.*) 1. sour; tart. 2. harsh; stern.

bitterly (*adv.*) sternly, harshly.

bitterness (*n.*) 1. tartness. 2. grief. 3. spite.

bitumen (*n.*) asphalt; pitch.

bituminous (*adj.*) containing pitch.

bivouac (*n.*) an open-air camp. BIVOUAC (*v.*) to sleep by a campfire.

bizarre (*adj.*) ridiculous; fantastic.

blab (*v.*) to give away secrets. BLAB (*n.*) thoughtless talk.

black (*adj.*) 1. opposite to white; dark. 2. gloomy; mournful. 3. wicked.

blackberry (*n.*) fruit of the bramble. (*pl.* BLACKBERRIES).

blackbird (*n.*) the black song-thrush.

blackguard (*n.*) a scamp. BLACKGUARDLY (*adj.*).

blacking (*n.*) black polish.

blacklead (*n.*) pencil-lead; plumbago.

blackmail (*n.*) money, goods or service obtained from a person by threatening injury. BLACKMAIL (*v.*) to obtain anything from another by threats.

blacksmith (*n.*) an iron-worker.

bladder (*n.*) 1. a bag-like organ in the body of a mammal. 2. a thin bag which can be inflated with air, as that in a football.

blade (*n.*) 1. the flat, cutting part of a knife, sword, etc. 2. the broad part of a bat, an oar, etc. 3. the flat part of a leaf, or of the shoulderbone.

blame (*v.*) to find fault with; to fix the responsibility on. BLAME (*n.*) a reproof; censure. BLAMELESS; BLAMEWORTHY (*adjs.*).

bland (*adj.*) mild and polite.

blank (*adj.*) not written or printed on. BLANK (*n.*) an empty surface. BLANKNESS (*n.*).

blanket (*n.*) a woollen bed-covering. BLANKET (*v.*) to cover with a blanket; to protect.

blare (*v.*) to make a trumpeting sound.

blasphemy (*n.*) mocking or irreverent words about God, or sacred things. BLASPHEME (*v.*). BLASPHEMOUS (*adj.*).

blast (*n.*) a strong gust. BLAST (*v.*) 1. to blow up. 2. to blight.

blatant (*adj.*) loud-voiced; vulgar.

blaze (*n.*) 1. a bright flame. 2. a storm of anger. BLAZE (*v.*) to flame. BLAZING (*adj.*).

bleach (*v.*) to make white.

bleak (*adj.*) dreary; windswept. BLEAKNESS (*n.*).

bleat (*v.*) to utter cry of sheep, goat or calf. BLEAT (*n.*).

bleed (*v.*) 1. to lose blood. 2. to extort money from.

blemish (*v.*) to spoil the beauty of. BLEMISH (*n.*) a defect; stain.

blend (*v.*) to mix; to mingle. BLEND (*n.*) a mixture of kinds of tea, etc.

bless (*v.*) 1. to make holy; to consecrate. 2. to ask for God's protection for oneself and others. 3. to wish success to. BLESSING (*n.*).

blight (*n.*) a disease of plants. BLIGHT (*v.*) to wither.

blind (*adj.*) 1. sightless. 2. unknowing, or indifferent to. 3. closed at one end. 4. offering no future success. BLIND (*n.*) 1. a window-screen. 2. a pretence intended to deceive. BLIND (*v.*) 1. to make sightless. 2. to dazzle. 3. to deceive; to mislead.

bliss (*n.*) joy. BLISSFUL (*adj.*).

blister (*n.*) 1. a painful, bubble-like swelling filled with fluid, on the skin. 2. a similar swelling on a plant-leaf, paint-work, etc. BLISTER (*v.*) to cause a blister.

blithe (*adj.*) gay; joyous.

blizzard (*n.*) a violent snowstorm with an icy, raging wind.

bloat (*v.*) 1. to swell or puff up. 2. to cure herring by smoking until slightly swollen. BLOATED (*adj.*).

bloater (*n.*) a herring cured by bloating.

block (*n.*) 1. a solid mass of material. 2. a row of connected buildings. 3. a stoppage. BLOCK (*v.*) to obstruct.

blockade (*v.*) to cut off an enemy's supplies. BLOCKADE (*n.*) a siege.

blockhead (*n.*) a dunce; simpleton.

blond (*n.*) a fair-haired man. BLONDE (*n.*) a fair-haired woman.

blood (*n.*) a red fluid flowing in the arteries and veins of men and animals.

bloodshed (*n.*) slaughter.

bloodshot (*adj.*) tinged with blood.

bloodthirsty (*adj.*) cruel; savage.

bloom (*n.*) 1. a flower; blossom. 2. freshness; vigour. BLOOM (*v.*) 1. to flower. 2. to flourish; to glow.

blooming (*adj.*) 1. blossoming. 2. healthy.

blossom (*v.*) to flower; to bloom. BLOSSOM (*n.*) a flower; bloom.

blot (*v.*) 1. to spot with ink. 2. to disgrace. BLOT (*n.*) 1. an ink-spot. 2. a blemish; stain.

blouse (*n.*) a loose upper garment.

blow (*v.*) 1. to force air from the lungs. 2. to cause air to move. BLOW (*n.*) 1. a puff from the lungs. 2. a gust of wind. 3. a knock; rap. 4. a shock; disaster.

blown (*adj.*) 1. breathless; exhausted. 2. inflated.

blowy (*adj.*) windy; breezy.

blubber (*n.*) whale fat. BLUBBER (*v.*) to sob noisily.

bludgeon (*n.*) a heavy-headed stick; cudgel.

blue (*adj.*) 1. clear; sky-coloured. 2. dismal; downhearted.

bluebell (*n.*) the wild hyacinth; harebell.

bluebottle (*n.*) a large, noisy fly.

bluejacket (*n.*) a naval seaman.

bluff (*adj.*) 1. steep. 2. frank; hearty. BLUFF (*v.*) to deceive; to pretend. BLUFF (*n.*) 1. a pretence. 2. a headland.

blunder (*v.*) to make a mistake. BLUNDER (*n.*) a mistake; an oversight. BLUNDERER (*n.*). BLUNDERING (*adj.*).

blunt (*adj.*) 1. dull; thick. 2. plainspoken; frank. BLUNT (*v.*) to dull the edge or point; to deaden.

bluntness (*n.*) 1. dullness. 2. outspokenness.

blur (*v.*) to smear; to smudge. BLUR (*n.*) a smudge.

blurred (*adj.*) indistinct; confused.

blurt (*v.*) to speak hastily; to burst out with.

blush (*v.*) to flush; to become rosy-faced. BLUSH (*n.*) a red face-glow.

blushingly (*adv.*) 1. with a blush. 2. shyly; modestly.

bluster (*v.*) 1. to blow gustily. 2. to bully; to fume. BLUSTER (*n.*) empty talk; swagger.

blustery (*adj.*) stormy; gusty.

boa (*n.*) a large, crushing snake.

boar (*n.*) a male pig.

board (*n.*) 1. a plank. 2. a table. 3. daily meals. 4. a committee. BOARD (*v.*) 1. to cover with boards. 2. to supply with meals. 3. to embark on a ship, train, etc.

boast (*v.*) to brag; to glorify oneself. BOAST (*n.*) brag; self-praise. BOASTFUL (*adj.*).

boat (*n.*) a small vessel or ship.

bobbin (*n.*) a reel; spool for holding thread.

bode (*v.*) to foretell; to predict.

bodily (*adv.*) 1. physically. 2. completely; entirely.

body (*n.*) 1. a person. 2. a group; crowd (*pl.* BODIES).

bog (*n.*) a swamp; marsh. BOGGY (*adj.*).

bogus (*adj.*) sham; false.

bogy (*n.*) a goblin. (*pl.* BOGIES).

boil (*v.*) to turn water into steam; to seethe. BOIL (*n.*) a hard, painful swelling.

boiler (*n.*) a strong, metal container in which steam is made.

boisterous (*adj.*) 1. violent; rough. 2. cheerful.

bold (*adj.*) 1. brave; venturesome. 2. clear; well-marked.

boldness (*n.*) 1. courage; enterprise. 2. clearness; prominence.

bolster (*n.*) a long bed-pillow. BOLSTER (*v.*) to prop; to support.

bolt (*n.*) 1. a metal securing rod. 2. a dart. BOLT (*v.*) 1. to fasten. 2. to flee away; to run off. 3. to gulp; to swallow hastily.

bomb (*n.*) a metal case filled with explosive. BOMB (*v.*) to drop or hurl bombs.

bombard (*v.*) 1. to batter with shot and shell. 2. to question again and again. BOMBARDMENT (*n.*).

bombast (*n.*) boasting; bluster.

bombastic (*adj.*) boastful; high-sounding.

bomber (*n.*) a bomb-carrying aircraft.

bond (*n.*) 1. a contract; an agreement. 2. a link; tie.

bondage (*n.*) slavery; serfdom.

bone (*n.*) a hard substance forming parts of the body. BONY (*adj.*).

boneshaker (*n.*) an early bicycle with hard tyres.

bonfire (*n.*) a large, open-air fire.

bonny (*adj.*) healthy; chubby.

bonus (*n.*) an extra goodwill payment.

booby (*n.*) a dunce; simpleton.

book (*n.*) written or printed sheets bound together. BOOK (*v.*) to engage beforehand. BOOKSELLER; BOOKBINDER (*nn.*).

bookish (*adj.*) studious.

book-worm (*n.*) one very fond of reading.

boom (*n.*) 1. a long spar. 2. a barrier across a harbour mouth. 3. the sound from an explosion. 4. a sudden increase of trade or prosperity. BOOM (*v.*) 1. to make a deep, hollow sound. 2. to advertise; make known.

boomerang (*n.*) Australian weapon which, when thrown, returns to its thrower.

boon (*n.*) a gift or blessing asked for. BOON (*adj.*) merry; bountiful.

boor (*n.*) a lout; rude fellow.

boorish (*adj.*) rude; ill-bred.

boot (*n.*) 1. leather footwear coming above the ankle. 2. place for luggage on a vehicle.

booth (*n.*) a stall or tent.

bootless (*adj.*) useless; worthless.

booty (*n.*) plunder; loot.

border (*n.*) the edge; boundary. BORDERING (*adj.*).

borderland (*n.*) 1. land forming a frontier. 2. an uncertain or doubtful matter, proposal, etc.

bore (*v.*) 1. to pierce through. 2. to weary. BORE (*n.*) 1. a hole. 2. the width of a hole. 3. anything wearisome. 4. a tidal wave.

boredom (*n.*) dullness; weariness.

borough (*n.*) a town governed by a Council, or one sending a member to Parliament.

borrow (*v.*) to obtain on loan. BORROWER (*n.*).

bosom (*n.*) 1. the breast; heart. 2. the centre; midst. BOSOM (*adj.*) loved; cherished.

botanist (*n.*) a student of plant-life.

botany (*n.*) the study of plants. BOTANICAL (*adj.*).

botch (*v.*) to do badly; to bungle.

bother (*v.*) to disturb when busy; to annoy. BOTHER (*n.*) fuss; annoyance.

bothersome (*adj.*) troublesome.

bottle (*n.*) a hollow, narrow-necked vessel. BOTTLE (*v.*) to put into bottles.

bottom (*n.*) the lowest part; base.
bottomless (*adj.*) unfathomable; very deep.
boudoir (*n.*) a woman's private room.
bough (*n.*) a branch or limb of a tree.
boulder (*n.*) a large stone or rock.
boulevard (*n.*) a broad, tree-lined street.
bounce (*v.*) to leap back; to rebound. BOUNCE (*n.*) 1. a rebound. 2. impudence.
bouncing (*adj.*) bonny; energetic.
bound (*v.*) to leap. BOUND (*n.*) 1. a leap. 2. a boundary.
boundary (*n.*) line dividing one property from another.
boundless (*adj.*) unlimited.
bountiful (*adj.*) liberal; generous.
bounty (*n.*) 1. generosity. 2. a reward.
bouquet (*n.*) 1. a bunch of flowers. 2. the perfume of wine.
bout (*n.*) a fight.
bow (*v.* pron. BOUGH) 1. to bend the head or body forward in respect or greeting. 2. to yield; to submit. BOW (*n.*) 1. an inclination of the head or body. 2. the curved front part of a ship; the prow.
bow (*n.* pron. BO) 1. a weapon which shoots arrows. 2. a particular knot in a tie or ribbon. 3. stick used to play various stringed instruments. 4. anything curved, as a rainbow.
bowels (*n. pl.*) the intestines; part of the digestive organs.
bower (*n.*) an arbour; a shady nook.
bowl (*n.*) a basin-like vessel to hold liquids.
bowls (*n.*) an outdoor game with heavy, wooden balls. BOWLER (*n.*). BOWLING (*n. & adj.*).
bowman (*n.*) an archer.
box (*n.*) 1. an evergreen shrub. 2. a wooden case. 3. a smack, especially on the ear. (*pl.* BOXES). BOX (*v.*) 1. to encase. 2. to fight with gloved fists.
boxer (*n.*) a fighter with gloved fists; a pugilist.
boxing (*n.*) fighting according to strict rules; pugilism.
boy (*n.*) a male child.
boycott (*v.*) to shun; to ignore.
boyhood (*n.*) the years between birth and youth.

boyish (*adj.*) young; immature. BOYISHLY (*adv.*).
brace (*v.*) to prop; to support. BRACE (*n.*) 1. a support. 2. a pair; couple. 3. an implement for holding a bit or drill.
bracken (*n.*) a coarse variety of wild fern, common on hillsides.
bracket (*n.*) 1. a small wall-shelf. 2. marks enclosing words, etc., as ( ).
brag (*n.*) self-praise. BRAG (*v.*) to boast.
braggart (*n.*) a boaster.
braid (*v.*) 1. to weave or entwine together. 2. to plait the hair. BRAID (*n.*) 1 a cord or tape made by weaving different strands together. 2. plaited hair. BRAIDED (*adj.*).
braille (*n.*) a system enabling blind people to read and work. See appendix.
brain (*n.*) an organ in the skull which thinks and remembers.
brainless (*adj.*) stupid.
brake (*n.*) an apparatus for stopping or slowing a moving vehicle. BRAKE (*v.*) to check; to slow down.
bramble (*n.*) a rough, prickly shrub bearing blackberries.
bran (*n.*) husks of grain, separated from flour after grinding.
branch (*n.*) 1. the bough of a tree. 2. an offshoot of a family, business, etc. (*pl.* BRANCHES). BRANCH (*v.*) to form offshoots.
brand (*n.*) 1. mark made with a hot iron. 2. a burning or charred log or stick; a fiery torch. 3. a trade-mark. 4. a sword. BRAND (*v.*) to mark with a hot iron.
brandish (*v.*) to shake; to wave.
brandy (*n.*) a spirit made from wine. (*pl.* BRANDIES).
brass (*n.*) a mixture of copper and zinc.
brat (*n.*) a neglected child; an urchin.
bravado (*n.*) defiance; a show of bravery.
brave (*adj.*) valiant. BRAVE (*n.*) a Red-Indian warrior.
bravery (*n.*) courage; valour. BRAVELY (*adv.*).
brawl (*v.*) to quarrel. BRAWL (*n.*) a noisy quarrel; row. BRAWLER; BRAWLING (*nn.*).
brawn (*n.*) 1. pressed, cooked pork. 2. muscular strength.
brawny (*adj.*) strong; muscular.

bray (*v.*) 1. to make a harsh sound as that of the ass or trumpet. 2. to pound into powder. BRAY (*n.*) the cry of an ass; the trumpet's blare.

brazen (*adj.*) 1. made of brass. 2. impudent.

brazenly (*adv.*) boldly; impudently.

brazier (*n.*) 1. an iron frame for holding fire. 2. a brass-worker.

breach (*n.*) 1. a break; gap. 2. a quarrel. BREACH (*v.*) to make a gap in.

bread (*n.*) food made from flour; food in general.

breadth (*n.*) width; the measurement across.

break (*v.*) to shatter; to fracture. BREAK (*n.*) a pause; an interruption. BREAKAGE (*n.*). BREAKABLE (*adj.*).

breakdown (*n.*) a collapse; failure.

breaker (*n.*) a foam-topped wave.

breakfast (*n.*) the first meal of the day. BREAKFAST (*v.*).

breakneck (*adj.*) hasty; headlong.

breakwater (*n.*) a jetty; mole.

bream (*n.*) a river fish.

breast (*n.*) 1. the chest; bosom. 2. the front of anything. BREAST (*v.*) to face; to withstand.

breastwork (*n.*) a low defensive wall or earthwork.

breath (*n.*) 1. the air breathed. 2. a light wind; a puff.

breathe (*v.*) 1. to use the lungs. 2. to whisper. 3. to live.

breather (*n.*) a short rest; a spell of hard exercise.

breathing (*n.*) respiration. BREATHING (*adj.*) living.

breathless (*adj.*) 1. lifeless. 2. winded.

breech (*n.*) the loading end of a gun.

breeches (*n. pl.*) short-legged trousers.

breed (*v.*) to have young; to rear. BREED (*n.*) the race; family.

breeding (*n.*) the result of rearing or training.

breeze (*n.*) 1. a light wind. 2. a show of temper. BREEZY (*adj.*).

breezily (*adv.*) heartily; in a friendly way.

brevity (*n.*) shortness; conciseness. (*pl.* BREVITIES).

brew (*v.*) to make beer, tea, etc. BREW (*n.*) a single brewing. BREWER; BREWERY (*nn.*).

briar, brier (*n.*) 1. the prickly wild rose. 2. the white heath plant and the tobacco pipes made from it.

bribe (*n.*) money offered to gain a favour. BRIBE (*v.*) to tempt with a bribe.

bribery (*n.*) the taking of a bribe.

brick (*n.*) a moulded block of fire-hardened clay; a building material.

bridal (*n.*) a wedding. BRIDAL (*adj.*) concerning a wedding or bride.

bride (*n.*) a newly-married woman.

bridegroom (*n.*) a newly-married man.

bridesmaids (*n. pl.*) unmarried women attending a bride at her wedding.

bridge (*n.*) 1. a structure spanning a gap. 2. a card game. BRIDGE (*v.*) 1. to span a gap. 2. to overcome.

bridle (*n.*) headgear for a horse; a check; restraint. BRIDLE (*v.*).

brief (*adj.*) short. BRIEF (*n.*) a summary. BRIEF (*v.*) to instruct a barrister. BRIEFNESS (*n.*). BRIEFLY (*adv.*).

brigand (*n.*) a bandit; an outlaw.

brigandage (*n.*) armed robbery.

bright (*adj.*) 1. shining. 2. clever. BRIGHTNESS (*n.*).

brighten (*v.*) to make. 1. bright. 2. cheerful.

brilliance (*n.*) great brightness or cleverness.

brilliant (*adj.*) 1. sparkling. 2. talented. BRILLIANT (*n.*) a diamond; gem.

brilliantly (*adv.*) splendidly; cleverly.

brim (*n.*) the edge; lip.

brimful (*adj.*) overflowing.

brimming (*adj.*) full to the brim.

brimstone (*n.*) sulphur.

brine (*n.*) salt water; pickle. BRINY (*adj.*).

bring (*v.*) to fetch; to carry to.

brink (*n.*) the edge of a cliff or steep place; the margin.

brisk (*adj.*) active; lively. BRISKLY (*adv.*).

briskness (*n.*) smartness; agility.

bristle (*n.*) a stiff, coarse hair. BRISTLE (*v.*) 1. to stand up straight, like an angry animal's hair. 2. to show temper or indignation. BRISTLY (*adj.*).

brittle (*adj.*) easy to break; fragile.

broach (*v.*) 1. to pierce a hole for a tap; to open. 2. to begin to speak of. BROACH (*n.*) a spit for roasting.

broad (*adj.*) wide; extensive. BROAD (*n.*) a flooded fen.

broadcast (*n.*) a wireless transmission. BROADCAST (*v.*) 1. to scatter. 2. to transmit by wireless.

broaden (*v.*) to make wide or wider.

brocade (*n.*) woven cloth having a raised pattern.

broccoli (*n.*) a variety of cauliflower.

broil (*n.*) a noisy quarrel. BROIL (*v.*) to cook over hot coals.

broker (*n.*) one who does business for others; an agent; a dealer.

bronchitis (*n.*) inflammation of the air tubes in the lungs.

bronze (*n.*) a mixture of copper and tin. BRONZE (*v.*) to tan. BRONZE (*adj.*) made of bronze.

brooch (*n.*) an ornamental clasp or pin. (*pl.* BROOCHES).

brood (*n.*) 1. a hatch of young birds. 2. a swarm. BROOD (*v.*) to worry sullenly.

broody (*adj.*) 1. hatching. 2. thoughtful; worried.

brook (*n.*) a small stream. BROOK (*v.*) to put up with; tolerate.

broom (*n.*) 1. a brush. 2. a yellow-flowered shrub.

broth (*n.*) vegetable soup.

brother (*n.*) 1. a son of the same parents. 2. a friend; comrade. (*pl.* BROTHERS or BRETHREN). BROTHERLY (*adj.*).

brotherhood (*n.*) 1. brotherly feeling. 2. a men's society founded on fellow-feeling.

brow (*n.*) 1. the forehead. 2. the top of a hill.

browbeat (*v.*) to scold; to bully. BROW-BEATEN (*adj.*).

brown (*adj.*) red and yellow mixed. BROWN (*v.*) 1. to make brown; to toast. 2. to tan; to sunburn.

browse (*v.*) to nibble here and there; to graze.

bruise (*n.*) a skin injury caused by a blow. BRUISE (*v.*) to press; to crush.

brunette (*n.*) a dark-haired woman.

brunt (*n.*) the strength of a blow or attack.

brush (*n.*) 1. an implement for sweeping or scrubbing. 2. a short fight; a skirmish. 3. a fox's tail. BRUSH (*v.*) 1. to sweep. 2. to touch in passing; to ignore.

brusque (*adj.*) abrupt; blunt in speech and manner.

brusquely (*adv.*) abruptly; gruffly.

brutal (*adj.*) cruel.

brutality (*n.*) ill-treatment.

brute (*n.*) 1. a beast. 2. anyone cruel or savage.

bubble (*n.*) a thin, ball-shaped film of liquid full of air. BUBBLE (*v.*) 1. to rise in bubbles. 2. to flow with a gurgling noise.

buccaneer (*n.*) a pirate; sea-robber.

buck (*n.*) the male of many animals, deer, goat, rabbit, etc. BUCK (*v.*) to jump with arched back.

bucket (*n.*) a vessel for carrying water; a pail.

bucketful (*n.*) a full bucket. (*pl.* BUCKETFULS).

buckle (*n.*) a metal clasp. BUCKLE (*v.*) 1. to crumple. 2. to fasten with a buckle.

bud (*n.*) a leaf or flower not fully open. BUD (*v.*) to begin growing.

budge (*v.*) to move slightly.

budgerigar (*n.*) a small bird which can be trained to talk.

budget (*n.*) a calculation to make sure that expenses will not be more than income. BUDGET (*v.*) to plan to keep within one's income. THE BUDGET (*n.*) the annual financial statement of the Chancellor of the Exchequer.

buff (*n.*) a pale yellow colour.

buffalo (*n.*) a wild ox. (*pl.* BUFFALOES).

buffer (*n.*) anything that softens a blow; a fender.

buffet (*v.*) to cuff; to beat. BUFFET (*n.*) 1. a cuff; blow. 2. a refreshment counter.

buffoon (*n.*) a jester; clown.

buffoonery (*n.*) antics; silly jokes. (*pl.* BUFFOONERIES).

bug (*n.*) a small, bloodsucking insect.

bugbear (*n.*) a nuisance; a dreaded person, event or thing.

bugle (*n.*) a small trumpet. BUGLER (*n.*).

bulb (*n.*) 1. a ball-shaped root. 2. a ball-like shape.

bulbous (*adj.*) ball-shaped.

bulge (*v.*) to swell outwards. BULGE (*n.*) a swelling. BULGING (*adj.*).

bulk (*n.*) the size; volume.

bulkiness (*n.*) the amount of volume.

bulky (*adj.*) of great size; cumbersome.

bull (*n.*) the male of cattle, elephant, etc.

bulldog (*n.*) a strong, fearless dog.

bulldozer (*n.*) a large self-propelled machine for levelling or clearing land.

bullet (*n.*) a missile shot from rifle or pistol.

bulletin (*n.*) a short, official news report.

bullion (*n.*) gold or silver bars before being made into coins.

bullock (*n.*) an ox.

bull's eye (*n.*) the centre of a target.

bully (*n.*) one who ill-treats someone weaker. BULLY (*v.*) to frighten; to ill-treat.

bulrush (*n.*) a tall, reed-like water plant.

bulwark (*n.*) 1. a defensive wall or bank. 2. a protection. 3. a ship's side above the deck.

bump (*n.*) 1. a slight knock; collision. 2. a swelling. BUMP (*v.*) to knock into.

bumptious (*adj.*) self-praising; conceited.

bun (*n.*) a small, round cake.

bunch (*n.*) a cluster. BUNCH (*v.*) to cluster; to gather together.

bundle (*n.*) a package; parcel. BUNDLE (*v.*) to bind together.

bungalow (*n.*) a one-storied house.

bungle (*v.*) to blunder; to do clumsily.

bungler (*n.*) a clumsy person.

bunion (*n.*) an inflamed swelling on the large joint of the great toe.

bunk (*n.*) a box-like bed; a sleeping-berth.

bunker (*n.*) 1. a ship's coal-bin. 2. a sandy hollow on a golf links.

bunkum (*n.*) humbug; nonsense.

bunting (*n.*) 1. a small bird. 2. a flag. 3. flag-making material.

buoy (*n.*) a large, anchored float to guide ships. BUOY (*v.*) 1. to keep afloat. 2. to cheer; to comfort.

buoyancy (*n.*) 1. lightness. 2. gaiety.

buoyant (*adj.*) 1. floating. 2. light-hearted; gay.

burden (*n.*) a load; weight. BURDEN (*v.*) to lay weight upon; to load.

burdensome (*adj.*) heavy; wearisome.

bureau (*n.*) 1. a writing-desk with drawers. 2. an office; a government department. (*pl.* BUREAUS or BUREAUX).

burgess (*n.*) an inhabitant of a borough; a citizen.

burglar (*n.*) one who burgles.

burglary (*n.*) housebreaking and robbery at night. (*pl.* BURGLARIES).

burgle (*v.*) to break into at night to rob.

burial (*n.*) a funeral; an interment.

burlesque (*n.*) a laughable imitation. BURLESQUE (*v.*) to make fun of.

burly (*adj.*) lusty; strong.

burn (*n.*) 1. a sore caused by fire. 2. a small stream. BURN (*v.*) to blaze; to flame.

burning (*adj.*) 1. flaming. 2. eager. BURNER (*n.*).

burnish (*v.*) to polish; to brighten. BURNISH (*n.*) a polish; gloss. BURNISHED (*adj.*)

burr (*n.*) 1. a prickly seed-case. 2. a whirring sound.

burrow (*n.*) a tunnel in the earth dug by an animal as a home and refuge. BURROW (*v.*) to tunnel in the earth. BURROWING (*adj.*).

burst (*v.*) to fly into pieces; to split. BURST (*n.*) a splitting; flying apart.

bury (*v.*) 1. to cover over; to hide in the earth. 2. to forgive and forget. BURIAL (*n.*).

bus (*n.*) a public, passenger-carrying motor vehicle.

bush (*n.*) 1. a shrub. 2. a forest country.

bushel (*n.*) an Imperial measure of capacity (8 gallons).

bushy (*adj.*) abounding in bushes; overgrown.

business (*n.*) work; trade; profession. BUSINESS (*adj.*) concerning business; practical.

business-like (*adj.*) practical; organized.

bust (*n.*) a sculpture of a person's head, shoulders and chest.

bustard (*n.*) a large, slow-running bird.

bustle (*n.*) fuss; noisy stir. BUSTLE (*v.*) to hurry about fussily. BUSTLING (*adj.*).

busy (*adj.*) fully occupied; active. BUSILY (*adv.*).

busybody (*n.*) a meddler; interferer. (*pl.* BUSYBODIES).

butcher (*n.*) 1. one who kills animals for food. 2. one who sells meat. BUTCHER (*v.*) to kill; to slaughter.

butchery (*n.*) slaughter; massacre.

butler (*n.*) a chief manservant.

butt (*n.*) 1. the thicker end of anything. 2. a large cask. 3. a blow from an

animal's head. 4. anyone ridiculed.
BUTT (*v.*) to strike with the head.
butter (*n.*) a food obtained from milk.
BUTTER (*v.*) 1. to spread with butter.
2. to flatter.
buttercup (*n.*) a wild plant bearing yellow,
cup-shaped flowers.
butterfly (*n.*) 1. an insect with large,
coloured wings. 2. a gay, flighty
person.
button (*n.*) a round, flat disc or knob for
fastening clothing. BUTTON (*v.*) to
fasten with buttons.
buttonhole (*n.*) 1. a slit made to take a
button. 2. a flower worn in the buttonhole. BUTTONHOLE (*v.*) to stop or delay
a person.
buttress (*n.*) building giving support to a
wall. (*pl.* BUTTRESSES). BUTTRESS (*v.*)
to support; to prop.
buxom (*adj.*) plump and cheerful; jolly.
buy (*v.*) to purchase. BUYER (*n.*).
buzz (*n.*) 1. the humming sound made
by a flying bee. 2. the hum of many
people talking. BUZZ (*v.*) to hum.
buzzard (*n.*) a bird of prey, falcon or
hawk.
buzzer (*n.*) a factory whistle; siren.
bye (*n.*) a term used in games.
bye-law (*n.*) a local law.
bypass (*v.*) to go round, not through.
BYPASS (*n.*) a road round.
bystander (*n.*) an onlooker; a spectator.
by-way (*n.*) a short cut; little-used track.
byword (*n.*) 1. a proverb. 2. a name
held in disrepute.

C

cab (*n.*) a public carriage.
cabbage (*n.*) a large, green vegetable.
cabin (*n.*) 1. a hut. 2. a room in a ship.
cabinet (*n.*) a wooden case having
drawers.
cable (*n.*) 1. a strong rope, wire or chain.
2. rubber-covered electric wires. 3. a
submarine telegraph line. CABLE (*v.*)
to telegraph overseas.
cablegram (*n.*) a message sent by telegraph
cable.
cachou (*n.*) a scented sweet or pill.
cackle (*n.*) 1. the noise of a hen. 2. a

giggle; idle prattle. CACKLE (*v.*) 1. to
cluck. 2. to giggle.
cactus (*n.*) a spiny desert plant.
cad (*n.*) an ill-mannered person; a lout.
cadaverous (*adj.*) pale; lean-faced.
caddie (*n.*) one who carries a golfer's
clubs.
caddish (*adj.*) rude.
caddy (*n.*) a small tea-box. (*pl.* CADDIES).
cadence (*n.*) the rise and fall of the voice.
cadet (*n.*) a young man training as an
officer in the armed services or police.
café (*n.*) a coffee or tea shop; a
restaurant.
cafeteria (*n.*) a café in which customers
serve themselves.
cage (*n.*) a barred prison for birds or
beasts. CAGE (*v.*) to imprison.
cairn (*n.*) a conical heap of stones.
cajole (*v.*) to coax; to wheedle.
cajolery (*n.*) coaxing; flattery. (*pl.*
CAJOLERIES).
calamitous (*adj.*) dreadful; ruinous.
calamity (*n.*) a disaster. (*pl.* CALAMITIES).
calcium (*n.*) a yellow metal not found in
nature, but in substances like lime.
calculate (*v.*) to count. CALCULATION (*n.*).
calendar (*n.*) a list showing days, weeks
and months.
calf (*n.*) 1. the young of certain animals,
as cow, elephant. 2. the back, bulging
part of the leg. (*pl.* CALVES).
calibre (*n.*) 1. the inside width of a gun-
barrel; the bore. 2. degree of
importance.
calico (*n.*) white cotton cloth. (*pl.*
CALICOES).
call (*v.*) 1. to shout out. 2. to name.
3. to summon. 4. to visit. CALL (*n.*)
1. a shout. 2. an invitation. 3. a visit.
CALLER (*n.*).
calling (*n.*) one's profession or business.
callous (*adj.*) unfeeling; hard-hearted.
callow (*adj.*) young; inexperienced.
calm (*adj.*) still; windless. CALM (*v.*) to
make peaceful; to quieten.
calmness (*n.*) stillness; peace.
calorie (*n.*) 1. the energy value of food.
2. a unit measure of heat.
camber (*n.*) the slope of a road from the
middle.
cambric (*n.*) fine, white linen.
camel (*n.*) a large, humped, domestic
Eastern animal.

cameo (*n.*) a stone formed of coloured layers in which figures are carved standing out in relief.

camera (*n.*) an apparatus for taking photographs.

camouflage (*v.*) to disguise. CAMOUFLAGE (*n.*) disguise.

camp (*v.*) to live in tents. CAMP (*n.*) a group of inhabited tents. CAMPER (*n.*).

campaign (*n.*) a series of military operations in one area. CAMPAIGN (*v.*) to carry on warfare.

camphor (*n.*) a white, oily juice, or crystalline substance, from the camphor tree.

camphorated (*adj.*) containing camphor.

campion (*n.*) a flowering wild plant.

can (*n.*) a small, metal container. CAN (*v.*) 1. to be able. 2. to preserve in tins.

canal (*n.*) a man-made watercourse.

canard (*n.*) a false report; a hoax.

canary (*n.*) a yellow song-bird. (*pl.* CANARIES). CANARY (*adj.*) bright yellow.

cancel (*v.*) to cross out.

cancellation (*n.*) a striking out.

cancer (*n.*) a harmful growth in the body.

candid (*adj.*) frank; straightforward.

candidate (*n.*) an applicant for a post.

candied (*adj.*) soaked in sugar.

candle (*n.*) a rod of wax through which a wick runs for giving light.

candle-power (*n.*) a measure of the brightness of light.

candour (*n.*) honesty; sincerity.

candy (*n.*) a sugary sweet. CANDY (*v.*) to boil in sugar.

cane (*n.*) a thin, flexible stick. CANE (*v.*) to beat with a cane.

canine (*adj.*) of the dog tribe.

caning (*n.*) a beating with a cane.

canister (*n.*) a small, metal box.

canker (*n.*) 1. a sore. 2. a plant disease. CANKER (*v.*) to eat away; to corrode.

canned (*adj.*) preserved in tins.

cannery (*n.*) a preserving factory.

cannibal (*n.*) a man-eating savage.

cannon (*n.*) a large gun. CANNON (*v.*) to collide.

cannonade (*n.*) a continuous gunfire. CANNONADE (*v.*) to fire fast at; to bombard.

canny (*adj.*) shrewd; cautious.

canoe (*n.*) a light, open boat. CANOE (*v.*) to sail or paddle a canoe. CANOEIST (*n.*).

canon (*n.*) 1. a religious law. 2. a cathedral clergyman.

canopy (*n.*) a light, overhead covering. (*pl.* CANOPIES).

cant (*n.*) 1. hypocritical talk. 2. a leaning to one side. CANT (*v.*) 1. to tilt to one side. 2. to talk insincerely, without conviction.

cantankerous (*adj.*) headstrong; quarrelsome.

canteen (*n.*) 1. a factory dining-room. 2. a case for cutlery. 3. a soldier's mess-tin.

canter (*n.*) a slow gallop. CANTER (*v.*) to gallop slowly.

canticle (*n.*) a little song; a psalm.

cantilever (*n.*) 1. a bracket to support a balcony. 2. one of the two bracket-like arms placed on opposite banks of a river to support a bridge.

canting (*adj.*) 1. tilting; sloping. 2. shamming.

canton (*n.*) a small district having a separate government, as in the cantons of Switzerland.

canvas (*n.*) strong, coarse cloth for sails, sacks, etc.

canvass (*v.*) to seek votes or subscriptions. CANVASSER (*n.*).

canyon (*n.*) a deep, narrow gorge.

cap (*n.*) 1. a soft, peaked headcovering. 2. the top. CAP (*v.*) 1. to cover. 2. to surpass.

capability (*n.*) ability; power. (*pl.* CAPABILITIES).

capable (*adj.*) able to do; efficient.

capacious (*adj.*) roomy; large enough.

capacity (*n.*) 1. the volume; size. 2. the ability. (*pl.* CAPACITIES).

cape (*n.*) 1. a headland. 2. a short cloak.

caper (*v.*) to jump about in play. CAPER (*n.*) 1. a frolicsome jumping. 2. the flower-bud of the caper-bush used for pickling and for flavouring sauces.

capital (*n.*) 1. a chief city. 2. money used for business. 3. a large letter. CAPITAL (*adj.*) excellent.

capitalist (*n.*) one who has capital or money.

Capitol (*n.*) 1. the Temple of Jupiter, Rome, and the fort protecting it.

2. the House of Assembly, Washington, of the United States Congress.

capitulate (*v.*) to give in.

capitulation (*n.*) a surrender.

caprice (*n.*) a sudden impulse; a whim.

capricious (*adj.*) fickle; changeable.

capsize (*v.*) to overturn.

capstan (*n.*) a machine for winding in a cable.

capsule (*n.*) 1. a pill. 2. a seed-pod. 3. part of a space vehicle.

captain (*n.*) 1. an officer qualified to command a ship. 2. a military officer commanding a company. 3. the leader of a sports team or club. CAPTAIN (*v.*) to lead; to command.

captivate (*v.*) to charm; to delight. CAPTIVATING (*adj.*).

captive (*n.*) a prisoner.

captivity (*n.*) imprisonment.

capture (*v.*) 1. to catch. 2. to imprison. CAPTOR (*n.*).

carafe (*n.*) a glass water-bottle.

caramel (*n.*) a brown-sugar sweet.

carat (*n.*) 1. a jeweller's weight. 2. a 24th part, pure gold being 24 carats.

caravan (*n.*) 1. a home on wheels. 2. a desert convoy.

caraway (*n.*) a plant bearing spicy seeds.

carbolic acid (*n.*) a strong disinfectant.

carbon (*n.*) pure charcoal.

carbonic (*adj.*) obtained from carbon.

carbon paper (*n.*) paper used for taking copies of letters.

carbuncle (*n.*) 1. a painful boil. 2. a deep-red gem.

carburettor (*n.*) that part of a motor engine which turns petrol into vapour.

carcase(-ass) (*n.*) the body of a person or animal, and especially a dead body.

card (*n.*) 1. a piece or sheet of very stiff paper. 2. an instrument for combing wool or flax. 3. a droll, original fellow. CARD (*v.*) to comb or disentangle.

cardigan (*n.*) a knitted, woollen jacket. See appendix.

cardinal (*n.*) a member of the Pope's Council. CARDINAL (*adj.*) most important; chief.

care (*n.*) 1. attention. 2. worry. 3. caution. CARE (*v.*) 1. to be interested. 2. to be anxious. 3. to be watchful.

career (*n.*) one's profession or course in life. CAREER (*v.*) to run swiftly and heedlessly.

careful (*adj.*) painstaking; watchful. CAREFULLY (*adv.*).

careless (*adj.*) thoughtless; heedless. CARELESSNESS (*n.*).

caress (*n.*) a friendly touch. (*pl.* CARESSES). CARESS (*v.*) to pet; to hug.

cargo (*n.*) the load carried by a ship; freight. (*pl.* CARGOES).

caricature (*n.*) a laughable drawing or description. CARICATURE (*v.*) to make fun of. CARICATURIST (*n.*).

carillon (*n.*) a chime of bells.

carmine (*adj. & n.*) crimson.

carnage (*n.*) slaughter.

carnation (*n.*) 1. a garden-flower of the pink family. 2. a pink colour.

carnival (*n.*) a merrymaking; festivity.

carnivora (*n. pl.*) flesh-eating animals. (*sing.* CARNIVORE).

carnivorous (*adj.*) flesh or meat-eating.

carol (*n.*) a joyful song. CAROL (*v.*) to sing gaily. CAROLLING (*adj.*).

carp (*n.*) a freshwater fish. CARP (*v.*) to find fault. CARPING (*adj.*).

carpenter (*n.*) a joiner; cabinet maker. CARPENTRY (*n.*).

carpet (*n.*) a woven floor-covering. CARPET (*v.*) to cover with carpet.

carriage (*n.*) 1. a wheeled vehicle. 2. one's bearing; deportment. 3. the cost of transport.

carrier (*n.*) a conveyor of goods, etc.

carrot (*n.*) a reddish-brown root vegetable.

carry (*v.*) 1. to convey. 2. to gain.

cart (*n.*) a waggon. CART (*v.*) to convey by cart or waggon. CARTER (*n.*).

cartage (*n.*) the cost of carting.

carton (*n.*) a cardboard box.

cartoon (*n.*) a comic drawing. CARTOONIST (*n.*).

cartridge (*n.*) a case containing explosive for use in a firearm.

cartridge paper (*n.*) thick, strong paper.

carve (*v.*) 1. to shape by cutting. 2. to slice meat. CARVER (*n.*).

carving (*n.*) a sculpture.

cascade (*n.*) a little waterfall. CASCADE (*v.*) to fall step by step.

case (*n.*) 1. a container. 2. a lawsuit. CASE (*v.*) to enclose.

casement (*n.*) a window opening outwards.

cash (*n.*) money. CASH (*v.*) to turn into money.

cashier (*n.*) one who has charge of money in a bank or office. CASHIER (*v.*) to dismiss in disgrace.

cashmere (*n.*) a fine woollen fabric first brought to England from Cashmere, India.

casing (*n.*) the outside covering.

cask (*n.*) a barrel.

casket (*n.*) a small ornamental box.

casserole (*n.*) an earthenware cooking-vessel.

cassock (*n.*) a clergyman's gown.

cast (*v.*) 1. to throw. 2. to shape in a mould. 3. to drop; to shed. CAST (*n.*) 1. a throw. 2. anything moulded. 3. the actors in a play.

castaway (*n.*) a shipwrecked sailor.

caste (*n.*) 1. one's respect; dignity. 2. a class of people.

castigate (*v.*) to punish.

castigation (*n.*) a whipping.

castle (*n.*) 1. a stronghold. 2. a chess-piece.

castor (*n.*) 1. a small wheel fitted under furniture. 2. an oil used in medicine.

casual (*adj.*) easygoing; unplanned.

casualty (*n.*) 1. an accident. 2. an injured person. (*pl.* CASUALTIES).

cat (*n.*) a common domestic animal; a feline.

catalogue (*n.*) a complete list. CATALOGUE (*v.*) to make a list.

catapult (*n.*) an instrument once used for hurling heavy stones in warfare, but now a toy, its power coming from the recoil, or spring back, of strong elastic. CATAPULT (*v.*) to shoot forward as from a catapult.

cataract (*n.*) 1. a waterfall. 2. an eye complaint.

catarrh (*n.*) a severe head cold.

catastrophe (*n.*) a disaster. CATASTROPHIC (*adj.*).

catch (*v.*) 1. to capture. 2. to grasp. 3. to overtake. 4. to understand. CATCH (*n.*) 1. a capture. 2. a fastening-clasp or hook. 3. a sudden, short stoppage of breath.

category (*n.*) a class or kind.

cater (*v.*) to supply. CATERER (*n.*).

caterpillar (*n.*) the grub of moth or butterfly.

cathedral (*n.*) a chief church with a bishop's throne.

cathode (*n.*) the negative pole of an electric current.

catholic (*adj.*) world-wide; universal. CATHOLIC (*n.*) a member of the Catholic Church.

catkin (*n.*) a down-covered flower of the willow-tree.

cat's-paw (*n.*) 1. a tool or dupe. 2. a light breeze.

cattle (*n, pl.*) oxen and cows.

cauldron (*n.*) a large, basin-like boiling-pot.

cauliflower (*n.*) a flowering cabbage.

cause (*n.*) 1. a beginning. 2. a reason. 3. a purpose. CAUSE (*v.*) to make happen.

causeway (*n.*) a raised path or road.

caustic (*adj.*) able to injure the skin, like a burn.

caution (*n.*) 1. watchfulness; prudence. 2. a warning. CAUTION (*v.*) to warn.

cautious (*adj.*) heedful; prudent. CAUTIOUSLY (*adv.*).

cavalcade (*n.*) a company or procession of horsemen.

cavalier (*n.*) a horseman. CAVALIER (*adj.*) haughty.

cavalry (*n.*) horse-soldiers; troopers.

cave (*n.*) a hole in a cliff or hillside.

cavern (*n.*) a large, underground cave.

cavernous (*adj.*) cave-like.

cavity (*n.*) a hollow; pocket. (*pl.* CAVITIES).

caw (*n.*) the harsh cry of a rook. CAW (*v.*) to imitate a rook's cry.

cayenne (*n.*) red pepper.

cease (*v.*) to stop; to come to an end.

ceaseless (*adj.*) endless.

cedar (*n.*) a fragrant, cone-bearing tree.

cede (*v.*) to give up; to surrender.

ceiling (*n.*) 1. the flat roof of a room. 2. an aeroplane's greatest height.

celebrate (*v.*) to honour; to praise.

celebration (*n.*) a special festivity; merry-making.

celebrity (*n.*) a notable person. (*pl.* CELEBRITIES).

celerity (*n.*) swiftness.

celery (*n.*) a white vegetable, having long, edible stalks.

celestial (*adj.*) heavenly.

cell (*n.*) 1. a prison room. 2. a one-roomed dwelling. 3. a single storage-space in a honeycomb. 4. a unit in an electric battery.

cellar (*n.*) an underground room; a vault.

cello (*n.* pron. CHEL-oh) a musical instrument like a large violin.

Celsius (*n.*) a thermometer scale having a hundred degrees between 0° freezing-point of water and 100° boiling-point. See appendix.

Celt (*n.* with capital C) a member of an ancient race, the ancestors of the Welsh, Cornish, Manx, Highlanders and Irish.

cellular (*adj.*) honey-combed; formed of cells.

celluloid (*n.*) a hard substance, usually ivory-coloured.

cellulose (*n.*) a woody, plant-forming substance.

cement (*n.*) mortar. CEMENT (*v.*) to join securely.

cemetery (*n.*) a burial-ground.

cenotaph (*n.*) a monument to one, or many, buried elsewhere.

censor (*n.*) an official who prohibits offensive books, plays or films. CENSOR (*v.*) to prohibit; to ban. CENSORSHIP (*n.*).

censorious (*adj.*) fault-finding.

censure (*v.*) to blame; to reprove. CENSURE (*n.*) blame; reproof.

census (*n.*) an official numbering of the population.

cent (*n.*) 1. 100, as in 10 per cent, or 10 in each hundred. 2. a United States coin which is one-hundredth part of a dollar.

centenarian (*n.*) a person 100 years old or over.

centenary (*n.*) the 100th anniversary.

centigrade (*adj.*) divided into 100 degrees. See CELSIUS.

centimetre (*n.*) the 100th part of a metre.

centipede (*n.*) a many-footed insect.

central (*adj.*) 1. in the middle. 2. chief; leading. CENTRALLY (*adv.*).

centre (*n.*) the middle. CENTRE (*v.*) to place in the middle.

century (*n.*) 1. 100 years. 2. a score of 100. (*pl.* CENTURIES).

cereal (*n.*) any grain used for food.

cerebral (*adj.*) belonging to the brain.

ceremonial (*adj.*) official; exact.

ceremonious (*adj.*) with the right formal behaviour.

ceremony (*n.*) a solemn or stately celebration. (*pl.* CEREMONIES).

cerise (*adj.*) cherry-coloured.

certain (*adj.*) sure.

certainly (*adv.*) willingly.

certainty (*n.*) a fact.

certificate (*n.*) a written proof.

certify (*v.*) to inform truthfully; accurately.

certitude (*n.*) the certainty; sureness.

cessation (*n.*) a stopping; ceasing.

cesspool (*n.*) a pool for drainage.

chafe (*v.*) 1. to wear away. 2. to annoy. 3. to rub. CHAFING (*adj.*).

chaff (*v.*) to make fun of. CHAFF (*n.*) 1. husks of grain. 2. mockery. 3. anything worthless. CHAFFING (*adj.*).

chaffinch (*n.*) a small, grain-eating bird.

chagrin (*n.*) ill-humour; annoyance. CHAGRINED (*adj.*).

chain (*n.*) 1. a length of joined links or rings. 2. a measure of length (22 yards). 3. a series of events. CHAIN (*v.*) to bind; to secure with a chain.

chair (*n.*) a backed, four-legged seat for one. CHAIR (*v.*) to raise and carry in a chair as an honour.

chairman (*n.*) one who presides over a meeting. (*pl.* CHAIRMEN). A woman who presides is called the CHAIRMAN, but is addressed as MADAM CHAIRMAN.

chalet (*n.*) a wooden cottage built in the Swiss style.

chalice (*n.*) a stemmed cup; a Communion-cup.

chalk (*n.*) soft, white limestone. CHALK (*v.*) to mark with chalk. CHALKY (*adj.*).

challenge (*v.*) to defy; to dare. CHALLENGE (*n.*) a defiance. CHALLENGER (*n.*).

chamber (*n.*) a room.

chamberlain (*n.*) the head official of a royal household.

chameleon (*n.*) a lizard-like reptile able to change its colour.

chamois (*n.* pron. SHAM-wah) a goat-like Alpine antelope.

chamois (*adj.* pron. SHAMMY) made of soft, yellow leather.

champ (*v.*) to munch noisily.

champagne (*n.*) a sparkling French wine.

champion (*n.*) 1. one who defends others. 2. a victor over all competitors. CHAMPION (*v.*) to uphold; to defend. CHAMPIONSHIP (*n.*).

chance (*n.*) 1. an unplanned event. 2. a risk. CHANCE (*v.*) to risk. CHANCY (*adj.*).

chancel (*n.*) the east end of a church, where the altar stands.

chancellor (*n.*) 1. a high officer of state. 2. the head of a university.

chandelier (*n.*) a hanging frame to hold lights.

change (*n.*) 1. an alteration. 2. money received back from a sum offered. CHANGE (*v.*) to alter; to substitute.

changeable (*adj.*) unsettled.

changeless (*adj.*) without change; steadfast.

channel (*n.*) 1. a waterway. 2. a groove. CHANNEL (*v.*) 1. to groove. 2. to cut a canal. THE CHANNEL (*n.*) the English Channel.

chant (*v.*) to sing. CHANT (*n.*) a sacred song.

chaos (*n.* pron. KAY-oss) disorder.

chaotic (*adj.*) greatly confused.

chap (*v.*) to crack; to split. CHAP (*n.*) a boy; man; fellow. CHAPPED (*adj.*).

chapel (*n.*) a house of worship.

chaplain (*n.*) the minister of a private chapel, ship, regiment, etc.

chaplet (*n.*) a wreath worn on the head.

chapter (*n.*) 1. a division of a book. 2. the cathedral clergy.

char (*v.*) to burn partially; to scorch.

character (*n.*) 1. a person's own nature. 2. a reputation. 3. a person in a story or play.

characteristic (*n.*) a special mark; something distinctive.

characterize (*v.*) to distinguish specially.

charade (*n.*) a game in which some of the players guess words the syllables of which are acted by the others.

charcoal (*n.*) partially burnt wood; carbon.

charge (*v.*) 1. to rush at. 2. to fill up. 3. to ask a price. 4. to accuse. CHARGE (*n.*) 1. an onslaught. 2. a filling. 3. a price. 4. an accusation.

charily (*adv.*) cautiously; doubtfully.

chariot (*n.*) an ancient war-cart. CHARIOTEER (*n.*).

charitable (*adj.*) kind; forgiving.

charity (*n.*) kindness; goodwill. (*pl.* CHARITIES).

charm (*n.*) 1. ability to please. 2. a magic spell. 3. a good-luck trinket. CHARM (*v.*) 1. to delight. 2. to enchant.

charming (*adj.*) pleasing.

chart (*n.*) a sailor's sea-map. CHARTLESS (*adj.*) unguided.

charter (*n.*) a document granting certain rights. CHARTER (*v.*) to hire for a period.

chary (*adj.*) cautious; doubtful.

chase (*v.*) to pursue; to hunt. CHASE (*n.*) a pursuit; the hunt.

chasm (*n.*) a gorge; deep opening.

chassis (*n.*) the base-frame of a car or carriage.

chaste (*adj.*) pure.

chasten (*v.*) to teach by punishing.

chastisement (*n.*) punishment.

chastity (*n.*) purity.

chat (*v.*) to gossip. CHAT (*n.*) a friendly talk.

chattels (*n. pl.*) goods; belongings.

chatter (*v.*) to talk fast or idly. CHATTER (*n.*) idle talk.

chatterbox (*n.*) one constantly talking.

chauffeur (*n.* pron. SHOW-fer) a motorcar driver.

cheap (*adj.*) of little value. CHEAPNESS (*n.*).

cheapen (*v.*) 1. to lower in value. 2. to belittle.

cheat (*v.*) to swindle. CHEAT (*n.*) a swindler.

check (*v.*) 1. to slow down or stop. 2. to rebuke. 3. to make sure. CHECK (*n.*) 1. a hindrance. 2. a pass. 3. a making sure. 4. cloth patterned in squares.

cheek (*n.*) 1. each side of the face. 2. impudence.

cheeky (*adj.*) impudent. CHEEKINESS (*n.*). CHEEKILY (*adv.*).

cheer (*v.*) 1. to applaud by shouting. 2. to gladden. CHEER (*n.*) 1. a cry of applause or welcome. 2. happiness.

cheerful (*adj.*) jolly. CHEERFULNESS (*n.*).

cheerily (*adv.*) merrily.

cheeriness (*n.*) good spirits.

cheerless (*adj.*) sad; gloomy. CHEERLESSNESS (*n.*).

cheery (*adj.*) gay; lively.

cheese (*n.*) a food made from milk curd pressed and dried.

chef (*n.* pron. SHEF) a head cook.

chemical (*n. & adj.*) made by chemistry. CHEMICALLY (*adv.*).

chemist (*n.*) 1. one skilled in chemistry. 2. a seller of medicine.

chemistry (*n.*) the study and science of the elements.

cheque (*n.*) a written order to a banker to pay money.

cherish (*v.*) to care for; to guard.

cherry (*n.*) a small, sweet stone-fruit. (*pl.* CHERRIES). CHERRY (*adj.*) reddish; ruddy.

cherub (*n.*) an angel-child. (*pl.* CHERUBS or CHERUBIM). CHERUBIC (*adj.*) angelic.

chess (*n.*) indoor game for two played on a squared board. CHESS-BOARD (*n.*).

chest (*n.*) 1. the breast. 2. a large box.

chestnut (*n.*) 1. a tree bearing red-brown nuts. 2. a red-brown horse. 3. a stale joke. CHESTNUT (*adj.*) red-brown.

chew (*v.*) to crush with the teeth.

chick (*n.*) a newly-hatched bird.

chicken (*n.*) a young fowl. CHICKEN-HEARTED (*adj.*) timid.

chicory (*n.*) ground root of a plant often mixed with coffee.

chide (*v.*) to find fault with a person; to reprove.

chief (*n.*) a leader; head. CHIEF (*adj.*) most important.

chieftain (*n.*) 1. head of a clan. 2. a military chief.

chilblain (*n.*) a blister caused by frost.

child (*n.*) an infant. (*pl.* CHILDREN).

childhood (*n.*) infancy.

childish (*adj.*) playful; silly.

chill (*n.*) 1. a coolness. 2. a shivery cold. CHILL (*v.*) 1. to make cold. 2. to dishearten.

chilly (*adj.*) 1. cold; bleak. 2. unfriendly. CHILLINESS (*n.*).

chime (*n.*) the music of bells. CHIME (*v.*) to ring tunefully.

chimney (*n.*) a tube-like passage to carry smoke away; a flue.

chimpanzee (*n.*) a man-like ape.

chin (*n.*) the face below the mouth.

china (*n.*) fine, thin pottery.

chinchilla (*n.*) animal bearing soft, grey fur.

chink (*n.*) a narrow slit. CHINK (*v.*) to jingle.

chintz (*n.*) gay-patterned cotton cloth.

chip (*n.*) a tiny piece. CHIP (*v.*) to break off a fragment. CHIPPED (*adj.*).

chipmunk (*n.*) the American squirrel.

chiropodist (*n.*) one who treats foot-complaints.

chirp (*n.*) a shrill bird-note. CHIRP (*v.*) to call like a young bird. CHIRPING (*n.*).

chirpy (*adj.*) cheerful. CHIRPINESS (*n.*).

chisel (*n.*) a wood or stone-cutting tool. CHISEL (*v.*) to cut or carve with a chisel.

chivalrous (*adj.*) manly; courteous.

chivalry (*n.*) manly gentleness; courtesy.

chlorine (*n.*) a poisonous, bleaching gas.

chloroform (*n.*) a vapour causing insensibility. CHLOROFORM (*v.*) to make insensible with chloroform.

chocolate (*n.*) a sweet or beverage made from cocoa. CHOCOLATE (*adj.*) deep brown.

choice (*n.*) anything chosen or selected. CHOICE (*adj.*) rare; excellent.

choir (*n.*) 1. a band of singers. 2. that part of a church occupied by the choir; the chancel.

choke (*v.*) 1. to smother. 2. to block up. 3. to catch the breath.

cholera (*n.*) a serious disease of the stomach or bowels.

choose (*v.*) to select; to pick.

chop (*v.*) to cut with short down-strokes. CHOP (*n.*) a pork or mutton rib.

choppy (*adj.*) having short, broken waves; rough.

choral (*adj.*) belonging to a chorus or choir.

chord (*n.*) 1. two or more musical notes in harmony. 2. string of a musical instrument. 3. straight line joining the ends of an arc of a circle.

chorister (*n.*) a member of a choir.

chortle (*v.*) to chuckle. CHORTLE (*n.*) a chuckle.

chorus (*n.*) music which all join in singing.

chosen (*adj.*) picked; selected.

christen (*v.*) to baptize and name. CHRISTENING (*n.*).

Christendom (*n.*) Christian countries and people.

Christian (*adj.*) concerning Christ and His teaching. CHRISTIAN (*n.*) a believer in Christ's teaching.

Christianity (*n.*) Christ's teaching.

Christmas (*n.*) the festival celebrating Christ's birth. (December 25).

chrome (*adj.*) deep yellow.

chromium (*n.*) a bright metal.

chronic (*adj.*) lasting; lingering.

chronicle (*n.*) an historical record. CHRONICLE (*v.*) to record.

chronological (*adj.*) arranged in order of happening.

chronology (*n.*) the study of dated records.

chronometer (*n.*) an accurate time-keeper for ships.

chrysalis (*n.*) an insect's form while growing its wings.

chub (*n.*) a freshwater fish.

chubby (*adj.*) plump. CHUBBINESS (*n.*).

chuckle (*v.*) to laugh quietly. CHUCKLE (*n.*) an amused laugh held back or suppressed.

chum (*n.*) a close friend. CHUMMY (*adj.*).

chunk (*n.*) a short, thick piece. CHUNKY (*adj.*).

church (*n.*) 1. a building set apart for worship (small c). 2. the whole body of Christians (capital C).

churchyard (*n.*) a burial-ground around a church.

churl (*n.*) a rough, surly man. CHURLISH-NESS (*n.*).

churn (*n.*) a butter-making machine. CHURN (*v.*) to make butter.

chute (*n.*) a sloping trough or slide.

cicerone (*n.*) a guide. See appendix.

cider (*n.*) a drink made from apples.

cigar (*n.*) tobacco leaf rolled for smoking.

cigarette (*n.*) tobacco rolled in paper for smoking.

cinder (*n.*) a substance burnt, but not to ashes. CINDERY (*adj.*).

cinema (*n.*) a moving-picture theatre.

cinematograph (*n.*) a machine that throws moving pictures on a screen; a projector.

cinnamon (*n.*) the fragrant bark of a tree used as spice.

cipher (*n.*) 1. the symbol 0. 2. a code. 3. a nonentity; nothing. CIPHER (*v.*) 1. to write in code. 2. to count; to calculate.

circle (*n.*) a perfect ring. CIRCLE (*v.*) to revolve.

circuit (*n.*) a roundabout journey.

circuitous (*adj.*) indirect; roundabout.

circular (*adj.*) round; ring-like. CIRCULAR (*n.*) a notice distributed around.

circulate (*v.*) to distribute; to spread around.

circulation (*n.*) 1. a distribution. 2. the movement of blood in the body.

circumference (*n.*) the line enclosing a circle; distance round anything circular in form.

circumscribe (*v.*) to surround; to encircle.

circumspect (*adj.*) cautious; careful. CIRCUMSPECTION (*n.*).

circumstance (*n.*) a particular incident; a fact.

circumstances (*n. pl.*) 1. the conditions. 2. the state of one's own affairs.

circumvent (*v.*) to outwit; to gain advantage over.

circus (*n.*) a travelling company of horse riders, acrobats, etc. (*pl.* CIRCUSES).

cistern (*n.*) a water-storage tank.

citadel (*n.*) a stronghold in a city.

cite (*v.*) 1. to quote. 2. to summon to a law court to prove something.

citizen (*n.*) 1. an inhabitant of a city. 2. a member of a country or nation.

citizenship (*n.*) being, or having the rights of, a citizen.

citron (*n.*) lemon-like fruit of the citron-tree.

city (*n.*) an important town which is or has been a bishop's seat. (*pl.* CITIES). THE CITY = LONDON.

civic (*adj.*) concerned with a citizen or city.

civil (*adj.*) 1. concerned with a nation; national. 2. courteous.

civilian (*n.*) one not serving in the armed forces.

civility (*n.*) politeness; courtesy. CIVILLY (*adv.*).

civilization (*n.*) the way of life of an enlightened, cultured people.

civilize (*v.*) to educate and enlighten.

claim (*v.*) to demand a due. CLAIM (*n.*) a demand for one's due.

claimant (*n.*) one who demands his due.

clamber (*v.*) to climb by clinging; to scramble.

clammy (*adj.*) cold; slimy.

clamorous (*adj.*) loud-calling; noisy.

clamour (*n.*) noisy outcry. CLAMOUR (*v.*) to shout noisily.

clamp (*v.*) to grip together. CLAMP (*n.*) a clasp for holding things together firmly.

clan (*n.*) a tribe united under a chieftain. CLANNISH (*adj.*).

clang (*n.*) the loud, harsh sound of heavy bell or cymbal. CLANG (*v.*) to make a harsh, metallic sound.

clap (*v.*) to smack the hands together. CLAP (*n.*) 1. the sound of clapping. 2. a peal of thunder. CLAPPING (*adj.*).

clapper (*n.*) the tongue of a bell.

claret (*n.*) a French red wine. CLARET (*adj.*) purple-red.

clarification (*n.*) a purifying; making clear.

clarify (*v.*) to purify; to make clear.

clarity (*n.*) clearness; brightness.

clash (*v.*) to strike together noisily; to collide. CLASH (*n.*) a collision.

clasp (*v.*) 1. to grasp. 2. to embrace. 3. to buckle. CLASP (*n.*) 1. a grasp. 2. an embrace. 3. a buckle.

class (*n.*) a group of persons or things of the same kind.

classic (*n.*) a model; the best kind.

classical (*adj.*) of the highest rank, especially in literature.

classics (*n. pl.*) ancient Latin and Greek literature.

classification (*n.*) a placing with its own kind; a sorting.

classify (*v.*) to sort into kinds or groups.

clatter (*v.*) to rattle noisily. CLATTER (*n.*) a repeated rattling noise.

clause (*n.*) 1. a part of a sentence. 2. a paragraph in an agreement.

claw (*n.*) an animal's hooked nail; a talon. CLAW (*v.*) to tear or scratch with claws.

clay (*n.*) moist, sticky earth.

claymore (*n.*) two-handed sword once used by Scottish Highlanders.

clean (*v.*) to free from dirt. CLEAN (*adj.*) unsoiled. CLEAN (*adv.*) altogether; completely.

cleanliness (*n.*) being clean.

cleanly (*adv.*) neatly; tidily.

cleanse (*v.*) to purify; to wash free from dirt.

cleansing (*n.*) a purifying; a washing.

clear (*v.*) 1. to free from impurity. 2. to make bright. 3. to prove innocent. CLEAR (*adj.*) 1. distinct. 2. open. 3. transparent.

clearance (*n.*) 1. a setting free. 2. a removal of anything unwanted.

clearly (*adv.*) undoubtedly; evidently.

clearness (*n.*) 1. distinctness. 2. transparency.

cleavage (*n.*) a splitting; separation.

cleave (*v.*) 1. to cling to. 2. to split; to cut through.

cleaver (*n.*) a butcher's chopper.

cleft (*n.*) a split; rift. CLEFT (*adj.*) split; cut through.

clematis (*n.*) a flowering, climbing shrub.

clemency (*n.*) mercy; leniency.

clement (*adj.*) mild; gentle.

clench (*v.*) to close teeth or fingers tightly. CLENCHED (*adj.*).

clergy (*n. pl.*) ministers of the Church.

clergyman (*n.*) a minister. (*pl.* CLERGYMEN).

cleric (*n.*) a minister; clergyman.

clerical (*adj.*) 1. concerning the Church or clergy. 2. written.

clerk (*n.*) a secretary; scribe.

clever (*adj.*) intelligent.

cleverly (*adv.*) skilfully.

cleverness (*n.*) talent; skill.

click (*n.*) a snapping sound. CLICK (*v.*) to make a snapping sound. CLICKING (*adj.*).

client (*n.*) one who employs a lawyer.

cliff (*n.*) a precipice.

climate (*n.*) the weather over a region or zone.

climatic (*adj.*) concerning the weather.

climax (*n.*) the highest point; turning-point.

climb (*v.*) to ascend, using hands and feet. CLIMBER (*n.*).

cling (*v.*) to hold to firmly. CLINGING (*adj.*).

clink (*v.*) to jingle. CLINKING (*adj.*).

clip (*v.*) to cut; to trim. CLIP (*n.*) 1. a hair-cut. 2. a fastener.

clipper (*n.*) a fast sailing-ship.

cloak (*v.*) to screen; to hide. CLOAK (*n.*) 1. a sleeveless outer garment. 2. a pretence.

clock (*n.*) a time-piece.

clockwise (*adj.*) from left to right.

clockwork (*n.*) spring-driven machinery.

clod (*n.*) a piece of turf; a sod.

clodhopper (*n.*) a stupid person.

clog (*v.*) to block; to choke. CLOG (*n.*) 1. a hindrance. 2. a wooden shoe. CLOGGED (*adj.*).

cloister (*n.*) 1. a sheltered walk. 2. a monastery.

cloistral (*adj.*) sheltered; quiet.

close (*v.* pron. KLOZ) 1. to shut. 2. to end. 3. to draw nearer. CLOSE (*n.*) the end. CLOSED (*adj.*).

close (*adj.* pron. KLOS) 1. private. 2. near. 3. mean. 4. stuffy. CLOSENESS (*n.*). CLOSELY (*adv.*).

clot (*v.*) to thicken; to curdle. CLOT (*n.*) a soft lump.

cloth (*n.*) a woven fabric.

clothe (*v.*) to dress; to garb.

clothes (*n. pl.*) garments. CLOTHIER (*n.*).

clothing (*n.*) bodily covering.

clotted (*adj.*) curdled; thickened.

cloud (*v.*) to hide; to obscure. CLOUD (*n.*) an overhead mass of vapour from which rain falls.

cloudless (*adj.*) 1. clear. 2. unclouded.

cloudy (*adj.*) 1. gloomy. 2. muddy. CLOUDINESS (*n.*).

clout (*n.*) 1. a piece of cloth. 2. a blow from a clout or the flat of the hand. CLOUT (*v.*) to slap.

clove (*n.*) a plant-bud used as spice.

cloven (*adj.*) split into two parts.

clover (*n.*) a plant grown as fodder.

clown (*n.*) a jester; fool. CLOWNING (*n.*).

clownish (*adj.*) boorish.

cloy (*v.*) to glut; to feel discomfort from richness or sweetness. CLOYING (*adj.*).

club (*n.*) 1. a heavy-headed stick; cudgel. 2. a society or its meeting place. CLUB (*v.*) 1. to beat with a club. 2. to unite together.

clue (*n.*) a guide; key to overcoming a difficulty.

clump (*n.*) a group of trees. CLUMP (*v.*) to walk heavily.

clumsiness (*n.*) awkwardness; ungainliness.

clumsy (*adj.*) awkward; bungling. CLUMSILY (*adv.*).

cluster (*v.*) to form a group. CLUSTER (*n.*) a bunch; group.

clutch (*v.*) to grasp at; to snatch at. CLUTCH (*n.*) 1. a grip. 2. a set of eggs. 3. part of a motor-car's driving device.

clutter (*v.*) to litter. CLUTTER (*n.*) untidiness; disorder.

coach (*n.*) a large, covered carriage. COACHMAN (*n.*).

coach (*v.*) to teach. COACH (*n.*) a teacher. COACHING (*n.*).

coal (*n.*) a hard, black mineral used as fuel.

coalition (*n.*) an alliance; a union.

coarse (*adj.*) 1. rough. 2. vulgar. COARSELY (*adv.*).

coarseness (*n.*) 1. roughness. 2. vulgarity.

coast (*n.*) where land and sea meet. COASTAL (*adj.*).

coaster (*n.*) a vessel trading at home ports.

coat (*v.*) to cover; to spread over. COAT (*n.*) 1. an outer garment. 2. an animal's fur or hair. 3. a layer of paint.

coax (*v.*) to wheedle; to cajole. COAXING (*n. & adj.*).

cob (*n.*) 1. a small loaf. 2. a young horse. 3. an ear of maize.

cobalt (*n.*) 1. a steel-grey metal. 2. a deep-blue pigment.

cobble (*v.*) to mend.

cobbler (*n.*) a boot-repairer.

cobra (*n.*) a deadly, hooded snake.

cobweb (*n.*) a spider's web. COBWEBBY (*adj.*).

cochineal (*n.*) a scarlet dye.

cock (*n.*) 1. a male bird. 2. a water-tap.

cockatoo (*n.*) a crested parrot.

cockchafer (*n.*) the loud-humming beetle.

cockerel (*n.*) a young cock.

cockle (*n.*) an edible shellfish.

cockney (*n.*) a London-born person.

cockpit (*n.*) 1. pilot's seat in an aeroplane. 2. a fighting arena.

cockroach (*n.*) a large, black housebeetle.

cock-sure (*adj.*) oversure.

coco (*n.*) a tropical palm-tree.

cocoa (*n.*) a drink made from the powdered seeds of the cacao-palm.

coconut (*n.*) large, milk-containing fruit of the coco-palm.

cocoon (*n.*) a silky case spun by many insects.

cod (*n.*) a large, edible sea-fish.

coddle (*v.*) to pamper; to pet. CODDLED (*adj.*).

41

code (*n.*) 1. a set of laws or rules. 2. words or signs having a secret meaning. CODE (*v.*) to give words a secret meaning.

codify (*v.*) to write down laws or rules.

coerce (*v.*) to compel. COERCION (*n.*).

coffee (*n.*) 1. a tropical shrub. 2. the beverage made from its ground and roasted seeds.

coffer (*n.*) a treasure-chest.

coffin (*n.*) a box in which a dead body is placed for burial or cremation. COFFIN (*v.*) to place in a coffin.

cog (*n.*) a tooth-like projection on the rim of a wheel.

cogitate (*v.*) to think about. COGITATION (*n.*).

coherent (*adj.*) sensible.

cohesion (*n.*) unity.

cohesive (*adj.*) united.

coil (*v.*) to wind in loops. COIL (*n.*) a length wound in loops.

coin (*n.*) a metal piece of money. COIN (*v.*). 1. to make into money; to mint. 2. to invent.

coinage (*n.*) the metal money in general use.

coincide (*v.*) 1. to agree or fit exactly. 2. to happen at the same time.

coincidence (*n.*) 1. exact agreement. 2. events which puzzle by happening at the same time.

coiner (*n.*) one who makes or mints coins, true or false.

coke (*n.*) the remains of coal after making gas from it.

cold (*adj.*) 1. chilly. 2. unfeeling. COLD (*n.*) a chill.

coldness (*n.*) 1. chilliness. 2. unfriendliness.

collaborate (*v.*) to work with another.

collaboration (*n.*) united work. COLLABORATOR (*n.*).

collapse (*n.*) a sudden failure. COLLAPSE (*v.*) to break down.

collar (*n.*) a neckband. COLLAR (*v.*) to seize; to grasp.

colleague (*n.*) a partner; an associate.

collect (*n.* pron. COLL-ect) a short prayer.

collect (*v.* pron. col-LECT) to gather together; to store.

collected (*adj.*) 1. gathered; assembled. 2. calm; unmoved.

collection (*n.*) 1. the whole gathering;

assembly. 2. the offertory taken in a church.

collective (*adj.*) as a whole; all together. COLLECTOR (*n.*).

college (*n.*) 1. an educational institution. 2. a society whose members are learned in the arts or sciences. COLLEGIAN (*n.*).

collide (*v.*) to knock together or against.

collie (*n.*) a Scottish sheep-dog.

collier (*n.*) 1. a coal miner. 2. a coal-carrying ship.

colliery (*n.*) a coal mine. (*pl.* COLLIERIES).

colon (*n.*) a punctuation mark (:).

colonel (*n.*) the commander of a regiment.

colonial (*adj.*) concerning a colony.

colonist (*n.*) an inhabitant of a colony.

colonize (*v.*) to settle in a new land.

colony (*n.*) 1. a settlement formed in a new land by emigrants. 2. a settled swarm of insects.

colossal (*adj.*) immense.

colossus (*n.*) a giant. See appendix.

colour (*v.*) to dye; to paint. COLOUR (*n.*) a dye; paint.

colour-blind (*adj.*) unable to tell one colour from another.

colourful (*adj.*) bright; gay.

colourless (*adj.*) dull; drab.

colt (*n.*) 1. a young horse. (*fem.* FILLY). 2. a young cricket professional. COLT (*v.*) to frisk; to frolic. COLTISH (*adj.*).

column (*n.*) 1. a round pillar. 2. a strip of printing. 3. troops in marching order.

coma (*n.*) a deep sleep.

comb (*v.*) to dress the hair. COMB (*n.*) 1. a toothed implement for dressing the hair. 2. a cock's crest. 3. bees' storage-place for honey.

combat (*v.*) to fight against. COMBAT (*n.*) a fight.

combatant (*n.*) a fighter; an antagonist.

combative (*adj.*) fight-loving; quarrelsome.

combination (*n.*) an alliance; a league.

combine (*v.* pron. com-BINE) to unite; to co-operate. COMBINE (*n.* pron. COM-bine) a union of business firms.

combustible (*adj.*) taking fire easily.

combustion (*n.*) a burning; consuming.

come (*v.*) to move towards; to arrive.

comedian (*n.*) a fun-maker.

comedy (*n.*) an amusing play or incident.

comeliness (*n.*) grace; charm.

comely (*adj.*) pleasing.

comet (*n.*) a starlike body having a shining tail.

comfort (*v.*) to console; to cheer. COMFORT (*n.*) ease; contentment.

comfortable (*adj.*) cosy; happy.

comforter (*n.*) 1. one who consoles. 2. a scarf.

comfortless (*adj.*) uneasy; wretched.

comic (*adj.*) funny; laughable.

comically (*adv.*) amusingly; mirthfully.

coming (*adj.*) approaching; future.

comma (*n.*) a mark of punctuation (,).

command (*v.*) to order; to direct. COMMAND (*n.*) an order.

commander (*v.*) to take; to seize.

commander (*n.*) a leader.

commanding (*adj.*) able; impressive.

commandment (*n.*) a divine law.

commando (*n.*) 1. a soldier trained for dangerous service. 2. a small body of swiftly-moving, picked troops.

commemorate (*v.*) to honour by remembering.

commemoration (*n.*) an act of remembrance.

commence (*v.*) to begin.

commencement (*n.*) a beginning.

commend (*v.*) to praise; to recommend.

commendable (*adj.*) praiseworthy.

commendation (*n.*) praise; approval.

comment (*v.*) to remark; to say.

commentary (*n.*) a series of remarks. (*pl.* COMMENTARIES).

commentator (*n.*) one who explains; describes.

commerce (*n.*) trade, especially with foreign countries.

commercial (*adj.*) concerning trade and commerce.

commission (*n.*) 1. the act of committing (see COMMIT). 2. an appointment to an office of trust and authority. 3. a body appointed to investigate and report upon some public matter. 4. money paid in accordance with business done. COMMISSION (*v.*) to give a commission; to empower.

commit (*v.*) 1. to do. 2. to entrust. 3. to imprison.

commitment (*n.*) 1. an engagement. 2. a responsibility.

committal (*n.*) imprisonment.

committee (*n.*) a body of people chosen for some special work.

commodious (*adj.*) roomy; spacious.

commodities (*n. pl.*) goods; wares. (*sing.* COMMODITY).

common (*adj.*) 1. ordinary. 2. public. 3. vulgar. COMMON (*n.*) a tract of public land.

commoner (*n.*) one who is not a noble.

commonly (*adv.*) usually; generally.

commonplace (*n.*) anything very ordinary. COMMONPLACE (*adj.*) well-known; uninteresting.

Commons (*n. pl.*) 1. Members of the House of Commons as a body. 2. the House of Commons.

commonwealth (*n*) a self-governing state or states.

commotion (*n.*) a bustle; disturbance.

communal (*adj.*) public.

commune (*v.*) to talk one with another.

communicate (*v.*) to inform; to correspond with.

communication (*n.*) news; information.

communion (*n.*) 1. fellowship; union in worship. 2. the Lord's Supper.

community (*n.*) the public. (*pl.* COMMUNITIES).

compact (*adj.* pron. kom-PACT) 1. closely packed. 2. concise. COMPACT (*n.* pron. KOM-pact) an agreement; a covenant.

companion (*n.*) a friend; an associate. COMPANIONSHIP (*n.*).

companionable (*adj.*) friendly; agreeable.

company (*n.*) a group; an assembly. (*pl.* COMPANIES).

comparable (*adj.*) alike; similar.

compare (*v.*) to liken.

comparison (*n.*) likeness; similarity.

compartment (*n.*) a part shut off from the rest by partitions.

compass (*n.*) a direction finder. COMPASS (*v.*) to walk round; to encircle.

compasses (*n. pl.*) an instrument for drawing circles.

compassion (*n.*) sympathy; pity.

compassionate (*adj.*) sympathetic; pitying.

compatriot (*n.*) a fellow-countryman.

compel (*v.*) to force; to make. COMPELLING (*adj.*).

compensate (*v.*) to make amends. COMPENSATORY (*adj.*).

compensation (*n.*) a recompense; amends.

compete (*v.*) to strive against another; to vie with.

competence (*n.*) 1. ability; fitness. 2. a suitable amount.

competent (*adj.*) capable; fit.

competition (*n.*) a contest; rivalry. COMPETITOR (*n.*).

competitive (*adj.*) rival.

compile (*v.*) to collect; to make a book by collecting extracts from other books. COMPILATION (*n.*).

complacence (*n.*) contentment.

complacent (*adj.*) satisfied.

complain (*v.*) to grumble.

complaint (*n.*) 1. a grievance. 2. an ailment.

complement (*n.*) the amount needed to make anything full, whole or complete; the difference between the part and the whole. COMPLEMENTARY (*adj.*).

complete (*adj.*) whole. COMPLETE (*v.*) to finish.

completion (*n.*) the ending; conclusion.

complex (*adj.*) composed of many parts.

complexion (*n.*) colouring and texture of a person's face.

complexity (*n.*) anything composed of many parts.

complicate (*v.*) to entangle; to make difficult.

complication (*n.*) a difficulty; problem.

compliment (*v.*) to praise. COMPLIMENT (*n.*) a tribute.

complimentary (*adj.*) given as praise.

comply (*v.*) to consent; to yield. COMPLIANCE (*n.*).

component (*n.*) a part necessary to make up a complete machine, instrument, etc.

compose (*v.*) 1. to invent. 2. to make calm.

composition (*n.*) 1. a piece of original writing or music. 2. a mixture.

compositor (*n.*) one who sets up type for printing.

composure (*n.*) calmness; coolness.

compound (*v.*) to mix. COMPOUND (*n.*) a mixture.

comprehend (*v.*) to understand.

comprehensible (*adj.*) understandable.

comprehension (*n.*) intelligence; understanding.

comprehensive (*adj.*) wide; all-including.

compress (*v.*) to press or squeeze tightly together. COMPRESSION (*n.*).

comprise (*v.*) to contain; to include.

compromise (*n.*) a settlement made by both sides giving way a little. COMPROMISE (*v.*) to settle by agreement; to bargain.

compulsion (*n.*) force.

compulsory (*adj.*) unavoidable; enforced.

compunction (*n.*) regret; remorse.

computation (*n.*) a calculation; reckoning.

compute (*v.*) to count; to calculate.

computer (*n.*) an electrical calculating machine.

comrade (*n.*) a friend. COMRADESHIP (*n.*).

con (*v.*) to study; to read.

concave (*adj.*) hollow; saucer-like in shape; opposite to convex.

conceal (*v.*) to hide.

concealment (*n.*) a hiding.

concede (*v.*) to allow; to grant.

conceit (*n.*) vanity. CONCEITED (*adj.*).

conceive (*v.*) to suppose; to think. CONCEIVABLE (*adj.*).

concentrate (*v.*) 1. to pack closely together. 2. to fix one's mind on.

concentration (*n.*) close attention; fixity. CONCENTRATED (*adj.*).

conception (*n.*) a thought; an idea.

concern (*v.*) to take interest in; to be anxious about. CONCERN (*n.*) 1. interest; anxiety. 2. an enterprise; business.

concerning (*prep.*) about.

concert (*n.*) a musical entertainment.

concerted (*adj.*) planned; arranged.

concession (*n.*) a grant; an allowance.

conciliate (*v.*) to make friendly. CONCILIATOR (*n.*).

conciliation (*n.*) a peace-making.

conciliatory (*adj.*) soothing; calming.

concise (*adj.*) brief; short.

conciseness (*n.*) brevity.

conclude (*v.*) 1. to end. 2. to decide.

conclusion (*n.*) 1. a finish. 2. a decision.

conclusive (*adj.*) 1. final. 2. definite.

concoct (*v.*) to make up; to invent.

concoction (*n.*) 1. a mixture. 2. a made-up story.

concord (*n.*) unity; agreement.

concourse (*n.*) a crowd; multitude.

concrete (*adj.*) real. CONCRETE (*n.*) a mixture of cement, stones and water.

concur (*v.*) to agree; to assent.

concurrence (*n.*) co-operation.

concussion (*n.*) 1. a violent shock. 2. a brain injury.

condemn (*v.*) to hold guilty.

condemnation (*n.*) judgment given against a person or action.

condensation (*n.*) 1. a reduction. 2. a cooling.

condense (*v.*) 1. to reduce. 2. to cool.

condenser (*n.*) 1. apparatus for cooling vapour into liquid. 2. appliance for collecting or condensing electricity.

condescend (*v.*) to stoop; to patronize.

condescension (*n.*) patronage.

condiment (*n.*) a seasoning; relish.

condition (*n.*) the state a thing is in.

conditional (*adj.*) depending on something else; limited.

condole (*v.*) to sympathize. CONDOLENCE (*n.*).

condone (*v.*) 1. to pardon; to forgive. 2. to overlook a wrongdoing which ought to be punished. CONDONATION (*n.*).

conduct (*n.* pron. KON-duct) behaviour. CONDUCT (*v.* pron. kon-DUCT) 1. to lead; to guide. 2. to carry; to transmit.

conductor (*n.*) 1. a guide; leader. 2. a carrier; transmitter. (*fem.* CONDUCT-RESS).

conduit (*n.*) a water-channel.

cone (*n.*) anything shaped like a steeple. CONICAL (*adj.*).

confection (*n.*) a sweet; a sugared fruit. CONFECTIONER (*n.*).

confectionery (*n.*) sweets and fancy cakes.

confederate (*v.*) to unite in a league; to support one another. CONFEDERATE (*n.*) an ally; a supporter.

confederation (*n.*) a league; an alliance.

confer (*v.*) to discuss with; to bestow upon.

conference (*n.*) a meeting for discussion.

confess (*v.*) to own up; to admit. CON-FESSOR (*n.*).

confession (*n.*) an admission; avowal.

confide (*v.*) to trust to or in. CONFIDENT (*adj.*).

confidence (*n.*) trust; belief in.

confidential (*adj.*) not to be repeated or disclosed.

confine (*v.*) to keep within bounds; to shut up.

confinement (*n.*) imprisonment; detention.

confirm (*v.*) 1. to strengthen. 2. to make sure.

confirmation (*n.*) 1. proof; certainty. 2. admission to Church membership. CONFIRMATIVE (*adj.*).

confiscate (*v.*) 1. to take for public use. 2. to take forcibly.

confiscation (*n.*) a taking; seizing.

conflagration (*n.*) a great fire.

conflict (*n.* pron. KON-flict) a struggle; fight. CONFLICT (*v.* pron. kon-FLICT) to disagree; to oppose.

confliction (*n.*) disagreement; opposition. CONFLICTING (*adj.*).

conform (*v.*) to behave according to rule or law; to comply.

conformity (*n.*) agreement; likeness. CONFORMABLE (*adj.*).

confound (*v.*) to mix up; to defeat.

confounded (*adj.*) upset; defeated.

confront (*v.*) to face. CONFRONTING (*adj.*). CONFRONTATION (*n.*).

confuse (*v.*) 1. to jumble together. 2. to bewilder.

confusion (*n.*) 1. a mixture; disorder. 2. tumult; ruin.

congeal (*v.*) to curdle; to become solid.

congenial (*adj.*) 1. alike; akin. 2. pleasing; sympathetic.

congest (*v.*) to pack together; to overcrowd. CONGESTED (*adj.*).

congestion (*n.*) an overcrowding.

conglomerate (*adj.*) mixed up; confused.

conglomeration (*n.*) a higgledy-piggledy mixture.

congratulate (*v.*) to offer good wishes. CONGRATULATORY (*adj.*).

congratulation (*n.*) an expression of goodwill.

congregate (*v.*) to gather together; to assemble.

congregation (*n.*) an assembly for religious worship.

congress (*n.*) 1. an assembly of representatives who discuss and decide. 2. (capital C) the national legislature of the United States.

conical (*adj.*) cone-shaped.

conifer (*n.*) a cone-bearing tree.

conjecture (*v.*) to suppose; to guess. CONJECTURE (*n.*) a guess; supposition.

conjunction (*n.*) 1. a connection. 2. a word used to join sentences.

conjure (*v.*) to work magic; to mystify.

conjure(o)r (*n.*) a magician; wizard; a juggler.

connect (*v.*) to join; to unite. CONNECTION (*n.*).

conquer (*v.*) to gain the victory; to overcome.

conqueror (*n.*) a victor.

conquest (*n.*) a victory; capture.

conscience (*n.*) a knowledge of right and wrong.

conscientious (*adj.*) upright; honourable.

conscious (*adj.*) awake; knowing.

consciousness (*n.*) ability to use one's senses.

conscript (*n.*) one compelled to serve in the national forces. CONSCRIPT (*adj.*).

conscription (*n.*) compulsory service.

consecrate (*v.*) to make sacred. CONSECRATED (*adj.*).

consecration (*n.*) a making holy.

consecutive (*adj.*) following in correct order.

consent (*v.*) to agree. CONSENT (*n.*) permission.

consequence (*n.*) a result; an effect.

consequent (*adj.*) following after.

consequently (*adv.*) therefore.

conservation (*n.*) preservation.

conservative (*adj.*) able to preserve.

conservatory (*n.*) a greenhouse.

conserve (*v.*) to preserve; to keep. CONSERVE (*n.*) jam.

consider (*v.*) to think about; to reflect.

considerable (*adj.*) large; notable.

considerate (*adj.*) thoughtful; mindful of others.

consideration (*n.*) thoughtfulness; care for others.

consign (*v.*) to send goods or a person to a destination.

consignee (*n.*) the receiver.

consignment (*n.*) a load; shipment.

consignor (*n.*) the sender.

consist (*v.*) to be made of.

consistency (*n.*) the thickness; firmness.

consistent (*adj.*) in agreement with.

consolation (*n.*) comfort; relief.

console (*v.*) to comfort.

consolidate (*v.*) to make solid or firm.

consolidation (*n.*) soundness; solidity.

consonant (*adj.*) in agreement or harmony with. CONSONANT (*n.*) a letter or sound which cannot be spoken without a vowel.

consort (*v.*) to keep company with. CONSORT (*n.*) a husband or wife.

conspicuous (*adj.*) clearly seen; outstanding.

conspicuously (*adv.*) plainly; prominently.

conspiracy (*n.*) a plot. (*pl.* CONSPIRACIES). CONSPIRATOR (*n.*).

conspire (*v.*) to plot.

constable (*n.*) a policeman.

constabulary (*n.*) the police force.

constancy (*n.*) faithfulness; steadfastness.

constant (*adj.*) unchanging.

constantly (*adv.*) always; often.

constellation (*n.*) a group of fixed stars having a name.

consternation (*n.*) terror; dismay.

constituency (*n.*) a body of voters who elect a Member of Parliament.

constituent (*n.*) 1. a part. 2. a voter.

constitute (*v.*) to compose; to form.

constitution (*n.*) 1. the rules which a society or government must keep. 2. the state of one's natural health.

constitutional (*adj.*) lawful. CONSTITUTIONAL (*n.*) a health-giving walk.

constrain (*v.*) to compel.

constraint (*n.*) compulsion.

constrict (*v.*) to contract; to squeeze.

constricted (*adj.*) cramped.

constriction (*n.*) a tightness; contraction.

construct (*v.*) to make; to build.

construction (*n.*) anything made.

constructive (*adj.*) uplifting; encouraging.

consul (*n.*) a state's agent in a foreign town, who protects its subjects there. CONSULATE (*n.*). CONSULAR (*adj.*).

consult (*v.*) to ask advice.

consultant (*n.*) one able to advise.

consultation (*n.*) a meeting to consider something.

consume (*v.*) 1. to use up. 2. to eat.

consumer (*n.*) a user; buyer.

consumption (*n.*) 1. the amount used. 2. a lung disease.

contact (*v.*) to touch; to meet.

contagion (*n.*) the spreading of disease by touching sufferers.

contagious (*adj.*) catching; spread by touching.

contain (*v.*) to hold within; to include. CONTAINER (*n.*).

contaminate (*v.*) 1. to infect. 2. to stain.

contamination (*n.*) 1. infection. 2. uncleanness.

contemplate (*v.*) 1. to think about. 2. to study.

contemplation (*n.*) thought; study.

contemporary (*adj.*) belonging to the same generation.

contempt (*n.*) scorn; disdain.

contemptible (*adj.*) worthless; despicable.

contemptuous (*adj.*) scornful; disdainful.

contend (*v.*) 1. to fight. 2. to try to gain. CONTENDER (*n.*).

content (*n.* pron. KON-tent) all within a vessel (volume), or within a boundary (area). CONTENT (*adj.* pron. kon-TENT) satisfied; pleased. CONTENT (*v.*) to satisfy.

contentious (*adj.*) quarrelsome.

contentment (*n.*) happiness; satisfaction.

contents (*n. pl.*) 1. all contained within anything. 2. a list of matters written about in a book.

contest (*v.*) to strive; to compete. CONTEST (*n.*) 1. a struggle. 2. a competition.

contestant (*n.*) a competitor; rival.

context (*n.*) the words of a speech or writing which precede and follow any words quoted.

continent (*n.*) one of the large land masses on the globe. CONTINENTAL (*adj.*).

continual (*adj.*) going on without a break or stop.

continually (*adv.*) ceaselessly.

continuation (*n.*) an extension; addition.

continue (*v.*) to add to; to prolong.

continuous (*adj.*) unbroken; unceasing.

continuously (*adv.*) endlessly.

contort (*v.*) to twist out of shape; to distort.

contortion (*n.*) a twisting of the body or limbs.

contour (*n.*) an outline.

contraband (*n.*) smuggled goods. CONTRABAND (*adj.*) forbidden; prohibited by law.

contract (*v.* pron. kon-TRACT) to shorten.

contract (*v.* pron. KON-tract) to agree; to undertake. CONTRACT (*n.*) an agreement.

contraction (*n.*) a shortening.

contractor (*n.*) one who undertakes to do certain work.

contradict (*v.*) to deny; to gainsay.

contradiction (*n.*) a statement opposite to one already made.

contradictory (*adj.*) opposite; denying.

contrary (*adj.*) opposite; against. CONTRARY (*n.*) the opposite or different opinion, intention or action.

contrast (*n.* pron. KON-trast) a difference; an unlikeness.

contrast (*v.* pron. kon-TRAST) to find or show differences.

contribute (*v.*) to give something; to help.

contribution (*n.*) a gift; donation.

contributor (*n.*) a supporter. CONTRIBUTORY (*adj.*).

contrite (*adj.*) sorry for; penitent.

contrition (*n.*) regret; sorrow.

contrivance (*n.*) a device; machine.

contrive (*v.*) to plan; to manage.

control (*v.*) to regulate; to guide. CONTROL (*n.*) the mastery.

controllable (*adj.*) manageable. CONTROLLER (*n.*).

controversial (*adj.*) concerned with disputes; doubtful.

controversy (*n.*) dispute, debate.

contumely (*n.*) insulting words; abuse.

contusion (*n.*) a bruise.

conundrum (*n.*) a riddle.

convalesce (*v.*) to recover health. CONVALESCENT (*adj.*).

convalescence (*n.*) a gradual recovery of health.

convene (*v.*) to call a meeting. CONVENER (*n.*).

convenience (*n.*) the fitness; suitability.

convenient (*adj.*) fit; suitable.

convent (*n.*) a house of nuns.

convention (*n.*) 1. an assembly of representatives. 2. a general custom.

conventional (*adj.*) not original; customary.

converge (*v.*) to approach a point from different directions.

conversant (*adj.*) acquainted with.

conversation (*n.*) talk between two or more people.

converse (*v.* pron. kon-VERSE) to talk to. CONVERSE (*n.* pron. KON-verse) the opposite.

conversely (*adv.*) the other way round; otherwise.

conversion (*n.*) a change from one belief, side, etc., to another.

convert (*v.* pron. kon-VERT) to change. CONVERT (*n.* pron. KON-vert) one who has changed.

convertible (*adj.*) can be changed into something else.

convex (*adj.*) curved outwards; the opposite of concave.

convey (*v.*) 1. to carry; to transport. 2. to transfer property.

conveyance (*n.*) 1. the means of transport; a vehicle. 2. the legal transfer of property from one person to another.

convict (*v.* pron. kon-VICT) to prove guilty. CONVICT (*n.* pron. KON-vict) an imprisoned criminal.

conviction (*n.*) 1. a proving guilty. 2. a firm belief.

convince (*v.*) to make one feel sure; to satisfy.

convincing (*adj.*) satisfying. CONVINCINGLY (*adv.*).

convivial (*adj.*) festive.

conviviality (*n.*) good-fellowship.

convolvulus (*n.*) a quick-growing climbing plant.

convoy (*n.*) a protected fleet of ships. CONVOY (*v.*) to guard on a journey.

convulse (*v.*) to shake severely.

convulsion (*n.*) 1. a fit; spasm. 2. a tumult. 3. an earthquake.

convulsive (*adj.*) spasmodic.

con(e)y (*n.*) a rabbit. (*pl.* CONIES).

cook (*v.*) to prepare food by heat. COOK (*n.*) one who cooks food.

cookery (*n.*) skill in making food edible.

cool (*adj.*) 1. slightly cold. 2. quiet; calm. COOL (*v.*) 1. to make colder. 2. to become calmer.

coolly (*adv.*) quietly; without excitement.

coolness (*n.*) 1. coldness. 2. unconcern.

cooper (*n.*) a maker of barrels, casks, etc.

co-operate (*v.*) to work together; to help one another.

co-operation (*n.*) a working to help one another.

co-operative (*adj.*) ready to help.

co-ordinate (*adj.*) of the same rank or authority. CO-ORDINATE (*v.*) to make equal; to bring to the same level.

CO-ORDINATES (*n. pl.*) lines which fix the exact position of a point.

coot (*n.*) a small black water fowl of the duck family.

cope (*v.*) to handle successfully. COPE (*n.*) a priest's mantle or vestment.

copious (*adj.*) abundant.

copper (*n.*) a hard, reddish metal. COPPERY (*adj.*).

coppers (*n. pl.*) pence and halfpence.

copse or **coppice** (*nn.*) a grove of trees.

copy (*v.*) to imitate. COPY (*n.*) a likeness. (*pl.* COPIES).

copyright (*n.*) the sole right to print or sell a book, etc.

coracle (*n.*) a light, portable boat of wickerwork covered over with leather or skins (as used by the ancient Britons).

coral (*n.*) a red, stony substance formed by tiny creatures in warm seas.

cord (*n.*) strong, thick string.

cordage (*n.*) ropes.

cordial (*adj.*) friendly; heartfelt.

cordiality (*n.*) friendliness.

cordially (*adv.*) warmly; gladly.

cordon (*n.*) a ring of guards. CORDON (*v.*) to surround with guards.

corduroy (*n.*) a strong, hard-wearing cloth.

core (*n.*) the centre; heart.

cork (*n.*) the bark of the cork tree and the stopper made from it. CORK (*v.*) to stop or plug with a cork.

cormorant (*n.*) a greedy diving-bird.

corn (*n.*) 1. grain. 2. a painful, hard growth upon the toe.

corner (*n.*) a sharp bend where two lines. walls, streets, etc., meet. CORNER (*v.*) to drive into a trap.

cornered (*adj.*) trapped.

cornet (*n.*) a brass or silver trumpet

coronation (*n.*) the ceremony of crowning a sovereign.

coroner (*n.*) an official who tries to find the cause of a sudden or violent death.

coronet (*n.*) a small crown.

corporal (*n.*) army non-commissioned officer. CORPORAL (*adj.*) bodily.

corporation (*n.*) 1. the body of persons governing a city or town. 2. a united body of persons.

corps (*n.*) a large body of troops.

corpse (*n.*) a dead body.

corpulent (*adj.*) stout; bulky.

corral (*n.*) an enclosure for cattle or horses. CORRAL (*v.*).

correct (*adj.*) exact; accurate. CORRECT (*v.*) 1. to set right. 2. to punish.

correction (*n.*) 1. a making right. 2. punishment.

correspond (*v.*) 1. to match; to fit. 2. to write letters to.

correspondence (*n.*) 1. agreement. 2. letters.

correspondent (*n.*) a letter-writer.

corridor (*n.*) a covered passage in a building.

corroborate (*v.*) to strengthen; to make more certain.

corroboration (*n.*) a strengthening; proving.

corrode (*v.*) to crumble away; to rust.

corrosion (*n.*) 1. rust. 2. action of wearing away.

corrugate (*v.*) to furrow; to wrinkle. CORRUGATED (*adj.*).

corrupt (*v.*) 1. to decay. 2. to bribe, or tempt to do wrong. CORRUPT (*adj.*) 1. rotten. 2. evil.

corruption (*n.*) 1. decay. 2. dishonesty.

corruptly (*adv.*) dishonestly.

corsair (*n.*) a pirate; sea-rover.

corset (*n.*) a close-fitting undergarment worn to support the trunk. CORSET (*v.*) to enclose in a corset.

corvette (*n.*) a small, speedy warship.

cosily (*adv.*) snugly; comfortably.

cosiness (*n.*) comfort; snugness.

cosmetic (*n.*) skin powder or cream.

cosmic rays (*n. pl.*) radio-active particles which reach the earth from outer space.

cosmonaut (*n.*) one who travels in space (U.S.S.R.).

cosmopolitan (*adj.*) world-wide; universal.

cost (*v.*) to have a price or value. COST (*n.*) the price.

costermonger or coster (*n.*) a street fruit-seller.

costliness (*n.*) a high value.

costly (*adj.*) highly priced; expensive.

costume (*n.*) a dress; uniform.

costumier (*n.*) a maker or seller of costumes.

cosy (*adj.*) snug; comfortable. COSY (*n.*) a padded covering for a tea-pot.

cot (*n.*) a child's bed; a crib.

coterie (*n.*) a brotherhood; a band.

cotillion (*n.*) a lively dance.

cotton (*n.*) 1. a plant bearing soft, white down. 2. cloth made from this.

cottage (*n.*) a small house, often with thatched roof.

couch (*v.*) to lie down. COUCH (*n.*) a sofa; a bed.

cough (*n.*) a sudden, noisy outburst of air from the lungs. COUGH (*v.*).

council (*n.*) an assembly which discusses and decides.

councillor (*n.*) a member of a council.

counsel (*v.*) to advise. COUNSEL (*n.*) 1. a lawyer; barrister. 2. advice.

counsellor (*n.*) an adviser.

count (*v.*) to number; to reckon. COUNT (*n.*) a nobleman. (*fem.* COUNTESS).

countenance (*v.*) to support; to permit. COUNTENANCE (*n.*) the face or expression.

counter (*v.*) to oppose. COUNTER (*n.*) 1. serving bench in a shop. 2. an imitation coin.

counteract (*v.*) to defeat by doing the opposite; to hinder.

counterfeit (*v.*) 1. to make an imitation. 2. to sham. COUNTERFEIT (*adj.*) false; sham.

counterpane (*n.*) a coverlet for a bed.

counterpart (*n.*) a copy; twin.

counterpoise (*v.*) to balance. COUNTER-POISE (*n.*) a weight equal to another.

countersign (*n.*) a watchword; password.

countless (*adj.*) numberless; innumerable.

country (*n.*) 1. one's native land. 2. open land outside towns. (*pl.* COUNTRIES). COUNTRY (*adj.*) belonging to the country; rural.

countryman (*n.*) 1. a fellow-citizen or native. 2. a dweller in the country-side.

countryside (*n.*) a country district.

county (*n.*) a shire. (*pl.* COUNTIES).

coup (*n.*) a successful stroke or action, usually long prepared.

couple (*v.*) to join two things together. COUPLE (*n.*) a pair; two.

coupling (*n.*) a connecting link.

coupon (*n.*) a ticket exchangeable for money or goods.

courage (*n.*) bravery.

courageous (*adj.*) brave. COURAGEOUSLY (*adv.*).

courier (*n.*) a swift messenger.

course (*n.*) 1. the route; direction. 2. one's progress; method. COURSE (*v.*) to hunt.

court (*v.*) to try to please. COURT (*n.*) 1. a place of justice. 2. a ruler's palace. 3. a yard.

courteous (*adj.*) respectful; polite.

courtesy (*n.*) politeness; civility.

courtier (*n.*) 1. one who attends a ruler's court. 2. a well-mannered person.

courtly (*adj.*) well-mannered.

cousin (*n.*) the child of an uncle or aunt.

covenant (*n.*) a written agreement.

cover (*v.*) 1. to spread over. 2. to hide. 3. to include. COVER (*n.*) 1. anything placed over something else. 2. a shelter.

covering (*n.*) a protection.

covet (*v.*) to desire greatly; to envy.

covetous (*adj.*) over-eager for gain; greedy.

cow (*n.*) female of many animals, the ox, elephant, etc. COW (*v.*) to make afraid; to intimidate.

coward (*n.*) a person without courage.

cowardice (*n.*) fear; timidity.

cowardly (*adj.*) afraid; timid.

cower (*v.*) to shrink from; to cringe.

cowl (*n.*) 1. a chimney cover. 2. a monk's hood.

cowslip (*n.*) a yellow meadow-flower.

cox (*v.*) to steer.

coxswain (*n.*) a boat's steersman.

coy (*adj.*) shy; modest. COYLY (*adv.*).

crab (*n.*) a round-backed shellfish.

crabbed (*adj.*) 1. surly. 2. ill-written.

crack (*v.*) 1. to split without breaking completely. 2. to make a sharp, whip-like sound. CRACK (*n.*) 1. a small opening or split. 2. a snapping noise. CRACK (*adj.*) first-rate. CRACKED (*adj.*).

cracker (*n.*) 1. a biscuit. 2. a firework.

crackle (*v.*) to make snapping noises. CRACKLE (*n.*) the noise of dry sticks burning.

cradle (*n.*) 1. a rocking bed for a baby. 2. the timber framework supporting a vessel when building. CRADLE (*v.*) to lay, or rock, in a cradle, or in the arms.

craft (*n.*) 1. skill. 2. a ship. 3. an occupation. 4. cunning.

craftily (*adv.*) cunningly.

craftiness (*n.*) cunning; slyness.

craftsman (*n.*) a skilled workman. CRAFTSMANSHIP (*n.*).

crafty (*adj.*) sly; cunning.

crag (*n.*) a steep, rugged rock.

cram (*v.*) to ram in; to overfill.

crammed (*adj.*) tightly packed; overfull.

cramp (*v.*) to squeeze; to tighten. CRAMP (*n.*) a sudden, severe pain in a muscle; a spasm.

cranberry (*n.*) a red, sour berry used in jam and sauce-making. (*pl.* CRANBERRIES).

crane (*n.*) 1. a long-necked wading-bird. 2. a machine for raising heavy weights. CRANE (*v.*) to thrust the chest and neck forward.

cranium (*n.*) the skull. CRANIAL (*adj.*).

crank (*v.*) to wind; to turn. CRANK (*n.*) 1. a bend; turn. 2. an odd, faddy person.

cranky (*adj.*) 1. unsteady. 2. faddy; whimsical.

cranny (*n.*) a slit; chink. (*pl.* CRANNIES).

crash (*n.*) 1. the loud noise of things breaking. 2. sudden failure or ruin, especially in business. CRASH (*v.*) 1. to break noisily. 2. to fail; to become bankrupt.

crass (*adj.*) stupid; dense.

crate (*n.*) a large packing-case.

crater (*n.*) 1. the mouth of a volcano. 2. a cup-shaped hole in the ground.

cravat (*n.*) a neckcloth or tie.

crave (*v.*) to beg for; to long for.

craven (*adj.*) cowardly. CRAVEN (*n.*) a coward.

crawl (*v.*) to creep on all fours. CRAWL (*n.*).

crayfish (*n.*) a freshwater shellfish like a small lobster.

crayon (*n.*) 1. a pencil or stick of coloured chalk. 2. a drawing made with crayons. CRAYON (*v.*) to sketch with crayons.

craze (*n.*) a popular fashion; a fad.

craziness (*n.*) madness; folly. CRAZILY (*adv.*).

crazy (*adj.*) 1. unsound; foolish. 2. jumbled.

creak (*n.*) a sharp, harsh noise. CREAK (*v.*) to make such a noise.

cream (*n.*) 1. the rich, oily substance

which rises to the surface of milk. 2. the richest and best part of anything. CREAM (v.) to skim off, or separate, cream from milk. CREAMY (adj.).

crease (n.) 1. a line or mark made by folding. 2. a limiting line marked on a cricket pitch. CREASE (v.) to mark by folding, squeezing, etc. CREASED (adj.).

create (v.) to make; to invent.

creation (n.) 1. all that God has made; the universe. 2. anything made or invented.

creative (adj.) inventive.

creator (n.) 1. one who invents; originates. 2. THE CREATOR = GOD.

creature (n.) 1. a living, moving being. 2. a wretch, vagabond.

credence (n.) belief; trust.

credentials (n. pl.) papers proving the truth of a person's statements or claims.

credibility (n.) truth; reliability.

credible (adj.) believable; trustworthy.

credit (n.) 1. reputation. 2. goods sold to one who is trusted to pay later. 3. the time allowed for payment. CREDIT (v.) to believe; to trust.

creditable (adj.) honourable.

creditor (n.) one to whom a debt is owing.

credulity (n.) ready belief; trust.

credulous (adj.) too ready to believe; simple.

creed (n.) a statement of belief; faith.

creek (n.) a narrow, coastal inlet.

creep (v.) 1. to move on hands and knees. 2. to move silently on tiptoe.

creeper (n.) 1. one who creeps. 2. a climbing plant.

cremate (v.) to burn.

cremation (n.) a burning to ashes.

crematorium (n.) a place where bodies of the dead are cremated.

creosote (n.) an oily fluid taken from tar.

crescent (adj.) shaped like the new moon.

cress (n.) a water plant bearing edible leaves.

crest (n.) 1. a tuft or comb on a bird's head. 2. a design on a coat of arms. 3. the top; summit.

crestfallen (adj.) downcast; disappointed.

cretonne (n.) unglazed cotton cloth,

printed on one side with coloured patterns.

crevasse (n.) a deep crack in a glacier.

crevice (n.) a crack, or fissure, especially in rock.

crew (n.) 1. the body of men manning a ship. 2. a gang; crowd.

crib (n.) 1. a baby's bed. 2. a manger. CRIB (v.) 1. to cheat; to copy unfairly. 2. to cage; to coop.

cricket (n.) 1. outdoor game for two teams, eleven a side, played with ball, bats and wickets. (CRICKETER, n.). 2. a small, jumping, chirping insect.

crime (n.) wrongdoing; sin.

criminal (adj.) illegal. CRIMINAL (n.) a lawbreaker.

crimson (adj.) deep red in colour.

cringe (v.) to crouch; to shrink from in fear.

crinkle (v.) to wrinkle; to curl. CRINKLE (n.) a wrinkle.

cripple (v.) to disable; to ruin. CRIPPLE (n.) a lame person.

crisis (n.) a turning-point; a decisive moment. (pl. CRISES).

crisp (adj.) curly; brittle.

critic (n.) one who examines and judges.

critical (adj.) fault-finding; decisive for good or evil.

criticism (n.) an opinion; a judgment.

criticize (v.) to examine and judge.

croak (n.) the noise made by frog or raven. CROAK (v.) to look on the worse side of things.

crochet (n.) fine knitting worked with a hooked needle. CROCHET (v.) to knit with a crochet needle.

crockery (n.) earthenware vessels.

crocodile (n.) a large, lizard-like reptile.

crocus (n.) a dwarf bulbous plant with bright flowers.

crony (n.) a bosom friend.

crook (n.) a hook; a hooked staff. CROOK (v.) to bend; to curve.

crooked (adj.) 1. bent. 2. dishonest.

croon (v.) 1. to sing softly to oneself. 2. to sing in a low, moaning tone. CROONER (n.).

crop (v.) 1. to harvest. 2. to cut short. CROP (n.) 1. the produce of field or farm. 2. a haircut. 3. a riding-whip. 4. the first stomach of many birds; the craw.

cross (*n.*) 1. anything X-shaped. 2. a misfortune; worry. CROSS (*v.*) 1. to pass from one side to the other. 2. to oppose; to make angry. CROSS (*adj.*) annoyed. CROSSLY (*adv.*).

crotchet (*n.*) a whimsical fancy; a black-headed note in music; half a minim.

crouch (*v.*) to stoop with the knees bent; to bend down. CROUCH (*n.*) a stooping; bending.

crow (*v.*) 1. to boast. 2. to triumph. CROW (*n.*) 1. a large, black bird. 2. a cock's cry.

crowd (*n.*) a multitude; throng. CROWD (*v.*) 1. to pack closely together; to cram. 2. to gather in a large number.

crown (*n.*) 1. the symbol of sovereignty placed on a monarch's head at a coronation. 2. a head-wreath, or symbol of victory. 3. the top of many objects, e.g., the head, a hill. CROWN (*v.*) 1. to place a crown on a sovereign's head. 2. to establish the complete success of one's purpose or career.

crucial (*adj.*) 1. cross-shaped. 2. important; decisive.

crucible (*n.*) a melting-pot.

crucifixion (*n.*) a crucifying. THE CRUCIFIXION (*n.*) the putting to death on a cross of Jesus Christ.

crucify (*v.*) to put to death on a cross.

crude (*adj.*) raw; rough. CRUDELY (*adv.*).

cruel (*adj.*) hurtful; inhuman. CRUELLY (*adv.*).

cruelty (*n.*) brutality; savagery.

cruet (*n.*) 1. a small glass table-bottle for holding vinegar or oil. 2. a table-set holding cruet, salt-cellar, and mustard and pepper-pots.

cruise (*v.*) to sail; to voyage. CRUISE (*n.*) a pleasure voyage.

cruiser (*n.*) a warship with a high rate of speed.

cruising (*n.*) sailing for health or pleasure.

crumb (*n.*) a small fragment, especially of bread. CRUMB (*v.*) to break into, or cover with, crumbs.

crumble (*v.*) to break into little pieces.

crumbling (*adj.*) falling to pieces.

crumple (*v.*) to crush gently. CRUMPLE (*n.*) a wrinkle; crease.

crunch (*v.*) 1. to crush with the teeth. 2. to grind underfoot. CRUNCH (*n.*) the noise of chewing or grinding.

crusade (*v.*) to fight in a good cause. CRUSADE (*n.*) 1. a war of Christians against infidels. 2. a campaign against evil.

crusader (*n.*) a warrior who fights in a crusade.

crush (*v.*) 1. to injure by pressing or squeezing. 2. to overcome; to ruin. CRUSH (*n.*) a closely-packed crowd.

crust (*n.*) a hard coating, rind or shell.

crusty (*adj.*) 1. rough and hard. 2. irritable.

crutch (*n.*) a staff, with cross-piece, placed under the arm to support the lame when walking.

crux (*n.*) a difficult or puzzling matter.

cry (*v.*) 1. to weep; to sob. 2. to shout; to yell. CRY (*n.*) a sob; a shout. (*pl.* CRIES).

crying (*adj.*) 1. weeping. 2. calling for notice. CRYING (*n.*) lamentation.

crypt (*n.*) a cellar under a church; a vault.

cryptic (*adj.*) hidden; secret.

crystal (*n.*) 1. a glassy stone having all its sides flat. 2. a clear, bright glass. CRYSTAL (*adj.*) clear; transparent.

crystalline (*adj.*) 1. crystal-shaped. 2. transparent.

crystallize (*v.*) 1. to form into crystals. 2. to boil in sugar.

cub (*n.*) the young of some animals as the bear, fox, etc.

cube (*n.*) a body with six equal square sides or faces.

cubic (*adj.*) having volume; capacity.

cubicle (*n.*) a small bedroom.

cuckoo (*n.*) 1. a bird that lays its eggs in the nests of other birds. 2. a simpleton.

cucumber (*n.*) a long, green, juicy salad vegetable.

cubit (*n.*) an ancient measure of length (45–55 centimetres).

cud (*n.*) food chewed a second time by animals called ruminants, as the cow.

cuddle (*v.*) to snuggle against; to hug lovingly. CUDDLE (*n.*) a close hug.

cudgel (*n.*) a heavy stick.

cue (*n.*) 1. a sign; hint. 2. a rod used in playing billiards.

cuff (*n.*) 1. a slap. 2. the banded end of a sleeve. CUFF (*v.*) to slap with the hand.

cuisine (*n.*) cookery.

culinary (*adj.*) concerned with the kitchen and cooking.

cull (*v.*) to pick here and there; to gather.

culminate (*v.*) to reach the top; to end.

culmination (*n.*) the top; finish.

culpability (*n.*) the guilt; fault.

culpable (*adj.*) blameworthy; guilty.

culprit (*n.*) an offender; a guilty person.

cultivate (*v.*) 1. to till the ground; to grow crops. 2. to train the mind.

cultivated (*adj.*) 1. cared for. 2. trained.

cultivation (*n.*) 1. agriculture. 2. education. 3. giving care to.

cultural (*adj.*) civilizing.

culture (*n.*) the trained state of mind; method of cultivation.

cumber (*v.*) to get in the way of; to hamper.

cumbersome (*adj.*) troublesome; unwieldy.

cumulative (*adj.*) heaped up; increasing.

cumulus (*n.*) a white, woolly cloud. (*pl.* CUMULI).

cunning (*adj.*) skilful; crafty. CUNNING (*n.*) skill; deceit.

cup (*n.*) a small, bell-shaped drinking vessel, standing on a slender shaft and base, or provided with a handle. CUP (*v.*) to place the hands in the form of a cup.

cupidity (*n.*) greed; over-eagerness.

cur (*n.*) a snappy dog; an unworthy man.

curable (*adj.*) can be cured; healed.

curacy (*n.*) the office of a curate.

curate (*n.*) an assisting clergyman.

curative (*n.*) anything that aids healing. CURATIVE (*adj.*) healing.

curator (*n.*) head of a museum, art gallery, etc.

curb (*v.*) to check; to control. CURB (*n.*) a check; bridle. CURBING (*adj.*).

curd (*n.*) thick, sour milk.

curdle (*v.*) to turn sour; to thicken.

cure (*v.*) 1. to heal: to restore. 2. to preserve. CURE (*n.*) 1. a remedy. 2. a recovery.

curfew (*n.*) an order to remain indoors after a stated time.

curio (*n.*) anything rare.

curiosity (*n.*) 1. eagerness to learn. 2. inquisitiveness. 3. a marvel; freak. (*pl.* CURIOSITIES).

curious (*adj.*) 1. interesting. 2. prying; inquisitive. 3. strange; queer. CURIOUSLY (*adv.*).

curl (*v.*) to coil into ringlets. CURL (*n.*) a ringlet.

curlew (*n.*) a long-billed wading-bird.

curling (*n.*) a game played on ice.

curmudgeon (*n.*) a surly, grumpy person.

currant (*n.*) 1. a small, dried grape. 2. shrub bearing clusters of edible berries.

currency (*n.*) 1. anything passed from hand to hand. 2. money in use in a country. 3. publicity.

current (*n.*) the flowing of a liquid (stream), of air (wind), or of electricity. CURRENT (*adj.*) 1. popular; widespread. 2. in the present time; now.

curry (*n.*) a peppery seasoning used with food, chiefly in India. CURRY (*v.*) 1. to rub down a horse with a comb. 2. to seek favour by flattery or servility.

curse (*v.*) 1. to utter wishes that evil befall a person or thing; to swear or blaspheme. 2. to afflict with evil. CURSE (*n.*) 1. an utterance wishing evil to befall. 2. suffering due to human error, as warfare, or to a natural cause, as an epidemic.

cursorily (*adv.*) hastily.

cursory (*adj.*) quick; hasty.

curt (*adj.*) short; abrupt.

curtail (*v.*) to cut short; to lop.

curtailment (*n.*) a shortening; reduction.

curtain (*n.*) 1. a hanging cloth used to darken or conceal. 2. the cloth concealing the stage from the audience in a theatre. CURTAIN (*v.*) to enclose or provide with a curtain.

curtness (*n.*) abruptness; rudeness.

curts(e)y (*n.*) a woman's salutation made by bending the knees and lowering the body. CURTS(E)Y (*v.*) to make a curtsy.

curvature (*n.*) the amount of curving or bending.

curve (*n.*) a line no part of which is straight. CURVE (*v.*) to bend out of the straight.

cushion (*n.*) a bag stuffed with soft material; a pillow. CUSHION (*v.*) to lessen a shock or blow.

custard (*n.*) a dish of milk and eggs, sweetened and baked or boiled.

custodian (*n.*) 1. a guardian; keeper. 2. one who has the care of anything.

custody (*n.*) 1. care; safe-keeping. 2. imprisonment.

custom (*n.*) 1. a habit; rule. 2. a tax on imports. 3. support given to a tradesman.

customary (*adj.*) ordinary; usual.

customer (*n.*) a regular buyer.

cut (*v.*) 1. to open, divide or sever with anything sharp-edged. 2. to divide a pack of cards. 3. to play a particular stroke in various games. 4. to refuse to recognize a person. CUT (*n.*) 1. a wound from a sharp edge. 2. a piece of meat. 3. a games-stroke. 4. an insult.

cutlass (*n.*) a short, curved sword.

cutler (*n.*) a maker or seller of knives and edged tools.

cutlery (*n.*) edged implements and tools.

cutlet (*n.*) a slice of meat.

cuttlefish (*n.*) a fish with ten long arms or feelers.

cycle (*n.*) 1. a period of time. 2. a bicycle or tricycle. CYCLE (*v.*) to ride a bicycle or tricycle. CYCLIST (*n.*).

cyclone (*n.*) a violent storm in which the wind moves round in circles.

cyclotron (*n.*) an apparatus for splitting atoms.

cygnet (*n.*) a young swan.

cylinder (*n.*) a roller.

cylindrical (*adj.*) roller-shaped.

cymbal (*n.*) one of a pair of round brass plates which clang when struck together.

cynic (*n.*) one who sneers at good intentions or deeds.

cynical (*adj.*) sneering; unbelieving.

cynicism (*n.*) fault-seeking.

cypress (*n.*) a dark-leaved, evergreen tree.

cyst (*n.*) a small, hard lump which forms on the skin.

D

dab (*v.*) to pat gently. DAB (*n.*) 1. a gentle pat. 2. a flatfish.

dabble (*v.*) 1. to splash. 2. to meddle.

dace (*n.*) a small fresh-water fish.

dachshund (*n.*) a long-bodied, badger-hunting dog.

dacoit (*n.*) a robber; bandit (Eastern).

daffodil (*n.*) yellow, bell-shaped flower of narcissus family.

dagger (*n.*) a short-bladed stabbing weapon.

dahlia (*n.*) plant bearing large, coloured flowers. See appendix.

daily (*adj.*) everyday; often. DAILY (*n.*) a newspaper. (*pl.* DAILIES).

daintily (*adv.*) tenderly; delicately.

daintiness (*n.*) neatness; niceness.

dainty (*adj.*) 1. neat. 2. particular. DAINTY (*n.*) a tasty foodstuff.

dairy (*n.*) a place where milk is kept and sold. (*pl.* DAIRIES). Beware DIARY.

dais (*n.*) a raised platform.

daisy (*n.*) a common meadow-flower.

dale (*n.*) a valley; glen.

dalliance (*n.*) a delay; dawdling.

dally (*n.*) to dawdle; to waste time.

dalmatian (*n.*) a large, spotted dog.

dam (*v.*) to block a flow of water. DAM (*n.*) a bank or barrier stopping a flow of water.

damage (*v.*) to injure, to hurt. DAMAGE (*n.*) injury.

damages (*n. pl.*) compensation for injury or wrong.

damask (*n.*) rich silk or fine linen fabric.

Dame (*n.*) title of honour conferred on a woman.

dame (*n.*) the mistress of a household or school; a matron.

damn (*v.*) 1. to doom to eternal punishment for sin. 2. to condemn; to censure. DAMN (*n.*) 1. an uttered curse. 2. a worthless trifle.

damp; dampness (*nn.*) moisture; slight wetness. DAMP (*v.*) 1. to moisten. 2. to discourage.

damper (*n.*) 1. a draught regulator in a flue. 2. a discouragement.

damson (*n.*) a small, purple plum.

dance (*v.*) 1. to move to music with measured steps. 2. to move nimbly or merrily for joy. DANCE (*n.*) 1. the act of moving in time with music. 2. an assembly in which all dance; a ball. DANCER (*n.*).

dandelion (*n.*) a yellow-flowered plant with toothed leaves.

dandy (*n.*) a man who wears fine clothes.

danger (*n.*) peril.

dangerous (*adj.*) unsafe; perilous.

dangle (v.) to suspend, or hang down loosely.

dank (adj.) damp; moist.

dapper (adj.) 1. small and active. 2. trim and neat.

dappled (adj.) spotted in different colours.

dare (v.) to attempt; to challenge.

daring (adj.) bold; venturesome. DARING (n.) boldness.

dark (adj.) 1. without light; sunless. 2. ignorant. 3. cheerless.

darkness (n.) 1. blackness. 2. ignorance.

darling (adj.) dearly loved. DARLING (n.) one dearly loved.

dart (v.) 1. to fly off; to spring away. 2. to fling; to hurl. DART (n.) 1. a quick dash away. 2. a pointed missile.

dash (v.) 1. to run off quickly. 2. to smash against. 3. to discourage. DASH (n.) 1. a quick run. 2. a small amount. 3. a stroke (—).

dashing (adj.) 1. daring. 2. showy; gay.

dastard (n.) a coward; poltroon.

dastardly (adj.) cowardly; sneaking.

data (n. pl.) facts; information. (sing. DATUM = a fact).

date (n.) 1. the number of the day in the month and year. 2. the time when an event happened. 3. a North African palm-tree and its fruit.

daub (v.) 1. to smear. 2. to paint badly. DAUB (n.) 1. a smear. 2. a worthless painting.

daughter (n.) a female child. DAUGHTERLY (adj.).

daughter-in-law (n.) a son's wife. (pl. DAUGHTERS-IN-LAW).

daunt (v.) to frighten; to dismay.

dauntless (adj.) fearless.

davits (n. pl.) apparatus for lowering a ship's boat.

dawdle (v.) to loiter; to stroll slowly. DAWDLING (adj.).

dawn (v.) 1. to begin to grow light. 2. to grow clear. DAWN (n.) 1. daybreak. 2. a beginning.

day (n.) 1. 24 hours. 2. daylight time between sunrise and sunset.

daybreak (n.) dawn; sunrise.

daydream (n.) a castle in the air. DAYDREAM (v.) to fancy; to imagine.

daytime (n.) the daylight hours.

daze (v.) to confuse; to bewilder. DAZE (n.) confusion. DAZED (adj.).

dazzle (v.) to confuse with light; to blind. DAZZLE (n.) a glare; blinding light.

dazzling (adj.) brilliant; blinding.

deacon (n.) 1. a clergyman ranking next below a priest. 2. a church official.

dead (adj.) lifeless; no longer living. DEAD (n. pl.) all those no longer living.

deaden (v.) 1. to lose use or feeling; to numb. 2. to soften; to lessen. DEADENING (adj.).

deadlock (n.) a stoppage; standstill.

deadly (adj.) causing death; fatal.

deaf (adj.) unable or unwilling to hear; heedless.

deafen (v.) to make deaf.

deafness (n.) inability to hear.

deal (v.) 1. to share; to handle. 2. to trade with. 3. to deliver. DEAL (n.) 1. a business act. 2. a pinewood plank. 3. a handing-out.

dealer (n.) a trader; shopkeeper.

dean (n.) head of a cathedral and its clergy; next in rank below a bishop.

deanery (n.) 1. the residence of a dean. 2. district over which a dean has authority.

dear (adj.) 1. beloved. 2. costly. DEAR (n.) a darling; favourite.

dearly (adv.) 1. very much. 2. expensively.

dearth (n.) a scarcity; famine.

death (n.) the end of life.

deathless (adj.) undying; immortal.

deathly (adj.) like death; fatal.

debar (v.) to shut out; to exclude.

debase (v.) to lower in value; to degrade.

debasement (n.) shame; dishonour.

debasing (adj.) dishonouring.

debatable (adj.) doubtful; questionable.

debate (v.) to argue; to discuss. DEBATE (n.) a discussion.

debit (v.) to note the sum owing. DEBIT (n.) a debt.

debonair (adj.) bright; gay.

debris (n. pron. day-bree) wreckage; rubbish.

debt (n.) anything one owes.

debtor (n.) one who owes.

decade (n.) a period of ten years.

decadence (n.) a weakening; a decay.

decadent (adj.) failing; weakening.

decamp (v.) to take oneself off; to break up camp.

decay (v.) to wither; to rot. DECAY (n.) rottenness. DECAYED (adj.).

decease (n.) death.

deceased (adj.) dead.

deceit (n.) trickery; fraud.

deceitful (adj.) false; underhand. DECEITFULLY (adv.).

deceive (v.) to mislead; to cheat. DECEIVER (n.).

December (n.) the twelfth and last month in the year; the Roman tenth month.

decency (n.) respectability; modesty.

decent (adj.) becoming; proper. DECENTLY (adv.).

deception (n.) pretence; falsity.

deceptive (adj.) misleading. DECEPTIVELY (adv.).

decibel (n.) a measure of the loudness of sound.

decide (v.) to settle; to resolve.

decided (adj.) firm; determined. DECIDEDLY (adv.).

deciduous (adj.) falling off, or away; shedding. (Trees shedding their leaves yearly are deciduous).

decimal (adj.) counted by tens or tenths.

decipher (v.) to read ill-written writing, or a code.

decision (n.) 1. a final judgment. 2. firmness.

decisive (adj.) settled; firm.

decisively (adv.) firmly; unalterably.

deck (n.) the flooring covering a ship's hull. DECK (v.) to cover; to decorate.

declaim (v.) to speak in public.

declaration (n.) 1. a proclamation. 2. a true statement.

declare (v.) to announce; to state.

decline (v.) to refuse. DECLINE (n.) a weakening; loss of strength.

declining (adj.) wasting away; growing older.

declivity (n.) a steep, downhill slope.

decompose (v.) to decay; to rot.

decomposing (adj.) decaying.

decomposition (n.) decay; crumbling.

decorate (v.) to beautify; to adorn. DECORATOR (n.).

decoration (n.) 1. an award or honour. 2. adornment.

decorative (adj.) ornamental.

decorous (adj.) seemly; proper. DECOROUSLY (adv.).

decorum (n.) proper behaviour.

decoy (v.) to snare; to trap. DECOY (n.) a bait; temptation.

decrease (v.) to lessen. DECREASE (n.) a lessening; reduction.

decree (n.) 1. a judge's decision. 2. an order. DECREE (v.) to command; to ordain.

decrepit (adj.) feeble; unsteady.

decrepitude (n.) weakness caused by old age.

decry (v.) to belittle; to find fault with.

dedicate (v.) 1. to make sacred. 2. to devote oneself to a special work.

dedication (n.) a consecration; devotion.

deduce (v.) to learn, or find out by reasoning.

deduct (v.) to subtract; to take away from.

deduction (n.) 1. whatever is learned by reasoning. 2. the part taken away.

deed (n.) 1. an action; a doing. 2. a legal document.

deep (adj.) 1. extending far down or far back. 2. hard to understand; mysterious. 3. thick; dark. THE DEEP (n.) the sea.

deer (n.) swift-running, grass-eating quadrupeds with branching horns. (pl. DEER).

deface (v.) to disfigure; to scratch out. DEFACEMENT (n.).

defamation (n.) slander; abuse.

defamatory (adj.) abusive; slanderous.

defame (v.) to injure a reputation unjustly; to slander.

default (v.) to fail in one's duty; to neglect. DEFAULT (n.) failure; negligence.

defaulter (n.) one absent from duty without permission.

defeat (v.) to overcome; to beat. DEFEAT (n.) an overthrow.

defect (n.) a fault; flaw.

defective (adj.) 1. imperfect. 2. incomplete.

defence (n.) 1. protection. 2. resistance.

defenceless (adj.) unguarded; unresisting.

defend (v.) to maintain against attackers.

defensible (adj.) can be defended.

defensive (adj.) shielding; resisting.

defer (v.) 1. to postpone; to delay. 2. to give in to another's wishes.

deference (n.) friendly submission.

deferential (*adj.*) respectful; courteous.

deferment (*n.*) a delay; postponement.

defiance (*n.*) 1. open disobedience. 2. a challenge.

defiant (*adj.*) boldly disobedient.

defiantly (*adv.*) fearlessly.

deficiency (*n.*) a lack; shortage. (*pl.* DEFICIENCIES).

deficient (*adj.*) lacking; short.

deficit (*n.*) the amount lacking; shortage.

defile (*v.*) 1. to dirty; to taint. 2. to move one behind another. DEFILE (*n.*) a narrow pass or gorge.

defilement (*n.*) a stain; an uncleanness.

define (*v.*) to make clear; to explain.

definite (*adj.*) exact; fixed.

definitely (*adv.*) certainly.

definition (*n.*) 1. a clearness. 2. an explanation of a word's meaning.

deflect (*v.*) to turn aside; to swerve.

deflection (*n.*) a bending away; a swerving. DEFLECTED (*adj.*).

deform (*v.*) to misshape. DEFORMED (*adj.*).

deformity (*n.*) a disfigurement.

defraud (*v.*) to cheat; to deceive.

defray (*v.*) to pay the cost.

deft (*adj.*) skilful; nimble-fingered.

deftness (*n.*) skill.

defy (*v.*) 1. to disregard; to flout. 2. to dare; to challenge.

degeneracy (*n.*) a sinking down; a growing worse.

degenerate (*adj.*) base. DEGENERATE (*v.*) to sink lower.

degeneration (*n.*) a slow sinking down to baseness.

degradation (*n.*) disgrace; dishonour.

degrade (*v.*) to disgrace; to dishonour.

degrading (*adj.*) unworthy; dishonourable.

degree (*n.*) 1. a step; stage. 2. a rank. 3. a university title. 4. a measured space; an interval.

deify (*v.*) to worship; to idolize.

deign (*v.*) to stoop; to condescend.

deity (*n.*) a god. (*pl.* DEITIES). THE DEITY (*n.*) = GOD.

deject (*v.*) to sadden. DEJECTED (*adj.*).

dejection (*n.*) sadness; depression.

delay (*v.*) 1. to linger. 2. to postpone. DELAY (*n.*) 1. slowness. 2. a postponement.

delectable (*adj.*) delightful.

delegate (*v.*) to send as a representative; to depute. DELEGATE (*n.*) a representative.

delegation (*n.*) a body of representatives.

delete (*v.*) to erase; to cross out.

deletion (*n.*) an erasure.

deliberate (*v.*) to consider; to talk over. DELIBERATE (*adj.*) intentional.

deliberation (*n.*) 1. careful thought. 2. discussion; counsel.

deliberately (*adv.*) purposely.

delicacy (*n.*) 1. weakness. 2. tenderness. 3. fineness; daintiness. 4. a tasty morsel. (*pl.* DELICACIES).

delicate (*adj.*) 1. fine; frail. 2. requiring care. 3. subject to ill-health. DELICATELY (*adv.*).

delicious (*adj.*) delightful. DELICIOUSLY (*adv.*).

delight (*v.*) to please; to charm. DELIGHT (*n.*) joy; gladness.

delightful (*adj.*) pleasant; charming.

delinquency (*n.*) 1. neglect of duty. 2. wrongdoing. (*pl.* DELINQUENCIES).

delinquent (*n.*) a wrong-doer. DELINQUENT (*adj.*) faulty; guilty.

delirious (*adj.*) 1. fevered. 2. highly excited.

delirium (*n.*) madness aroused by fever.

deliver (*v.*) 1. to set free. 2. to hand over. 3. to speak; to address.

deliverance (*n.*) release; rescue. DELIVERER (*n.*).

delivery (*n.*) 1. a distribution of articles. 2. the manner of speaking; addressing.

dell (*n.*) a glade; a glen.

delta (*n.*) land drained by all the mouths of a river.

delude (*v.*) to mislead; to deceive.

delusion (*n.*) a deception; false opinion. DELUSIVE (*adj.*).

deluge (*n.*) a great flood. DELUGE (*v.*) to flood; to pour down. THE DELUGE (*n.*) Noah's great Flood.

delve (*v.*) 1. to dig. 2. to search or inquire into.

demand (*v.*) to ask firmly; to claim. DEMAND (*n.*) a claim.

demean (*v.*) 1. to behave. 2. to degrade.

demeanour (*n.*) the outward appearance; manner.

demented (*adj.*) insane; mad.

democracy (*n.*) government by representatives elected by the people.

democrat (*n.*) a supporter of democracy. DEMOCRATIC (*adj.*).

demolish (*v.*) to pull down. DEMOLITION (*n.*).

demon (*n.*) an evil spirit; a fiend. DEMONIACAL (*adj.*).

demonstrate (*v.*) to show; to prove. **demonstration** (*n.*) an illustration; exhibition.

demonstrative (*adj.*) 1. giving proof. 2. freely showing one's feelings.

demoralization (*n.*) 1. corruption. 2. confusion.

demoralize (*v.*) to destroy the character; to corrupt.

demur (*v.*) 1. to waver; to hesitate. 2. to raise objections.

demure (*adj.*) modest; grave.

den (*n.*) a wild animal's lair.

denial (*n.*) a refusal; contradiction.

denizen (*n.*) a resident; an inhabitant.

denote (*v.*) to indicate; to point out.

denounce (*v.*) to accuse publicly.

dense (*adj.*) 1. thick. 2. stupid.

densely (*adv.*) closely; compactly.

density (*n.*) 1. thickness. 2. stupidity.

dent (*n.*) a shallow mark or impression made by a blow; a dinge. DENT (*v.*) to impress with a blow.

dental (*adj.*) concerning the teeth.

dentist (*n.*) a tooth doctor.

denture (*n.*) a set of false teeth.

denude (*v.*) to make bare or naked; to strip off. DENUDATION (*n.*).

denunciation (*n.*) a threat; an accusation.

deny (*v.*) 1. to gainsay; to contradict. 2. to refuse.

depart (*v.*) to go; to leave.

department (*n.*) a separate part; a section.

departure (*n.*) a leaving; going away.

depend (*v.*) to rely on; to trust.

dependable (*adj.*) reliable; trustworthy.

dependant (*n.*) one who is supported by another.

dependence (*n.*) reliance; trust.

dependency (*n.*) a country which is governed by another.

depict (*v.*) to picture; to describe. DEPICTION (*n.*).

deplete (*v.*) to drain out; to empty. DEPLETION (*n.*).

deplorable (*adj.*) sad; regrettable.

deplore (*v.*) to regret.

deport (*v.*) to banish; to expel from a country. DEPORTATION (*n.*).

deportment (*n.*) conduct; behaviour.

depose (*v.*) 1. to dismiss from a high position. 2. to state.

deposit (*v.*) 1. to lay down. 2. to place in safety. 3. to pledge. DEPOSIT (*n.*) 1. a sediment. 2. a pledge.

deposition (*n.*) 1. a dismissal; dethronement. 2. a statement.

depositor (*n.*) one who places money, etc. in safety, as in a bank.

depot (*n.* pron. DEP-oh) a storage place; headquarters.

deprave (*v.*) to make bad; to corrupt. DEPRAVED (*adj.*).

depravity (*n.*) wickedness.

deprecate (*v.*) 1. to regret deeply. 2. to pray to be free from. DEPRECATION (*n.*).

depreciate (*v.*) 1. to lose value or worth. 2. to undervalue.

depreciation (*n.*) a fall in value.

depress (*v.*) 1. to press down or in. 2. to dishearten.

depressed (*adj.*) gloomy.

depression (*n.*) 1. a dent; hollow. 2. sadness.

deprive (*v.*) to be prevented from having; to take away from. DEPRIVATION (*n.*).

depth (*n.*) the deepness; distance from top to bottom.

deputation (*n.*) a group of persons representing others.

depute (*v.*) to appoint a substitute or agent.

deputize (*v.*) to act on behalf of another.

deputy (*n.*) a representative.

derange (*v.*) 1. to disorder; to confuse. 2. to drive mad. DERANGEMENT (*n.*).

derelict (*adj.*) forsaken; abandoned. DERELICT (*n.*) anything abandoned by its owner.

dereliction (*n.*) neglect; failure.

deride (*v.*) to laugh at; to mock.

derision (*n.*) ridicule; mockery.

derisive (*adj.*) scornful; mocking. DERISIVELY (*adv.*).

derive (*v.*) 1. to gain from. 2. to trace from the beginning. DERIVATION (*n.*).

derrick (*n.*) a machine for raising heavy weights; a crane.

descant (*n.*) melody; a variation on the

main air. DESCANT (v.) to talk about fully.

descend (v.) to go down.

descendant (n.) a child; offspring.

descent (n.) 1. a going down. 2. the way down. 3. a line of forefathers; ancestors.

describe (v.) to speak or write about.

description (n.) an account; a report.

descriptive (adj.) explanatory.

descry (v.) to catch sight of or glimpse.

desert (v. pron. dez-ERT) to forsake; to abandon. DESERT (n. pron. DEZ-ert) a waste; waterless place.

deserted (adj.) forsaken.

deserter (n.) one who leaves his duty, post, etc.

desertion (n.) a leaving; forsaking.

deserts (n. pl.) what one deserves.

deserve (v.) to earn; to merit.

deserving (adj.) worthy; meritorious.

design (v.) to plan; to prepare. DESIGN (n.) 1. a plan. 2. an intention. 3. a pattern.

designate (v.) to name; to indicate.

designed (adj.) planned; intended.

designedly (adv.) purposely; intentionally.

desirability (n.) the worth; value.

desirable (adj.) worth wishing for; wanted.

desire (v.) to wish for; to crave.

desirous (adj.) wishful; eager.

desist (v.) to stop; to cease.

desolate (adj.) 1. alone; forlorn. 2. lonely; deserted.

desolation (n.) 1. loneliness. 2. a wilderness.

despair (v.) to lose hope. DESPAIR (n.) hopelessness.

despatch (v.) 1. to send away. 2. to do business. 3. to kill. DESPATCH (n.) 1. a message or messenger; a sending away. 2. prompt dealing.

despatches (n. pl.) official or government letters; messages.

desperado (n.) a villain; ruffian.

desperate (adj.) 1. beyond cure. 2. rash.

desperately (adv.) recklessly.

desperation (n.) hopelessness.

despicable (adj.) vile; contemptible. DESPICABLY (adv.).

despise (v.) to look down upon; to scorn.

despite (prep.) in spite of; notwithstanding.

despoil (v.) to plunder. DESPOILER (n.).

despond (v.) to lose hope; to despair.

despondency (n.) despair.

despondent (adj.) downcast. DESPONDENTLY (adv.).

despot (n.) an oppressor; a tyrant.

despotic (adj.) oppressive.

despotism (n.) tyranny.

dessert (n.) fruit or sweetmeats ending a meal.

destination (n.) the end of a journey.

destine (v.) to fix the future of; to arrange.

destiny (n.) fate.

destitute (adj.) 1. in great need. 2. penniless. DESTITUTION (n.) poverty; need.

destroy (v.) to kill; to ruin.

destruction (n.) ruin; extinction.

destructive (adj.) 1. causing ruin. 2. fatal.

destructiveness (n.) the wish or power to destroy.

detach (v.) to take off; to disconnect.

detachable (adj.) removable.

detachment (n.) 1. the part taken away. 2. inattention. 3. a body of troops taken from their usual duties.

detail (v.) to give full particulars. DETAIL (n.) an item; a particular.

detailed (adj.) described item by item.

detain (v.) to withhold; to keep waiting.

detect (v.) to find; to discover.

detection (n.) discovery.

detective (n.) person trained to investigate wrongdoing.

detention (n.) restraint; confinement.

deter (v.) to hold back; to prevent.

detergent (n.) a cleansing substance.

deteriorate (v.) to grow worse.

deterioration (n.) a worsening.

determination (n.) firmness; decision.

determine (v.) to decide; to resolve. DETERMINED (adj.).

deterrent (n.) a warning; a prevention.

detest (v.) to loathe; to hate.

detestable (adj.) hateful; vile.

detestation (n.) hatred; loathing.

detonate (v.) to explode.

detonation (n.) an explosion.

detonator (n.) a contrivance for exploding.

detour (n.) a roundabout way.

detract (v.) to take away; to lower.

detraction (n.) a slander.

detriment (*n.*) an injury; a loss.

detrimental (*adj.*) harmful.

devastate (*v.*) to lay waste; to ruin.

devastation (*n.*) desolation; ruin. DEVAS-
TATED (*adj.*).

develop (*v.*) to grow or improve gradually.

development (*n.*) growth; progress.

deviate (*v.*) to turn aside; to stray from.

deviation (*n.*) a turning aside; a mistake.

device (*n.*) 1. a contrivance; an invention.
2. an emblem.

devil (*n.*) an evil spirit or power; a
demon.

devise (*v.*) 1. to plan; to invent. 2. to
give by will.

devoid (*adj.*) without; empty.

devolve (*v.*) to deliver to another; to hand
over to a successor.

devote (*v.*) to give full attention to.

devotion (*n.*) love; worship.

devour (*v.*) to eat greedily; to consume.

devout (*adj.*) religious; sincere.

dew (*n.*) water-drops which gather on the
ground when it is colder than the
air.

dexterity (*n.*) skill; quickness.

dexterous (*adj.*) skilful; clever. DEX-
TEROUSLY (*adv.*).

diabolic (*adj.*) devilish.

diabolically (*adv.*) very wickedly; devil-
ishly.

diadem (*n.*) a crown.

diagnose (*v.*) to discover the nature of an
illness.

diagnosis (*n.*) a doctor's opinion or
recognition of a disease. (*pl.* DIAG-
NOSES).

diagonal (*n.*) a line joining opposite
corners.

diagonally (*adv.*) slantingly; obliquely.

diagram (*n.*) a plan; sketch. DIAGRAM-
MATIC (*adj.*).

dial (*v.*) to call a number on an automatic telephone. DIAL (*n.*) the face of
a clock, watch, etc.

dialect (*n.*) the speech of a district.

dialogue (*n.*) conversation; discourse.

diameter (*n.*) the width of, or distance
across, a circle.

diamond (*n.*) an extremely hard and
valuable gem.

diaphragm (*n.* pron. DI-a-fram) a thin
partition or. shutter.

diarist (*n.*) writer of a daily record.

diary (*n.*) a daily record; journal.
Beware DAIRY.

dictaphone (*n.*) an apparatus which records
speech for future repetition.

dictate (*v.*) 1. to compel obedience.
2. to tell another what to write. DIC-
TATOR (*n.*). DICTATION (*n.*).

dictatorial (*adj.*) overbearing; domineering.

diction (*n.*) choice of words and manner
of speaking them.

dictionary (*n.*) a book which explains the
meanings of words.

die (*n.*) a stamp used for making coins
or patterns. DIE (*v.*) to cease to live.

diesel engine (*n.*) a motor engine using
heavy oil.

diet (*n.*) 1. food; nourishment. 2. a
parliament.

differ (*v.*) 1. to be unlike. 2. to disagree.

difference (*n.*) 1. disagreement. 2. a
quarrel.

different (*adj.*) unlike; dissimilar.

differentiate (*v.*) to know one from
another; to distinguish between.

difficult (*adj.*) 1. hard to do. 2. unmanageable.

difficulty (*n.*) anything hard to overcome;
a problem. (*pl.* DIFFICULTIES).

diffidence (*n.*) modesty; shyness.

diffident (*adj.*) shy; bashful. DIFFIDENTLY
(*adv.*).

diffuse (*v.* pron. diff-UZE) to scatter; to
spread. DIFFUSE (*adj.* pron. diff-USE)
scattered.

diffusion (*n.*) a spreading; scattering.

dig (*v.*) 1. to cast up soil. 2. to thrust.
3. to search. DIGGER (*n.*).

digest (*v.*) 1. to dissolve food in the
stomach. 2. to absorb. DIGEST (*n.*) a
short version.

digestible (*adj.*) easily digested.

digestion (*n.*) the stomach's ability to
digest.

digit (*n.*) 1. a finger or toe. 2. a single
figure or numeral.

dignified (*adj.*) noble; stately.

dignify (*v.*) to make worthy or stately.

dignitary (*n.*) person of high rank. (*pl.*
DIGNITARIES).

dignity (*n.*) worthiness; eminence. (*pl.*
DIGNITIES).

digress (*v.*) to turn aside; to wander from.

digression (*n.*) a turning aside.

dike (*n.*) 1. a ditch. 2. a bank built to hold back flood-water.

dilapidated (*adj.*) tumbledown; shabby.

dilapidation (*n.*) decay; shabbiness.

dilate (*v.*) to swell. DILATED (*adj.*).

dilation (*n.*) a swelling; enlarging.

dilatorily (*adv.*) lazily; sluggishly.

dilatoriness (*n.*) slowness.

dilatory (*adj.*) slow; lazy.

dilemma (*n.*) a fix; predicament.

diligence (*n.*) attention to work and duty; a foreign stage-coach.

diligent (*adj.*) hard working; industrious.

diligently (*adv.*) attentively.

dilute (*v.*) to weaken by adding water. DILUTED (*adj.*).

dilution (*n.*) the weakening of a liquid.

dim (*adj.*) faint, indistinct. DIM (*v.*) to make faint or fainter.

dimension (*n.*) the measure of length, breadth and depth.

diminish (*v.*) to decrease; to lessen. DIMINISHED (*adj.*).

diminution (*n.*) a reduction; lessening.

diminutive (*adj.*) very small; tiny.

dimly (*adv.*) faintly; vaguely.

dimness (*n.*) faintness; vagueness.

dimple (*n.*) a small hollow on the cheek or chin.

din (*n.*) uproar; clamour.

dinghy (*n.*) a small boat.

dinginess (*n.*) griminess; dreariness.

dingle (*n.*) a little glen.

dingy (*adj.*) faded; grimy.

dinner (*n.*) the main meal of the day.

dint (*n.*) 1. a mark made by a blow; a dent. 2. the force of a blow. DINT (*v.*) to dent; to dinge.

diocese (*n.*) the district under a bishop; a see.

diocesan (*adj.*) concerning a diocese.

dip (*v.*) 1. to immerse in liquid for a moment. 2. to bathe. 3. to slope steeply downwards. DIP (*n.*) 1. a quick immersion. 2. a bathe.

diphtheria (*n.* pron. dif-THEER-i-a) a dangerous throat disease.

diphthong (*n.* pron. DIF-thong) a union of two vowels into one sound.

diploma (*n.*) a certificate proving success.

diplomacy (*n.*) skill in making people of nations friendly.

diplomatic (*adj.*) tactful; prudent. DIPLOMATICALLY (*adv.*).

dire (*adj.*) terrible; disastrous.

direct (*adj.*) 1. straight. 2. outspoken. DIRECT (*v.*) 1. to aim. 2. to govern. 3. to guide. 4. to address.

direction (*n.*) 1. the way towards. 2. management. 3. an order.

directly (*adv.*) at once; immediately.

director (*n.*) a manager; controller.

directory (*n.*) a book giving people's addresses. (*pl.* DIRECTORIES).

dirge (*n.*) a mournful tune; a lament.

dirigible (*n.*) an airship. DIRIGIBLE (*adj.*) controllable.

dirt (*n.*) matter that soils, as mud, soot, etc. DIRTY (*adj.*).

disability (*n.*) inability; powerlessness. (*pl.* DISABILITIES).

disable (*v.*) to make powerless; to cripple.

disadvantage (*n.*) a drawback; an inconvenience.

disadvantageous (*adj.*) harmful; unfavourable.

disaffect (*v.*) to fill with discontent.

disaffected (*adj.*) disloyal.

disagree (*v.*) to differ; to quarrel.

disagreeable (*adj.*) unpleasant.

disagreement (*n.*) a difference; a quarrel.

disappear (*v.*) to vanish.

disappearance (*n.*) a vanishing from sight.

disappoint (*v.*) to fail to fulfil one's hopes or desires.

disappointing (*adj.*) failing to please.

disappointment (*n.*) displeasure caused by failure.

disapproval (*n.*) dislike.

disapprove (*v.*) to show dislike or dissent.

disarm (*v.*) to take away weapons; to render harmless.

disarmament (*n.*) the reduction or abolition of arms.

disaster (*n.*) a great misfortune; a calamity.

disastrous (*adj.*) destructive; ruinous.

---

*NOTE.—Some words beginning with DIS are omitted. DIS is a prefix and is used in front of a word when it means *the opposite of.* For instance, *disallow* means *to refuse to allow.* You would therefore look up the word *allow.*

disband (v.) to dismiss; break up.
disbelief (n.) doubt; distrust.
disbelieve (v.) to refuse to believe.
disc (n.) see DISK.
discard (v.) to throw away; to reject.
discern (v.) to see; to choose.
discernible (adj.) visible; clear.
discerning (adj.) understanding; wise.
discernment (n.) 1. recognition. 2. wisdom.
discharge (v.) 1. to shoot. 2. to dismiss. 3. to unload cargo. 4. to do. DISCHARGE (n.) 1. gunfire. 2. dismissal. 3. an outflow. 4. a completion.
disciple (n.) 1. a follower. 2. a scholar.
disciplinary (adj.) concerned with discipline.
discipline (n.) obedience; training. DISCIPLINE (v.) to train to give strict obedience.
disclose (v.) to uncover; to reveal.
disclosure (n.) a discovery; revelation.
discolour (v.) to spoil the colour of; to stain. DISCOLOURED (adj.).
discoloration (n.) a stain; disfigurement.
discomfit (v.) to upset; to make uneasy.
discomfiture (n.) uneasiness; embarrassment.
discomfort (n.) lack of comfort.
disconcert (v.) to take unawares; to embarrass.
disconnect (v.) to unfasten. DISCONNECTED (adj.).
disconnection (n.) a separation; severance.
disconsolate (adj.) unhappy.
discontent (v.) to make dissatisfied. DISCONTENT (n.) dissatisfaction; disquiet.
discontinue (v.) to stop; to cease. DISCONTINUANCE (n.).
discord (n.) 1. disagreement; strife. 2. a harsh or jarring sound.
discordant (adj.) 1. harsh. 2. contradictory.
discount (n.) an allowance; a sum deducted from a bill. DISCOUNT (v.) to reduce; to allow.
discourage (v.) to lower one's hope; to try to prevent. DISCOURAGEMENT (n.).
discourse (v.) to talk; to converse. DISCOURSE (n.) a conversation; speech.
discourteous (adj.) uncivil; impolite. DISCOURTEOUSLY (adv.).
discourtesy (n.) rudeness; incivility.
discover (v.) to find. DISCOVERER (n.).

discovery (n.) whatever is found or learned.
discredit (v.) 1. to disbelieve. 2. to dishonour. DISCREDIT (n.) dishonour; disgrace. DISCREDITED (adj.).
discreditable (adj.) disgraceful.
discreet (adj.) heedful; prudent. DISCREETLY (adv.).
discrepancy (n.) 1. a difference in two accounts of the same happening. 2. a shortage. (pl. DISCREPANCIES).
discretion (n.) judgment; wisdom.
discriminate (v.) to notice small differences; to judge; to show preference.
discrimination (n.) insight; judgment.
discursive (adj.) roundabout; rambling.
discuss (v.) to talk over with others; to debate.
discussion (n.) a debate; reasoning.
disdain (v.) to despise; to scorn. DISDAIN (n.) scorn; contempt.
disdainful (adj.) haughty; contemptuous.
disease (n.) an illness.
disembark (v.) to put on shore; to land from a ship. DISEMBARKATION (n.).
disengage (v.) to release; to free oneself from.
disentangle (v.) to unravel; to unfold. DISENTANGLED (adj.).
disfigure (v.) to spoil the appearance of.
disfigured (adj.) marred; defaced.
disfigurement (n.) a blemish; defacement.
disgorge (v.) to give back what has been taken. DISGORGED (adj.).
disgrace (v.) to dishonour; to shame. DISGRACE (n.) dishonour; discredit.
disgraceful (adj.) shameful; infamous.
disguise (v.) to alter the appearance; to hide the truth.
disgust (v.) to cause loathing; to repel. DISGUST (n.) loathing.
disgusting (adj.) loathsome; repulsive.
dish (n.) 1. a shallow plate or vessel for holding food. 2. a particular kind of food. DISH (v.) 1. to place on a dish ready to serve. 2. to disappoint; to damage.
dishearten (v.) to sadden; to discourage.
dishevel (v.) to tangle; to muddle. DISHEVELLED (adj.).
dishonest (adj.) not honest; false.
dishonestly (adv.) unfairly.
dishonesty (n.) falseness; unfairness.
dishonour (v.) to disgrace; to shame.

DISHONOUR (*n.*) a loss of honour or reputation.

disillusion (*v.*) to set free from false ideas or hopes; to disenchant.

disinclined (*adj.*) unwilling; undesirous.

disinfect (*v.*) to cleanse from infection; to purify.

disinfectant (*n.*) anything that destroys germs.

disinherit (*v.*) to take away an heir's rights or inheritance.

disintegrate (*v.*) to fall to pieces; to crumble.

disintegration (*n.*) a breaking up; a crumbling. DISINTEGRATED (*adj.*).

disinterested (*adj.*) not seeking anything for oneself; impartial.

disk (*n.*) a flat, circular object.

dislike (*v.*) to have no liking for; to feel displeasure. DISLIKE (*n.*) displeasure; aversion.

dislocate (*v.*) to put out of joint.

disloyal (*adj.*) unfaithful; treacherous. DISLOYALTY (*n.*).

dismal (*adj.*) dreary; cheerless.

dismally (*adv.*) sadly; dolefully.

dismantle (*v.*) to take to pieces; to strip. DISMANTLED (*adj.*).

dismay (*v.*) to daunt; to frighten. DISMAY (*n.*) fear; alarm.

dismiss (*v.*) to send away; to discharge. DISMISSED (*adj.*).

dismissal (*n.*) a sending away; a discharge from work.

dismount (*v.*) to get off anything ridden.

disobedience (*n.*) a refusal to obey.

disobedient (*adj.*) unwilling or refusing to obey; undutiful.

disobey (*v.*) to disregard or ignore an order.

disoblige (*v.*) to be unhelpful or ungracious.

disorder (*v.*) to upset; to disarrange. DISORDER (*n.*) 1. confusion. 2. a slight sickness. DISORDERED (*adj.*).

disorderly (*adj.*) unruly.

disorganize (*v.*) to throw out of order; to cause disorder.

disown (*v.*) to deny; to reject.

disparage (*v.*) to belittle; to run down.

disparagement (*n.*) a belittling; despising.

disparity (*n.*) the difference; unlikeness.

dispassionate (*adj.*) calm; unexcited.

dispatch (*v.*) see DESPATCH.

dispel (*v.*) to drive away; to banish.

dispensary (*n.*) place where medicines are made up for sick people.

dispense (*v.*) 1. to give out. 2. to do without. 3. to make up medicines.

dispenser (*n.*) a chemist; one who makes up medicines.

disperse (*v.*) to scatter; to spread. DISPERSED (*adj.*).

dispersion (*n.*) a scattering.

displace (*v.*) to take, or change, the place of; to remove.

display (*v.*) to show; to exhibit. DISPLAY (*n.*) a parade; an exhibition.

displease (*v.*) to offend; to anger. DISPLEASURE (*n.*).

disport (*v.*) to play; to frolic.

dispose (*v.*) 1. to arrange. 2. to get rid of; to sell.

disposition (*n.*) 1. an arrangement; a settlement. 2. one's character; manner.

dispossess (*v.*) to put out of possession; to eject.

disprove (*v.*) to prove wrong or false; to refute.

disputable (*adj.*) doubtful; debatable.

disputation (*n.*) an argument; a debate.

dispute (*v.*) 1. to discuss. 2. to quarrel. DISPUTE (*n.*) 1. a discussion. 2. a quarrel.

disqualify (*v.*) to make unable or incapable. DISQUALIFIED (*adj.*).

disquiet (*v.*) to make uneasy; to worry. DISQUIET (*n.*) uneasiness; anxiety.

disregard (*v.*) to ignore. DISREGARD (*n.*) unconcern; indifference.

disrepair (*n.*) the bad condition; the need for repair.

disreputable (*adj.*) 1. dishonourable. 2. shabby.

disrepute (*n.*) discredit.

disrespect (*n.*) rudeness; incivility.

disrespectful (*adj.*) rude; discourteous.

disrupt (*v.*) to tear apart; to burst.

dissatisfaction (*n.*) displeasure; discontent. DISSATISFIED (*adj.*).

dissatisfy (*v.*) to displease.

dissect (*v.*) to cut up for examination. DISSECTION (*n.*).

dissemble (*v.*) to say one thing and mean another; to pretend.

dissension (*n.*) disagreement; strife.

dissent (*v.*) to differ; to disagree.

dissenter (*n.*) one who disagrees.

dissimilar (*adj.*) unlike.

dissimulate (*v.*) to pretend; to deceive.

dissipate (*v.*) 1. to scatter. 2. to waste in pleasure.

dissipation (*n.*) extravagance; loose conduct.

dissolute (*adj.*) disorderly; shameless.

dissolve (*v.*) 1. to break up or disappear in a liquid. 2. to bring to an end.

dissuade (*v.*) to advise against; to discourage.

dissuasion (*n.*) discouragement; opposition.

distance (*n.*) the measure of length between one point and another.

distant (*adj.*) 1. far away; remote. 2. shy; reserved.

distaste (*n.*) dislike; disgust. DISTASTEFUL (*adj.*).

distemper (*n.*) 1. an ailment. 2. a dog's disease. 3. a water paint.

distend (*v.*) to enlarge; to swell.

distension (*n.*) a swelling; an enlargement.

distil (*v.*) to purify a liquid by boiling and then cooling its vapour.

distilled (*adj.*) pure.

distillery (*n.*) a place where spirit is distilled.

distinct (*adj.*) 1. clear; plain. 2. separate.

distinction (*n.*) 1. fame. 2. difference from others.

distinctive (*adj.*) notable; outstanding.

distinguish (*v.*) 1. to make or notice a difference. 2. to honour highly.

distinguishable (*adj.*) observable; noticeable.

distinguished (*adj.*) famous; renowned.

distort (*v.*) to turn out of shape; to twist. DISTORTED (*adj.*).

distortion (*n.*) a twisting; a grimace.

distract (*v.*) to draw one's attention away. DISTRACTED (*adj.*).

distraction (*n.*) 1. inattention. 2. bewilderment.

distraught (*adj.*) very distressed; frantic.

distress (*v.*) to ₁cause pain or sorrow. DISTRESS (*n.*) trouble; grief.

distribute (*v.*) to deal out; to share among.

distribution (*n.*) a giving; sharing.

distributor (*n.*) 1. one who gives or shares. 2. part of a motor-engine.

district (*n.*) an undefined area explained by its name, e.g., Lake District.

distrust (*v.*) to doubt; to misbelieve. DISTRUST (*n.*) doubt; suspicion.

distrustful (*adj.*) doubtful; suspicious.

disturb (*v.*) 1. to bother; to molest. 2. to agitate; to upset.

disturbance (*n.*) 1. molestation. 2. disorder; riot.

disuse (*v.* pron. dis-UZE) to stop employing. DISUSE (*n.* pron. dis-USE) neglect; abandonment.

ditch (*n.*) a drainage-trench. DITCH (*v.*).

ditto (*n.*) as before; also; the same.

ditty (*n.*) a little song. (*pl.* DITTIES).

divan (*n.*) a low seat or bed.

dive (*v.*) 1. to plunge head foremost into water. 2. to drop suddenly (aircraft).

diver (*n.*) one equipped to sink to and examine sunken vessels, etc.

diverge (*v.*) to move away from a point in different directions.

divergence (*n.*) 1. a moving apart. 2. a difference.

divers (*adj.*) several; various.

diverse (*adj.*) different; varied.

diversity (*n.*) a difference; variety. (*pl.* DIVERSITIES).

divert (*v.*) 1. to amuse. 2. to turn in another direction.

divest (*v.*) 1. to take off; to undress. 2. to dispossess.

divide (*v.*) 1. to cut into parts; to break up. 2. to separate.

dividend (*n.*) a share; part of a profit.

dividers (*n.*) an instrument for dividing.

divine (*adj.*) 1. due to God; holy. 2. supreme; exalted. DIVINE (*n.*) a clergyman. DIVINE (*v.*) to foretell; to predict.

divinity (*n.*) 1. a god. 2. the study of religion.

division (*n.*) 1. a disunion. 2. the process of dividing. 3. section of an army or a fleet.

divorce (*v.*) to separate; to part. DIVORCE (*n.*) 1. separation. 2. a legal ending of marriage.

divulge (*v.*) to tell; to reveal.

dizziness (*n.*) giddiness; faintness. DIZZY (*adj.*). DIZZILY (*adv.*).

do (*v.*) to make; to act; to accomplish.

docile (*adj.*) tame; obedient.

docility (*n.*) tameness; quietness.

dock (*n.*) 1. a basin in which ships berth. 2. a healing herb. DOCK (*v.*) 1. to sail a ship into a dock. 2. to cut short.

docker (*n.*) workman who loads and unloads ships.

dockyard (*n.*) a place where ships are repaired.

doctor (*n.*) one qualified to treat the sick and injured; a physician.

doctrine (*n.*) something one has been taught to believe.

document (*n.*) a written deed; a certificate.

dodge (*v.*) to move aside quickly; to avoid. DODGE (*n.*) 1. a plan; trick. 2. a movement to avoid something.

doe (*n.*) the female of many animals, as the deer, rabbit, etc.

doff (*v.*) to take off; to remove.

dog (*n.*) a domestic animal. DOG (*v.*) to follow closely; to track.

dogged (*adj.*) determined; stubborn. DOGGEDNESS (*n.*).

doggerel (*n.*) poor poetry.

dogma (*n.*) a firm belief.

dogmatic (*adj.*) unshakable; stubborn.

doldrums (*n. pl.*) the ocean belt near the equator where calms prevail.

dole (*n.*) 1. a small portion. 2. unhappiness; distress. DOLE (*v.*) to deal out in small portions.

doleful (*adj.*) sorrowful.

doll (*n.*) 1. a puppet. 2. a toy baby for a child.

dollar (*n.*) United States and Canadian coin worth 100 cents.

dolphin (*n.*) a sea-mammal of the whale family.

dolt (*n.*) a stupid person; blockhead. DOLTISH (*adj.*).

domain (*n.*) 1. one's estate; property. 2. one's native country.

dome (*n.*) a basin-shaped roof.

domestic (*adj.*) 1. belonging to the home. 2. private.

domesticate (*v.*) to make home-loving; to settle. DOMESTICATED (*adj.*).

domesticity (*n.*) family life or affairs.

domicile (*n.*) a house; dwelling. DOMICILED (*adj.*).

dominate (*v.*) to rule; to master. DOMINATED (*adj.*).

domination (*n.*) rule; mastery.

domineer (*v.*) to bully.

dominion (*n.*) 1. rule; government. 2. the territory over which a government has authority.

domino (*n.*) 1. a loose cloak with hood, used as a disguise. 2. one of the 28 pieces of wood marked with spots used in the game of dominoes.

don (*v.*) to put on. DON (*n.*) 1. a university college tutor or fellow. 2. a Spanish gentleman.

donate (*v.*) to give; to contribute.

donation (*n.*) a contribution; gift.

donkey (*n.*) 1. an ass, a patient beast of burden. 2. a stupid or obstinate person.

donor (*n.*) a contributor; giver.

doom (*v.*) to pass sentence on; to condemn. DOOM (*n.*) 1. judgment; ruin. 2. fate; destiny.

doomsday (*n.*) the day of final judgment.

dormant (*adj.*) 1. sleeping. 2. quiet; inactive.

dormer (*n.*) a window in a sloping roof.

dormitory (*n.*) a bedroom with many beds. (*pl.* DORMITORIES).

dormouse (*n.*) a small field-rodent that sleeps a great deal. (*pl.* DORMICE).

dose (*n.*) quantity of medicine taken at one time. DOSE (*v.*) to give medicine.

dot (*n.*) a tiny spot; a speck. DOT (*v.*) to mark with tiny spots. DOTTED (*adj.*).

dote (*v.*) 1. to love too well. 2. to become weaker in mind when old.

dotage (*n.*) weakness of mind.

double (*v.*) 1. to multiply by two. 2. to fold over. 3. to turn back to escape pursuers. 4. to sail round. DOUBLE (*n.*) 1. twice as much. 2. a person or thing much like another. 3. a counterpart.

doubt (*v.*) to be uncertain. DOUBT (*n.*) uncertainty; distrust.

doubtful (*adj.*) undecided; wavering.

doubtless (*adv.*) without doubt; certainly.

dough (*n.*) moist flour, kneaded but not baked.

doughty (*adj.*) gallant; valiant.

dove (*n.*) bird of the pigeon family.

dovetail (*v.*) to fit one thing into another.

dowdily (*adv.*) shabbily; out of date.

dowdiness (*n.*) shabbiness.

dowdy (*adj.*) old-fashioned.

dower (*n.*) a wife's marriage portion. DOWER (*v.*) to provide with a dower or dowry; to endow.

down (*n.*) 1. open high land. 2. fine hair or feathers. DOWN (*adv. & prep.*) from above to below.

downcast (*adj.*) sad; discouraged.

downfall (*n.*) 1. heavy rain. 2. destruction; ruin.

down-hearted (*adj.*) unhappy; depressed.

downright (*adj.*) thorough; straightforward.

doze (*v.*) to drowse; to be half-asleep. DOZE (*n.*) a nap; short sleep.

dozen (*n.*) a group of twelve things.

dozy (*adj.*) sleepy; drowsy.

drab (*adj.*) dull; dreary.

draft (*v.*) 1. to prepare a letter or statement. 2. to send troops elsewhere. DRAFT (*n.*) 1. a rough copy of a document. 2. a picked body of troops. 3. an order to a banker to pay money.

drag (*v.*) to haul or pull along.

dragon (*n.*) a fabulous fiery monster.

dragoon (*n.*) a horse-soldier. DRAGOON (*v.*) to compel.

drain (*v.*) to carry away waste water; to empty. DRAIN (*n.*) a waste-pipe; gutter.

drainage (*n.*) the system of carrying away waste water.

drake (*n.*) a male duck.

dram (*n.*) a small measure of weight (60 grains or minims); one-sixteenth ounce avoirdupois.

drama (*n.*) a play.

dramatic (*adj.*) thrilling; full of action.

dramatist (*n.*) a writer of plays.

dramatize (*v.*) to turn a story into a play.

drape (*v.*) to cover with cloth. DRAPED (*adj.*).

draper (*n.*) a cloth seller.

drapery (*n.*) clothing and fabrics.

drastic (*adj.*) powerful; violent.

drastically (*adv.*) strongly; severely, as in an emergency.

draught (*n.*) 1. a current of air. 2. a drink. 3. a rough sketch or plan. 4. the depth of water a ship draws.

draughts (*n. pl.*) game for two with counters and a chequered board.

draughtsman (*n.*) one skilled in drawing plans.

draughty (*adj.*) breezy.

draw (*v.*) 1. to pull. 2. to attract. 3. to sketch. DRAW (*n.*) an attraction.

drawback (*n.*) a hindrance; disadvantage.

drawing (*n.*) a sketch.

drawl (*v.*) to speak slowly or lazily. DRAWL (*n.*) a slowness in speech.

dray (*n.*) a low, four-wheeled cart or lorry for heavy goods.

dread (*v.*) to fear greatly. DREAD (*n.*) terror; alarm.

dreadful (*adj.*) terrible; fearful.

dreadfully (*adv.*) greatly; awfully.

dream (*n.*) 1. the mind-pictures of a sleeper. 2. recalled memories or idle fancies. DREAM (*v.*) to fancy things as real during sleep. DREAMER (*n.*). DREAMILY (*adv.*).

drearily (*adv.*) dismally; gloomily.

dreary (*adj.*) cheerless; bleak.

dredge (*v.*) to scoop mud from a channel; to deepen.

dredger (*n.*) 1. a ship having apparatus to deepen channels. 2. a flour sifter.

dregs (*n.*) 1. particles lying at the bottom of a liquid; sediment. 2. the waste; refuse.

drench (*v.*) to wet through; to soak. DRENCHED (*adj.*).

dress (*n.*) clothing; apparel. DRESS (*v.*) 1. to put on clothes. 2. to prepare food for cooking.

dribble (*v.*) 1. to throw down in drops. 2. to keep a ball moving slowly in football by giving light kicks. 3. to slaver as a child. DRIBBLE (*n.*) a few drops; a trickle.

drift (*v.*) to wander or float aimlessly. DRIFT (*n.*) 1. a heap of wind-blown sand, snow, etc. 2. the meaning or purpose of a remark or talk.

drill (*v.*) 1. to exercise. 2. to bore a hole. DRILL (*n.*) 1. physical exercises. 2. a boring tool.

drink (*v.*) to swallow liquid. DRINK (*n.*) liquor of any kind to be swallowed.

drip (*v.*) to fall drop by drop.

dripping (*n.*) the fat from meat when roasting.

drive (*v.*) 1. to force or urge along. 2. to guide and control a moving animal or vehicle. DRIVE (*n.*) a car-road to a house. DRIVER (*n.*).

drivel (*n.*) nonsense; idle chatter.

drizzle (*n.*) a fine or gentle rain. DRIZZLE (*v.*) to rain gently.

droll (*adj.*) amusing; comical.

dromedary (*n.*) a one-humped camel. (*pl.* DROMEDARIES).

drone (*n.*) 1. a bee that collects no honey. 2. a lazy person. 3. a low hum. DRONE (*v.*) to hum; to buzz.

droop (*v.*) to hang limply; to sag. DROOPING (*adj.*).

drop (*n.*) 1. a tiny ball-shaped quantity of liquid; a globule. 2. a distance from a higher to a lower place, or a fall through such distance. 3. a sip; a taste. DROP (*v.*) 1. to pour in drops. 2. to fall or let fall. DROPPING (*n.*).

drought (*n.*) continuous dry weather.

drove (*n.*) a band of driven animals. DROVER (*n.*).

drown (*v.*) 1. to suffocate under water. 2. to use too much water; to flood.

drowse (*v.*) to doze; to sleep lightly.

drowsily (*adv.*) sleepily.

drowsiness (*n.*) sleepiness.

drudge (*v.*) to toil; to slave. DRUDGE (*n.*) a toiler; labourer.

drug (*n.*) a substance used to make medicine. DRUG (*v.*) to give or take medicine which causes insensibility. DRUGGED (*adj.*).

druggist (*n.*) a seller of medicines; a chemist.

druid (*n.*) an ancient British priest.

drum (*n.*) 1. a round, hollow instrument, having skins stretched over its open ends, which gives a loud booming or rattling sound when beaten. 2. a drum-like organ within the ear. DRUM (*v.*) 1. to beat a drum; to beat on anything with the fingers. 2. to throb.

drunk (*past participle of verb* to drink) overcome or excited by drinking wine, spirits or beer, or by much success or power; intoxicated. DRUNKARD (*n.*). DRUNKEN (*adj.*).

dry (*v.*) to free from moisture. DRY (*adj.*) 1. waterless. 2. thirsty. 3. uninteresting.

dryness (*n.*) the amount of drying or thirstiness.

dual (*adj.*) twofold; double.

dub (*v.*) 1. to strike with a sword and make a knight; to entitle. 2. to give a new name to.

dubious (*adj.*) doubtful; uncertain.

duck (*n.*) 1. a domestic and wild water-fowl of the mallard family. 2. no score by a batsman in cricket. 3. a dip of the head under water. 4. a quick bob of head or body to escape a blow. 5. a light, cotton fabric made into clothing in hot countries. DUCK (*v.*) 1. to plunge, dive or dip the head under water. 2. to bob to avoid a blow.

duct (*n.*) a pipe; tube.

due (*n.*) 1. a right. 2. a debt. DUE (*adj.*) 1. owing. 2. suitable. 3. expected.

duel (*n.*) a fight between two armed people.

duellist (*n.*) a fighter in a duel.

duet (*n.*) music performed by two people.

dugout (*n.*) 1. an underground shelter. 2. a boat made from a hollowed-out tree-trunk.

duke (*n.*) a noble or peer of the highest rank. (*fem.* DUCHESS). DUCAL (*adj.*). DUCHY (*n.*).

dull (*v.*) to dim; to deaden. DULL (*adj.*) 1. blunt. 2. stupid. 3. cloudy; sunless.

dullness (*n.*) 1. bluntness. 2. stupidity. 3. dimness.

duly (*adv.*) rightly; properly.

dumb (*adj.*) unable to speak; mute. DUMBNESS (*n.*).

dumbfound (*v.*) to astonish.

dummy (*n.*) a puppet; a sham.

dump (*v.*) to unload; to pile. DUMP (*n.*) a rubbish or storage heap.

dumps (*n. pl.*) sadness; depression.

dun (*v.*) to press for payment. DUN (*adj.*) dull brown.

dunce (*n.*) one slow to learn; a dullard. See appendix.

dune (*n.*) a low sandhill.

dung (*n.*) animal-manure used to fertilize soil.

dungeon (*n.*) a dark, underground prison.

dupe (*v.*) to cheat. DUPE (*n.*) one easily deceived. DUPED (*adj.*).

duplicate (*n.*) a copy; a double. DUPLICATE (*v.*) to reproduce; to repeat.

duplication (*n.*) a repetition.

duplicator (*n.*) a machine for making copies.

duplicity (*n.*) double-dealing; deceit.
durability (*n.*) endurance; permanence.
durable (*adj.*) lasting; abiding.
duration (*n.*) the time anything takes, or lasts.
duress (*n.*) hardship; compulsion.
during (*prep.*) while; throughout.
dusk (*n.*) twilight; nightfall.
dusky (*adj.*) dark; swarthy.
dust (*n.*) fine dry particles of earth. DUSTY (*adj.*).
dutiable (*adj.*) liable to be taxed.
dutiful (*adj.*) obedient; faithful.
duty (*n.*) 1. anything due or owing. 2. a tax on goods.
dwarf (*n.*) anything much undersized. DWARF (*v.*) to make nearby objects appear small.
dwell (*v.*) 1. to live in; reside. 2. to think about fondly.
dwindle (*v.*) to lessen or shrink gradually.
dwindling (*adj.*) gradually becoming smaller.
dye (*v.*) to colour; to stain. DYE (*n.*) a colouring substance.
dyer (*n.*) one who dyes cloth. DYEING (*n.*).
dynamic (*adj.*) powerful; vigorous.
dynamite (*n.*) an explosive.
dynamo (*n.*) a machine for generating electricity.
dynasty (*n.*) a line of rulers of the same family.
dyne (*n.*) a measure of the force of electricity.
dyspepsia (*n.*) indigestion.

E

each (*adj. and pron.*) every one of a number taken singly or separately.
eager (*adj.*) keen; enthusiastic. EAGERLY (*adv.*).
eagerness (*n.*) enthusiasm; zeal.
eagle (*n.*) large, powerful bird of prey.
eaglet (*n.*) a young eagle.
ear (*n.*) 1. the organ of hearing. 2. a head or spike of corn.
earache (*n.*) a pain in the ear.
earl (*n.*) nobleman ranking next below a marquis. (*fem.* COUNTESS). EARLDOM (*n.*).

early (*adj.*) long ago; in bygone days. EARLY (*adv.*) before the usual time; beforehand.
earn (*v.*) to gain by one's own effort or worth.
earnest (*adj.*) serious; determined.
earnestly (*adv.*) intently.
earnestness (*n.*) 1. zeal; determination. 2. seriousness.
earnings (*n. pl.*) money earned; wages.
earth (*n.*) 1. the world; globe. 2. the soil; loam.
earthen (*adj.*) made or built of earth.
earthenware (*n.*) utensils made of fire-hardened clay; pottery.
earthly (*adj.*) belonging to the world.
earthquake (*n.*) an underground shock which makes the earth tremble.
earwig (*n.*) a small, dark-coloured insect which was supposed to creep into the ear.
ease (*n.*) rest; comfort.
easel (*n.*) a wooden frame to support a picture, blackboard, etc.
easily (*adv.*) without difficulty.
east (*n.*) the point where the sun rises. EAST (*adj.*) towards the rising sun. EASTWARD (*adv.*).
easy (*adj.*) restful; not difficult.
eat (*v.*) to swallow or consume food.
eatable (*adj.*) fit for food; edible.
eatables (*n. pl.*) foodstuffs.
eaves (*n. pl.*) the lower edges of a roof, which overhang the walls.
eavesdrop (*v.*) to listen secretly, or to a private talk. EAVESDROPPER (*n.*).
ebb (*v.*) to go lower slowly; to drain away. EBB (*n.*) a decrease; decline.
ebbing (*adj.*) failing; weakening.
ebony (*n.*) a dark, heavy, durable wood.
eccentric (*adj.*) odd; unreliable.
eccentricity (*n.*) 1. odd behaviour. 2. a habit. (*pl.* ECCENTRICITIES).
ecclesiastic (*n.*) a clergyman.
echo (*v.*) to throw back or reflect a sound; to resound. ECHO (*n.*) a sound reflected from afar. (*pl.* ECHOES). See appendix.
echoing (*adj.*) reflecting; resounding.
eclipse (*n.*) a darkening of the sun or moon. ECLIPSE (*v.*) 1. to darken; to overshadow. 2. to do better than another; to surpass. ECLIPSING (*adj.*).

economic (*adj.*) concerned with economics.

economical (*adj.*) thrifty; frugal.

economically (*adv.*) carefully; sparingly.

economics (*n. pl.*) the study of careful management.

economist (*n.*) one skilled in planning ahead; an expert in economics.

economize (*v.*) to reduce expense; to save.

economy (*n.*) wise management; thrift. (*pl.* ECONOMIES).

ecstasy (*n.*) great joy; rapture.

ecstatic (*adj.*) jumping for joy. ECSTATICALLY (*adv.*).

eczema (*n.*) a skin complaint.

eddy (*v.*) to whirl round. EDDY (*n.*) a whirling current of air or water; a little whirlpool (*pl.* EDDIES).

edge (*v.*) 1. to sharpen. 2. to move little by little. EDGE (*n.*) 1. the rim; brink. 2. the sharpness. 3. the cutting part of a blade.

edging (*n.*) the border; fringe.

edible (*adj.*) eatable; wholesome.

edict (*n.*) a proclaimed law or order.

edification (*n.*) enlightenment; moral instruction.

edifice (*n.*) a building; structure.

edify (*v.*) to build up; to improve. EDIFYING (*adj.*).

edit (*v.*) to prepare material for publication; to revise.

edition (*n.*) the number of copies printed at one time.

editor (*n.*) one who edits. (*fem.* EDITRESS).

editorial (*adj.*) about an editor and his work. EDITORIAL (*n.*) an article written by the editor, or giving his views.

educate (*v.*) to teach; to train.

education (*n.*) instruction; training. EDUCATOR (*n.*).

educational (*adj.*) concerned with teaching.

eel (*n.*) a snake-like fish.

eerie (*adj.*) causing awe or fear. EERILY (*adv.*).

eeriness (*n.*) a feeling of awe or fear.

efface (*v.*) to make unreadable; to erase.

effaceable (*adj.*) can be rubbed out.

effacement (*n.*) a rubbing out; an erasure.

effect (*v.*) to do; to complete. EFFECT (*n.*) a result; consequence.

effective (*adj.*) 1. able; capable. 2. striking; taking the eye.

effectiveness (*n.*) ability; efficiency.

effects (*n. pl.*) 1. goods; belongings. 2. stage imitations of sounds, etc.

effectual (*adj.*) suitable; competent.

effectuate (*v.*) to do; to accomplish.

effeminate (*adj.*) womanish. EFFEMINACY (*n.*).

effervesce (*v.*) 1. to bubble; to boil. 2. to be excited.

effervescence (*n.*) 1. a bubbling. 2. high spirits. EFFERVESCENT (*adj.*).

effete (*adj.*) worn out; exhausted.

efficacious (*adj.*) able; efficient.

efficacy (*n.*) capability; effectiveness.

efficiency (*n.*) ability; skill. EFFICIENT (*adj.*).

effigy (*n.*) an image; a statue. (*pl.* EFFIGIES).

effort (*n.*) an attempt; endeavour.

effortless (*adj.*) with ease; without exertion.

effrontery (*n.*) impudence; audacity.

effusive (*adj.*) overflowing; gushing. EFFUSIVENESS (*n.*).

egg (*v.*) to urge on; to stir into action. EGG (*n.*) the round or oval body from which birds and fish are hatched.

egoism (*n.*) love of oneself; vanity.

egoist (*n.*) a vain, selfish person.

egotistic (*adj.*) vain; conceited.

egress (*n.*) a going out; departure.

egret (*n.*) a small, white heron.

eiderdown (*n.*) a bedcover stuffed with the soft feathers of the eider duck.

eight (*n.*) a number or unit, one more than seven; the symbol 8 or VIII.

eisteddfod (*n.*) an assembly of bards and minstrels held in Wales.

either (*adj.*) one or the other of two persons or things.

ejaculate (*v.*) to cry out suddenly; to exclaim.

ejaculation (*n.*) an exclamation.

eject (*v.*) to throw out; to expel.

ejection (*n.*) an expulsion.

elaborate (*adj.*) decorative; overdone. ELABORATE (*v.*) 1. to overdo; to ornament. 2. to explain; to exaggerate.

elaboration (*n.*) exaggeration.

elapse (v.) to slip by; to pass (applied to time).

elastic (adj.) able to spring back or rebound, if stretched. ELASTIC (n.) rubber cord or tape.

elasticity (n.) ability to spring back; springiness.

elate (v.) to raise the spirits; to excite. ELATED (adj.).

elation (n.) great joy; satisfaction.

elbow (v.) to thrust aside with the elbows; to jostle. ELBOW (n.) 1. joint between fore and upper arm. 2. an angle; a corner.

elder (n. & adj.) the older of two persons. ELDER (n.) 1. tree bearing clusters of purple berries. 2. a leading official in certain Churches.

elderly (adj.) getting old.

eldest (adj.) the oldest of three or more persons.

elect (v.) to choose by voting. ELECT (adj.) chosen. ELECT (n.) the best; most worthy.

election (n.) the act of choosing by vote.

elector (n.) a voter.

electorate (n.) the whole body of voters; all entitled to vote.

electric (adj.) concerned with electricity.

electrically (adv.) by electricity.

electrician (n.) one who has studied electricity, and who attends to electrical apparatus.

electricity (n.) a power which produces light and heat.

electrification (n.) the act of providing or charging with electric power.

electrify (v.) 1. to charge with electricity. 2. to change from the power in use to electric power. 3. to enliven; to amaze.

electron (n.) a unit of negative electricity contained in an atom.

electronics (n.) the behaviour of electrons applied to science and industry.

elegance (n.) grace; beauty.

elegant (adj.) graceful; accomplished.

elegy (n.) a sad poem; a dirge.

element (n.) the simplest form of anything. ELEMENTARY (adj.).

elephant (n.) the largest land animal. ELEPHANTINE (adj.).

elevate (v.) 1. to lift up. 2. to inspire.

elevation (n.) 1. a height; hill. 2. a promotion; advancement. 3. liveliness; inspiration. 4. a drawing showing the height.

elevator (n.) a machine for raising grain to a higher level; a lift.

elf (n.) a mischievous fairy. (pl. ELVES). ELFIN (adj.).

elicit (v.) to find out; to learn. Beware ILLICIT.

eligible (adj.) suitable; qualified. ELIGIBLY (adv.).

eliminate (v.) to leave out.

elimination (n.) a removal; erasure.

élite (n.) the best; most choice.

elk (n.) a giant deer.

ellipse (n.) an oval-shaped figure. ELLIPTICAL (adj.).

elm (n.) a rough-barked forest tree.

elocution (n.) the art or manner of speaking.

elocutionist (n.) a teacher of elocution.

elongate (v.) to lengthen; to stretch out.

elope (v.) to run away and escape, especially with a lover. ELOPEMENT (n.).

eloquence (n.) apt or fluent speech.

eloquent (adj.) well-spoken; fluent.

else (adv.) besides; otherwise.

elsewhere (adv.) in another place.

elucidate (v.) to make clear; to explain.

elucidation (n.) an explanation; a solution. ELUCIDATORY (adj.).

elude (v.) to dodge; to avoid.

elusive (adj.) hard to catch; evasive.

elusory (adj.) on the tip of one's tongue; evasive.

emaciate (v.) to grow thin and lean; to waste away. EMACIATED (adj.).

emaciation (n.) leanness; gauntness.

emanate (v.) to flow from.

emanation (n.) anything that flows from another like light from the sun.

emancipate (v.) to set free; to liberate. EMANCIPATED (adj.).

emancipation (n.) freedom; liberty. EMANCIPATOR (n.).

embalm (v.) to preserve a dead body.

embankment (n.) a strong earthen bank, built to hold back water, etc. EMBANK (v.).

embargo (n.) an official forbidding; a prohibition.

embark (v.) to go on board a ship or aeroplane. EMBARKATION (n.).

embarrass (*v.*) 1. to make to feel uncomfortable. 2. to confuse.

embarrassing (*adj.*) causing discomfort; unease.

embarrassment (*n.*) 1. uneasiness. 2. shortage of money.

embassy (*n.*) 1. the mission or duties entrusted to an ambassador. 2. an ambassador's residence. (*pl.* EMBASSIES).

embellish (*v.*) to adorn; to beautify.

embellishment (*n.*) an adornment; a decoration.

ember (*n.*) a glowing or smouldering coal.

embezzle (*v.*) to steal from one who trusts you.

embezzlement (*n.*) stealing what one is trusted to guard. EMBEZZLER (*n.*).

embitter (*v.*) to cause ill-feeling.

embitterment (*n.*) ill-feeling; enmity.

emblem (*n.*) a badge; a symbol.

embody (*v.*) to join the main body; to include. EMBODIED (*adj.*).

embolden (*v.*) to encourage.

emboss (*v.*) to decorate with a raised pattern; to work in relief. EMBOSSER (*n.*).

embossing (*n.*) art of working in relief.

embrace (*v.*) 1. to clasp in the arms; to hug. 2. to include. EMBRACE (*n.*) a hug; clasp.

embrocation (*n.*) a lotion for rubbing on sprains.

embroider (*v.*) to ornament with needlework.

embroidery (*n.*) ornamental needlework.

embroil (*v.*) to draw into a quarrel.

embryo (*n.*) the beginning; first stage. EMBRYO (*adj.*) imperfect; budding.

emend (*v.*) to correct; to reform. See AMEND.

emendation (*n.*) a correction; a reform.

emerald (*n.*) a green gem. EMERALD (*adj.*) green.

emerge (*v.*) to come out of; to appear.

emergence (*n.*) an appearance.

emergency (*n.*) a happening which must be dealt with at once.

emery (*n.*) a hard stone used for edging tools.

emigrant (*n.*) one who emigrates.

emigrate (*v.*) to leave one's country and settle in another.

emigration (*n.*) a departure to settle anew.

eminence (*n.*) 1. a height; a hill. 2. renown; fame. 3. a cardinal's title.

eminent (*adj.*) famous; celebrated. EMINENTLY (*adv.*).

emissary (*n.*) a spy.

emit (*v.*) to send out; to give off.

emolument (*n.*) a payment; salary.

emotion (*n.*) a feeling of joy, pity, etc.

emotional (*adj.*) full of feeling; sensitive.

emperor (*n.*) the ruler of an empire. (*fem.* EMPRESS).

emphasis (*n.*) an added stress or force given to the voice.

emphasize (*v.*) to stress important words.

emphatic (*adj.*) spoken with firmness or force.

empire (*n.*) a union of countries under the rule of a single sovereign or government.

employ (*v.*) to use; to give work to.

employed (*adj.*) busy; occupied. EMPLOYABLE (*adj.*).

employee (*n.*) one who works for another.

employer (*n.*) one who gives work to another.

employment (*n.*) work; occupation.

emporium (*n.*) a large shop; a store.

empower (*v.*) to give power to; to authorize.

empties (*n. pl.*) empty containers.

emptiness (*n.*) a complete lack; a void.

empty (*v.*) to take out until nothing remains. EMPTY (*adj.*) containing nothing.

emu (*n.*) a large Australian, wingless bird.

emulate (*v.*) to try to equal or excel; to rival.

emulation (*n.*) competition; rivalry. EMULATOR (*n.*).

enable (*v.*) to give ability to; to strengthen.

enact (*v.*) to make into law. ENACTMENT (*n.*).

enamel (*n.*) a smooth, hard coating. ENAMEL (*v.*) to coat with enamel. ENAMELLER (*n.*).

enamour (*v.*) to inspire or fill with love; to charm.

encamp (*v.*) to erect or pitch tents; to form a camp. ENCAMPMENT (*n.*).

enchant (*v.*) 1. to charm; to delight. 2. to bewitch.

enchanting (*adj.*) charming; pleasing.

enchantment (*n.*) 1. delight; bliss. 2. witchcraft.

encircle (*v.*) to surround; to embrace. ENCIRCLEMENT (*n.*).

enclose (*v.*) 1. to surround. 2. to fence in. 3. to wrap in.

enclosure (*n.*) 1. ground within a fence. 2. the object within a wrapper or envelope.

encompass (*v.*) to encircle; to surround.

encore (*v.*) to ask to be repeated. ENCORE (*n.*) a demand for a repetition.

encounter (*v.*) 1. to meet as enemies. 2. to meet by chance. ENCOUNTER (*n.*) 1. a fight. 2. a chance meeting. ENCOUNTERED (*adj.*).

encourage (*v.*) to embolden; to stimulate.

encouragement (*n.*) strength; support. ENCOURAGING (*adj.*).

encroach (*v.*) to trespass; to intrude.

encroachment (*n.*) a trespass; an intrusion. ENCROACHING (*adj.*).

encumber (*v.*) to overload; to burden.

encumbrance (*n.*) a burden; hindrance.

encyclopædia (*n.*) a book containing items of information in alphabetical order.

end (*n.*) 1. the last part; the termination. 2. the limit; extrem'ty. 3. the result; aim. 4. the close of life. END (*v.*) 1. to finish; to conclude. 2. to destroy; to put to death.

endanger (*v.*) to place in danger; to imperil.

endearment (*n.*) loving conduct; a loving word or phrase.

endeavour (*v.*) to try; to attempt. ENDEAVOUR (*n.*) an effort; attempt.

ending (*n.*) the result; conclusion.

endless (*adj.*) everlasting; perpetual.

endorse (*v.*) to approve; to agree to.

endorsement (*n.*) an approval; agreement.

endow (*v.*) to provide for; to grant.

endowment (*n.*) 1. a gift to found or maintain a cause. 2. a natural talent.

endurable (*adj.*) bearable; supportable.

endurance (*n.*) ability to bear; fortitude.

endure (*v.*) 1. to bear. 2. to hold out. ENDURING (*adj.*).

endwise (*adv.*) on end.

enemy (*n.*) a foe; an adversary. (*pl.* ENEMIES).

energetic (*adj.*) active; vigorous. ENERGETICALLY (*adv.*).

energy (*n.*) power; vigour. (*pl.* ENERGIES).

enervate (*v.*) to weaken; to lose strength. ENERVATING (*adj.*).

enfeeble (*v.*) to weaken; to tire. ENFEEBLING (*adj.*).

enfold (*v.*) 1. to wrap up. 2. to clasp; to embrace.

enforce (*v.*) to compel to do.

enforceable (*adj.*) compulsory.

enforcement (*n.*) compulsion.

enfranchise (*v.*) 1. to set free. 2. to give the right to vote.

engage (*v.*) 1. to employ. 2. to undertake. 3. to begin to fight.

engagement (*n.*) 1. a contract. 2. an appointment. 3. a fight. 4. a betrothal or promise to marry.

engaging (*adj.*) pleasing; interesting.

engine (*n.*) a machine which produces power, or enables work to be done.

engineer (*n.*) one expert in designing, constructing or using machines or power.

engineering (*n.*) the science of planning and doing work which requires machines or power.

engrave (*v.*) to cut a design in a metal plate or in glass.

engraver (*n.*) an artist who engraves.

engraving (*n.*) a picture printed from an engraved plate.

engross (*v.*) 1. to take one's whole attention. 2. to write a document in legal form. ENGROSSER (*n.*).

engulf (*v.*) to swallow up; to overwhelm.

enhance (*v.*) to raise higher; to grow in value.

enhancement (*n.*) an increase; a betterment.

enigma (*n.*) a puzzle; a problem.

enigmatic (*adj.*) puzzling.

enjoy (*v.*) 1. to like. 2. to possess.

enjoyable (*adj.*) bringing joy.

enjoyment (*n.*) 1. pleasure. 2. possession.

enlarge (*v.*) to make larger; to magnify.

enlargement (*n.*) an increase; expansion.

enlighten (*v.*) 1. to give light. 2. to teach.

enlightened (*adj.*) educated; informed.

enlightenment (*n.*) knowledge; understanding.

enlist (*v.*) to join the army; to gain the support of.

enliven (*v.*) to rouse; to excite.

enmesh (*v.*) to catch in a net; to snare.

enmity (*n.*) ill-will; hatred.

ennoble (*v.*) 1. to make noble. 2. to create a peer or nobleman.

enormity (*n.*) a great wrong. (*pl.* ENORMITIES).

enormous (*adj.*) huge; vast. ENORMOUSLY (*adv.*).

enough (*adj.*) sufficient; ample.

enquire (*v.*) see INQUIRE.

enrage (*v.*) to anger; to infuriate. ENRAGED (*adj.*).

enrapture (*v.*) to fill with joy.

enrich (*v.*) to make rich with any kind of wealth; to make fertile; to adorn.

enrol, enroll (*v.*) 1. to write or enter in a register. 2. to join a class, society, etc. ENROL(L)MENT (*n.*).

enshrine (*v.*) to regard as sacred; to treasure.

ensign (*n.*) a banner; standard.

enslave (*v.*) to bring into slavery or bondage. ENSLAVEMENT (*n.*).

ensnare (*v.*) to trap.

ensue (*v.*) to follow from what has been done; to result.

ensuing (*adj.*) following; succeeding.

ensure (*v.*) to make sure or safe.

entail (*v.*) to include; to make necessary.

entangle (*v.*) to mix up; to tie in knots.

entanglement (*n.*) a muddle; complication.

enter (*v.*) 1. to go or come into. 2. to record in a book.

enterprise (*n.*) 1. a bold venture. 2. readiness to take risks.

enterprising (*adj.*) daring; audacious.

entertain (*v.*) 1. to amuse. 2. to consider. 3. to maintain as a guest. ENTERTAINER (*n.*).

entertaining (*adj.*) amusing; interesting.

entertainment (*n.*) 1. amusement. 2. hospitality.

enthral (*v.*) 1. to enslave. 2. to delight; to thrill. Also ENTHRALL.

enthralling (*adj.*) most interesting.

enthrone (*v.*) to place on a throne. EN-THRONEMENT (*n.*).

enthusiasm (*n.*) eagerness; zeal.

enthusiast (*n.*) a keen, zealous person.

enthusiastic (*adj.*) zealous; whole-hearted.

entice (*v.*) to tempt; to lure.

enticement (*n.*) a temptation; an attraction.

enticing (*adj.*) attractive; tempting.

entire (*adj.*) whole; complete.

entirely (*adv.*) wholly; perfectly.

entitle (*v.*) to give a right to; to allow.

entrance (*n.* pron. EN-trance) the way in; gateway. ENTRANCE (*v.* pron. en-TRANCE) to charm; to delight.

entrant (*n.*) one who enters.

entreat (*v.*) to beg; to implore.

entreaty (*n.*) a prayer; an earnest request.

entrust (*v.*) to place in another's care.

entry (*n.*) 1. admission into. 2. an entrance. 3. an item written in a book.

entwine (*v.*) to twist together.

enumerate (*v.*) to number; to count.

enumeration (*n.*) a counting; numbering.

enunciate (*v.*) to speak; to pronounce.

enunciation (*n.*) clear speaking; distinct pronunciation.

envelop (*v.*) to wrap up; to enclose.

envelope (*n.*) an outer case; a wrapper.

enviable (*adj.*) causing jealousy; desirable.

envious (*adj.*) jealous. ENVIOUSLY (*adv.*).

environ (*v.*) to surround.

environs (*n. pl.*) the surroundings of a place; the suburbs.

envoy (*n.*) a special representative.

envy (*v.*) to grudge; to be jealous of. ENVY (*n.*) jealousy.

eon (*n.*) an era; an age.

epic (*n.*) a poem describing a heroic deed. EPIC (*adj.*) heroic; mighty.

epicure (*n.*) a lover of pleasure and luxury.

epicurean (*adj.*) luxury-loving. See appendix.

epidemic (*n.*) a quickly spreading outbreak of disease.

epigram (*n.*) a short, witty saying.

epigrammatic (*adj.*) brief; cleverly-worded.

epilogue (*n.*) a speech ending a play; the closing words or scene.

episode (*n.*) an incident; an event.

epistle (*n.*) a letter; message.

epitaph (*n.*) words inscribed on a tomb.

epithet (*n.*) a descriptive word or name; an adjective.

epoch (*n.*) an historical period or age.

equable (*adj.*) even-tempered; well-balanced.

equal (*adj.*) alike in size, number, worth, etc.

equality (*n.*) sameness; likeness. (*pl.* EQUALITIES).

equalize (*v.*) to make equal.

equally (*adv.*) to the same extent.

equanimity (*n.*) calmness; steadiness.

equator (*n.*) an imaginary circle round the earth, midway between the north and south poles.

equatorial (*adj.*) on or near the equator.

equerry (*n.*) an official in charge of the royal horses.

equestrian (*n.*) a horseman; rider. EQUESTRIAN (*adj.*) about horsemanship. (*fem.* EQUESTRIENNE).

equilateral (*adj.*) having all sides equal.

equilibrium (*n.*) balance; steadiness.

equinoctial (*adj.*) at or near the equinox.

equinox (*n.*) times in the year when day and night are equal in length. (March 20–21; Sept. 22–23).

equip (*v.*) to provide all required.

equipage (*n.*) a company travelling with all supplies.

equipment (*n.*) outfit; baggage.

equitable (*adj.*) fair; just. EQUITABLY (*adv.*).

equity (*n.*) justice; fairness.

equivalent (*adj.*) equal in value, usefulness, strength, etc. EQUIVALENT (*n.*) a thing equal in value, or in any other quality, to another.

era (*n.*) a long period of time; an age.

eradicate (*v.*) to uproot; to destroy.

erase (*v.*) to rub out.

erasure (*n.*) a rubbing out; an effacement.

ere (*adv.*) sooner than. ERE (*prep.*) before, in respect to time.

erect (*v.*) to build; to construct. ERECT (*adj.*) upright.

erection (*n.*) a building; construction.

ermine (*n.*) a weasel-like animal.

erode (*v.*) to wear away. ERODED (*adj.*).

erosion (*n.*) a slow wearing by weather; weathering.

erosive (*adj.*) wearing; eating away.

err (*v.*) 1. to do wrong; to sin. 2. to make a mistake.

errand (*n.*) the journey with, and delivery of, a message.

errant (*adj.*) wandering; lost.

errata (*n. pl.*) errors; misprints. (*sing.* ERRATUM).

erratic (*adj.*) changeable; unreliable. ERRATICALLY (*adv.*).

erroneous (*adj.*) wrong; inaccurate. ERRONEOUSLY (*adv.*).

error (*n.*) a mistake; blunder.

erupt (*v.*) to burst out; to explode.

eruption (*n.*) 1. an outburst. 2. a skin rash. ERUPTIVE (*adj.*).

escalator (*n.*) a moving stairway.

escapade (*n.*) an adventure; a prank.

escape (*v.*) 1. to free oneself. 2. to avoid danger, disease, etc. 3. to leak. ESCAPE (*n.*) 1. a release. 2. an avoidance. 3. a leakage.

escort (*v.*) to go with and protect. ESCORT (*n.*) an accompanying guard.

Eskimo (*n.*) one of a race of primitive people inhabiting lands chiefly within the Arctic zone.

especial (*adj.*) special; particular.

espionage (*n.*) spying.

esplanade (*n.*) a public walk, or drive; a promenade.

espousal (*n.*) 1. a marriage. 2. support; sympathy.

espouse (*v.*) 1. to marry. 2. to support; to uphold.

espy (*v.*) to catch sight of; to see.

essay (*v.*) to try; to attempt. ESSAY (*n.*) 1. an attempt. 2. a written composition. ESSAYIST (*n.*).

essence (*n.*) 1. the heart or core of a thing. 2. a perfume.

essential (*adj.*) necessary; important. ESSENTIALLY (*adv.*).

establish (*v.*) 1. to make firm; to found. 2. to prove.

establishment (*n.*) anything firmly founded. ESTABLISHED (*adj.*).

estate (*n.*) one's lands, property or rank.

esteem (*v.*) to value highly. ESTEEM (*n.*) respect; regard.

estimable (*adj.*) worthy; honourable. ESTEEMED (*adj.*).

estimate (*v.*) to judge; to form an opinion. ESTIMATE (*n.*) an opinion. ESTIMATED (*adj.*).

estimation (*n.*) good opinion; esteem.

estrange (*v.*) to make unfriendly. ESTRANGED (*adj.*).

estrangement (*n.*) unfriendliness; indifference.

estuary (*n.*) a river mouth.

et cetera (**etc.**) and the rest.

etch (*v.*) to engrave on a metal plate. ETCHED (*adj.*).

etching (*n.*) a print from an etched plate.

eternal (*adj.*) everlasting.

eternally (*adv.*) always; perpetually.

eternity (*n.*) 1. all time. 2. a very long time.

ether (*n.*) 1. an invisible substance that fills all space. 2. a liquid anæsthetic.

ethereal (*adj.*) pure; heavenly.

ethical (*adj.*) relating to conduct and duty.

ethics (*n. pl.*) the study of right and wrong conduct.

ethnology (*n.*) the study of human races.

etiquette (*n.*) rules of polite conduct.

etymology (*n.*) the study of words.

eucalyptus (*n.*) an Australian gum tree and the oil from its leaves.

Eucharist (*n.*) the sacrament of the Lord's Supper.

Europe (*n.*) the smallest of the five continents or great land masses of the world. EUROPEAN (*adj.*). See appendix.

evacuate (*v.*) to leave; to empty. EVACUATED (*adj.*).

evacuation (*n.*) a withdrawal; quitting.

evacuee (*n.*) one ordered to leave a dangerous area in wartime.

evade (*v.*) to avoid; to dodge.

evaporate (*v.*) to turn into vapour; to disappear. EVAPORATED (*adj.*).

evaporation (*n.*) a turning into vapour; disappearance.

evasion (*n.*) dishonest avoidance.

evasive (*adj.*) misleading.

eve (*n.*) 1. the close of day; evening. 2. the evening before a saint's day. 3. the period just before an important event.

even (*adj.*) 1. level; exact. 2. divisible by two without remainder. EVEN (*n.*) evening.

evening (*n.*) the day's end; nightfall.

evenly (*adv.*) 1. smoothly. 2. exactly.

evenness (*n.*) flatness; smoothness.

event (*n.*) a notable happening.

eventful (*adj.*) important; memorable.

eventual (*adj.*) last; final.

eventually (*adv.*) at last.

eventuate (*v.*) to happen; to end.

ever (*adv.*) always; at all times.

everlasting (*adj.*) ceaseless; undying.

evermore (*adv.*) always.

every (*adj.*). It means EACH and ALL. For example, "I heard every word," means, "I heard EACH word and ALL the words."

everyday (*adj.*) frequent; usual.

evict (*v.*) to expel a person, especially a tenant, from a property by legal order or process; to dispossess. EVICTION (*n.*).

evidence (*n.*) 1. proof. 2. the statement of a witness.

evident (*adj.*) plain; clear.

evidently (*adv.*) undoubtedly; surely.

evil (*n.*) wrongdoing; sin. EVIL (*adj.*) sinful; base.

evilly (*adv.*) wickedly; sinfully.

evince (*v.*) to show; to prove.

evoke (*v.*) to call up; to summon.

evolution (*n.*) a gradual growth; development.

evolve (*v.*) to grow slowly; to develop. EVOLUTIONARY (*adj.*).

ewe (*n.*) a female sheep.

ewer (*n.*) a water-jug.

exact (*v.*) to demand and enforce; to insist upon. EXACT (*adj.*) true; correct.

exacting (*adj.*) severe; compelling.

exactitude (*n.*) correctness; precision.

exactly (*adv.*) precisely.

exactness (*n.*) correctness; accuracy.

exaggerate (*v.*) to overstate; to magnify.

exaggeration (*n.*) an overstatement.

exalt (*v.*) to praise; to honour. EXALTED (*adj.*).

exaltation (*n.*) light-heartedness; joy.

examination (*n.*) 1. a test. 2. an investigation.

examine (*v.*) to test; to inquire. EXAMINER (*n.*).

example (*n.*) a pattern; model.

exasperate (*v.*) to vex; to provoke. EXASPERATING (*adj.*).

exasperation (*n.*) anger; vexation.

excavate (*v.*) to dig out. EXCAVATED (*adj.*).

excavation (*n.*) a hole; trench.

excavator (*n.*) a digger; digging-machine.

exceed (*v.*) to be more or larger; to surpass.

exceedingly (*adv.*) extremely.

excel (*v.*) to be better than; to beat.

excellence (*n.*) perfection; merit. EXCEL-
LENT (*adj.*).

except (*v.*) to leave out; to omit. EXCEPT
(*prep.*) leaving out; omitting.

exception (*n.*) that left out; an omission.

exceptional (*adj.*) rare; unusual.

excerpt (*n.*) an extract from; a selection.

excess (*n.*) 1. the extra amount; surplus.
2. extravagance.

excessive (*adj.*) overmuch; unreasonable.

exchange (*v.*) to give one thing for
another; to barter. EXCHANGE (*n.*)
1. barter; trade. 2. a place where
merchants meet. 3. a telephone headquarters.

exchequer (*n.*) a treasury. THE EXCHEQUER
(*n.*) the government department dealing
with the nation's money affairs.

excise (*n.*) a tax on home-manufactured
goods.

excise (*v.*) to cut out; to notch. EXCISED
(*adj.*).

excision (*n.*) a cutting out; a notch.

excitability (*n.*) an eager, lively feeling.

excitable (*adj.*) lively; eager. EXCITING
(*adj.*).

excite (*v.*) to enliven; to arouse.

excitement (*n.*) liveliness; eager expectation.

exclaim (*v.*) to cry out suddenly.

exclamation (*n.*) a sudden cry expressing
pain or surprise.

exclude (*v.*) to leave out.

exclusion (*n.*) a shutting out; an omission.

exclusive (*adj.*) outside the ordinary;
select.

exclusively (*adv.*) solely; only.

excommunicate (*v.*) to shut out or expel
from fellowship with others in the
Church. EXCOMMUNICATION (*n.*).

excursion (*n.*) a pleasure-trip; an outing.
EXCURSIONIST (*n.*).

excusable (*adj.*) permissible; allowable.

excusably (*adv.*) pardonably.

excuse (*v.* pron. ex-CUZE) to pardon.
EXCUSE (*n.* pron. ex-CUSE) reason for
one's fault or failure.

execrable (*adj.*) hateful; abominable.

execrate (*v.*) to hate; to detest.

execration (*n.*) hatred; detestation.

execute (*v.*) 1. to do; to carry out. 2. to
put to death.

execution (*n.*) 1. the doing; carrying out.
2. the putting to death of a criminal.

executive (*adj.*) having power to do or
manage.

executor (*n.*) person appointed to carry
out the terms of a will. (*fem.*
EXECUTRIX).

exemplary (*adj.*) worthy; admirable.

exemplify (*v.*) to show by example.

exempt (*v.*) to free from; to excuse.

exemption (*n.*) release; freedom from a
task or duty.

exercise (*v.*) to train the muscles or mind
by systematic work or drill. EXERCISE
(*n.*).

exert (*v.*) to use one's strength; to strive.

exertion (*n.*) an effort; endeavour.

exhalation (*n.*) a vapour; mist.

exhale (*v.*) to breathe out. EXHALED
(*adj.*).

exhaust (*v.*) to tire; to use up. EXHAUST
(*n.*) used steam or gas from an engine;
tube for exit of used steam or gas.

exhaustion (*n.*) weariness; collapse.

exhaustive (*adj.*) tiring; prostrating;
leaving nothing more to be done or
said.

exhaustively (*adv.*) completely; thoroughly.

exhibit (*v.*) to display; to show.

exhibition (*n.*) 1. a show; display. 2. a
scholarship; an award.

exhilarate (*v.*) to enliven; to excite.
EXHILARATING (*adj.*).

exhort (*v.*) to advise; to urge.

exhortation (*n.*) advice; encouragement.

exile (*v.*) to send from home and
country; to banish. EXILE (*n.*) 1. a
banished person. 2. long absence from
home and country.

exist (*v.*) to live; to endure. EXISTENT
(*adj.*).

existence (*n.*) life.

exit (*n.*) 1. a way out. 2. a departure;
withdrawal.

exodus (*n.*) departure of a large number;
an emigration. THE EXODUS (*n.*) departure of the Israelites from Egypt under
Moses and Aaron.

exonerate (*v.*) to free from blame; to
acquit.

exorbitant (*adj.*) excessive; unreasonable.

expand (*v.*) to stretch; to enlarge.

expanse (*n.*) a wide, open space.

expansion (*n.*) growth; increase.

expansive (*adj.*) extensive; vast; genial.

expect (*v.*) to look forward to; to await.
expectant (*adj.*) waiting; hopeful.
expectation (*n.*) hope; anticipation.
expectations (*n. pl.*) hopes for the future.
expedience (*n.*) suitability; fitness.
expedient (*n.*) a means; method. EX-PEDIENT (*adj.*) advisable; profitable.
expedite (*v.*) to hasten.
expedition (*n.*) a journey for a particular purpose; speed.
expeditious (*adj.*) speedy.
expel (*v.*) to turn or drive out.
expend (*v.*) to spend; to use.
expenditure (*n.*) the sum spent.
expense (*n.*) the cost.
expensive (*adj.*) dear; costly.
experience (*v.*) to learn from what happens to oneself. EXPERIENCE (*n.*) a happening in one's own life.
experienced (*adj.*) skilled; expert.
experiment (*v.*) to try to find out or prove. EXPERIMENT (*n.*) a test; trial.
experimental (*adj.*) trying; testing.
expert (*n.*) a skilled person; a specialist. EXPERT (*adj.*) skilful; trained.
expiration (*n.*) 1. the end. 2. a breathing out.
expire (*v.*) 1. to die; to end. 2. to breathe out.
expiry (*n.*) the end.
explain (*v.*) to make clear or understandable.
explanation (*n.*) that which makes clear.
explanatory (*adj.*) meant to make clear.
explicit (*adj.*) plain; undoubted.
explicitly (*adv.*) plainly.
explode (*v.*) to burst noisily; to blow up.
exploit (*v.*) to use to benefit oneself. EXPLOIT (*n.*) a brave, striking act.
exploitation (*n.*) an undue use; an abuse.
exploration (*n.*) a search; discovery. EXPLORER (*n.*).
explore (*v.*) to examine; to search.
explosion (*n.*) a noisy burst.
explosive (*n.*) a substance that will explode. EXPLOSIVE (*adj.*) liable to explode.
export (*n.*) merchandise sent abroad. EXPORT (*v.*) to send goods abroad. EXPORTER (*n.*).
expose (*v.*) 1. to uncover. 2. to endanger. 3. to discredit.
exposed (*adj.*) 1. unprotected. 2. unmasked; revealed.

expostulate (*v.*) to object; to protest.
exposure (*n.*) 1. bareness. 2. danger. 3. a showing up.
expound (*v.*) to explain; to make clear.
express (*v.*) to state; to declare. EXPRESS (*adj.*) quick; swift.
expression (*n.*) 1. a statement. 2. a look. 3. a show of feeling. 4. emphasis; stress.
expressionless (*adj.*) without emphasis or feeling.
expressive (*adj.*) with feeling; with effect.
expressly (*adv.*) 1. clearly; firmly. 2. specially.
expulsion (*n.*) a driving out; banishment.
expunge (*v.*) to wipe out.
exquisite (*adj.*) acute; keen; delicate. EXQUISITELY (*adv.*).
extempore (*adj.*) unprepared; without preparation.
extend (*v.*) to stretch; to spread.
extension (*n.*) a lengthening; an addition.
extensive (*adj.*) wide; spacious.
extent (*n.*) the size; amount.
exterior (*n.*) the outside. EXTERIOR (*adj.*) outward; external.
exterminate (*v.*) to destroy completely.
extermination (*n.*) destruction; extinction.
external (*adj.*) outside; outward.
externally (*adv.*) outwardly.
extinct (*adj.*) 1. quenched. 2. not now existing.
extinction (*n.*) 1. a riddance. 2. a quenching.
extinguish (*v.*) 1. to put an end to. 2. to quench.
extinguisher (*n.*) apparatus for quenching fires.
extol (*v.*) to praise; to glorify.
extort (*v.*) to take forcibly; to wring from.
extortion (*n.*) an unjust gain.
extortionate (*adj.*) harsh; oppressive.
extra (*adj.*, *adv.*, *n.*) additional; more than usual or necessary.
extract (*v.* pron. EX-TRACT) 1. to draw or pull out. 2. to distil. EXTRACT (*n.* pron. EX-tract) 1. anything taken or copied from something else. 2. an essence; a juice.
extraction (*n.*) a pulling, or taking out.
extraordinarily (*adv.*) remarkably.
extraordinary (*adj.*) strange; rare.
extravagance (*n.*) foolish waste.

extravagant (*adj.*) wasteful; lavish.

extreme (*adj.*) farthest; utmost. EXTREME (*n.*) the opposite end; the farthest point.

extremely (*adv.*) exceedingly.

extremist (*n.*) one who overdoes things.

extremity (*n.*) the end; the edge. (*pl.* EXTREMITIES).

extricate (*v.*) to free; to disentangle.

extrication (*n.*) a disentanglement; an escape.

exuberance (*n.*) 1. abundance. 2. high spirits.

exuberant (*adj.*) plenty; overflowing.

exude (*v.*) to ooze out, like perspiration.

exult (*v.*) to rejoice; to crow.

exultant (*adj.*) joyous; triumphant.

eye (*n.*) 1. the organ of sight or vision. 2. a small hole as in a needle. EYE (*v.*) 1. to view; to observe. 2. to watch carefully.

eyeball (*n.*) the ball of the eye.

eyebrow (*n.*) an arch of hair above the eye.

eyed (*v.*) looked at; caught sight of.

eyelash (*n.*) line of hairs edging the eye-lid.

eyelet (*n.*) a small hole as for a shoelace.

eyelid (*n.*) the movable skin covering the eye.

eye-opener (*n.*) a marvellous story; a shock.

eyesore (*n.*) anything offensive to the sight; a nuisance.

eyot (*n.*) a small island in a river.

eyrie (*n.*) the nest of a bird of prey.

F

fable (*n.*) a story with a moral; a legend. FABLED (*adj.*).

fabric (*n.*) 1. the walls, floors and roof of a building. 2. a woven material.

fabricate (*v.*) 1. to make; to construct. 2. to lie; to invent.

fabrication (*n.*) 1. a construction. 2. an untruth. FABRICATED (*adj.*).

fabulous (*adj.*) unreal; fanciful; legendary.

façade (*n.*) the face or front of a building.

face (*n.*) 1. the front of the head. 2. the front surface of anything. FACE (*v.*) 1. to look towards. 2. to oppose firmly.

facet (*n.*) a tiny face or surface, as on a jewel.

facetious (*adj.*) witty; amusing.

facial (*adj.*) about the face.

facile (*adj.*) easy; light.

facilitate (*v.*) to make easy; to help.

facility (*n.*) a readiness; a help. (*pl.* FACILITIES).

facing (*n.*) an outer covering.

facsimile (*n.*) an exact copy; a replica.

fact (*n.*) a truth; reality.

faction (*n.*) a dissatisfied party or group.

factious (*adj.*) discontented; quarrelsome.

factor (*n.*) 1. a steward. 2. a partaker. 3. a number which divides into another number exactly.

factory (*n.*) buildings in which goods are manufactured; a works.

factual (*adj.*) true; real.

faculty (*n.*) an ability; a knack. (*pl.* FACULTIES).

fad (*n.*) a whim; fancy.

faddy (*adj.*) 1. fanciful; whimsical. 2. over-particular.

fade (*v.*) to grow dim; to wither. FADED (*adj.*).

faggot (*n.*) a stick or bundle of sticks.

Fahrenheit (*n.*) a thermometer scale having 32° and 212° marked at the freezing and boiling points of water.

fail (*v.*) to disappoint; to miss.

failure (*n.*) a lack of success; a break-down.

faint (*v.*) to swoon; to droop. FAINT (*n.*) a swoon. FAINT (*adj.*) dim; weak.

faintly (*adv.*) dimly; indistinctly.

faintness (*n.*) 1. dimness. 2. a feeling of dizziness.

fair (*adj.*) 1. just; right. 2. light-coloured. 3. bright; sunny. 4. pleasing. FAIR (*n.*) a market with side-shows.

fairly (*adv.*) justly; moderately.

fairness (*n.*) 1. justice. 2. cleanliness.

fairy (*n.*) an imaginary little person with magic powers. (*pl.* FAIRIES). FAIRY (*adj.*) lovely; dainty.

faith (*n.*) belief; trust.

faithful (*adj.*) true; loyal.

faithfulness (*n.*) loyalty; steadfastness.

faithless (*adj.*) disloyal; untrustworthy.

fake (*v.*) to sham; to deceive. FAKE (*n.*) a sham; a fraud.

falcon (*n.*) a powerful bird of prey.

fall (*v.*) to drop; to pass from high to low. FALL (*n.*) 1. a drop; a descent. 2. a stumble.

fallacious (*adj.*) mistaken; misleading.

fallacy (*n.*) a mistake; an error.

fallible (*adj.*) uncertain; liable to make mistakes.

fallow (*adj.*) 1. untilled; unused. 2. pale brown in colour.

false (*adj.*) 1. untrue; faithless. 2. sham; artificial.

falsehood (*n.*) a lie; an untruth.

falsify (*v.*) to make untrue; to misrepresent.

falter (*v.*) to stumble; to be tonguetied.

faltering (*adj.*) hesitating; weak.

fame (*n.*) renown; honour.

familiar (*adj.*) well-known to; friendly with.

familiarity (*n.*) friendliness; experience of.

familiarize (*v.*) to learn all about; to accustom.

family (*n.*) 1. a household. 2. related or kindred people. 3. persons, plants and animals of the same kind. (*pl.* FAMILIES).

famine (*n.*) scarcity of food; starvation.

famish (*v.*) to starve; to hunger. FAMISHED (*adj.*).

famous (*adj.*) celebrated.

famously (*adv.*) excellently.

fan (*n.*) an instrument for making air currents. FAN (*v.*) to stir the air; to agitate.

fanatic (*n.*) an enthusiast; a zealot.

fanatical (*adj.*) zealous; enthusiastic.

fanaticism (*n.*) zeal; enthusiasm.

fancied (*adj.*) 1. supposed; imagined. 2. desired.

fanciful (*adj.*) 1. unreal. 2. ornamental.

fancy (*v.*) to suppose; to imagine. FANCY (*n.*) an idea; a notion. (*pl.* FANCIES).

fanfare (*n.*) a flourish of trumpets.

fang (*n.*) a long, pointed tooth.

fantastic (*adj.*) fanciful; absurd.

fantasy (*n.*) a fancy; an absurdity.

far (*adj.*) distant; remote.

far-fetched (*adj.*) unbelievable; exaggerated.

farad (*n.*) a measure of the amount of electricity. See appendix.

farce (*n.*) 1. a silly, but amusing play. 2. a futile proceeding.

farcical (*adj.*) comical; droll.

fare (*v.*) 1. to live. 2. to manage. 3. to journey. FARE (*n.*) 1. food. 2. the price of passage.

farewell (*n.*) a leave-taking. FAREWELL (*inter.*) good-bye.

farm (*v.*) to till; to cultivate. FARM (*n.*) a tract or holding of cultivated land. FARMER (*n.*).

farrier (*n.*) one who shoes horses; a smith.

farther (*adv.*) to or at a more advanced point or distance; in addition; also. FARTHER (*adj.*) more distant; more extended.

farthing (*n.*) a coin valued at a quarter of a penny.

fascinate (*v.*) to attract; to charm. FASCINATING (*adj.*).

fascination (*n.*) attraction; charm.

fashion (*v.*) to make; to shape. FASHION (*n.*) a style; model.

fashionable (*n.*) in general use.

fashionably (*adv.*) in the right style.

fast (*adj.*) 1. rapid. 2. secure. 3. reckless. FAST (*v.*) to go without food; to hunger. FAST (*n.*) a period during which little or no food is eaten.

fasten (*v.*) to make secure; to tie. FASTENER (*n.*).

fastening (*n.*) anything that secures, as a bolt, knot, etc.

fastidious (*adj.*) hard to please; particular.

fat (*n.*) a solid, greasy substance found in the body. FAT (*adj.*) 1. plump. 2. rich.

fatal (*adj.*) deadly; ruinous.

fatality (*n.*) a calamity; a disaster which causes death. (*pl.* FATALITIES). FATALLY (*adv.*).

fate (*n.*) an event bound to happen. See appendix.

fated (*adj.*) bound to happen; destined.

fateful (*adj.*) unavoidable; inevitable.

father (*n.*) a male parent or ancestor. FATHERLY (*adj.*).

father-in-law (*n.*) the father of one's husband or wife. (*pl.* FATHERS-IN-LAW).

fatherland (*n.*) one's native country.

fathom (*n.*) a measure (6 feet) of the depth of water. FATHOM (*v.*) 1. to find the depth. 2. to learn the truth. 3. to get to the bottom of.

fathomless (*adj.*) bottomless; unsolvable.

fatigue (*n.*) tiredness; exhaustion. FATIGUE (*v.*) to tire out.

fatness (*n.*) the amount of fat; plumpness.

fatten (*v.*) to make fat; plump.

fatuity (*n.*) foolishness; uselessness.

fatuous (*adj.*) silly; useless.

fault (*n.*) 1. a flaw; defect. 2. a sin; an offence.

faultless (*adj.*) 1. perfect; flawless. 2. innocent.

faulty (*adj.*) imperfect; defective.

fauna (*n.*) the animals of a region. See appendix.

favour (*v.*) to befriend; to prefer. FAVOUR (*n.*) a kindness; a token of goodwill.

favourable (*adj.*) friendly; beneficial.

favourite (*adj.*) best-loved. FAVOURITE (*n.*) the dearest; the best-loved.

favouritism (*n.*) partiality; bias.

fawn (*n.*) a young deer. FAWN (*adj.*) yellowish-brown. FAWN (*v.*) to seek favour; to flatter.

fay (*n.*) a fairy; an elf.

fealty (*n.*) loyalty; faithfulness.

fear (*n.*) a feeling of dread; terror. FEAR (*v.*) to feel terror; dismay. FEARED (*adj.*).

fearful (*adj.*) 1. afraid; timid. 2. dreadful; awful.

fearless (*adj.*) bold; undaunted.

fearlessness (*n.*) courage; boldness.

fearsome (*adj.*) causing fear; dreadful.

feasible (*adj.*) possible; believable.

feast (*n.*) 1. a banquet; festive meal. 2. a holiday; anniversary. FEAST (*v.*) to entertain with a banquet.

feat (*n.*) a notable deed; an exploit.

feather (*n.*) a fringed quill which grows on a bird. FEATHERED (*adj.*).

feathery (*adj.*) feather-like.

feature (*n.*) 1. a distinctive part of the face. 2. an outstanding part of anything. FEATURE (*v.*) to make prominent.

features (*n.*) the face. FEATURED (*adj.*).

February (*n.*) the second month in the year.

feckless (*adj.*) feeble; irresponsible.

federal (*adj.*) united; allied.

federate (*v.*) to unite; to band together.

federation (*n.*) a league; alliance.

fee (*n.*) a payment for service; a remuneration.

feeble (*adj.*) weak; slight.

feebleness (*n.*) weakness; inability.

feebly (*adv.*) badly; half-heartedly.

feed (*v.*) 1. to supply with food or materials; to nourish. 2. to take food; to eat.

feel (*v.*) 1. to touch. 2. to be moved or affected. FEEL (*n.*) the knowledge gained by touching.

feeler (*n.*) an insect's organ of touch.

feeling (*n.*) 1. the sense of touch. 2. a thought; an emotion.

feelings (*n. pl.*) the sensations or emotions produced by one's five senses.

feign (*v.*) to sham; to pretend.

feint (*n.*) a mock attack in boxing, etc. FEINT (*v.*) to make a mock attack.

felicitate (*v.*) to express pleasure; to congratulate.

felicitous (*adj.*) 1. delightful; fortunate. 2. well-said.

felicity (*n.*) great happiness; bliss.

feline (*n.*) an animal of the cat family. FELINE (*adj.*) cat-like; stealthy.

fell (*v.*) to knock down; to hew. FELL (*n.*) 1. a hill. 2. a skin with hair on it. FELL (*adj.*) fierce; inhuman.

fellow (*n.*) 1. a companion. 2. a member of a learned society.

fellowship (*n.*) 1. companionship. 2. a university appointment.

felon (*n.*) a criminal.

felony (*n.*) a serious crime. (*pl.* FELONIES).

felt (*v.*) past tense of FEEL. FELT (*n.*) cloth made of pressed wool, used chiefly for laying under carpets.

female (*n.*) 1. a woman or girl. 2. an animal of the sex that has young. 3. a fruit-bearing plant.

feminine (*adj.*) concerned with women.

fen (*n.*) a marsh; bog.

fence (*n.*) a boundary hedge or railing. FENCE (*v.*) 1. to enclose. 2. to engage in swordplay. 3. to evade giving a true answer.

fend (*v.*) to keep or ward off; to protect from injury.

fender (*n.*) an object placed between two things to protect one or both of them.

ferment (*v.*) 1. to make sour. 2. to stir up; to excite. FERMENT (*n.*) a state of excitement.

fermentation (*n.*) excitement; commotion.

fern (*n.*) a plant having feathery leaves.

ferocious (*adj.*) fierce; savage.

ferocity (*n.*) wildness; fury.

ferret (*n.*) a weasel-like animal. FERRET (*v.*) to drive out of a hiding-place; to search.

ferry (*v.*) to carry over a river. FERRY (*n.*) a boat which carries across a river. (*pl.* FERRIES)

fertile (*adj.*) fruitful; productive.

fertility (*n.*) fruitfulness; richness.

fertilize (*v.*) to make fruitful; to enrich.

fertilizer (*n.*) material put into the soil to enrich it.

fervency (*n.*) eagerness; zeal.

fervent (*adj.*) keen; zealous.

fervour (*n.*) keenness; enthusiasm.

fester (*v.*) 1. to be filled with poisonous matter. 2. to rankle.

festival (*n.*) a feast; merrymaking.

festive (*adj.*) jolly; gay.

festivity (*n.*) a celebration; gala. (*pl.* FESTIVITIES).

festoon (*n.*) a hanging garland of flowers or ribbons. FESTOON (*v.*) to decorate with garlands.

fetch (*v.*) to bring; to carry from.

fête (*n.*) a gala; carnival. FÊTE (*v.*) to entertain gaily.

fetish (*n.*) a charm; talisman.

fetlock (*n.*) the tuft of hair and the place on the back of a horse's leg where it grows.

fetter (*n.*) a chain binding the ankles. FETTER (*v.*) to chain; to hinder.

fettle (*v.*) to repair; to work with activity. FETTLE (*n.*) fitness or readiness for work.

feud (*n.*) a lasting quarrel.

feudalism (*n.*) a system under which land was held in return for military service.

fever (*n.*) 1. a disease which overheats the blood. 2. eager excitement.

feverish (*adj.*) affected with fever.

feverishly (*adv.*) eagerly; excitedly.

few (*adj.*) not many. FEW (*n. & pro.*) a small number; the minority.

fiasco (*n.*) a complete failure.

fib (*n.*) a lie; falsehood. FIB (*v.*) to lie.

fibre (*n.*) a thread of mineral or vegetable material from which fabrics are manufactured.

fickle (*adj.*) inconstant; changeable.

fickleness (*n.*) changeableness; unreliability.

fiction (*n.*) a story; an invention. FICTIONAL (*adj.*).

fictitious (*adj.*) imagined; invented.

fiddle (*n.*) a violin. FIDDLER (*n.*).

fidelity (*n.*) loyalty; devotion.

fidget (*v.*) to be restless; to fret. FIDGETY (*adj.*)

field (*n.*) 1. a large enclosed piece of land. 2. a battleground; sportsground. 3. the extent or range of anything.

fiend (*n.*) a devil; monster. FIENDISH (*adj.*).

fierce (*adj.*) savage; ferocious. FIERCELY (*adv.*).

fiery (*adj.*) 1. flaming; burning. 2. quick-tempered.

fife (*n.*) a small, shrill flute. FIFE (*v.*) to play a fife.

fig (*n.*) the soft, pear-shaped fruit of the fig-tree.

fight (*v.*) 1. to struggle with another. 2. to battle with. FIGHT (*n.*) a combat; battle. FIGHTER (*n.*).

figment (*n.*) a fiction; invention.

figure (*n.*) 1. a shape; image. 2. a number; digit. FIGURE (*v.*) to calculate; to act.

filament (*n.*) a very fine thread.

filbert (*n.*) a hazel-nut. See appendix.

filch (*v.*) to steal; to pilfer.

file (*n.*) 1. a steel tool for smoothing by rubbing. 2. a case in which to store documents. 3. a single line of people. FILE (*v.*) 1. to use a file. 2. to place in a file. 3. to move one behind another.

filial (*adj.*) relating to a son or daughter.

filigree (*n.*) ornament of gold or silver wire.

filings (*n.*) metal fragments rubbed off by filing.

fill (*v.*) to become, or make, full; to provide all a container of any kind (cup, box, room, etc.) will hold. FILL (*n.*) a full supply.

fillet (*n.*) 1. a hair band. 2. fish or meat with the bone removed. FILLET (*v.*) to take bones out.

film (*n.*) 1. a thin coating or skin. 2. ribbon on which photographs are taken. FILM (*v.*) 1. to coat thinly. 2. to photograph.

filmy (*adj.*) thin; cobweb-like.

filter (*v.*) to purify by straining. FILTER (*n.*) a fine-meshed strainer.

filth (*n.*) 1. foulness. 2. foul language.

filthy (*adj.*) dirty; foul.

filtrate (*n.*) a filtered liquid.

fin (*n.*) an organ enabling a fish to swim, balance, etc.

final (*adj.*) last; conclusive.

finale (*n.*) the end; conclusion.

finality (*n.*) the completeness; certainty.

finally (*adv.*) lastly; in conclusion.

finance (*n.*) money matters or dealings. FINANCE (*v.*) to supply with money.

financial (*adj.*) concerned with money.

financier (*n.*) a manager of large sums of money.

finch (*n.*) one of many kinds of small singing-birds.

find (*v.*) 1. to discover. 2. to recover or come across something lost or mislaid. FIND (*n.*) 1. a discovery. 2. a thing restored.

fine (*adj.*) 1. very thin. 2. choice; excellent. 3. dry; sunny. FINE (*n.*) money paid as a penalty. FINE (*v.*) to impose a penalty.

finely (*adv.*) 1. thinly; closely. 2. excellently; well said or done.

fineness (*n.*) 1. the thinness; slenderness. 2. the keenness. 3. the splendour; elegance.

finery (*n.*) showy dress or decoration. (*pl.* FINERIES).

finesse (*n.*) great skill; cunning.

finger (*n.*) one of the four (or five with thumb) jointed, nail-tipped members or digits of the hand. FINGER (*v.*) 1. to touch or handle with the fingers. 2. to use the fingers in playing an instrument.

finish (*v.*) to end; to complete. FINISH (*n.*) 1. a completion. 2. a high polish. FINISHED (*adj.*).

finite (*adj.*) limited; bounded.

fir (*n.*) a resinous, cone-bearing tree.

fire (*n.*) 1. flame and heat from burn-ing. 2. passion; excitement. FIRE (*v.*) 1. to cause to burn. 2. to shoot off a gun. 3. to make enthusiastic; to inspire.

fireless (*adj.*) 1. without fire. 2. dull; lifeless.

fireproof (*adj.*) unburnable.

firm (*adj.*) fixed; steadfast. FIRM (*n.*) a company; business.

firmament (*n.*) the heavens; sky.

firmness (*n.*) steadfastness; resolution.

first (*adj.*) in front of all others; the foremost or earliest. FIRST (*adv.*) before anything else. FIRST (*n.*) 1. the foremost in position. 2. the earliest in time. 3. the chief; head.

firth (*n.*) a narrow inlet of the sea into which a river flows, especially in Scotland.

fiscal (*adj.*) concerning public wealth; revenue.

fish (*n.*) an animal living entirely in water and breathing through gills. FISH (*v.*) to catch fish; to angle. FISHERMAN (*n.*).

fishery (*n.*) the business of catching fish.

fishmonger (*n.*) one who sells fish.

fission (*n.*) a splitting into parts.

fissure (*n.*) a deep, narrow cleft; a crevice.

fist (*n.*) a hand tightly closed. FIST (*v.*) to strike or thrust aside with the fist.

fit (*v.*) to agree exactly; to suit. FIT (*n.*) 1. a sudden seizure; a spasm. 2. a whim; notion. FIT (*adj.*) suitable; right.

fitful (*adj.*) irregular; unreliable.

fitness (*n.*) 1. suitability. 2. healthiness.

fitting (*adj.*) suitable; right.

fittings (*n. pl.*) fixtures in a room or shop.

five (*n.*) a number one more than four; the figure or numeral 5 or V.

fix (*v.*) 1. to make firm; to secure. 2. to decide; to settle. FIX (*n.*) a difficulty; predicament.

fixed (*adj.*) firm; immovable. FIXEDLY (*adv.*).

fixture (*n.*) 1. anything unmovable. 2. the date of a future event.

fizz (*v.*) to make a hissing sound; to effervesce. FIZZ (*n.*) a hissing sound, especially that made by gas escaping from a liquid.

flabbergast (*v.*) to astonish; to amaze.

flabbiness (*n.*) softness; looseness.

flabby (*adj.*) limp; slack.

flaccid (*adj.*) soft; limp.

flag (*n.*) 1. a banner; an ensign. 2. a paving stone. FLAG (*v.*) 1. to tire. 2. to signal with flags. 3. to pave.

flagon (*n.*) large, narrow-mouthed flask.

flagrant (*adj.*) disgraceful; notorious.

flail (*n.*) instrument for threshing corn.

flake (*n.*) a shaving; a light, fleecy tuft or piece; thin scale. FLAKE (*v.*) to scale off.

flaky (*adj.*) in scales or layers.

flamboyant (*adj.*) flaming; bold.

flame (*n.*) 1. a tongue of fire; a blaze. 2. eagerness; enthusiasm. FLAME (*v.*) 1. to blaze; to flare. 2. to show eagerness; temper.

flaming (*adj.*) 1. blazing. 2. excited.

flamingo (*n.*) a long-necked wading-bird.

flange (*n.*) a raised rim on a wheel.

flank (*n.*) the side. FLANK (*v.*) to be at one side; to border on one side.

flannel (*n.*) a soft woollen cloth of loose texture. FLANNEL (*v.*) to clothe or rub with flannel.

flap (*n.*) a hanging strip. FLAP (*v.*) to flutter; to wave.

flare (*v.*) to blaze; to flame. FLARE (*n.*) 1. a sudden flaming. 2. a signal-light.

flash (*n.*) 1. a quick gleam of light. 2. an instant; a moment. FLASH (*v.*) to break into flame or sparks.

flat (*adj.*) 1. level; smooth. 2. stale; tasteless. FLAT (*n.*) 1. a dwelling having all rooms on a single floor. 2. a musical sign.

flatfish (*n.*) a broad, flattened fish, having both eyes on its upper side.

flatten (*v.*) to lay flat; to make level.

flatter (*v.*) to praise insincerely. FLATTERER (*n.*).

flattery (*n.*) false praise; blarney. (*pl.* FLATTERIES).

flaunt (*v.*) to show off; to brag.

flavour (*n.*) the taste; relish. FLAVOUR (*v.*) to season; to salt.

flavouring (*n.*) the seasoning.

flavourless (*adj.*) tasteless; insipid.

flaw (*n.*) a defect; weakness. FLAWLESS (*adj.*).

flax (*n.*) plant whose fibre provides linen.

flaxen (*adj.*) fair; golden.

flay (*v.*) to strip off the skin.

fleck (*n.*) a spot; speck. FLECK (*v.*) to speckle; to dapple.

fledgeling (*n.*) 1. a young bird. 2. an inexperienced person.

flee (*v.*) to run away.

fleece (*n.*) a sheep's coat of wool. FLEECE (*v.*) 1. to shear; to clip. 2. to swindle.

fleecy (*adj.*) woolly; soft.

fleet (*n.*) a group of ships. FLEET (*adj.*) quick; swift.

fleeting (*adj.*) swiftly passing; momentary.

fleetness (*n.*) rapidity; swiftness.

flesh (*n.*) all the soft matter covering the framework of bones in animals.

flex (*v.*) to bend; to twist. FLEX (*n.*) rubber-covered wire which conveys electricity.

flexibility (*n.*) suppleness; pliancy.

flexible (*adj.*) 1. easily bent; pliable. 2. tractable; manageable.

flick (*n.*) a light, whiplike stroke. FLICK (*v.*) to strike lightly.

flicker (*v.*) to waver; to flutter. FLICKER (*n.*) a wavering light.

flickering (*adj.*) wavering; fluctuating.

flight (*n.*) 1. a running away; fleeing. 2. an aeroplane journey. 3. the flying of birds. 4. distance a missile travels in the air. 5. a series of steps or hurdles.

flightiness (*n.*) lightheartedness; fickleness.

flighty (*adj.*) changeable; capricious.

flimsiness (*n.*) 1. fragility. 2. worthlessness.

flimsy (*adj.*) 1. easily torn. 2. poor; worthless.

flinch (*v.*) to wince; to shrink from.

fling (*v.*) to hurl; to throw. FLING (*n.*) 1. a throw; cast. 2. a Highland dance.

flint (*n.*) a hard stone from which steel strikes fire.

flip (*v.*) to toss with the fingers. FLIP (*n.*) a flick; snap.

flippancy (*n.*) inconsiderate talk; pertness.

flippant (*adj.*) taking serious things lightly.

flirt (*v.*) to play with. FLIRT (*n.*) one who plays at lovemaking.

flirtation (*n.*) lovemaking for amusement.

flit (*v.*) to dart from place to place; to flutter.

float (*v.*) 1. to rest on the surface of a

liquid. 2. to start a new enterprise or business. FLOAT (*n.*) anything that does not sink in a liquid.

floatation (*n.*) the starting of a new company. Also FLOTATION (*n.*).

floating (*adj.*) buoyant.

flock (*n.*) 1. a group of sheep or birds. 2. a Christian congregation. FLOCK (*v.*) to gather in crowds.

floe (*n.*) a large or extensive sheet of ice floating in the sea.

flog (*v.*) to strike with rod or whip.

flogging (*n.*) a severe thrashing.

flood (*n.*) 1. an overflow of water. 2. over-abundance of anything. 3. the flowing in of the tide. FLOOD (*v.*) 1. to cover with water; to swamp. 2. to overwhelm.

flooding (*n.*) an overflowing; inundation.

floor (*n.*) 1. the level portion on which one walks in a building. 2. a storey of a building. FLOOR (*v.*) 1. to lay a floor. 2. to silence in argument. 3. to knock to the floor.

flop (*v.*) 1. to sit or lie down suddenly and heavily. 2. to collapse.

flora (*n.*) the plants of a region. See appendix.

floral (*adj.*) concerning flowers.

florid (*adj.*) flowery; red in colour.

florin (*n.*) a two-shilling piece.

florist (*n.*) one who sells flowers.

floss (*n.*) rough silk.

flotilla (*n.*) a fleet of small vessels.

flotsam (*n.*) goods and wreckage floating on the sea.

flounce (*v.*) to jerk away suddenly. FLOUNCE (*n.*) 1. a sudden jerk or spring. 2. a border on a dress.

flounder (*v.*) to struggle helplessly. FLOUNDER (*n.*) a flatfish.

flour (*n.*) finely-ground meal or wheat.

flourish (*v.*) 1. to prosper; to succeed. 2. to wave about; to brandish. FLOURISH (*n.*) 1. a waving; brandishing. 2. a fanfare of trumpets. 3. an ornamental curve.

flourishing (*adj.*) thriving; prosperous.

flout (*v.*) to treat with contempt; to insult. FLOUT (*n.*) an insult.

flow (*v.*) to move easily as a liquid; to glide. FLOW (*n.*) 1. the outpouring of a liquid, talk, etc. 2. the rise of the tide.

flower (*n.*) 1. a bloom; blossom. 2. the choicest part of anything. FLOWER (*v.*) to blossom. FLOWERY (*adj.*).

flowing (*adj.*) 1. running smoothly. 2. in-coming; rising.

fluctuate (*v.*) to rise and fall; to vary.

fluctuation (*n.*) variation; unsteadiness.

flue (*n.*) a chimney; ventilating shaft.

fluency (*n.*) readiness of speech.

fluent (*adj.*) smooth-flowing.

fluff (*n.*) tiny pieces of downy matter.

fluid (*n.*) a substance that flows; a liquid or gas. FLUID (*adj.*) able to flow.

fluidity (*n.*) the ease or difficulty of flowing.

fluke (*n.*) 1. a flatfish; flounder. 2. one of the pointed parts in an anchor and a whale's tail. 3. an unexpected and lucky success.

flume (*n.*) an artificial water-channel to a mill-wheel, or power-station.

flurried (*adj.*) flustered; excited.

flurry (*v.*) to fluster; to bustle. FLURRY (*n.*) bustle; confusion.

flush (*v.*) 1. to blush; to redden. 2. to flood with water. FLUSH (*n.*) a rush of colour to the face. FLUSH (*adj.*) level with the top; full.

fluster (*v.*) to confuse; to upset. FLUSTER (*n.*) confusion; agitation. FLUSTERED (*adj.*).

flute (*n.*) 1. a tubular wind-instrument with finger-holes. 2. a shallow groove cut in a pillar.

flutist (*n.*) a flute-player. Also FLAUTIST.

flutter (*v.*) 1. to flap the wings without flying. 2. to hurry about in confusion. FLUTTER (*n.*) 1. a hovering. 2. a confusion; flurry.

flux (*n.*) any substance which helps metal to melt or fuse.

fly (*v.*) 1. to move through the air with wings, or in an aeroplane. 2. to run away; to flee. FLY (*n.*) a winged insect, but especially the house-fly. 2. a tent flap. (*pl.* FLIES).

foal (*n.*) a young horse; a colt or filly.

foam (*n.*) froth; spume. FOAM (*v.*) 1. to gather froth. 2. to be angry.

fob (*n.*) a little pocket for a watch. FOB (*v.*) to cheat; to deceive, or put a person off with an inferior article.

focal (*adj.*) having a central point.

focus (*n.*) the point from which rays of light seem to spread; the centre point. (*pl.* FOCI). FOCUS (*v.*) 1. to draw attention to. 2. to regulate a lens or camera to give a clear image.

fodder (*n.*) cattle-food.

foe (*n.*) an enemy; antagonist.

fog (*n.*) a dirt or smoke-laden mist.

fog(e)y (*n.*) an old-fashioned man; an old man behind the times.

foggy (*adj.*) misty; murky.

foible (*n.*) a weakness; a little fault, or failing.

foil (*v.*) to outwit; to baffle. FOIL (*n.*) 1. a fencing weapon. 2. paper-thin metal sheets used for wrapping. 3. a background which improves the appearance.

foist (*v.*) to pass off a spurious thing as genuine.

fold (*v.*) to double over; to enclose. FOLD (*n.*) 1. the part doubled over. 2. a pen for sheep.

folder (*n.*) a stiff sheet doubled over to contain papers.

foliage (*n.*) the leaves of trees.

folio (*n.*) 1. a sheet of paper once folded. 2. a book made of such sheets.

folk (*n.*) people; kindred.

folklore (*n.*) old-time learning, customs, etc.

folksong (*n.*) an old-time song.

follow (*v.*) 1. to come behind. 2. to support. 3. to understand.

follower (*n.*) a supporter; disciple.

following (*n.*) all who support. FOLLOWING (*adj.*) succeeding; next after.

folly (*n.*) foolishness; lack of good sense. (*pl.* FOLLIES).

foment (*v.*) 1. to bathe with hot water. 2. to stir up or excite.

fomentation (*n.*) 1. a hot-water bathing. 2. encouragement; agitation.

fond (*adj.*) 1. affectionate; loving. 2. doting.

fondle (*v.*) to caress; to pet.

fondly (*adv.*) lovingly.

fondness (*n.*) love; liking.

font (*n.*) 1. the basin holding baptismal water. 2. the spring or source.

food (*n.*) 1. anything eaten by living creatures to nourish them. 2. provisions.

fool (*n.*) a silly person; simpleton

FOOL (*v.*) 1. to jest. 2. to deceive; to hoodwink.

foolery (*n.*) folly; nonsense.

foolhardy (*adj.*) reckless; risky.

fooling (*n.*) silly behaviour. FOOLISH (*adj.*).

foolishly (*adv.*) stupidly; unwisely.

foolproof (*adj.*) 1. extremely simple. 2. guarding against misuse by stopping automatically.

foolscap (*n.*) a size of paper.

foot (*n.*) 1. that part of a limb on which an animal stands or walks. 2. a measure of length (12 inches). 3. the bottom or base of an object. (*pl.* FEET).

football (*n.*) a team game, and the inflated leather ball kicked by the players.

footfall (*n.*) a footstep or its sound.

foothold (*n.*) a firm support for the foot.

footlights (*n. pl.*) lights along the front of a theatre stage.

footnotes (*n. pl.*) notes placed at the bottom of a page.

footprint (*n.*) the mark left by the foot on soft soil.

fop (*n.*) a vain man; a dandy.

for (*prep.*) 1. instead of. 2. toward. 3. during. 4. on behalf of. 5. in search of. FOR (*conj.*) because.

forage (*v.*) to search for food. FORAGE (*n.*) cattle-food; fodder. FORAGER (*n.*).

foray (*n.*) a plundering raid.

forbear (*v.*) to hold back; to be patient. FORBEAR (*n.*) an ancestor; forefather.

forbearance (*n.*) moderation; patience.

forbearing (*adj.*) patient; long-suffering.

forbid (*v.*) to tell not to do; to prohibit.

forbidden (*adj.*) prohibited; banned.

forbidding (*adj.*) unpleasant; threatening.

force (*v.*) to make; to compel. FORCE (*n.*) 1. power. 2. compulsion. 3. naval or military strength. 4. a body of troops or police.

forced (*adj.*) 1. compulsory. 2. unnatural; strained.

forceful (*adj.*) firm; vigorous.

forceps (*n. pl.*) small pincers for removing thorns, etc.

forcible (*adj.*) done by force; strength.

ford (*n.*) place where a river can be crossed on foot. FORD (*v.*) to wade across a river.

fore (*n.*) the front. FORE (*adj.*) at the front.

forearm (*n.* pron. FORE-arm) the arm between wrist and elbow. FOREARM (*v.* pron. fore-ARM) to be ever ready against attack.

forebode (*v.*) to foretell; to predict.

foreboding (*n.*) a feeling of coming evil a presentiment.

forecast (*n.* pron. FORE-cast) a statement of what may be expected. FORECAST (*v.* pron. fore-CAST) to foresee; to plan beforehand.

foreclose (*v.*) to stop; to shut up.

forefather (*n.*) an ancestor.

for(e)go (*v.*) to give up; to renounce.

foregoing (*adj.*) earlier; former.

foregone (*adj.*) already settled or decided.

forehead (*n.*) the face between the hair and eyes.

foreign (*adj.*) 1. concerning another country; alien. 2. strange; belonging elsewhere. FOREIGNER (*n.*).

foreland (*n.*) a headland; cape.

foreman (*n.*) 1. an overseer. 2. a jury's spokesman.

foremost (*adj.*) chief; first.

foresee (*v.*) to look ahead; to anticipate.

foresight (*n.*) wise forethought; prudence.

forest (*n.*) a large tract of woodland.

forestall (*v.*) to be before others; to thwart.

forester (*n.*) official in charge of a forest.

forestry (*n.*) the art of managing forests.

foretell (*v.*) to prophesy; to predict.

forethought (*n.*) a planning beforehand; prudence.

forfeit (*v.*) to give up, or lose as a penalty. FORFEIT (*n.*) anything yielded to or taken by another as a punishment, or through neglect.

forge (*v.*) 1. to hammer into shape. 2. to imitate dishonestly; to counterfeit. 3. to thrust forward. FORGE (*n.*) a smithy.

forger (*n.*) a counterfeiter.

forgery (*n.*) a copy made to defraud.

forget (*v.*) to fail to remember; to overlook.

forgetful (*adj.*) apt to forget; unmindful.

forgetfulness (*n.*) inability to remember; heedlessness.

forgivable (*adj.*) pardonable; excusable.

forgive (*v.*) to let off; to pardon.

forgiveness (*n.*) pardon.

forgo (*v.*) to give up; to renounce.

forgotten (*adj.*) 1. unremembered. 2. neglected; slighted.

fork (*n.*) 1. a tossing, digging or eating implement having two or more prongs fitted into a handle. 2. the place where a road or stream divides into two or more branches. 3. the place where a branch leaves the trunk of a tree. FORK (*v.*) 1. to use or to impale upon a fork. 2. to branch from.

forlorn (*adj.*) friendless; forsaken.

form (*v.*) to shape; to fashion. FORM (*n.*) 1. a shape; figure. 2. a seat; bench. 3. a class. 4. an official paper to be filled in. 5. a method; system or style.

formal (*adj.*) precise; exact.

formality (*n.*) a rule; ceremony.

formation (*n.*) 1. an orderly arrangement. 2. a building up; composing.

former (*adj.*) earlier.

formerly (*adv.*) in time past; once.

formidable (*adj.*) powerful; mighty.

formless (*adj.*) 1. shapeless. 2. vague; indefinite.

formula (*n.*) a set form of words; recipe. (*pl.* FORMULÆ).

formulate (*v.*) to state clearly.

forsake (*v.*) to leave; to abandon.

forsaken (*adj.*) deserted.

fort (*n.*) a stronghold.

forte (*n.*) one's strong point; special talent. FORTE (*adj.*) very loud.

forth (*adv.*) forward; in front.

forthcoming (*adj.*) coming; arriving.

forthwith (*adv.*) immediately.

fortification (*n.*) a fortress; stronghold.

fortify (*v.*) to strengthen; to reinforce.

fortissimo (*adv.*) a musical direction meaning very loud.

fortitude (*n.*) endurance; strength.

fortress (*n.*) a fort; stronghold.

fortuitous (*adj.*) accidental; happening by chance.

fortunate (*adj.*) lucky; prosperous.

fortune (*n.*) 1. luck; fate. 2. wealth; success. See appendix.

forum (*n.*) 1. a place of public assembly in ancient Rome. 2. a law court; a place of judgment.

forward (*adv.*) ahead; onward. FORWARD (*adj.*) 1. early; progressive. 2. bold;

impudent. FORWARD (*v.*) 1. to encourage; to foster. 2. to hasten. 3. to send by ship, post, etc.

fossil (*n.*) remains of plant or animal life dug out of the earth.

fossilize (*v.*) to turn into stone.

foster (*v.*) 1. to rear; to nourish. 2. to aid; to encourage.

foul (*adj.*) 1. dirty. 2. vulgar. 3. unfair. 4. stormy. FOUL (*n.*) an unfair attack; an advantage. FOUL (*v.*) to soil; to sully.

foulness (*n.*) 1. filthiness. 2. unfairness.

found (*v.*) to start; to originate.

foundation (*n.*) 1. the base; groundwork. 2. an institution; establishment.

founder (*n.*) 1. the author; originator. (*fem.* FOUNDRESS). FOUNDER (*v.*) 1. to be wrecked. 2. to fall to pieces.

foundry (*n.*) a cast-metal works.

fount (*n.*) 1. a spring or well of water; a fountain. 2. the origin or beginning. 3. a set of printers' type of the same face.

fountain (*n.*) 1. a spring; jet of water. 2. the cause; origin.

fowl (*n.*) 1. a bird. 2. the barnyard cock or hen.

fowler (*n.*) a bird-catcher.

fox (*n.*) a wild animal of the dog family. FOX (*v.*) to sham; to pretend.

foxtrot (*n.*) a ballroom dance.

foxy (*adj.*) wily; cunning.

fracas (*n.*) a noisy quarrel; a brawl.

fraction (*n.*) a part.

fractional (*adj.*) very small.

fractious (*adj.*) naughty; fretful.

fracture (*v.*) to break; to snap. FRACTURE (*n.*) a break; a snap.

fragile (*adj.*) easily broken; breakable.

fragility (*n.*) brittleness; flimsiness.

fragment (*n.*) a bit; morsel.

fragmentary (*adj.*) in pieces; broken up.

fragrance (*n.*) the smell; perfume.

fragrant (*adj.*) sweet-smelling.

frail (*adj.*) weak; delicate.

frailty (*n.*) feebleness.

frame (*v.*) 1. to make; to fashion. 2. to invent; compose. FRAME (*n.*) 1. the fabric; construction. 2. one's temper; mood.

framework (*n.*) the supports round which something is built.

franchise (*n.*) the right to vote in an election; freedom.

frank (*adj.*) sincere; straightforward.

frankincense (*n.*) a dry resin used as a perfume.

frankly (*adv.*) openly; truthfully.

frankness (*n.*) straightforwardness.

frantic (*adj.*) mad; desperate.

fraternal (*adj.*) brotherly.

fraternity (*n.*) a brotherhood.

fraternize (*v.*) to make friends with.

fraud (*n.*) 1. trickery; deception. 2. a cheat; trickster.

fraudulent (*adj.*) dishonest; deceitful.

fraught (*adj.*) full; laden.

fray (*n.*) a fight; contest. FRAY (*v.*) to wear away by rubbing; to chafe.

frayed (*adj.*) rubbed; worn.

freak (*n*) 1. anything very odd. 2. a whim; prank.

freakish (*adj.*) 1. odd; strange. 2. whimsical; fanciful.

freckle (*n.*) a brownish spot on the skin, especially one caused by the sun. FRECKLE (*v.*) to become covered with freckles.

free (*adj.*) 1. at liberty; loose. 2. open; frank. 3. generous; liberal. 4. costing nothing. FREE (*v.*) to liberate; to unloose.

freedom (*n.*) 1. liberty; independence. 2. room; scope.

freehold (*n.*) land held free from payments except rates and taxes. FREEHOLDER (*n.*).

freely (*adv.*) 1. openly. 2. without cost.

freeze (*v.*) to turn from a liquid into a solid; to chill.

freight (*v.*) to load; to burden. FREIGHT (*n.*) a load; cargo.

freighter (*n.*) a cargo vessel.

frenzied (*adj.*) enraged; infuriated.

frenzy (*n.*) fury; madness.

frequency (*n.*) 1. the number of times. 2. the number of wave vibrations a second.

frequent (*adj.* pron. FREE-quent) happening often. FREQUENT (*v.* pron. free-QUENT) to visit often; to haunt.

frequently (*adv.*) many times; often.

fresco (*n.*) a picture painted on a wall.

fresh (*adj.*) 1. new; recent. 2. brisk; refreshing. 3. lively. 4. unskilled; inexperienced.

freshen (*v.*) to revive; to brighten up.

freshness (*n.*) briskness; vigour.

fret (*v.*) 1. to worry. 2. to vex. 3. to wear away.

fretful (*adj.*) irritable; peevish.

fretfulness (*n.*) ill-humour; crossness.

fretwork (*n.*) woodwork cut into ornamental designs.

friar (*n.*) a priest who travelled from place to place preaching and healing, and who kept himself by begging.

friary (*n.*) a headquarters for friars.

friction (*n.*) 1. the hindrance caused by things rubbing together. 2. disagreement; wrangling.

Friday (*n.*) the sixth day of the week. See appendix.

friend (*n.*) a person drawn to another by affection.

friendliness (*n.*) affection; goodwill.

friendly (*adj.*) affectionate; attached.

friendship (*n.*) attachment to another.

frieze (*n.*) ornamental border round walls of a room.

frigate (*n.*) a small, swift warship.

fright (*n.*) fear; dread.

frighten (*v.*) to make afraid; to terrify.

frightened (*adj.*) scared; terrified.

frightful (*adj.*) dreadful; shocking.

frigid (*adj.*) 1. cold; icy. 2. cold in manner; unwelcoming.

frigidity (*n.*) 1. coldness. 2. stiffness; primness.

frill (*n.*) a pleated or ruffled edging.

fringe (*n.*) 1. a border trimmed with loose, hanging threads. 2. the edge; margin.

frisk (*v.*) to romp; to frolic.

friskiness (*n.*) playfulness.

frisky (*adj.*) frolicsome.

fritter (*v.*) to throw away little by little; to waste.

frivolity (*n.*) 1. a trifle. 2. fun; gaiety.

frivolous (*adj.*) 1. foolish; flippant. 2. fond of fun.

fro (*adv.*) shortened form of from, or away. TO and FRO, backwards and forwards.

frock (*n.*) 1. a monk's long gown with loose sleeves. 2. a woman's or child's dress or gown.

frog (*n.*) a four-footed amphibian noted for jumping.

frolic (*v.*) to romp. FROLIC (*n.*) a romp; prank.

frolicsome (*adj.*) lively; playful.

from (*prep.*) away; out of.

front (*n.*) foremost part of anything; the face. FRONT (*v.*) to face; to encounter.

frontage (*n.*) ground in front of a building.

frontal (*adj.*) belonging to the forehead.

frontier (*n.*) the boundary between two countries.

frontispiece (*n.*) a picture at the beginning of a book.

frost (*n.*) frozen drops of water or dew. FROSTY (*adj.*).

frostbite (*n.*) an injury like a burn caused by severe frost.

froth (*n.*) 1. bubbles caused by stirring a liquid; foam. 2. nonsense; frivolous talk.

frothy (*adj.*) 1. foamy. 2. vain.

frown (*v.*) 1. to wrinkle the forehead; to scowl. 2. to discourage; to disapprove. FROWN (*n.*) a wrinkling of the brows; a scowl.

frozen (*adj.*) 1. ice-cold; turned into ice. 2. food preserved by freezing.

fructify (*v.*) 1. to bear fruit. 2. to bring reward.

frugal (*adj.*) thrifty; economical.

frugality (*n.*) thrift; economy.

fruit (*n.*) 1. the seed-container of a plant. 2. the produce; crop.

fruiterer (*n.*) a dealer in fruit.

fruitful (*adj.*) 1. bearing fruit. 2. profitable.

fruitfulness (*n.*) ability to produce fruit.

fruition (*n.*) 1. the harvesting; reaping. 2. the attainment.

fruitless (*adj.*) useless; unsuccessful.

frump (*n.*) a dowdy person.

frustrate (*v.*) to thwart; to defeat.

frustration (*n.*) a defeat; disappointment.

fry (*v.*) to cook in a pan over a fire. FRY (*n.*) young fish.

fuchsia (*n.*) a garden shrub with long, drooping flowers. See appendix.

fuel (*n.*) material which will burn.

fugitive (*n.*) one who runs away; flees. FUGITIVE (*adj.*) not fixed; unstable.

fulcrum (*n.*) the point on which a lever balances.

fulfil (*v.*) to carry out; to accomplish.

fulfilled (*adj.*) completed; accomplished.

fulfilment (*n.*) a completion; satisfaction.
full (*adj.*) complete.
fully (*adv.*) completely.
fulminate (*v.*) 1. to explode; to burst. 2. to shout at; to threaten.
fulsome (*adj.*) overdone; sickening.
fumble (*v.*) to grope; to bungle.
fumbler (*n.*) a bungler; mismanager.
fumbling (*adj.*) clumsy-fingered; awkward.
fume (*v.*) 1. to steam; to smoke. 2. to rage; to bluster. FUME (*n.*) smelly smoke or vapour.
fumigate (*v.*) to disinfect with fumes.
fuming (*adj.*) 1. giving out fumes. 2. angry.
fun (*n.*) amusement; merriment. FUNNY (*adj.*). FUNNILY (*adv.*).
function (*v.*) to work properly; to act. FUNCTION (*n.*) 1. one's work; duty. 2. a ceremony; an event.
functional (*adj.*) designed for working regularly and properly.
functionary (*n.*) an official.
fund (*n.*) a supply of money to be used or reserved. THE FUNDS (*n. pl.*) the National Debt.
fundamental (*adj.*) necessary; essential. FUNDAMENTAL (*n.*) 1. a foundation. 2. an essential.
funeral (*n.*) a burial ceremony.
funereal (*adj.*) mournful; sad.
fungus (*n.*) a spongy, mushroom-like plant. (*pl.* FUNGI).
funnel (*n.*) 1. an instrument for pouring liquid into narrow-necked bottles. 2. a smoke-flue on a locomotive or ship.
funny (*adj.*) 1. amusing; comical. 2. strange; queer.
fur (*n.*) 1. the soft hair of many animals. 2. a strong, hard coating inside boilers.
furious (*adj.*) wild; raging.
furl (*v.*) to roll up; to fold up.
furlong (*n.*) an Imperial measure of length (220 yards).
furnace (*n.*) an intensely hot oven in which metals are smelted.
furnish (*v.*) to supply; to provide.
furnished (*adj.*) provided with furniture.
furnishings (*n.*) fittings; supplies.
furniture (*n.*) the equipment necessary in a house, ship or trade.
furrier (*n.*) a dresser, or seller of furs.

furrow (*n.*) 1. a trench cut by a plough. 2. a wrinkle. FURROW (*v.*) 1. to plough. 2. to wrinkle the brow.
further (*adj.*) 1. more distant. 2. additional. FURTHER (*adv.*) 1. to a greater distance. 2. moreover; also. FURTHER (*v.*) to encourage; to help onward.
furtherance (*n.*) promotion; advancement.
furthermore (*adv.*) besides; moreover.
furthest (*adj.*) the most.
furtive (*adj.*) secret; sly.
furtively (*adv.*) secretly; stealthily.
fury (*n.*) ungovernable rage; frenzy. See appendix (FURIES).
furze (*n.*) a thorny evergreen shrub with yellow flowers
fuse (*v.*) 1. to melt with heat. 2. to blend; to intermingle. FUSE (*n.*) 1. a safety device to protect electrical apparatus. 2. a device to explode explosives.
fused (*adj.*) melted by heat.
fuselage (*n.*) the framework of an aeroplane.
fusion (*n.*) 1. a melting. 2. a blending by melting.
fuss (*n.*) excitement over little things; bustle. FUSS (*v.*) to worry over trifles; to bother.
fussy (*adj.*) worrying; fidgety.
fusty (*adj.*) mouldy; mildewed.
futile (*adj.*) useless; worthless.
futility (*n.*) uselessness.
future (*n.*) the time to come; the hereafter. FUTURE (*adj.*) coming.
futurity (*n.*) the future time; future events.

G

gabble (*v.*) to talk nonsense; to chatter. GABBLE (*n.*) silly talk.
gaberdine (*n.*) a coarse, loose upper garment.
gable (*n.*) part of a wall enclosed by sloping sides of roof.
gad (*v.*) to ramble, or rove about idly.
gadfly (*n.*) a stinging fly which pesters cattle.
gadget (*n.*) any small helpful device.
gag (*n.*) something stuffed into the mouth. GAG (*v.*) to silence with a gag.

gage (*n.*) a thrown-down glove; a pledge. GAGE (*v.*) to challenge; to pledge.

gaiety (*n.*) mirth; merriment. (*pl.* GAIETIES).

gaily (*adv.*) gleefully.

gain (*n.*) a profit; an advantage. GAIN (*v.*) 1. to profit. 2. to reach; to attain.

gainful (*adj.*) profitable.

gainsay (*v.*) to contradict; to dispute.

gait (*n.*) one's manner of walking; a step; pace.

gaiters (*n. pl.*) cloth coverings over legs and ankles.

gala (*n.*) a festivity; rejoicing.

galaxy (*n.*) 1. the Milky Way, a band of stars across the sky. 2. a company of talented people.

gale (*n.*) a storm; tempest.

gall (*n.*) 1. a bitter substance in the liver; bile. 2. a bitter nut. 3. spite; malice. 4. a painful sore. GALL (*v.*) 1. to chafe; to hurt. 2. to vex; to torment.

gallant (*adj.*) brave; heroic. GALLANT (*n.*) one courteous to women.

gallantly (*adv.*) bravely; valiantly.

gallantry (*n.*) 1. bravery. 2. politeness and courtesy.

galleon (*n.*) an old-time Spanish warship.

gallery (*n.*) 1. a long corridor. 2. a theatre balcony. 3. a room in which paintings are exhibited.

galley (*n.*) 1. a ship driven by sails and oars. 2. a ship's cook-house; a caboose.

galling (*adj.*) 1. chafing; irritating. 2. vexing.

gallon (*n.*) an Imperial measure of capacity (8 pints).

gallop (*n.*) a horse's fastest pace. GALLOP (*v.*) to run by leaps and bounds.

gallows (*n. pl.*) a wooden erection on which criminals sentenced to death are hanged.

galore (*adv.*) in plenty; abundantly.

galvanism (*n.*) electricity produced by chemical means. See appendix.

galvanize (*v.*) 1. to give an electric shock. 2. to give metals a rust-proof coating by means of electricity.

gamble (*v.*) to bet; to take risks. GAMBLE (*n.*) a risk.

gambling (*n.*) playing games for money; betting. GAMBLER (*n.*).

gamboge (*n.*) a deep yellow colour. See appendix.

gambol (*v.*) to leap and jump; to frisk. GAMBOL (*n.*) a frolicsome romp. GAMBOLLING (*adj.*).

game (*n.*) 1. a sport of any kind. 2. wild animals hunted for food or sport. GAME (*adj.*) plucky.

gamekeeper (*n.*) one who protects game from illegal hunting.

gamester (*n.*) a gambler.

gaming (*n.*) gambling.

gammon (*n.*) 1. a smoked ham. 2. a hoax; nonsense. GAMMON (*v.*) 1. to make bacon of. 2. to hoax; to humbug.

gamp (*n.*) a large umbrella. See appendix.

gander (*n.*) a male goose.

gang (*n.*) a crew; band; company.

ganger (*n.*) a foreman of a gang of workmen.

gangrene (*n.*) wound-poisoning.

gangster (*n.*) a member of a criminal gang.

gangway (*n.*) 1. a movable bridge between dockside and ship. 2. a passage between rows of seats.

gannet (*n.*) a large northern seabird.

gaol (*n.*) a prison; jail.

gaoler (*n.*) a prison warder.

gap (*n.*) an opening; a break.

gape (*v.*) 1. to yawn. 2. to stare at open-mouthed. GAPING (*adj.*).

garage (*n.*) a building for housing one or more motor-cars.

garb (*n.*) dress; attire. GARB (*v.*) to dress.

garbage (*n.*) rubbish; refuse.

garble (*v.*) to pick out pieces here and there; to cut out; to mutilate.

garden (*n.*) ground attached to a house in which flowers and vegetables are cultivated.

gargle (*v.*) to wash the throat. GARGLE (*n.*) a throat-wash.

gargoyle (*n.*) a strangely carved spout projecting from a roof-gutter.

garish (*adj.*) showy; gaudy.

garland (*n.*) a wreath of flowers.

garlic (*n.*) a plant with a strong smell used in cookery.

garment (*n.*) an article of clothing.

garner (*v.*) to gather in; to store. GARNER (*n.*) a granary.

garnet (*n.*) a deep-red gem.

garnish (*v.*) to beautify; to adorn. GARNISHED (*adj.*).

garret (*n.*) a top-floor room; an attic.

garrison (*n.*) troops defending a fortress or town. GARRISON (*v.*) to provide with defending troops.

garrulity (*n.*) talkativeness; wordiness. GARRULOUS (*adj.*).

garter (*n.*) a narrow elastic band for holding up a stocking.

gas (*n.*) 1. any air-like vapour. 2. the vapour given off by a substance when heated. (*pl.* GASES). GAS (*v.*) to make unconscious or to kill with a gas.

gaseous (*adj.*) in the form of a gas; vaporous.

gash (*v.*) to cut deep. GASH (*n.*) a deep cut; a slash. GASHED (*adj.*).

gas mask (*n.*) a device for protection against breathing poisonous gases.

gasoline (*n.*) American word for petrol.

gasometer (*n.*) a large tank for storing coal gas.

gasp (*v.*) to breathe in gulps with wide-open mouth. GASP (*n.*) a gulp; a laboured breath. GASPING (*adj.*).

gastric (*adj.*) concerning the stomach.

gastritis (*n.*) inflammation of the stomach.

gate (*n.*) a hinged barrier across an entrance.

gateway (*n.*) an entrance.

gather (*v.*) 1. to assemble. 2. to pluck. 3. to fasten. 4. to get. 5. to understand. 6. to plait or pucker.

gathering (*n.*) 1. an assemblage. 2. an abscess or festering sore.

gaudiness (*n.*) showiness; finery.

gaudy (*adj.*) showy; gay. GAUDILY (*adv.*).

gauge (*n.*) a measure; a standard. GAUGE (*v.*) to measure; to estimate.

gaunt (*adj.*) lean; hungry-looking. See appendix.

gauntlet (*n.*) a glove that covers the wrist.

gauss (*n.*) a measure of magnetic strength. See appendix.

gauze (*n.*) a thin, light cloth used in surgical dressings; a transparent sheet of silk or wire, etc. GAUZY (*adj.*).

gawk (*n.*) a simpleton. GAWKY (*adj.*).

gay (*adj.*) jolly; cheerful.

gaze (*v.*) to look at intently. GAZE (*n.*) an intent look.

gazelle (*n.*) a small antelope.

gazette (*n.*) a newspaper; journal. GAZETTE (*v.*) to announce; to publish.

gazetteer (*n.*) a geographical dictionary.

gear (*n.*) 1. equipment; tools. 2. toothed or cogged wheels.

gearing (*n.*) an arrangement of toothed wheels in a machine which enables its speed to be changed.

gelatine (*n.*) a jelly-like substance made from bones. GELATINOUS (*adj.*).

gem (*n.*) 1. a jewel. 2. something prized.

gender (*n.*) the grammatical form given to a noun or pronoun to indicate the sex of the person or object it names.

general (*adj.*) 1. relating to a whole class, not to one or a few. 2. widespread; unlimited. GENERAL (*n.*) 1. the whole. 2. a high-ranking military commander.

generality (*n.*) the main body; the bulk.

generalization (*n.*) a rule that applies to all things of the same kind.

generalize (*v.*) to include all.

generally (*adv.*) commonly; upon the whole.

generate (*v.*) to make; to produce.

generation (*n.*) 1. a creation; production. 2. a period of about 30 years. One's own generation is that of all persons born about the same time. Most individuals live in three generations. You live partly in that of your parents; wholly in your own; and partly in that of your children.

generator (*n.*) 1. a vessel in which steam is produced. 2. a machine which makes electricity; a dynamo.

generosity (*n.*) liberality; munificence.

generous (*adj.*) 1. liberal; open-handed. 2. kind; forgiving.

genesis (*n.*) a creation; beginning.

genial (*adj.*) pleasant; jovial. GENIALLY (*adv.*).

geniality (*n.*) joviality; cordiality.

genius (*n.*) 1. great intelligence; talent. 2. a highly intelligent person.

genteel (*adj.*) well-bred; well-mannered.

gentility (*n.*) gentlemanly qualities.

gentle (*adj.*) 1. tender; mild. 2. merciful; humane. 3. soft; light.

gentleness (*n.*) 1. tenderness; meekness. 2. mildness; lightness.

gently (*adv.*) lightly; without violence.

genuine (*adj.*) real; true.

genuineness (*n.*) the soundness; reality.

genus (*n.*) a race; class, especially of animals or plants.

geographical (*adj.*) concerning geography.

geography (*n.*) the science concerned with the earth's surface, climates, etc.

geological (*adj.*) concerned with geology.

geologist (*n.*) one versed in geology.

geology (*n.*) the science of studying the earth's structure.

geometrical (*adj.*) concerned with geometry.

geometry (*n.*) a mathematical science concerned with the measurement of lines, surfaces and solids.

geranium (*n.*) a plant bearing strongly-scented flowers.

germ (*n.*) 1. a microbe which causes disease. 2. a seed from which a living thing grows.

germicide (*n.*) anything that destroys disease germs.

germinate (*v.*) to sprout: to begin to grow.

germination (*n.*) a coming to life; a sprouting.

gesticulate (*v.*) to signal with the hands; to gesture.

gesticulation (*n.*) a gesture; hand-signal.

gesture (*n.*) a bodily movement which has a meaning.

get (*v.*) 1. to obtain. 2. to become. 3. to arrive.

getting (*n.*) an obtaining; gaining.

geyser (*n.*) 1. a hot-water spring or fountain. 2. a water-heating appliance.

ghastliness (*n.*) pallor; hideousness.

ghastly (*adj.*) pale; death-like.

ghost (*n.*) a spirit; an apparition.

ghostliness (*n.*) weirdness; eeriness.

ghostly (*adj.*) weird; supernatural.

giant (*n.*) a man of unusual size and strength. (*fem.* GIANTESS). GIANT (*adj.*) giant-like.

gibberish (*n.*) nonsense; drivel.

gibe (*v.*) to sneer; to scoff. GIBE (*n.*) a sneer; taunt.

giblets (*n. pl.*) the neck and internal eatable parts of a fowl.

giddiness (*n.*) 1. dizziness. 2. flightiness.

giddy (*adj.*) 1. dizzy; dazed. 2. flighty; fickle.

gift (*n.*) 1. anything given; a present. 2. a natural power; talent.

gifted (*adj.*) intelligent; talented.

gig (*n.*) a light, two-wheeled vehicle.

gigantic (*adj.*) huge; enormous. GIGANTICALLY (*adv.*).

giggle (*v.*) to laugh in a silly way. GIGGLE (*n.*) a silly, nervous laugh. GIGGLER (*n.*).

gild (*v.*) 1. to cover with gold leaf or gold paint. 2. to soften anything unpleasant.

gilding (*n.*) an overlaying with gold.

gill (*n.*) 1. an Imperial measure of capacity (quarter-pint). 2. the breathing organ of a fish.

gilt (*n.*) gold laid on the surface; gilding.

gimlet (*n.*) a small wood-boring tool with a screw point.

gin (*n.*) 1. a snare; trap. 2. an intoxicating liquor.

ginger (*n.*) the hot, spicy root of the ginger-plant.

gingerly (*adv.*) 1. cautiously; warily. 2. daintily.

gipsy (*n.*) a wandering caravan-dweller. (*pl.* GIPSIES).

giraffe (*n.*) a long-necked African animal.

gird (*v.*) to bind round; to encircle.

girder (*n.*) a steel beam supporting a floor.

girdle (*n.*) a waistband or belt.

girl (*n.*) female child.

girth (*n.*) 1. the measurement round anything. 2. a saddle-band.

gist (*n.*) the substance; main point.

give (*v.*) 1. to present, or hand over, to another; to bestow. 2. to begin to bend or collapse under pressure; to yield.

gizzard (*n.*) a bird's muscular second stomach where its food is ground.

glacial (*adj.*) 1. about glaciers. 2. icy.

glacier (*n.*) a slow-moving river of ice.

glad (*adj.*) 1. pleased; delighted. 2. happy; contented.

gladden (*v.*) to make happy; to cheer.

glade (*n.*) an open place in a wood.

gladiator (*n.*) a Roman swordsman who fought in the arena.

gladly (*adv.*) cheerfully; with pleasure.

gladness (*n.*) joy; cheerfulness.

glamorous (*adj.*) beautiful; bewitching.

glamour (*n.*) charm; attraction.

glance (*n.*) a quick look; a glimpse.

GLANCE (v.) 1. to look quickly at. 2. to glide off an object instead of hitting it full.

gland (n.) a bodily organ able to take and store substances from the blood.

glare (v.) 1. to shine with dazzling light. 2. to look at fiercely. GLARE (n.) 1. a dazzling light. 2. an angry look.

glaring (adj.) 1. dazzling. 2. fierce-looking. 3. obvious; bare-faced.

glass (n.) 1. a brittle, transparent substance. 2. a mirror. 3. a drinking-vessel. GLASSY (adj.). GLASSFUL (n.).

glasses (n. pl.) spectacles.

glassware (n.) articles or utensils made of glass.

glaze (n., a glassy surface given to earthenware. GLAZE (v.) 1. to fit with glass. 2. to coat with glaze.

glazier (n.) a glass-fitter or dealer.

gleam (n.) a tiny flash of light. GLEAM (v.) to give light.

glean (v.) 1. to gather grain left by reapers. 2. to collect or save little by little. GLEANER (n.).

glee (n.) 1. merriment; jollity. 2. a part song or round.

gleeful (adj.) merry; mirthful.

glen (n.) a narrow valley; a dale.

glib (adj.) smooth-tongued; fluent.

glibness (n.) persuasiveness; readiness.

glide (v.) to move gently and smoothly. GLIDE (n.) a swift, smooth motion.

glider (n.) an engineless aeroplane.

glimmer (v.) to shine faintly and unsteadily. GLIMMER (n.) a faint, unsteady light.

glimmering (adj.) faint; dawning. GLIMMERING (n.) a trace; suspicion.

glimpse (n.) a quick look; a glance. GLIMPSE (v.) to catch sight of.

glint (v.) to sparkle; to glisten. GLINT (n.) a sparkle; gleam.

glisten (v.) to gleam; to glitter. GLISTEN (n.) a glitter; sparkle.

glistening (adj.) gleaming; shining.

glitter (v.) to sparkle; to glisten. GLITTER (n.) brightness; lustre.

glittering (adj.) sparkling; beaming.

gloaming (n.) the time of dusk; twilight.

gloat (v.) to look at or think about with glee or satisfaction.

gloating (adj.) self-satisfied; exultant.

globe (n.) a ball; sphere.

globule (n.) a little ball; a drop.

gloom (n.) 1. dimness. 2. sadness.

gloomily (adv.) 1. dimly. 2. dismally.

gloomy (adj.) 1. dusky; dim. 2. sad; cheerless.

glorification (n.) a giving of glory; praise.

glorify (v.) to praise; to honour.

glorious (adj.) 1. splendid; brilliant. 2. famous; distinguished.

glory (n.) 1. brightness; splendour. 2. fame; renown. GLORY (v.) to rejoice; to triumph.

gloss (n.) a shiny surface on paint or varnish.

glossary (n.) a dictionary of words having a special meaning; a vocabulary.

glossy (adj.) gleaming; shiny.

glove (n.) a covering for the hand, each finger having its sheath.

glow (v.) 1. to spread light and heat. 2. to be eager. 3. to feel hot; flushed.

glower (v.) to scowl. GLOWER (n.) a scowl.

glowing (adj.) 1. warm and bright. 2. enthusiastic. 3. flushed.

glow-worm (n.) an insect having wings and wing-cases. At night the wingless female's tail shines with a pale green light.

glucose (n.) grape-sugar.

glue (n.) a very sticky substance.

glum (adj.) downcast; dejected.

glut (n.) an over-supply; a surfeit. GLUT (v.) to supply too much; to flood.

glutinous (adj.) like glue; sticky.

glutted (adj.) crammed; stuffed.

glutton (n.) 1. one who eats too much. 2. the wolverine, an American animal.

gluttony (n.) excess in eating; voracity.

glycerine (n.) a thick, sweet, colourless liquid.

gnarl (n.) a knot in wood; a snag.

gnarled (adj.) knotty; distorted.

gnash (v.) to grind the teeth.

gnashing (n.) the grinding of teeth.

gnat (n.) a tiny, two-winged insect.

gnaw (v.) to wear away or bore through by biting.

gnome (n.) an underground dwarf; a goblin.

gnu (n.) a South African antelope.

go (v.) 1. to move from one place to another; to depart from. 2. to be in motion, as a watch, machine, etc. GO (*n.*) 1. energy; vitality. 2. a spell of action; a turn.

goad (*n.*) a pointed rod for driving cattle; a spur. GOAD (*v.*) 1. to prod; to spur. 2. to anger; to provoke.

goal (*n.*) 1. the aim; objective. 2. in football, the space marked by two upright posts and a crossbar, and the act of kicking a ball through or over this goal.

goat (*n.*) a horned animal of the sheep family.

gobbet (*n.*) a small piece of meat or other food; a mouthful.

gobble (*v.*) 1. to gulp; to swallow greedily. 2. to make a noise like a turkey. GOBBLE (*n.*) the noise of a turkey.

goblet (*n.*) a drinking-vessel.

goblin (*n.*) a mischievous fairy; a gnome.

God (*n.*) the Creator; Supreme Being. GOD (*n.*) the idol or supposed power worshipped by heathens.

godless (*adj.*) living without God; irreligious.

godliness (*n.*) goodness; piety.

godly (*adj.*) religious; devout.

godsend (*n.*) an unexpected gain; a stroke of good fortune.

godspeed (*n.*) a wishing success, or a safe journey.

goggles (*n. pl.*) large spectacles which protect the eyes.

gold (*n.*) a heavy, yellow, precious metal. GOLD (*adj.*) made of gold.

golden (*adj.*) 1. made of gold. 2. gold-coloured. 3. the best; highest.

goldfield (*n.*) an area containing several gold mines.

goldsmith (*n.*) a skilled craftsman in gold.

golf (*n.*) an outdoor game played with club-headed sticks and a small, hard ball. GOLFER (*n.*).

gondola (*n.*) a long, narrow, Venetian boat.

gondolier (*n.*) a man who propels a gondola.

gong (*n.*) a metal plate or strip (for clocks) giving a booming sound when struck.

good (*adj.*) 1. right; true. 2. beneficial; profitable. 3. clever; skilful. GOOD (*n.*) welfare; benefit.

good-natured (*adj.*) kindly; obliging.

goodness (*n.*) 1. honesty; uprightness. 2. kindliness; friendliness.

goods (*n. pl.*) merchandise; possessions.

goodwill (*n.*) 1. friendliness. 2. the value of a firm's success and reputation.

goose (*n.*) 1. a large, web-footed, farmyard bird. (*pl.* GEESE). 2. a tailor's iron. 3. a silly person.

gooseberry (*n.*) a thorny garden shrub and its fruit. (*pl.* GOOSEBERRIES).

gore (*n.*) 1. blood. 2. a section of a parachute canopy. GORE (*v.*) to pierce as with a spear or an animal's horn.

gored (*adj.*) pierced.

gorge (*n.*) 1. a narrow mountain pass. 2. the throat; gullet. GORGE (*v.*) to swallow greedily.

gorgeous (*adj.*) brilliant; magnificent.

gorgeously (*adv.*) richly; splendidly.

gorgon (*n.*) anything extremely hideous or repulsive. See appendix.

gorilla (*n.*) a strong, fierce ape.

gormandize (*v.*) to eat greedily. GORMANDIZER (*n.*).

gorse (*n.*) a prickly shrub bearing yellow flowers; furze.

gory (*adj.*) bloodstained.

goshawk (*n.*) a short-winged, slender falcon.

gosling (*n.*) a young goose.

gospel (*n.*) an account of the work of Jesus; one of the first four books in the New Testament.

gossamer (*n.*) a fine substance like cobweb found floating in the air in summer. GOSSAMER (*adj.*) flimsy; unsubstantial.

gossip (*n.*) 1. talk; tittle-tattle. 2. a chatterer; tale-bearer. GOSSIP (*v.*) to talk or tattle. GOSSIPER (*n.*).

gossiping (*n.*) tale-bearing.

gouge (*v.*) to scoop out. GOUGE (*n.*) a chisel for cutting grooves.

gout (*n.*) a painful malady in the joints and toes.

govern (*v.*) to rule; to command.

governable (*adj.*) manageable; controllable.

governess (*n.*) a woman having the care and teaching of children in a private family.

government (*n.*) 1. control; rule. 2. the body of people ruling a country.

governor (*n.*) 1. an official appointed to rule. 2. a device for driving a machine at a steady speed.

gown (*n.*) a woman's loose upper garment.

grab (*v.*) to seize; to clutch. GRABBER (*n.*).

grace (*v.*) to adorn; to dignify. GRACE (*n.*) 1. beauty; refinement. 2. kindness; love. 3. a prayer; blessing.

graceful (*adj.*) beautiful in movement and manner. GRACELESS (*adj.*).

gracious (*adj.*) courteous; gentle. GRACIOUSLY (*adv.*).

grade (*n.*) 1. a step; degree. 2. the steepness of a slope. GRADE (*v.*) to arrange in classes, sizes, etc.

gradient (*n.*) a slope.

gradual (*adj.*) by degrees. GRADUALLY (*adv.*).

graduate (*v.*) 1. to mark in degrees. 2. to receive a university degree. GRADUATE (*n.*) one who has a university degree.

graduated (*adj.*) marked in degrees or equal intervals.

graft (*v.*) to reset a plant shoot into a tree upon which it will grow; to transplant. GRAFT (*n.*) 1. a plant which grows from another. 2. a piece of living skin taken from one part of the body and grafted to a raw or wounded part. 3. dishonest dealing.

grain (*n.*) 1. corn. 2. a particle. 3. a pattern made by wood fibres. 4. the smallest measure of weight (1 lb. = 7,000 grains). GRAIN (*v.*) to make a wood pattern in paint.

grammar (*n.*) rules which enable one to speak and write a language correctly.

grammatical (*adj.*) by the rules of grammar.

gramme (*n.*) a metric unit of mass.

gramophone (*n.*) an instrument for recording the human voice and other sounds.

grampus (*n.*) a large dolphin.

granary (*n.*) a grain storehouse. (*pl.* GRANARIES).

grand (*adj.*) 1. splendid. 2. chief.

grandchild (*n.*) child of one's son or daughter.

grandeur (*n.*) splendour; magnificence.

grandiose (*adj.*) imposing; impressive.

grandparent (*n.*) a parent of one's father or mother.

grandsire (*n.*) 1. one's grandfather. 2. any male ancestor.

grange (*n.*) a country house having a farm with a granary attached to it.

granite (*n.*) a very hard building stone.

granny (*n.*) a grandmother.

grant (*v.*) to give; to allow. GRANT (*n.*) a gift; an allowance.

granulate (*v.*) to grind into grains. GRANULATED (*adj.*).

grape (*n.*) the fruit of the vine.

grapefruit (*n*) a bitter fruit like a large orange.

graph (*n.*) a diagram giving information by means of lines drawn on squared paper.

graphic (*adj.*) lifelike; striking.

graphite (*n.*) blacklead.

grapnel (*n.*) a light anchor with four flukes.

grapple (*v.*) to grip and hold; to wrestle.

grasp (*v.*) 1. to grip; to clasp. 2. to understand. GRASP (*n.*) a grip; clasp.

grasping (*adj.*) greedy; avaricious.

grass (*n.*) the green herbage which provides food for cattle, etc.

grasshopper (*n.*) a small jumping insect.

grate (*n.*) the iron fire bars and frame of a fireplace. GRATE (*v.*) 1. to rub together harshly; to rasp. 2. to jar; to irritate.

grateful (*adj.*) thankful.

gratification (*n.*) satisfaction; delight.

gratify (*v.*) to gladden; to satisfy.

grating (*n.*) 1. a lattice of metal bars; a grid. 2. the sound of rubbing rough surfaces. GRATING (*adj.*) 1. harsh. 2. jarring; irritating.

gratis (*adv.*) for nothing; freely.

gratitude (*n.*) thankfulness.

gratuitous (*adj.*) 1. free. 2. without cause; baseless.

gratuity (*n.*) a gift; a present, usually for services rendered.

grave (*v.*) to cut into; to engrave. GRAVE (*n.*) a burial-place. GRAVE (*adj.*) serious; important.

gravel (*n.*) tiny pebbles. GRAVELLY (*adj.*).

gravely (*adv.*) seriously; solemnly.

gravitation (*n.*) the attraction due to gravity. GRAVITATIONAL (*adj.*).

gravity (*n.*) 1. the force which draws all bodies to the earth's centre. 2. weight. 3. seriousness; importance.

gravy (*n.*) the juices flowing from meat while cooking, and the sauces made from them.

graze (*v.*) 1. to eat grass. 2. to rub gently. 3. to scrape the skin. GRAZE (*n.*) a slight rub; a scrape.

grease (*n.*) a thick, soft, fatty substance. GREASE (*v.*) to rub with grease; to lubricate.

greasy (*adj.*) 1. oily; fatty. 2. slippery.

great (*adj.*) 1. big; large. 2. long in time. 3. gifted. 4. notable; eminent.

greatness (*n.*) 1. largeness; magnitude. 2. fame, grandeur.

greed (*n.*) a never-satisfied desire; avarice.

greediness (*n.*) covetousness; rapacity.

greedy (*adj.*) avaricious; grasping. GREEDILY (*adv.*).

green (*adj.*) 1. grass-coloured. 2. fresh; new. 3. unskilled. GREEN (*n.*) a grassplot; lawn.

greenery (*n.*) foliage; leafage.

greengage (*n.*) a variety of plum, green-coloured when ripe.

greengrocer (*n.*) one who sells vegetables.

greenhouse (*n.*) a glasshouse for rearing plants.

greet (*v.*) to welcome; to salute.

greeting (*n.*) a welcome; salutation.

gregarious (*adj.*) fond of company; sociable.

grenade (*n.*) a hand-thrown bomb.

grenadier (*n.*) 1. a soldier who threw grenades. 2. a soldier in the Grenadier Guards, first regiment of household infantry.

grey (*adj.*) 1. mingled black and white in colour. 2. dull; gloomy. Also GRAY.

greybeard (*n.*) an elderly man.

greyhound (*n.*) a swift, slender, long-legged hound.

grid (*n.*) 1. a grating. 2. the supply of electricity over a large area.

gridiron (*n.*) a utensil for cooking meat over a fire.

grief (*n.*) 1. sorrow; distress. 2. failure; disaster.

grieve (*v.*) 1. to lament; to mourn. 2. to hurt; to afflict.

grievous (*adj.*) painful; distressing.

griffin (*n.*) fabulous monster with eagle's head and lion's body, which guarded hidden treasure. Also GRYPHON.

grill (*v.*) to cook on a gridiron; to broil.

grim (*adj.*) stern; sinister.

grimace (*n.*) a facial distortion. GRIMACE (*v.*) to pull a face.

grime (*n.*) dirt; filth.

grimly (*adv.*) sullenly; fiercely.

grimness (*n.*) severity; dreadfulness.

grimy (*adj.*) dirty; filthy.

grin (*v.*) 1. to smile broadly. 2. to show the teeth in pain or scorn. GRIN (*n.*) 1. a broad smile. 2. an expression of pain.

grind (*v.*) 1. to crush to powder. 2. to sharpen on a grindstone. 3. to overwork.

grinding (*n.*) the work of powdering or sharpening.

grindstone (*n.*) a flat, circular sandstone able to revolve rapidly.

grip (*v.*) to hold fast; to grasp. GRIP (*n.*) a secure hold.

gripe (*v.*) to cause a sharp bowel pain.

grisly (*adj.*) dreadful; horrible.

grist (*n.*) 1. ground corn. 2. gain; profit.

gristle (*n.*) a smooth, elastic substance in animal bodies. GRISTLY (*adj.*).

grit (*n.*) 1. fine sand; dust. 2. courage; determination.

gritty (*adj.*) coarse; clogging.

grizzly (*n.*) a fierce bear. GRIZZLY (*adj.*) greyish.

groan (*v.*) to moan; to complain. GROAN (*n.*) a moaning sound.

groat (*n.*) a silver fourpence.

groats (*n. pl.*) crushed oats.

grocer (*n.*) a tradesman who sells provisions. GROCERIES (*n. pl.*).

groin (*n.*) 1. the part of the body between the abdomen and the thigh. 2. the curve made by two arches which cross one another.

groom (*n.*) 1. a bridegroom. 2. a man who attends to horses. GROOM (*v.*) 1. to brush and curry horses. 2. to make oneself trim and tidy.

groomsman (*n.*) a bridegroom's attendant.

groove (*n.*) 1. a channel; rut. 2. a routine. GROOVED (*adj.*).

grope (*v.*) to feel in the dark; to seek blindly.

gropingly (*adv.*) by groping.

gross (*adj.*) 1. big; bulky. 2. coarse; vulgar. 3. clear; plain. 4. whole; entire. GROSS (*n.*) 12 dozen (144).

grossness (*n.*) coarseness; vulgarity.

grotesque (*adj.*) 1. curiously shaped. 2. nonsensical. GROTESQUE (*n.*) a figure fantastically carved.

grotesquely (*adv.*) absurdly; ridiculously.

grotto (*n.*) a small cave; a cavern.

ground (*n.*) 1. the earth's surface. 2. the surface on which a design is drawn. 3. a reason. GROUND (*v*) 1. to run a ship ashore. 2. to land an aeroplane.

groundless (*adj.*) unfounded; baseless.

groundsel (*n.*) kind of weed used as food for cage-birds.

groundwork (*n.*) 1. the part undecorated. 2. the chief ingredient. 3. the preparatory work.

group (*n.*) a small company; a cluster. GROUP (*v.*) to arrange in order.

grouse (*n.*) a game bird. GROUSE (*v.*) to grumble; to complain.

grove (*n.*) a cluster of trees; a small wood.

grovel (*v.*) to lie face downwards.

grovelling (*adj.*) 1. lying face down. 2. base; despicable.

grow (*v.*) 1. to sprout; to shoot. 2. to increase in size. 3. to cultivate; to plant. GROWER (*n.*).

growing (*n.*) the gradual increase in size. GROWING (*adj.*) encouraging.

growl (*v.*) to grumble; to snarl. GROWL (*n.*) the snarling sound of an angry dog.

growling (*n.*) the grumbling; snarling.

grown (*adj.*) 1. enlarged. 2. at full growth; mature.

growth (*n.*) 1. the increase; progress. 2. the vegetation; produce.

grub (*v.*) to dig up; to uproot. GRUB (*n.*) a newly-hatched insect; a maggot.

grubbiness (*n.*) dirtiness; uncleanness.

grubby (*adj.*) 1. grimy. 2. full of grubs; maggoty.

grudge (*v.*) 1. to bear ill-will; to envy. 2. to give unwillingly. GRUDGE (*n.*) a spite; an ill-will.

grudgingly (*adv.*) unwillingly; reluctantly.

gruel (*n.*) a light, liquid food of meal boiled in water.

gruelling (*adj.*) difficult; exhausting.

gruesome (*adj.*) repulsive; causing horror.

gruff (*adj.*) surly; uncivil.

gruffness (*n.*) churlishness; incivility.

gruffly (*adv.*) roughly; rudely.

grumble (*v.*) to voice discontent; to complain. GRUMBLE (*n.*) a fault-finding; complaint.

grumbler (*n.*) one who complains or murmurs.

grumbling (*n.*) a discontent; murmuring.

grumpiness (*n.*) surliness; irritability.

grumpy (*adj.*) surly; snappy.

grunt (*n.*) 1. noise made by a pig. 2. a hog-like sound. GRUNT (*v.*) to express discontent.

guarantee (*v.*) 1. to promise faithfully; to undertake. 2. to be responsible for. GUARANTEE (*n.*) an assurance; pledge.

guaranteed (*adj.*) certified as true; real.

guarantor (*n.*) one who certifies.

guard (*v.*) to defend; to protect. GUARD (*n.*) 1. a protection; shield. 2. a protector; defender. 3. a bus or tram conductor; person in charge of a passenger train.

guarded (*adj.*) cautious; wary. GUARDEDLY (*adv.*).

guardian (*n.*) one responsible for the care of another. GUARDIAN (*adj.*) protecting; watching.

guardianship (*n.*) work or duty of a guardian.

guards (*n. pl.*) picked regiments of troops forming a sovereign's bodyguard.

gudgeon (*n.*) 1. a small fresh-water fish. 2. a bait.

guess (*v.*) 1. to estimate. 2. to imagine; to suppose. GUESS (*n.*) an estimate; a surmise.

guess-work (*n.*) a surmise; supposition.

guest (*n.*) 1. a visitor in one's home. 2. one lodged in an hotel.

guffaw (*n.*) an overloud outburst of laughter; a horse-laugh.

guidance (*n.*) the direction; management.

guide (*v.*) to lead; to direct. GUIDE (*n.*) a leader; pilot.

guild (*n.*) a fellowship; society.

guildhall (*n.*) hall in which a guild or corporation assembles; a town hall.

guile (*n.*) deception; slyness.

guileful (*adj.*) deceitful; treacherous.

guileless (*adj.*) innocent; blameless. GUILELESSLY (*adv.*).

guillotine (*n.*) a machine for trimming books, paper, etc., or (in France) for beheading. See appendix.

guilt (*n.*) crime; sin.

guiltless (*adj.*) innocent.

guilty (*adj.*) proved to be a wrongdoer.

guinea (*n.*) English gold coin last minted in 1813. Also a sum of money, twenty-one shillings.

guise (*n.*) 1. dress; garb. 2. behaviour.

guitar (*n.*) a six-stringed musical instrument.

gulf (*n.*) 1. a wide bay. 2. a deep chasm; cleft.

gull (*v.*) to cheat; to deceive. GULL (*n.*) a seabird.

gullet (*n.*) the food passage inside the throat.

gullibility (*n.*) the ease or difficulty with which one is cheated.

gullible (*adj.*) easily cheated; over-trustful.

gully (*n.*) a deep channel worn by a swift stream.

gulp (*v.*) to swallow greedily. GULP (*n.*) a gasp; choke.

gum (*n.*) 1. the flesh containing the teeth. 2. a thin, sticky liquid; a mucilage.

gumboil (*n.*) a painful abscess caused by a decaying tooth.

gummy (*adj.*) sticky; adhesive.

gumption (*n.*) common sense.

gun (*n.*) a weapon fired by an explosive; a firearm.

gunner (*n.*) operator of a gun.

gunnery (*n.*) science of operating guns or artillery.

gunpowder (*n.*) an explosive once used in guns.

gunsmith (*n.*) a maker or seller of small guns.

gunwale (*n.*) upper edge of a ship's side.

gurgle (*n.*) noise of bubbling or boiling water. GURGLE (*v.*) to boil or bubble noisily.

gurgling (*n.*) a bubbling; boiling.

gush (*v.*) to make a show of affection. GUSH (*n.*) an outrush of water.

gushing (*adj.*) 1. outrushing. 2. soft-hearted; sentimental.

gust (*n.*) a blast of wind; a squall.

gusty (*adj.*) windy; squally.

gut (*n.*) violin strings. GUT (*v.*) to destroy the interior.

gutted (*adj.*) 1. completely burnt out. 2. emptied.

gutter (*n.*) a channel for carrying off rainwater. GUTTER (*v.*) to fall in drops.

guttural (*adj.*) hoarse; throaty. GUTTURAL (*n.*) a throat sound.

guy (*n.*) 1. a steadying rope or wire. 2. a person of queer appearance. 3. an effigy of Guy Fawkes. GUY (*v.*) to ridicule. See appendix.

guzzle (*v.*) to eat and drink to excess. GUZZLER (*n.*).

gymkhana (*n.*) athletic sports and the place where they are held.

gymnasium (*n.*) a room set apart for physical exercises. (*pl.* GYMNASIA).

gymnast (*n.*) one skilled in physical training or exercises.

gymnastic (*adj.*) concerning athletics.

gymnastics (*n. pl.*) athletics.

gypsum (*n.*) mineral used in plaster of Paris.

gyrate (*v.*) to spin; to whirl.

gyro-compass (*n.*) a compass not affected by magnetism.

gyroscope (*n.*) a spinning balance-wheel.

H

haberdasher (*n.*) a dealer in small articles of dress.

haberdashery (*n.*) small articles of dress.

habit (*n.*) 1. anything done regularly; a custom. 2. dress.

habitable (*adj.*) fit to live in.

habitation (*n.*) a dwelling; home.

habitual (*adj.*) usual; regular.

hack (*v.*) to chop carelessly. HACK (*n.*) a hired horse.

hackle (*n.*) 1. toothed instrument for separating coarse fibre from fine. 2. a feather in a cock's neck. 3. a fly for angling. HACKLE (*v.*) 1. to draw through a hackle. 2. to tear asunder roughly.

hackneyed (*adj.*) worn out; heard or done too often.

haddock (*n.*) a sea-fish of the cod family.

haft (*n.*) handle of a tool or weapon.

hag (*n.*) an ugly old woman.

haggard (*adj.*) wrinkled; careworn.

haggis (*n.*) a Scottish dish made of a sheep's heart chopped fine with herbs and seasoning and boiled with oatmeal, etc.

haggle (*v.*) 1. to bargain. 2. to dispute; to wrangle. HAGGLER (*n.*).

hail (*v.*) to be pleased to see; to greet. HAIL (*n.*) frozen rain-drops. HAIL (*v.*) to fall as hail.

hair (*n.*) fine filaments or threads growing from the skin of many mammals. HAIRY (*adj.*).

hairbreadth (*n.*) the tiniest distance; a shave. HAIRBREADTH (*adj.*) very narrow.

hairsplitting (*n. & adj.*) being too particular; overclever.

hake (*n.*) a sea-fish of the cod family.

hale (*adj.*) healthy; robust.

half (*n.*) one of two equal parts. (*pl.* HALVES).

halibut (*n.*) a flatfish like a giant plaice.

hall (*n.*) 1. an entrance passage or room. 2. a large room for public meetings. 3. residence of a landowner or squire.

hall-mark (*n.*) mark stamped on gold and silver articles to guarantee their quality.

hallow (*v.*) to hold holy; sacred. Beware HOLLOW.

Hallowe'en (*n.*) the evening before All Hallows or All Saints' Day. (Evening of October 31st).

hallucination (*n.*) a vision; delusion.

halo (*n.*) a circle of light round (1), the sun or moon, or (2), a saint's head. (*pl.* HALOES).

halt (*v.*) to stop; to hesitate. HALT (*n.*) a stop. HALT (*adj.*) lame; limping.

halter (*n.*) a rope for leading a horse.

halve (*v.*) to divide into two equal parts.

halyard (*n.*) a thin rope for hoisting a flag.

ham (*n.*) the salted and cured thigh of the pig.

hamlet (*n.*) a small village.

hammer (*v.*) to drive in or beat with a hammer; to forge. HAMMER (*n.*) a tool for driving nails and beating metal. HAMMERED (*adj.*).

hammock (*n.*) a hanging net on which to lie or sleep.

hamper (*v.*) to get in the way; to hinder. HAMPER (*n.*) a large, lidded, wicker basket.

hand (*n.*) the end part of the arm below the wrist.

handcuffs (*n. pl.*) chained bracelets to secure a prisoner's hands.

handful (*n.*) 1. as much as the hand can hold. (*pl.* HANDFULS). 2. a difficult person to manage.

handicap (*n.*) 1. a disadvantage. 2. an allowance given to enable all competitors to start on equal terms. HANDICAP (*v.*) to hinder. HANDICAPPER (*n.*).

handicraft (*n.*) work done by hand. HANDICRAFTSMAN (*n.*).

handiwork (*n.*) work done by one's own hands.

handkerchief (*n.*) a small square of cotton or linen for blowing the nose, etc.

handle (*v.*) 1. to undertake; to deal with. 2. to discuss. 3. to touch or feel with the hands. HANDLE (*n.*) the part by which an article, etc., is held; the haft.

handle-bar (*n.*) the steering bar of a cycle.

handsome (*adj.*) 1. good-looking; well-built. 2. generous.

handsomely (*adv.*) generously; liberally.

handwriting (*n.*) one's own particular writing.

handy (*adj.*) 1. skilled with the hands; dexterous. 2. within reach; near by.

hang (*v.*) 1. to suspend; to drape. 2. to droop (the head).

hangar (*n.*) a shed for aircraft.

hank (*n.*) a skein, or length of yarn.

hanker (*v.*) to long for; to desire. HANKERING (*n.*).

hap (*n.*) a chance; an accident.

haphazard (*adj.*) unplanned; at random. HAPHAZARDLY (*adv.*).

haply (*adv.*) maybe; perhaps.

happen (*v.*) to come to pass; to occur.

happening (*n.*) an event; occurrence.

happily (*adv.*) 1. joyfully. 2. fortunately.

happiness (*n.*) joy; bliss.

happy (*adj.*) delighted; contented.

happy-go-lucky (*adj.*) easy-going.

harangue (v.) to address an audience. HARANGUE (n.) a public speech.

harass (v.) to plague; to annoy. HARASSING (adj.).

harbinger (n.) a forerunner; an announcer.

harbour (v.) to shelter; to lodge. HARBOUR (n.) a refuge for ships; a haven.

harbourage (n.) 1. lodging. 2. a shelter; an anchorage for ships.

hard (adj.) 1. firm; unyielding. 2. difficult. 3. unkind.

harden (v.) to strengthen; to toughen.

hardheaded (adj.) shrewd; cautious.

hardhearted (adj.) harsh; unfeeling.

hardihood (n.) daring; determination.

hardly (adv.) nearly; only just.

hardness (n.) 1. solidity; firmness. 2. harshness; cruelty.

hardship (n.) trouble; misfortune.

hardware (n.) metal goods, cutlery, etc.

hardy (adj.) strong; enduring.

hare (n.) a wild, rabbit-like animal which does not burrow.

harebell (n.) wild plant with blue, bell-shaped flowers.

harem (n.) the women's apartments in Eastern countries.

haricot (n.) the dried kidney-bean.

hark (v.) listen.

harlequin (n.) a jester; clown.

harlequinade (n.) a merry, fantastic show.

harm (v.) to hurt; to damage. HARM (n.) an injury; a wrong.

harmful (adj.) hurtful; damaging.

harmless (adj.) inoffensive; innocent.

harmonious (adj.) 1. sweet-sounding; tuneful. 2. friendly.

harmonize (v.) 1. to be in tune. 2. to agree; to match.

harmony (n.) 1. melody. 2. agreement. 3. friendship.

harness (n.) 1. horse-fittings. 2. armour. 3. equipment. HARNESS (v.) to dress in harness; to equip.

harp (n.) a triangle-shaped, stringed musical instrument. HARPIST (n.).

harpoon (n.) a whale-killing spear. HARPOONER (n.).

harpy (n.) 1. a fabulous winged monster having a woman's face and a vulture's body. 2. a plunderer. See appendix.

harrier (n.) a hare-hunting hound, a beagle; a cross-country runner.

harrow (n.) an iron-toothed frame dragged on soil to break it up. HARROW (v.) 1. to break under a harrow. 2. to wound; to torment.

harrowing (adj.) heart-rending; distressful.

harry (v.) 1. to lay waste; to plunder. 2. to worry. HARRYING (adj.).

harsh (adj.) 1. jarring; grating. 2. severe; cruel. HARSHLY (adv.).

harshness (n.) roughness; severity.

hart (n.) a male deer; stag.

harvest (n.) the full crop; the yield. HARVEST (v.) to gather in; to reap. HARVESTER (n.).

hash (v.) 1. to cut to bits. 2. to spoil; to muddle. HASH (n.) 1. a meat stew. 2. a muddle; mess.

hasp (n.) a fastening secured by a padlock.

hassock (n.) 1. a tuft of coarse grass. 2. a thick mat or cushion for kneeling on.

haste (n.) speed; quickness.

hasten (v.) to hurry.

hasty (adj.) quick; speedy. HASTILY (adv.).

hat (n.) an outdoor head-covering having a brim.

hatch (v.) 1. to bring young from eggs. 2. to plot; to scheme. HATCH (n.) 1. the brood of young. 2. an opening in a ship's deck.

hatchery (n.) a place for hatching eggs.

hatchet (n.) a small, short-handled axe.

hate (v.) to dislike intensely; to detest. HATE (n.) strong dislike; aversion.

hateful (adj.) destestable; loathsome. HATEFULLY (adv.).

hatred (n.) enmity; detestation.

hatter (n.) a maker or seller of hats.

haughtiness (n.) pride; disdain.

haughty (adj.) disdainful; arrogant. HAUGHTILY (adv.).

haul (v.) to pull; to draw. HAUL (n.) 1. a pull. 2. a catch of fish.

haulage (n.) carriage; transport. HAULER or HAULIER (n.).

haunch (n.) the hip, and thickest part of the thigh.

haunt (v.) 1. to visit often. 2. to follow; to dog. HAUNT (n.) a favourite retreat; a den.

haunted (adj.) visited by ghosts.

hauteur (*n.*) arrogance; scorn.

have (*v.*) to possess; to hold.

haven (*n.*) a refuge; a harbour.

haversack (*n.*) a bag slung from the shoulder.

havoc (*n.*) destruction; ruin.

haw (*n.*) 1. the hawthorn berry and seed. 2. a hesitation in speech. HAW (*v.*) to hesitate or stop a moment in speech.

hawk (*v.*) to sell goods from door to door; to peddle.

hawk (*n.*) a sharp-eyed bird of prey. HAWK (*v.*) to hunt with hawks.

hawker (*n.*) a pedlar.

hawking (*n.*) the sport of hunting with hawks.

hawser (*n.*) a ship's cable; a tow-rope.

hawthorn (*n.*) a thorny shrub with white or red blossom.

hay (*n.*) grass cut and dried for fodder.

hazard (*v.*) to place in danger; to risk. HAZARD (*n.*) a risk; danger. HAZARDOUS (*adj.*).

haze (*n.*) a light, thin mist.

hazel (*n.*) 1. a nut-bearing tree. 2. a red-brown colour.

hazy (*adj.*) 1. misty. 2. doubtful; vague.

he (*pron.*) 1. the male person already mentioned in speech or writing. 2. the male of many mammals, as he-goat, etc.

head (*n.*) 1. that part of the body containing the brain. 2. the chief; principal. 3. the source; origin. HEAD (*v.*) 1. to be first; to lead. 2. to hit with the head. HEAD (*adj.*) 1. chief; main. 2. contrary; adverse.

headache (*n.*) a pain in the head.

headland (*n.*) a cape; promontory.

headlong (*adj.*) head first; hasty.

headstrong (*adj.*) stubborn; wilful.

headway (*n.*) motion forward; progress.

heal (*v.*) to cure; to restore. HEALER (*n.*). HEALING (*adj.*).

health (*n.*) freedom from sickness; fitness. HEALTHFUL (*adj.*).

healthiness (*n.*) fitness; robustness.

healthy (*adj.*) 1. well; robust. 2. wholesome; hygienic.

heap (*n.*) a pile; mound. HEAP (*v.*) to pile; to collect.

hear (*v.*) to catch the sound of; to listen to.

hearer (*n.*) a listener.

hearing (*n.*) 1. the sense by which sound is perceived. 2. the ability to hear. 3. a public trial.

hearken (*v.*) to listen; to attend to.

hearsay (*n.*) common talk; rumour.

hearse (*n.*) a carriage for conveying the dead to the grave.

heart (*n.*) 1. organ that forces blood to flow through the body. 2. the centre; core.

heartache (*n.*) sorrow; yearning.

heartburn (*n.*) a burning feeling in the chest.

heartbroken (*adj.*) overcome by grief.

hearten (*v.*) to encourage; to comfort.

heartfelt (*adj.*) deeply felt; sincere.

hearth (*n.*) the floor of a fireplace.

heartily (*adv.*) from the heart; sincere.

heartiness (*n.*) cheerfulness; good nature.

heartless (*adj.*) unfeeling; uncaring.

heartlessness (*n.*) indifference; cruelty.

hearty (*adj.*) 1. honest; sincere. 2. cordial; jovial.

heat (*n.*) 1. hotness; warmth. 2. anger; zeal. HEAT (*v.*) 1. to make warm. 2. to excite; to arouse.

heater (*n.*) an appliance for heating.

heath (*n.*) moorland.

heathen (*n.*) one who does not worship God; a pagan.

heathenism (*n.*) paganism.

heather (*n.*) a low-growing moorland shrub.

heave (*v.*) 1. to lift and throw. 2. to rise and fall like the sea. 3. to pant. HEAVE (*n.*) an upward motion.

heaven (*n.*) 1. the abode or presence of God. 2. the sky.

heavenly (*adj.*) divine; perfect.

heavens (*n. pl.*) the sky with all its stars, planets, etc.

heavily (*adv.*) forcefully; with great weight.

heaviness (*n.*) 1. weight. 2. sadness. 3. dullness. 4. oppressiveness.

heavy (*adj.*) 1. weighty; massive. 2. downcast; gloomy. 3. sluggish. 4. oppressive.

Hebrew (*n.*) 1. an Israelite; a Jew. 2. the language of the Jews. HEBREW (*adj.*) concerning the Hebrews or their language.

heckle (*v.*) 1. to worry or annoy with questions. 2. to interrupt frequently.

heckler (*n.*) a persistent questioner.

hectare (*n.*) metric unit of area; 10 000m².

hectic (*adj.*) 1. feverish; flushed. 2. exciting.

hector (*v.*) to bully; to browbeat. See appendix. HECTORING (*adj.*).

hedge (*v.*) 1. to fence; to enclose. 2. to dodge; to evade. HEDGE (*n.*) a fence of growing shrubs.

hedgehog (*n.*) a quill-covered, little animal which can roll itself into a ball.

hedgerow (*n.*) shrubs forming a hedge.

heed (*v.*) to take notice of; to regard. HEED (*n.*) attention; mindfulness.

heedful (*adj.*) attentive; watchful.

heedless (*adj.*) inattentive; negligent.

heel (*n.*) the back part of the foot or of footwear. HEEL (*v.*) to lean to one side.

hefty (*adj.*) big and strong; heavy.

heifer (*n.*) a young cow.

height (*n.*) 1. distance from bottom to top; the altitude. 2. a hill, mountain. 3. the top; summit.

heighten (*v.*) to raise higher; to elevate.

heinous (*adj.*) wicked; infamous.

heir (*n.*) an inheritor; a successor. (*fem.* HEIRESS).

heirloom (*n.*) a family possession inherited by each heir.

helicopter (*n.*) an aircraft able to take off and alight vertically.

heliotrope (*n.*) small plant with fragrant purple flowers.

helium (*n.*) a very light gas which will not burn.

hell (*n.*) 1. the evil place ruled by Satan; the abode of souls that do not enter heaven. 2. any place of misery, torture or evil.

helm (*n.*) 1. the rudder by which a ship is steered. 2. a helmet. HELMSMAN (*n.*).

help (*v.*) to aid; to assist. HELP (*n.*) aid; support. HELPER (*n.*).

helpful (*adj.*) giving aid; useful.

helpless (*adj.*) powerless; useless.

helpmate (*n.*) 1. a wife. 2. a partner; companion.

helter-skelter (*adv.*) in disorderly haste.

hem (*v.*) 1. to fold over and sew. 2. to surround; to enclose. HEM (*n.*) the doubled edge of a dress.

hemisphere (*n.*) one-half of (1) a sphere or globe, and (2) the world.

hemlock (*n.*) a poisonous plant.

hemp (*n.*) a plant of the nettle family. Its strong fibres are used for making rope.

hen (*n.*) female of any kind of bird, especially the domestic fowl.

hence (*adv.*) from this place or time; therefore.

henceforth (*adv.*) from this time.

henna (*n.*) a thorny tree producing an orange dye.

heptagon (*n.*) a seven-sided figure.

her (*pron.*) the objective and possessive case of the pronoun she. HER (*adj.*) of, or belonging to, a female.

herald (*n.*) 1. an official who regulates royal ceremonies. 2. a forerunner; an announcer. HERALD (*v.*) to proclaim; to usher in.

heraldic (*adj.*) concerning heraldry.

heraldry (*n.*) the study of coats of arms.

herb (*n.*) any plant with a soft, juicy stem.

herbaceous (*adj.*) concerned with herbs.

herbage (*n.*) grass; pasture.

herbalist (*n.*) a seller of medicinal herbs.

Herculean (*adj.*) 1. powerful; mighty. 2. difficult; laborious. See appendix.

herd (*v.*) to crowd together. HERD (*n.*) 1. a drove or flock of animals. 2. a crowd of people; a rabble. HERDSMAN (*n.*).

here (*adv.*) in, or to, this place.

hereabouts (*adv.*) somewhere near.

hereafter (*n.*) the future.

hereditary (*adj.*) passed on; inherited.

heredity (*n.*) the passing of qualities or resemblances from parents to children.

herein (*adv.*) in this; within.

heresy (*n.*) a wrong belief.

heretic (*n.*) one who holds wrong beliefs.

heretofore (*adv.*) up to the present.

heritage (*n.*) an inheritance; a right.

hermetic (*adj.*) air-tight. See appendix.

hermit (*n.*) one who leaves his fellow-men to live alone.

hermitage (*n.*) a hermit's dwelling.

hero (*n.*) a brave man or boy. (*fem.* HEROINE. *pl.* HEROES).

heroic (*adj.*) brave; valiant. HEROICALLY (*adv.*).

heroism (*n.*) gallantry; valour.

heron (*n.*) a long-legged wading-bird.

herring (*n.*) a small food-fish, which moves in vast shoals.

hesitancy (*n.*) uncertainty; suspense.

hesitate (*v.*) to pause; to be reluctant.

hesitation (*n.*) indecision; doubt. HESI-TATINGLY (*adv.*).

Hesperus (*n.*) the evening star. See appendix.

hew (*v.*) to cut with an axe; to fell. HEWER (*n.*).

hexagon (*n.*) a six-sided figure. HEXAGONAL (*adj.*).

heyday (*n.*) prosperity; vigour.

hibernate (*v.*) to pass the winter in sleep.

hibernation (*n.*) a winter-long sleep.

hiccup (*n.*) a curious catch in the breath; a throat spasm. HICCUP (*v.*) to suffer from breath spasms.

hickory (*n.*) an American nut-tree noted for its tough timber.

hidden (*adj.*) 1. concealed. 2. mysterious.

hide (*v.*) 1. to conceal. 2. to keep secret. HIDE (*n.*) an animal's skin.

hideous (*adj.*) ugly; horrible. HIDEOUSNESS (*n.*).

hie (*v.*) to hasten; to hurry on.

hieroglyphics (*n. pl.*) ancient Egyptian picture-writing.

high (*adj.*) 1. lofty; elevated. 2. proud; haughty. 3. strong; shrill.

high-handed (*adj.*) overbearing; arrogant.

highlands (*n. pl.*) mountainous parts of a country. HIGHLANDERS (*n.*).

high-minded (*adj.*) proud; arrogant; having noble ideas.

high-road (*n.*) a highway; main road.

highway (*n.*) a public road.

highwayman (*n.*) a robber on the highway.

hilarious (*adj.*) laughing; jolly.

hilarity (*n.*) merriment; fun.

hill (*n.*) a little mountain; a mount. HILLY (*adj.*).

hillock (*n.*) a small hill; a mound.

hilt (*n.*) half of a sword or dagger.

him (*pron.*) the objective case of the pronoun he.

hind (*n.*) a female deer. HIND (*adj.*) at the back.

hinder (*v.*) to check; to delay.

hindmost (*adj.*) last; rear.

hindrance (*n.*) a check; restraint.

Hindu (*n.*) a native of India, whose religion is Hinduism.

hinge (*n.*) 1. a movable joint on which a door or lid swings. 2. that on which something depends. HINGE (*v.*) 1. to turn upon. 2. to depend upon.

hint (*v.*) to indicate in a roundabout way. HINT (*n.*) an indirect suggestion.

hip (*n.*) 1. the upper part of the thigh. 2. the fruit of the wild dog-rose.

hippodrome (*n.*) ancient Greek racecourse or circus.

hippopotamus (*n.*) huge African river-animal. (*pl.* HIPPOPOTAMI).

hire (*n.*) 1. payment for work done; a wage. 2. payment for the use of something; a rent; fare. HIRE (*v.*) 1. to engage for pay or wages. 2. to obtain from another for temporary use.

his (*pron.*) belonging to him.

hiss (*n.*) sound of the letter S. HISS (*v.*) to express disapproval.

historian (*n.*) a writer of history.

historic (*adj.*) relating to the past; famous in history.

history (*n.*) the record of past events. (*pl.* HISTORIES).

hit (*v.*) to strike; to collide. HIT (*n.*) 1. a stroke; blow. 2. a success.

hitch (*v.*) 1. to fasten with a loop or hook. 2. to jerk. HITCH (*n.*) 1. a fastening; tethering. 2. a difficulty; check.

hither (*adv.*) to this place.

hitherto (*adv.*) up to now.

hive (*n.*) a home for bees; a place full of busy workers.

hoar (*adj.*) grey or white with age.

hoar-frost (*n.*) white frost.

hoard (*n.*) 1. a hidden or reserve store. 2. hidden treasure. HOARD (*v.*) to store; to collect. HOARDER (*n.*).

hoarding (*n.*) 1. a large board for advertisements. 2. a fence of boards.

hoarse (*adj.*) harsh-voiced; husky. HOARSELY (*adv.*).

hoarseness (*n.*) huskiness; harshness of voice.

hoary (*adj.*) white with age; ancient.

hoax (*n.*) a trick played in joke. HOAX (*v.*) to fool; to bamboozle.

hoaxer (*n.*) a joker.

hob (*n.*) 1. the flat part of a grate at the side where things are placed to keep warm. 2. the pin, or mark, in quoits.

hobble (v.) to walk lamely; to limp. HOBBLING (adj.).

hobby (n.) a favourite pastime; recreation. (pl. HOBBIES).

hobgoblin (n.) a mischievous sprite; a bogey.

hock (n.) a German white wine.

hockey (n.) team game played with a hard ball and curved sticks.

hoe (n.) garden tool for weeding.

hog (n.) 1. a pig. 2. a greedy person.

hoggish (adj.) greedy; brutish.

Hogmanay (n.) the last day of the year, and a gift given on that day.

hogshead (n.) large cask containing 52½ gallons.

hoist (v.) to lift up; to raise. HOIST (n.) a goods-lift.

hoity-toity (adj.) haughty; stuck up.

hold (v.) 1. to grasp; to keep fast. 2. to stop; to arrest. 3. to believe; to declare. HOLD (n.) 1. a grasp; clasp. 2. cargo space in a ship.

holder (n.) 1. an occupier; tenant. 2. a device for grasping something.

holding (n.) a possession; a small farm.

hole (n.) 1. a pit; cavity. 2. a fix; difficulty.

holiday (n.) a rest; vacation. HOLIDAY-MAKER (n.).

holily (adv.) sacredly; with holy intentions.

holiness (n.) goodness; devotion.

hollow (adj.) 1. not solid; empty inside. 2. insincere; empty. HOLLOW (n.) a crease, indentation, or concavity in the surface of anything, as a wrinkle, a furrow, a dell, etc. HOLLOW (v.) to make hollow; to excavate.

holly (n.) an evergreen tree with glossy, pickly leaves and red berries.

hollyhock (n.) a tall plant with large flowers in various colours.

holy (adj.) godly; sacred.

Holy Writ (n.) The Bible.

homage (n.) duty; loyalty.

home (n.) one's own dwelling-place.

homeless (adj.) without a home.

homeliness (n.) plainness; simplicity.

homely (adj.) plain; simple.

homesick (adj.) yearning to return home.

homicide (n.) the killing or killer of a human being.

hone (n.) a sharpening-stone.

honest (adj.) upright; true. HONESTLY (adv.).

honesty (n.) uprightness; integrity.

honey (n.) a sweet juice collected by bees.

honeycomb (n.) group of waxen cells in which bees store honey.

honeymoon (n.) first month after marriage.

honeysuckle (n.) wild, climbing plant; the woodbine.

honorarium (n.) a payment or gift given in gratitude.

honorary (adj.) done for honour, not payment.

honour (n.) 1. a high reputation or rank. 2. regard for everything worthy. HONOUR (v.) to respect; to esteem.

honourable (adj.) 1. worthy; illustrious. 2. title given to a peer's child.

honours (n. pl.) titles or rewards granted for outstanding national service.

hood (n.) a head-covering; a cowl. HOODED (adj.).

hoodwink (v.) 1. to blindfold. 2. to cheat.

hoof (n.) horny cap on the feet of certain animals. (pl. HOOFS or HOOVES). HOOFED (adj.).

hook (n.) a curved instrument. HOOK (v.) to catch and hold.

hooligan (n.) a street rough; a ruffian. HOOLIGAN (adj.) disorderly; destructive.

hooliganism (n.) rowdiness; destructiveness.

hoot (n.) 1. the sound of a steam whistle. 2. an owl's cry. HOOT (v.) to make an owl-like cry in disapproval or derision.

hop (v.) to jump on one foot. HOP (n.) 1. a spring on one foot. 2. a climbing plant used in beer-making.

hope (v.) to wish something good will happen; to expect. HOPE (n.) belief; expectation.

hopeful (adj.) 1. expectant. 2. promising.

hopeless (adj.) 1. impossible. 2. despairing.

hopelessness (n.) 1. impossibility. 2. despair.

horde (n.) a rough, wandering crowd.

horizon (n.) distant line where earth and sky seem to meet.

horizontal (*adj.*) level; flat.

horn (*n.*) 1. pointed weapon some animals grow on the head. 2. a wind-instrument of music; an oboe.

horned (*adj.*) armed with horns. HORNY (*adj.*).

hornet (*n.*) wasp-like insect with a painful sting.

hornpipe (*n.*) a lively sailors' dance; a reel.

horrible (*adj.*) dreadful; terrible.

horrid (*adj.*) hateful; shocking.

horrify (*v.*) to terrify; to shock.

horror (*n.*) terror; dread.

hors-de-combat (*adj.*) unable to fight; disabled.

horse (*n.*) a four-legged animal now used chiefly for riding or hauling loads.

horse-guards (*n. pl.*) cavalry forming the life-guard of a sovereign.

horsemanship (*n.*) ability to ride and manage horses.

horse-play (*n.*) rough, boisterous play.

horse-power (*n.*) the measure of work a machine or engine can do.

horseshoe (*n.*) an iron shoe for horses.

hose (*n.*) 1. stockings. 2. a rubber tube for conveying water.

hosiery (*n.*) stockings and socks. HOSIER (*n.*).

hospitable (*adj.*) kind; friendly. HOS-PITABLY (*adv.*).

hospital (*n.*) a building for the care of the sick.

hospitality (*n.*) friendly treatment; neigh-bourliness.

host (*n.*) 1. a multitude. 2. one who entertains guests. 3. an hotel keeper. (*fem.* HOSTESS).

hostage (*n.*) a prisoner kept until promises made are fulfilled; a pledge.

hostel (*n.*) a lodging for students.

hostile (*adj.*) unfriendly; threatening.

hostilities (*n. pl.*) warfare.

hostility (*n.*) enmity; unfriendliness.

hot (*adj.*) very warm; burning. 2. hasty; eager.

hotchpotch (*n.*) a mixture; jumble.

hotel (*n.*) an inn; a public house.

hotfoot (*adv.*) in great haste; at speed.

hot-head (*n.*) a hasty, dashing person. HOT-HEADED (*adj.*).

hot-house (*n.*) a greenhouse.

hot-tempered (*adj.*) having a violent temper.

hound (*n.*) 1. a hunting-dog. 2. a base, contemptible person. HOUND (*v.*) 1. to urge on; to pursue. 2. to persecute; to harry.

hour (*n.*) 1. the twenty-fourth part of a natural day. 2. the fixed or appointed time.

hourly (*adj.*) happening each hour; often. HOURLY (*adv.*) every hour; frequently.

house (*n.*) 1. a building in which people live. 2. a family. 3. a notable firm. HOUSE (*v.*) to shelter; to protect.

household (*n.*) a family.

householder (*n.*) the occupier of a house; tenant.

housekeeper (*n.*) a woman manager of a household.

housewife (*n.*) the mistress of a family.

hovel (*n.*) a poor, wretched house.

hover (*v.*) 1. to hang poised in the air. 2. to move to and fro near by; to hang about.

how (*adv.*) 1. in what manner or way. 2. by what means. 3. for what price. 4. to what extent.

however (*adv.*) but; still. HOWEVER (*conj.*) though; nevertheless.

howl (*n.*) a long wailing cry; a yowl. HOWL (*v.*) to wail; to yowl.

howler (*n.*) an amusing mistake.

hub (*n.*) the centre of (1) a wheel, (2) interest; attention.

hubbub (*n.*) clamour; tumult.

huckster (*n.*) a hawker; a pedlar.

huddle (*v.*) to crowd together. HUDDLE (*n.*) a confused crowd.

hue (*n.*) 1. a tint; shade of colour. 2. a complexion.

huff (*n.*) a fit of temper; sulks.

huffy (*adj.*) angered; sulky.

hug (*v.*) 1. to clasp in the arms; to embrace. 2. to keep near to. HUG (*n.*) an embrace; squeeze.

huge (*adj.*) large; enormous. HUGELY (*adv.*).

hugeness (*n.*) the bulk; vastness.

hulk (*n.*) the hull of an old ship.

hulking (*adj.*) overgrown; unwieldy.

hull (*n.*) 1. the body of a ship. 2. a husk; shell.

hullabaloo (*n.*) an uproar.

hum (*n.*) noise of a bee in flight. HUM

(v.) 1. to buzz. 2. to sing quietly with closed lips.

human (*adj.*) concerned with man or mankind.

humane (*adj.*) merciful; sympathetic.

humanely (*adv.*) with goodwill.

humanitarian (*n.*) a lover of mankind.

humanity (*n.*) 1. all mankind. 2. kindness; mercy.

humanize (*v.*) to soften; to civilize.

humanly (*adv.*) by human means.

humble (*adj.*) meek; modest. HUMBLE (*v.*) to shame; to abash.

humbly (*adv.*) meekly; modestly.

humbug (*n.*) 1. an impostor; a nuisance. 2. deceit: quackery.

humdrum (*adj.*) dull; dreary.

humid (*adj.*) damp; moist.

humidity (*n.*) dampness; moisture.

humiliate (*v.*) to shame; to humble.

humiliated (*adj.*) made to feel ashamed.

humiliation (*n.*) a feeling of shame; disgrace.

humility (*n.*) meekness; modesty.

humorist (*n.*) an amusing talker; writer.

humorous (*adj.*) funny; witty. HUMOROUSLY (*adv.*).

humour (*n.*) 1. fun; amusement. 2. a state of mind. HUMOUR (*v.*) to pamper; to fall in with.

hump (*n.*) a lump; knoll.

humus (*n.*) decayed or rotted vegetation; leaf-mould.

hunch (*n.*) a lump; a thick slice.

hundred (*adj.*) ten times ten. HUNDRED (*n.*) the product of ten times ten; the symbol or numeral 100, C.

hunger (*n.*) a craving for food. HUNGER (*v.*) to desire; to crave.

hungry (*adj.*) needing food.

hunk (*n.*) a large lump or piece.

hunt (*v.*) 1. to search. 2. to chase and kill wild animals. HUNT (*n.*) 1. a search. 2. an assembly of huntsmen.

hunter (*n.*) 1. a searcher. 2. a huntsman. 3. a horse trained for hunting.

hurdle (*n.*) a movable framework used as a fence or obstacle.

hurl (*v.*) to throw; to fling with force.

hurly-burly (*n.*) tumult; uproar.

hurrah (*inter.*) a shout of joy.

hurricane (*n.*) a severe gale; a tempest.

hurried (*adj.*) quick; hasty.

hurry (*v.*) to hasten; to speed. HURRY (*n.*) haste; speed.

hurt (*v.*) 1. to harm; to wound. 2. to cause offence; grief. HURT (*n.*) an injury; a pain.

hurtful (*adj.*) harmful; injurious. HURTFULLY (*adv.*).

hurtle (*v.*) to rush or fall headlong.

husband (*n.*) a married man. HUSBAND (*v.*) to manage frugally.

hush (*v.*) to silence; to make quiet. HUSH (*n.*) a stillness; silence. HUSHED (*adj.*).

husk (*n.*) a seed-case; rind.

huskily (*adv.*) harshly; hoarsely.

husky (*adj.*) harsh; hoarse. HUSKY (*n.*) an Eskimo dog.

hussy (*n.*) an impudent girl.

hustle (*v.*) to hurry; to push through.

hut (*n.*) a small wooden house, or cabin.

hutch (*n.*) a box in which to keep tame rabbits. HUTCH (*v.*) to hoard.

hyacinth (*n.*) a bell-shaped spring flower. See appendix.

hybrid (*n.*) a plant or an animal whose parents are not of the same species; a mongrel.

hydrangea (*n.*) a shrub bearing large clusters of white, blue or pink flowers.

hydrant (*n.*) a pipe from street mains which supplies water to fire engines.

hydraulic (*adj.*) worked by water-power.

hydrogen (*n.*) a gas which quickly takes fire; the lightest substance known.

hydrophobia (*n.*) disease caused by a mad dog's bite.

hydroplane (*n.*) 1. a flat-bottomed speedboat. 2. an aeroplane that alights on water.

hydrosphere (*n.*) the watery portion of the earth's crust; the seas, lakes, etc.

hyena (*n.*) a savage, wolf-like, wild animal.

hygiene (*n.*) knowledge about good health. See appendix.

hygienic (*adj.*) good for the health.

hymn (*n.*) a song of praise; sacred song. HYMN (*v.*) to praise in song.

hymnal (*n.*) a hymn book.

hyphen (*n.*) a short dash between two words (-).

hyphenate (*v.*) to join with a hyphen.

hypnotic (*adj.*) causing deep sleep.

hypnotism (*n.*) power to send into deep sleep.

hypnotist (*n.*) person able to hypnotize.

hypnotize (*v.*) to send into a deep sleep.

hypocrisy (*n.*) an outward show of goodness.

hypocrite (*n.*) person who pretends to be good.

hypocritical (*adj.*) false; deceitful.

hypotenuse (*n.*) the longest side of a right-angled triangle.

hysteria (*n.*) a nervous complaint.

hysterical (*adj.*) subject to hysterics; emotional.

hysterics (*n.*) a nervous outburst.

I

ibex (*n.*) the Alpine wild goat. (*pl.* IBEXES).

ice (*n.*) frozen or solid water.

iceberg (*n.*) a floating mass of ice.

icicle (*n.*) a hanging spike of ice.

icy (*adj.*) 1. ice-covered. 2. unfriendly. ICILY (*adv.*).

idea (*n.*) a thought; fancy.

ideal (*n.*) a perfect example. IDEAL (*adj.*) perfect.

idealism (*n.*) a desire for the best. IDEALIST (*n.*).

idealize (*v.*) to find what is good in a thing.

identical (*adj.*) exactly alike. IDENTICALLY (*adv.*).

identification (*n.*) knowing; recognizing.

identify (*v.*) to know; to recognize.

identity (*n.*) a sameness; likeness.

idiocy (*n.*) mental weakness.

idiot (*n.*) a weak-minded person.

idiotic (*adj.*) stupid; silly.

idle (*adj.*) 1. unoccupied. 2. vain; useless. 3. lazy.

idleness (*n.*) inactivity; sloth.

idler (*n.*) a lazy person; sluggard.

idling (*adj.*) dawdling; lounging. IDLY (*adv.*).

idol (*n.*) 1. an image which is worshipped. 2. a hero.

idolater (*n.*) an idol-worshipper. (*fem.* IDOLATRESS).

idolatrous (*adj.*) heathen; pagan.

idolatry (*n.*) idol-worship.

idolize (*v.*) to worship; to adore.

idyll (*n.*) poem about simple country life.

idyllic (*adj.*) pleasant; perfect.

igneous (*adj.*) volcanic.

ignite (*v.*) to take fire.

ignition (*n.*) 1. a setting on fire. 2. apparatus for igniting the explosive mixture in an internal combustion engine cylinder.

ignoble (*adj.*) dishonourable; base. IGNOBLY (*adv.*).

ignominious (*adj.*) disgraceful; shameful.

ignominy (*n.*) disgrace; dishonour.

ignoramus (*n.*) an ignorant person. (*pl.* IGNORAMUSES).

ignorance (*n.*) a want of knowledge.

ignorant (*adj.*) knowing little; uneducated.

ignore (*v.*) to refuse to notice; to disregard.

ill (*adj.*) 1. sick; unwell. 2. bad; evil. 3. unfortunate.

ill-advised (*adj.*) badly advised; unwise.

ill-disposed (*adj.*) unfriendly.

illegal (*adj.*) against the law; unlawful. ILLEGALLY (*adv.*).

illegality (*n.*) an unlawful act.

illegible (*adj.*) unreadable.

ill-favoured (*adj.*) plain; ugly.

ill-gotten (*adj.*) not obtained honestly.

ill-health (*n.*) poor health; sickliness.

ill-humour (*n.*) bad temper. ILL-HUMOURED (*adj.*).

illicit (*adj.*) not allowed; forbidden. ILLICITLY (*adv.*).

illiteracy (*n.*) the state of being unable to read or write.

illiterate (*adj.*) unable to read or write.

ill-judged (*adj.*) unwise.

ill-nature (*n.*) bad temper; churlishness. ILL-NATURED (*adj.*).

illness (*n.*) poor health; sickness.

illogical (*adj.*) faulty; against reason. ILLOGICALLY (*adv.*).

ill-starred (*adj.*) unfortunate; unlucky.

illuminant (*n.*) anything that gives light.

illuminate (*v.*) to throw light upon; to shine upon.

illumination (*n.*) light.

illusion (*n.*) something that deceives the eye.

illusive (*adj.*) false; deceptive. Beware ELUSIVE.

illusory (*adj.*) imaginary; unreal.

illustrate (*v.*) to make clear; to explain by pictures.

illustration (*n.*) an example; a drawing. ILLUSTRATOR (*n.*).

illustrative (*adj.*) helping to make clear.

illustrious (*adj.*) famous; celebrated. ILLUSTRIOUSLY (*adv.*).

ill-will (*n.*) enmity; hatred.

image (*n.*) 1. a picture in one's mind. 2. a' likeness; statue.

imaginary (*adj.*) unreal; fanciful.

imagination (*n.*) ability to make mind-pictures.

imaginative (*adj.*) inventive; fanciful.

imagine (*v.*) to suppose; to fancy.

imbecile (*n.*) a weak-minded person. IMBECILE (*adj.*) weak-minded.

imbecility (*n.*) feeble-mindedness.

imitate (*v.*) to copy; to mimic.

imitation (*n.*) 1. a copy; likeness. 2. a counterfeit.

imitative (*adj.*) inclined to copy. IMITATOR (*n.*).

immaculate (*adj.*) spotless; pure.

immaterial (*adj.*) unimportant; trivial.

immature (*adj.*) not fully grown; crude.

immaturity (*n.*) unripeness; imperfection.

immeasurable (*adj.*) vast; limitless. IMMEASURABLY (*adv.*).

immediate (*adj.*) 1. near; close. 2. prompt. IMMEDIATELY (*adv.*).

immemorial (*adj.*) beyond memory; ancient.

immense (*adj.*) enormous; vast. IMMENSELY (*adv.*).

immensity (*n.*) a vastness; greatness. (*pl.* IMMENSITIES).

immerse (*v.*) 1. to plunge into liquid; to submerge. 2. to be absorbed in.

immersion (*n.*) 1. a dip; soaking. 2. an absorption.

immigrant (*n.*) a settler in a new country.

immigrate (*v.*) to enter a country and settle there.

immigration (*n.*) an entrance of settlers.

imminence (*n.*) the nearness; closeness. Beware EMINENCE.

imminent (*adj.*) near; about to happen.

immobile (*adj.*) motionless; stopped.

immodest (*adj.*) bold; impudent. IMMODESTLY (*adv.*).

immodesty (*n.*) boldness; brazenness.

immoral (*adj.*) wicked; sinful.

immorality (*n.*) wrongdoing.

immortal (*adj.*) deathless; everlasting.

immortality (*n.*) 1. deathlessness. 2. undying fame.

immortalize (*v.*) to make famous for ever.

immovable (*adj.*) 1. cannot be moved. 2. stubborn.

immune (*adj.*) free from; exempt.

immunity (*n.*) a permission to be absent, or not to do; an exemption.

immunization (*n.*) a protection from disease.

immunize (*v.*) to make safe against disease; to vaccinate.

immure (*v.*) to imprison; to confine.

immutability (*n.*) changelessness; constancy.

immutable (*adj.*) unalterable; unchangeable.

imp (*n.*) a little demon; a mischievous child.

impact (*n.*) a knocking together; collision.

impair (*v.*) to weaken; to injure.

impale (*v.*) to fix on a stake; to put to death by this means.

impart (*v.*) 1. to tell; to reveal. 2. to give.

impartial (*adj.*) not one-sided; fair.

impartiality (*n.*) fairness; neutrality.

impassable (*adj.*) cannot be passed; blocked.

impasse (*n.*) something one cannot escape; a blind alley.

impassioned (*adj.*) eager; earnest; with great feeling.

impassive (*adj.*) calm; unmoved. IMPASSIVELY (*adv.*).

impatience (*n.*) annoyance at delay; restlessness.

impatient (*adj.*) restless; fidgety.

impeach (*v.*) to accuse of wrongdoing.

impeachment (*n.*) an accusation; charge.

impeccable (*adj.*) perfect; faultless.

impecunious (*adj.*) poor; penniless.

impede (*v.*) to get in the way. IMPEDIMENT (*n.*).

impel (*v.*) 1. to push; to urge. 2. to persuade. IMPELLED (*adj.*).

impend (*v.*) 1. to approach. 2. to threaten. IMPENDING (*adj.*).

impenetrable (*adj.*) cannot be passed, or seen through; dense.

impenitent (*adj.*) not sorry for one's offence. IMPENITENCE (*n.*).

imperative (*adj.*) commanding; essential. IMPERATIVELY (*adv.*).

imperceptible (*adj.*) 1. cannot be seen; invisible. 2. small; slight.

imperfect (*adj.*) not perfect; faulty.

imperfection (*n.*) a blemish; fault.

imperial (*adj.*) concerning an empire or emperor; majestic.

imperil (*v.*) to place in peril; to endanger. IMPERILMENT (*n.*).

imperious (*adj.*) domineering; overbearing. IMPERIOUSLY (*adv.*).

imperishable (*adj.*) indestructible; everlasting.

impersonal (*adj.*) referring to no person particularly.

impersonate (*v.*) to pretend to be someone else.

impertinence (*n.*) impudence; rudeness.

impertinent (*adj.*) insolent; saucy. IMPERTINENTLY (*adv.*).

impervious (*adj.*) 1. waterproof. 2. deaf to; unheedful.

impetigo (*n.*) an infectious skin complaint.

impetuosity (*n.*) hastiness; impulsiveness.

impetuous (*adj.*) eager; headlong.

impetus (*n.*) the force driving a thing forward; energy.

impiety (*n.*) sin; irreverence.

impinge (*v.*) to touch; to strike against.

impious (*adj.*) ungodly; profane.

impish (*adj.*) cheeky; mischievous.

implacability (*n.*) mercilessness; pitilessness.

implacable (*adj.*) unforgiving; relentless.

implant (*v.*) 1. to take root; to grow. 2. to teach; to train.

implement (*n.*) a tool; instrument. IMPLEMENT (*v.*) 1. to add to; to complete. 2. to carry into effect.

implicate (*v.*) to mix up in; to entangle.

implication (*n.*) a hint; something understood though not said.

implicit (*adj.*) 1. understood or gathered from words not plainly expressed; implied. 2. undoubted; complete.

implore (*v.*) to beseech; to entreat.

imply (*v.*) to hint; to suggest.

impolite (*adj.*) unmannerly; uncivil.

impoliteness (*n.*) rudeness; discourtesy.

import (*v.*) 1. to bring in from other countries. 2. to convey a meaning. IMPORT (*n.*) the meaning; importance. IMPORTED (*adj.*). IMPORTS (*n. pl.*)

goods brought from abroad. IMPORTER (*n.*).

important (*adj.*) mattering very much. IMPORTANCE (*n.*).

impose (*v.*) to put upon; to tax.

imposing (*adj.*) grand; impressive.

imposition (*n.*) 1. a fraud; deception. 2. a tax; levy.

impossible (*adj.*) cannot be done. IMPOSSIBILITY (*n.*).

impostor (*n.*) one who pretends to be another; a deceiver.

imposture (*n.*) a pretence; deception.

impotence (*n.*) helplessness; inability.

impotent (*adj.*) helpless; unable.

impoverish (*v.*) to make poor; to beggar.

impoverishment (*n.*) poverty; ruin.

impracticable (*adj.*) impossible; unthinkable.

impregnable (*adj.*) cannot be overcome or conquered.

impress (*v.*) 1. to mark by pressing or stamping. 2. to fix in the mind.

impression (*n.*) 1. a stamped or printed mark. 2. an idea; a recollection. 3. a feeling; sensation.

impressionable (*adj.*) easily influenced; quick to learn.

impressive (*adj.*) striking; imposing.

imprint (*v.* pron. im-PRINT) to mark by pressure; to print. IMPRINT (*n.* pron. IM-print) any mark made by pressure or by printing.

imprison (*v.*) to put in prison; to confine. IMPRISONMENT (*n.*).

improbability (*n.*) an unlikelihood.

improbable (*adj.*) unlikely; doubtful.

impromptu (*adj.*) unprepared; off-hand.

improper (*adj.*) wrong; unsuitable.

improve (*v.*) to make or become better.

improvement (*n.*) a betterment; change for the better.

improvidence (*n.*) waste; extravagance. IMPROVIDENT (*adj.*).

improvise (*v.*) to speak or do off-hand, or without preparation. IMPROVISATION (*n.*).

imprudence (*n.*) carelessness; thoughtlessness.

imprudent (*adj.*) unwise; rash.

impudent (*adj.*) disrespectful; rude; cheeky. IMPUDENCE (*n.*).

impugn (*v.*) to contradict; to gainsay.

impulse (*n.*) 1. a sudden thrust. 2. something done hastily. IMPULSIVE (*adj.*).

impulsiveness (*n.*) impatience; rashness.

impunity (*n.*) safety; a knowledge that punishment will not follow words or act.

impure (*adj.*) mixed with other things; not pure. IMPURITY (*n.*).

impute (*v.*) to regard as the cause; to place the blame upon. IMPUTATION (*n.*).

inability (*n.*) lack of ability; powerlessness.

inaccessible (*adj.*) out of reach.

inaccuracy (*n.*) a mistake; an error.

inaccurate (*adj.*) not correct; wrong.

inaction (*n.*) stillness; quietness.

inactive (*adj.*) still; at rest.

inactivity (*n.*) idleness; inertness.

inadequacy (*n.*) a shortage; lack.

inadequate (*adj.*) not enough; insufficient.

inadvertence (*n.*) an oversight; a slip.

inadvertent (*adj.*) not intentional.

inane (*adj.*) silly; stupid.

inanimate (*adj.*) lifeless; dead.

inanity (*n.*) foolishness; stupidity.

inarticulate (*adj.*) speechless; dumb.

inartistic (*adj.*) not interested in art.

inattention (*n.*) lack of attention; disregard.

inattentive (*adj.*) heedless; regardless.

inaudible (*adj.*) cannot be heard; unheard.

inaugurate (*v.*) to begin; to do for the first time. INAUGURATION (*n.*).

inborn (*adj.*) given by nature; inbred.

incalculable (*adj.*) cannot be counted; uncertain.

incandescence (*n.*) heat-glow; brightness. INCANDESCENT (*adj.*).

incantation (*n.*) a spell; charm.

incapability (*n.*) inability; incompetence.

incapable (*adj.*) unable; unfitted.

incapacity (*n.*) inability; powerlessness.

incarnate (*adj.*) clothed with, or enclosed in, flesh.

incautious (*adj.*) unwise; rash.

incendiary (*n.*) 1. one who purposely sets fire to property. 2. one who stirs people to strife by his speeches. INCENDIARY (*adj.*) intended to destroy by burning, or to cause strife.

incense (*v.*) to anger; to enrage. INCENSE (*n.*) a mixture of spices giving fragrance when burned.

incentive (*n.*) 1. a good reason. 2. an aim; urge.

inception (*n.*) a beginning; commencement.

incessant (*adj.*) unceasing; continual.

inch (*n.*) an Imperial measure of length; a twelfth part of a foot.

incident (*n.*) an event; happening.

incidental (*adj.*) slight; occasional.

incision (*n.*) a cut; gash.

incisor (*n.*) a biting tooth.

incite (*v.*) to urge on; to prod.

incitement (*n.*) a prodding; urging.

incivility (*n.*) rudeness; disrespect.

inclemency (*n.*) the roughness; severity.

inclement (*adj.*) stormy; violent.

inclination (*n.*) 1. a slope; slant. 2. a liking for.

incline (*v.*) to slope; to lean towards. INCLINE (*n.*) a slope; slant. INCLINED (*adj.*).

include (*v.*) 1. to be among others. 2. to be contained in.

inclusion (*n.*) a containing; enclosing.

incombustible (*adj.*) unburnable; fire-proof. INCOMBUSTIBLE (*n.*) an unburnable substance.

income (*n.*) total money received or gained annually.

incomparable (*adj.*) matchless; unequalled.

incompatible (*adj.*) opposite in character, nature or meaning; contradictory. INCOMPATIBILITY (*n.*).

incompetent (*adj.*) unsatisfactory; unskilful.

incomplete (*adj.*) imperfect; unfinished.

incompleteness (*n.*) imperfection; faultiness.

incomprehensible (*adj.*) cannot be understood; puzzling.

incomprehension (*n.*) failure to understand.

inconceivable (*adj.*) unbelievable; unimaginable.

inconclusive (*adj.*) unconvincing; indecisive.

incongruous (*adj.*) ridiculously unsuitable; out of harmony. INCONGRUITY (*n.*).

inconsiderable (*adj.*) trivial; small.

inconsiderate (*adj.*) thoughtless.

inconsistent (*adj.*) changeable; variable.

inconsolable (*adj.*) cannot be comforted.

inconspicuous (*adj.*) not noticeable; overlooked.

inconstancy (*n.*) changeableness; fickleness.

inconstant (*adj.*) ever-changing; fickle.

incontestable (*adj.*) undeniable; certain.

inconvenience (*n.*) awkwardness; disturbance. INCONVENIENCE (*v.*) to trouble; to upset.

inconvenient (*adj.*) troublesome; disturbing.

incorporate (*v.*) to form into a single society or body; to unite together as one. INCORPORATE (*adj.*) united in one body; combined. INCORPORATION (*n.*).

incorrect (*adj.*) wrong; inaccurate.

incorrigible (*adj.*) undisciplined; unmanageable.

incorruptible (*adj.*) 1. sound; honest. 2. free from decay. 3. cannot be bribed.

increase (*v.*) 1. to make greater; to enlarge. 2. to grow; to gain. INCREASE (*n.*) a growth; gain. INCREASED (*adj.*).

incredibility (*n.*) disbelief; impossibility.

incredible (*adj.*) hard to believe; surprising.

incredulity (*n.*) distrust; doubt.

incredulous (*adj.*) unwilling to believe.

increment (*n.*) an addition; increase.

incriminate (*v.*) to charge with a crime or fault; to accuse. INCRIMINATORY (*adj.*). INCRIMINATION (*n.*).

incubate (*v.*) to hatch.

incubation (*n.*) 1. a hatching. 2. period taken by germs to give signs of disease.

incubus (*n.*) a burden; nuisance.

inculcate (*v.*) to impress on the mind; to teach.

incur (*v.*) to become responsible for; to meet.

incurable (*adj.*) cannot be cured.

incursion (*n.*) an invasion; a trespass.

indebted (*adj.*) obliged to; owing.

indebtedness (*n.*) one's debt of money, or thanks.

indecency (*n.*) coarseness; vulgarity.

indecent (*adj.*) coarse; disgusting.

indecision (*n.*) hesitation; irresolution.

indecisive (*adj.*) unsettled; uncertain.

indeed (*adv.*) in truth; really.

indefatigable (*adj.*) tireless; industrious.

indefinite (*adj.*) uncertain; vague.

indelible (*adj.*) cannot be rubbed out; fixed.

indemnify (*v.*) to make amends; to compensate.

indemnity (*n.*) a compensation; insurance.

indent (*v.*) to press in; to notch.

indenture (*n.*) a legal agreement; a contract.

independence (*n.*) freedom; liberty.

independent (*adj.*) thinking and acting for oneself; uncontrolled.

indescribable (*adj.*) cannot be described; wonderful.

indestructible (*adj.*) everlasting; endurable. INDESTRUCTIBILITY (*n.*).

index (*v.*) to make an index. INDEX (*n.*) 1. hour-hand on a timepiece. 2. the forefinger. 3. list of contents of a book.

indicate (*v.*) 1. to point out; to show. 2. to hint.

indication (*n.*) 1. a sign; mark. 2. a hint. INDICATOR (*n.*).

indicative (*adj.*) giving signs; showing.

indict (*v.*) 1. to accuse of a crime. 2. to summon for trial. INDICTMENT (*n.*). INDICTABLE (*adj.*).

indifference (*n.*) 1. unconcern. 2. tolerance.

indifferent (*adj.*) 1. uninterested. 2. passable; moderate.

indigent (*adj.*) poor; destitute.

indigestion (*n.*) pain due to improper digestion. INDIGESTIBLE (*adj.*).

indignant (*adj.*) angry; furious. INDIGNANTLY (*adv.*).

indignation (*n.*) resentment; anger.

indignity (*n.*) a slight; an insult.

indigo (*n.*) a deep blue dye.

indirect (*adj.*) not direct; roundabout. INDIRECTLY (*adv.*).

indirectness (*n.*) unfairness.

indiscreet (*adj.*) thoughtless in speech and behaviour; injudicious. INDISCRETION (*n.*).

indiscriminate (*adj.*) mixed; confused. INDISCRIMINATELY (*adv.*).

indispensable (*adj.*) necessary; essential.

indisputable (*adj.*) certain; undeniable. INDISPUTABILITY (*n.*).

indistinct (*adj.*) not clear; blurred.

indistinguishable (*adj.*) showing no difference.

individual (*adj.*) single; special. INDIVIDUAL (*n.*) a single person, animal or thing.

individuality (*n.*) one's distinctive character.

individually (*adv.*) separately; one by one.

indolence (*n.*) idleness; laziness.

indolent (*adj.*) idle; lazy.

indomitable (*adj.*) unyielding; unsubdued.

induce (*v.*) to tempt; to persuade.

inducement (*n.*) anything that attracts or tempts.

indulge (*v.*) 1. to satisfy one's desires. 2. to humour others; to pamper.

indulgence (*n.*) forbearance; satisfaction.

indulgent (*adj.*) tender; easy-going. INDULGENTLY (*adv.*).

industrial (*adj.*) manufacturing.

industrious (*adj.*) busy; hard-working.

industry (*n.*) 1. diligence. 2. a branch of trade or business.

inedible (*adj.*) unfit as food; uneatable.

ineffective (*adj.*) useless; vain.

ineffectual (*adj.*) weak; powerless. INEFFECTUALLY (*adv.*).

inefficient (*adj.*) unable or unqualified to do the work required; incompetent. INEFFICIENCY (*n.*).

inept (*adj.*) 1. foolish. 2. unfit; unsuitable.

ineptitude (*n.*) unfitness; unsuitability.

inert (*adj.*) 1. lifeless; powerless. 2. dozy; sluggish.

inertia (*n.*) unwillingness to move.

inescapable (*adj.*) certain; inevitable.

inestimable (*adj.*) priceless; precious.

inevitable (*adj.*) certain; sure.

inexact (*adj.*) inaccurate.

inexactitude (*n.*) inaccuracy; falseness.

inexhaustible (*adj.*) cannot be used up or emptied.

inexorable (*adj.*) unyielding; relentless.

inexpensive (*adj.*) cheap; not costly.

inexperience (*n.*) lack of practice; training.

inexperienced (*adj.*) untrained; unskilled.

inexplicable (*adj.*) cannot be explained; mysterious.

infallible (*adj.*) certain; unerring. INFALLIBILITY (*n.*).

infamous (*adj.*) shameful; disgraceful.

infamy (*n.*) baseness; disgrace.

infant (*n.* and *adj.*) 1. a baby; young child. 2. a person not of full or legal age; a minor. INFANCY (*n.*).

infantry (*n.*) foot-soldiers.

infatuate (*v.*) to fill with foolish liking or love. INFATUATION (*n.*).

infect (*v.*) 1. to spread disease to others; to taint. 2. to teach bad habits; to corrupt.

infection (*n.*) contagion; corruption.

infer (*v.*) to think out or learn from the known facts; to reason. INFERENCE (*n.*).

inferior (*adj.*) lower in rank, importance, etc.; secondary.

inferiority (*n.*) a lower state or condition.

infernal (*adj.*) fiendish; abominable.

infest (*v.*) to plague; to harass.

infidel (*adj.*) unbelieving; irreligious. INFIDEL (*n.*) a non-Christian; an unbeliever.

infidelity (*n.*) disloyalty; treachery.

infinite (*adj.*) limitless; immense. INFINITE (*n.*) eternity.

infinitesimal (*adj.*) extremely small; microscopic.

infirm (*adj.*) feeble or frail in health.

infirmary (*n.*) a hospital.

infirmity (*n.*) a malady; sickness. (*pl.* INFIRMITIES).

inflame (*v.*) 1. to set ablaze. 2. to rouse anger.

inflamed (*adj.*) 1. sore. 2. heated. 3. roused.

inflammable (*adj.*) easily set on fire.

inflammation (*n.*) a hot, painful sore.

inflate (*v.*) to puff up or swell; to distend. INFLATED (*adj.*).

inflation (*n.*) a swelling; an enlargement.

inflexibility (*n.*) 1. rigidity. 2. determination.

inflexible (*adj.*) 1. rigid; stiff. 2. stubborn; resolute.

inflict (*v.*) to give pain or punishment.

infliction (*n.*) anything that must be borne, hardship, illness, etc.

influence (*n.*) ability to affect others. INFLUENCE (*v.*) to affect; to sway.

influential (*adj.*) possessing influence.

influenza (*n.*) a severe feverish chill or cold.

influx (*n.*) an inflow.

inform (*v.*) to tell; to make known.

informal (*adj.*) not according to the rules

of behaviour, procedure, etc.; simple; unceremonious. INFORMALITY (n.).

informant; informer (nn.) one who tells.

information (n.) knowledge; news.

infra-red rays (n. pl.) rays invisible to the human eye, beyond the red in the spectrum.

infrequency (n.) rareness; uncommonness.

infrequent (adj.) rare; uncommon.

infringe (v.) to break rules; to transgress.

infringement (n.) an offence; transgression.

infuriate (v.) to make angry; to enrage. INFURIATED (adj.).

infuse (v.) 1. to soak in liquid without boiling; to steep. 2. to pour knowledge or ideas into the mind; to instil.

ingenious (adj.) 1. clever; gifted. 2. skilfully made.

ingenuity (n.) cleverness in thinking and doing.

ingenuous (adj.) 1. sincere. 2. artless.

ingle (n.) a fire or fireplace.

ingot (n.) a bar or block of cast metal.

ingratitude (n.) lack of thankfulness.

ingredient (n.) one of the materials in a mixture.

inhabit (v.) to live in. INHABITED (adj.).

inhabitable (adj.) fit to live in.

inhabitant (n.) a dweller; resident.

inhalation (n.) a breath taken in.

inhale (v.) to breathe in. INHALED (adj.)

inhere (v.) to be an inborn or natural part of; to be fixed in permanently.

inherent (adj.) inborn; natural.

inherit (v.) 1. to receive by another's death. 2. to receive by birth, a likeness, quality, character, etc., from a parent or ancestor. INHERITED (adj.).

inheritance (n.) anything inherited.

inheritor (n.) one who inherits. (fem. INHERITRIX).

inhibit (v.) to prevent; to forbid.

inhibited (adj.) held back; hindered.

inhibition (n.) a restraint; prohibition.

inhospitable (adj.) 1. unwelcoming; unfriendly. 2. wild; barren.

inhuman (adj.) unlike a human being; brutal.

inhumane (adj.) unkind; unfeeling.

inhumanity (n.) unkindness; cruelty.

inimitable (adj.) cannot be copied; matchless.

iniquitous (adj.) wicked; unjust.

iniquity (n.) 1. evil; sin. 2. crime.

initial (adj.) at the beginning or head. INITIAL (v.) to write one's initials. INITIAL (n.) first letter of a word.

initiate (v.) 1. to start; to begin. 2. to make a member.

initiation (n.) 1. an introduction. 2. an admission to membership.

initiative (n.) readiness to lead, to act.

inject (v.) to thrust or force into, especially with a syringe. INJECTION (n.).

injunction (n.) a command.

injure (v.) to hurt; to damage. INJURED (adj.).

injurious (adj.) harmful; hurtful.

injury (n.) 1. a hurt. 2. a loss; injustice. (pl. INJURIES).

injustice (n.) a wrong; unfairness.

ink (n.) 1. a coloured fluid used for writing. 2. a paste used in printing.

inkling (n.) 1. a hint; whisper. 2. a suspicion.

inky (adj.) 1. daubed with ink. 2. black; dark.

inlet (n.) a narrow creek or bay.

inmate (n.) dweller in a house, hospital, etc.

inmost (adj.) deepest or farthest within; innermost.

inn (n.) a house in which travellers obtain lodging and refreshment.

innate (adj.) born in or natural to; inborn; inherent.

innings (n. pl.) the time or turn for using the bat, especially in cricket.

innocence (n.) faultlessness; blamelessness.

innocent (adj.) guiltless; faultless.

innocuous (adj.) harmless.

innovate (v.) to change by introducing something new. INNOVATION (n.).

innumerable (adj.) countless; numberless.

inoculate (v.) to insert; to safeguard against disease.

inoculation (n.) the process of inoculating; vaccinating.

inoffensive (adj.) harmless; giving no offence.

inquest (n.) a legal inquiry into matters of fact.

inquire (v.) to question; to investigate. INQUIRER (n.).

inquiry (*n.*) 1. a question. 2. an investigation.

inquisition (*n.*) an official inquiry; a search.

inquisitive (*adj.*) curious; prying.

inquisitiveness (*n.*) curiosity; meddlesomeness.

insane (*adj.*) 1. demented; mad. 2. extremely unwise; rash. INSANITY (*n.*).

insatiable (*adj.*) never satisfied; greedy.

inscribe (*v.*) to write, print or engrave upon. INSCRIBED (*adj.*).

inscription (*n.*) anything inscribed.

inscrutable (*adj.*) hard to explain; mysterious.

insect (*n.*) small creature with six legs, and sometimes winged.

insecure (*adj.*) not safe; unguarded.

insecurity (*n.*) unsafeness; uncertainty.

inseparable (*adj.*) cannot be separated. INSEPARABLE (*n.*) a very close friend.

insert (*v.*) to put into or among.

insertion (*n.*) anything inserted.

inside (*prep.*) within the sides or boundaries of. INSIDE (*adj.*) contained within; internal. INSIDE (*n.*) the part within; the interior.

insidious (*adj.*) 1. secretly harmful. 2. sly; wily.

insight (*n.*) power to understand; discernment.

insignificance (*n.*) paltriness; smallness.

insignificant (*adj.*) little; unimportant.

insincere (*adj.*) false; hypocritical.

insincerity (*n.*) deceitfulness; hypocrisy.

insinuate (*v.*) to hint; to suggest.

insinuation (*n.*) a hint; suggestion.

insipid (*adj.*) 1. tasteless. 2. dull; uninteresting.

insipidity (*n.*) 1. tastelessness. 2. dullness.

insist (*v.*) to demand or maintain firmly; to press.

insistence (*n.*) a firm demand.

insistent (*adj.*) firm; determined.

insolence (*n.*) rudeness; impertinence.

insolent (*adj.*) impudent; insulting.

insoluble (*adj.*) cannot be dissolved.

insolvency (*n.*) inability to pay all debts; bankruptcy.

insomnia (*n.*) sleeplessness.

inspect (*v.*) to examine; to investigate.

inspection (*n.*) an examination. INSPECTOR (*n.*).

inspiration (*n.*) 1. an indrawn breath. 2. a divine influence. 3. a good idea.

inspire (*v.*) 1. to breathe in. 2. to encourage another.

inspired (*adj.*) moved or encouraged as if by a divine spirit.

instability (*n.*) 1. unsteadiness. 2. hesitation.

install (*v.*) 1. to place a thing where it is going to be used. 2. to place a person in a position or office, especially ceremoniously. INSTALLATION (*n.*).

instance (*n.*) an example.

instant (*adj.*) urgent; pressing. INSTANT (*n.*) 1. a moment. 2. the present month.

instantly (*adv.*) at once; immediately.

instead (*adv.*) in the place of.

instep (*n.*) the arch, or upper part of the foot near the ankle.

instigate (*v.*) to urge; to persuade.

instigation (*n.*) a goading; setting on. INSTIGATOR (*n.*).

instil (*v.*) to put in little by little; to teach.

instinct (*n.*) an inborn ability not controlled by one's own will; knowledge to act without being taught.

instinctive (*adj.*) doing by instinct; natural.

institute (*v.*) to found; to establish. INSTITUTE (*n.*) a meeting place for a society.

institution (*n.*) a society or its buildings.

instruct (*v.*) 1. to teach. 2. to order.

instruction (*n.*) 1. tuition; teaching. 2. a command. INSTRUCTOR (*n.*).

instructive (*adj.*) giving knowledge; informing.

instrument (*n.*) 1. a tool; implement. 2. apparatus for producing musical sounds.

instrumental (*adj.*) 1. helpful; useful. 2. produced by musical instruments. INSTRUMENTALIST (*n.*).

insubordinate (*adj.*) disobedient; rebellious.

insubordination (*n.*) disobedience; indiscipline.

insufferable (*adj.*) unbearable; detestable.

insular (*adj.*) 1. belonging to an island. 2. narrow-minded.

insularity (*n.*) 1. isolation. 2. narrow-mindedness.

insulate (*v.*) 1. to set apart; to isolate. 2. to prevent loss of heat or electricity by means of non-conductors.

insulation (*n.*) 1. an isolation. 2. a prevention of loss.

insulator (*n.*) a non-conductor of heat or electricity.

insult (*v.*) to offend; to affront. INSULT (*n.*) an affront; indignity.

insulting (*adj.*) insolent; abusive.

insupportable (*adj.*) unbearable; unendurable.

insurable (*adj.*) can be insured.

insurance (*n.*) a sum or premium paid to insure.

insure (*v.*) 1. to guarantee. 2. to arrange to receive compensation for loss by fire, burglary, etc.

insurgent (*adj.*) riotous; rebellious. INSURGENT (*n.*) a rioter; rebel.

insurrection (*n.*) a revolt; rebellion.

intact (*adj.*) 1. complete; whole. 2. unhurt; undamaged.

intangible (*adj.*) cannot be touched; imaginary.

integral (*adj.*) whole; complete.

integrity (*n.*) uprightness; reliability.

intellect (*n.*) 1. ability to think and reason. 2. sense and understanding.

intellectual (*adj.*) thoughtful; reasoning.

intelligence (*n.*) 1. mental alertness. 2. news; knowledge.

intelligent (*adj.*) 1. sensible; shrewd. 2. well-informed.

intelligible (*adj.*) clear; understandable. INTELLIGIBLY (*adv.*).

intend (*v.*) to mean; to purpose. INTENDED (*adj.*).

intense (*adj.*) earnest; concentrated.

intensify (*v.*) to strengthen; to emphasize.

intensity (*n.*) concentration; earnestness.

intent (*adj.*) fixed or bent upon; attentive to. INTENT (*n.*) purpose.

intention (*n.*) an aim; purpose.

intentional (*adj.*) done on purpose; deliberate.

inter (*v.*) to bury. INTERRED (*adj.*).

intercede (*v.*) to plead for; to mediate.

intercept (*v.*) to stop on the way; to interrupt.

interception (*n.*) an interruption; intervention.

intercession (*n.*) an effort to make peace.

intercourse (*n.*) dealings between people or nations; conversation; commerce, etc.

interest (*n.*) 1. payment for money loaned. 2. concern for. 3. attention to. 4. a share; part. INTEREST (*v.*) 1. to concern oneself. 2. to gain and hold attention.

interested (*adj.*) 1. having a share in. 2. attentive to.

interesting (*adj.*) pleasing; entertaining.

interfere (*v.*) to concern oneself with; to meddle.

interference (*n.*) meddlesomeness. INTERFERING (*adj.*).

interim (*n.*) the meantime; interval between two stated times.

interior (*n.*) the inside; inland portion of a country.

interject (*v.*) 1. to throw in; to insert. 2. to exclaim.

interjection (*n.*) 1. an interrupting word or comment. 2. an exclamation.

interloper (*n.*) an intruder; meddler.

intermediary (*n.*) an arbitrator; a go-between.

intermediate (*adj.*) middle; half-way between.

interment (*n.*) burial.

interminable (*adj.*) endless; unceasing.

intermingle (*v.*) to mix together; to blend.

intermingling (*n.*) a mixture; blend.

intermission (*n.*) a pause; an interval.

intermit (*v.*) to stop; to give up for a time.

intermittent (*adj.*) occurring at intervals.

intern (*v.*) to compel to live within fixed limits, as of a camp, town, etc.; to restrict freedom of movement.

internal (*adj.*) 1. inside; inner. 2. home; domestic.

international (*adj.*) concerning matters between nations.

interpret (*v.*) to explain; to translate.

interpretation (*n.*) an explanation; translation. INTERPRETER (*n.*).

interrogate (*v.*) to ask; to question.

interrogation (*n.*) a questioning.

interrogative (*adj.*) in the form of a question.

interrupt (*v.*) to break in between; to disturb.

interruption (*n.*) a hindrance; stoppage.

intersect (*v.*) to cut or lie across each other like crossroads.

intersection (*n.*) point at which lines, roads, etc., cross.

intersperse (*v.*) to set or scatter here and there. INTERSPERSION (*n.*).

interval (*n.*) gap between two times or events; a pause.

intervene (*v.*) to come between; to interfere.

intervention (*n.*) interference; mediation.

interview (*v.*) to meet and discuss. INTERVIEW (*n.*) a meeting for (1) discussion, or (2) information which may be published.

intimacy (*n.*) close friendship. (*pl.* INTIMACIES).

intimate (*adj.*) friendly; dear. INTIMATE (*n.*) a friend; crony.

intimate (*v.*) to hint; to suggest.

intimation (*n.*) a hint; suggestion.

intimidate (*v.*) to threaten; to menace.

intimidation (*n.*) a threatening; terrorizing.

intolerable (*adj.*) unbearable; unendurable.

intolerance (*n.*) narrow-mindedness; bigotry.

intolerant (*adj.*) unwilling to allow others to form their own opinions; narrowminded.

intoxicate (*v.*) 1. to make drunk. 2. to excite highly.

intoxication (*n.*) 1. drunkenness. 2. great excitement.

intrepid (*adj.*) brave; bold.

intrepidity (*n.*) courage; daring.

intricacy (*n.*) a tangle; complication. (*pl.* INTRICACIES).

intricate (*adj.*) tangled; complicated.

intrigue (*v.*) to plot secretly. INTRIGUE (*n.*) a plot; scheme.

intriguing (*adj.*) 1. deceitful. 2. interesting.

intrinsic (*adj.*) 1. contained within; innate. 2. true; genuine.

introduce (*v.*) 1. to make known to for the first time; to acquaint with. 2. to bring something new to notice, as a mode, fashion, etc. INTRODUCTION (*n.*).

intrude (*v.*) to enter without invitation; to encroach.

intruder (*n.*) a trespasser; meddler.

intrusion (*n.*) an entry without permission; a trespass.

intuition (*n.*) a feeling that one knows without understanding how or why; immediate insight.

intuitive (*adj.*) without reasoning.

inundate (*v.*) to flood; to swamp.

inundation (*n.*) a flood; deluge.

inure (*v.*) to get used to; to accustom.

invade (*v.*) to enter as an enemy.

invader (*n.*) an entering enemy.

invalid (*adj.*) without value; worthless.

invalid (*n.*) a sick person.

invalided (*adj.*) placed on the sick-list.

invaluable (*adj.*) of great value; priceless.

invariable (*adj.*) unchanging; constant.

invariably (*adv.*) without exception.

invasion (*n.*) a raid; incursion.

invective (*n.*) abuse.

inveigle (*v.*) to tempt; to wheedle.

invent (*v.*) 1. to devise something new; to create. 2. to make up; to concoct. INVENTOR (*n.*).

invention (*n.*) 1. a discovery; creation. 2. a romance; fabrication.

inventive (*adj.*) 1. able to invent. 2. quick at making things up.

inventory (*n.*) a list of goods or possessions. (*pl.* INVENTORIES).

invert (*v.*) to turn upside down.

invertebrate (*adj.*) without a vertebral column or backbone.

invest (*v.*) 1. to dress. 2. to besiege. 3. to use money to gain profit or interest.

investigate (*v.*) to inquire into; to search.

investigation (*n.*) an inquiry; search. INVESTIGATOR (*n.*).

investment (*n.*) 1. a siege. 2. the use of money to purchase property, etc., which will provide rent, interest, dividend, etc.

invigorate (*v.*) to strengthen; to refresh.

invigorating (*adj.*) bracing; health-giving.

invincibility (*n.*) unconquerableness.

invincible (*adj.*) unbeatable; irresistible.

invisibility (*n.*) inability to be seen.

invisible (*adj.*) cannot be seen; unseen.

invitation (*n.*) a request; bidding.

invite (*v.*) 1. to ask to come; to request. 2. to attract; to tempt.

inviting (*adj.*) attractive; tempting.

invocation (*n.*) a prayer; an entreaty.

invoice (*n.*) an account of goods supplied; a bill. INVOICE (*v.*) to make a detailed account.

invoke (*v.*) to ask for help; to pray.

involuntary (*adj.*) unintentional; not willed.

involve (*v.*) to tangle; to complicate.

invulnerable (*adj.*) cannot be harmed; unbeatable.

inward (*adj.*) within; internal. INWARD (*adv.*) toward the inside.

iodine (*n.*) a powerful antiseptic.

ion (*n.*) an electrified atom.

iota (*n.*) a particle; an atom.

irascibility (*n.*) bad-temper; irritation.

irascible (*adj.*) irritable; touchy.

irate (*adj.*) angry; furious.

ire (*n.*) fury; rage.

iridescence (*n.*) colouring like the rainbow.

iridescent (*adj.*) rainbow-coloured.

iris (*n.*) 1. the rainbow. 2. coloured ring of the eye. 3. a plant of the lily family. (*pl.* IRISES). See appendix.

irk (*v.*) to tire; to weary.

irksome (*adj.*) tiresome; tedious.

iron (*n.*) 1. a hard metal. 2. an instrument for pressing cloth. IRON (*adj.*) hard; strong. IRON (*v.*) to smooth with an iron.

ironic (*adj.*) saying one thing and meaning another; sarcastic.

ironmongery (*n.*) articles made of iron; hardware. IRONMONGER (*n.*).

irony (*n.*) mockery by saying the opposite to what is meant.

irradiate (*v.*) to shed light upon; to illuminate.

irradiation (*n.*) brightness; illumination.

irrational (*adj.*) absurd; unreasonable.

irreconcilable (*adj.*) can never agree.

irregular (*adj.*) 1. against the rules. 2. uneven; variable.

irregularity (*n.*) 1. a departure from rule. 2. fitfulness.

irreparable (*adj.*) cannot be repaired; without remedy.

irresistible (*adj.*) cannot be overcome.

irresolute (*adj.*) undecided; hesitant.

irresolution (*n.*) inability to make up one's mind.

irresponsible (*adj.*) without sense of duty; wayward.

irresponsive (*adj.*) unanswering.

irretrievable (*adj.*) lost beyond recovery.

irrigate (*v.*) to supply dry lands with water.

irrigation (*n.*) a system of supplying water for cultivation.

irritability (*n.*) annoyance; petulance.

irritable (*adj.*) fretful; peevish.

irritate (*v.*) 1. to annoy; to vex. 2. to itch; to chafe.

irritation (*n.*) 1. vexation; exasperation. 2. an itching.

island (*n.*) a piece of land surrounded by water. ISLE (*n.*).

isobar (*n.*) a line on a map connecting places having the same mean barometric or atmospheric pressure. ISOBARIC (*adj.*).

isolate (*v.*) to set apart or alone; to separate.

isolated (*adj.*) solitary; separated.

isolation (*n.*) solitude; separation.

isotherm (*n.*) a line on a map connecting places having the same mean monthly or annual temperature. ISOTHERMAL (*adj.*).

isotope (*n.*) atom with additional neutrons.

Israel (*n.*) 1. Jacob, father or founder of the Hebrews or Jews. 2. the Hebrew people or nation (Israelites). 3. the Hebrew or Jewish Republic in Palestine.

issue (*v.*) 1. to be born. 2. to flow from. 3. to publish. 4. to result. ISSUE (*n.*) 1. offspring. 2. outflow. 3. publication. 4. the consequence.

isthmus (*n.*) a narrow strip of land connecting larger pieces.

itch (*n.*) 1. an irritation of the skin. 2. a longing for. ITCH (*v.*) 1. to irritate. 2. to be eager for.

itching (*adj.*) 1. irritating. 2. eager.

item (*n.*) a single one out of a number; a separate thing.

iterate (*v.*) to repeat.

itinerant (*adj.*) wandering; roving.

itinerary (*n.*) the route of a journey.

ivory (*n.*) hard, white substance composing elephant tusk.

ivy (*n.*) evergreen climbing plant.

J

jab (*v.*) to poke. JAB (*n.*) a sharp stab with the finger.

jabber (v.) to chatter; to gabble.
jack (n.) 1. a tool for raising heavy weights. 2. a flag. 3. the aiming mark in bowls.
jackal (n.) wild animal of the dog family.
jackanapes (n.) an impertinent person.
jackass (n.) 1. the male of the ass. 2. a blockhead.
jackdaw (n.) a thievish and easily tamed black bird of the crow family.
jacket (n.) 1. a short coat. 2. an outside cover for many articles.
jade (v.) to tire; to fatigue. JADE (n.) 1. a green ornamental stone. 2. a saucy girl.
jaded (adj.) tired; weary.
jagged (adj.) rough-edged; notched. JAGGEDNESS (n.).
jaguar (n.) South American leopard.
jail (n.) a prison.
jam (v.) to squeeze; to wedge in. JAM (n.) 1. a preserve. 2. a blockage due to crowding.
jamb (n.) sidepost of door or window.
jangle (v.) to sound harshly. JANGLE (n.) a harsh sound; a discord. JANGLED (adj.).
janitor (n.) a door-keeper.
January (n.) the first month. See appendix.
jar (v.) 1. to jolt. 2. to grate. JAR (n.) 1. a jolt. 2. a harsh sound. 3. a glass or earthenware vessel; a jampot.
jargon (n.) special talk used in most professions; slang.
jarring (adj.) harsh; discordant.
jasmine (n.) a fragrant climbing shrub.
jaundice (n.) a malady which turns the skin yellow. JAUNDICED (adj.).
jaunt (n.) an outing; excursion.
jauntiness (n.) liveliness; gaiety. JAUNTY (adj.).
jaw (n.) either of the bones in the mouth in which the teeth are fixed.
jay (n.) a small, chattering bird with gay plumage.
jealous (adj.) suspicious; distrustful.
jealousy (n.) envy; distrust.
jean (n.) a twilled cotton cloth.
jeer (v.) to mock; to ridicule. JEER (n.) a taunt; jibe.
jelly (n.) a food made from gelatine.
jeopardize (v.) to endanger; to risk.
jeopardy (n.) danger; risk.

jerk (n.) a short, sharp pull; a twitch. JERK (v.) to pull sharply; to twitch. JERKY (adj.).
jerkin (n.) a man's tight-fitting jacket or short coat.
jersey (n.) a close-fitting, knitted garment.
jest (v.) to joke. JEST (n.) a joke. JESTER (n.).
Jesus (n.) the name of the founder of the Christian Faith and Religion, who is worshipped by Christians as the Son of God and the Saviour of Mankind.
jet (n.) 1. a stream of water or gas shot from a nozzle. 2. a hard, black stone. JET (adj.) deep black.
jet-propelled (v.) driven by powerful jets of gas.
jetsam (n.) cargo thrown overboard to lighten a ship in danger.
jettison (v.) to throw overboard; to abandon.
jetty (n.) a landing pier; a mole. (pl. JETTIES).
Jew (n.) a man of the Hebrew race; an Israelite. (fem. JEWESS).
jewel (n.) a precious stone; a gem.
jewellery (n.) gems; ornaments of gold and silver. JEWELLER (n.).
jib (v.) 1. to jump sharply away from. 2. to move restively. JIB (n.) a triangular foresail.
jig (n.) a brisk dance with rapid up and down movement. JIG (v.) to dance a jig.
jilt (n.) a woman who breaks her promise to marry the man to whom she is betrothed. JILT (v.) to break one's betrothal promises; to cast aside.
jingle (v.) to clink or tinkle. JINGLE (n.) sound of rattling coins.
jinks (n. pl.) merrymaking; noisy fun.
job (n.) 1. a piece of work. 2. employment; business.
jockey (n.) a racehorse rider.
jocular (adj.) fond of joking.
jocund (adj.) gay; jolly.
jog (v.) 1. to push; to nudge. 2. to remind. 3. to trot.
join (v.) 1. to connect; to fasten. 2. to make contact with a person, society, etc.
joiner (n.) a wood or timber worker.
joinery (n.) 1. timber-work required in a building. 2. a joiner's work.

joint (*n.*) 1. a connection made between two pieces. 2. a large piece of meat. JOINT (*adj.*) combined.

jointly (*adv.*) working together; combined.

joist (*n.*) beam supporting floor or roof.

joke (*v.*) to jest. JOKE (*n.*) a jest; prank. JOKER (*n.*).

jollification (*n.*) a merrymaking; festivity.

jollity (*n.*) mirth; fun.

jolly (*adj.*) lively; jovial. JOLLILY (*adv.*).

jolt (*v.*) to jerk; to bump. JOLT (*n.*) 1. a bump. 2. a shock.

jonquil (*n.*) plant of the daffodil family.

joss (*n.*) a Chinese idol.

jostle (*v.*) to knock against. JOSTLE (*n.*) a knock when being pushed or bustled.

jot (*n.*) a trifle; a dot. JOT (*v.*) to write down.

jotter (*n.*) a note-book; writing-pad.

joule (*n.*) a measure of electrical work or energy. See appendix.

journal (*n.*) 1. a daily, weekly or quarterly publication. 2. a diary.

journalism (*n.*) work of writing and producing a newspaper.

journalist (*n.*) editor of or writer for a newspaper or journal.

journalistic (*adj.*) concerned with newspapers.

journey (*v.*) to travel; to voyage. JOURNEY (*n.*) a single trip; voyage.

joust (*n.*) a sporting combat between two mounted knights armed with lances; a tilt. JOUST (*v.*) to ride against another in armed combat; to tilt.

jovial (*adj.*) jolly; cheerful. JOVIALLY (*adv.*).

joviality (*n.*) good-humour; cordiality. See appendix.

jowl (*n.*) the jaw; cheek.

joy (*n.*) happiness; delight. JOYFUL (*adj.*). JOYFULLY (*adv.*).

joyless (*adj.*) unenjoyable; dull.

joyous (*adj.*) buoyant; elated.

jubilant (*adj.*) rejoicing; triumphant. JUBILANTLY (*adv.*).

jubilation (*n.*) triumph.

jubilee (*n.*) 1. the 50th anniversary. 2. a celebration.

judge (*v.*) to adjudicate; to decide. JUDGE (*n.*) one who decides.

judgment (*n.*) 1. a judge's decision. 2. one's ability to decide.

judicial (*adj.*) concerning courts and judges.

jug (*n.*) a deep vessel, with handle, for holding liquids. JUG (*v.*) to boil or stew, especially hare, in a jug or jar.

juggle (*v.*) to conjure; to play tricks. JUGGLER (*n.*).

jugglery (*n.*) the art of conjuring.

jugular (*adj.*) concerning the throat and neck.

juice (*n.*) liquid contained in fruits and vegetables.

juiciness (*n.*) the quality of being juicy.

juicy (*adj.*) tasty; succulent.

July (*n.*) the seventh month. See appendix.

jumble (*v.*) to mix up; to muddle. JUMBLE (*n.*) a muddle of oddments; confusion. JUMBLED (*adj.*).

jump (*v.*) 1. to leap; to spring. 2. to start; to wince. JUMP (*n.*) 1. a leap. 2. a start.

jumper (*n.*) 1. one who jumps. 2. a knitted garment.

jumpiness (*n.*) nervousness.

junction (*n.*) place where things join or meet.

juncture (*n.*) 1. a linking point. 2. a particular moment.

June (*n.*) the sixth month.

jungle (*n.*) a wild, tangled forest.

junior (*n.*) 1. younger in age. 2. lower in position.

juniper (*n.*) an evergreen shrub and its oil.

junk (*n.*) 1. discarded oddments; waste. 2. a Chinese ship. 3. salt meat.

junket (*n.*) curds and whey. JUNKET (*v.*) to feast.

Jupiter (*n.*) the largest of the planets. See appendix.

jurisdiction (*n.*) 1. the legal authority of an official. 2. the area in which he has authority.

juror (*n.*) a member of a jury; a juryman.

jury (*n.*) a body of persons sworn to hear evidence in a law case and to give a decision or verdict.

just (*adj.*) right; fair.

justice (*n.*) 1. rightness; fairness. 2. a judge; magistrate.

justifiable (*adj.*) allowable; excusable.

justification (*n.*) a defence.

justify (*v.*) 1. to prove something is right. 2. to defend oneself.

justness (*n.*) fairness; rightness.

jut (*v.*) to stick out; to project.

jute (*n.*) a vegetable fibre used in mat-making.

juvenile (*adj.*) young; youthful. JUVENILE (*n.*) a young person; one not adult.

K

kale (*n.*) a kind of cabbage.

kangaroo (*n.*) an Australian animal with short front legs and long back legs.

kaolin (*n.*) China clay for pottery making.

kayak (*n.*) a light Eskimo canoe of wooden framework covered with seal-skins.

kedge (*n.*) a small ship's anchor.

keel (*n.*) the long bottom beam on which a ship's frame is built.

keen (*adj.*) 1. sharp-edged. 2. quick-witted; eager.

keenness (*n.*) 1. sharpness. 2. eagerness; zeal. KEENLY (*adv.*).

keep (*v.*) 1. to hold. 2. to feed. 3. to fulfil. KEEP (*n.*) a castle; stronghold.

keeper (*n.*) a guard; guardian.

keepsake (*n.*) anything kept for the giver's sake; a souvenir.

keg (*n.*) a small cask.

kennel (*n.*) an outdoor dog-house.

kerchief (*n.*) a head or neck cloth.

kernel (*n.*) 1. seed within a nutshell. 2. the heart or core of anything.

kerosene (*n.*) paraffin oil.

kestrel (*n.*) a small, slender hawk.

ketch (*n.*) small, two-masted ship.

ketchup (*n.*) sauce made from mushrooms, tomatoes, etc.

kettle (*n.*) metal vessel for boiling water.

kettledrum (*n.*) bowl-shaped copper vessel covered with skin.

key (*n.*) 1. implement for operating a lock. 2. a musical scale. 3. finger-lever on piano or organ.

khaki (*n.*) a dull-yellow cloth used for military uniforms.

kick (*v.*) to strike with the foot. KICK (*n.*) a blow from the foot.

kid (*n.*) 1. a young goat. 2. leather made from kidskin.

kidnap (*v.*) to seize and carry off a person; to abduct.

kidnapper (*n.*) one who kidnaps.

kidney (*n.*) a gland in the body.

kill (*v.*) 1. to put to death. 2. to calm; to quieten.

kiln (*n.*) a large oven for burning or drying.

kilogramme (*n.*) metric measure of mass.

kilometre (*n.*) metric measure of distance, equal to 1000 metres.

kilowatt (*n.*) measure of quantity of electricity used (1,000 watts).

kilt (*n.*) short skirt of tartan cloth.

kin or **kindred** (*n.*) family and blood relations.

kind (*n.*) 1. a family; race. 2. a sort; way. KIND (*adj.*) gentle; loving.

kindergarten (*n.*) nursery school for very young children.

kindle (*v.*) 1. to set on fire. 2. to catch fire. 3. to influence; to excite.

kindliness (*n.*) gentleness; affection.

kindly (*adj.*) helpful; good-natured. KINDLY (*adv.*) gently.

kindness (*n.*) tenderness; goodwill.

kine (*n. pl.*) cows.

kinematograph (*n.*) see CINEMATOGRAPH.

king (*n.*) 1. a male sovereign; monarch. 2. the chief chesspiece.

kingdom (*n.*) territory ruled by a king.

kingfisher (*n.*) small, gaily-coloured diving-bird.

kingly (*adj.*) royal; majestic.

kink (*n.*) a twist or bend in a rope; a mental twist.

kiosk (*n.*) a telephone-box, summer-house or small stall.

kipper (*n.*) a herring, split and cured by smoke.

kirk (*n.*) a church.

kismet (*n.*) fortune; fate.

kiss (*v.*) to touch with the lips. KISS (*n.*) a touch of the lips; a caress.

kit (*n.*) an outfit; equipment.

kitchen (*n.*) cooking-room in a house.

kite (*n.*) 1. a falcon-like bird of prey. 2. a light, paper-covered framework flown in the air.

kith (*n.*) kindred; relatives.

kitten (*n.*) a young cat.

kittiwake (*n.*) small gull with long wings.

knack (*n.*) ability to do some particular thing cleverly; dexterity.

knapsack (*n.*) a kit-bag carried on the shoulder.

knave (*n.*) a rascal; scamp.

knavery (*n.*) rascality; roguery. KNAVISH (*adj.*).

knead (*v.*) 1. to work up flour into dough. 2. to massage.

knee (*n.*) joint between thigh and foreleg.

kneel (*v.*) to rest or fall on bent knees.

knell (*n.*) sound of a tolling or funeral bell.

knick-knack (*n.*) a trifle; toy.

knife (*n.*) an instrument for cutting. (*pl.* KNIVES).

knight (*n.*) one who has received the honour of knighthood. KNIGHT (*v.*) to dub or create a knight.

knighthood (*n.*) rank and dignity conferred on a man by his sovereign in recognition of his personal merit.

knightly (*adj.*) chivalrous; courteous. KNIGHTLY (*adv.*) bravely; boldly.

knit (*v.*) 1. to weave with long needles. 2. to join; to unite.

knitter (*n.*) one who knits. KNITTING (*n.*).

knob (*n.*) a rounded lump; a handle.

knobby (*adj.*) lumpy.

knock (*v.*) to strike; to rap upon. KNOCK (*n.*) a blow; rap.

knocker (*n.*) hinged metal hammer fixed on a door.

knoll (*n.*) a low, rounded hillock; a mound.

knot (*n.*) 1. a tie or tangle in a rope. 2. a hard bulge in wood. 3. a small group of people. 4. a difficulty; problem. 5. measure of a ship's speed. 1 knot = 1 sea mile (6,080 feet) per hour. N.B. Say so many knots. Never add, an hour, or per hour.

knotted (*adj.*) 1. tied; tangled. 2. gnarled.

knotty (*adj.*) difficult; perplexing.

know (*v.*) 1. to be sure; certain. 2. to understand. 3. to be told; informed. 4. to recognize.

knowable (*adj.*) easy to get on with.

knowing (*adj.*) sharp; shrewd.

knowingly (*adv.*) intelligently; deliberately.

knowledge (*n.*) learning; understanding.

knuckle (*n.*) a finger-joint. KNUCKLE (*v.*) to strike with the knuckles.

kudos (*n.*) 1. fame; reputation. 2. credit.

L

label (*n.*) a slip of paper or card for fastening on parcels. LABEL (*v.*) to affix a label to. LABELLED (*adj.*).

labial (*adj.*) about the lips. LABIAL (*n.*) letter sounded by the lips (b, p, m.).

laboratory (*n.*) a scientist's workroom. (*pl.* LABORATORIES).

laborious (*adj.*) tiring; toilsome.

labour (*n.*) work; industry. LABOUR (*v.*) to work.

labourer (*n.*) worker at heavy, unskilled work.

laburnum (*n.*) tree and its hanging, yellow flowers.

labyrinth (*n.*) a muddle of winding passages; a maze. THE LABYRINTH. That of King Minos at Cnossus, Crete.

lace (*n.*) 1. cord passed through eyelets. 2. a fine, openwork fabric. LACE (*v.*) fasten with laces.

lacerate (*v.*) 1. to tear; to rend. 2. to hurt the feelings; to distress.

laceration (*n.*) 1. a rip; rent. 2. a distress; harrowing.

lack (*v.*) to be without; to need. LACK (*n.*) a need; shortage.

lackadaisical (*adj.*) easy-going; happy-go-lucky.

lackey (*n.*) a footman; attendant.

laconic (*adj.*) brief; short. LACONICALLY (*adv.*).

lacquer (*n.*) a hard, glossy varnish.

lacrosse (*n.*) open-air team game played with ball and long-handled racquet.

lad (*n.*) a boy; youth.

ladder (*n.*) 1. two lengths of wood, rope, etc., connected by wooden bars or rungs which form steps. 2. a line of loosened stitches in a stocking.

lade (*v.*) to load a ship; to burden. LADEN (*adj.*).

lading (*n.*) cargo; freight.

ladle (*n.*) long-handled cup for serving liquids.

lady (*n.*) a courteous, well-educated woman. (*pl.* LADIES).

ladybird (*n.*) a tiny, vari-coloured beetle, which eats plant-lice.

lag (*v.*) to linger; to dawdle.

laggard (*n.*) a sluggard; loiterer.

lagging (*adj.*) slow; backward.

lagoon (*n.*) 1. the water inside an atoll. 2. a sea-water lake.

lair (*n.*) a wild beast's den.

laird (*n.*) Scottish squire or landowner.

laity (*n.*) people who are not clergy.

lake (*n.*) a body of water surrounded by land.

lamb (*n.*) a young sheep.

lambert (*n.*) measure of the brightness of light. See appendix.

lame (*adj.*) 1. crippled; limping. 2. imperfect; unsatisfactory.

lameness (*n.*) 1. a disability. 2. an imperfection.

lament (*v.*) to mourn; to bewail. LAMENT (*n.*) a mournful song; a dirge.

lamentable (*adj.*) pitiful; miserable. LAMENTABLY (*adv.*).

Lammas (*n.*) a harvest festival; August 1st.

lamp (*n.*) a device for giving light.

lamplight (*n.*) light shed by a lamp.

lampoon (*n.*) a writing ridiculing someone. LAMPOON (*v.*) to ridicule. LAMPOONIST (*n.*).

lamprey (*n.*) an eel-like fish.

lance (*n.*) a long-shafted spear. LANCE (*v.*) 1. to pierce with a spear. 2. to cut with a lancet.

lancet (*n.*) 1. a two-edged surgical knife. 2. a pointed or lance-shaped window.

land (*n.*) 1. any solid part of earth's surface. 2. a country; territory. 3. an estate. LAND (*v.*) to get on shore.

landed (*adj.*) owning land.

landfall (*n.*) a ship's destination.

landing (*n.*) 1. a disembarkation. 2. level place between two flights of stairs.

landlord (*n.*) 1. owner of a rented house. 2. host of an inn. (*fem.* LANDLADY).

land-lubber (*n.*) person not used to the sea; a landsman.

landmark (*n.*) object visible from a distance.

landscape (*n.*) a scene; view.

landslide (*n.*) a fall of part of a hill-side or cliff.

lane (*n.*) narrow road or passage.

language (*n.*) the speech or tongue of a person, nation or race.

languid (*adj.*) faint; drooping.

languish (*v.*) to droop; to flag.

languor (*n.*) weariness; exhaustion.

lank (*adj.*) long and lean.

lankiness (*n.*) thinness; leanness.

lanky (*adj.*) thin; lean.

lantern (*n.*) a case containing a light.

lap (*v.*) 1. to wrap over. 2. to lick up. LAP (*n.*) 1. the clothes on the knee when seated. 2. once round a race track.

lapel (*n.*) that part of a coat folded back.

lapse (*n.*) 1. a slip; an error. 2. a passage of time. LAPSE (*v.*) 1. to err. 2. to pass slowly. 3. to come to an end.

lapwing (*n.*) the peewit or pewit.

larceny (*n.*) theft; pilfering.

larch (*n.*) a cone-bearing tree.

lard (*n.*) pig-fat melted and purified.

larder (*n.*) household food store.

large (*adj.*) big in size; great.

largely (*adv.*) chiefly; mostly.

lark (*n.*) 1. a soaring song-bird. 2. a frolic; prank. LARK (*v.*) to frolic; to joke.

larva (*n.*) a grub that will become an insect. (*pl.* LARVÆ).

laryngitis (*n.*) inflammation of the larynx.

larynx (*n.*) cavity in the throat holding the vocal chords; the voice-box.

laser (*n.*) powerful light beam used in science and industry (light amplification by stimulated emission of radiation).

lash (*v.*) 1. to whip. 2. to hit. 3. to move the tail angrily. 4. to fasten; bind. 5. to speak angrily; to unbraid. LASH (*n.*) 1. a hair edging the eyelid. 2. a whip's cord.

lassitude (*n.*) unwillingness to move; listlessness.

lasso (*n. pron.* las-SOO) a noosed, rawhide rope for catching cattle.

last (*n.*) 1. a cobbler's model of the foot. 2. a measure of weight. 3. the final; hindmost. LAST (*v.*) 1. to endure. 2. to hold out. LAST (*adj.*) final; latest. LAST (*adv.*) at the end.

lasting (*adj.*) enduring; permanent. LASTING (*n.*) endurance.

lastly (*adv.*) finally; in the last place.

latch (*n.*) a door catch. LATCH (*v.*) to fasten with a latch.

latchet (*n.*) a shoe-string.

late (*adj.*) 1. behind time; overdue. 2. not now alive; deceased. 3. near the day's end.

lately (*adv.*) recently; not long ago.

lateness (*n.*) 1. nearness to the day's end. 2. tardiness; delay.

latent (*adj.*) hidden; not developed.

lateral (*adj.*) relating to the side.

lath (*n.*) a narrow strip of wood.

lathe (*n.*) machine which shapes wooden or metal articles.

lather (*n.*) foam made of soap and water. LATHER (*v.*) to cover with lather.

Latin (*n.*) 1. language of the ancient Romans. 2. a Roman citizen.

latitude (*n.*) 1. distance north or south of the equator. 2. a freedom from rules; laxity. 3. the extent; scope.

latter (*adj.*) the second of two.

latterly (*adv.*) not long ago; of late.

lattice (*n.*) a window with glass set in crossed strips or bars.

laud (*v.*) to praise; to extol. LAUDABLE (*adj.*).

laudation (*n.*) praise; commendation.

laudatory (*adj.*) full of praise.

laugh (*n.*) a noisy expression of amusement. LAUGH (*v.*) to show amusement with mouth and voice.

laughable (*adj.*) amusing; funny.

laughingly (*adv.*) jokingly; with a laugh.

laughter (*n.*) the sound of laughing.

launch (*v.*) 1. to hurl. 2. to begin. 3. to set afloat. LAUNCH (*n.*) a small motor-boat. LAUNCHING PAD (*n.*) site used to launch rockets.

launder (*v.*) to wash and get up linen, etc.

laundress (*n.*) woman who launders.

laundry (*n.*) establishment where fabrics are laundered.

laureate (*adj.*) laurel-crowned. The Poet Laureate is the national poet. The Laureateship is the highest literary honour in Britain.

laurel (*n.*) a glossy-leaved, evergreen shrub; a wreath made of laurel; the bay-tree.

laurels (*n. pl.*) honours; victories.

lava (*n.*) molten rock from a volcano.

lavatory (*n.*) a wash room.

lave (*v.*) to wash; to bathe.

lavender (*n.*) fragrant shrub and its flowers.

lavish (*adj.*) extravagant; wasteful.

lavishness (*n.*) prodigality; profusion.

law (*n.*) a rule ordered by an act of parliament; a statute; a rule established by a community. Beware STATUE.

law-abiding (*adj.*) obedient to the law.

lawful (*adj.*) allowed by law; legal.

lawfulness (*n.*) legality; validity.

lawless (*adj.*) disorderly; rebellious.

lawlessness (*n.*) revolt; anarchy.

lawn (*n.*) 1. a grass-grown open space. 2. fine linen or cambric.

lawsuit (*n.*) a trial in a lawcourt.

lawyer (*n.*) one skilled in law and legal work; a solicitor.

lax (*adj.*) slack; negligent. LAXLY (*adv.*).

laxity (*n.*) carelessness; negligence.

lay (*v.*) 1. to put down. 2. to place; to put. 3. to produce eggs. LAY (*n.*) a poem; song. LAY (*adj.*) not professional or expert.

layman (*n.*) one without professional or expert knowledge.

layer (*n.*) a substance spread evenly over another; a stratum.

layette (*n.*) a complete outfit for a new-born baby.

lazily (*adv.*) idly; sluggishly.

laziness (*n.*) idleness; slothfulness.

lazy (*adj.*) indolent; idle.

lea (*n.*) grassland; meadow.

lead (*v.*) 1. to guide; to conduct. 2. to be in front; to excel. LEAD (*n.*) the guidance; control.

lead (*n.*) a dull, heavy metal.

leaded (*adj.*) lead-covered.

leaden (*adj.*) 1. made of lead. 2. dull; lifeless.

leader (*n.*) a guide; head.

leadership (*n.*) ability to lead.

leading (*adj.*) foremost; principal. LEADING (*n.*) direction; guidance.

leadline (*n.*) a lead-weighted line used to find the depth of water.

leadsman (*n.*) sailor who heaves the lead, or finds the depth.

leaf (*n.*) 1. thin, flat shoot from a stem. 2. two pages, or one sheet, of a book. 3. one side of a double-door. (*pl.* LEAVES).

leafage (*n.*) the abundance of leaves; foliage.

leafless (*adj.*) without leaves; bare.
leaflet (*n.*) a printed handbill; circular.
leafy (*adj.*) abounding in leaves.
league (*n.*) 1. old measure of length (three miles). 2. an association; confederation. LEAGUE (*v.*) to unite; to confederate.
leaguer (*n.*) 1. member of a league. 2. a siege-camp.
leak (*n.*) a tiny crack through which liquid passes. 2. a disclosure of information. LEAK (*v.*) to let liquid enter or escape. LEAKING (*adj.*).
leakage (*n.*) 1. the quantity that leaks. 2. a disclosure.
leaky (*adj.*) having leaks.
lean (*v.*) 1. to incline towards. 2. to rest against. LEAN (*adj.*) 1. having little fat. 2. thin; lank. LEAN (*n.*) fatless meat.
leaning (*n.*) an inclination; a bias.
leanness (*n.*) want of flesh; thinness.
leap (*v.*) to jump; to spring. LEAP (*n.*) 1. a bound; a jump. 2. the space leapt over. LEAPER (*n.*).
leap-year (*n.*) year containing 366 days; year divisible exactly by four, except that beginning each century.
learn (*v.*) to gain new knowledge or skill. LEARNED (*adj.*).
learner (*n.*) a student; novice.
learning (*n.*) knowledge gained; scholarship.
lease (*n.*) an agreement to let land for rent.
leasehold (*adj.*) held by lease.
leaseholder (*n.*) a tenant holding by lease.
leash (*n.*) a cord or thong to hold a dog. LEASH (*v.*) to hold on a leash.
least (*adj., adv., & n.*) 1. the smallest. 2. the meanest, or lowest in importance.
leather (*n.*) the tanned hide of an animal. LEATHER (*v.*) to thrash.
leathern (*adj.*) made of leather.
leathery (*adj.*) like leather; tough.
leave (*v.*) 1. to depart. 2. to give by will; to bequeath. LEAVE (*n.*) 1. permission. 2. an absence; holiday.
leaven (*n.*) a substance that makes dough rise; yeast. LEAVEN (*v.*) to ferment or lighten dough.
leavings (*n. pl.*) things left; the remains.
lectern (*n.*) a church reading-desk.

lecture (*n.*) 1. an instructive address. 2. a scolding. LECTURE (*v.*) 1. to address. 2. to scold. LECTURER (*n.*).
lectureship (*n.*) appointment as a lecturer.
ledge (*n.*) a shelf; ridge.
ledger (*n.*) the chief account book.
lee (*n.*) the sheltered side.
leech (*n.*) a blood-sucking worm once used by physicians in treating diseases.
leek (*n.*) herb of the onion family. National emblem of Wales.
lees (*n. pl.*) the dregs; sediment
leeward (*adj., n., adv.*) on, towards the side turned from the wind.
leeway (*n.*) lost ground.
left (*adj.*) same side of the body as the heart.
leg (*n.*) limb used in standing or walking.
legacy (*n.*) a gift by will; a bequest. (*pl.* LEGACIES).
legal (*adj.*) allowed by law; lawful.
legality (*n.*) the lawfulness; validity.
legalize (*v.*) to make lawful; to authorize.
legate (*n.*) 1. a representative sent on a mission to a foreign state. 2. an ambassador of the Pope.
legatee (*n.*) one who receives a legacy.
legation (*n.*) a legate's residence.
legend (*n.*) 1. an ancient story; a fable. 2. an inscription on a coin or medal.
legendary (*adj.*) fabulous; wonderful.
legerdemain (*n.*) sleight-of-hand; conjuring.
legging (*n.*) a stiff cover for the leg.
legibility (*n.*) distinctness; readableness.
legible (*adj.*) plain; easily read. Beware ELIGIBLE.
legion (*n.*) a host; multitude.
legionary (*adj.*) numerous. LEGIONARY (*n.*) a member of a legion.
legislate (*v.*) to make laws; to enact.
legislation (*n.*) the making of laws.
legislative (*adj.*) by law; properly.
legislator (*n.*) a law-maker.
legislature (*n.*) an assembly having power to make laws.
legitimate (*adj.*) lawful; right.
leisure (*n.*) spare time; ease.
leisurely (*adj.*) slow; easy-going.
lemon (*n.*) a tree and its bitter, yellow fruit.
lemur (*n.*) a small, night-loving monkey.
lend (*v.*) to allow to have or use for a time. LENDER (*n.*).

length (*n.*) 1. the extent of anything from end to end. 2. a space of time.

lengthen (*v.*) to make longer; to extend.

lengthily (*adv.*) at great length.

lengthwise (*adv.*) in the direction of the length.

leniency (*n.*) mildness; mercy. LENIENT (*adj.*).

lens (*n.*) a curved glass used for spectacles, etc. (*pl.* LENSES).

Lent (*n.*) the period between Ash-Wednesday and Easter Day, the forty weekdays in which are fast days. LENTEN (*adj.*).

lentil (*n.*) the edible seed of a plant of the bean family.

leonine (*adj.*) lion-like; kingly.

leopard (*n.*) yellowish, black-spotted jungle-cat. (*fem.* LEOPARDESS).

leper (*n.*) a sufferer from leprosy.

leprechaun (*n.*) an Irish fairy or sprite.

leprosy (*n.*) a loathsome disease.

less (*adj.*) smaller; reduced. LESS (*adv.*) not so much. LESS (*n.*) 1. a smaller portion. 2. the younger.

lessee (*n.*) one to whom a lease is granted.

lessen (*v.*) 1. to reduce. 2. to humble.

lesson (*n.*) 1. a piece of instruction. 2. something to be learnt. 3. a reading from the Bible.

lessor (*n.*) one who grants a lease.

lest (*conj.*) that not; for fear that.

let (*v.*) 1. to permit; to allow. 2. to offer a house for rent.

lethal (*adj.*) causing death; fatal.

lethargy (*n.*) slowness; sleepiness. LETHARGIC (*adj.*).

letter (*n.*) 1. character or symbol which represents a sound. 2. a written message; a missive.

lettered (*adj.*) well-read; educated.

letterpress (*n.*) printed contents of a book or paper.

letters (*n. pl.*) education; learning.

lettuce (*n.*) a crisp-leaved salad plant.

level (*n.*) 1. a flat, even surface. 2. instrument for testing flatness. LEVEL (*v.*) 1. to make flat. 2. to pull down. 3. to make equal.

level-headed (*adj.*) shrewd; sensible.

lever (*n.*) a rigid bar for raising weights.

leverage (*n.*) power needed to use a lever.

leviathan (*n.*) 1. a whale. 2. anything very large.

levity (*n.*) frivolity; flightiness.

levy (*v.*) 1. to collect a tax. 2. to assemble men for war. LEVY (*n.*) the tax or men raised. (*pl.* LEVIES).

lexicon (*n.*) a dictionary.

liability (*n.*) anything owed; a debt.

liable (*adj.*) 1. likely to be. 2. responsible for.

liar (*n.*) one who wilfully utters lies or falsehoods.

libel (*v.*) to write falsely about anyone; to defame. LIBEL (*n.*) a false writing intended to injure character; a slander.

libellous (*adj.*) damaging to character; defaming.

liberal (*adj.*) 1. plentiful; abundant. 2. generous; bounteous. LIBERALLY (*adv.*).

liberality (*n.*) generosity; kindness.

liberate (*v.*) to set free; to release.

liberation (*n.*) release; deliverance. LIBERATOR (*n.*).

liberty (*n.*) 1. freedom. 2. leave; permission.

librarian (*n.*) person having charge of a library.

library (*n.*) 1. a collection of books. 2. room or building holding a book-collection.

licence (*n.*) 1. an official permit to keep, use or do. 2. an abuse of freedom.

license (*v.*) to permit by law; to grant a licence. LICENSED (*adj.*).

licentious (*adj.*) disorderly; unruly.

lichen (*n.*) a green moss growing on stones and tree-trunks.

lick (*v.*) to draw the tongue over; to lap. LICK (*n.*) a stroke with the tongue.

lid (*n.*) the cover of (1) a container, and (2) the eye. LIDDED (*adj.*).

lido (*n.*) a bathing beach or resort.

lie (*v.*) 1. to rest at full length on anything horizontal. 2. to speak falsely. LIE (*n.*) an untruth; a falsehood.

lieutenant (*n.*) 1. a naval, army or flying officer. 2. a deputy.

life (*n.*) 1. the vital power enabling animals and plants to exist as active beings. 2. the period between birth and the present time, or between birth and death. 3. activity; animation; vitality. 4. a person's history; biography. LIFELESS; LIFELIKE (*adjs.*).

lift (*v.*) to raise; to hoist. LIFT (*n.*) 1. an aid; a help. 2. machine carrying people from floor to floor in a building.

ligament (*n.*) string-like tissue binding bones together.

light (*n.*) 1. brightness shining from anything burning. 2. knowledge; understanding. LIGHT (*v.*) to cause light to shine; to illumine. LIGHT (*adj.*) 1. of little weight. 2. pale in colour. 3. slight; trivial. 4. gentle; flimsy. 5. unburdened; empty. LIGHTLY (*adv.*).

lighten (*v.*) 1. to brighten; to illumine. 2. to make less heavy; to ease.

light-headed (*adj.*) 1. dizzy; giddy. 2. thoughtless.

light-hearted (*adj.*) carefree; cheerful.

lighthouse (*n.*) tower showing a powerful light to guide ships.

lightness (*n.*) lack of weight.

lightning (*n.*) an electric flash across the sky.

light year (*n.*) distance light travels in a year.

lik(e)able (*adj.*) lovable; attractive.

like (*v.*) to be pleased with. LIKE (*adj.*) resembling; similar. LIKE (*n.*) 1. an equal. 2. a copy; counterpart. LIKE (*prep.*) in the same way as.

likelihood (*n.*) the possibility; probability.

likely (*adj.*) possible; believable. LIKELY (*adv.*) most probably.

liken (*v.*) to compare.

likeness (*n.*) 1. a sameness; resemblance. 2. a portrait.

likewise (*adv.*) also; moreover.

liking (*n.*) a fondness for.

lilac (*n.*) 1. a shrub and its white or purple flowers. 2. a pale-violet colour. LILAC (*adj.*).

Lilliputian (*n.*) a dwarf; pigmy. LILLI-PUTIAN (*adj.*) tiny.

lilt (*n.*) a merry dance or song. LILTING (*adj.*).

lily (*n.*) flowering plant growing from a bulb. (*pl.* LILIES).

limb (*n.*) 1. a leg or arm. 2. a paw. 3. a branch. 4. a scapegrace child.

limber (*adj.*) easily bent; flexible; supple.

lime (*n.*) 1. burnt limestone. 2. tree and its small, lemon-like fruit.

limelight (*n.*) 1. brilliant light made by a flame on lime. 2. publicity.

limestone (*n.*) a hard, waterproof building stone.

limit (*n.*) a boundary; border. LIMIT (*v.*) to keep within bounds; to restrict.

limitation (*n.*) 1. a boundary. 2. a rule which restricts.

limited (*adj.*) bounded; restricted.

limitless (*adj.*) unbounded; unrestricted.

limousine (*n.*) motor-car with closed body.

limp (*adj.*) without stiffness; easily twisted. LIMP (*v.*) to walk lamely.

limpet (*n.*) shellfish which sticks tightly to a rock.

limpid (*adj.*) clear as crystal; transparent.

limpidity (*n.*) clearness; transparency.

line (*n.*) 1. a pen or pencil mark. 2. a cord; string. 3. a family; descent. 4. an occupation; a business. 5. a class of goods. THE LINE, the equator. LINE (*v.*) to cover the inside.

lineage (*n.*) a family line; descent.

lineal (*adj.*) 1. having length. 2. hereditary.

lineament (*n.*) features; one of the lines which shape the face.

linear (*adj.*) straight from end to end.

linen (*n.*) cloth woven from flax.

ling (*n.*) 1. heather. 2. a cod-like fish.

linger (*v.*) to delay; to tarry. LINGERER (*n.*).

lingering (*adj.*) slow; loitering. LINGERING (*n.*) slowness; delay.

lingual (*adj.*) formed by the tongue.

linguist (*n.*) one skilled in speaking languages.

liniment (*n.*) a liquid ointment; an embrocation.

lining (*n.*) covering of an inner surface.

link (*n.*) 1. a single ring in a chain. 2. a measure of length (1/100 part of Gunter's Chain). 3. a connection. LINK (*v.*) to join; to connect. LINKED (*adj.*).

links (*n. pl.*) a golf course.

linnet (*n.*) small, brown songbird.

linoleum (*n.*) a floor-covering made of canvas thickly coated with linseed oil, on which a coloured pattern is printed.

linseed (*n.*) flax-seed and its oil.

lint (*n.*) soft linen for dressing wounds.

lintel (*n.*) beam over a door or window.

lion (*n.*) 1. large, powerful animal of the cat family; the king of beasts. National

emblem of Britain. (*fem.* LIONESS).
2. a celebrity.

lion-hearted (*adj.*) brave; valiant.

lionize (*v.*) to treat a person as a hero.

lions (*n. pl.*) the sights worth seeing.

lion's share (*n.*) largest share; nearly all.

lip (*n.*) edge or brim of anything. LIPS (*n. pl.*) edges of the mouth.

liquefy (*v.*) to make liquid; to melt. LIQUEFACTION (*n.*).

liquid (*n.*) any substance that flows like water. LIQUID (*adj.*) flowing.

liquidate (*v.*) to pay a debt; to settle.

liquidation (*n.*) settlement of a bankrupt's debts. LIQUIDATOR (*n.*).

liquor (*n.*) any liquid, but especially any containing alcohol.

liquorice (*n.*) a plant root used as a sweet-meat and medicine.

lisle (*n.*) a fine stocking-thread.

lisp (*v.*) to pronounce imperfectly; to be unable to pronounce certain sounds, notably, s, z and sh. LISP (*n.*) a childish or imperfect pronunciation.

lissom (*adj.*) supple; slender.

list (*n.*) 1. a roll or register. 2. a catalogue; inventory. LIST (*v.*) 1. to lean to one side. 2. to listen.

listen (*v.*) 1. to try to hear. 2. to hear and attend. 3. to eavesdrop. LISTENER (*n.*).

listless (*adj.*) 1. slack; weary. 2. inattentive; bored. LISTLESSNESS (*n.*).

literacy (*n.*) ability to read and write; education.

literal (*adj.*) strictly as stated; word for word. Beware LITTORAL.

literally (*adv.*) exactly; precisely.

literary (*adj.*) learned in literature; scholarly.

literate (*adj.*) instructed; educated.

literature (*n.*) written or printed works or books.

lithe (*adj.*) easily bent; flexible.

lithium (*n.*) the lightest metal known.

lithograph (*n.*) a print from a design drawn on a kind of stone. LITHO-GRAPHER (*n.*).

lithography (*n.*) art of drawing designs on stone and printing from them.

litigant (*n.*) one who takes legal proceedings.

litigate (*v.*) to go to law; to take legal proceedings.

litigation (*n.*) the settling of disputes by a law-court.

litre (*n.*) metric unit of capacity (1 litre = 1000 cm³).

litter (*n.*) 1. an untidy jumble. 2. a number of animals born together. 3. a portable bed. LITTER (*v.*) to scatter untidily.

little (*adj.*) small in size or amount. LITTLE (*n.*) a small quantity. LITTLE (*adv.*) not much; slightly.

littoral (*n.*) the region along the shore. Beware LITERAL.

live (*v.*) 1. to have life; to exist. 2. to dwell. LIVE (*adj.*) 1. having life; active. 2. vivid; glowing.

livelihood (*n.*) one's means of living; work.

liveliness (*n.*) briskness; brightness.

livelong (*adj.*) long in passing.

lively (*adj.*) active; gay.

liven (*v.*) to brighten; to cheer up.

liver (*n.*) a gland which purifies the blood.

liverish (*adj.*) bad-tempered; irritable.

livery (*n.*) a uniform. (*pl.* LIVERIES).

livid (*adj.*) black and blue; discoloured. LIVIDNESS (*n.*).

living (*adj.*) 1. having life or liveliness. 2. life-giving; invigorating. LIVING (*n.*) 1. a clergyman's livelihood. 2. all who are alive.

lizard (*n.*) four-footed reptile with a long tail.

llama (*n.*) South American camel-like animal.

load (*n.*) 1. a burden; weight. 2. a cargo; freight. LOAD (*v.*) 1. to fill. 2. to take cargo. 3. to put a missile into a gun. LOADED (*adj.*).

loadstone (*n.*) an iron ore which is magnetic.

loaf (*n.*) a portion of bread of standard weight. (*pl.* LOAVES). LOAF (*v.*) to hang about; to idle. LOAFING (*adj.*).

loafer (*n.*) an idler; a lounger.

loam (*n.*) fertile soil. LOAMY (*adj.*).

loan (*n.*) anything lent. LOAN (*v.*) to lend.

loath (*adj.*) unwilling; reluctant.

loathe (*v.*) to detest; to hate.

loathing (*n.*) hatred; detestation.

loathsome (*adj.*) hateful; repulsive.

lob (*n.*) a slow, high-pitched ball at cricket or tennis. LOB (*v.*) to bowl slowly.

lobby (*n.*) an entrance hall.

lobe (*n.*) the rounded base of the ear.

lobster (*n.*) large shellfish with powerful claws.

local (*adj.*) belonging to a particular place. LOCALLY (*adv.*).

locality (*n.*) a particular place or district. (*pl.* LOCALITIES).

localize (*v.*) to limit to a locality.

locate (*v.*) to place; to situate.

location (*n.*) 1. the place; situation. 2. the site of a film performance and its shooting.

loch (*n.*) a Scottish lake, or an inlet of the sea.

lock (*n.*) 1. a door-bolt worked by a key. 2. a canal basin where ships may rise and fall to different water-levels. 3. a curl of hair. LOCK (*v.*) to fasten with lock and key. LOCKSMITH (*n.*).

locker (*n.*) small cupboard secured with a lock.

locket (*n.*) a small, flat metal case worn as an ornament.

locomotion (*n.*) ability to move from place to place; travel.

locomotive (*n.*) a railway engine. LOCO-MOTIVE (*adj.*) moving; travelling.

locust (*n.*) 1. destructive grasshopper-like insect. 2. the carob-tree.

lode (*n.*) a vein of metallic ore.

lodestar (*n.*) sailors' guiding star, the Pole Star, or Polaris.

lodge (*v.*) 1. to live in hired rooms. 2. to leave in another's care. 3. to enter and remain. LODGE (*n.*) 1. a small house. 2. a society or its meeting place.

lodger (*n.*) one living in hired rooms.

lodgings (*n.*) accommodation in hired rooms.

loft (*n.*) room directly beneath a roof.

loftiness (*n.*) 1. height; tallness. 2. nobility; stateliness.

lofty (*adj.*) 1. high; towering. 2. proud; stately. LOFTILY (*adv.*).

log (*n.*) 1. a felled tree-trunk. 2. instrument for measuring a ship's speed. 3. an official journal or diary.

loggerheads (*n. pl.*) a dispute; argument; quarrel.

logging (*n.*) business of cutting down timber.

logic (*n.*) science of correct reasoning.

logical (*adj.*) sound; true. LOGICALLY (*adv.*).

logwood (*n.*) tropical tree and the red dye it yields.

loin (*n.*) 1. part of the body just above the hips. 2. ribs of sheep or lamb.

loiter (*v.*) to hang about; to dilly-dally. LOITERER (*n.*). LOITERING (*adj.*).

loll (*v.*) to sprawl; to lounge. LOLLING (*adj.*).

lollipop (*n.*) a large sweet.

lone (*adj.*) alone; companionless. LONELY (*adj.*).

loneliness (*n.*) isolation; solitude.

lonesome (*adj.*) dreary; making one feel lonely.

long (*adj.*) lengthy; far-reaching. LONG (*v.*) to yearn for; to desire.

longevity (*n.*) long life.

long-headed (*adj.*) far-seeing; shrewd.

longing (*n.*) a yearning; an eagerness for.

longitude (*n.*) distance east or west of Greenwich.

longitudinal (*adj.*) about length or distance.

long-run (*n.*) the final result.

long-stop (*n.*) cricketer behind the wicket-keeper.

long-suffering (*adj.*) patient; enduring.

long-winded (*adj.*) talkative; tedious.

look (*v.*) 1. to set eye upon; to regard. 2. to seem; to appear. 3. to seek; to search. LOOK (*n.*) 1. a glance; peep. 2. a facial expression.

loom (*n.*) machine for weaving cloth. LOOM (*v.*) 1. to appear in the distance. 2. to lour; to threaten. LOOMING (*adj.*).

loon (*n.*) 1. a rascal. 2. a diving-bird.

loop (*n.*) ring or noose formed by doubling a rope. LOOP (*v.*) 1. to make a loop. 2. to fasten in a loop. LOOPED (*adj.*).

loophole (*n.*) 1. a small opening in a wall. 2. a way of escape.

loose (*adj.*) 1. free; at liberty. 2. slack; untied. LOOSELY (*adv.*).

loosen (*v.*) 1. to release. 2. to untie. 3. to make less tight.

looseness (*n.*) slackness; carelessness.

loot (*n.*) plunder; spoil. LOOT (*v.*) to pillage; to rob. LOOTER (*n.*).

lop (*v.*) 1. to cut off a part; to amputate. 2. to hang limply; to droop.

lop-sided (*adj.*) leaning to one side.

lopsidedness (*n.*) instability; ricketiness.
loquacious (*adj.*) talkative; garrulous. LOQUACIOUSLY (*adv.*).
loquacity (*n.*) talkativeness; garrulity.
lord (*n.*) 1. a master; ruler. 2. a peer; noble. LORD (*v.*) to domineer; to rule over.
lordliness (*n.*) nobility; pride.
lordly (*adj.*) haughty; imperious.
lore (*n.*) learning; knowledge.
lorry (*n.*) a long, weight-carrying waggon without sides.
lose (*v.*) 1. to fail to keep. 2. to be defeated. 3. to miss; to mislay. LOSER (*n.*).
loss (*n.*) 1. anything lost. 2. damage; injury.
lost (*adj.*) 1. missing; mislaid. 2. deep in thought; dreamy. 3. bad; wicked. LOST (*n.*) those killed in battle.
lot (*n.*) 1. the total number; all. 2. an item offered at auction. 3. one's luck; fate. 4. a chance in a lottery.
lotion (*n.*) a healing liquid for the skin.
lottery (*n.*) a distribution of prizes won by chance or lot. (*pl.* LOTTERIES).
lotus (*n.*) an Eastern water-lily, which, in legend, brought sleep to those eating it, and caused them to hate every form of active life.
loud (*adj.*) 1. noisy; deafening. 2. showy; gaudy. LOUDLY (*adv.*).
loudness (*n.*) uproar; clamour.
loudspeaker (*n.*) a device making speech or music audible out of doors or in a large hall.
lough (*n.*) the Irish form of loch or lake.
lounge (*v.*) to behave idly and lazily; to loll. LOUNGE (*n.*) 1. a place in which to lounge. 2. a restful, comfortable room.
lounger (*n.*) an idler; a loafer. LOUNGING (*adj.*).
lour (*v.*) 1. to grow dark. 2. to frown; to scowl.
louring (*adj.*) 1. gloomy; threatening. 2. frowning; scowling.
lout (*n.*) a good-for-nothing; a boor. LOUTISH (*adj.*). LOUTISHNESS (*n.*).
lovable (*adj.*) worthy of love. LOVABLENESS (*n.*).
love (*n.*) fondness; affection. LOVE (*v.*) to hold dear.
loveliness (*n.*) beauty; charm.

lovelorn (*adj.*) lovesick; pining.
lovely (*adj.*) beautiful; pleasing.
lover (*n.*) one who loves; a sweetheart.
loving (*adj.*) affectionate; devoted. LOVINGLY (*adv.*).
low (*adj.*) 1. near the ground; not high. 2. coarse; vulgar. 3. feeble; weak. 4. soft; subdued. LOW (*v.*) to moo like a cow. LOW (*n.*) the cry of a cow.
lower (*v.*) 1. to let down. 2. to humble. 3. to reduce in value.
lowing (*n.*) the cry of cattle.
lowlands (*n. pl.*) 1. flat, level country. 2. southern portion of Scotland.
lowliness (*n.*) meekness; humility.
lowly (*adj.*) meek; modest.
lowness (*n.*) ill-health; depression.
low water (*n.*) low-tide; the lowest point to which the tide ebbs or goes out.
loyal (*adj.*) faithful; true. LOYALLY (*adv.*). LOYALIST (*n.*).
loyalty (*n.*) fidelity; devotion.
lozenge (*n.*) 1. small, flat sweet. 2. a diamond-shaped figure.
lubber (*n.*) a clumsy, awkward person.
lubberly (*adj.*) clumsy; bungling.
lubricant (*n.*) a substance that lubricates.
lubricate (*v.*) to oil; to make slippery.
lubricating (*adj.*) oily; greasy.
lubrication (*n.*) an oiling; a greasing.
lucid (*adj.*) 1. clear; straightforward. 2. sensible; understandable. LUCIDLY (*adv.*).
lucidity (*n.*) clearness; sense.
luck (*n.*) fortune; chance.
luckily (*adv.*) happily; fortunately.
luckless (*adj.*) unfortunate; ill-fated. LUCKLESSNESS (*n.*).
lucky (*adj.*) fortunate; favoured.
lucrative (*adj.*) profitable; money-making. LUCRATIVELY (*adv.*).
lucre (*n.*) money; riches.
ludicrous (*adj.*) ridiculous; absurd. LUDICROUSLY (*adv.*).
lug (*v.*) to pull; to drag.
luggage (*n.*) baggage; trunks.
lugger (*n.*) a small, square-sailed ship.
lugubrious (*adj.*) gloomy; sad. LUGUBRIOUSLY (*adv.*).
lukewarm (*adj.*) 1. slightly warm; tepid. 2. indifferent; unconcerned. LUKEWARMNESS (*n.*).
lull (*v.*) to soothe; to quieten. LULL (*n.*)

a calm period between storms; a peaceful interval.

lullaby (*n.*) a song softly sung to lull a child to sleep. (*pl.* LULLABIES).

lumbago (*n.*) rheumatism in the back.

lumber (*n.*) 1. sawn timber. 2. discarded furniture; junk. LUMBER (*v.*) to go heavily and clumsily.

lumbering (*n.*) tree-felling. LUMBERING (*adj.*) clumsy; blundering.

lumen (*n.*) measure of the brightness of light.

luminary (*n.*) a light-giving body. THE LUMINARY, the sun.

luminosity (*n.*) brightness; radiance.

luminous (*adj.*) light-giving; shining. LUMINOUSLY (*adv.*).

lump (*n.*) 1. a piece; morsel. 2. a swelling.

lumpy (*adj.*) having lumps; knobby.

lunacy (*n.*) madness.

lunar (*adj.*) concerning the moon.

lunatic (*n.*) a mad person.

lunch (*n.*) a midday meal; a repast. LUNCH (*v.*) to eat a midday meal. LUNCHEON (*n.*).

lung (*n.*) one of the two breathing organs in the chest.

lunge (*v.*) to thrust forward. LUNGE (*n.*) a forward thrust, especially with sword or bayonet.

lupin (*n.*) a tall plant bearing long spikes of brightly-coloured flowers.

lurch (*v.*) to roll to one side; to stagger. LURCH (*n.*) a sudden roll; a stagger.

lurcher (*n.*) a game-dog.

lure (*v.*) to tempt; to entice. LURE (*n.*) a bait; drag.

lurid (*adj.*) glowing like fire; sensational. LURIDLY (*adv.*).

lurk (*v.*) to lie in wait; to hide. LURKER (*n.*).

luscious (*adj.*) delicious; sweet.

lusciousness (*n.*) sweetness; richness.

lush (*adj.*) fresh; juicy.

lustily (*adv.*) vigorously; energetically.

lustre (*n.*) 1. brightness; splendour. 2. fame; renown.

lustreless (*adj.*) dull; dim.

lustrous (*adj.*) bright; radiant.

lusty (*adj.*) healthy; robust.

lute (*n.*) a guitar-like stringed instrument.

lux (*n.*) a measure of the brightness of light.

luxuriance (*n.*) greatness; abundance of growth.

luxuriant (*adj.*) rich in growth. LUXURIANTLY (*adv.*).

luxurious (*adj.*) living richly and extravagantly; splendid.

luxury (*n.*) anything costly, but not necessary for reasonable comfort or pleasure. (*pl.* LUXURIES).

lying (*n.*) the habit of telling lies. LYING (*adj.*) untruthful.

lymph (*n.*) a colourless fluid in animal bodies.

lynch (*v.*) to put to death by a mob and without a legal trial.

lynx (*n.*) a keen-sighted, cat-like animal. (*pl.* LYNXES). See appendix.

lyre (*n.*) a small harp used in ancient times.

lyric (*n.*) a song. LYRICAL (*adj.*).

M

macabre (*adj.*) grim; gruesome.

macadam (*n.*) a modern road-surface. MACADAMIZE (*v.*). See appendix.

macaroni (*n.*) flour paste made into long, slender tubes.

macaroon (*n.*) a small, sweet cake.

macaw (*n.*) a large parrot.

mace (*n.*) 1. a war club. 2. a symbol of authority. 3. dried nutmeg husks.

machination (*n.*) a plot; conspiracy.

machine (*n.*) an apparatus for doing work.

machinery (*n.*) machines, or their working parts. MACHINIST (*n.*).

mackerel (*n.*) a sea-fish.

mackintosh (*n.*) a rain-proof coat. See appendix.

mad (*adj.*) 1. insane. 2. angry. MADLY (*adv.*).

madam or **madame** (*n.*) title of respect given to married or elderly woman. (*pl.* MADAMS or MESDAMES).

madcap (*n.*) a wild, rash person. MADCAP (*adj.*) harum-scarum.

madden (*v.*) to make mad; to enrage.

maddening (*adj.*) annoying; provoking.

madder (*n.*) plant and the red dye its root yields.

mademoiselle (*n.*) the title, Miss, given to a foreign unmarried woman.

madness (*n.*) 1. insanity. 2. folly; rashness. MADMAN (*n.*).

Madonna (*n.*) 1. the Virgin Mary. 2. a picture or statue of the Virgin Mary.

madrigal (*n.*) a love-song; part-song.

magazine (*n.*) 1. warehouse. 2. storehouse for explosives. 3. a periodical.

magenta (*n.*) a crimson dye. MAGENTA (*adj.*) crimson.

maggot (*n.*) 1. a grub. 2. a whim; fancy. MAGGOTY (*adj.*).

magic (*n.*) 1. strange happenings once thought to be the work of evil spirits. 2. conjuring.

magical (*adj.*) 1. enchanted; supernatural. 2. mystifying; conjured. MAGICALLY (*adv.*).

magician (*n.*) 1. a conjuror; juggler. 2. man formerly thought to have magic powers.

magisterial (*adj.*) relating to magistrates; judicial.

magistracy (*n.*) magistrates as a body.

magistrate (*n.*) a justice who tries police-court cases.

magnanimity (*n.*) greatness of mind; generosity. MAGNANIMOUS (*adj.*).

magnate (*n.*) an eminent or wealthy man; a leading business man.

magnesia (*n.*) a medicine obtained from magnesium.

magnesium (*n.*) a metal that burns with a bright light.

magnet (*n.*) iron or steel which is magnetized.

magnetic (*adj.*) 1. acting like a magnet. 2. attractive; compelling.

magnetism (*n.*) 1. a natural force which attracts iron and steel. 2. a personal charm; attraction.

magnetize (*v.*) to fill with magnetism.

magneto (*n.*) a small dynamo, sparks from which ignite petrol.

magnification (*n.*) 1. an enlargement. 2. an exaggeration.

magnificence (*n.*) splendour; pomp.

magnificent (*adj.*) grand; superb.

magnified (*adj.*) 1. enlarged. 2. exaggerated.

magnify (*v.*) 1. to make greater; to enlarge. 2. to praise; to glorify. 3. to exaggerate. MAGNIFYING (*adj.*).

magnitude (*n.*) 1. the size; largeness. 2. the greatness; importance. 3. the measure of the brightness of stars.

magnolia (*n.*) a flowering laurel-tree.

magpie (*n.*) black and white bird of crow family.

mahogany (*n.*) a tree and its hard, red wood.

Mahomet (*n.*) Arab prophet (A.D. 570–632), who founded the Muslim religion.

maid (*n.*) 1. a girl; lass. 2. a servant-girl.

maiden (*n.*) 1. an unmarried woman. 2. a cricket over in which no runs are scored. 3. a frame for drying clothes.

maidenhood (*n.*) girlhood.

maiden speech (*n.*) one's first speech.

maiden voyage (*n.*) a ship's first voyage.

mail (*n.*) 1. metal armour. 2. the postal service; letters carried by post. MAIL (*v.*) to post.

mailed (*adj.*) 1. armoured. 2. posted.

maim (*v.*) to disable; to cripple. MAIMED (*adj.*).

main (*n.*) 1. strength; force. 2. the chief part; the bulk. 3. the ocean; sea. MAIN (*adj.*) chief; leading.

mainland (*n.*) 1. the coast. 2. the continent, without off-lying islands.

mainly (*adv.*) chiefly; firstly.

maintain (*v.*) 1. to provide for; to sustain. 2. to uphold; to support.

maintainable (*adj.*) can be said; supported.

maintenance (*n.*) 1. a provision; upkeep. 2. an upholding; support.

maize (*n.*) Indian corn.

majestic (*adj.*) stately; regal.

majesty (*n.*) 1. sovereignty. 2. dignity; grandeur. 3. title given to a sovereign.

major (*n.*) an army officer. MAJOR (*adj.*) the greater; the more important.

majority (*n.*) 1. the bulk; mass. 2. legal age (21 years); adulthood. (*pl.* MAJORITIES).

make (*v.*) 1. to construct; to manufacture. 2. to compel. 3. to add up to; to amount to.

make-believe (*n.*) a sham; pretence.

maker (*n.*) a doer; manufacturer. THE MAKER. God, the Creator.

makeshift (*n.*) something that does for the time being; an expedient.

makings (*n. pl.*) 1. the profits. 2. materials required to manufacture.

malady (*n.*) an ailment or disease. (*pl.* MALADIES).

malaria (*n.*) fever caused by mosquito bites. MALARIAL (*adj.*).

malcontent (*adj.*) discontented; dissatisfied. MALCONTENT (*n.*) a discontented person; grumbler.

male (*n.*) 1. a man; boy. 2. a masculine animal.

malediction (*n.*) a curse; a ban.

malefactor (*n.*) a wrongdoer.

malevolence (*n.*) spitefulness; malice. MALEVOLENT (*adj.*).

malice (*n.*) ill-will; spite. MALICIOUS (*adj.*).

malign (*adj.*) evil; hurtful. MALIGN (*v.*) to speak evil of; to defame.

malignancy (*n.*) an intense hatred; virulence. MALIGNANT (*adj.*).

malignity (*n.*) hatred; resentment.

malinger (*v.*) to sham illness. MALINGERER (*n.*).

mallet (*n.*) a wooden or rubber hammer.

malpractice (*n.*) a wrongdoing; a cheating.

malt (*n.*) barley made ready for brewing. MALTSTER (*n.*).

maltreat (*v.*) to ill-treat; to abuse. MALTREATMENT (*n.*).

mammal (*n.*) an animal that nourishes its young. MAMMALIAN (*adj.*).

mammon (*n.*) great wealth, if sought and used chiefly for its power. See appendix.

mammoth (*n.*) hairy elephant now extinct. MAMMOTH (*adj.*) gigantic; enormous.

man (*n.*) an adult male person. (*pl.* MEN)

manacle (*n.*) a handcuff; fetter. MANACLE (*v.*) to put handcuffs on. MANACLED (*adj.*).

manage (*v.*) 1. to make do; to get along. 2. to control; to direct.

manageable (*adj.*) controllable; docile.

management (*n.*) 1. control; direction. 2. the governing body.

manager (*n.*) the director; supervisor. (*fem.* MANAGERESS).

managerial (*adj.*) concerned with management.

mandate (*n.*) 1. an order. 2. an instruction to act on behalf of another. MANDATORY (*adj.*).

mandible (*n.*) 1. the lower jaw-bone. 2. the upper and lower beak.

mandolin (*n.*) stringed musical instrument.

mandrill (*n.*) a large baboon.

mane (*n.*) long hair on the neck of many animals, e.g. horse, lion. MANED (*adj.*).

manfully (*adv.*) nobly; bravely.

mange (*n.*) a disease in dogs and cattle.

manger (*n.*) a box or trough from which farm-animals feed.

mangle (*v.*) 1. to tear; to rend. 2. to press; to squeeze. MANGLE (*n.*) a machine for pressing fabrics.

mangled (*adj.*) 1. torn in pieces; rent. 2. pressed.

manhood (*n.*) adulthood; maturity; manliness.

mania (*n.*) 1. madness; delirium. 2. an intense desire. 3. a prevailing craze.

maniac (*n.*) a madman. MANIACAL (*adj.*).

manicure (*n.*) the care of the hands. MANICURE (*v.*) to treat the hands. MANICURIST (*n.*).

manifest (*adj.*) plain; evident. MANIFEST (*v.*) to show; to reveal. MANIFESTLY (*adv.*).

manifestation (*n.*) a display; revelation.

manifesto (*n.*) a declaration; proclamation.

manifold (*adj.*) many in number and kind. MANIFOLD (*v.*) to make copies.

manilla (*n.*) 1. a cheroot or cigar made in Manilla, capital of the Philippine Islands. 2. rope made from hemp.

manipulate (*v.*) 1. to make work; to operate. 2. to use the hands.

manipulation (*n.*) skill in handling; operating. MANIPULATOR (*n.*).

mankind (*n.*) the human race; humanity.

manliness (*n.*) having manly qualities.

manly (*adj.*) strong; brave.

manner (*n.*) 1. a way; method. 2. a kind; style. 3. one's behaviour; bearing. 4. a mode; fashion.

mannerism (*n.*) a habit or trick of one's own.

mannerless (*adj.*) rude; boorish.

mannerly (*adj.*) well-behaved; courteous.

manners (*n. pl.*) one's behaviour and habits.

manoeuvre (*n.*) 1. a movement of troops. 2. a well-planned action. MANOEUVRE (*v.*) to act as planned.

manoeuvres (*n. pl.*) 1. naval or military exercises. 2. steps in planning.

manor (*n.*) land belonging to a lord.

manse (*n.*) house of a minister of religion.

mansion (*n.*) a large house.

manslaughter (*n.*) causing death by carelessness and without intention.

mantel (*n.*) a shelf above a fireplace.

mantle (*n.*) loose, sleeveless cloak. MANTLE (*v.*) 1. to cover; to hide. 2. to blush.

manual (*adj.*) anything done by the hands. MANUAL (*n.*) 1. an instruction book. 2. an organ keyboard.

manufactory (*n.*) a factory; place of manufacture.

manufacture (*v.*) 1. to make; to construct. 2. to make by machinery.

manufactured (*adj.*) 1. factory-made. 2. invented; made up.

manufacturer (*n.*) 1. a factory owner. 2. producer of goods on a large scale.

manure (*n.*) a substance which enriches the soil; a fertilizer.

manuscript (*n.*) a book or paper written by hand. MANUSCRIPT (*adj.*) handwritten.

many (*adj.*) large in number; numerous. MANY (*n.*) the crowd; multitude.

map (*n.*) a drawing showing features of the earth's surface; a chart. MAP (*v.*) 1. to make a map. 2. to plan.

maple (*n.*) tree of the sycamore kind.

mapped (*adj.*) 1. shown on a map. 2. planned.

mar (*v.*) to damage; to spoil. MARRED (*adj.*).

Marathon (*n.*) long-distance foot-race; a test of endurance.

maraud (*v.*) to rob; to plunder. MARAUDER (*n.*). MARAUDING (*adj.*).

marble (*n.*) 1. a limestone which takes a high polish. 2. a small stone or glass ball. MARBLE (*adj.*) cold; unfeeling.

March (*n.*) the third month. See appendix.

march (*n.*) 1. a movement onward, in step, as soldiers. 2. the distance traversed. 3. piece of music suitable to

march to. MARCH (*v.*) to move onward in regular step.

marconigram (*n.*) a wireless telegram. See appendix.

mare (*n.*) a female horse.

margarine (*n.*) a butter substitute.

margin (*n.*) the edge; brink.

marginal (*adj.*) on or near the edge; border.

marguerite (*n.*) a large daisy.

marigold (*n.*) plant bearing yellow flowers.

marine (*adj.*) living in the sea. MARINE (*n.*) a soldier serving on a ship.

mariner (*n.*) a sailor; seaman.

marionette (*n.*) 1. a puppet moved by strings. 2. a person easily led or influenced.

maritime (*adj.*) relating to the sea.

mark (*v.*) 1. to observe; to regard. 2. to stamp; to label. MARK (*n.*) 1. a label; imprint. 2. a target; token. 3. fame; renown.

marked (*adj.*) 1. written on; priced. 2. noticed; seen. 3. notable; important. MARKER (*n.*).

market (*n.*) 1. a public buying and selling place. 2. the district where particular goods are sal(e)able. MARKET (*v.*) to sell; to trade.

marketable (*adj.*) sal(e)able.

marksman (*n.*) a skilled shot; a sharpshooter.

marmalade (*n.*) a preserve made of orange, lemon or quince.

marmoset (*n.*) small S. American monkey.

marmot (*n.*) a squirrel-like rodent.

maroon (*v.*) to abandon on an uninhabited island. MAROON (*n.*) 1. a warning rocket. 2. a brownish red colour.

marquee (*n.*) a very large tent.

marquis (*n.*) nobleman next above an earl. (*fem.* MARCHIONESS). Also MARQUESS.

marriage (*n.*) 1. life together of husband and wife; wedlock. 2. the ceremony uniting husband and wife.

marriageable (*adj.*) old enough to marry.

married (*adj.*) joined in marriage; wedded.

marrow (*n.*) 1. soft substance found in bones. 2. a large, pulpy vegetable.

marry (*v.*) 1. to become husband and wife; to wed. 2. to perform the marriage ceremony.

Mars (*n.*) planet with two moons lying between Earth and Jupiter. See appendix. MARTIAN (*adj.*).

marsh (*n.*) a swamp; bog. MARSHY (*adj.*).

marshal (*v.*) to arrange in order. MARSHAL (*n.*) 1. an army or air-force officer of highest rank. 2. high official who directs royal ceremonies.

mart (*n.*) a market.

marten (*n.*) a weasel-like animal.

martial (*adj.*) warlike; soldierly. See appendix.

martin (*n.*) bird of swallow family.

martinet (*n.*) one who enforces strict discipline.

martyr (*n.*) one who dies for his belief; cause.

martyrdom (*n.*) sufferings or death of a martyr.

marvel (*v.*) to wonder; to be amazed. MARVEL (*n.*) a wonder; miracle.

marvellous (*adj.*) extraordinary; unbelievable. MARVELLOUSLY (*adv.*).

mascot (*n.*) any person, animal or object expected to bring good luck.

masculine (*adj.*) male; concerning men.

mash (*v.*) to pound into pulp; to crush. MASH (*n.*) pulpy food given to animals.

mask (*n.*) a face-covering; a disguise. MASK (*v.*) to hide; to conceal.

mason (*n.*) 1. a builder in stone. 2. a freemason.

masonic (*adj.*) concerning the freemasons, a brotherly society.

masonry (*n.*) building work and materials.

masquerade (*n.*) a masked ball. MASQUERADE (*v.*) to disguise; to conceal.

mass (*n.*) 1. the quantity; size. 2. the weight. 3. a crowd. (*pl.* MASSES).

massacre (*n.*) a great slaughter. MASSACRE (*v.*) to slay many.

massage (*n.*) treatment of ailments by rubbing and kneading. MASSAGE (*v.*) to rub and knead the muscles.

masseur (*n.*) one skilled in massage. (*fem.* MASSEUSE).

massive (*adj.*) having size and weight; ponderous. MASSIVENESS (*n.*).

mast (*n.*) 1. a pole supporting a ship's sails. 2. acorns.

master (*n.*) 1. man in charge. 2. an employer. 3. head of a household. (*fem.* MISTRESS). 4. an expert.

masterful (*adj.*) firm; commanding.

masterly (*adj.*) skilful; expert.

masterpiece (*n.*) 1. an excellent work. 2. one's best achievement.

mastery (*n.*) the control; command.

mast-head (*n.*) the top of the mast.

masticate (*v.*) to chew thoroughly. MASTICATED (*adj.*).

mastication (*n.*) chewing.

mastiff (*n.*) a large, powerful hound.

mat (*n.*) 1. a rug for foot-wiping. 2. a thin pad to protect a surface. MAT (*v.*) to twist; to tangle. MATTED (*adj.*).

match (*n.*) 1. a wood splinter heated to give a flame. 2. an equal. 3. a marriage. 4. a games contest. MATCH (*v.*) 1. to equal or overcome. 2. to agree; to tally.

matchless (*adj.*) unequalled; unrivalled.

mate (*v.*) to marry; to wed. MATE (*n.*) 1. a wife or husband. 2. a friend; pal. 3. ship's officer next in command to captain. 4. a checkmate or win in chess.

material (*n.*) substance of which a thing is made. MATERIAL (*adj.*) 1. real; actual. 2. bodily; personal. 3. worldly; earthly. 4. essential; important.

materialize (*v.*) 1. to happen; to occur. 2. to appear; to become real.

materially (*adv.*) essentially; vitally.

maternal (*adj.*) motherly.

maternity (*n.*) motherhood.

mathematical (*adj.*) accurate; precise.

mathematician (*n.*) one expert in mathematics.

mathematics (*n.*) science dealing with numbers and measurements.

matins (*n.*) morning service in a church.

matriculate (*v.*) to admit to university membership.

matriculation (*n.*) admission to university membership.

matrimony (*n.*) marriage. MATRIMONIAL (*adj.*).

matron (*n.*) 1. an elderly married woman. 2. the woman head of a hospital. 3. housekeeper in a boarding-school.

matronly (*adj.*) elderly; grave.

matter (*n.*) 1. any substance. 2. yellow

fluid from a wound; pus. 3. a happening; an event. 4. a subject. MATTER (v.) to be of importance.

matter-of-fact (adj.) calm; unexcited.

mattress (n.) a large, flat bag stuffed with soft material to form a bed.

mature (adj.) ripe; full-grown. MATURE (v.) to ripen.

maturity (n.) ripeness; perfection.

maudlin (adj.) tearful; sentimental.

maul (v.) to beat or handle roughly.

Maundy (n.) an ancient ceremony on Maundy Thursday (day before Good Friday) at which loaves and specially minted money are given to certain poor people by the Royal Almoner.

mausoleum (n.) a splendid tomb. (pl. MAUSOLEA). See appendix.

mauve (n.) a purple dye. MAUVE (adj.) purple.

maxim (n.) a wise saying; a proverb.

maximum (n.) the greatest; utmost. (pl. MAXIMA).

May (n.) the fifth month. MAY (v.) to be permitted; to be possible.

maybe (adv.) possibly; perhaps.

mayor (n.) chief magistrate of a city or borough. (fem. MAYORESS).

mayoralty (n.) mayor's period of office.

maze (n.) a puzzle-path full of turnings; a labyrinth. MAZE (v.) to bewilder; to perplex.

mead (n.) 1. a meadow. 2. a drink made of honey and water.

meadow (n.) grassland mown for hay. MEADOWY (adj.).

meagre (adj.) poor; small. MEAGRELY (adv.).

meagreness (n.) littleness; scantiness.

meal (n.) 1. food taken at one time; a repast. 2. ground grain.

mealy (adj.) soft; smooth.

mealy-mouthed (adj.) unwilling to speak openly or straightforwardly.

mean (v.) to intend; to purpose. MEAN (adj.) 1. poor; small. 2. coarse; vulgar. 3. base; vile. 4. niggardly; stingy. MEAN (n.) the middle; the average.

meander (v.) to wander aimlessly; to wind at random, as does the river Meander in Phrygia, Asia Minor.

meaning (n.) 1. an explanation. 2. an intention; aim.

meaningless (adj.) senseless; useless.

meaningly (adv.) pointedly; significantly.

meanly (adv.) basely; ignobly.

meanness (n.) miserliness; stinginess.

means (n. pl.) 1. one's money; possessions. 2. the way; method.

mean-spirited (adj.) worthless; contemptible.

meantime (n.) the time between; interval.

measles (n.) an infectious fever.

measurable (adj.) easy; moderate.

measure (n.) 1. a measuring instrument; a ruler. 2. the extent; size. 3. a law. 4. a dance and its music. MEASURE (v.) to find the size or extent.

measured (adj.) 1. steady; regular. 2. fixed; limited.

measureless (adj.) unlimited; boundless.

measurement (n.) the extent; size.

measures (n. pl.) 1. the means; course. 2. the methods; plans.

meat (n.) 1. flesh used as food. 2. food; a meal.

mechanic (n.) a worker skilled with tools, and with machines.

mechanical (adj.) machine-like; automatic.

mechanically (adv.) unthinkingly; blindly.

mechanics (n.) study of machines and motion.

mechanism (n.) a machine's working parts; the works.

mechanize (v.) to fit with machines.

medal (n.) a coin-shaped piece of metal struck to reward merit, or to commemorate an event.

medallist (n.) winner of a medal.

meddle (v.) to interfere; to busy oneself with.

meddler (n.) an interferer; a busybody.

meddlesome (adj.) 1. interfering; officious. 2. curious; prying.

mediæval (adj.) concerning the Middle Ages (5th to 15th century A.D.).

mediate (v.) to try to settle disputes; to help opponents to agree.

mediation (n.) an effort to help; an intervention.

mediator (n.) a peacemaker; an arbitrator.

medical (adj.) concerning doctors and healing.

medicinal (adj.) able to cure or restore.

medicine (*n.*) 1. substance used to cure or heal. 2. the science of healing.

mediocre (*adj.*) neither good nor bad; middling.

mediocrity (*n.*) moderation; ordinariness.

meditate (*v.*) to think about; to ponder.

meditation (*n.*) deep thought; study.

meditative (*adj.*) inclined to ponder. MEDITATIVELY (*adv.*).

Mediterranean (*n.*) great, almost inland, sea lying between Southern Europe and Northern Africa, which once formed the middle of the Roman Earth or Empire.

medium (*adj.*) in between; moderate. MEDIUM (*n.*) the means; instrument. (*pl.* MEDIA).

medley (*n.*) a mixture; jumble.

meek (*adj.*) gentle; humble. MEEKLY (*adv.*).

meekness (*n.*) humility; submission.

meet (*v.*) 1. to come face to face; to encounter. 2. to assemble; to muster. 3. to satisfy; to fulfil. MEET (*adj.*) right; proper. MEET (*n.*) as assembly of huntsmen.

meeting (*n.*) 1. an encounter. 2. an assembly; conference. 3. a joining together; junction.

megaphone (*n.*) a large speaking-trumpet.

melancholy (*n.*) sadness; unhappiness. MELANCHOLY (*adj.*) sad; moody.

mellow (*adj.*) 1. ripe; juicy. 2. genial; cordial. MELLOW (*v.*) to ripen; to mature.

mellowness (*n.*) 1. ripeness; perfection. 2. geniality.

melodious (*adj.*) sweet-sounding; tuneful. MELODIOUSLY (*adv.*).

melodrama (*n.*) a thrilling play.

melodramatic (*adj.*) thrilling; exciting.

melody (*n.*) 1. a musical air; tune. 2. harmony.

melon (*n.*) a large juicy fruit.

melt (*v.*) 1. to change from solid to liquid; to liquefy. 2. to soften hard feelings; to mollify.

melting (*adj.*) 1. liquefying; thawing. 2. appeasing; calming.

member (*n.*) 1. a body organ; limb. 2. one belonging to a family or society.

membership (*n.*) all the members.

membrane (*n.*) thin layer of skin or tissue.

memento (*n.*) a keepsake; souvenir.

memoir (*n.*) a record of an event; a journal.

memorable (*adj.*) worth remembering; noteworthy.

memorandum (*n.*) a few words written as a reminder. (*pl.* MEMORANDA).

memorial (*n.*) anything recalling a person or event to memory; a monument.

memorize (*v.*) to learn by heart.

memory (*n.*) ability to remember; recollection.

menace (*v.*) to alarm; to threaten. MENACE (*n.*) a threat; danger.

menacing (*adj.*) frightening; alarming. MENACINGLY (*adv.*).

menagerie (*n.*) a collection of wild animals.

mend (*v.*) 1. to repair; to restore. 2. to improve; to correct. MEND (*n.*) a repair; restoration.

mendacious (*adj.*) untruthful; lying.

mendacity (*n.*) deception; double-dealing.

mendicant (*n.*) a beggar.

menial (*adj.*) slave-like; base. MENIAL (*n.*) an inferior servant.

meningitis (*n.*) a severe brain malady.

mensuration (*n.*) measurement of lengths, areas and volumes.

mental (*adj.*) relating to the mind or intellect. MENTALLY (*adv.*).

mentality (*n.*) intellect; brain-power.

mention (*v.*) to speak of; to name. MENTION (*n.*) a remark about; a reference to.

mentor (*n.*) an adviser; counsellor. See appendix.

menu (*n.*) a list of dishes served; a bill of fare.

mercantile (*adj.*) concerned with trade; commercial.

mercenary (*adj.*) 1. money-loving; avaricious. 2. hired soldier in foreign service.

mercer (*n.*) a dealer in silks.

merchandise (*n.*) goods; wares.

merchant (*n.*) buyer and seller of goods; a trader.

merchantman (*n.*) a trading vessel.

merciful (*adj.*) forgiving; humane. MERCIFULLY (*adv.*).

merciless (*adj.*) unforgiving; pitiless.

mercurial (*adj.*) light-hearted; gay.

mercury (*n.*) 1. a heavy, liquid metal.

2. the planet nearest to the sun. See appendix.

mercy (*n.*) forgiveness; lenience. (*pl.* MERCIES).

mere (*n.*) a pool; lake. MERE (*adj.*) simple; trifling.

merely (*adv.*) solely; only.

merge (*v.*) 1. to be mixed with; to be absorbed. 2. to combine; to unite.

merger (*n.*) a combining of two or more businesses into one.

meridian (*n.*) 1. midday; noon. 2. a line of longitude, that is, a circle passing through the North and South Poles. 3. the top; summit.

meringue (*n.*) a light confection of eggs and sugar.

merino (*n.*) a fine-woolled sheep, and the cloth woven from it.

merit (*n.*) worth; excellence.

merited (*adj.*) deserved; earned. MERITEDLY (*adv.*).

meritorious (*adj.*) praiseworthy; deserving reward.

mermaid (*n.*) a fabled sea-animal, partly woman, partly fish. (*masc.* MERMAN).

merriment (*n.*) mirth; jollity.

merry (*adj.*) happy; gay. MERRILY (*adv.*).

mesh (*n.*) 1. openwork in lace and netting. 2. a snare. MESH (*v.*) to catch in a net.

mesmerize (*v.*) to make a person sleep by will-power; to hypnotize. MESMERISM (*n.*). See appendix.

mess (*n.*) 1. disorder; muddle. 2. dirtiness. 3. a meal taken with others. MESS (*v.*) 1. to dirty; to soil. 2. to eat with others.

message (*n.*) information sent from one person to another; a communication.

messenger (*n.*) one who bears a message.

Messiah (*n.*) the deliverer God promised to the Jews, whom Christians believe to be Jesus.

metal (*n.*) a substance smelted from ore. METALLIC (*adj.*).

metals (*n. pl.*) the rails of a railway.

metamorphosis (*n.*) a change of shape; transformation.

metaphor (*n.*) a comparison in which one person or thing is described as being another, e.g., That GIRL is an ANGEL.

metaphorical (*adj.*) not literally true; figurative.

mete (*n.*) a measure; boundary. METE (*v.*) to measure; to allot.

meteor (*n.*) a shooting star.

meteoric (*adj.*) 1. relating to meteors. 2. short-lived; dazzling only for a moment.

meteorite (*n.*) a meteor that has fallen on the earth.

meteorologist (*n.*) one skilled in meteorology.

meteorology (*n.*) the study of the earth's weather and atmosphere.

meter (*n.*) instrument that measures quantities.

method (*n.*) 1. a way or manner of doing things. 2. orderliness; system.

methodical (*adj.*) orderly; systematic. METHODICALLY (*adv.*).

methodism (*n.*) the system of religious worship founded by John Wesley.

methodist (*n.*) a believer in methodism.

methylated spirit (*n.*) spirit of wine mixed with crude wood-alcohol to make it unfit for drinking.

meticulous (*adj.*) over-careful about small details.

metre (*n.*) 1. a metric unit of length (1 metre = 100 cm = 1000 mm). 2. the rhythm or swing of a verse.

metric (*adj.*) a decimal system of weights and measures.

metrical (*adj.*) written in verses; having rhythm.

metropolis (*n.*) chief city of a country; the capital. METROPOLITAN (*adj.*).

mettle (*n.*) courage; pluck. METTLESOME (*adj.*).

mew (*v.*) to cage; to confine. MEW (*n.*) a seagull's or a cat's cry.

mewed (*adj.*) shut up; caged.

mica (*n.*) a mineral which splits into thin sheets.

Michaelmas (*n.*) the Feast of St. Michael (29th September), and the autumn quarter-day.

microbe (*n.*) a germ invisible to the eye.

microphone (*n.*) an instrument which enables sounds to be transmitted by wireless.

microscope (*n.*) a magnifying instrument. MICROSCOPIC (*adj.*).

mid (*n. & adj.*) the middle. MID (*prep.*) amid; among.

midday (*n.*) noon.

middle (*n.*) point at equal distance from each end or side; the centre.

middling (*adj.*) moderate.

midge (*n.*) a gnat.

midget (*n.*) a small person or thing; a dwarf.

midnight (*n.*) 12 o'clock at night.

midst (*n.*) the middle. MIDST (*prep.*) amidst.

mien (*n.*) one's manner and appearance.

might (*n.*) energy; force.

mightily (*adv.*) with great strength.

mightiness (*n.*) strength; power.

mighty (*adj.*) strong; powerful.

migrant (*n.*) a migrating animal or bird.

migrate (*v.*) to change one's abode with the seasons; to move from cold to warmer lands, and vice versa.

migration (*n.*) flight of birds and animals to warmer lands.

migratory (*adj.*) roving; wandering; given to migrating.

mild (*adj.*) gentle; light. MILDLY (*adv.*).

mildew (*n.*) downy substance growing on damp things.

mildness (*n.*) gentleness; tenderness.

mile (*n.*) an Imperial measure of distance (1760 yards).

mileage (*n.*) distance in miles. MILESTONE (*n.*).

militancy (*n.*) quarrelsomeness; hostility.

militant (*adj.*) fighting; contending; warlike.

military (*adj.*) 1. soldierly. 2. warlike; martial. MILITARY (*n.*) the army; soldiery.

militate (*v.*) to fight against; to oppose.

milk (*n.*) a liquid on which mammals feed their young.

milkiness (*n.*) amount of milk in a food.

milksop (*n.*) a timorous person.

milk-teeth (*n. pl.*) a child's first teeth.

milky (*adj.*) like or containing milk.

mill (*n.*) 1. a grinding machine. 2. a factory. 3. a fight.

millboard (*n.*) a thick cardboard.

milled (*adj.*) having a grooved edge like a coin.

millennium (*n.*) period of 1,000 years.

miller (*n.*) owner or worker of a grinding-mill.

millet (*n.*) a hardy grass.

milliard (*n.*) a thousand millions.

millilitre (*n.*) metric unit of capacity; 1/1000 of a litre.

millimetre (*n.*) metric unit of length; 1/1000 of a metre.

milliner (*n.*) a maker or seller of women's hats. MILLINERY (*n.*).

million (*n.*) a thousand thousand. MILLIONAIRE (*n.*).

millstone (*n.*) hard, round stone which grinds grain.

mime (*v.*) to mimic; to act without speaking.

mimic (*v.*) to imitate; to ape. MIMIC (*n.*) one who imitates or copies. MIMIC (*adj.*) mocking; imitative.

mince (*v.*) 1. to cut into tiny pieces. 2. to walk with short steps.

mincemeat (*n.*) finely cut meat and fruit mixed and spiced.

mind (*n.*) the intellect; understanding. MIND (*v.*) 1. to take care of. 2. to heed; to obey. 3. to remember.

mindful (*adj.*) heedful; attentive.

mindless (*adj.*) stupid; careless.

mine (*n.*) 1. a pit from which minerals are dug. 2. an explosive placed under ground or water. MINE (*pron.*) belonging to me. MINE (*v.*) 1. to dig in the earth. 2. to lay explosives.

miner (*n.*) one who mines; a collier.

mineral (*n.*) any substance obtained by mining.

mineralogist (*n.*) one skilled in a knowledge of minerals.

mineralogy (*n.*) the study of minerals.

mingle (*v.*) to mix; to blend.

miniature (*adj.*) tiny; small. MINIATURE (*n.*) a small painted portrait.

minim (*n.*) 1. a small measure of liquid; drop. 2. a musical note.

minimize (*v.*) 1. to make as small as possible. 2. to underestimate.

minimum (*n.*) the least amount. (*pl.* MINIMA). MINIMUM (*adj.*) smallest.

minister (*n.*) 1. a clergyman; pastor. 2. one trusted by a sovereign to assist in government. MINISTER (*v.*) 1. to help; to care for. 2. to serve.

ministration (*n.*) the helping; supplying.

ministry (*n.*) the duties of (1) a clergyman, and (2) a minister of state.

mink (*n.*) weasel-like, fur-bearing animal.

minnow (*n.*) tiny freshwater fish.

minor (*adj.*) smaller; less important. MINOR (*n.*) 1. the younger. 2. one under 21 years of age.

minority (*n.*) 1. the smaller number. 2. the state of being a minor.

minster (*n.*) an abbey; a cathedral. Beware MINISTER.

minstrel (*n.*) a singer and harper; a bard. MINSTRELSY (*n.*).

mint (*n.*) 1. place where coins are made or struck. 2. a strong-smelling herb. MINT (*v.*) to coin. MINT (*adj.*) new; unused.

minuet (*n.*) a graceful dance.

minus (*adj.*) less; negative. MINUS (*n.*) the sign (—) which indicates a deduction or a negative.

minute (*adj.*) 1. small. 2. exact. MINUTE (*n.*) a measure of (1) time (1/60 hour), and of (2) angle (1/60 degree).

minutely (*adv.*) closely; thoroughly.

minuteness (*n.*) smallness; fineness.

minutes (*n. pl.*) written notes of business done at a meeting.

minx (*n.*) a pert girl; a hussy.

miracle (*n.*) something beyond human power; a marvel.

miraculous (*adj.*) divine; amazing. MIRACULOUSLY (*adv.*).

mirage (*n.*) image of a distant object seen in the air.

mire (*n.*) mud; slime.

mirror (*n.*) 1. a looking-glass. 2. an example. MIRROR (*v.*) to reflect; to copy.

mirth (*n.*) merriment; gaiety.

mirthful (*adj.*) merry; frolicsome. MIRTHFULLY (*adv.*).

mirthfulness (*n.*) fun; jollity.

mirthless (*adj.*) unhappy; joyless.

miry (*adj.*) muddy; slushy.

misadventure (*n.*) an accident; a mishap.

misanthrope (*n.*) a hater of mankind; a sour recluse.

misanthropy (*n.*) rejection of human society.

misapply (*v.*) to misuse; to use dishonestly.

misapprehend (*v.*) to misunderstand; to mistake.

misapprehension (*n.*) a misunderstanding.

misbehave (*v.*) to behave badly.

misbehaviour (*n.*) misconduct; rudeness.

misbelieve (*v.*) to believe wrongly. MISBELIEF (*n.*).

miscalculate (*v.*) to reckon wrongly; to underestimate.

miscalculation (*n.*) a mistake; an error.

miscellaneous (*adj.*) mixed; varied.

miscellany (*n.*) 1. a collection of works on different subjects. 2. a medley; jumble.

mischance (*n.*) a mishap; an accident.

mischief (*n.*) 1. childish misdoing. 2. damage done on purpose.

mischief-maker (*n.*) one who stirs up quarrels; a trouble-maker.

mischievous (*adj.*) annoying; trouble-making. MISCHIEVOUSLY (*adv.*)

misconceive (*v.*) to misjudge; to mistake.

misconception (*n.*) a wrong idea; false opinion.

misconduct (*n.*) 1. misbehaviour. 2. mismanagement.

miscount (*v.*) to reckon wrongly; to miscalculate. MISCOUNT (*n.*) a wrong calculation.

miscreant (*n.*) a scamp; rascal.

misdeal (*v.*) to make a mistake in dealing cards. MISDEAL (*n.*) a faulty distribution of cards.

misdeed (*n.*) an offence; a sin.

misdemeanour (*n.*) a wrong; crime.

misdirect (*v.*) to direct wrongly.

misdirection (*n.*) 1. an error of judgment. 2. a wrong address.

miser (*n.*) one who saves money and lives wretchedly.

miserable (*adj.*) unhappy; distressed. MISERABLY (*adv.*).

miserly (*adj.*) mean; greedy.

misery (*n.*) sorrow; affliction.

misfit (*n.*) a garment that does not fit the person it is meant for.

misfortune (*n.*) failure; disaster.

misgive (*v.*) to fill with doubt.

misgiving (*n.*) uncertainty; doubt.

misgovern (*v.*) to rule badly; to mismanage. MISGOVERNMENT (*n.*).

misguidance (*n.*) bad advice.

misguide (*v.*) to mislead; to deceive.

mishandle (*v.*) to maltreat; to mismanage.

mishap (*n.*) a mischance; an accident.

misinform (*v.*) to inform wrongly; to mislead.

misinterpret (*v.*) to misunderstand; to misconstrue. MISINTERPRETATION (*n.*).

misjudge (*v.*) to judge wrongly; to get a wrong opinion. MISJUDGMENT (*n.*).

mislay (*v.*) to misplace; to lose.

mislead (*v.*) to lead astray; to deceive.

misleading (*adj.*) causing mistakes; deceptive.

misplace (*v.*) to put in the wrong place; to mislay.

misprint (*n.*) a mistake in printing.

mispronounce (*v.*) to pronounce wrongly. MISPRONUNCIATION (*n.*).

misquote (*v.*) to quote or repeat wrongly. MISQUOTATION (*n.*).

misrepresent (*v.*) to describe falsely; to deceive.

misrepresentation (*n.*) a false description; deception.

misrule (*n.*) misgovernment; disorder.

miss (*n.*) a girl; an unmarried woman. MISS (*v.*) 1. to fail to hit. 2. to leave out. 3. to regret the loss of.

missal (*n.*) book containing the service of Mass for the whole year; the Roman Catholic book of prayers.

missile (*n.*) a weapon thrown or fired; or launched by a rocket.

missing (*adj.*) absent; lost.

mission (*n.*) 1. persons entrusted with a special task or duty. 2. the task or duty undertaken.

missionary (*n.*) one sent to convert the heathen. (*pl.* MISSIONARIES).

missive (*n.*) a letter; dispatch.

mis-spelling (*n.*) a wrong spelling. MIS-SPELT (*adj.*).

mis-statement (*n.*) an incorrect statement.

mist (*n.*) fine water-vapour filling the air; fog. MIST (*v.*) to cloud; to obscure.

mistakable (*adj.*) liable to be wrong.

mistake (*n.*) a fault; an error. MISTAKE (*v.*) to be wrong; to err.

mistaken (*adj.*) wrong; incorrect. MISTAKENLY (*adv.*).

mistiness (*n.*) the thickness or density of the mist.

mistletoe (*n.*) a berry-bearing plant which grows on apple and other trees.

mistress (*n.*) woman head of a family, school, etc. (*pl.* MISTRESSES).

mistrial (*n.*) a trial that cannot result in a lawful decision because a mistake has occurred.

mistrust (*v.*) to doubt; to distrust. MISTRUST (*n.*) doubt; misgiving.

mistrustful (*adj.*) suspicious; doubting. MISTRUSTFULLY (*adv.*).

misty (*adj.*) hazy; foggy.

misunderstand (*v.*) to mistake; to misinterpret.

misunderstanding (*n.*) 1. a mistake. 2. a disagreement; quarrel.

misuse (*v.*) to maltreat; to abuse.

mite (*n.*) 1. a tiny insect. 2. a trifle; nothing. 3. a small child.

mitigate (*v.*) to make lighter; to ease.

mitigation (*n.*) a reduction; decrease.

mitre (*n.*) a bishop's head-dress.

mitten (*n.*) a kind of glove without thumb and fingers; covering for the wrist and palm.

mix (*v.*) to mingle; to blend.

mixture (*n.*) a medley of substances; a jumble.

moan (*n.*) a low sound denoting pain or sorrow; groan. MOAN (*v.*) to groan; to lament.

moat (*n.*) deep ditch round a castle.

mob (*n.*) a disorderly crowd; a rabble. MOB (*v.*) to crowd around and follow.

mobile (*adj.*) moving; active.

mobility (*n.*) movement; activity.

mobilization (*n.*) preparations made for warfare.

mobilize (*v.*) 1. to gather together. 2. to summon and equip men for warfare.

mock (*v.*) to make fun of; to deride. MOCK (*adj.*) sham; imitation.

mockery (*n.*) ridicule; derision.

mocking (*adj.*) ridiculing; jeering.

mode (*n.*) 1. the way; method. 2. the fashion; style.

model (*n.*) 1. an example; a pattern. 2. a small copy. MODEL (*v.*) to shape; to mould. MODEL (*adj.*) perfect. MODELLER (*n.*).

moderate (*v.*) to make less violent; to soothe. MODERATE (*adj.*) fair; reasonable. MODERATELY (*adv.*).

moderation (*n.*) forbearance; restraint.

modern (*adj.*) new; current.

modernize (*v.*) to bring up-to-date; to renew.

modest (*adj.*) meek; shy. MODESTLY (*adv.*).

modesty (*n.*) meekness; reticence.

modification (*n.*) 1. an alteration. 2. an easing; a softening.

modify (*v.*) 1. to alter; to vary. 2. to make less severe; to tone down.

modish (*adj.*) fashionable; stylish.

modulate (*v.*) 1. to regulate; to adjust. 2. to bring into tune; to harmonize.

modulation (*n.*) 1. an alteration. 2. an attuning.

modulator (*n.*) a tonic sol-fa chart.

module (*n.*) 1. part of a space-ship. 2. a proportionate unit of measurement.

mohair (*n.*) hair of the angora goat, and the fabric made from it.

moist (*adj.*) 1. damp; wet. 2. rainy; humid.

moisten (*v.*) to damp; to wet slightly.

moisture (*n.*) wetness; humidity.

molar (*n.*) a grinding tooth.

molasses (*n.*) syrup; treacle.

mole (*n.*) 1. a spot on the skin. 2. a furry, burrowing animal. 3. a jetty; pier. MOLESKIN (*n.*).

molecule (*n.*) a tiny particle.

molest (*v.*) to disturb; to pester.

molestation (*n.*) interference; disturbance.

mollification (*n.*) a soothing; calming.

mollify (*v.*) to soothe; to pacify.

molten (*adj.*) melted; made liquid.

moment (*n.*) 1. a tiny length of time; an instant. 2. importance.

momentary (*adj.*) lasting only an instant. MOMENTARILY (*adv.*).

momentous (*adj.*) very important; serious. MOMENTOUSLY (*adv.*).

momentum (*n.*) the amount of force that moves a body, which is shown by its speed or velocity; impetus gained by movement.

monarch (*n.*) a sovereign; ruler.

monarchy (*n.*) a country ruled by a monarch. (*pl.* MONARCHIES).

monastery (*n.*) buildings in which monks live or lived. (*pl.* MONASTERIES).

monastic (*adj.*) relating to monks and monasteries.

Monday (*n.*) the second day of the week.

monetary (*adj.*) relating to money.

money (*n.*) 1. coin; banknotes. 2. wealth; riches. (*pl.* MONEYS). MONEYED (*adj.*).

mongoose (*n.*) a rat-like, snake-killing animal.

mongrel (*n.*) an animal of mixed breed; a hybrid. MONGREL (*adj.*) of mixed origin, nature or character.

monitor (*n.*) 1. an instructor; adviser.

2. pupil who assists a teacher. 3. a small warship, mounting heavy guns.

monk (*n.*) man who lives a religious life in a monastery.

monkey (*n.*) a small ape.

monocle (*n.*) a single eyeglass or lens.

monogram (*n.*) a design made by intermingling letters.

monolith (*n.*) a single standing stone; a pillar.

monologue (*n.*) entertainment by a single performer; a recitation.

monoplane (*n.*) aeroplane with one pair of wings.

monopolist (*n.*) one who has sole control.

monopolize (*v.*) to take for oneself; to have sole control.

monopoly (*n.*) exclusive control by a single person or firm.

monotonous (*adj.*) 1 regular; unchanging. 2. boring; wearisome. MONOTONOUSLY (*adv.*).

monotony (*n.*) 1. regularity; sameness. 2. dullness; boredom.

monsoon (*n.*) rain-bearing wind that blows over India and Burma.

monster (*n.*) 1. a fierce, terrifying beast. 2. a cruel, inhuman person. MONSTER (*adj.*) very large.

monstrosity (*n.*) anything frightful or unnatural in appearance.

monstrous (*adj.*) tremendous; horrible. MONSTROUSLY (*adv.*).

month (*n.*) one of the year's twelve divisions.

monthly (*adj.*) each month. MONTHLY (*adv.*) once a month. MONTHLY (*n.*) periodical published each month.

monument (*n.*) anything erected in memory of a person or event; a memorial.

monumental (*adj.*) 1. large; imposing. 2. important; outstanding.

mood (*n.*) one's frame of mind; temper.

moodiness (*n.*) glumness; sulkiness.

moody (*adj.*) sullen; peevish. MOODILY (*adv.*).

moon (*n.*) the satellite, or heavenly body, that revolves round the earth. MOON (*v.*) to wander about; to idle.

moonbeam (*n.*) a ray of moonlight.

moonlit (*adj.*) illumined by the moon.

moonshine (*n.*) 1. moonlight. 2. nonsense; humbug.

moonstruck (*adj.*) affected by the moon; sentimental.

moor (*n.*) a heath. MOOR (*v.*) to secure or berth a ship. MOORLAND (*n.*).

mooring (*n.*) a ship's berth or anchorage.

moose (*n.*) a giant American deer.

mop (*n.*) 1. a bundle of rags on a handle for wiping floors. 2. untidy mass of hair. MOP (*v.*) to use a mop.

mope (*v.*) to be silent and dull.

moping (*adj.*) listless; dispirited.

moral (*adj.*) knowing right conduct and duty; well-conducted. MORAL (*n.*) lesson taught by a fable or by experience.

morale (*n.*) courage and spirit to do one's duty.

morality (*n.*) right and dutiful conduct; integrity.

moralize (*v.*) to think about right and wrong.

morals (*n. pl.*) goodness or badness of character.

morass (*n.*) a marsh; swamp.

morbid (*adj.*) unhealthy; sickly. MORBIDLY (*adv.*).

moreover (*adv.*) besides; also.

moribund (*adj.*) dying.

morn or **morning** (*n.*) the first part of the day, from midnight to noon.

morose (*adj.*) surly; gruff. MOROSELY (*adv.*).

moroseness (*n.*) sullenness; surliness.

morphia or **morphine** (*n.*) drug which eases pain. See appendix.

morrow (*n.*) the next following day; to-morrow.

morse (*n.*) a telegraphic code. See appendix.

morsel (*n.*) a small piece; a bit.

mortal (*adj.*) 1. human. 2. causing death. MORTAL (*n.*) a human being.

mortality (*n.*) 1. death. 2. loss of life in accidents, etc. 3. the death-rate.

mortally (*adv.*) fatally; extremely.

mortar (*n.*) 1. cement. 2. a bowl in which substances are finely ground. 3. a short, wide-mouthed cannon.

mortgage (*n.*) 1. property given in security for money lent. 2. a pledge. MORTGAGE (*v.*) to pledge a property.

mortgagee (*n.*) person who grants the loan; creditor.

mortgagor (*n.*) person who receives the loan; debtor.

mortification (*n.*) 1. decay. 2. shame; humiliation.

mortify (*v.*) 1. to decay. 2. to shame; to humiliate. MORTIFYING (*adj.*).

mortuary (*n.*) place where dead bodies are received to await burial or identification. MORTUARY (*adj.*) concerning the burial of the dead.

mosaic (*n.*) a design made with small pieces of glass or stone. MOSAIC (*adj.*) of Moses. See appendix.

Moslem (*n.*) Muslim; a believer in the teachings of Mohammed.

mosque (*n.*) a Muslim place of worship.

mosquito (*n.*) a gnat whose bite infects with fever. (*pl.* MOSQUITOES).

moss (*n.*) tiny plant growing in marshy soil. MOSSY (*adj.*).

most (*n.*) the greatest number, quantity, etc. MOST (*adv.*) in the greatest or highest degree. MOST (*adj.*) greatest.

mote (*n.*) a spot; speck.

moth (*n.*) a night-flying insect: some kinds eat cloth, fur, etc.

mother (*n.*) 1. female parent, especially of a human being. 2. superior or head of a nunnery or convent.

motion (*n.*) 1. movement; action. 2. a suggestion at a meeting to do something; proposal.

motionless (*adj.*) still; stationary.

motive (*adj.*) causing movement. MOTIVE (*n.*) a reason for doing a thing.

motley (*n.*) a jester's dress. MOTLEY (*adj.*) two-coloured.

motor (*n.*) 1. an engine which drives a machine. 2. an automobile. MOTOR (*v.*) to travel by motor-car.

motorway (*n.*) a road designed to take fast moving traffic.

mottle (*v.*) to spot with different colours; to variegate. MOTTLED (*adj.*).

motto (*n.*) a wise saying; maxim.

mould (*v.*) to shape; to cast. MOULD (*n.*) 1. loose soil. 2. mildew; dry-rot. 3. container which gives its shape to whatever is poured or pressed into it.

moulder (*n.*) one who casts from a mould. MOULDER (*v.*) to crumble; to decay.

moulding (*n.*) ornamental projection on a wall or picture-frame.

mouldy (*adj.*) musty; mildewed.

moult (*v.*) to shed feathers, hair, etc.

mound (*n.*) a low hillock; heap of soil or stones.

mount (*n.*) 1. a hill. 2. a horse. MOUNT (*v.*) 1. to rise; to ascend. 2. to bestride a horse or bicycle. 3. to prepare specimens for display. MOUNTED (*adj.*).

mountain (*n.*) a high hill. MOUNTAINOUS (*adj.*).

mountaineer (*n.*) a mountain-climber.

mountebank (*n.*) an impostor; a quack.

mourn (*v.*) to grieve; to lament. MOURNER (*n.*).

mournful (*adj.*) sad; sorrowful. MOURNFULLY (*adv.*).

mourning (*n.*) 1. sorrow; woe. 2. dress worn by mourners.

mouse (*n.*) small gnawing animal infesting houses and fields. (*pl.* MICE).

moustache (*n.*) hair grown on the upper lip.

mouth (*n.*) 1. the opening between the lips. 2. any opening or orifice, cave, river, etc. MOUTHFUL (*n.*).

movable (*adj.*) 1. light; portable. 2. changeable; variable.

move (*v.*) 1. to change a position. 2. to do; to act. 3. to arouse; to agitate. MOVE (*n.*) a motion; an action.

movement (*n.*) 1. motion. 2. mechanism of a watch or clock. 3. a cause; crusade.

moving (*adj.*) 1. in motion. 2. touching; pathetic.

mow (*v.*) to cut down grain or grass.

mower (*n.*) 1. one who mows. 2. a mowing-machine.

much (*n.*) a great quantity. MUCH (*adj.*) great in quantity; abundant; long in time. MUCH (*adv.*) to a great extent; almost.

mud (*n.*) water-soaked earth; mire. MUDDY (*adj.*).

muddiness (*n.*) 1. dirtiness; impurity. 2. cloudiness; obscurity.

muddle (*v.*) to mix up; to confuse. MUDDLE (*n.*) disorder; disarray.

muddle-headed (*adj.*) blundering; confused.

muff (*v.*) to bungle; to spoil. MUFF (*n.*) 1. a bungler. 2. a fur hand-wrap.

muffin (*n.*) a flat, round, spongy cake.

muffle (*v.*) 1. to wrap up. 2. to deaden the sound; to stifle.

muffled (*adj.*) dulled; suppressed.

muffler (*n.*) 1. a scarf; neck-wrap. 2. a wrapping to deaden sound.

mug (*n.*) a cylindrical drinking vessel of earthenware or metal.

mulberry (*n.*) tree on whose leaves silkworms feed, and its fruit. (*pl.* MULBERRIES).

mulct (*v.*) to fine; to penalize.

mule (*n.*) 1. offspring of the horse and ass. 2. an obstinate person. 3. a thread-spinning machine.

mulish (*adj.*) headstrong; obstinate.

mulishness (*n.*) stubbornness; obstinacy.

mullet (*n.*) a fish which delves in the sand.

mullion (*n.*) an upright division between the lights of windows.

multifarious (*adj.*) of many kinds; various.

multilateral (*adj.*) many-sided.

multiple (*adj.*) having many parts; manifold. MULTIPLE (*n.*) the product of two or more numbers multiplied together.

multiply (*v.*) to make a quantity greater; to increase.

multitude (*n.*) a crowd; a throng. MULTITUDINOUS (*adj.*).

mum (*v.*) to act in dumb show; to mime. MUM (*adj.*) silent; tongue-tied. MUM (*inter.*) silence.

mumble (*v.*) to speak indistinctly; to mutter. MUMBLER (*n.*).

mumbling (*adj.*) muttering.

mumps (*n.*) 1. a painful neck complaint. 2. the sulks.

munch (*v.*) to chew noisily; to crunch.

mundane (*adj.*) worldly; earthly.

municipal (*adj.*) concerning the affairs of a city or borough.

municipality (*n.*) a borough or city governed by a corporation.

munificence (*n.*) generosity; liberality.

munificent (*adj.*) generous; lavish. MUNIFICENTLY (*adv.*).

munitions (*n. pl.*) war materials; supplies.

mural (*adj.*) concerned with, or on, a wall.

murder (*n.*) an unlawful intentional killing. MURDER (*v.*) intentionally to kill a person unlawfully.

murk (*n.*) darkness; gloom. MURKINESS (*n.*). MURKY (*adj.*).

murmur (*n.*) 1. a low, gentle sound. 2. a grumble; complaint. MURMUR (*v.*) 1. to mutter; to grumble. 2. to mutter softly.

murmuring (*adj.*) 1. grumbling; complaining. 2. soft-sounding.

muscle (*n.*) any movement-causing organ in the body.

muscular (*adj.*) sturdy; athletic.

muse (*v.*) to be wrapped in thought; to meditate. MUSE (*n.*) one of the nine goddesses of learning and art.

museum (*n.*) a building in which a collection of objects of historical interest is shown. See appendix.

mushroom (*n.*) an eatable fungus which grows in a night.

music (*n.*) a pleasing arrangement of sounds; melody.

musical (*adj.*) 1. melodious; tuneful. 2. fond of music.

musician (*n.*) one skilled in composing or performing music.

musing (*n.*) meditation; contemplation. MUSINGLY (*adv.*).

musk (*n.*) a fragrant perfume. MUSKY (*adj.*).

muslin (*n.*) a thin, gauzy, cotton cloth.

mussel (*n.*) a small shell-fish.

must (*v.*) 1. to be obliged or compelled. 2. to be essential to the end desired. MUST (*n.*) mouldiness; sourness.

mustang (*n.*) an American wild horse.

mustard (*n.*) a plant whose seeds are ground to make a condiment or plaster.

muster (*v.*) 1. to assemble. 2. to gather troops for war. 3. to meet; to rally. MUSTER (*n.*) an assembly; a rally.

mustiness (*n.*) staleness; mouldiness.

musty (*adj.*) stale; mouldy.

mutable (*adj.*) changeable; unsettled.

mute (*adj.*) dumb; silent.

mutely (*adv.*) silently.

mutilate (*v.*) 1. to cut; to slash. 2. to cripple; to disfigure.

mutilation (*n.*) an impairment; a disfigurement.

mutineer (*n.*) one guilty of mutiny.

mutinous (*adj.*) insubordinate; disobedient. MUTINOUSLY (*adv.*).

mutiny (*n.*) a revolt of soldiers or sailors. (*pl.* MUTINIES). MUTINY (*v.*) to refuse to obey; to revolt.

mutter (*v.*) to speak in an undertone; to murmur. MUTTER (*n.*) a murmur; mumble.

mutton (*n.*) the flesh of sheep.

mutual (*adj.*) felt or done in the same way by two persons, for or towards each other.

muzzle (*n.*) 1. an animal's long nose and mouth. 2. a light cage which prevents an animal biting. 3. open end of a gun-barrel. MUZZLE (*v.*) 1. to fasten in a muzzle. 2. to impose silence on a person.

muzzled (*adj.*) 1. placed in a muzzle. 2. silenced.

myriad (*n.*) an immense number. MYRIAD (*adj.*) countless; innumerable.

myrrh (*n.*) a fragrant gum used as incense.

myrtle (*n.*) an evergreen shrub with white, sweet-scented flowers.

mysterious (*adj.*) unknown; unexplained.

mystery (*n.*) something beyond human understanding; an enigma.

mystic (*adj.*) awe-inspiring; supernatural.

mystification (*n.*) bewilderment; perplexity.

mystify (*v.*) 1. to bewilder; to perplex. 2. to puzzle; to hoax.

myth (*n.*) a fable; legend.

mythical (*adj.*) fanciful; imaginary.

mythological (*adj.*) legendary; fabled.

mythology (*n.*) the study of myths.

N

nab (*v.*) to catch; to grab.

nag (*v.*) to give no peace; to pester. NAG (*n.*) a horse.

naiad (*n.*) a water-nymph.

naive (*adj.* pron. NA-EVE) unaffected; artless. NAIVELY (*adv.*).

nail (*n.*) 1. horny growth on finger-tips and toes. 2. small metal spike. 3. measure of length (2¼ inches). NAIL (*v.*) to fasten with nails.

naked (*adj.*) unclothed; bare. NAKEDNESS (*n.*).

name (*n.*) 1. word by which a person or thing is known; appellation. 2. reputation. NAME (*v.*) 1. to give a name to; to baptize. 2. to mention by name; to nominate.

nameless (*adj.*) anonymous; obscure.

namely (*adv.*) that is to say.

namesake (*n.*) one having the same name as another.

nap (*n.*) 1. a short sleep; a doze. 2. woolly surface on fabrics.

nape (*n.*) the back of the neck.

naphtha (*n.*) an oil obtained from wood and coal.

napkin (*n.*) 1. a small cloth or towel. 2. a serviette.

narcissus (*n.*) fragrant flower of daffodil family. (*pl.* NARCISSI). See appendix.

narcotic (*n.*) medicine that eases pain and causes sleep.

narrate (*v.*) to tell; to relate.

narration (*n.*) the telling of a story. NARRATOR (*n.*).

narrative (*n.*) a tale or history.

narrow (*adj.*) 1. of little breadth. 2. prejudiced. NARROW (*v.*) to lessen the breadth; to contract.

narrowly (*adv.*) by a small distance; barely.

narrow-minded (*adj.*) having fixed ideas.

narrowness (*n.*) thinness; straitness.

nasal (*adj.*) 1. relating to the nose. 2. spoken partly through the nose. NASALLY (*adv.*).

nasal organ (*n.*) the nose.

nastiness (*n.*) 1. dirtiness. 2. unpleasantness.

nasturtium (*n.*) bright-flowered garden plant with peppery leaves.

nasty (*adj.*) 1. dirty; unclean. 2. unpleasant. NASTILY (*adv.*).

nation (*n.*) whole body of people who are citizens of the same country.

national (*adj.*) relating to a nation; public.

nationalism (*n.*) support of one's nation; patriotism.

nationalist (*n.*) one who upholds his nation; a patriot.

nationality (*n.*) membership of a particular nation; citizenship. (*pl.* NATIONALITIES).

nationalize (*v.*) to make a thing national property. NATIONALIZATION (*n.*).

nationally (*adv.*) throughout the nation.

native (*adj.*) 1. belonging to by birth; inborn. 2. as found in nature. NATIVE (*n.*) 1. an original or early inhabitant. 2. a person born as a citizen.

nativity (*n.*) birth. THE NATIVITY, the Birth of Jesus.

natty (*adj.*) neat; tidy. NATTILY (*adv.*).

natural (*adj.*) 1. occurring in nature; inborn. 2. usual; normal. 3. simple; unaffected.

natural history (*n.*) study of the earth's productions, especially animal life and vegetation.

naturalist (*n.*) a student of natural history.

naturalize (*v.*) to make a foreigner a native or citizen; to adopt. NATURALIZATION (*n.*).

naturally (*adv.*) as might be expected; of course.

nature (*n.*) 1. all Creation, that is, all that exists and happens that is not the work of man. 2. the character and qualities of living beings and things.

naught (*n.*) nothing.

naughtiness (*n.*) misbehaviour; mischief.

naughty (*adj.*) ill-behaved; troublesome. NAUGHTILY (*adv.*).

nausea (*n.*) a feeling of (1) sickness, or (2) disgust; loathing. NAUSEOUS (*adj.*).

nauseate (*v.*) to sicken; to feel disgust.

nautical (*adj.*) concerning ships and navigation.

nautical mile (*n.*) a sea-mile (6080 feet).

naval (*adj.*) relating to the navy and shipping.

nave (*n.*) the body, or central part of a church.

navigable (*adj.*) suitable for ships to sail on.

navigate (*v.*) to manage a ship or aircraft and direct its course. NAVIGATOR (*n.*).

navigation (*n.*) 1. the work of navigation. 2. seamanship.

navvy (*n.*) a labourer. (*pl.* NAVVIES).

navy (*n.*) 1. a fleet of ships. 2. a nation' war vessels. (*pl.* NAVIES).

nay (*n.*) no, the negative answer to question.

neap tides (*n. pl.*) the lowest tides, soon after new and full moon.

near (*adj.*) 1. not far away; nigh. 2. closely related. 3. mean; miserly.

nearly (*adv.*) closely; almost.

nearness (*n.*) 1. closeness. 2. meanness.

neat (*adj.*) 1. tidy. 2. deft. 3. pure; unmixed with water.

neatness (*n.*) 1. tidiness. 2. skill; dexterity.

nebula (*n.*) a cloudy light-patch in the sky; it consists of distant stars. (*pl.* NEBULÆ).

nebulous (*adj.*) 1. dim. 2. uncertain.

necessarily (*adv.*) without fail; certainly.

necessary (*adj.*) needful. NECESSARY (*n.*) something that cannot be done without; an essential. (*pl.* NECESSARIES).

necessitate (*v.*) to make necessary; to compel.

necessitous (*adj.*) needy; poor.

necessity (*n.*) a want; need. (*pl.* NECESSITIES).

neck (*n.*) 1. part of body joining head to shoulders. 2. narrow part of a vessel, implement, etc. 3. an isthmus.

necklace (*n.*) a string of beads or jewels worn round the neck.

nectar (*n.*) 1. wine the gods drank. 2. honey found in flowers. 3. any delicious drink.

nectarine (*n.*) a kind of peach with a smooth rind.

need (*v.*) to want; to require. NEED (*n.*) 1. a lack; want. 2. poverty; distress. NEEDILY (*adv.*).

needful (*adj.*) 1. necessary; requisite. 2. needy; poor.

needle (*n.*) 1. small instrument for sewing or knitting. 2. a compass magnet. 3. a pinnacle of rock.

needless (*adj.*) unnecessary.

needy (*adj.*) in need; poor.

ne'er (*adv.*) never.

ne'er-do-well (*n.*) a failure; wastrel.

nefarious (*adj.*) wicked. NEFARIOUSLY (*adv.*).

negation (*n.*) a denial; refusal.

negative (*adj.*) denying; refusing. NEGATIVE (*n.*) 1. the words NO and NOT. 2. a photographic film or plate. NEGATIVE (*v.*) to refuse; to forbid.

neglect (*v.*) to leave undone or uncared for. NEGLECT (*n.*) carelessness; disregard.

neglectful (*adj.*) thoughtless; remiss.

negligence (*n.*) slackness; want of proper care.

negligent (*adj.*) careless; heedless. NEGLIGENTLY (*adv.*).

negligible (*adj.*) not worth noticing; trifling.

negotiable (*adj.*) can be discussed or exchanged.

negotiate (*v.*) 1. to try to reach agreement; to bargain. 2. to exchange; to transfer.

negotiation (*n.*) a business transaction; agreement.

negro (*n.*) an African black man. (*fem.* NEGRESS). (*pl.* NEGROES). NEGRO (*adj.*) of the negro race.

neigh (*n.*) the cry of a horse; a whinny. NEIGH (*v.*).

neighbour (*n.*) one who lives near. NEIGHBOUR (*v.*) to be near; to adjoin.

neighbourhood (*n.*) the district around one's dwelling; the vicinity.

neighbouring (*adj.*) near; adjoining.

neighbourly (*adj.*) friendly; obliging.

neighing (*adj.*) whinnying.

neither (*pron.* & *conj.*) not either; not one or the other.

nemesis (*n.*) vengeance; punishment. See appendix

neon (*n.*) a gas which electricity causes to glow brightly.

nephew (*n.*) son of a brother or sister.

Neptune (*n.*) 1. god of the sea. 2. distant planet with one moon. See appendix.

nerve (*n.*) 1. fibre that carries feelings or sensations to and from the brain. 2. pluck; resolution. NERVE (*v.*) to pluck up courage; to brave.

nerveless (*adj.*) weak; irresolute

nervous (*adj.*) 1. excitable; highly-strung. 2. afraid; timid.

nervousness (*n.*) fear; dread. NERVOUSLY (*adv.*).

ness (*n.*) a cape; headland.

nest (*n.*) 1. a bird's home. 2. a snug resting-place. 3. a group of objects which fit into each other. NEST (*v.*) to build a nest; to settle down.

nest-egg (*n.*) money saved for emergency.

nestle (*v.*) to lie or sit closely and warmly; to snuggle.

nestling (*n.*) bird too young to leave the nest.

net (*n.*) 1. twine knotted into meshes. 2. a snare. NET (*v.*) to snare; to capture. NET (*adj.*) without deduction; actual.

nether (*adj.*) lower. NETHERMOST (*adj.*).

netted (*adj.*) meshed.

netting (*n.*) any net-like fabric.

nettle (*n.*) a stinging weed. NETTLE (*v.*) to vex; to provoke.

nettled (*adj.*) annoyed; angry.

net-work (*n.*) a net-like system of roads, railways, etc.

neuralgia (*n.*) a severe nerve-pain in the head.

neuritis (*n.*) pain from an inflamed nerve.

neurotic (*adj.*) suffering from disordered nerves.

neuter (*adj.*) neutral; of neither masculine nor feminine gender.

neutral (*adj.*) neither for nor against; impartial. NEUTRAL (*n.*) a person or nation taking no part in a dispute or war; a non-partisan.

neutrality (*n.*) a refusal to join either side; impartiality.

neutralize (*v.*) to balance; to make inactive.

neutron (*n.*) an atom-particle which has no electricity.

never (*adv.*) not ever; not at any time.

nevertheless (*conj.*) all the same; for all that.

new (*adj.*) 1. hitherto unknown; unused. 2. unfamiliar; strange.

newly (*adv.*) freshly; recently.

newness (*n.*) freshness; novelty.

news (*n. pl.*) fresh or additional tidings or information.

newscaster (*n.*) one who broadcasts news on radio or television.

newspaper (*n.*) a printed paper circulating news, advertisements, etc.

newsvendor (*n.*) a seller of newspapers.

newt (*n.*) small, lizard-like creature living on land or in water (amphibian); an eft.

newton (*n.*) a measure of force. See appendix.

next (*adj.*) nearest; immediately following.

nib (*n.*) point of a pen.

nibble (*v.*) 1. to take tiny bites. 2. to bite at bait. NIBBLE (*n.*) a little bite; a bite at bait. NIBBLER (*n.*).

niblick (*n.*) a kind of golf-club.

nice (*adj.*) 1. delicious. 2. exact. 3. fine; delicate. NICELY (*adv.*).

nicety (*n.*) the accuracy; precision.

niche (*n.*) a recess in a wall.

nick (*n.*) a notch. NICK (*v.*) to cut in notches.

nickel (*n.*) 1. a hard, white metal. 2. an American coin.

nickname (*n.*) a popular or friendly name.

nicotine (*n.*) a poisonous substance found in tobacco.

niece (*n.*) daughter of a brother or sister.

niggard (*n.*) a mean person; a miser.

niggardly (*adj.*) mean; stingy.

nigh (*prep.*) near. NIGH (*adv.*) almost.

night (*n.*) between sunset and sunrise; darkness.

nightfall (*n.*) sunset; evening.

nightingale (*n.*) bird that sings sweetly at night.

nightly (*adj. & adv.*) done by night, or every night.

nightmare (*n.*) a terrifying, realistic dream.

nil (*n.*) nothing.

nimble (*adj.*) 1. quick in movement; sprightly. 2. ready-tongued; quick-witted.

nimbleness (*n.*) 1. agility. 2. readiness; aptness.

nimbly (*adv.*) briskly; smartly.

nimbus (*n.*) 1. the circle of light round (i) the sun or moon; (ii) the head of a saint; a halo. 2. a storm-cloud. (*pl.* NIMBUSES).

nincompoop (*n.*) a blockhead.

nine (*adj.*) one more than eight. NINE (*n.*) the figure or symbol 9 or IX.

ninepins (*n.*) indoor game of skittles.

nip (*v.*) to pinch; to bite. NIP (*n.*) 1. a pinch; bite. 2. a small drink.

nippers (*n. pl.*) 1. small pincers. 2. claws of a crab.

nipping (*adj.*) damaging; blighting.

nitre (*n.*) saltpetre, a rich fertilizer.

nitrogen (*n.*) a gas which makes up four-fifths of the air.

no (*adv.*) 1. a word of denial. 2. not at all. NO (*adj.*) not any; not one. NO (*n.*) a denial; refusal.

nobility (*n.*) 1. worthiness of mind and character; greatness. 2. the whole body of nobles or peers.

noble (*n.*) a lord; peer. NOBLE (*adj.*) 1. lordly. 2. distinguished; eminent. 3. brave.

nobly (*adv.*) 1. bravely. 2. splendidly; magnificently.

nobody (*n.*) 1. no person; no one. 2. a person of no importance. (*pl.* NOBODIES).

nocturnal (*adj.*) 1. relating to night. 2. awake or active at night; night-loving. NOCTURNALLY (*adv.*).

nocturne (*n.*) a dreamy piece of music.

nod (*v.*) 1. to bend the head forward in greeting. 2. to droop the head in sleep. NOD (*n.*) a bend or droop of the head.

nodule (*n.*) a small, rounded swelling; a lump.

noggin (*n.*) a gill or quarter-pint measure.

noise (*n.*) din; clamour. NOISE (*v.*) to talk about; to spread rumours.

noiseless (*adj.*) silent.

noisiness (*n.*) loudness; rowdiness.

noisy (*adj.*) loud; clamorous. NOISILY (*adv.*).

nomad (*n.*) a wanderer; roamer. NOMADIC (*adj.*).

no-man's-land (*n.*) unclaimed territory.

nominal (*adj.*) existing only in name; trivial.

nominally (*adv.*) in name only.

nominate (*v.*) to propose someone by name; to designate.

nomination (*n.*) a proposal; recommendation.

nominator (*n.*) the one who names; proposer.

nominee (*n.*) the one named; recommended.

nonagenarian (*n.*) one ninety years of age or over.

nonagon (*n.*) figure having nine sides.

nonchalance (*n.*) coolness; indifference.

nonchalant (*adj.*) calm; unconcerned.

nonconformist (*n.*) a Protestant who is not a member of the Church of England.

nondescript (*adj.*) hard to classify. NONDESCRIPT (*n.*) a thing hard to describe.

none (*n. & pron.*) no one; nothing. NONE (*adj.*) not any; not one.

nonentity (*n.*) 1. an unimportant person. 2. a thing that doesn't exist. (*pl.* NONENTITIES).

nonesuch (*n.*) a thing without equal.

nonplus (*v.*) to puzzle; to dumbfound.

nonsense (*n.*) foolish talk; silliness.

nonsensical (*adj.*) meaningless; absurd. NONSENSICALLY (*adv.*).

noodle (*n.*) a simpleton.

nook (*n.*) a secluded corner.

noose (*n.*) a loop with a running knot. NOOSE (*v.*) to snare in a noose.

nor (*conj.*) and not; and no more.

norm (*n.*) a rule; typical example.

normal (*adj.*) according to rule; usual.

normality (*n.*) regularity; usualness.

Norse (*adj.*) concerning ancient Scandinavia (Norway and Sweden). NORSE (*n.*) language of ancient Scandinavia.

north (*n.*) direction opposite the sun at midday (look at the sun, then the north is behind you).

northerly or **northern** (*adj.*) in or belonging to the north. NORTHWARD (*adv.*).

nose (*n.*) the organ of smell. NOSE (*v.*) to smell; to detect by smell; to scent.

nosegay (*n.*) a bunch of flowers; a posy.

nostalgia (*n.*) home-sickness. NOSTALGIC (*adj.*).

nostril (*n.*) one of the two openings in the nose.

nostrum (*n.*) a patent medicine.

not (*adv.*) word expressing denial or refusal; a negative.

notability (*n.*) a famous or eminent person.

notable (*adj.*) famous; renowned.

notably (*adv.*) chiefly; especially.

notch (*n.*) a nick; dent. NOTCH (*v.*) to nick; to dent.

note (*n.*) 1. a letter. 2. a single musical sound. 3. words jotted down to remind. 4. a piece of paper-money. 5. fame; renown. NOTE (*v.*) 1. to observe; to notice. 2. to write down; to record.

noted (*adj.*) famous; distinguished.

noteworthy (*adj.*) remarkable; memorable.

nothing (*n.*) 1. not anything. 2. a nonentity. NOTHING (*adv.*) in no degree.

notice (*v.*) to observe; to see. NOTICE (*n.*) 1. a displayed announcement. 2. a warning. 3. respectful treatment; attention.

noticeable (*adj.*) easily seen; outstanding.

noticeably (*adv.*) clearly; undoubtedly.

notifiable (*adj.*) must be told to the Health Authority.

notification (*n.*) a telling; a giving notice.

notify (*v.*) to inform; to advertise.

notion (*n.*) an idea; opinion.

notoriety (*n.*) a being known to all as discreditable.

notorious (*adj.*) known to have a bad name; infamous.

notoriously (*adv.*) undoubtedly; certainly.

notwithstanding (*conj.*) however; nevertheless. NOTWITHSTANDING (*prep.*) in spite of.

nougat (*n.*) a sweetmeat containing almonds.

noun (*n.*) a part of speech; the name of a thing.

nourish (*v.*) to care for; to feed.

nourishing (*adj.*) strengthening; sustaining.

nourishment (*n.*) food; nutriment.

novel (*adj.*) new; original. NOVEL (*n.*) a work of fiction; a story. NOVELIST (*n.*).

novelty (*n.*) a new thing. (*pl.* NOVELTIES).

November (*n.*) the eleventh month.

novice (*n.*) a beginner; learner.

now (*adv.*) at the present time; immediately.

nowadays (*adv.*) in the present day.

nowhere (*adv.*) not in any place.

noxious (*adj.*) harmful; poisonous.

nozzle (*n.*) the nose or mouth-piece fitted to a hose; an outlet tube.

nuclear (*adj.*) relating to a nucleus. NUCLEAR ENERGY (*n.*) from reaction in atomic nuclei.

nucleus (*n.*) 1. the centre round which something gathers; the core. 2. the central point of an atom. (*pl.* NUCLEI).

nudge (*v.*) to push; to poke. NUDGE (*n.*) a gentle touch with fist or elbow.

nugget (*n.*) a small, rough lump of native gold.

nuisance (*n.*) an annoyance; a pest.

null (*adj.*) wiped out; cancelled.

nullify (*v.*) to cancel; to extinguish.

numb (*adj.*) without feeling; dulled.

number (*n.*) 1. a figure; digit. 2. a crowd. NUMBER (*v.*) to find how many; to count.

numberless (*adj.*) countless; innumerable.

numbness (*n.*) loss of feeling.

numeral (*n.*) a figure; digit.

numerate (*v.*) to count; to number.

numeration (*n.*) a counting; numbering.

numerator (*n.*) the number above the line in a vulgar fraction.

numerous (*adj.*) many; abundant.

nun (*n.*) a woman devoted to a religious life.

nunnery (*n.*) building in which nuns live; a convent.

nurse (*v.*) 1. to tend children and the sick. 2. to care for; to cherish. 3. to save; to economize. NURSE (*n.*) one trained to tend children and the sick.

nursery (*n.*) 1. a room set apart for young children. 2. a place for rearing plants. (*pl.* NURSERIES).

nurture (*v.*) to nourish; to tend.

nut (*n.*) 1. a seed within a hard shell. 2. a metal collar screwed to fit a bolt.

nutcrackers (*n. pl.*) instrument for cracking nuts.

nutmeg (*n.*) kernel of an Indian fruit used as spice.

nutriment (*n.*) food; nourishment. NUTRITION (*n.*).

nutritious (*adj.*) wholesome; strengthening.

nylon (*n.*) a strong fibre made from artificial plastic material.

nymph (*n.*) 1. a fabled sea, wood or river goddess. 2. a girl; damsel.

O

oaf (*n.*) a lout; dolt.

oak (*n.*) the acorn-bearing tree. OAKEN (*adj.*).

oar (*n.*) flat-bladed instrument for rowing boats. OARSMAN (*n.*).

oasis (*n.*) fertile place in a desert. (*pl.* OASES).

oast (*n.*) kiln to dry hops or malt.

oat (*n.*) an edible grain; a cereal. OATEN (*adj.*).

oath (*n.*) 1. a solemn promise made in God's name to speak truth. 2. a swear word; profanity.

oatmeal (*n.*) ground oats, used in making porridge.

obdurate (*adj.*) stubborn; unfeeling. OBDURATELY (*adv.*).

obedience (*n.*) submission; dutifulness.
obedient (*adj.*) submissive; yielding. OBEDIENTLY (*adv.*).
obeisance (*n.*) a bow; homage.
obelisk (*n.*) a tapering, four-sided column.
obese (*adj.*) fat; stout.
obesity (*n.*) fatness; corpulence.
obey (*v.*) to do as told; to submit.
object (*n.* pron. OB-ject) 1. an aim; purpose. 2. a thing; an article. OBJECT (*v.* pron. ob-JECT) to disapprove; to protest.
objection (*n.*) a protest; opposition. OBJECTOR (*n.*).
objectionable (*adj.*) unpleasant; offensive.
objective (*n.*) the aim; goal. OBJECTIVE (*adj.*) real; actual.
oblation (*n.*) an offering; a sacrifice.
obligation (*n.*) a binding promise; duty.
obligatory (*adj.*) binding; compulsory.
oblige (*v.*) 1. to compel. 2. to do a favour; to help.
obliging (*adj.*) helpful; kind. OBLIGINGLY (*adv.*).
oblique (*adj.*) slanting; inclined.
obliquely (*adv.*) 1. slantingly. 2. indirectly; in a roundabout way.
obliquity (*n.*) 1. slant; slope. 2. indirectness.
obliterate (*v.*) to destroy; to efface.
obliteration (*n.*) an effacement; erasure.
oblivion (*n.*) forgetfulness; disregard.
oblivious (*adj.*) heedless; forgetful.
oblong (*n.*) a four-sided, right-angled figure longer than it is broad. OBLONG (*adj.*) having greater length than breadth.
obnoxious (*adj.*) nasty; offensive. OBNOXIOUSLY (*adv.*).
oboe (*n.*) a wooden wind instrument.
obscene (*adj.*) unsavoury; disgusting. OBSCENELY (*adv.*).
obscenity (*n.*) coarseness; foul language.
obscure (*adj.*) 1. dark; gloomy. 2. unknown; hidden. OBSCURELY (*adv.*).
obscurity (*n.*) 1. darkness; indistinctness. 2. doubt; vagueness.
obsequies (*n. pl.*) funeral ceremonies.
obsequious (*adj.*) trying to win favour; flattering.
observance (*n.*) 1. careful notice; attention. 2. a religious rule or ceremony.
observant (*adj.*) 1. watchful. 2. regardful. 3. obedient to.

observation (*n.*) 1. study; notice. 2. a remark; comment. 3. obedience.
observatory (*n.*) building in which astronomers study the stars.
observe (*v.*) 1. to see; to notice. 2. to keep; to follow. 3. to comment; to remark. OBSERVER (*n.*).
obsess (*v.*) to fill one's mind; to have all one's interest.
obsession (*n.*) a thought or intention which overcomes all others.
obsolete (*adj.*) not now used; extinct.
obstacle (*n.*) a hindrance; an obstruction.
obstinacy (*n.*) stubbornness; mulishness.
obstinate (*adj.*) headstrong; stubborn. OBSTINATELY (*adv.*).
obstruct (*v.*) to bar; to block.
obstruction (*n.*) a barrier; an obstacle. OBSTRUCTIVE (*adj.*).
obtain (*v.*) to get; to procure. OBTAINABLE (*adj.*).
obtrude (*v.*) 1. to enter where not wanted; to intrude. 2. to interfere.
obtrusion (*n.*) an intrusion; interference.
obtrusive (*adj.*) too ready to interfere; officious.
obtuse (*adj.*) 1. greater than a right angle. 2. blunt; rounded. 3. slow-witted; dull. OBTUSELY (*adv.*).
obtuseness (*n.*) dullness; slowness.
obverse (*adj.*) opposite; facing. OBVERSE (*n.*) the face or front of a coin or medal.
obviate (*v.*) to clear away; to remove.
obvious (*adj.*) easily seen; unmistakable. OBVIOUSLY (*adv.*).
obviousness (*n.*) clearness; certainty.
occasion (*n.*) 1. the reason; need. 2. the happening; occurrence. OCCASION (*v.*) to cause; to start.
occasional (*adj.*) infrequent; happening now and then.
occasionally (*adv.*) sometimes.
Occident (*n.*) the West. OCCIDENTAL (*adj.*).
occult (*adj.*) mysterious; ghostly.
occupant (*n.*) a dweller in; a user of. Also OCCUPIER (*n.*).
occupation (*n.*) 1. possession; residence. 2. one's business; work.
occupy (*v.*) 1. to live in. 2. to take possession of. 3. to take up room or time.
occur (*v.*) 1. to happen. 2. to enter the mind.

occurrence (*n.*) an event; incident.

ocean (*n.*) a large sea; the deep. OCEANIC (*adj.*).

ochre (*n.*) a yellow or red earth.

o'clock (*abbrev.*) of the clock; clock-time.

octagon (*n.*) an eight-sided figure. OCTAGONAL (*adj.*).

octave (*n.*) 1. an eight-lined verse. 2. a scale of eight notes. 3. a sound eight notes higher than another.

octavo (*n.*) sheet of paper folded to make eight leaves.

October (*n.*) the tenth month. (In Roman times the eighth.)

octogenarian (*n.*) person eighty years old.

octopus (*n.*) sea-creature with eight arms; a cuttlefish. (*pl.* OCTOPUSES).

ocular (*adj.*) relating to the eyes or sight; visual.

ocularly (*adv.*) by means of the eye; by sight.

oculist (*n.*) an eye-doctor.

odd (*adj.*) 1. not even; not divisible exactly by two. 2. strange; unusual. ODDLY (*adv.*).

oddity (*n.*) a queer person or thing; curiosity. (*pl.* ODDITIES).

oddments (*n. pl.*) odds and ends; scraps.

oddness (*n*). strangeness; peculiarity.

odds (*n. pl.*) 1. chances that something will or will not happen. 2. the difference; variance.

ode (*n.*) a short poem or song.

odious (*adj.*) nasty; loathsome.

odium (*n.*) the blame; unpopularity.

odorous (*adj.*) fragrant; scented.

odour (*n.*) fragrance; perfume.

odourless (*adj.*) scentless.

o'er (*abbrev.*) over.

oersted (*n.*) a unit of magnetism. See appendix.

offence (*n.*) 1. a wrong; an illegal act. 2. a misdeed; sin.

offend (*v.*) 1. to hurt; to displease. 2. to sin.

offender (*n.*) the culprit; sinner.

offending (*adj.*) hurtful; annoying.

offensive (*adj.*) unpleasant; disgusting. OFFENSIVE (*n.*) an attack; assault. OFFENSIVELY (*adv.*).

offensiveness (*n.*) 1. unpleasantness. 2. annoyance; insolence.

offer (*v.*) 1. to hold out for one to take;

to proffer. 2. to say what one is willing to pay or do. 3. to sacrifice.

offering (*n.*) 1. anything offered; a gift. 2. a sacrifice.

offertory (*n.*) a church collection.

off-hand (*adj.*) 1. without preparation. 2. careless; easy-going.

office (*n.*) 1. a business-room. 2. an official post; a duty.

officer (*n.*) 1. one who commands in the national forces. 2. an official.

official (*n.*) one who performs public duties. OFFICIAL (*adj.*) public; authorized.

officiate (*v.*) to perform the duties of a position or office.

officious (*adj.*) offering unwanted help; interfering. OFFICIOUSLY (*adv.*).

offing (*n.*) the sea, or a point therein, distant from the shore, or from a ship at sea.

offset (*v.*) to make up for; to balance.

offshoot (*n.*) a twig; branch.

offspring (*n.*) a child or children.

oft; often (*advs.*) frequently; many times.

ogle (*v.*) to look at with side glances. OGLE (*n.*) a side glance or look.

ogre (*n.*) a fairy-tale giant; a monster. (*fem.* OGRESS).

ohm (*n.*) a unit of electrical resistance. See appendix.

oil (*n.*) 1. a liquid fat. 2. a liquid mineral. OIL (*v.*) to put oil on moving machinery; to lubricate.

oiliness (*n.*) greasiness; slipperiness.

oilcloth (*n.*) a shiny, coated canvas fabric.

oilskin (*n.*) cloth waterproofed with oil. OILSKINS (*n. pl.*).

oily (*adj.*) containing oil; greasy.

ointment (*n.*) a greasy paste for healing or softening the skin.

old (*adj.*) 1. long existing; ancient. 2. worn; decayed.

olden (*adj.*) long past; ancient. OLD-FASHIONED (*adj.*).

olive (*n.*) 1. evergreen tree and its small, oily berries. OLIVE (*adj.*) yellowish-green.

olive-branch (*n.*) a symbol of peace.

Olympic (*adj.*) 1. of or at Olympia, Greece, and the games held there every four years. 2. about similar international games held in the present day.

omega (*n.*) last letter in Greek alphabet; the end.

omelet (*n.*) beaten eggs fried and folded over.

omen (*n.*) a sign of a future event; an augury.

ominous (*adj.*) foretelling misfortune; threatening. OMINOUSLY (*adv.*).

omission (*n.*) 1. something left out or not done. 2. careless neglect.

omit (*v.*) to leave out or undone; to exclude.

omnibus (*n.*) a bus; motor-coach. (*pl.* OMNIBUSES).

omnipotence (*n.*) infinite power; invincibility. OMNIPOTENT (*adj.*).

omniscience (*n.*) knowledge of everything. OMNISCIENT (*adj.*).

omnivorous (*adj.*) able to eat all kinds of food.

once (*adv.*) at one time; on one occasion.

one (*adj., n.* and *pron.*) any single person or thing; unity.

onerous (*adj.*) burdensome; heavy. ONEROUSLY (*adv.*).

onion (*n.*) an edible bulbous root.

onlooker (*n.*) a spectator; witness.

only (*adj.*) alone; by itself. ONLY (*adv.*) solely; singly. ONLY (*conj.*) but.

onset (*n.*) an attack; a hasty beginning.

onslaught (*n.*) an attack; assault.

onus (*n.*) the responsibility of proving or accomplishing something.

onward (*adj.*) forward; advanced.

onyx (*n.*) precious stone having colours in layers or streaks.

ooze (*n.*) slush; slime. OOZE (*v.*) to leak slowly; to sweat. OOZY (*adj.*).

opacity (*n.*) cloudiness; denseness.

opal (*n.*) precious stone which changes colour as light falls on it.

opaque (*adj.*) not transparent; dense.

open (*adj.*) 1. unshut; unhidden. 2. undefended. 3. sincere; frank. OPEN (*v.*) 1. to unclose; to unfasten. 2. to disclose; to reveal. 3. to begin; to start.

open-eyed (*adj.*) watchful; vigilant.

open-handed (*adj.*) generous; liberal.

open-hearted (*adj.*) candid; honest.

opening (*n.*) 1. a gap; an aperture. 2. a beginning; start in life. 3. an opportunity.

openly (*adv.*) in full view; publicly.

open-minded (*adj.*) fair; unbiassed.

opera (*n.*) a musical drama. OPERATIC (*adj.*).

operate (*v.*) 1. to make to work. 2. to give surgical treatment.

operation (*n.*) 1. an action; a performance. 2. surgical treatment.

operative (*adj.*) working; efficient. OPERATIVE (*n.*) a workman.

opiate (*n.*) medicine that soothes or sends to sleep.

opine (*v.*) to think; to suppose.

opinion (*n.*) a belief; what one thinks about something.

opinionated (*adj.*) cock-sure; conceited.

opium (*n.*) a sleep-causing drug.

opossum (*n.*) small, American, pouched animal.

opponent (*n.*) 1. a foe. 2. a rival; competitor.

opportune (*adj.*) just right; well-timed. OPPORTUNELY (*adv.*).

opportunist (*n.*) one who acts to suit himself.

opportunity (*n.*) a good chance; an opening.

oppose (*v.*) to be against; to resist. OPPOSER (*n.*).

opposite (*adj.*) 1. face to face. 2. entirely different. OPPOSITE (*n.*) the contrary.

opposition (*n.*) the antagonism; party of opponents.

oppress (*v.*) to treat severely; to overburden.

oppression (*n.*) severity; persecution.

oppressive (*adj.*) 1. severe; inhuman. 2. close; sultry.

oppressiveness (*n.*) closeness; sultriness.

oppressor (*n.*) a severe ruler; a persecutor.

optical (*adj.*) relating to eyesight and vision.

optician (*n.*) 1. an adviser on eyesight. 2. a maker of optical instruments.

optics (*n.*) study of light and vision.

optimism (*n.*) belief that all that happens is for the best.

optimist (*n.*) one who looks on the bright side. OPTIMISTIC (*adj.*).

option (*n.*) a choice. OPTIONAL (*adj.*).

opulence (*n.*) wealth; riches. OPULENT (*adj.*).

oracle (*n.*) 1. sacred place where Greek gods gave advice. 2. a wise person. ORACULAR (*adj.*).

oral (*adj.*) spoken; verbal. ORALLY (*adv.*).

orange (*n.*) a tree and its round, yellow fruit. ORANGE (*adj.*) reddish-yellow.

orang-outang (*n.*) large, long-armed ape.

oration (*n.*) a public speech; an address. ORATOR (*n.*).

oratorio (*n.*) a sacred dramatic musical composition.

oratory (*n.*) 1. a speaker's eloquence. 2. a small private chapel.

orb (*n.*) 1. a globe; sphere. 2. a symbol of sovereignty.

orbit (*n.*) the path in which a heavenly body moves.

orchard (*n.*) a fruit-garden.

orchestra (*n.*) 1. a band of musicians. 2. their place in a theatre.

orchestral (*adj.*) performed by an orchestra.

orchid (*n.*) tropical plant bearing huge flowers, often brilliantly coloured and fantastically shaped.

ordain (*v.*) 1. to order; to enact. 2. to admit to holy orders.

ordained (*adj.*) 1. settled; decided. 2. given authority as a minister.

ordeal (*n.*) a severe trial or experience.

order (*n.*) 1. a command. 2. a method; rule. 3. a grade; rank.

orderly (*adj.*) 1. well-arranged; methodical. 2. well-behaved.

ordinance (*n.*) a law; decree. Beware ORDNANCE.

ordinary (*adj.*) 1. usual; common. 2. plain; homely. ORDINARILY (*adv.*).

ordination (*n.*) the act of making a man a deacon or priest.

ordnance (*n.*) weapons of warfare, guns, etc. Beware ORDINANCE.

ore (*n.*) a mineral, or rock containing metal.

organ (*n.*) 1. a part of the body fitted to do special work. 2. a musical instrument.

organic (*adj.*) produced by living organs.

organism (*n.*) a living body.

organist (*n.*) an organ-player.

organization (*n.*) 1. a system; plan of work. 2. a society; business.

organize (*v.*) to arrange; to plan. ORGANIZER (*n.*).

orgy (*n.*) a riotous merrymaking. (*pl.* ORGIES).

oriel (*n.*) a projecting upper window.

Orient (*n.*) the East.

oriental (*adj.*) eastern. ORIENTAL (*n.*) inhabitant of an eastern country.

orifice (*n.*) 1. an opening; a hole. 2. a mouth; entrance.

origin (*n.*) a source; beginning.

original (*adj.*) first; new. ORIGINAL (*n.*) the first copy; the source. ORIGINALLY (*adv.*).

originality (*n.*) the newness; freshness.

originate (*v.*) 1. to cause to exist. 2. to invent; to devise.

origination (*n.*) the beginning; starting-point.

Orion (*n.*) 1. a great hunter famous in Greek legend. 2. bright constellation or group of stars named after him. See appendix.

orison (*n.*) a prayer; supplication.

ornament (*n.*) a decoration; adornment. ORNAMENT (*v.*) to adorn; to beautify.

ornamental (*adj.*) decorative. ORNAMENTALLY (*adv.*).

ornamentation (*n.*) a beautifying; an adorning.

ornate (*adj.*) richly decorated. ORNATELY (*adv.*).

ornateness (*n.*) richness; floridness.

orphan (*n.*) a child who has lost one or both parents.

orphanage (*n.*) a home for orphans.

orthodox (*adj.*) thinking or behaving as most people do.

orthodoxy (*n.*) obedience to the general rule.

orthography (*n.*) spelling.

oscillate (*v.*) to swing; to vibrate. OSCILLATORY (*adj.*).

oscillation (*n.*) a swing; variation.

ostensible (*adj.*) seemingly; pretended.

ostentation (*n.*) a rich display; pomp.

ostentatious (*adj.*) fond of display; showy. OSTENTATIOUSLY (*adv.*).

ostler (*n.*) a man in charge of horses.

ostrich (*n.*) large, swift-running African bird.

other (*adj.*) not the same; different. OTHER (*pron.*) other person or thing.

otherwise (*adv.*) in a different way. OTHERWISE (*conj.*) but for this; else.

otter (*n.*) furry, weasel-like, fish-eating animal.

ought (*v.*) to be compelled to do or say by duty, or by what one knows is right and proper.

ounce (*n.*) 1. an Imperial measure of weight. 2. a leopard-like animal.

our (*pron.*) belonging to us. When no noun is expressed, OURS is used, e.g. (*a*) This is OUR house. (*b*) These are OURS.

oust (*v.*) to turn out; to eject.

out (*adv.*) 1. not at home; or inside. 2. in foliage or bloom. 3. not in office or employment. 4. not in fashion. 5. not burning or lighted. 6. exhausted; finished. 7. in error. 8. to the end. OUT (*prep.*) forth from; outside of.

outbid (*v.*) to offer more than another.

outbreak (*n.*) a sudden bursting out.

outburst (*n.*) a breaking or rushing out, especially of sound; an explosion.

outcast (*n.*) an exile; a vagabond.

outcome (*n.*) a result; consequence.

outcry (*n.*) a sudden loud cry; a clamour. (*pl.* OUTCRIES).

outdo (*v.*) to excel; to surpass.

outfit (*n.*) 1. necessaries required by a ship, expedition, etc., for journey. 2. a set of tools, clothes, etc. OUTFIT (*v.*) to supply special needs; to equip. OUTFITTER (*n.*).

outflank (*v.*) to get the better of.

outgoing (*n.*) the expenditure.

outgrow (*v.*) to grow too big or too old for a thing; to surpass.

outing (*n.*) an excursion; a trip.

outlandish (*adj.*) unusual; strange.

outlaw (*n.*) a robber; bandit.

outlay (*n.*) the cost; expenditure.

outlet (*n.*) a way out; an exit.

outlive (*v.*) 1. to continue to live after another's death; to survive. 2. to exist as a thing of no further use or service; to encumber.

outlook (*n.*) the view; prospect.

outlying (*adj.*) distant; remote.

out-of-date (*adj.*) old-fashioned; dowdy.

outpost (*n.*) any position beyond a camp's boundaries, and the guard placed there.

output (*n.*) the quantity of goods made; the production.

outrage (*n.*) a shocking crime. OUTRAGE (*v.*) to shock; to offend.

outrageous (*adj.*) shocking; inexcusable.

outright (*adv.*) completely; at once.

outset (*n.*) the beginning.

outshine (*v.*) to excel in brightness or ability; to surpass.

outside (*n.*) the outer part.

outspoken (*adj.*) candid; frank.

outstanding (*adj.*) greatly above other persons or things in situation, ability, reputation, etc.

outstrip (*v.*) to outrun; to leave behind.

outward (*adj.*) 1. external. 2. on the surface; superficial.

outwit (*v.*) to beat by skill or cunning.

oval (*adj.*) egg-shaped.

ovation (*n.*) applause; a welcome.

oven (*n.*) brick, stone, or metal box or chamber for baking, heating, or drying any substance.

over (*prep.*) 1. across; from side to side. 2. above, in position, authority, value, etc. 3. more than. OVER (*adv.*) 1. on the opposite side. 2. from one to another. 3. more than required. 4. ended; finished. OVER (*adj.*) upper; covering. OVER (*n.*) one period of bowling in cricket.

overawe (*v.*) to frighten; to daunt.

overbearing (*adj.*) domineering; dictatorial.

overboard (*adv.*) out of, or over the side of a ship.

overcast (*adj.*) cloudy; threatening.

overcharge (*v.*) 1. to charge too much. 2. to load or burden with too much. OVERCHARGE (*n.*) the amount above the right price, load, etc.; excess.

overdue (*adj.*) past the time fixed for arrival, payment, etc.; late.

overflow (*v.*) 1. to flow over the edges or sides of a container. 2. to flood; to inundate. OVERFLOW (*n.*) 1. the excess; superabundance. 2. the flood; inundation.

overhaul (*v.*) 1. to overtake. 2. to examine and repair.

overlap (*v.*) to extend beyond the edge of something above or below; to overhang. OVERLAP (*n.*) the amount of extension beyond an edge or boundary.

overlook (*v.*) 1. to superintend. 2. to pass by; to pardon.

overpower (*v.*) to overcome; to vanquish. OVERPOWERING (*adj.*).

overseer (*n.*) a superintendent; supervisor.

oversight (*n.*) 1. a mistake; inadvertence. 2. the care; protection.

overstep (*v.*) to go too far; to exceed.

overthrow (*v.*) to destroy; to ruin. OVERTHROW (*n.*) defeat; destruction.

overture (*n.*) 1. an offer; invitation. 2. a musical prologue.

overturn (*v.*) 1. to upset; to turn upside down. 2. to defeat; to destroy.

overweening (*adj.*) vain; conceited.

overwhelm (*v.*) 1. to conquer; to defeat. 2. to flood; to sweep away.

overwrought (*adj.*) excited; overworked.

owe (*v.*) to be in debt.

owl (*n.*) a night bird of prey. OWLET (*n.*).

own (*v.*) 1. to possess. 2. to admit; to confess. 3. to acknowledge; to recognize. OWN (*adj.*) belonging to oneself.

ox (*n.*) the male of cattle. (*pl.* OXEN).

oxygen (*n.*) the life-supporting gas in the air.

oyster (*n.*) shellfish esteemed as food.

ozone (*n.*) a form of oxygen.

P

pace (*v.*) to walk step by step. PACE (*n.*) a step.

pacific (*adj.*) peaceful; calm.

pacification (*n.*) a peace-making; reconciliation.

pacifist (*n.*) an upholder of peace.

pacify (*v.*) to make calm; to soothe.

pack (*n.*) 1. a bundle. 2. a number of hounds. 3. a set of cards. PACK (*v.*) to crowd together; to compress.

package (*n.*) a bundle; parcel.

packet (*n.*) 1. a small package. 2. mail-boat. PACKET (*n.*).

pact (*n.*) an agreement; a treaty.

pad (*v.*) to stuff with soft material. PAD (*n.*) 1. small, soft cushion, or anything like such. 2. fleshy cushion forming sole of foot of some quadrupeds. 3. a writing- or drawing-block. 4. guard for parts of body in cricket, etc.

paddle (*n.*) short, wide-bladed oar. PADDLE (*v.*) 1. to propel with a paddle. 2. to row gently. 3. to wade.

paddock (*n.*) a small pasture.

padlock (*n.*) a detachable lock. PADLOCK (*v.*) to fasten with a padlock.

pagan (*adj.*) barbarian; heathen. PAGAN (*n.*) a heathen; idolator.

paganism (*n.*) heathenism; idolatry.

page (*n.*) 1. a boy attendant. 2. one side of a book-leaf.

pageant (*n.*) a colourful parade.

pageantry (*n.*) splendour; pomp.

pagoda (*n.*) Chinese sacred temple.

pail (*n.*) a bucket.

pain (*n.*) suffering. PAIN (*v.*) to cause suffering; to distress.

painful (*adj.*) 1. hurtful; sore. 2. toilsome; hard. PAINLESS (*adj.*).

painstaking (*adj.*) industrious; plodding.

paint (*n.*) oily liquid for colouring. PAINT (*v.*) 1. to coat with paint. 2. to make a picture.

painter (*n.*) 1. one who paints. 2. a rope for securing a boat.

painting (*n.*) a painted picture.

pair (*n.*) two like things; a couple. PAIR (*v.*) to unite; to join.

palace (*n.*) a magnificent house.

palatable (*adj.*) tasty; delicious.

palate (*n.*) 1. roof of the mouth. 2. sense of taste.

palatial (*adj.*) royal; like a palace.

palaver (*n.*) 1. idle talk. 2. a conference. PALAVER (*v.*) to confer.

pale (*adj.*) colourless; wan. PALE (*n.*) 1. a pointed stake. 2. a boundary. PALE (*v.*) to turn white; to fade.

palette (*n.*) thin board on which artist mixes colours.

palfrey (*n.*) small, gentle horse; a pony.

paling (*n.*) a fence of stakes.

palisade (*n.*) defensive fence built of stakes.

pall (*v.*) to weary; to bore. PALL (*n.*) 1. a coffin covering. 2. a priestly or royal mantle.

pallet (*n.*) a small bed.

palliate (*v.*) to cover up a fault; to excuse.

palliation (*n.*) an excuse; a cloak.

palliative (*n.*) a pain-relieving medicine. PALLIATIVE (*adj.*) soothing.

pallid (*adj.*) pale; wan.

pallor (*n.*) paleness.

palm (*n.*) 1. a tropical tree. 2. emblem of victory. 3. the flat of the hand. PALM (*v.*) to hide in the hand.

palmy (*adj.*) happy; prosperous.

palpable (*adj.*) actual; real. PALPABLY (*adv.*).

palpitate (*v.*) to beat rapidly; to throb.

palpitation (*n.*) a beating; quivering.

palsy (*n.*) numbness; paralysis. PALSIED (*adj.*).

palter (*v.*) to play with; to trifle with.

paltry (*adj.*) trifling; worthless.

pampas (*n.*) vast, grassy plains in South America.

pamper (*v.*) to spoil with too much kindness; to indulge. PAMPERED (*adj.*).

pamphlet (*n.*) a booklet.

pan (*n.*) 1. a shallow, metal vessel or container. 2. the god of nature. See appendix.

panacea (*n.*) a cure for all complaints.

pancake (*n.*) thin, flat cake fried in a pan.

pandemonium (*n.*) uproar; disorder.

pane (*n.*) a plate of glass.

panel (*n.*) 1. a thin sheet of wood. 2. a list of jurors.

panelling (*n.*) panelled work; wainscotting.

pang (*n.*) sudden shoot of pain; a throe.

panic (*n.*) wild fear; terror.

pannier (*n.*) a wicker basket.

panorama (*n.*) complete view in every direction.

pansy (*n.*) flower like a large violet.

pant (*v.*) 1. to gasp for breath. 2. to yearn for.

pantechnicon (*n.*) a furniture-removal van.

panther (*n.*) a leopard.

pantomime (*n.*) amusing stage play with nursery-rhyme characters.

pantry (*n.*) household foodstore. (*pl.* PANTRIES).

papacy (*n.*) the office and authority of the Pope. PAPAL (*adj.*).

paper (*n.*) material used for writing or printing on.

papyrus (*n.*) an Egyptian reed and the paper-like material made from it. (*pl.* PAPYRI).

par (*n.*) equality; a fixed sum or standard by which a gain or loss is measured.

parable (*n.*) a story which teaches a lesson.

parachute (*n.*) an appliance for descending from an aeroplane in flight. PARACHUTIST (*n.*).

parade (*n.*) 1. an assembly of troops, etc., for inspection. 2. a procession or marching for display. 3. a public promenade. PARADE (*v.*) 1. to muster. 2. to walk slowly up and down.

paradise (*n.*) 1. the Garden of Eden. 2. happiness; bliss.

paraffin (*n.*) an oil distilled from coal and shale used as illuminant, fuel, lubricant, and in making candle-wax.

paragon (*n.*) a perfect example; a model.

paragraph (*n.*) 1. a distinct passage in any book or writing. 2. a newspaper item.

parallel (*adj.*) 1. alike; similar. 2. the same distance apart; equidistant. PARALLEL (*n.*) 1. a line marking latitude. 2. a likeness; similarity. 3. a line equidistant from another.

parallelogram (*n.*) a quadrilateral having its opposite sides parallel.

paralyse (*v.*) to make powerless.

paralysis (*n.*) malady causing inability to speak or move.

paramount (*adj.*) first; chief.

parapet (*n.*) a low protecting wall.

paraphernalia (*n.*) belongings of all kinds.

parasite (*n.*) animal, or plant, living upon another.

parasol (*n.*) a sunshade.

parcel (*n.*) a bundle; package. PARCEL (*v.*) to divide into parts.

parch (*v.*) to scorch; to shrivel. PARCHED (*adj.*).

parchment (*n.*) skin, dried and prepared for writing on.

pardon (*v.*) to forgive; to set free. PARDON (*n.*) forgiveness; release. PARDONER (*n.*).

pardonable (*adj.*) permissible; excusable. PARDONABLY (*adv.*).

pare (*v.*) to cut off a little; to trim.

parent (*n.*) a father or mother. PARENTAL (*adj.*).

parentage (*n.*) forefathers; ancestors.

pariah (*n.*) an outcast; a vagabond.

paring (*n.*) a clipping; shaving.

parish (*n.*) 1. a local government district.

2. a district ministered to by a clergyman.

parishioner (*n.*) one living in a parish.

parity (*n.*) equality.

parley (*v.*) to discuss peace terms. PARLEY (*n.*) a meeting to settle a dispute.

parliament (*n.*) a supreme, lawmaking council. PARLIAMENTARY (*adj.*).

parlour (*n.*) family sitting-room.

parochial (*adj.*) concerning a parish; narrow-minded.

parody (*n.*) a comical imitation; a burlesque. PARODY (*v.*) to imitate humorously; to mock. PARODIST (*n.*).

parole (*n.*) a word of honour; an unbreakable promise.

parrot (*n.*) gay-feathered bird able to talk. PARROT (*v.*) to repeat words without understanding them.

parry (*v.*) to turn a blow aside; to evade.

parsimonious (*adj.*) miserly; frugal.

parsimony (*n.*) meanness; frugality.

parsley (*n.*) a garden herb.

parsnip (*n.*) vegetable with edible root.

parson (*n.*) a clergyman.

parsonage (*n.*) a parson's residence.

part (*v.*) 1. to separate. 2. to divide. PART (*n.*) 1. a portion; share. 2. character in a play; a rôle. PARTLY (*adv.*).

partake (*v.*) to take part in; to share. PARTAKER (*n.*).

partial (*adj.*) 1. incomplete. 2. favouring; biassed.

partiality (*n.*) a liking for; one-sidedness.

participant (*n.*) a sharer; partaker.

participate (*v.*) to share with others. PARTICIPATION (*n.*).

particle (*n.*) a speck; an atom.

participle (*n.*) a verbal adjective which can also indicate tense and govern an object.

particular (*n.*) a small thing; an item. PARTICULAR (*adj.*) 1. distinct; special. 2. careful; faddy.

particularly (*adv.*) especially; one by one.

partisan (*n.*) a supporter of a party or cause; a disciple.

partition (*v.*) to divide into compartments. PARTITION (*n.*) a screen; a dividing-wall.

partly (*adv.*) to some extent; in parts.

partner (*n.*) 1. person who shares another's work; an associate. 2. a husband or wife.

partnership (*n.*) an association; co-operation.

partridge (*n.*) a grey game-bird.

party (*n.*) 1. a body of people with same interests. 2. a merry-making. (*pl.* PARTIES).

pass (*v.*) 1. to go onward or by. 2. to succeed in an examination. PASS (*n.*) 1. a passage through mountains. 2. an admission-ticket.

passable (*adj.*) 1. can be crossed. 2. fairly good.

passage (*n.*) 1. a narrow lane; corridor. 2. a voyage; journey.

pass-book (*n.*) a bank-book.

passenger (*n.*) a traveller by train, ship, etc.

passion (*n.*) 1. suffering. 2. strong feeling; emotion.

passionate (*adj.*) emotional; enthusiastic.

passive (*adj.*) quiet; submissive.

passport (*n.*) document permitting travel in a foreign country.

password (*n.*) a secret word marking friend from foe.

past (*adj.*) gone; spent. PAST (*n.*) the time already gone.

paste (*n.*) 1. a sticky mixture of flour and water. 2. dough. 3. an artificial gem. PASTE (*v.*) to stick with paste.

paste-board (*n.*) a stiff, thick paper.

pastel (*n.*) a coloured chalk; a drawing in chalk or crayon. PASTEL (*adj.*) a pale shade or colour.

pastime (*n.*) a sport; recreation.

pastor (*n.*) a minister of a church.

pastoral (*adj.*) concerning rural life. PASTORAL (*n.*) a poem about country life.

pastry (*n.*) dough, rolled out and baked; pies and tarts. (*pl.* PASTRIES).

pasture (*n.*) grassland; herbage. PASTURE (*v.*) to graze cattle. PASTURAGE (*n.*).

pat (*n.*) 1. a light touch. 2. a small piece; lump. PAT (*v.*) to hit or touch lightly. PAT (*adj.*) quick; apt.

patch (*n.*) 1. material used to mend a hole. 2. a small plot of land. PATCH (*v.*) to mend; to cobble.

patchwork (*n.*) 1. work made of bits of vari-coloured cloth. 2. a clumsy piece of work.

patchy (*adj.*) 1. having patches. 2.

clumsy; slipshod. 3. sometimes good, sometimes poor or bad.

pate (*n.*) top of the head.

paten (*n.*) plate used for consecrated bread.

patent (*adj.*) plain; evident. PATENT (*n.*) a right given an inventor to prevent anyone using his invention without payment. PATENT (*v.*) to obtain a patent.

patently (*adv.*) obviously; unmistakably.

paternal (*adj.*) 1. fatherly. 2. related through one's father.

paternity (*n.*) being a father; fatherhood.

path (*n.*) 1. a track. 2. a trodden way. PATHLESS (*adj.*).

pathologist (*n.*) a specialist in diseases.

pathology (*n.*) study of disease.

pathos (*n.*) a feeling of sympathy; pity.

pathway (*n.*) a footway; track.

patience (*n.*) ability to endure or wait without discontent.

patient (*adj.*) enduring; uncomplaining. PATIENT (*n.*) one receiving medical treatment. PATIENTLY (*adv.*).

patly (*adv.*) fitly; aptly.

patriarch (*n.*) 1. founder or father of a tribe. 2. a respected old man. PATRIARCHAL (*adj.*).

patrician (*n.*) a nobleman.

patriot (*n.*) one who loves his country. PATRIOTIC (*adj.*).

patriotism (*n.*) love of country; loyalty.

patrol (*v.*) to walk round on watch; to protect. PATROL (*n.*) a person or body marching round on watch.

patron (*n.*) 1. a supporter; helper. 2. a customer.

patronage (*n.*) support; encouragement.

patronize (*v.*) 1. to help; to encourage. 2. to act as though doing a favour.

patronizing (*adj.*) 1. helping. 2. acting in a favouring manner; condescending.

patter (*n.*) 1. sound of raindrops or running feet. 2. glib talk. PATTER (*v.*) 1. to sound like raindrops. 2. to talk glibly. PATTERING (*adj.*).

pattern (*n.*) 1. an example; a model. 2. a sample specimen. 3. a design to copy.

patty (*n.*) a little pie. (*pl.* PATTIES).

paucity (*n.*) a fewness; scantiness.

pauper (*n.*) a poor person.

pauperism (*n.*) poverty; need.

pauperize (*v.*) to make poor; to ruin.

pause (*v.*) to rest for a time; to stop. PAUSE (*n.*) a short rest; an interval.

pave (*v.*) 1. to cover with flat stones. 2. to prepare; to smoothe.

pavement (*n.*) a paved footway.

pavilion (*n.*) 1. a large tent. 2. a club-house.

paw (*n.*) an animal's clawed foot. PAW (*v.*) 1. to scrape with the forefoot. 2. to handle clumsily; to maul.

pawl (*n.*) a short bar which prevents a wheel running back.

pawn (*v.*) to pledge; to give as security for a loan. PAWN (*n.*) a chess-piece of lowest value.

pawnbroker (*n.*) one who lends money on goods pledged.

pay (*v.*) 1. to give money in return for goods bought, or work done; to remunerate. 2. to suffer for neglect or misdoing. 3. to discharge one's debts; to requite. PAY (*n.*) wages; salary.

payable (*adj.*) must be paid; justly due.

payment (*n.*) 1. the sum paid; settlement. 2. the punishment.

pea (*n.*) plant and the round seed that grows in its pod.

peace (*n.*) freedom from war or disturbance; concord.

peaceable (*adj.*) peace-loving; undisturbed. PEACEABLY (*adv.*).

peaceful (*adj.*) calm; quiet. PEACEFULLY (*adv.*).

peach (*n.*) tree and its soft, round, stoned fruit.

peacock (*n.*) bird with a long, gay, spreading tail. (*fem.* PEAHEN).

peak (*n.*) 1. pointed top of a hill or mountain. 2. the highest point. 3. the brim of a cap. PEAK (*v.*) to waste away.

peaked (*adj.*) 1. pointed. 2. looking ill.

peaky (*adj.*) pale; sickly.

peal (*n.*) 1. clang of bells. 2. roll of thunder. PEAL (*v.*) 1. to clang; to resound. 2. to thunder; to roll.

peanut (*n.*) ground-nut; monkey-nut.

pear (*n.*) tree and its pointed, juicy fruit.

pearl (*n.*) smooth, round gem made by an oyster. PEARLY (*adj.*).

peasant (*n.*) a farm-worker; countryman.

peasantry (*n.*) the countryfolk; farm-workers.

peat (*n.*) turf cut from bogland and used as fuel. PEATY (*adj.*).

pebble (*n.*) a tiny, round stone. PEBBLY (*adj.*).

peccadillo (*n.*) a slight offence; a naughtiness. (*pl.* PECCADILLOES).

peck (*n.*) 1. poke from a bird's beak. 2. an Imperial measure of capacity (two gallons). PECK (*v.*) 1. to strike with the beak; to jab. 2. to nibble at food.

peckish (*adj.*) hungry.

peculiar (*adj.*) 1. strange; unusual. 2. belonging specially to oneself; personal. PECULIARLY (*adv.*).

peculiarity (*n.*) 1. a strangeness; curiosity. 2. a personal habit; mannerism. (*pl.* PECULIARITIES).

pecuniary (*adj.*) relating to money.

pedagogue (*n.*) a schoolmaster. PEDAGOGIC (*adj.*).

pedal (*v.*) to work with the foot. PEDAL (*n.*) bar or lever pressed by the foot. PEDAL (*adj.*) relating to, or operated by, the foot.

pedant (*n.*) a lover of extreme accuracy.

pedantic (*adj.*) too precise. PEDANTICALLY (*adv.*).

peddle (*v.*) to go from place to place selling goods; to hawk.

peddlar or **pedlar** (*n.*) a hawker.

pedestal (*n.*) a stand at the base of a column or statue.

pedestrian (*n.*) a walker. PEDESTRIAN (*adj.*) 1. going on foot. 2. dull; slow.

pedigree (*n.*) descent; a list of ancestors.

peel (*n.*) 1. the rind of many fruits. 2. a fortified tower. PEEL (*v.*) to strip off the rind or skin.

peeling (*n.*) a piece stripped off.

peep (*v.*) 1. to look at slyly or cautiously. 2. to look at through an opening. PEEP (*n.*) 1. a quick or sly look. 2. a first appearance. 3. a chick's cry.

peeping (*adj.*) looking at slyly or secretly.

peer (*n.*) 1. an equal. 2. a nobleman. (*fem.* PEERESS). PEER (*v.*) to look at intently.

peerage (*n.*) the whole body of nobles.

peerless (*adj.*) unequalled; unmatched.

peevish (*adj.*) fretful; snappish. PEEVISHLY (*adv.*).

peevishness (*n.*) fretfulness; irritability.

peewit (*n.*) the lapwing. Also PEWIT.

peg (*n.*) 1. a wooden spike. 2. a clothes clip. PEG (*v.*) to fasten with a peg; to clip.

pelican (*n.*) large water-bird having a pouch beneath its bill.

pellet (*n.*) a tiny ball; pill.

pell-mell (*adj.*) headlong; in confusion.

pelt (*n.*) a hide; skin. PELT (*v.*) 1. to attack by throwing things at; to bombard. 2. to fall heavily like rain.

pelting (*adj.*) pouring down heavily.

pen (*n.*) 1. enclosure for animals; a pinfold. 2. an instrument for writing. PEN (*v.*) 1. to shut in; to coop. 2. to write; to compose.

penal (*adj.*) relating to punishment.

penalize (*v.*) 1. to punish. 2. to handicap.

penalty (*n.*) a punishment; fine. (*pl.* PENALTIES).

penance (*n.*) punishment suffered in order to gain forgiveness.

pence (*n. pl.*) pennies, or their amount in value.

pencil (*n.*) instrument for writing or drawing. PENCIL (*v.*) to write or draw with a pencil. PENCILLED (*adj.*).

pendant (*n.*) ornament hanging from a necklet, or bracelet.

pendent (*adj.*) dangling; suspended.

pending (*adj.*) awaiting; undecided.

pendulum (*n.*) swinging weight which regulates a clock.

penetrate (*v.*) 1. to pass through; to pierce. 2. to enter one's mind.

penetrating (*adj.*) 1. piercing. 2. wise; shrewd.

penetration (*n.*) 1. a piercing. 2. sharpness; intelligence.

penguin (*n.*) Antarctic bird which swims but cannot fly.

penicillin (*n.*) a drug which quickly kills the germs of many diseases.

peninsula (*n.*) piece of land almost an island. THE PENINSULA, Spain and Portugal.

peninsular (*adj.*) concerning a peninsula.

penitence (*n.*) sorrow for wrongdoing; remorse.

penitent (*adj.*) sorry; regretful. PENITENTLY (*adv.*).

penitential (*adj.*) sorrowful; remorseful.

penknife (*n.*) a small pocket-knife.

penmanship (*n.*) 1. the art of writing. 2. kind or style of writing.

pennant (*n.*) a long, narrow flag.

penniless (*adj.*) very poor; without money.

pennon (*n.*) a short, pointed flag.

Penny, new (*n.*) decimal coin worth 1/100 of a £.

penny (*n.*) to 1971 a bronze coin worth 1/12 of a shilling.

pennyweight (*n.*) unit of Troy Weight (24 grains).

pennyworth (*n.*) what can be got for one penny.

pension (*n.*) an allowance paid regularly for past services. PENSIONER (*n.*).

pensionable (*adj.*) carrying a pension.

pensive (*adj.*) thoughtful; dreamy. PEN-SIVELY (*adv.*).

pentagon (*n.*) a five-sided figure. PEN-TAGONAL (*adj.*).

Pentecost (*n.*) 1. Jewish harvest festival of fiftieth day after the Passover. 2. the Christian Whitsuntide.

penurious (*adj.*) miserly; niggardly.

penury (*n.*) need; poverty.

peony (*n.*) plant with large flowers. See appendix.

people (*n.*) human beings; the populace. PEOPLE (*v.*) to provide with inhabitants; settlers.

pepper (*n.*) plant whose seeds are ground into a hot spice. PEPPER (*v.*) to season with pepper. PEPPERY (*adj.*).

peppercorn (*n.*) a pepper-berry or seed.

peppermint (*n.*) plant and its pungent oil.

peradventure (*adv.*) by chance; perhaps.

perambulate (*v.*) to walk around; to ramble. PERAMBULATION (*n.*).

perambulator (*n.*) a baby-carriage. (*abbrev.* PRAM).

perceive (*v.*) 1. to see; to observe. 2. to know; to understand.

perceptible (*adj.*) 1. noticeable; visible. 2. understandable.

perception (*n.*) 1. recognition; sight. 2. understanding; discernment.

perceptive (*adj.*) 1. observant. 2. understanding.

perch (*n.*) 1. an Imperial measure of land (5½ yards). 2. bird's rest-bar. 3. a spiny-finned fish. PERCH (*v.*) to rest upon; to roost.

perchance (*adv.*) perhaps.

percussion (*n.*) a blow; collision.

percussive (*adj.*) hitting; colliding.

perdition (*n.*) extreme misery and ruin.

peregrinate (*v.*) to travel about; to wander through.

peregrination (*n.*) a tour; journey.

peremptory (*adj.*) spoken firmly, or with decision.

perennial (*adj.*) living long. PERENNIAL (*n.*) a long-lived plant.

perfect (*adj.* pron. PER-fect) 1. excellent; faultless. 2. completed. PERFECT (*v.* pron. per-FECT) to complete; to make excellent.

perfection (*n.*) excellence; faultlessness.

perfectly (*adv.*) totally; without mistake.

perfidy (*n.*) disloyalty; treachery. PER-FIDIOUS (*adj.*).

perforate (*v.*) to pierce with holes; to punch. PERFORATED (*adj.*).

perforation (*n.*) a punched or drilled hole.

perforce (*adv.*) by force; of necessity.

perform (*v.*) 1. to do; to achieve. 2. to act or sing on a stage.

performance (*n.*) 1. an action; achievement. 2. an exhibition; production. PERFORMER (*n.*).

performing (*adj.*) trained to act.

perfume (*n.*) a pleasing smell; scent. PERFUME (*v.*) to give out a sweet smell.

perfumed (*adj.*) fragrant; scented.

perfumer (*n.*) a maker or seller of perfumes.

perfumery (*n.*) scents of every kind.

perfunctory (*adj.*) careless; easy-going.

perhaps (*adv.*) maybe; possibly.

peril (*n.*) a danger; risk.

perilous (*adj.*) dangerous; risky. PERIL-OUSLY (*adv.*).

perimeter (*n.*) the boundary and its measurement; the circumference.

period (*n.*) 1. an interval of time. 2. a full stop.

periodical (*adj.*) happening at intervals; systematic. PERIODICAL (*n.*) a magazine; journal.

periscope (*n.*) a mirror instrument used in submarines to see objects above water.

perish (*v.*) 1. to die; to expire. 2. to decay; to wither.

perishable (*adj.*) 1. destructible; mortal. 2. likely to spoil.

periwinkle (*n.*) 1. edible shellfish. 2. flowering plant.

perjure (*v.*) to give false evidence on oath. PERJURED (*adj.*).

perjurer (*n.*) giver of false witness; an oath-breaker.

perjury (*n.*) false witness; oath-breaking.

perk (*v.*) 1. to push the head forward saucily. 2. to trim; to smarten oneself.

perkiness (*n.*) cheekiness; sauce. PERKY (*adj.*). PERKILY (*adv.*).

permanency (*n.*) endurance; constancy.

permanent (*adj.*) lasting; enduring. PERMANENTLY (*adv.*).

permeate (*v.*) to soak into; to saturate. PERMEATION (*n.*).

permissible (*adj.*) allowed; lawful. PERMISSIBLY (*adv.*).

permission (*n.*) leave; consent.

permit (*v.*) to let; to allow. PERMIT (*n.*) a pass; passport.

pernicious (*adj.*) destructive; injurious.

perpendicular (*adj.*) upright; vertical.

perpetrate (*v.*) to do unlawfully; to be guilty.

perpetration (*n.*) a wrong-doing; crime.

perpetrator (*n.*) a wrong-doer.

perpetual (*adj.*) unending; everlasting.

perpetuate (*v.*) to make remembered for ever; to preserve.

perplex (*v.*) to puzzle; to bewilder. PERPLEXING (*adj.*).

perplexity (*n.*) puzzlement; bewilderment. (*pl.* PERPLEXITIES).

persecute (*v.*) to ill-treat; to torment. PERSECUTED (*aaj.*). PERSECUTOR (*n.*).

persecution (*n.*) ill-treatment; oppression.

perseverance (*n.*) steadfastness; persistence.

persevere (*v.*) to persist; to strive.

persist (*v.*) to last; to continue firm.

persistence (*n.*) endurance; doggedness. PERSISTENT (*adj.*).

person (*n.*) a human being; an individual.

personable (*adj.*) well-built; good-looking.

personage (*n.*) a notable person.

personal (*adj.*) one's own; private.

personality (*n.*) 1. character; behaviour. 2. an important person. (*pl.* PERSONALITIES).

personnel (*n. pl.*) employees; staff.

perspective (*n.*) a method of drawing which gives a correct idea of distance, and of the relation in size of one object to another.

perspire (*v.*) to sweat. PERSPIRATION (*n.*).

persuade (*v.*) to lead another to agree with oneself; to sway.

persuasion (*n.*) ability to win another's agreement.

persuasive (*adj.*) influencing; winning. PERSUASIVELY (*adv.*).

pert (*adj.*) impudent; saucy. PERTLY (*adv.*).

pertain (*v.*) to belong to; to be part of.

pertinacious (*adj.*) stubborn; unshakable. PERTINACIOUSLY (*adv.*).

pertinacity (*n.*) determination; obstinacy.

pertinency (*n.*) fitness; suitability.

pertinent (*adj.*) concerned with; to the point.

pertness (*n.*) rudeness; impudence.

perturb (*v.*) to upset; to disquiet. PERTURBING (*adj.*).

perturbation (*n.*) worry; anxiety.

peruse (*v.*) to read; to study. PERUSAL (*n.*).

pervade (*v.*) to fill; to saturate. PERVADING (*adj.*).

pervasion (*n.*) a filling; an overspreading.

perverse (*adj.*) wayward; naughty. PERVERSELY (*adv.*).

perversion (*n.*) a change for the worse.

perversity (*n.*) contrariness; naughtiness.

pervert (*v.*) to misuse; to use wrongly. PERVERTED (*adj.*).

pessimism (*n.*) a readiness to see the worst side of things.

pessimist (*n.*) a gloomy, despondent person.

pessimistic (*adj.*) glum; dismal. PESSIMISTICALLY (*adv.*).

pest (*n.*) a nuisance; an annoyance. THE PEST, plague; pestilence.

pester (*v.*) to worry; to annoy.

pestiferous (*adj.*) disease-bringing; infectious.

pestilence (*n.*) an epidemic; plague.

pestilent (*adj.*) tormenting; vexing. PESTILENTIAL (*adj.*).

pet (*n.*) a loved child or animal; a favourite. PET (*v.*) to fondle; to caress.

petal (*n.*) the leaf of a flower, or corolla.

petition (*n.*) 1. a prayer; entreaty. 2. a written request to a sovereign or parliament.

petitioner (*n.*) one who prays or asks.

petrel (*n.*) strong-winged sea-bird that seems to walk on the water. See appendix.

petrified (*adj.*) 1. turned to stone. 2. amazed; stupefied.

petrify (*v.*) 1. to turn to stone. 2. to paralyse with terror.

petrol (*n.*) refined petroleum; motor-fuel.

petroleum (*n.*) a mineral-oil; rock-oil.

pettifogging (*adj.*) paltry; worthless.

pettiness (*n.*) littleness; paltriness.

petty (*adj.*) trivial; unimportant. PETTILY (*adv.*).

petulance (*n.*) peevishness; impatience. PETULANT (*adj.*).

pew (*n.*) a seat in church.

pewit (*n.*) a small bird so named from its cry; the lapwing. Also PEEWIT.

pewter (*n.*) a dull metal composed of tin and lead.

phantom (*n.*) an apparition; a ghost.

pharmacist (*n.*) one who makes up medicines; a chemist.

pharmacy (*n.*) 1. the work of preparing medicines. 2. a chemist's shop.

phase (*n.*) one of the stages a growing thing passes through.

pheasant (*n.*) a woodland game-bird.

phenomenal (*adj.*) remarkable; miraculous. PHENOMENALLY (*adv.*).

phenomenon (*n.*) a rare event; a marvel. (*pl.* PHENOMENA).

phial (*n.*) a small glass flask; a vial.

philanthropic (*adj.*) humane; charitable. PHILANTHROPICALLY (*adv.*).

philanthropist (*n.*) one eager to help others.

philanthropy (*n.*) kindness; benevolence.

philatelist (*n.*) a postage-stamp collector.

philately (*n.*) postage-stamp collecting. PHILATELIC (*adj.*).

philharmonic (*adj.*) music-loving.

philologist (*n.*) a student of philology.

philology (*n.*) study of languages, their nature and history.

philosopher (*n.*) a student of philosophy; a thinker.

philosophic (*adj.*) 1. wise; reasoning. 2. cool; calm.

philosophize (*v.*) to think about things; to reason.

philosophy (*n.*) love of wisdom and knowledge. (*pl.* PHILOSOPHIES).

phlegm (*n.*) 1. a substance coughed up from the throat. 2. coolness; indifference.

phlegmatic (*adj.*) 1. unfeeling; cold-blooded. 2. slow; dull.

phœnix (*n.*) a fabled bird which burnt itself to ashes, then rose again to a new life.

phon (*n.*) unit of the loudness of sound.

'phone (*n. & v. abbrev.*) telephone.

phonograph (*n.*) early form of gramophone.

phosphorescent (*adj.*) glowing without heat.

phosphorus (*n.*) waxy substance that glows without giving heat.

phot (*n.*) a measure of the brightness of light.

photo (*n. & v. abbrev.*) photograph.

photograph (*n.*) a picture taken by a camera. PHOTOGRAPHER (*n.*).

photography (*n.*) the work of taking photographs. PHOTOGRAPHIC (*adj.*).

phrase (*n.*) a part of a sentence. PHRASE (*v.*) to express a thought grammatically.

physic (*n.*) medicine; remedies.

physical (*adj.*) 1. relating to the body. 2. according to the laws of nature.

physically (*adv.*) 1. bodily; visibly. 2. naturally.

physician (*n.*) a skilled healer; a doctor.

physics (*n. pl.*) the study of natural forces.

physique (*n.*) a person's bodily build and fitness.

pianist (*n.*) a piano player.

piano (*n. abbrev.*) pianoforte. PIANO (*adj.*) soft; gentle.

pianoforte (*n.*) instrument giving music from wires struck by hammers.

pianola (*n.*) a piano which plays automatically.

piccalilli (*n.*) pickle of chopped vegetables and spices.

piccaninny (*n.*) a negro baby.

piccolo (*n.*) a small, shrill flute.

pick (*v.*) 1. to choose; to select. 2. to pluck; to collect. 3. to use a pickaxe; to peck. PICK (*n.*) 1. a choice; selection. 2. a tool for breaking hard ground.

picket (*n.*) 1. a guard; sentry. 2. a pointed peg. PICKET (*v.*) 1. to place on guard duty. 2. to tie up a horse; to tether.

pickle (v.) to preserve in brine or other liquid. PICKLE (n.) 1. food preserved in liquid. 2. a predicament; a plight.

pickup (n.) a device that changes sounds into electric signals; a microphone.

picnic (n.) an outdoor meal on a pleasure excursion.

pictorial (adj.) illustrated by pictures.

picture (n.) 1. a painting; photograph. 2. a vivid description.

picturesque (adj.) 1. beautiful, like a picture. 2. vivid, like a description.

picture-tube (n.) the image-forming tube in a television receiver.

pie (n.) a dish of fruit or meat cooked in pastry.

piebald (adj.) marked with white and black; streaked.

piece (n.) a part; bit. PIECE (v.) to put parts together to make a whole.

piecemeal (adj.) made of pieces. PIECE-MEAL (adv.) little by little; in pieces.

pied (adj.) of various colours; variegated.

pier (n.) 1. a landing-place or promenade built out to sea. 2. a bridge or arch support.

pierce (v.) 1. to bore through; to puncture. 2. to offend the ears; to go through one.

piercing (adj.) 1. penetrating. 2. shrill. 3. cold; bitter. PIERCINGLY (adv.).

piety (n.) obedience to God's will; devotion.

pig (n.) a hog; swine.

pigeon (n.) a bird which coos; a dove.

pigeon-hole (n.) small division in a cabinet for storing papers. PIGEON-HOLE (v.) to put aside and forget.

pig-headed (adj.) stubborn; perverse. PIGHEADEDNESS (n.).

pig-iron (n.) impure iron melted from ore in a furnace; cast iron.

pigment (n.) a paint which colours the surface.

pigmented (adj.) coloured.

pigtail (n.) a long plait of hair.

pike (n.) 1. a lance; spear. 2. a fierce freshwater fish.

pikelet (n.) a light, thin cake; a crumpet.

pilchard (n.) small sea-fish of herring family.

pile (v.) to heap up; to amass. PILE (n.) 1. a heap; mound. 2. a large building.

3. a pointed post. 4. surface of a fabric; nap.

pilfer (v.) to steal trifles. PILFERER (n.).

pilgrim (n.) person who visits a holy place, or shrine.

pilgrimage (n.) a pilgrim's journey.

pill (n.) medicine made up in a tiny ball; pellet.

pillage (v.) to plunder; to loot. PILLAGE (n.) the plunder taken. PILLAGER (n.).

pillar (n.) an upright post; a column.

pillar-box (n.) short, usually hollow structure for receiving letters.

pillion (n.) seat behind the saddle on horse or bicycle.

pillory (n.) wooden frame having holes to hold the head and hands of a wrong-doer. PILLORY (v.) to lock in the pillory; to expose to shame.

pillow (n.) a cushion for the head. PILLOW (v.) to rest the head upon.

pilot (n.) one who steers a ship or flies an aeroplane; a guide. PILOT (v.) to guide; to direct. PILOTED (adj.).

pilotless (adj.) 1. unguided; lost. 2. needing no pilot.

pimpernel (n.) small scarlet flower.

pimple (n.) a tiny, hard swelling. PIMPLY (adj.).

pin (n.) short, pointed piece of wire for fastening papers, etc. PIN (v.) to fasten with a pin.

pinafore (n.) a child's apron.

pincers (n. pl.) tool with jaws for gripping.

pinch (v.) 1. to nip; to squeeze between. 2. to live sparingly. PINCH (n.) 1. a nip; sharp squeeze. 2. a tiny amount. 3. an emergency; a crisis.

pine (n.) evergreen, cone-bearing tree. PINE (v.) 1. to long for; to yearn. 2. to waste away; to languish.

pine-apple (n.) tropical plant and its juicy fruit.

pinhole (n.) hole made by a pin's point.

pinion (n.) 1. a bird's wing. 2. a small, toothed wheel. PINION (v.) to bind a person's arms, or a bird's wings.

pink (n.) 1. a garden flower. 2. a pale red colour. 3. good health. PINK (v.) to pierce; to puncture. PINK (adj.) pale red.

pinnace (n.) a ship's small boat.

pinnacle (*n.*) 1. a slender, pointed turret. 2. a spire. 3. a high point; summit.

pin-prick (*n.*) an annoyance; irritation.

pint (*n.*) an Imperial measure of capacity (⅛ gallon).

pioneer (*n.*) first who explores a new land, or tries a new method. PIONEER (*v.*) to lead the way.

pious (*adj.*) righteous; devout. PIOUSLY (*adv.*).

pip (*n.*) a fruit-seed.

pipe (*n.*) 1. a tube. 2. tube-like musical instrument. 3. bowl with a hollow stem for smoking tobacco. PIPE (*v.*) 1. to fill from a pipe. 2. to cry out or whistle shrilly.

piping (*n.*) 1. system of pipes laid in a building. 2. sound of pipes playing.

pippin (*n.*) a kind of apple.

piquancy (*n.*) 1. a sharp flavour; tartness. 2. keen wit.

piquant (*adj.*) 1. sharp; tart. 2. witty; sparkling.

pique (*n.*) a feeling of hurt pride; resentment. PIQUE (*v.*) to displease; to nettle.

piqued (*adj.*) hurt in feelings; resentful.

piracy (*n.*) robbing on the sea.

pirate (*n.*) a sea-robber; buccaneer. PIRATICAL (*adj.*).

pirouette (*n.*) a whirl round on the toes.

pistil (*n.*) part of a flower which produces seeds.

pistol (*n.*) small gun fired from one hand.

piston (*n.*) round plug fitting exactly into a tube or cylinder.

piston-rod (*n.*) rod which slides a piston to and fro in a cylinder.

pit (*n.*) 1. a deep hole in the ground. 2. ground floor of a theatre. PIT (*v.*) to mark with shallow holes; to indent.

pitch (*v.*) 1. to hurl. 2. to fling headlong. 3. to rise and fall on waves. 4. to cover with pitch. 5. to erect tents; to encamp. PITCH (*n.*) 1. boiled tar. 2. a headlong tumble. 3. a throw; cast. 4. ground used by games' players, campers, etc. 5. keynote in music.

pitcher (*n.*) 1. a thrower; bowler. 2. an urn-shaped vessel.

pitching (*n.*) 1. bowling. 2. up and down motion of a ship or aircraft.

pitchfork (*n.*) 1. long-handled fork for lifting hay, etc. 2. a tuning-fork.

piteous (*adj.*) 1. arousing pity, sorrowful. 2. showing pity; compassionate. PITEOUSLY (*adv.*).

pitfall (*n.*) a hidden pit to entrap animals; a trap.

pith (*n.*) 1. spongy substance in many plant stems. 2. the real or important matter.

pithily (*adv.*) briefly; pointedly.

pitiable (*adj.*) deserving pity. PITIABLY (*adv.*).

pitiful (*adj.*) 1. moved by sorrow; humane. 2. deserving scorn; trivial; miserable.

pitiless (*adj.*) hard-hearted; merciless. PITILESSLY (*adv.*).

pittance (*n.*) a small allowance; a little.

pitted (*adj.*) marked with shallow holes; indented.

pity (*n.*) 1. a feeling of sympathy; compassion. PITY (*v.*) to feel sorry for; to offer kindness; comfort.

pityingly (*adv.*) tenderly; compassionately.

pivot (*n.*) short, pointed support on which a compass-needle or other body rotates. PIVOT (*v.*) to place or rotate on a pivot. PIVOTED (*adj.*).

pixy (*n.*) a fairy; an elf. (*pl.* PIXIES).

placable (*adj.*) 1. can be soothed; pacified. 2. willing to forgive.

placard (*n.*) a large notice; a poster. PLACARD (*v.*) to post up in a public place; to advertise.

place (*n.*) 1. a particular spot. 2. a locality, town, etc. 3. a job; position. PLACE (*v.*) 1. to put in a special spot. 2. to appoint; to fix. 3. to recognize; to remember.

placid (*adj.*) calm; unruffled. PLACIDLY (*adv.*).

placidity (*n.*) calmness; tranquillity.

plague (*n.*) a pestilence; any widespread affliction. PLAGUE (*v.*) 1. to afflict with disease. 2. to vex; to tease.

plaice (*n.*) a flat-bodied sea-fish.

plaid (*n.*) wrap of woollen cloth with a check or tartan pattern. PLAID (*adj.*) tartan; striped with colour.

plain (*adj.*) 1. simple; undecorated. 2. easily seen; visible. 3. level. 4. obvious; unmistakable. 5. straightforward; blunt. PLAIN (*n.*) stretch of flat country; a prairie. PLAINLY (*adv.*).

plain clothes (*n. pl.*) private, or non-official clothes.

plain-dealing (*n.*) honesty; sincerity.

plainness (*n.*) 1. simplicity. 2. obviousness. 3. distinctness.

plaint (*n.*) 1. a sad song; lament. 2. a complaint; grievance.

plaintiff (*n.*) person who brings a lawsuit against another.

plaintive (*adj.*) sad; mournful. PLAINTIVELY (*adv.*).

plait (*v.*) 1. to twine together; to braid. 2. to fold. PLAIT (*n.*) 1. length of braided strands of hair. 2. a crease; fold. PLAITED (*adj.*).

plan (*n.*) 1. drawing showing the arrangement of rooms, streets, etc. 2. a scheme; proposal. PLAN (*v.*) 1. to draw a plan. 2. to think out; to prepare.

plane (*n.*) 1. a flat surface. 2. tool for smoothing wood. 3. a tall, spreading tree. 4. abbrev. for AEROPLANE. PLANE (*v.*) 1. to level. 2. to glide down in an aeroplane.

planet (*n.*) heavenly body which revolves round the sun. PLANETARY (*adj.*).

plank (*n.*) a wide, flat length of timber.

plant (*n.*) 1. living thing growing from a root in the soil. 2. machinery and equipment of a factory. PLANT (*v.*) 1. to place in the soil; to sow. 2. to found a business.

plantation (*n.*) 1. land planted with trees. 2. estate for growing cotton or tobacco.

planting (*n.*) a crop. PLANTER (*n.*).

plaster (*n.*) 1. cement-like substance spread on walls. 2. strip of linen treated with a healing substance. PLASTER (*v.*) to coat with plaster. PLASTERER (*n.*).

plastic (*adj.*) easily moulded into shape.

plastics (*n. pl.*) substances easily moulded by heat.

plate (*n.*) 1. flat sheet of metal or glass. 2. a round, shallow dish. 3. articles of gold or silver. PLATE (*v.*) to cover with a thin coating of gold or silver.

plateau (*n.*) tract of high, flat land; a tableland. (*pl.* PLATEAUS or PLATEAUX).

platform (*n.*) 1. a raised floor; a stage. 2. a station landing-place.

platinum (*n.*) heavy, silvery, rare metal.

platter (*n.*) large, shallow dish.

plaudit (*n.*) loud praise; applause.

plausibility (*n.*) persuasiveness; glibness.

plausible (*adj.*) persuasive; glib. PLAUSIBLY (*adv.*).

play (*v.*) 1. to join in games. 2. to act a part. 3. to perform on a musical instrument. PLAY (*n.*) 1. a game; an amusement. 2. a dramatic performance.

playful (*adj.*) fond of fun; lively. PLAYFULLY (*adv.*).

plaything (*n.*) a toy.

playwright (*n.*) a writer of plays.

plea (*n.*) a defendant's answer to the charge against him.

plead (*v.*) 1. to beg; to entreat. 2. to answer a charge brought in a law court.

pleasant (*adj.*) agreeable; delightful. PLEASANTLY (*adv.*).

pleasantry (*n.*) anything done in fun.

please (*v.*) to make glad; to delight. PLEASING (*adj.*).

pleasure (*n.*) enjoyment; delight.

pleat (*n.*) a fold of cloth. PLEAT (*v.*) to fold.

plebeian (*adj.*) common; vulgar.

plebiscite (*n.*) a vote on a special matter by all electors.

pledge (*n.*) 1. a promise; bond. 2. anything given to another as security. PLEDGE (*v.*) 1. to promise; to guarantee. 2. to pawn; to mortgage.

plentiful (*adj.*) ample; sufficient. PLENTIFULLY (*adv.*).

plenty (*n.*) an abundance; sufficiency. PLENTY (*adv.*) quite.

pliability (*n.*) flexibility; suppleness.

pliable (*adj.*) 1. easily bent; flexible. 2. easily influenced; manageable.

pliant (*adj.*) 1. bendable; flexible. 2. docile; tractable.

pliers (*n. pl.*) small pincers.

plight (*v.*) to promise; to engage. PLIGHT (*n.*) 1. one's condition or state. 2. a predicament.

plighted (*adj.*) promised; betrothed.

plod (*v.*) 1. to walk heavily; to trudge. 2. to work steadily; to study.

plodder (*n.*) a diligent worker; a student. PLODDING (*adj.*).

plot (*n.*) 1. a piece of ground; an allotment. 2. a scheme; conspiracy. 3. thread of a play. PLOT (*v.*) to scheme; to conspire. PLOTTER (*n.*).

plough (*n.*) farm implement for cutting and turning soil. PLOUGH (*v.*) to turn with a plough. PLOUGHMAN (*n.*).

ploughshare (*n.*) blade of a plough.

plover (*n.*) a marsh-loving bird.

pluck (*n.*) bravery; daring. PLUCK (*v.*) 1. to pull away; to snatch. 2. to gather flowers.

plucky (*adj.*) brave; bold. PLUCKILY (*adv.*).

plug (*v.*) to stop up a hole or leak. PLUG (*n.*) a stopper. PLUGGED (*adj.*).

plum (*n.*) tree and its pulpy, stoned fruit.

plumage (*n.*) a bird's feathers.

plumb (*adj.*) upright; vertical. PLUMB (*n.*) lead-weighted line used to test the uprightness of building-work. PLUMB (*v.*) 1. to test. 2. to find the depth of water; to sound.

plumbago (*n.*) blacklead.

plumber (*n.*) a fitter of water and gas pipes.

plumbing (*n.*) lead-work and piping in a building.

plume (*n.*) a large, gay feather. PLUME (*v.*) 1. to adorn with feathers. 2. to pride oneself.

plummet (*n.*) a small lead weight.

plump (*adj.*) chubby; fat.

plunder (*v.*) to ravage; to sack. PLUNDER (*n.*) booty; spoil.

plunderer (*n.*) a brigand; pirate.

plunge (*v.*) to thrust under water; to dive. PLUNGE (*n.*) a dive; immersion.

plural (*adj.*) two or more in number.

plus (*n.*) the sign of addition (+).

plush (*n.*) a thick velvet cloth.

Pluto (*n.*) planet farthest from the sun. See appendix.

plutonium (*n.*) a radio-active element.

ply (*v.*) 1. to keep busy. 2. to make regular trips. PLY (*n.*) a thickness.

plywood (*n.*) strong board made by gluing sheets of wood together.

pneumatic (*adj.*) 1. air-filled. 2. operated by air-power.

pneumonia (*n.*) inflammation of the lungs.

poach (*v.*) 1. to seek game without a licence. 2. to cook an egg by breaking it into boiling water.

poacher (*n.*) person who hunts game unlawfully. POACHING (*n.*).

pocket (*n.*) 1. small bag sewn in a gar-

ment. 2. place where an aeroplane in flight drops suddenly. POCKET (*v.*) 1. to place in a pocket. 2. to take secretly.

pod (*n.*) a long seed-case or shell.

podgy (*adj.*) short and fat; thick.

poem (*n.*) thoughts written in verse.

poet (*n.*) a writer of verse. (*fem.* POETESS).

poetic (*adj.*) 1. about poets and poetry. 2. written in verse; versified.

poetry (*n.*) the art or work of a poet.

poignant (*adj.*) piercing; painful. POIGNANCY (*n.*).

point (*n.*) 1. a sharp end; tip. 2. an aim; purpose. 3. a place; position. 4. each punctuation mark. 5. a headland; cape. 6. an item; idea. POINT (*v.*) 1. to sharpen. 2. to aim at. 3. to show with the finger.

pointed (*adj.*) 1. sharpened. 2. stressed; emphasized.

pointer (*n.*) 1. a rod for pointing. 2. dog trained to point to game with his head.

points (*n. pl.*) 1. a railway switch. 2. divisions on a mariner's compass.

poise (*n.*) 1. balance; steadiness. 2. one's carriage; bearing. POISE (*v.*) to balance or hover in the air.

poison (*n.*) substance that kills living things; venom. POISON (*v.*) 1. to kill with poison. 2. to infect; to envenom.

poisoned (*adj.*) containing poison; infected.

poisonous (*adj.*) harmful; deadly.

poke (*v.*) to prod; to thrust with a finger or rod. POKE (*n.*) a thrust; push.

poker (*n.*) rod for stirring a fire.

poky (*adj.*) narrow; cramped.

polar (*adj.*) concerning the North and South Poles.

pole (*n.*) 1. a wooden rod. 2. measure of length (5½ yards). 3. the North or South of the earth's axis. 4. the end of a magnet.

Pole Star (*n.*) Polaris, a star fixed almost directly above the North Pole; a guide.

police (*n.*) body of men and women appointed to enforce law and order.

policy (*n.*) 1. a settled plan. 2. a method of action or procedure. 3. an insurance agreement.

polish (*v.*) 1. to make smooth and

glossy; to burnish. 2. to acquire good manners. POLISH (*n.*) 1. glossiness. 2. politeness; courtesy.

polished (*adj.*) 1. bright; shining. 2. well-mannered.

polite (*adj.*) courteous; civil. POLITELY (*adv.*).

politeness (*n.*) courtesy; civility.

politic (*adj.*) careful not to offend; prudent.

political (*adj.*) concerning the plans and acts of government.

politician (*n.*) one who takes part in politics.

politics (*n. pl.*) art of national government.

polka (*n.*) a lively dance.

poll (*n.*) 1. part of the head on which hair grows. 2. a register of voters. POLL (*v.*) 1. to cut; to shear. 2. to vote at an election.

pollen (*n.*) fine dust found in flowers.

polling (*n.*) voting.

pollute (*v.*) to make unfit; to taint. POLLUTED (*adj.*).

pollution (*n.*) 1. an impurity; infection. 2. a stain; taint.

polo (*n.*) team game played on ponies.

polonaise (*n.*) music for a slow dance.

polonium (*n.*) a radio-active metal.

poltroon (*n.*) a coward.

polygon (*n.*) a many-sided figure. POLYGONAL (*adj.*).

pomade (*n.*) perfumed hair-ointment.

pomegranate (*n.*) tree and its seed-filled fruit.

pommel (*n.*) a round knob on a saddle or sword-hilt. POMMEL (*v.*) to beat with the fists; to belabour.

pomp (*n.*) splendour; magnificence.

pomposity (*n.*) vanity; self-importance.

pompous (*adj.*) self-important; swollen-headed. POMPOUSLY (*adv.*).

pond (*n.*) a small pool.

ponder (*v.*) to think about; to study.

pondering (*adj.*) thoughtful; meditative.

ponderous (*adj.*) 1. heavy; massive. 2. clumsy; awkward. PONDEROUSLY (*adv.*).

poniard (*n.*) a dagger.

pontoon (*n.*) wide, flat-bottomed boat used to support a bridge.

pony (*n.*) a small horse. (*pl.* PONIES).

poodle (*n.*) small, long-haired dog.

pool (*n.*) small patch of water; a pond.

poor (*adj.*) 1. possessing little; needy. 2. infertile; barren.

poorly (*adj.*) ill; ailing. POORLY (*adv.*) badly; miserably.

poorness (*n.*) weakness; worthlessness.

pop (*v.*) 1. to make an explosive sound. 2. to move suddenly in and out. POP (*n.*) an explosive sound.

Pope (*n.*) Bishop of Rome, and head of Roman Catholic Church.

poplar (*n.*) tall, quick-growing tree.

poplin (*n.*) woven fabric of silk and worsted.

poppy (*n.*) plant with large-petalled flowers. (*pl.* POPPIES).

populace (*n.*) the people; multitude.

popular (*adj.*) liked by many; favourite. POPULARLY (*adv.*).

popularity (*n.*) a general regard; esteem.

popularize (*v.*) to make well-known.

populate (*v.*) to fill or settle with inhabitants.

population (*n.*) inhabitants; citizens. POPULATED (*adj.*).

porcelain (*n.*) fine, delicate earthenware.

porch (*n.*) covered entrance to a doorway; a portico.

porcupine (*n.*) kind of giant rat covered with long spines.

pore (*n.*) tiny hole in the skin. PORE (*v.*) to read attentively.

pork (*n.*) pig-flesh.

porker (*n.*) a pig.

porous (*adj.*) having pores; absorbent.

porpoise (*n.*) sea-mammal of the whale family.

porridge (*n.*) oatmeal boiled in water.

port (*n.*) 1. a harbour-town; haven. 2. a Portuguese wine. 3. one's bearing, behaviour. 4. left-hand side of a ship or aeroplane facing forward.

portable (*adj.*) made to be carried; movable. PORTABILITY (*n.*).

portal (*n.*) an entrance door or gate.

portend (*v.*) to foreshadow; to betoken.

portent (*n.*) an evil sign; omen of ill-fortune.

portentous (*adj.*) 1. warning; threatening. 2. very important.

porter (*n.*) 1. a gatekeeper. 2. one who handles luggage; a carrier.

portfolio (*n.*) small, folding case for carrying documents.

portico (*n.*) a covered porch. (*pl.* PORTICOS).

portion (*n.*) a part; share. PORTION (*v.*) to share among; to distribute. Beware POTION.

portly (*adj.*) 1. dignified; stately. 2. stout; corpulent.

portmanteau (*n.*) a stiff travelling-bag. (*pl.* PORTMANTEAUS or PORTMANTEAUX).

portrait (*n.*) 1. a likeness 2. a description.

portraiture (*n.*) art of portrait-painting, or of vivid description.

portray (*v.*) 1. to paint or draw a likeness. 2. to describe.

pose (*n.*) a fixed attitude; posture. POSE (*v.*) 1. to assume and hold an attitude. 2. to puzzle; to perplex.

poser (*n.*) a riddle; puzzle.

position (*n.*) 1. a place; spot. 2. a job; situation. 3. an attitude; posture. 4. a rank; status.

positive (*adj.*) sure; certain. POSITIVE (*n.*) 1. a photograph. 2. a plus; an added quantity. POSITIVELY (*adv.*).

possess (*v.*) 1. to have; to occupy. 2. to own. POSSESSOR (*n.*).

possession (*n.*) anything one holds, occupies, or owns.

possessions (*n. pl.*) all one's property; assets.

possibility (*n.*) something that may or may not happen.

possible (*adj.*) can happen or be done.

possibly (*adv.*) maybe; perhaps.

post (*n.*) 1. a heavy beam; stake. 2. a fixed place; position. 3. a job; situation. 4. a letter-carrying system; mail. POST (*v.*) 1. to place in a fixed position; to station. 2. to affix a poster. 3. to send by mail.

postage (*n.*) fee for mail service.

postal (*adj.*) relating to the mail service. POSTALLY (*adv.*).

post-date (*v.*) to date a letter or document later than the date of writing or signing.

poster (*n.*) printed notice for public display.

posterior (*adj.*) later; behind.

posterity (*n.*) 1. future generations. 2. descendants.

postern (*n.*) a small door in or near a large one.

post-haste (*adv.*) at great speed; without delay.

postpone (*v.*) to put off until later; to defer. POSTPONED (*adj.*).

postponement (*n.*) a delaying; deferment.

postscript (*n.*) words added to a letter after it is signed; an afterthought.

posture (*n.*) carriage of the body; attitude. POSTURE (*v.*) to assume a special attitude; to pose.

posy (*n.*) bunch of flowers; a nosegay. (*pl.* POSIES).

pot (*n.*) 1. an earthenware container. 2. metallic cooking vessel. POT (*v.*) to plant or preserve in pots.

potassium (*n.*) a soft, white metal.

potato (*n.*) plant, and its edible, ball-like roots. (*pl.* POTATOES).

potency (*n.*) strength; power.

potent (*adj.*) strong; powerful.

potentate (*n.*) a ruler; monarch.

potential (*adj.*) can be; possible.

potentiality (*n.*) something that can be; a possibility.

potion (*n.*) a dose of medicine. Beware PORTION.

potter (*n.*) a maker of pottery. POTTER (*v.*) to do odd jobs in a haphazard way. POTTERER (*n.*).

Potteries (*n.*) North Staffordshire, the seat of the pottery industry.

pottery (*n.*) 1. earthenware. 2. its place of manufacture.

pouch (*n.*) a loose bag or pocket.

poulterer (*n.*) a dealer in poultry.

poultice (*n.*) soft mass of healing substance put on a sore place.

poultry (*n.*) all farmyard fowls.

pounce (*v.*) to seize suddenly; to swoop. POUNCE (*n.*) a sudden seizing.

pound (*n.*) 1. pen for strayed animals. 2. an Imperial measure of weight (16 oz. av.; 12 oz. tr). 3. a money value (100p). POUND (*v.*) to beat into powder; to pulverize.

pour (*v.*) 1. to flow out. 2. to rain heavily. 3. to rush with a crowd; to stream.

pout (*v.*) to push out the lips in displeasure.

pouter (*n.*) a kind of pigeon.

poverty (*n.*) 1. need; want. 2. shortage; scarcity. 3. infertility.

powder (*v.*) 1. to pound into dust. 2. to sprinkle; to dab. POWDER (*n.*) anything fine, as dust or sand.

powdery (*adj.*) fine; dust-like.

power (*n.*) 1. ability to do; to act. 2. strength; energy. 3. control; mastery. 4. magnifying strength of a lens.

powerful (*adj.*) mighty; forceful. POWERFULLY (*adv.*).

powerless (*adj.*) unable; weak. POWERLESSLY (*adv.*).

practicable (*adj.*) possible; likely.

practical (*adj.*) 1. fit for use; usable. 2. skilled; efficient.

practically (*adv.*) 1. efficiently. 2. nearly; almost.

practice (*n.*) 1. a habit. 2. a repeated exercise.

practise (*v.*) to do repeatedly; to exercise.

practised (*adj.*) skilled; trained.

practitioner (*n.*) a doctor.

prairie (*n.*) immense stretch of grassland.

praise (*v.*) 1. to speak well of; to commend. 2. to worship; to extol. PRAISE (*n.*) 1. approval; commendation. 2. worship.

praiseworthy (*adj.*) deserving praise; laudable.

prance (*v.*) to spring; to jump about.

prancing (*adj.*) jumping; rearing.

prank (*n.*) a joke; trick.

prate (*v.*) to talk too much; to chatter.

prating (*n.*) chatter; prattle. PRATING (*adj.*) chattering.

prattle (*v.*) to talk childishly. PRATTLE (*n.*) childish talk. PRATTLER (*n.*).

prawn (*n.*) edible shellfish like a large shrimp.

pray (*v.*) 1. to speak to God. 2. to ask earnestly.

prayer (*n.*) a request, or thanksgiving to God.

preach (*v.*) to deliver a sermon. PREACHER (*n.*).

preamble (*n.*) a foreword; an introduction.

prearrange (*v.*) to arrange beforehand; to plan.

precarious (*adj.*) doubtful; uncertain. PRECARIOUSLY (*adv.*).

precaution (*n.*) care taken beforehand; forethought.

precautious (*adj.*) careful; prudent.

precede (*v.*) to go before.

precedence (*n.*) the lead; advantage.

precedent (*n.*) an example; a pattern. PRECEDENT (*adj.*) earlier.

precept (*n.*) a rule; an instruction.

preceptor (*n.*) a teacher.

precinct (*n.*) space enclosed within walls or boundaries of a building, especially of a church.

precious (*adj.*) 1. costly; valuable. 2. loved; prized.

precipice (*n.*) a cliff.

precipitant (*adj.*) hasty; reckless.

precipitate (*v.*) 1. to urge on; to expedite. 2. to hurl headlong. PRECIPITATE (*adj.*) rash; heedless. PRECIPITATELY (*adv.*).

precipitation (*n.*) rash haste; heedlessness.

precise (*adj.*) exact; fine. PRECISELY (*adv.*).

precision (*n.*) exactness; accuracy.

preclude (*v.*) to prevent from happening; to make impossible. PRECLUSION (*n.*).

precocious (*adj.*) too old for one's age; too forward.

precocity (*n.*) unexpected cleverness.

preconcerted (*adj.*) arranged beforehand; concocted.

precursor (*n.*) a forerunner; pioneer.

predatory (*adj.*) wild; destructive.

predecessor (*n.*) person whose place one takes.

predicament (*n.*) a difficulty; plight.

predict (*v.*) to foretell; to prophesy.

predictable (*adj.*) can be foretold.

prediction (*n.*) a forecast; prophecy.

predominance (*n.*) mastery; control.

predominant (*adj.*) chief; supreme.

predominantly (*adv.*) firstly; above all.

predominate (*v.*) to be master; to control.

pre-eminence (*n.*) supremacy; excellency.

pre-eminent (*adj.*) above all; supreme.

preen (*v.*) to trim; to smarten oneself.

preface (*n.*) a prologue; an introduction.

prefatory (*adj.*) introductory.

prefect (*n.*) one having authority over others.

prefer (*v.*). 1. to like better. 2. to promote

preferable (*adj.*) more desirable. PREFERABLY (*adv.*).

preference (*n.*) a choice; liking.

preferment (*n.*) promotion; advancement.

prefix (*n.*) 1. a syllable or word added to beginning of another word to change its meaning. 2. a title placed before a name, as Mr., Dr., etc. PREFIX (*v.*) to place at the beginning.

prehistoric (*adj.*) of a time before history was written; very early.

prejudge (*v.*) to condemn before hearing a case; to be unfair.

prejudice (*n.*) unfairness; bias. PREJUDICE (*v.*) 1. to turn a person against another unfairly. 2. to harm unfairly.

prejudicial (*adj.*) harmful; damaging.

prelate (*n.*) clergyman high in rank; a prince of the Church.

preliminary (*n.*) 1. a trial effort. 2. an introduction. PRELIMINARY (*adj.*) introductory; opening.

prelude (*n.*) music played before the main performance.

premature (*adj.*) happening too soon.

prematurely (*adv.*) hastily; unreadily.

premeditate (*v.*) to plan beforehand.

premeditated (*adj.*) deliberate; intended.

premeditation (*n.*) deliberateness; intention.

premier (*adj.*) first; chief. PREMIER (*n.*) 1. the first. 2. the Prime Minister.

premises (*n. pl.*) houses; buildings and their grounds.

premium (*n.*) 1. a reward; bonus. 2. annual sum paid to continue an insurance.

premonition (*n.*) feeling of danger or disaster soon to happen.

preoccupation (*n.*) absent-mindedness; engrossment.

preoccupied (*adj.*) absorbed; rapt.

preoccupy (*v.*) to take one's whole attention.

preparation (*n.*) 1. a readiness; provision. 2. a medicine or mixture already made up.

preparatory (*adj.*) introductory; preliminary.

prepare (*v.*) to make ready; to plan.

prepared (*adj.*) arranged; ready.

prepay (*v.*) to pay in advance. PREPAYMENT (*n.*).

preposition (*n.*) a word placed before a noun or pronoun to express relations of time, space, etc.: e.g. to, for, with, beyond, etc.

prepossessing (*adj.*) attractive; charming.

preposterous (*adj.*) absurd; ridiculous. PREPOSTEROUSLY (*adv.*).

prerogative (*n.*) a special right; a privilege.

presage (*v.*) to foretell; to warn; to forbode. PRESAGE (*n.*) a prediction; a warning; an omen.

prescribe (*v.*) to order; to give directions. PRESCRIBED (*adj.*).

prescription (*n.*) 1. an order. 2. doctor's instructions for medicine and treatment.

presence (*n.*) 1. a being present. 2. a personal appearance.

present (*n.* pron. PREZ-ent) a gift; an offer. PRESENT (*adj.*) now; immediate.

present (*v.* pron. pre-ZENT) 1. to give; to bestow. 2. to introduce; to name.

presentable (*adj.*) fit to be seen.

presentation (*n.*) 1. a giving; an offering. 2. introduction of one person to another.

presently (*adv.*) soon; shortly.

preservation (*n.*) protection; security.

preservative (*n.*) substance which delays or stops decay.

preserve (*v.*) 1. to keep safe. 2. to delay decay; to conserve. PRESERVE (*n.*) jam, pickles, etc.

preside (*v.*) to be in charge; to control.

presidency (*n.*) the office or work of a president.

president (*n.*) the head of a state, or of a society.

presidential (*adj.*) concerning a president or his work.

press (*v.*) 1. to squeeze; to crush. 2. to embrace. 3. to iron. 4. to urge; to compel. PRESS (*n.*) 1. a machine for compressing or squeezing. 2. a printing machine. 3. the business of printing. 4. a crowd.

pressing (*adj.*) urgent; immediate.

pressure (*n.*) 1. weight; force. 2. influence; compulsion.

prestige (*n.*) a high reputation.

presumably (*adv.*) as may be supposed; probably.

presume (*v.*) 1. to take for granted; to

suppose. 2. to take a liberty. 3. to give an opinion unasked.

presumption (*n.*) 1. opinion; surmise. 2. forwardness; impudence.

pretence (*n.*) 1. a sham; a false claim. 2. an excuse.

pretend (*v.*) to sham.

pretender (*n.*) 1. one who shams. 2. one who claims falsely.

pretext (*n.*) a pretence; an excuse.

prettily (*adv.*) pleasingly; nicely.

prettiness (*n.*) beauty; attractiveness.

pretty (*adj.*) pleasing; nice.

prevail (*v.*) to overcome; to win.

prevailing (*adj.*) usual; general.

prevalence (*n.*) the ordinariness; spread.

prevalent (*adj.*) common; usual.

prevaricate (*v.*) to evade the truth; to lie.

prevarication (*n.*) a lie; falsehood.

prevent (*v.*) 1. to stop; to check. 2. to go before; to foresee.

preventable (*adj.*) avoidable; can be stopped.

prevention (*n.*) a hindrance; stoppage.

preventive (*n.*) a protection against disease; an antidote.

previous (*adj.*) 1. former; earlier. 2. hasty; quick. PREVIOUSLY (*adv.*).

prey (*v.*) to hunt down and seize; to plunder. PREY (*n.*) 1. the quarry; victim. 2. the plunder; spoil.

price (*v.*) to fix the cost. PRICE (*n.*) the cost; value.

priceless (*adj.*) beyond price; valuable.

prick (*v.*) 1. to pierce slightly; to puncture. 2. to urge; to spur. PRICK (*n.*) a puncture; sting.

prickle (*v.*) to pierce with sharp points; to sting. PRICKLE (*n.*) a thorn; sting. PRICKLINESS (*n.*).

prickly (*adj.*) 1. thorny. 2. tingling.

pride (*n.*) 1. one's opinion of one's own worth; self-esteem. 2. a group of lions. PRIDE (*v.*) to feel pleased with oneself; to plume oneself.

priest (*n.*) an ordained clergyman.

priesthood (*n.*) whole body of clergy.

priestly (*adj.*) befitting a priest.

prig (*n.*) 1. conceited person; a know-all. 2. strait-laced; prim.

priggish (*adj.*) vain; conceited. PRIGGISH-NESS (*n.*).

prim (*adj.*) precise; formal. PRIMLY (*adv.*).

primary (*adj.*) first; most important. PRIMARY (*n.*) the first; chief.

primate (*n.*) the head clergyman; the Archbishop of Canterbury.

prime (*adj.*) 1. first; chief. 2. perfect; excellent. PRIME (*n.*) 1. the beginning; dawn. 2. fullness of health; ability.

primeval (*adj.*) earliest known; primitive.

primitive (*adj.*) 1. prehistoric. 2. rough; simple. PRIMITIVELY (*adv.*).

primness (*n.*) stiffness; formality.

primrose (*n.*) yellow spring flower.

prince (*n.*) 1. a ruler; monarch. 2. a sovereign's son. (*fem.* PRINCESS).

princely (*adj.*) 1. noble; regal. 2. rich; magnificent.

principal (*adj.*) chief, head. PRINCIPAL (*n.*) leader; master.

principally (*adv.*) chiefly; mainly.

principle (*n.*) a rule of conduct; a conviction; a basic truth.

print (*v.*) to impress; to stamp. PRINT (*n.*) 1. mark made by pressing; an impression. 2. a photograph. 3. cloth stamped with a design.

printer (*n.*) one who prints from types.

printing (*n.*) art of printing; typography.

prior (*adj.*) earlier; previous. PRIOR (*adv.*) previously. PRIOR (*n.*) head of a priory.

prioress (*n.*) head of a small nunnery or convent.

priority (*n.*) a first claim or place.

priory (*n.*) a small monastery; a convent.

prism (*n.*) solid glass rod with triangular ends.

prismatic (*adj.*) 1. like a prism. 2. many-coloured.

prison (*n.*) place of confinement for offenders or captives.

prisoner (*n.*) 1. an imprisoned wrong-doer. 2. a captive. 3. a caged animal.

pristine (*adj.*) 1. earliest; original. 2. unspoiled.

privacy (*n.*) solitude; seclusion.

private (*adj.*) 1. concerning oneself; personal. 2. hidden; secret. PRIVATE (*n.*) soldier of lowest rank.

privately (*adv.*) personally; confidentially.

privation (*n.*) 1. hardship. 2. poverty; distress.

privet (*n.*) an ornamental shrub.

privilege (*n.*) 1. one's own right. 2. a favour; an advantage.

privileged (*adj.*) 1. unhindered; unforbidden. 2. favoured.

privy (*adj.*) 1. private; personal. PRIVILY (*adv.*).

prize (*v.*) 1. to value; to esteem. 2. to force open. PRIZE (*n.*) a reward; an honour.

prized (*adj.*) valued; treasured.

probability (*n.*) a likelihood.

probable (*adj.*) likely to be.

probably (*adv.*) maybe; perhaps.

probation (*n.*) period of test or trial.

probationer (*n.*) a learner; pupil.

probe (*v.*) to search; to examine. PROBE (*n.*) surgical instrument for examining wounds.

probity (*n.*) honesty; integrity.

problem (*n.*) anything hard to decide or settle.

problematic (*adj.*) doubtful; unsettled.

procedure (*n.*) way something is done; the method.

proceed (*v.*) 1. to move forward. 2. to begin. 3. to act.

proceeding (*n.*) an action; a transaction.

proceedings (*n. pl.*) 1. a law-suit. 2. business of a meeting.

proceeds (*n. pl.*) the takings; profits.

process (*n.*) the method of manufacture.

procession (*n.*) a body of people marching in ranks; cavalcade. PROCESSIONAL (*adj.*).

proclaim (*v.*) to announce publicly; to declare.

proclamation (*n.*) public declaration ordered by a sovereign.

procrastinate (*v.*) to delay; to put off.

procrastination (*n.*) delay; postponement.

procurable (*adj.*) obtainable.

procure (*v.*) to obtain; to get.

prod (*v.*) 1. to poke; to thrust. 2. to rouse; to urge. PROD (*n.*) 1. a poke. 2. a reminder.

prodigal (*adj.*) wasteful; extravagant. PRODIGAL (*n.*) a spendthrift.

prodigality (*n.*) extravagance; lavishness.

prodigious (*adj.*) 1. enormous; monstrous. 2. marvellous.

prodigiously (*adv.*) immensely.

prodigy (*n.*) a wonder; marvel. (*pl.* PRODIGIES).

produce (*v.* pron. pro-DUCE) 1. to show. 2. to create; to make. 3. to yield crops. PRODUCE (*n.* pron. PROD-uce)

1. the quantity; yield. 2. the result of labour; goods.

producer (*n.*) 1. the grower; manufacturer. 2. director of stage, film or T.V. performances.

product (*n.*) 1. anything grown or manufactured. 2. answer given by multiplying two quantities.

production (*n.*) 1. the quantity; output. 2. a play; drama.

productive (*adj.*) fertile; fruitful.

productivity (*n.*) the growing or working capacity.

profanation (*n.*) ill-use of sacred things; irreverence.

profane (*adj.*) 1. not sacred; secular. 2. irreverent. PROFANE (*v.*) to ill-use sacred things.

profanity (*n.*) 1. foul language. 2. abuse.

profess (*v.*) 1. to show openly. 2. to claim; to pretend.

professed (*adj.*) self-declared; avowed.

profession (*n.*) 1. an open declaration. 2. a calling; occupation. 3. a pretence.

professor (*n.*) a learned teacher; a teacher of high rank, usually at a university.

proffer (*v.*) to offer; to volunteer.

proficiency (*n.*) skill; ability.

proficient (*adj.*) skilful; expert. PROFICIENTLY (*adv.*).

profile (*n.*) a side view; an outline of the head.

profit (*n.*) a gain; benefit. PROFIT (*v.*) to gain; to benefit.

profitable (*adj.*) beneficial; gainful. PROFITABLY (*adv.*).

profiteer (*n.*) one who makes excessive profit unfairly.

profitless (*adj.*) 1. unprofitable. 2. useless.

profound (*adj.*) 1. deep; bottomless. 2. learned; wise.

profoundly (*adv.*) intensely; thoroughly.

profundity (*n.*) depth or immensity of feeling and thought.

profuse (*adj.*) bountiful; unstinting. PROFUSELY (*adv.*).

profusion (*n.*) abundance; wealth.

progenitor (*n.*) a forefather; ancestor.

progeny (*n.*) children; offspring.

programme (*n.*) 1. a list of events. 2. plans for the future.

progress (*v.* pron. pro-GRESS) to move forward; to advance. PROGRESS (*n.*

pron. PRO-gress) improvement; development.

progressive (*adj.*) 1. advancing; gradually growing. 2. eager to make improvements.

prohibit (*v.*) to forbid; to stop.

prohibition (*n.*) order or law forbidding something.

prohibitive (*adj.*) too costly; impossible.

project (*v.* pron. pro-JECT) 1. to throw forward. 2. to jut out. PROJECT (*n.* pron. PRO-ject) a plan; an undertaking.

projected (*adj.*) 1. thrown. 2. proposed; planned.

projectile (*n.*) anything hurled through the air; a missile.

projecting (*adj.*) sticking out; jutting.

projector (*n.*) machine which throws pictures on a screen.

proletariat (*n.*) the poorer classes of people.

prolific (*adj.*) abundant; teeming. PRO-LIFICALLY (*adv.*).

prolix (*adj.*) wordy; lengthy.

prolixity (*n.*) wordiness; verbosity.

prologue (*n.*) introduction to a book or play; a foreword.

prolong (*v.*) to lengthen; to extend.

prolongation (*n.*) an extension; a continuation.

prolonged (*adj.*) lengthened; sustained.

promenade (*v.*) to walk for pleasure or display. PROMENADE (*n.*) a paved road suitable for promenading.

prominence (*n.*) 1. an outstanding object. 2. fame; celebrity.

prominent (*adj.*) 1. clearly seen; outstanding. 2. famous. PROMINENTLY (*adv.*).

promise (*n.*) an intention which must be fulfilled; an assurance. PROMISE (*v.*) to give one's word; to assure.

promised (*adj.*) agreed; assured.

promising (*adj.*) hopeful; encouraging.

promontory (*n.*) a cape; headland.

promote (*v.*) 1. to help; to encourage. 2. to raise to a higher position.

promoter (*n.*) founder of a new business.

promotion (*n.*) a rise in position; an advancement.

prompt (*adj.*) quick; without delay. PROMPT (*v.*) 1. to help; to encourage. 2. to help an actor who has forgotten his words.

prompter (*n.*) one who helps an actor or speaker.

promptitude (*n.*) quickness; readiness. PROMPTNESS (*n.*).

promptly (*adv.*) quickly; smartly.

prone (*adj.*) 1. lying face downwards. 2. having a liking for.

proneness (*n.*) a liking for; an inclination.

prong (*n.*) the spike of a fork.

pronounce (*v.*) to speak distinctly; to utter.

pronounceable (*adj.*) can be spoken.

pronounced (*adj.*) firm; definite.

pronouncement (*n.*) a statement; declaration.

pronunciation (*n.*) one's style in speaking words.

proof (*n.*) 1. a test; trial. 2. convincing evidence of the truth. 3. a printer's trial copy. PROOF (*adj.*) firm against; resisting.

prop (*v.*) to prevent from falling; to support. PROP (*n.*) a support; strut.

propaganda (*n.*) the spreading of opinions and beliefs.

propagandist (*n.*) one who spreads opinions.

propagate (*v.*) 1. to increase the number of living things; to multiply. 2. to spread abroad; to broadcast.

propagation (*n.*) increase; production.

propel (*v.*) to push forward; to urge on.

propellent (*n.*) a driving agent.

propeller (*n.*) revolving shaft with blades to propel a ship or aeroplane.

propensity (*n.*) a liking for certain things; tendency.

proper (*adj.*) 1. right; correct. 2. personal; special.

properly (*adj.*) 1. correctly. 2. suitably; decently.

property (*n.*) 1. anything owned; a possession. 2. a special ability or quality a person or thing has.

prophecy (*n.* pron. profi-SEE) 1. a revelation. 2. a forecast; prediction. (*pl.* PROPHECIES).

prophesy (*v.* pron. profi-SYE) 1. to reveal. 2. to foretell; to predict.

prophet (*n.*) 1. one who reveals God's will; a seer. 2. one who foretells future events. (*fem.* PROPHETESS).

prophetic (*adj.*) revealing; foretelling.

propitiate (*v.*) to make friendly; to pacify.

propitious (*adj.*) favourable; friendly.

proportion (*v.*) to share; to divide fairly. PROPORTION (*n.*) 1. a comparison of the amount of one thing with that of another. 2. a fair share.

proposal (*n.*) 1. a plan; suggestion. 2. an offer of marriage.

propose (*v.*) to offer; to suggest. PROPOSER (*n.*).

proposed (*adj.*) intended; recommended.

proposition (*n.*) a plan; suggestion.

proprietor (*n.*) an owner. (*fem.* PROPRIETRESS).

propriety (*n.*) correct behaviour; seemliness. (*pl.* PROPRIETIES).

propulsion (*n.*) a driving forward; motive-power.

prosaic (*adj.*) dull; wearisome. PROSAICALLY (*adv.*).

pros and cons (*n. pl.*) arguments for and against.

prose (*n.*) language written as it is spoken; not written in verse.

prosecute (*v.*) 1. to continue; to pursue. 2. to take action in a law court against someone; to summon.

prosecution (*n.*) the prosecuting party in a law court.

prosecutor (*n.*) one who takes action in criminal court.

prospect (*n.*) 1. the view; landscape. 2. a hope; an expectation. PROSPECT (*v.*) to explore; to search for minerals.

prospective (*adj.*) expected; coming.

prospector (*n.*) a searcher for minerals; an explorer.

prospectus (*n.*) a descriptive circular. (*pl.* PROSPECTUSES).

prosper (*v.*) to succeed; to thrive.

prosperity (*n.*) success; good fortune.

prosperous (*adj.*) successful; flourishing. PROSPEROUSLY (*adv.*).

prostrate (*adj.*) 1. lying at full length. 2. exhausted. PROSTRATE (*v.*) 1. to throw oneself down flat. 2. to exhaust.

prostration (*n.*) 1. a lying down flat. 2. exhaustion by illness.

prosy (*adj.*) dull; wearisome.

protect (*v.*) to shield; to defend. PROTECTOR (*n.*).

protected (*adj.*) guarded; fortified.

protection (*n.*) a defence; safe-guard.

protective (*adj.*) sheltering; watchful.

protectorate (*n.*) a country under another's care.

protest (*v.* pron. pro-TEST) to object; to oppose. PROTEST (*n.* pron. PRO-test) an objection; a complaint. PROTESTER (*n.*).

Protestant (*n.*) one who belongs to a church outside the Roman Church.

protestation (*n.*) a declaration against something; dissent.

proton (*n.*) an atom particle containing positive electricity.

prototype (*n.*) model from which something is copied; the original pattern.

protract (*v.*) 1. to draw out; to lengthen. 2. to delay.

protracted (*adj.*) 1. lengthened; prolonged. 2. delayed.

protractor (*n.*) instrument for making and measuring angles.

protrude (*v.*) 1. to jut out; to project. 2. to swell.

protrusion (*n.*) a projection; swelling.

protrusive (*adj.*) pushing forward; bulging.

protuberance (*n.*) a swelling; bulge.

protuberant (*adj.*) bulging; prominent.

proud (*adj.*) 1. thinking highly of oneself. 2. vain; haughty. 3. noble; stately.

proudly (*adv.*) 1. haughtily; arrogantly. 2. nobly; majestically.

prove (*v.*) 1. to test; to examine. 2. to show that a thing is true; to verify.

provender (*n.*) food for animals.

proverb (*n.*) a wise saying; an adage.

proverbial (*adj.*) well known as a proverb.

provide (*v.*) 1. to supply; to store. 2. to prepare; to arrange.

provided (*conj.*) on condition; if.

providence (*n.*) 1. God's care. 2. foresight; care.

provident (*adj.*) prudent; thrifty.

providential (*adj.*) fortunate; opportune. PROVIDENTIALLY (*adv.*).

province (*n.*) 1. a division of a country. 2. the limits of a person's duty or authority.

provincial (*adj.*) concerning a province. PROVINCIAL (*n.*) one not inhabiting the capital.

provision (*v.*) to supply; to equip.
provisional (*adj.*) 1. for the time being; temporary. 2. conditional.
provisions (*n. pl.*) foodstuffs; supplies.
proviso (*n.*) a condition.
provocation (*n.*) an insult; indignity.
provocative (*adj.*) annoying; vexing. PROVOCATIVELY (*adv.*).
provoke (*v.*) to anger; to vex.
provoking (*adj.*) vexing; irritating. PROVOKINGLY (*adv.*).
provost (*n.*) 1. chief magistrate or mayor of a Scottish town. 2. the heads of some colleges.
prow (*n.*) a ship's bow or forepart.
prowess (*n.*) valour; gallantry.
prowl (*v.*) to steal about in search of prey or mischief. PROWLER (*n.*). PROWLING (*adj.*).
proximity (*n.*) the nearness; neighbourhood.
proxy (*n.*) a representative; deputy.
prude (*n.*) a woman who is extremely proper in behaviour or speech. PRUDERY (*n.*).
prudence (*n.*) caution; foresight.
prudent (*adj.*) wary; farseeing. PRUDENTLY (*adv.*).
prune (*v.*) to cut off; to lop. PRUNE (*n.*) a dried plum.
pruning (*n.*) a cutting; trimming.
pry (*v.*) 1. to peer and search out of curiosity. 2. to ask impertinent questions about other people's affairs. PRY (*n.*) an inquisitive searcher or questioner.
psalm (*n.*) a sacred song.
psalmist (*n.*) a writer of psalms. THE PSALMIST, King David.
pseudonym (*n.*) an assumed name; a pen-name.
psychiatrist (*n.*) a mind-healer.
psychic (*adj.*) concerned with the mind and thought.
psychologist (*n.*) one skilled in psychology.
psychology (*n.*) study of the mind and how it thinks.
public (*adj.*) 1. concerning the people, or their welfare. 2. open; well-known. PUBLIC (*n.*) the people; community.
publication (*n.*) any method of making something widely known; a published book or journal.

publicity (*n.*) widespread knowledge; advertising.
publicly (*adv.*) openly; before all.
publish (*v.*) 1. to make known. 2. to issue printed matter. 3. to broadcast.
publisher (*n.*) person whose trade is the publishing of books.
puce (*adj.*) brownish-purple.
pucker (*v.*) to wrinkle; to crease. PUCKER (*n.*).
pudding (*n.*) 1. soft animal or vegetable ingredients mixed with, or enclosed in flour, and boiled, steamed, or baked, usually in a cloth, lidded basin, or pig's stomach. 2. one of several kinds of sausage.
puddle (*n.*) a small pool of water.
puerile (*adj.*) childish; silly.
puerility (*n.*) foolish talk and behaviour; childishness.
puff (*v.*) 1. to blow wind from the mouth. 2. to blow in gusts. 3. to swell; to inflate. PUFF (*n.*) 1. sudden, short blast of air; a whiff. 2. a light pastry. 3. a pad for powdering the skin.
puffin (*n.*) diving-bird with parrot-like beak.
puffy (*adj.*) swollen; inflated.
pug (*n.*) dog with a short, snub nose.
pugilism (*n.*) boxing.
pugilist (*n.*) a boxer; prize-fighter.
pugnacity (*n.*) readiness to fight. PUGNACIOUS (*adj.*).
pull (*v.*) to draw towards; to tug. PULL (*n.*) a tug; haul.
pullet (*n.*) a young hen.
pulley (*n.*) wheel having a grooved rim in which a rope runs.
pulp (*n.*) a mass of soft, often juicy substance. PULP (*v.*) 1. to make into pulp. 2. to remove the pulp from.
pulpit (*n.*) raised platform for a preacher.
pulpy (*adj.*) soft; fleshy.
pulsate (*v.*) to throb; to beat. PULSATION (*n.*).
pulse (*n.*) regular beating of the heart; a single beat.
pulverize (*v.*) to grind to powder.
puma (*n.*) American wild cat; the cougar.
pumice (*n.*) light, porous lava.
pummel (*v.*) to strike with the fists; to belabour.
pump (*n.*) 1. machine for drawing air or

liquid from a container, or for forcing them into one. 2. a light shoe. PUMP (v.) 1. to use a pump. 2. to extract information from. 3. to exhaust by violent effort.

pumpkin (n.) plant, and its large, melon-like fruit.

pun (n.) witty use of words having the same sound but a different meaning. PUN (v.) to make a pun.

punch (v.) 1. to strike with the fist. 2. to pierce. PUNCH (n.) 1. a blow with the fist. 2. a tool for making holes. 3. a drink made of spirits spiced and sweetened.

punctual (adj.) at the stated time; not late. PUNCTUALLY (adv.).

punctuality (n.) care in keeping strictly to time.

punctuate (v.) to mark written work with points or stops.

punctuation (n.) the marking of a written composition with points.

puncture (v.) to prick with a fine point; to pierce. PUNCTURE (n.) a fine hole; perforation.

pungency (n.) 1. sharpness; tartness. 2. bitterness; sarcasm.

pungent (adj.) 1. stinging to taste or smell. 2. sarcastic.

punish (v.) to make a wrongdoer suffer.

punishment (n.) a penalty; chastisement.

punt (n.) wide, flat-bottomed boat propelled by a pole. PUNT (v.) to use a punt.

puny (adj.) small; feeble.

pup (n.) young dog or seal.

pupil (n.) 1. a learner; scholar. 2. round opening in the iris of the eye.

puppet (n.) 1. doll moved by strings. 2. person led by others.

purchase (v.) to buy. PURCHASE (n.) anything bought. PURCHASER (n.).

pure (adj.) 1. unmixed with anything else; clean. 2. blameless; stainless.

purely (adv.) 1. innocently. 2. solely; quite.

purgatory (n.) in Roman Catholic belief a place where departed souls are purified wholly from sin before entering heaven.

purge (v.) 1. to cleanse. 2. to pardon.

purification (n.) 1. a cleansing. 2. an absolution.

purify (v.) 1. to make pure. 2. to cleanse from sin; to absolve.

puritan (n.) one who lives a strict, clean life.

purity (n.) 1. cleanness; perfection. 2. innocence; virtue.

purl (n.) 1. twisted cord of gold or silver wire for bordering. 2. a chain of small loops as edging to lace or ribbon. 3. inverted stitches in knitting. PURL (v.) 1. to decorate with fringe or embroidery. 2. to invert stitches.

purloin (v.) to pilfer; to steal. PURLOINER (n.).

purple (adj.) dark violet; reddish-blue. PURPLISH (adj.).

purport (v.) to mean; to intend. PURPORT (n.) the meaning.

purpose (v.) to mean; to plan. PURPOSE (n.) 1. the meaning; intention. 2. the aim; object.

purposeful (adj.) determined; intent. PURPOSEFULLY (adv.).

purposeless (adj.) aimless; undecided. PURPOSELESSLY (adv.).

purposely (adv.) knowingly; intentionally.

purr (n.) sound a pleased cat makes. PURR (v.).

purse (n.) a small money-bag.

purser (n.) ship's officer in charge of accounts.

pursue (v.) to hunt; to follow. PURSUER (n.).

pursuit (n.) 1. a chase; hunt. 2. one's business; employment.

purvey (v.) to supply with provisions. PURVEYOR (n.).

push (v.) 1. to thrust away; to shove. 2. to make an effort. PUSH (n.) 1. a thrust; shove. 2. an attack. 3. an endeavour.

pushing (adj.) energetic; enterprising.

pusillanimous (adj.) timid; cowardly.

puss or **pussy** (n.) a cat. (pl. PUSSIES).

put (v.) to place; to set down.

putrefy (v.) to go bad; to decay.

putrid (adj.) bad; decayed.

putt (v.) to attempt to hole a ball at golf. PUTT (n.) the stroke made in putting. PUTTER (n.).

putty (n.) waterproof paste used in glazing.

puzzle (n.) a hard problem; a poser.

PUZZLE (v.) to set a problem; to perplex.

puzzlement (n.) bewilderment; perplexity.

puzzling (adj.) perplexing; mystifying.

pygmy (n.) a dwarf; midget. PYGMY (adj.) tiny; dwarf-like.

pyjamas (n. pl.) a sleeping-suit.

pylon (n.) 1. an Egyptian temple gateway. 2. high, skeleton tower, which supports cables.

pyramid (n.) object having four equal triangular sides which meet at the top in a point. See appendix.

pyrotechnics (n. pl.) fireworks.

python (n.) large snake which crushes its prey. See appendix.

Q

quack (n.) 1. a duck's cry. 2. a humbug; an impostor. QUACK (v.) to cry as a duck.

quadrangle (n.) 1. a square or oblong. 2. a four-sided courtyard.

quadrant (n.) 1. a quarter-circle. 2. instrument for finding latitude.

quadrilateral (n.) a four-sided figure. QUADRILATERAL (adj.) four-sided.

quadruped (n.) a four-footed animal.

quadruple (n.) four times as great. QUADRUPLE (v.) to multipiy by four. QUADRUPLE (adj.) fourfold.

quadruplet (n.) one of four children born together.

quaff (v.) to drink in long draughts.

quaggy (adj.) boggy; swampy.

quagmire (n.) a bog; marsh.

quail (v.) to flinch; to cower. QUAIL (n.) a migratory game-bird.

quaint (adj.) odd; unusual. QUAINTLY (adv.).

quaintness (n.) oddness; queerness.

quake (v.) to tremble; to quiver. QUAKE (n.) 1. a shudder. 2. an earthquake.

quaking (adj.) shaking; trembling.

qualification (n.) fitness; suitability.

qualified (adj.) 1. fitted; suitable. 2. authorized; licensed.

qualify (v.) 1. to make fit. 2. to obtain a certificate proving ability.

quality (n.) 1. character or nature of anything. 2. the goodness or badness; the grade. (pl. QUALITIES).

qualm (n.) 1. a doubt; uneasiness. 2. a touch of sickness.

quandary (n.) a puzzling position; dilemma. (pl. QUANDARIES).

quantity (n.) the size; amount. (pl. QUANTITIES).

quarantine (v.) to keep persons suspected of infection away from healthy people; to isolate. QUARANTINE (n.) isolation.

quarrel (v.) to dispute; to wrangle. QUARREL (n.) an angry dispute.

quarrelling (n.) noisy strife.

quarrelsome (adj.) fond of quarrelling; unfriendly.

quarried (adj.) dug from a quarry.

quarry (n.) 1. place where stone is dug. 2. game hunted as prey. (pl. QUARRIES). QUARRY (v.) to dig stone from a quarry.

quarrying (n.) work of getting stone from a quarry.

quart (n.) an Imperial measure of capacity (two pints).

quarter (n.) 1. one of four equal parts. 2. a district in a town. 3. mercy shown to a foe. QUARTER (v.) 1. to divide into four equal parts. 2. to lodge soldiers.

quarterdeck (n.) ship's upper deck from mainmast to stern.

quarterly (adj.) happening at the end of each quarter-year. QUARTERLY (n.) periodical published each quarter.

quartermaster (n.) army official in charge of all supplies.

quarters (n. pl.) lodgings for soldiers.

quartet (n.) set of four musical performers and a composition suitable for them.

quarto (n.) a book size; sheet folded twice to make four leaves.

quartz (n.) a hard rock.

quash (v.) to crush; to subdue.

quaver (n.) a musical note. QUAVER (v.) to tremble; to shake.

quaveringly (adv.) shakily; timidly.

quay (n.) place to load and unload ships; a wharf.

queen (n.) 1. a woman sovereign. 2. a king's wife. 3. the chief or only female, as among bees. 4. a chief chesspiece.

queenly (adj.) like a queen; royal.

queer (*adj.*) unusual; peculiar.

queerly (*adv.*) oddly; strangely.

queerness (*n.*) strangeness; peculiarity.

quell (*v.*) 1. to overcome by force; to crush.

quench (*v.*) 1. to put out a fire or light; to extinguish. 2. to end a thirst; to slake.

quenchless (*adj.*) cannot be put out or slaked.

querulous (*adj.*) peevish; discontented. QUERULOUSLY (*adv.*).

query (*n.*) a question; inquiry. (*pl.* QUERIES). QUERY (*v.*) 1. to ask a question. 2. to doubt; to dispute.

quest (*n.*) a search. QUEST (*v.*) to seek; to search for.

question (*v.*) 1. to ask; to interrogate. 2. to doubt. QUESTION (*n.*) 1. an inquiry; interrogation. 2. a subject for discussion; topic. QUESTIONER (*n.*).

questionable (*adj.*) doubtful; uncertain.

questioning (*n.*) an examination; investigation.

questionnaire (*n.*) list of questions requiring written answers.

queue (*n.*) line of people waiting their turn for something. QUEUE (*v.*) to form, or wait in, a queue.

quibble (*v.*) to give a misleading answer. QUIBBLE (*n.*) a way of refusing to answer a question; an evasion.

quibbler (*n.*) one who doesn't wish to answer plainly.

quibbling (*adj.*) misleading; evasive.

quick (*n.*) all live things; the living. QUICK (*adj.*) 1. animated; alert. 2. swift; rapid. 3. clever; intelligent. 4. hot-tempered; impulsive.

quicken (*v.*) 1. to make alive. 2. to hasten; to smarten.

quicklime (*n.*) limestone burnt to a powder.

quickly (*adv.*) 1. swiftly; rapidly. 2. soon; at once.

quickness (*n.*) 1. speed; rapidity. 2. smartness; alertness.

quicksand (*n.*) loose, water-filled sand into which the feet sink deeply.

quicksilver (*n.*) the metal mercury.

quick-witted (*adj.*) intelligent.

quiescence (*n.*) peace of mind; contentment. QUIESCENT (*adj.*).

quiet (*adj.*) 1. noiseless; silent. 2. calm; restful. 3. solitary; secluded. QUIET (*v.*) 1. to make silent; to still. 2. to pacify; to lull.

quieten (*v.*) to make quiet; to soothe.

quietly (*adv.*) silently; softly.

quietness (*n.*) tranquillity; silence.

quill (*n.*) 1. a long feather. 2. pen made from a feather. 3. a porcupine's spine; prickle.

quilt (*n.*) a padded bed-cover. QUILT (*v.*) to pad; to stuff.

quilted (*adj.*) padded.

quince (*n.*) tree, and its hard, pear-shaped fruit.

quinine (*n.*) fever-easing medicine made from the bark of the cinchona.

quinquennial (*adj.*) every five years.

quinsy (*n.*) inflammation of the tonsils.

quintet (*n.*) group of five performers, or music suitable for them.

quip (*n.*) a jest; jeer. QUIP (*v.*) to jeer; to scoff.

quire (*n.*) 1. measure of paper (24 sheets). 2. see CHOIR.

quit (*v.*) 1. to leave; to forsake. 2. to free; to release. QUIT (*adj.*) free; acquitted.

quite (*adv.*) fully; entirely.

quits (*adj.*) on even terms with another; drawn.

quittance (*n.*) freedom from debt or blame, having made payment.

quitter (*n.*) one who gives up; a deserter.

quiver (*v.*) to tremble; to shiver. QUIVER (*n.*) 1. a flutter; shudder. 2. a case to hold arrows.

quivering (*adj.*) shaking; fluttering.

quiz (*v.*) to question; to try to puzzle. QUIZ (*n.*) a questioning; test.

quizzical (*adj.*) questioning; inquisitive.

quizzically (*adv.*) in a puzzled; doubtful manner.

quoit (*n.*) flat metal ring for throwing at a peg.

quoits (*n. pl.*) game of skill in which the quoit is used.

quota (*n.*) a fair share; an allowance.

quotation (*n.*) exact words of the saying or writing which is repeated.

quote (*v.*) 1. to repeat something said or written by another. 2. to give or state a price.

quotient (*n.*) number of times one number

divides into another; the answer to a division sum.

R

rabbi (*n.*) a Jewish doctor of the law, especially one authorised to perform certain religious functions.

rabbit (*n.*) small, white-tailed burrowing animal.

rabbit-warren (*n.*) underground home of a rabbit colony.

rabble (*n.*) a noisy mob.

rabid (*adj.*) furious; raging.

race (*n.*) 1. living things of same kind or family. 2. a running match. 3. rapid current. RACE (*v.*) to run or flow rapidly. RACER (*n.*). RACIAL (*adj.*).

rack (*n.*) frame for holding or drying articles. RACK (*v.*) to pain; to torment.

racket (*n.*) 1. a tennis bat. 2. an uproar; a din. RACKETY (*adj.*).

racoon (*n.*) small, fur-bearing animal of bear family.

radar (*n.*) electrical device which finds the position of ships, aeroplanes, etc.

radiance (*n.*) brightness; splendour.

radiant (*adj.*) 1. giving out light and heat; glowing. 2. happy; joyful.

radiate (*v.*) to scatter heat or light rays; to spread.

radiation (*n.*) the spreading of rays.

radiator (*n.*) 1. apparatus for warming a room. 2. a cooling device in motorcars.

radical (*adj.*) concerning a root or foundation; basic. RADICALLY (*adv.*).

radio (*n.*) wireless.

radio-active (*adj.*) giving off rays of force or energy.

radio-activity (*n.*) ability of certain substances to give off rays of energy.

radium (*n.*) rare radio-active metal used in medicine.

radius (*n.*) straight line from the centre of a circle to its edge or circumference.

raffle (*n.*) a lottery.

raft (*n.*) a floating, wooden platform.

rafter (*n.*) a roof-beam; roof-timber.

rag (*n.*) waste scrap of cloth.

rage (*n.*) anger; passion. RAGE (*v.*) to be furious or angry.

ragged (*adj.*) torn; tattered.

raging (*adj.*) furious; angry. RAGING (*n.*) fury; violence.

raid (*n.*) a sudden attack; an onslaught. RAID (*v.*) to attack for plunder or food. RAIDER (*n.*).

rail (*v.*) to scold; to abuse. RAIL (*n.*) wooden or metal bar.

railing (*adj.*) scolding. RAILING (*n.*) fence of rails fastened to posts.

railway (*n.*) track or road on which trains run.

raiment (*n.*) clothing; garments.

rain (*n.*) water-drops which fall from clouds. RAIN (*v.*) to fall from clouds as water. RAINY (*adj.*).

rainbow (*n.*) coloured arch formed in the sky by the sun shining through raindrops.

rainfall (*n.*) quantity of rain falling on a place in a given time.

rain-gauge (*n.*) instrument for measuring rainfall.

raise (*v.*) 1. to lift up; to elevate. 2. to rear; to bring up. 3. to collect troops, taxes, etc. 4. to stir up; to excite.

raisin (*n.*) a dried grape.

raising (*n.*) the lifting up; erection.

rake (*n.*) 1. toothed implement for scraping soil. 2. a loose-living person. RAKE (*v.*) to scrape, or collect, with a rake.

rally (*v.*) 1. to join together after separating; to reassemble. 2. to recover from illness. 3. to encourage. 4. to taunt. RALLY (*n.*) 1. assembly of people from all parts; a reunion. 2. a recovery.

ram (*v.*) 1. to run into; to sink. 2. to batter with a ram. RAM (*n.*) 1. a male sheep. 2. heavy beam for breaking down walls.

ramble (*v.*) 1. to walk for pleasure; to wander. 2. to stray from the subject; to digress. 3. to speak nonsense in illness. RAMBLE (*n.*) a walk for pleasure; a stroll.

rambler (*n.*) 1. a walker. 2. a climbing rose.

ramification (*n.*) a branching off; turning aside.

ramify (*v.*) to spread out like branches.

ramp (*n.*) sloping way to a higher level; an incline.

rampage (*v.*) to act in a wild, unruly manner. RAMPAGE (*n.*) unruly behaviour.

rampant (*adj.*) 1. rearing on the hind legs. 2. widespread.

rampart (*n.*) a defensive wall; a bulwark.

ramshackle (*adj.*) tumbledown; shaky.

ranch (*n.*) large cattle-farm. RANCHER (*n.*).

rancid (*adj.*) stale; musty.

rancorous (*adj.*) spiteful; revengeful. RANCOROUSLY (*adv.*).

rancour (*n.*) spite; bitterness.

random (*adj.*) unplanned; haphazard. RANDOM (*n.*) a chance; hazard.

range (*n.*) 1. a line; row. 2. extent of anything; scope. 3. a metal cooking fireplace. RANGE (*v.*) 1. to set in line. 2. to roam; to wander.

ranger (*n.*) keeper of a large, or a royal forest.

rank (*n.*) 1. a line; row. 2. a class; an order. RANK (*v.*) to class; to classify. RANK (*adj.*) 1. strong; tall. 2. coarse; rotting.

rankle (*v.*) 1. to fester. 2. to nurse unfriendly feelings.

ransack (*v.*) 1. to search everywhere. 2. to plunder.

ransom (*n.*) money paid for a captive's release. RANSOM (*v.*) to buy release or freedom; to redeem.

rant (*v.*) to shout; to rave. RANT (*n.*) noisy talk.

rap (*v.*) to strike a sharp blow. RAP (*n.*) 1. a blow. 2. the least bit; an atom.

rapacious (*adj.*) greedy. RAPACIOUSLY (*adv.*).

rapacity (*n.*) greed; voracity.

rapid (*adj.*) speedy; swift. RAPIDLY (*adv.*).

rapidity (*n.*) quickness; speed.

rapids (*n. pl.*) swift-running stretch of river.

rapier (*n.*) light fencing-sword.

rapine (*n.*) robbery; pillage.

rapping (*n.*) a knocking; striking.

rapt (*adj.*) lost in thought; intent.

rapture (*n.*) immense delight; joy.

rapturous (*adj.*) blissful; enchanting. RAPTUROUSLY (*adv.*).

rare (*adj.*) uncommon; unusual. RARELY (*adv.*).

rareness (*n.*) infrequency; uncommonness.

rarity (*n.*) a rare thing or event. (*pl.* RARITIES).

rascal (*n.*) a scamp; rogue. RASCALLY (*adj.*).

rascality (*n.*) villainy; knavery.

rash (*adj.*) hasty; reckless. RASH (*n.*) an eruption of spots on the skin.

rasher (*n.*) thin slice of bacon.

rashly (*adv.*) recklessly; audaciously.

rashness (*n.*) audacity; venturesomeness.

rasp (*n.*) 1. a coarse file. 2. a harsh sound. RASP (*v.*) to scrape; to grate.

raspberry (*n.*) shrub and its red, juicy fruit. (*pl.* RASPBERRIES).

rat (*n.*) a destructive rodent. RAT (*v.*) to hunt out rats.

ratable (*adj.*) having a fixed value.

ratchet (*n.*) short bar which catches in a toothed wheel and so prevents it running backwards.

rate (*n.*) 1. tax on property to pay public expenses. 2. a fixed price. 3. a speed; velocity. RATE (*v.*) 1. to value. 2. to impose a tax. 3. to scold; to rebuke.

ratepayer (*n.*) householder who pays rates.

rather (*adv.*) sooner; more willingly.

ratification (*n.*) an acceptance of an agreement; an approval.

ratify (*v.*) to approve; to confirm.

rating (*n.*) a scolding.

ratio (*n.*) a rate; proportion.

ration (*n.*) fixed allowance; a fair share. RATION (*v.*) to provide with rations.

rational (*adj.*) sensible; reasoning.

rationalize (*v.*) 1. to make fair; just. 2. to stop waste.

rationally (*adv.*) fairly; justly.

rattle (*v.*) to shake noisily. RATTLE (*n.*) 1. a sharp noise. 2. a baby's plaything.

rattle-snake (*n.*) snake which makes rattling sounds.

raucous (*adj.*) harsh; hoarse. RAUCOUSLY (*adv.*).

ravage (*v.*) to plunder; to lay waste. RAVAGE (*n.*) destruction by decay or violence; ruin. RAVAGER (*n.*).

ravaging (*adj.*) plundering; destroying.

rave (*v.*) to speak wildly; to rage.

ravel (*v.*) to entangle; to confuse. RAVELLED (*adj.*).

raven (*n.*) large, black bird of crow family. RAVEN (*adj.*) glossy black.

ravenous (*adj.*) extremely hungry; voracious. RAVENOUSLY (*adv.*).

ravine (*n.*) a gorge; defile.

raving (*n.*) wild talk in illness; delirium.

ravish (*v.*) 1. to delight; to charm. 2. to carry off by force.

ravishing (*adj.*) charming; entrancing. RAVISHINGLY (*adv.*).

raw (*adj.*) 1. uncooked; fresh. 2. untrained; unskilled. 3. cold; bleak.

rawness (*n.*) 1. freshness. 2. inexperience. 3. coldness.

ray (*n.*) 1. a beam of light. 2. large, flat sea-fish.

rayon (*n.*) artificial silk.

raze (*v.*) to level to the ground; to destroy.

razor (*n.*) implement for shaving the face.

reach (*v.*) 1. to stretch. 2. to arrive at; to obtain. REACH (*n.*) 1. a stretch. 2. part of a stream between two bends.

reachable (*adj.*) within reach.

react (*v.*) to act in opposite ways; to oppose each other.

reaction (*n.*) opposition; resistance.

read (*v.*) to understand the meaning of printed words.

readable (*adj.*) 1. plain; legible. 2. worth reading.

reader (*n.*) 1. one fond of reading. 2. an examiner of publishers' manuscripts. 3. a reading-book for schools.

readily (*adv.*) 1. quickly; promptly. 2. willingly.

readiness (*n.*) 1. quickness. 2. willingness. 3. handiness; convenience.

reading (*n.*) the study of books.

readjust (*v.*) to put in order again.

readjustment (*n.*) a new arrangement.

ready (*adj.*) 1. prompt; quick. 2. willing.

real (*adj.*) actual; genuine.

realist (*n.*) one interested in actual things, not ideas.

realistic (*adj.*) life-like; actual. REALISTICALLY (*adv.*).

reality (*n.*) a fact; truth.

realization (*n.*) 1. understanding. 2. a sale of goods for money.

realize (*v.*) 1. to understand. 2. to sell.

really (*adv.*) in truth; actually.

realm (*n.*) the land ruled; the kingdom.

reap (*v.*) 1. to cut grain. 2. to gather a crop. 3. to receive the reward or punishment for an earlier action.

reappear (*v.*) to appear again.

reappearance (*n.*) a fresh appearance.

reapply (*v.*) to apply again. REAPPLICATION (*n.*).

reappoint (*v.*) to appoint again. REAPPOINTMENT (*n.*).

rear (*n.*) back or hindmost part. REAR (*v.*) 1. to bring up; to raise. 2. to rise on the hind legs. 3. to build; to erect.

rearmost (*adj.*) farthest behind; last.

rearrange (*v.*) to arrange anew. REARRANGEMENT (*n.*).

reason (*n.*) right judgment; intelligence. REASON (*v.*) to think; to judge rightly.

reasonable (*adj.*) right; sensible. REASONABLY (*adv.*).

reasonableness (*n.*) moderation; properness.

reasoning (*n.*) right thinking.

reassemble (*v.*) to meet again; to put together again.

reassert (*v.*) to state again. REASSERTION (*n.*).

reassurance (*n.*) comfort; encouragement.

reassure (*v.*) to strengthen; to encourage. REASSURING (*adj.*).

reattempt (*v.*) to try again.

rebate (*n.*) a deduction; discount.

rebel (*v. pron.* re-BEL) to refuse to obey; to revolt. REBEL (*n. pron.* REB-el) a traitor; an insurgent.

rebellion (*n.*) a revolt; an insurrection.

rebellious (*adj.*) disobedient; defiant. REBELLIOUSLY (*adv.*).

rebound (*v. pron.* re-BOUND) to spring back; to recoil. REBOUND (*n. pron.* RE-bound) a bounce back; a result.

rebuff (*v.*) to refuse rudely; to snub. REBUFF (*n.*) a rude refusal; a repulse.

rebuild (*v.*) to reconstruct; to alter.

rebuilding (*n.*) the reconstruction; re-erection.

rebuke (*v.*) to check; to reprove. REBUKE (*n.*) a reproof.

recall (*v.*) 1. to call back. 2. to remember. 3. to take back; to withdraw. RECALL (*n.*) 1. an order to return. 2. a withdrawal of something said.

recapitulate (v.) to repeat often; to rehearse.

recapitulation (n.) 1. a short summary. 2. repetition.

recapture (v.) 1. to retake. 2. to remember. RECAPTURE (n.) 1. capture of an escaped prisoner. 2. a memory; recollection.

recede (v.) to retreat; to ebb. RECEDING (adj.).

receipt (n.) 1. an acceptance. 2. written acknowledgement that something has been received. RECEIPTED (adj.).

receive (v.) 1. to take a thing offered; to accept. 2. to take in; to admit.

receiver (n.) 1. one who receives. 2. telephone ear-piece. 3. a wireless set.

recent (adj.) 1. new; modern. 2. foregoing; preceding. RECENTLY (adv.).

receptacle (n.) a holder; container.

reception (n.) 1. an acceptance. 2. a welcoming of guests. 3. the receiving of wireless signals.

receptionist (n.) one who admits guests to a hotel, or patients to a doctor.

receptive (adj.) 1. ready to welcome. 2. good at remembering.

recess (n.) 1. a nook; an alcove. 2. a break; an interval.

recipe (n.) instructions for making a cake, toffee, etc.

recipient (n.) one who receives or accepts.

reciprocal (adj.) done by each to the other; given and received. RECIPROCAL (n.) the magnitude by which another magnitude is multiplied to make their product unity or 1. (If the product of two magnitudes is 1, each is the reciprocal of the other, e.g. $8 \times \frac{1}{8} = 1$).

recital (n.) 1. a narration. 2. a concert.

recitation (n.) a poem or work repeated before an audience.

recite (v.) to repeat aloud; to relate. RECITER (n.).

reck (v.) to watch; to heed.

reckless (adj.) rash; foolhardy. RECKLESSLY (adv.).

recklessness (n.) rashness; risk.

reckon (v.) to count; to calculate.

reckoner (n.) a book of tables.

reckoning (n.) 1. a calculation. 2. an account or bill.

reclaim (v.) 1. to demand the return of something. 2. to mend; to recover. 3. to improve; to reform.

reclaimable (adj.) returnable; recoverable.

reclamation (n.) 1. a recovery; restoration. 2. a rescue; reform.

recline (v.) to lie back; to repose.

recluse (n.) one who lives a lonely life; a hermit.

recognition (n.) a knowing or remembering what has been seen before.

recognizable (adj.) remembered; recalled.

recognize (v.) 1. to know again; to remember. 2. to own up; to admit.

recoil (v.) to spring back from. RECOIL (n.) 1. a flinching away from. 2. the return blow or force.

recollect (v.) to remember; to call to mind.

recollection (n.) a memory; remembrance.

recommence (v.) to begin again. RECOMMENCEMENT (n.).

recommend (v.) to speak favourably of another; to advise.

recommendation (n.) a letter in another's support; testimonial.

recompense (v.) to repay; to compensate. RECOMPENSE (n.) a repayment; settlement.

reconcilable (adj.) ready to be friendly.

reconcile (v.) to become or make others friendly again; to appease.

reconciliation (n.) a renewal of friendship.

reconnaissance (n.) an inspection before taking action; a survey.

reconnoitre (v.) to look around; to spy.

reconsider (v.) to think things over.

reconsideration (n.) further thought; second thoughts.

reconstruct (v.) 1. to replan; to remodel. 2. to put a broken thing together again.

reconstructed (adj.) replanned; restored.

reconstruction (n.) a replanning; restoration.

record (v. pron. re-KORD) 1. to write down. 2. to send sounds into a machine for reproduction. RECORD (n. pron. REK-ord) 1. a written account. 2. the best achievement yet known. 3. a gramophone disc. RECORDED (adj.).

recorder (n.) 1. one who keeps an official register of events and facts. 2. chief judicial officer in some cities. 3. a kind of flute.

recount (v.) to relate; to narrate.

re-count (v.) to count over again, a second time or oftener. RE-COUNT (n.) the second counting, especially of votes.

recoup (v.) to regain a loss; to get back.

recourse (n.) a source of help.

recover (v.) 1. to regain; to get back. 2. to regain health; to revive.

re-cover (v.) to put on a new cover.

recoverable (adj.) can be regained or restored.

recovery (n.) 1. a regaining of a loss. 2. a restoration to health.

recreate (v.) to renew one's strength.

recreation (n.) any leisure-time interest; games, sports, hobbies, etc.

recreative (adj.) refreshing; invigorating.

recriminate (v.) to accuse in return; to countercharge. RECRIMINATION (n.).

recruit (v.) 1. to gain fresh men and supplies. 2. to regain health; to recuperate. RECRUIT (n.) 1. a newcomer; beginner. 2. a newly-enlisted soldier.

recruitment (n.) a fresh supply; a reinforcement.

rectangle (n.) a figure having each angle a right angle; a square or oblong. RECTANGULAR (adj.).

rectification (n.) 1. the correction. 2. the process of refining or purifying.

rectified (adj.) 1. purified; refined. 2. put right.

rectify (v.) 1. to make right; to correct. 2. to purify; to refine.

rectitude (n.) uprightness; integrity.

rector (n.) 1. clergyman having charge of a parish. 2. head of a Scottish university.

rectory (n.) home of a rector.

recumbent (adj.) lying down; resting.

recuperate (v.) to recover health; to convalesce.

recuperation (n.) a recovery; convalescence.

recuperative (adj.) helping recovery; restorative.

recur (v.) to happen again.

recurrence (n.) a happening again and again; a repetition.

recurrent (adj.) frequent; repeated.

red (adj.) crimson; scarlet.

redden (v.) 1. to make red. 2. to blush.

redeem (v.) 1. to buy back; to re-purchase. 2. to ransom.

redeemer (n.) a rescuer; ransomer. THE REDEEMER, Jesus Christ.

redemption (n.) 1. a ransoming. 2. deliverance; salvation.

red-handed (adj.) caught in the act.

redirect (v.) to direct again; to re-address. REDIRECTED (adj.).

redness (n.) the amount of red colour.

redoubtable (adj.) valiant; formidable.

redound (v.) to roll, or surge back, as a wave; to come back as a result.

redress (v.) to put right; to remedy. REDRESS (n.) a remedy; relief.

Redskin (n.) a Red Indian.

reduce (v.) 1. to lessen; to contract. 2. to conquer.

reduction (n.) 1. a decrease. 2. a conquest.

redundancy (n.) an excess; a surplus. REDUNDANT (adj.).

reed (n.) 1. a tall water-plant. 2. thin piece of wood which causes windinstruments to sound.

reef (n.) a ridge of sand or rocks in the sea.

reek (v.) to give off or to smell of smoke. REEK (n.) smoke.

reel (n.) 1. a lively Scottish dance. 2. a spool; bobbin. 3. a stagger; totter. REEL (v.) 1. to wind on a bobbin. 2. to whirl. 3. to sway; to stagger. REELING (adj.).

re-elect (v.) to elect or appoint again. RE-ELECTION (n.).

re-embark (v.) to go on board ship again. RE-EMBARKATION (n.).

re-engage (v.) to employ again.

re-engagement (n.) a renewed employment.

re-establish (v.) to put back in its place; to restore.

re-establishment (n.) restoration; reinstatement.

refectory (n.) a dining-hall.

refer (v.) 1. to give to another for decision; to appeal to. 2. to speak about. 3. to consult a person or book.

referee (n.) one who decides; an umpire.

reference (n.) 1. mention. 2. a consulted book. 3. a testimonial.

refine (v.) 1. to purify. 2. to cleanse the mind from coarseness.

refined (*adj.*) 1. purified. 2. polite; courteous.

refinement (*n.*) courtesy.

refinery (*n.*) building in which materials are purified.

refit (*v.*) to provide or fit out a second time. REFIT (*n.*) the repairing of damages, especially to a ship.

reflect (*v.*) 1. to throw back rays of light. 2. to show a likeness; to mirror. 3. to think matters over; to consider.

reflected (*adj.*) mirrored.

reflection (*n.*) 1. a mirrored image. 2. a thought; meditation.

reflective (*adj.*) thoughtful; meditative.

reflector (*n.*) bright, metal surface that reflects light or heat.

reflex (*adj.*) automatic; uncontrolled by the will.

reform (*v.*) to change for the better; to improve. REFORM (*n.*) a betterment.

reformation (*n.*) a complete change for the better.

reformed (*adj.*) improved; corrected.

reformer (*n.*) one who strives to reform.

refractory (*adj.*) stubborn; unmanageable.

refrain (*v.*) to keep from doing; to hold back. REFRAIN (*n.*) a musical air; a tune.

refresh (*v.*) to freshen; to enliven. REFRESHING (*adj.*).

refreshment (*n.*) food; nourishment.

refrigerate (*v.*) to freeze; to chill.

refrigeration (*n.*) preservation by freezing.

refrigerator (*n.*) machine in which perishable goods are chilled.

refuge (*n.*) a place of safety; sanctuary.

refugee (*n.*) one who seeks safety from disaster or tyranny.

refund (*v.* pron. re-FUND) to pay back; to repay. REFUND (*n.* pron. RE-fund) a repayment.

refurnish (*v.*) to furnish anew.

refusal (*n.*) a rejection; denial.

refuse (*v.* pron. re-FUZE) to decline; to reject. REFUSE (*n.* pron. REF-use) rubbish; garbage.

refutal (*n.*) a disproof; a denial.

refute (*v.*) to prove a statement is wrong.

regain (*v.*) to get back; to recover something lost.

regal (*adj.*) royal; kingly. REGALLY (*adv.*).

regale (*v.*) to entertain splendidly.

regalia (*n. pl.*) the crown, and all symbols of regal authority.

regard (*v.*) 1. to look at; to behold. 2. to respect; to esteem. 3. to suppose; to judge. REGARD (*n.*) 1. heed; attention. 2. respect; liking.

regardful (*adj.*) heedful; attentive. REGARDFULLY (*adv.*).

regarding (*prep.*) concerning; respecting.

regardless (*adj.*) heedless; unconcerned. REGARDLESSLY (*adv.*).

regards (*n. pl.*) compliments; respects.

regatta (*n.*) organized boat and yacht races.

regency (*n.*) rule and authority of a regent.

regent (*n.*) one who rules when a sovereign is ill or absent.

régime (*n.*) a system of government.

regiment (*n.*) a body of soldiers bearing a distinguishing name, e.g., the Coldstream Guards.

regimental (*adj.*) concerning a regiment.

Regina (*n.*) the queen.

region (*n.*) a large area of land; country. REGIONAL (*adj.*).

register (*n.*) 1. an official list book. 2. a record containing information required by law. REGISTER (*v.*) 1. to record official information. 2. to have one's name entered on a record.

registered (*adj.*) 1. named in a register. 2. despatched by special posting.

registrar (*n.*) an official recorder, or keeper of records.

registration (*n.*) the entering of official information.

registry (*n.*) place where registers are written and kept.

regret (*v.*) to be sorry about; to bewail.

regretful (*adj.*) sorrowful. REGRETFULLY (*adv.*).

regrettable (*adj.*) sad; unfortunate. REGRETTABLY (*adv.*).

regular (*adj.*) 1. according to rule; methodical. 2. ordinary; usual. REGULARLY (*adv.*).

regularity (*n.*) orderliness; constancy.

regulate (*v̄.*) to control by rules; to keep in order.

regulated (*adj.*) controlled; managed.

regulation (*n.*) a rule; an order.

regulator (*n.*) contrivance to control the speed of a machine.

rehearsal (*n.*) practice in preparation for a public performance.

rehearse (*v.*) to make perfect beforehand; to practise. REHEARSED (*adj.*).

reign (*v.*) to rule; to govern. REIGN (*n.*) a sovereign's rule and its length of time.

reimburse (*v.*) to pay back money expended; to refund.

reimbursement (*n.*) a repayment; refund.

rein (*n.*) narrow strap for controlling a horse. REIN (*v.*) to control; to guide.

reindeer (*n.*) large deer inhabiting cold regions.

reinforce (*v.*) to give additional support; to strengthen. REINFORCED (*adj.*) strengthened.

reinforcement (*n.*) additional aid; support.

reinstate (*v.*) to place again in the position held before.

reinstatement (*n.*) a recovery of one's position.

reiterate (*v.*) to say or do again and again; to repeat.

reiteration (*n.*) repetition.

reject (*v.*) to refuse; to cast away. REJECTED (*adj.*).

rejection (*n.*) a refusal.

rejoice (*v.*) 1. to give joy; to delight. 2. to feel joy or gladness.

rejoicing (*n.*) a show of joy; rapture.

rejoin (*v.*) 1. to join again; to reunite. 2. to answer.

rejoinder (*n.*) an answer.

rejuvenate (*v.*) to make feel young again. REJUVENATED (*adj.*).

rejuvenation (*n.*) youthful freshness and vigour.

rekindle (*v.*) 1. to light again. 2. to rouse again.

relapse (*v.*) 1. to slip back; to return to former ways. 2. to fall back into illness after partial recovery. RELAPSE (*n.*) 1. a return to old ways; a backsliding. 2. a return of ill-health.

relate (*v.*) 1. to tell; to narrate. 2. to join; to connect.

related (*adj.*) 1. told; narrated. 2. connected by kinship.

relation (*n.*) 1. a narration. 2. a kinsman; connection.

relationship (*n.*) kinship; affinity.

relative (*n.*) a relation; kinsman. RELATIVE (*adj.*) connected with.

relatively (*adv.*) not completely; partly.

relax (*v.*) 1. to become less severe. 2. to rest.

relaxation (*n.*) 1. ease; rest. 2. recreation.

relaxed (*adj.*) eased; slackened.

relay (*v.*) 1. to bring fresh supplies. 2. to begin where another ends. RELAY (*n.*) 1. a fresh supply. 2. race carried on by successive runners.

release (*v.*) to free; to liberate. RELEASE (*n.*) 1. freedom; liberation. 2. relief from pain.

relegate (*v.*) 1. to transfer to a lower place. 2. to banish; to exile. RELEGATION (*n.*).

relent (*v.*) to become milder; to yield.

relentless (*adj.*) pitiless; unyielding. RELENTLESSLY (*adv.*).

relentlessness (*n.*) harshness; severity.

relevance (*n.*) fitness; suitability. RELEVANT (*adj.*).

reliability (*n.*) trustworthiness.

reliable (*adj.*) dependable. RELIABLY (*adv.*).

reliance (*n.*) trust in another. RELIANT (*adj.*).

relic (*n.*) 1. fragment of something holy. 2. a memorial; keepsake.

relief (*n.*) 1. help; aid. 2. easing of anxiety or pain. 3. release from duty. 4. a design which stands out from the surface. 5. one who follows another in a turn of duty.

relieve (*v.*) 1. to give help. 2. to ease; to soothe.

religion (*n.*) worship given to God.

religious (*adj.*) obedient to the teaching of religion.

religiously (*adv.*) 1. in a religious manner; devoutly. 2. faithfully; exactly.

relinquish (*v.*) to give up; to forsake.

relinquishment (*n.*) a surrender; abandonment.

relish (*v.*) to like; to enjoy the taste. RELISH (*n.*) a flavour; seasoning.

reluctance (*n.*) unwillingness.

reluctant (*adj.*) unwilling; loath.

rely (*v.*) to trust; to depend upon. See RELIABLE.

remain (*v.*) 1. to stay; to tarry. 2. to endure; to survive.

remainder (*n.*) the part unused; left over.

remand (*v.*) to send back to prison to await trial. REMAND (*n.*) the act of remanding.

remark (*v.*) 1. to say; to mention. 2. to notice; to observe. REMARK (*n.*) a mention; comment.

remarkable (*adj.*) unusual; extraordinary.

remarkably (*adv.*) extremely; exceptionally.

remedial (*adj.*) curative; healing.

remedy (*n.*) a cure; restorative. REMEDY (*v.*) to heal; to cure.

remember (*v.*) 1. to recall a past event; to recollect. 2. to reward.

remembrance (*n.*) 1. a memory; recollection. 2. a memento; memorial.

remind (*v.*) to cause to remember.

reminder (*n.*) anything causing one to remember.

reminiscence (*n.*) an account of a past event.

reminiscences (*n. pl.*) written account of one's memories.

reminiscent (*adj.*) recalling past events.

remiss (*adj.*) slack; negligent. REMISSLY (*adv.*).

remission (*n.*) pardon; forgiveness.

remit (*v.*) 1. to pardon. 2. to send by post.

remittance (*n.*) money sent by post or messenger.

remnant (*n.*) 1. piece left over; a remainder. 2. a scrap; fragment.

remodel (*v.*) to reshape; to refashion.

remonstrance (*n.*) a protest; an opposition.

remonstrate (*v.*) to protest; to object to.

remorse (*n.*) deep regret; repentance.

remorseful (*adj.*) sorry; penitent. REMORSEFULLY (*adv.*).

remorseless (*adj.*) pitiless; merciless. REMORSELESSLY (*adv.*).

remote (*adj.*) 1. far off; distant. 2. slight; faint. REMOTELY (*adv.*).

remoteness (*n.*) distance; isolation.

remount (*v.*) to mount again; to reascend.

removable (*adj.*) can be removed.

removal (*n.*) 1. a dismissal. 2. a transfer. 3. an extraction.

remove (*v.*) 1. to take from its place; to displace. 2. to take from one place to another; to transfer. 3. to take off;

to uncover. 4. to take from; to dismiss.

removed (*adj.*) taken away; separated.

remunerate (*v.*) to recompense; to reward.

remuneration (*n.*) payment; recompense.

remunerative (*adj.*) profitable; advantageous.

rend (*v.*) 1. to tear apart. 2. to split; to burst.

render (*v.*) 1. to give; to deliver. 2. to interpret; to translate.

rendering (*n.*) a translation; version.

rendezvous (*n.*) a meeting-place. RENDEZVOUS (*v.*) to arrange to meet.

renegade (*adj.*) false; disloyal. RENEGADE (*n.*) a deserter; traitor.

renew (*v.*) 1. to begin again. 2. to repair; to restore.

renewal (*n.*) a restoration; replacement.

renounce (*v.*) 1. to give up; to reject. 2. to disown; to forsake.

renovate (*v.*) to make as good as new; to restore.

renovation (*n.*) a restoration; renewal.

renown (*n.*) fame; honour.

renowned (*adj.*) celebrated; famous.

rent (*n.*) 1. payment for occupation of a house as tenant. 2. a tear; split.

rental (*n.*) a rent; the total rent of an estate.

renunciation (*n.*) a rejection; abandonment.

reopen (*v.*) to open again.

reorganization (*n.*) a rearrangement; a new system.

reorganize (*v.*) to change the system.

repair (*v.*) 1. to go elsewhere; to betake. 2. to mend; to patch. 3. to heal; to restore. REPAIR (*n.*) a mend; patch.

reparation (*n.*) money paid as compensation for injury or loss.

repartee (*n.*) a smart, witty reply.

repast (*n.*) a meal.

repatriate (*v.*) to restore to one's native land.

repatriation (*n.*) restoration to one's own country.

repay (*v.*) 1. to pay back anything borrowed. 2. to return a kindness.

repayment (*n.*) the sum repaid; a reimbursement.

repeal (*v.*) to abolish; to annul. REPEAL (*n.*) the abolition; cancellation.

repeat (*v.*) to say or do over again.

repeatedly (*adv.*) over and over again; often.

repel (*v.*) 1. to drive back; to repulse. 2. to cause dislike.

repellent (*adj.*) disgusting; distasteful.

repent (*v.*) to feel sorry for one's fault or sin.

repentance (*n.*) regret; penitence. REPENTANT (*adj.*).

repercussion (*n.*) a sound flung back; an echo.

repetition (*n.*) anything done over again.

repine (*v.*) to grumble; to fret.

repining (*n.*) a complaining; fretting.

replace (*v.*) 1. to put back in its place. 2. to put a person or thing in the place of another; to substitute.

replacement (*n.*) a transfer; substitution.

replenish (*v.*) to fill up again; to restock.

replenishment (*n.*) a supply of goods which replaces those used.

replete (*adj.*) full; complete.

repletion (*n.*) fullness; satisfaction.

replica (*n.*) an exact copy; a duplicate.

reply (*v.*) 1. to answer; to respond. 2. to echo. REPLY (*n.*) 1. an answer; a response. 2. an echo. (*pl.* REPLIES).

report (*v.*) 1. to tell the facts; to relate. 2. to spread news. 3. to announce one's arrival for duty. REPORT (*n.*) 1. a statement. 2. a rumour. 3. a declaration. 4. an echo. 5. an explosive noise.

reporter (*n.*) one who gathers news for the press.

repose (*v.*) to rest; to sleep. REPOSE (*n.*) 1. rest; sleep. 2. peace; ease.

reposeful (*adj.*) restful; peaceful.

repository (*n.*) storehouse for goods.

reprehend (*v.*) to blame; to rebuke.

reprehensible (*adj.*) blameworthy; guilty.

reprehension (*n.*) blame; censure.

represent (*v.*) 1. to show; to describe. 2. to draw; to picture. 3. to act on behalf of another.

representation (*n.*) 1. a likeness; model. 2. a dramatic performance. 3. the duty of a representative.

representative (*n.*) person who acts for another; an agent. REPRESENTATIVE (*adj.*) showing likeness; being an example.

repress (*v.*) to put down; to hold back.

repression (*n.*) a check; restraint.

repressive (*adj.*) checking; crushing.

reprieve (*v.*) 1. to delay; to postpone. 2. to remit or reduce punishment. REPRIEVE (*n.*) 1. a delay. 2. a release; respite.

reprieved (*adj.*) postponed; suspended.

reprimand (*v.*) to blame; to censure. REPRIMAND (*n.*) a good talking to; a rebuke.

reprint (*v.*) to print again; to print a second or new edition of. REPRINT (*n.*) a further printing of a printed work.

reprisal (*n.*) an act of revenge; retaliation.

reproach (*v.*) to blame; to scold. REPROACH (*n.*) an object of blame.

reproachful (*adj.*) shameful; disgraceful.

reproachfully (*adv.*) scornfully; contemptuously.

reprobate (*v.*) to blame; to condemn. REPROBATE (*n.*) a scamp; scoundrel. REPROBATE (*adj.*) wicked; shameless.

reprobation (*n.*) disownment; rejection.

reproduce (*v.*) 1. to have young. 2. to copy; to print.

reproduction (*n.*) 1. a copy; print. 2. a photograph; record.

reproof (*n.*) a rebuke; reprimand.

reprove (*v.*) to find fault with; to scold.

reptile (*n.*) animal that (1) glides without legs, a snake, or (2) moves on short legs, a lizard.

republic (*n.*) state governed by persons elected by its citizens.

republican (*n.*) one supporting a republic. REPUBLICAN (*adj.*) concerning a republic.

repudiate (*v.*) to have nothing to do with; to disown.

repudiation (*n.*) a rejection; disowning. REPUDIATOR (*n.*).

repugnance (*n.*) dislike; disgust.

repugnant (*adj.*) offensive; nasty.

repulse (*v.*) 1. to thrust back; to repel. 2. to make one dislike; to deter.

repulsion (*n.*) 1. defeat; disappointment. 2. dislike; disgust.

repulsive (*adj.*) hateful; odious. REPULSIVELY (*adv.*).

repurchase (*v.*) to buy back.

reputable (*adj.*) worthy; estimable. REPUTABLY (*adv.*).

reputation (*n.*) character; good name.

repute (*n.*) esteem; fame.

reputed (*adj.*) supposed; believed. RE-PUTEDLY (*adv.*).

request (*v.*) to ask; to require. REQUEST (*n.*) an asking; invitation.

require (*v.*) to want; to need.

requirement (*n.*) a need; desire.

requisite (*n.*) a necessity; an essential. REQUISITE (*adj.*) necessary; essential.

requisition (*v.*) to demand; to seize. REQUISITION (*n.*) 1. a list of things required. 2. a seizure of something essential.

requisitioned (*adj.*) seized because essential; demanded.

requite (*v.*) to return good or ill; to repay.

reredos (*n.*) screen behind an altar; an altar-piece.

rescind (*v.*) to reverse; to cancel.

rescue (*v.*) to free from danger; to save. RESCUE (*n.*) a deliverance; salvation. RESCUER (*n.*).

rescued (*adj.*) saved; preserved.

research (*n.*) the work of any who seek new knowledge.

resemblance (*n.*) a likeness; similarity.

resemble (*v.*) to have the same appearance; to be like.

resent (*v.*) to feel insulted; to bear ill-will.

resentful (*adj.*) indignant; offended. RE-SENTFULLY (*adv.*).

resentment (*n.*) indignation; rancour.

reservation (*n.*) 1. anything kept back or withheld. 2. a booked place or seat. 3. shyness; modesty.

reserve (*v.*) to withhold for emergency; to store. RESERVE (*n.*) 1. an emergency supply. 2. shyness; modesty.

reserved (*adj.*) 1. withheld. 2. booked. 3. shy; demure.

reservedly (*adv.*) 1. carefully. 2. thoughtfully. 3. shyly.

reservoir (*n.*) 1. a water-tank; cistern. 2. a city's water-supply.

reside (*v.*) to live in; to dwell.

residence (*n.*) a dwelling-house; home.

resident (*n.*) 1. an occupant; inmate. 2. a fellow-townsman.

residential (*adj.*) suitable for dwelling-houses.

residual (*adj.*) left over or remaining.

residue (*n.*) the rest; remainder.

resign (*v.*) 1. to leave; to give up. 2. to yield to; to surrender.

resignation (*n.*) 1. a giving up; relinquishment. 2. patience; submission.

resigned (*adj.*) submissive; uncomplaining. RESIGNEDLY (*adv.*).

resilience (*n.*) 1. springiness: elasticity. 2. sprightliness.

resilient (*adj.*) 1. springing back after stretching; elastic. 2. quickly overcoming troubles; buoyant.

resin (*n.*) gummy juice of certain trees. RESINOUS (*adj.*).

resist (*v.*) 1. to withstand; to oppose. 2. to check; to thwart.

resistance (*n.*) hindrance, opposition.

resistant (*adj.*) opposing; repelling.

resistless (*adj.*) unopposable; unconquerable.

resolute (*adj.*) steadfast; determined. RESOLUTELY (*adv.*).

resolution (*n.*) 1. determination. 2. a decision; resolve.

resolve (*v.*) to purpose; to decide. RESOLVE (*n.*) a purpose; decision.

resonance (*n.*) a re-echoing sound.

resonant (*adj.*) echoing; resounding.

resort (*v.*) 1. to go; to visit. 2. to have a reserve supply. RESORT (*n.*) 1. a much-visited place. 2. a reserve supply.

resound (*v.*) 1. to ring with sound. 2. to spread the fame of.

resource (*n.*) 1. a helpful contrivance. 2. a means of raising money. 3. enterprise; ingenuity.

resourceful (*adj.*) skilful; ingenious. RESOURCEFULLY (*adv.*).

resources (*n. pl.*) all one's possessions; assets.

respect (*v.*) to esteem; to honour. RESPECT (*n.*) esteem; regard.

respectability (*n.*) worthiness; importance.

respectable (*adj.*) 1. worthy; honourable. 2. decent.

respectful (*adj.*) courteous; dutiful. RESPECTFULLY (*adv.*).

respecting (*prep.*) concerning; regarding.

respective (*adj.*) individual; proper to each.

respectively (*adv.*) one at a time; separately.

respiration (*n.*) breathing.

respirator (*n.*) instrument which aids breathing.

respite (*n.*) a short pause; a rest. RESPITE (*v.*) to delay; to postpone.

resplendent (*adj.*) brilliant; glorious.

respond (*v.*) 1. to reply. 2. to agree. 3. to sympathize.

response (*n.*) 1. an answer; a reply. 2. the effect; result.

responsibility (*n.*) the trustworthiness; liability.

responsible (*adj.*) answerable; accountable.

responsive (*adj.*) quick (1) to reply, and (2) to show effects.

rest (*v.*) 1. to stop working; to relax. 2. to be still; quiet. 3. to sleep. REST (*n.*) 1. a pause; stop. 2. a sleep. 3. a support; prop. 4. the remainder; the others.

restaurant (*n.*) a place selling refreshments.

restful (*adj.*) quiet; peaceful. RESTFULLY (*adv.*).

restive (*adj.*) fidgety; fretful.

restless (*adj.*) uneasy; unsettled. RESTLESSNESS (*n.*).

restoration (*n.*) 1. a recovery. 2. a renewal.

restorative (*n.*) anything healing; a tonic.

restore (*v.*) 1. to give back; to bring back. 2. to repair. 3. to treat; to cure.

restrain (*v.*) to hold back; to check.

restraint (*n.*) 1. a check; hindrance. 2. self-control; patience.

restrict (*v.*) to keep within bounds; to confine.

restriction (*n.*) a condition; stipulation.

restrictive (*adj.*) hindering; hampering.

result (*v.*) to finish; to end. RESULT (*n.*) the outcome; consequence.

resulting (*adj.*) consequent; concluding.

resume (*v.*) to begin again.

resumption (*n.*) a fresh start.

resurrect (*v.*) to revive; to bring back again.

resurrection (*n.*) a rising again; a revival.

retail (*v.*) 1. to sell in a shop. 2. to tell to others; to gossip. RETAILER (*n.*).

retain (*v.*) 1. to keep. 2. to employ.

retainer (*n.*) 1. a fee paid to secure someone's services. 2. a servant and follower.

retaining (*adj.*) holding in position; supporting.

retaliate (*v.*) to get one's own back.

retaliation (*n.*) revenge; a tit for tat.

retard (*v.*) to make slower; to delay.

retardation (*n.*) a hindrance; brake.

reticence (*n.*) silence; reserve.

reticent (*adj.*) silent; reserved. RETICENTLY (*adv.*).

retina (*n.*) tissue within the eye which receives images.

retire (*v.*) 1. to withdraw. 2. to leave employment. 3. to go to bed.

retirement (*n.*) 1. a retreat. 2. withdrawal from employment. 3. seclusion; privacy.

retiring (*adj.*) shy; reserved.

retort (*v.*) to answer sharply. RETORT (*n.*) 1. a sharp reply. 2. vessel in which substances are distilled.

retouch (*v.*) to improve by new touches. RETOUCH (*n.*) an additional touch to improve any artistic work.

retrace (*v.*) to return the same way.

retract (*v.*) to take back one's words; to disown.

retracted (*adj.*) withdrawn; cancelled.

retraction (*n.*) a change of opinion.

retreat (*v.*) to go back; to retire. RETREAT (*n.*) 1. a retirement. 2. a refuge.

retrench (*v.*) to save; to economize.

retrenchment (*n.*) a saving; an economy.

retribution (*n.*) a just punishment; reckoning.

retrieve (*v.*) to recover anything lost; to regain.

retriever (*n.*) dog trained to find shot game.

return (*v.*) 1. to come or go back. 2. to give back; to restore. 3. to show a profit. RETURN (*n.*) 1. a reappearance. 2. a repayment. 3. a profit.

returnable (*adj.*) should be sent back.

reunion (*n.*) meeting of friends after absence.

reunite (*v.*) to join together again.

reveal (*v.*) 1. to show what was hidden; to unveil. 2. to tell a secret; to disclose.

revel (*v.*) to make merry; to celebrate. REVEL (*n.*) noisy merriment. REVELLER (*n.*).

revelation (*n.*) anything made known; a discovery.

revelry (*n.*) festivity; merriment.

revenge (*v.*) to get one's own back; to repay hurtfully. REVENGE (*n.*) a hurtful repayment; retaliation.

revengeful (*adj.*) spiteful; unforgiving.

revenue (*n.*) income of a person, business or nation.

reverberate (*v.*) to re-echo; to resound.

reverberation (*n.*) an echo; a vibration.

revere (*v.*) to respect; to honour. REVERED (*adj.*).

reverence (*v.*) to worship; to honour. REVERENCE (*n.*) worship.

reverend (*adj.*) worthy of respect. REVEREND (*n.*) title of respect given to clergymen.

reverent (*adj.*) respectful; meek. REVERENTLY (*adv.*).

reverie (*n.*) a day-dream; musing.

reversal (*n.*) 1. a change from front to back or inside out. 2. a defeat; disappointment.

reverse (*v.*) 1. to turn round about, or inside out. 2. to go backwards. 3. to undo; to cancel. REVERSE (*n.*) 1. a defeat; failure. 2. the other side; the opposite. REVERSE (*adj.*) opposite; backward.

reversible (*adj.*) 1. usable with either side outwards. 2. can be driven backwards.

revert (*v.*) to go back to the beginning.

review (*v.*) 1. to examine again; to revise. 2. to give an opinion; to criticize. REVIEW (*n.*) 1. an inspection. 2. a criticism.

reviewer (*n.*) one who examines a book, play, etc., and writes his opinions about it; a critic.

revile (*v.*) to abuse; to insult.

revise (*v.*) to read again and correct. REVISED (*adj.*).

revision (*n.*) a correction of errors.

revival (*n.*) restoration to use or health.

revive (*v.*) to restore to use or health.

revocation (*n.*) a cancellation; an annulment.

revoke (*v.*) to cancel; to wipe out.

revolt (*v.*) to rebel. REVOLT (*n.*) a rebellion.

revolting (*adj.*) shocking; horrible. REVOLTINGLY (*adv.*).

revolution (*n.*) 1. a rebellion. 2. a spin or rotation. 3. a sudden change in opinion, fashion, etc.

revolutionary (*adj.*) changing completely. REVOLUTIONARY (*n.*) a rebel; traitor.

revolutionize (*v.*) to change completely.

revolve (*v.*) 1. to spin; to whirl. 2. to ponder; to consider.

revolver (*n.*) a pistol.

revulsion (*n.*) a change of feeling; a dislike.

reward (*n.*) gift or honour earned by merit. REWARD (*v.*) to honour merit.

Reynard (*n.*) the fox.

rhapsody (*n.*) musical composition with no special melody.

rheumatism (*n.*) complaint bringing pain in joints and muscles.

rhinoceros (*n.*) large African animal with horned nose.

rhododendron (*n.*) large-flowered evergreen shrub.

rhubarb (*n.*) garden plant with acid, juicy stalks.

rhyme (*n.*) use by poets of words alike in sound. RHYME (*v.*) to use like-sounding words.

rhythm (*n.*) regular beat or accent in music or speech; metre.

rhythmic (*adj.*) regular; measured. RHYTHMICALLY (*adv.*).

rib (*n.*) one of the bones enclosing the chest.

ribald (*adj.*) coarse; vulgar.

ribbon (*n.*) long, narrow band of material.

rice (*n.*) a white, edible grain.

rich (*adj.*) 1. wealthy. 2. nourishing. 3. valuable. RICHLY (*adv.*).

riches (*n. pl.*) wealth; affluence.

richness (*n.*) the excellence; splendour.

rickets (*n.*) childhood disease of the bones.

rickety (*adj.*) shaky; tottery.

rid (*v.*) to make free from. RIDDANCE (*n.*).

riddle (*n.*) 1. a puzzling question. 2. a large sieve. RIDDLE (*v.*) 1. to sift. 2. to fill with holes.

riddled (*adj.*) full of holes; sifted.

ride (*v.*) to be carried by an animal or vehicle. RIDE (*n.*) a trip on an animal or in a vehicle. RIDER (*n.*).

ridge (*n.*) the earth between two furrows; a mountain range.

ridicule (*v.*) to make fun of; to mock. RIDICULE (*n.*) mockery.

ridiculous (*adj.*) silly; absurd. RIDICULOUSLY (*adv.*).

rife (*adj.*) found everywhere; general.

rifle (*v.*) 1. to rob; to ransack. 2. to cut spiral grooves. RIFLE (*n.*) gun having a grooved barrel. RIFLEMAN (*n.*).

rifled (*adj.*) 1. robbed; ransacked. 2. grooved.

rift (*n.*) 1. a narrow crack or cleft. 2. a quarrel.

rig (*v.*) 1. to provide a ship with spars, ropes and gear. 2. to provide dress or equipment. 3. to trick; to swindle. RIG (*n.*) 1. the particular fitting of a ship's masts and sails. 2. the look of a person or thing as determined by its dress, fancy costume, harness, etc. 3. the arranging of some matter of business to fraudulently advantage oneself.

right (*n.*) 1. the standard of truth, justice and duty. 2. correctness; properness. 3. thing each person is entitled to. RIGHT (*v.*) 1. to make straight. 2. to free from wrong; to correct. RIGHT (*adj.*) 1. just; true. 2. straight; correct. 3. real; direct. RIGHT (*adv.*) completely; exactly.

righteous (*adj.*) 1. just; upright. 2. devout; godly.

righteousness (*n.*) 1. goodness; uprightness. 2. piety.

rightful (*adj.*) just; fair. RIGHTFULLY (*adv.*).

rightly (*adv.*) justly; lawfully.

rigid (*adj.*) stiff; unbending. RIGIDLY (*adv.*).

rigidity (*n.*) firmness; stiffness.

rigmarole (*n.*) meaningless talk.

rigorous (*adj.*) severe; stern. RIGOROUSLY (*adv.*).

rigour (*n.*) harshness; severity.

rill (*n.*) a streamlet.

rim (*n.*) the outer edge; the brim.

rime (*n.*) hoar-frost. RIMY (*adj.*).

rind (*n.*) the hard outer coat; the crust.

ring (*n.*) 1. a hollow circle; a hoop. 2. the sound struck from metal. RING (*v.*) to make metal sound.

ringlet (*n.*) a curl.

rink (*n.*) level place prepared for skating or curling.

rinse (*v.*) to swill in clean water.

riot (*n.*) 1. lawless disorder. 2. a noisy feasting. RIOT (*v.*) to break out in disorder. RIOTER (*n.*).

riotous (*adj.*) lawless; turbulent. RIOTOUSLY (*adv.*).

rip (*v.*) to tear; to split. RIP (*n.*) 1. a rent; tear. 2. a wild, worthless fellow.

ripe (*adj.*) fully grown; ready for eating.

ripen (*v.*) to become mature.

ripeness (*n.*) complete growth; perfection.

ripple (*n.*) 1. a slow, gentle wave. 2. the rise and fall of voices. RIPPLE (*v.*) to ruffle the surface of water; to make tiny waves.

rippling (*n.*) the sound and movement of ripples.

rise (*v.*) 1. to stand. 2. to ascend; to soar. 3. to increase; to swell. 4. to revolt. RISE (*n.*) 1. an upward slope. 2. an increase. 3. an ascent.

rising (*n.*) a rebellion; revolt.

risk (*n.*) danger; peril. RISK (*v.*) to venture; to endanger.

risky (*adj.*) dangerous. RISKILY (*adv.*).

rite (*n.*) a religious ceremony.

ritual (*n.*) the form of worship.

rival (*n.*) an opponent; a competitor. RIVAL (*v.*) to strive against; to oppose.

rivalry (*n.*) competition; opposition.

riven (*adj.*) split asunder; burst.

river (*n.*) large or wide stream.

rivet (*n.*) metal bolt or pin used to clinch metal plates together tightly. RIVET (*v.*) to join with rivets. RIVETER (*n.*).

rivulet (*n.*) a small stream.

roach (*n.*) freshwater fish of carp family.

road (*n.*) a highway for traffic. ROADWAY (*n.*).

road-hog (*n.*) one who uses the road in a selfish manner.

roadstead (*n.*) place where ships safely ride at anchor.

roam (*v.*) to wander; to travel. ROAMER (*n.*).

roar (*n.*) loud, deep rolling sound like that of thunder. ROAR (*v.*) to make a sound as of thunder.

roast (*v.*) to cook before a fire or in an oven. ROAST (*n.*) joint of meat prepared for roasting.

rob (v.) to steal by force; to plunder. ROBBER (n.).

robbery (n.) stealing by force. (pl. ROBBERIES).

robe (n.) long, loose, outer gown. ROBE (v.) to dress.

robin (n.) a red-breasted bird.

robust (adj.) healthy; strong. ROBUSTLY (adv.).

robustness (n.) healthiness; sturdiness.

rock (n.) the fixed, solid part of the earth's crust. ROCK (v.) 1. to sway from side to side. 2. to soothe; to lull. 3. to reel; to stagger.

rockery (n.) ornamental mound for growing rock-loving plants.

rocket (n.) 1. firework. 2. used to launch a space-ship or a missile.

rocky (adj.) full of rocks.

rod (n.) 1. straight, slender bar. 2. a fishing-rod. 3. an Imperial measure of length (5½ yards).

rodent (n.) a gnawing animal.

roe (n.) 1. eggs or spawn of fish. 2. a species of deer. 3. a female deer.

roebuck (n.) species of small deer.

rogue (n.) 1. a rascal; scoundrel. 2. a mischievous lad. 3. a savage elephant.

roguery (n.) rascality; trickery. (pl. ROGUERIES).

roguish (adj.) 1. rascally. 2. mischievous. ROGUISHLY (adv.).

roguishness (n.) 1. knavery. 2. mischief; horseplay.

roister (v.) to have merry fun; to swagger.

roisterer (n.) a bully; swaggerer.

rôle (n.) part played by an actor.

roll (v.) 1. to turn over and over. 2. to level with a roller. 3. to wind or reel. ROLL (n.) 1. a turning over and over. 2. continued beat of drum. 3. a register; list. 4. anything wound.

roller (n.) rod or cylinder used for smoothing, pressing, etc.

roly-poly (n.) crust with jam rolled into a pudding.

Roman (adj.) 1. concerning Rome or the Roman people. 2. concerning the Roman Catholic religion. 3. erect, as letters which are not italic; ordinary printed letters. 4. expressed in letters, not figures, as V, X, for 5 and 10. ROMAN (n.) 1. a native citizen or resident of Rome. 2. a Roman Catholic.

romance (n.) any made-up story; fiction.

romancer (n.) an imaginative story-teller.

romances (n. pl.) 1. fanciful stories. 2. novels.

romantic (adj.) 1. fanciful; imaginative. 2. sentimental.

Romany (n.) 1. a gipsy. 2. language of the gipsies. ROMANY (adj.) belonging to the gipsies.

romp (v.) to frolic; to gambol. ROMP (n.) lively game with a child.

rood (n.) 1. large cross bearing the figure of Christ. 2. an Imperial measure of area (¼ acre).

roof (n.) 1. the cover of a building. 2. upper, or arched part of the mouth. ROOF (v.) to cover the top; to shelter.

rook (n.) 1. black bird of crow family. 2. a chesspiece, the castle.

rookery (n.) nesting-place of colony of rooks.

room (n.) 1. an apartment; chamber. 2. space anything occupies.

roominess (n.) spaciousness.

roomy (adj.) having plenty of space.

roost (n.) bird's perching place. ROOST (v.) to settle for sleep.

rooster (n.) a farm-yard cock.

root (n.) 1. that part of a plant growing in the soil. 2. a foundation; base. ROOT (v.) 1. to plant in the soil. 2. to fix firmly; to found.

rooted (adj.) 1. firmly fixed; embedded. 2. thorough; strong.

rope (n.) long length of cordage or cable. ROPE (v.) to catch or bind with rope.

rosary (n.) string of beads for counting prayers.

rose (n.) 1. prickly shrub and its fragrant flower. 2. English national flower; symbol of youth and beauty.

roseate (adj.) rose-coloured; lovely.

rosemary (n.) fragrant shrub and its perfume.

rosette (n.) rose-shaped ornament of ribbon; a badge.

rosily (adv.) happily; contentedly.

rosiness (n.) pinkness; bloom.

rostrum (n.) speaker's platform, or pulpit.

rosy (adj.) 1. pink. 2. bright; favourable.

rot (v.) to decay; to perish. ROT (n.) 1. decay; corruption. 2. nonsense.

rotary (*adj.*) wheeling; spinning.

rotate (*v.*) to turn on an axis; to revolve.

rotation (*n.*) 1. a turn; revolution. 2. taking a turn, one after another.

rote (*n.*) the mechanical repetition of anything learned by heart.

rotor (*n.*) 1. rotary part of a machine. 2. revolving blade which lifts a helicopter.

rotten (*adj.*) 1. bad; decayed. 2. untrustworthy; unsound.

rottenness (*n.*) 1. decay. 2. unsoundness.

rotund (*adj.*) round like a ball; plump.

rotundity (*n.*) 1. roundness. 2. plumpness.

rouge (*n.*) powder to redden the cheeks. ROUGE (*v.*) to apply rouge.

rough (*adj.*) 1. coarse; uneven. 2. wild; stormy. 3. harsh; severe. 4. rude; uncivil. ROUGH (*v.*) to live without comforts.

roughen (*v.*) to make rough. ROUGHLY (*adv.*).

roughness (*n.*) 1. coarseness. 2. severity.

round (*adj.*) 1. ball-shaped; spherical. 2. ring-shaped; circular. ROUND (*n.*) 1. a part-song. 2. visit to one person after another. 3. a cartridge. 4. timed period in boxing match; game of golf, etc.

roundabout (*adj.*) 1. indirect; out-of-the-way. ROUNDABOUT (*n.*) 1. a merry-go-round. 2. a road traffic-island.

roundel (*n.*) circular identification sign painted on aircraft.

rounders (*n.*) game played with bat and soft ball.

roundly (*adv.*) boldly; plainly.

roundness (*n.*) 1. rotundity. 2. plumpness. 3. plainness.

rouse (*v.*) to wake up; to stir up. ROUSE (*n.*) a wakening; stirring.

rousing (*adj.*) thrilling; exciting. ROUSINGLY (*adv.*).

rout (*n.*) 1. disorderly flight of beaten foe. 2. a mob. ROUT (*v.*) to put to flight.

route (*n.*) the way travelled; the course.

routine (*n.*) an orderly method; a system.

rove (*v.*) to roam; to sail the seas.

rover (*n.*) a wanderer; pirate.

roving (*adj.*) wandering.

row (*n.*) 1. line of people or things. 2. a sail in an oar-driven boat. ROW (*v.*) to propel with oars.

row (*n.*) an uproar; a riot. ROW (*v.*) to make a disturbance.

rowan (*n.*) mountain-ash and its berry.

rowdy (*adj.*) noisy; quarrelsome. ROWDY (*n.*) a brawler.

rowdyism (*n.*) disorderly behaviour.

rower (*n.*) an oarsman.

rowlock (*n.*) contrivance in which an oar rests.

royal (*adj.*) 1. regal; stately. 2. splendid; excellent. ROYALLY (*adv.*).

royalist (*n.*) supporter of rule by kings.

royalty (*n.*) 1. kingship. 2. king and his family. 3. money paid for the use of an invention or composition. (*pl.* ROYALTIES).

rub (*v.*) to slide and press one thing against another; to wipe. RUB (*n.*) a scrape; wipe.

rubber (*n.*) 1. tough, elastic substance obtained from a tropical tree. 2. an indiarubber eraser.

rubbing (*n.*) a scouring; polishing.

rubbish (*n.*) 1. refuse; waste. 2. nonsense.

rubble (*n.*) rough broken brick or stone.

rubicund (*adj.*) reddish, flushed.

ruby (*n.*) a red gem. RUBY (*adj.*) deep red.

ruck (*n.*) 1. a wrinkle; fold. 2. the crowd; multitude. RUCK (*v.*) to wrinkle; to pucker.

ruction (*n.*) an uproar; a row.

rudder (*n.*) the part of a ship or aircraft by which it is steered.

ruddiness (*n.*) rosiness; freshness.

ruddy (*adj.*) rosy; healthy-looking.

rude (*adj.*) 1. primitive; rough. 2. unmannerly; uncivil. RUDELY (*adv.*).

rudeness (*n.*) 1. roughness; coarseness. 2. incivility; vulgarity.

rudiment (*n.*) a seed; beginning.

rudimentary (*adj.*) imperfect; elementary.

rue (*v.*) to regret; to wish undone. RUE (*n.*) 1. sorrow; repentance. 2. plant with bitter taste.

rueful (*adj.*) woeful; pitiful. RUEFULLY (*adv.*).

ruffian (*n.*) a violent attacker; an assailant. RUFFIANLY (*adj.*).

ruffianism (*n.*) violence; brutality.

ruffle (*v.*) 1. to disturb the smoothness of anything; to disarrange. 2. to rub the wrong way; to irritate. 3. to swagger. RUFFLE (*n.*) a frill; trimming.

ruffled (*adj.*) 1. rumpled; shaken. 2. out of temper; upset. 3. frilled.

rug (*n.*) woollen wrap, coverlet or mat.

rugby (*n.*) form of football in which the ball may be seized and run with.

rugged (*adj.*) 1. rough; jagged. 2. robust; hardy.

ruggedness (*n.*) 1. roughness. 2. robustness.

ruin (*v.*) to wreck; to destroy. RUIN (*n.*) 1. remains of an abandoned building. 2. a destruction; collapse. 3. bankruptcy.

ruined (*adj.*) 1. finished; wrecked. 2. bankrupt.

ruination (*n.*) overthrow; destruction.

ruinous (*adj.*) causing ruin; wasteful. RUINOUSLY (*adv.*).

rule (*n.*) 1. government; authority. 2. leadership; command. 3. an order; regulation. RULE (*v.*) 1. to govern. 2. to control. 3. to draw straight lines.

ruler (*n.*) 1. a monarch. 2. a drawing and measuring instrument.

ruling (*n.*) a decision; judgment. RULING (*adj.*) 1. reigning. 2. widespread; prevalent.

rum (*n.*) spirit distilled from sugar-cane. RUM (*adj.*) peculiar; queer. RUMMILY (*adv.*).

rumba (*n.*) ballroom dance from Cuba.

rumble (*n.*) 1. low, rolling sound like thunder. 2. a growl; grumble. RUMBLE (*v.*) to thunder; to growl.

rumbling (*n.*) 1. a dull sound like distant thunder. 2. a low growl.

ruminant (*n.*) animal that chews food over again as a cow does.

ruminate (*v.*) 1. to chew again. 2. to reflect; to reconsider.

ruminative (*adj.*) thoughtful; meditative.

rummage (*v.*) to search by tumbling things about; to ransack. RUMMAGE (*n.*) odds and ends; junk. RUMMAGER (*n.*).

rumour (*n.*) doubtful news; gossip that spreads. RUMOUR (*v.*) to spread reports or hearsay.

rump (*n.*) an animal's tail end.

rumple (*v.*) to ruffle; to wrinkle. RUMPLE (*n.*) a fold; wrinkle.

rumpled (*adj.*) creased; puckered.

rumpus (*n.*) an uproar; a brawl.

run (*v.*) 1. to move swiftly; to race. 2. to flow. 3. to venture; to risk. RUN (*n.*) 1. a race. 2. a journey; trip. 3. an increased demand for goods.

runaway (*n.*) 1. a fugitive. 2. an uncontrollable animal or vehicle.

rung (*n.*) a crossbar on a ladder.

runner (*n.*) 1. one who runs; a racer. 2. a climbing bean.

runners (*n. pl.*) bars or rails on which things may slide or run easily.

running (*adj.*) 1. quickly moving; flowing. 2. continuous.

runway (*n.*) wide, hard path to enable aircraft to take off and land.

rupture (*n.*) 1. a break; burst. 2. a quarrel; a parting. RUPTURE (*v.*) 1. to burst; to split. 2. to quarrel.

rural (*adj.*) countrified; rustic.

ruse (*n.*) a trick; a wile.

rush (*v.*) 1. to run forward; to dash. 2. to run with a crowd; to stampede. 3. to enter eagerly; to venture. RUSH (*n.*) 1. haste; hurry. 2. a stampede. 3. eagerness. 4. a long-stemmed waterside plant.

russet (*adj.*) reddish-brown. RUSSET (*n.*) 1. a coarse, home-spun, reddish-brown cloth. 2. a rough-skinned, russet-coloured apple.

rust (*n.*) brownish coating formed on iron which is decaying; corrosion. RUST (*v.*) to be eaten away; to corrode.

rustic (*adj.*) countrified; pastoral. RUSTIC (*n.*) a countryman; peasant.

rustication (*n.*) retirement to a quiet place.

rusticity (*n.*) simplicity; plainness.

rustle (*n.*) sound of wind-blown leaves; a whisper. RUSTLE (*v.*) to blow lightly; to stir.

rusty (*adj.*) corroded; croaking.

rut (*n.*) 1. a wheel-track; furrow. 2. a fixed method; groove.

ruthless (*adj.*) pitiless; merciless. RUTHLESSLY (*adv.*).

ruthlessness (*n.*) cruelty; mercilessness.

rye (*n.*) grain which makes brown bread.

S

Sabbath (*n.*) the day of worship. Among Christians, the first day, Sunday; among Jews, the seventh day, Saturday.

sable (*n.*) weasel-like fur-bearing animal. SABLE (*adj.*) black; dusky.

sabotage (*n.*) damage done purposely. SABOTAGE (*v.*) to damage wilfully.

sabre (*n.*) heavy sword with curved blade.

sack (*v.*) 1. to dismiss from employment. 2. to loot. SACK (*n.*) 1. large, coarse bag. 2. the looting of a captured town

sackcloth (*n.*) mourning garment of certain races.

sacrament (*n.*) solemn religious ceremony; a rite. SACRAMENTAL (*adj.*).

sacred (*adj.*) holy; consecrated.

sacrifice (*v.*) 1. to give to God. 2. to suffer loss in helping others. SACRIFICE (*n.*) 1. an offering to God. 2. loss suffered for a cause or duty.

sacrilege (*n.*) abuse of sacred things; profanity. SACRILEGIOUS (*adj.*).

sad (*adj.*) unhappy; sorrowful. SADLY (*adv.*).

sadden (*v.*) to make unhappy.

saddle (*n.*) a rider's seat. SADDLE (*v.*) 1. to put a saddle upon. 2. to burden; to load.

saddler (*n.*) maker of saddles.

sadness (*n.*) sorrow; misery.

safe (*adj.*) 1. secure from harm. 2. trustworthy. SAFE (*n.*) strong steel chest for storage of valuables. SAFELY (*adv.*).

safeguard (*n.*) a defence; shield. SAFEGUARD (*v.*) to protect.

safety (*n.*) security; freedom from danger.

safety-pin (*n.*) pin with a protected point.

saffron (*n.*) a plant yielding an orange dye.

sag (*v.*) 1. to sink in the middle; to droop. SAG (*n.*) the downward droop of a slung wire or rope.

sagacious (*adj.*) wise; shrewd. SAGACIOUSLY (*adv.*).

sagacity (*n.*) wisdom; intelligence.

sage (*adj.*) wise; grave. SAGE (*n.*) 1. a wise man; a philosopher. 2. a garden herb.

sagely (*adv.*) wisely; prudently.

sagging (*n.*) the sinking; drooping.

sago (*n.*) edible pith of a sago-palm tree.

sail (*n.*) 1. a canvas sheet which catches the wind and propels a ship. 2. a sea-voyage; cruise. SAIL (*v.*) 1. to voyage. 2. to direct a ship; to navigate.

sailing (*n.*) voyaging; navigating.

sailor (*n.*) a seaman; mariner. SAILORLY (*adj.*).

saint (*n.*) holy or devout person. SAINTLY (*adj.*).

salable (*adj.*) can be sold; marketable.

salad (*n.*) seasoned mixture of chopped vegetables.

salamander (*n.*) fabled lizard which lived in fire.

salaried (*adj.*) earning a salary; stipend.

salary (*n.*) sum fixed for a year's work, a portion being paid monthly or quarterly.

sale (*n.*) exchange of anything in return for money.

salesman (*n.*) an experienced seller.

salesmanship (*n.*) ability to sell.

salient (*adj.*) noticeable; prominent.

saline (*adj.*) salty.

saliva (*n.*) fluid moistening the mouth.

sallow (*adj.*) pale; sickly-looking.

sallowness (*n.*) paleness.

sally (*n.*) 1. a sudden attack; a raid. 2. a quick answer; a retort.

salmon (*n.*) large, silver-scaled fish.

salon (*n.*) room in which paintings are exhibited.

saloon (*n.*) hall for public assemblies.

salt (*n.*) 1. white, mineral substance used to flavour and preserve food. 2. a sailor. SALT (*v.*) to season or preserve food.

saltpetre (*n.*) white, mineral substance used as a fertilizer.

salty (*adj.*) tasting of salt.

salubrious (*adj.*) wholesome; healthy.

salutary (*adj.*) beneficial; advantageous.

salutation (*n.*) a greeting; welcome.

salute (*n.*) a greeting. SALUTE (*v.*) to welcome; to hail.

salvage (*v.*) to save from destruction. SALVAGE (*n.*) goods recovered from shipwreck, fire or flood. SALVAGED (*adj.*).

salvation (*n.*) rescue from danger or sin.

salve (*n.*) a healing ointment. SALVE (*v.*) 1. to soothe; to heal. 2. to recover from fire or wreck.

same (*adj.*) identical; unchanging.

sameness (*n.*) 1. likeness. 2. tediousness; monotony.

sample (*n.*) a specimen; pattern. SAMPLE (*v.*) to test; to match.

sanatorium (*n.*) place where invalids receive treatment. (*pl.* SANATORIA).

sanctification (*n.*) sacredness; consecration.

sanctify (*v.*) to make holy; to consecrate. SANCTIFIED (*adj.*).

sanction (*v.*) to approve. SANCTION (*n.*) 1. approval; permission. 2. a penalty.

sanctity (*n.*) holiness; sacredness.

sanctuary (*n.*) 1. a church. 2. a protection; refuge. (*pl.* SANCTUARIES).

sanctum (*n.*) one's own room; a den.

sand (*n.*) fine grains of stone. SAND (*v.*) to spread with sand. SANDED (*adj.*).

sandal (*n.*) a sole strapped to the foot; an openwork shoe.

sandalwood (*n.*) tree and its fragrant wood.

sand-paper (*n.*) paper surfaced with sand and glue and used for smoothing.

sandstone (*n.*) coarse, sandy building-stone.

sandwich (*n.*) two pieces of buttered bread with a filling between. (*pl.* SANDWICHES). SANDWICH (*v.*) to jam between. See appendix.

sandy (*adj.*) 1. sand-covered. 2. yellowish-red.

sane (*adj.*) sound in mind; sensible. SANELY (*adv.*).

sanguine (*adj.*) hopeful; confident.

sanitary (*adj.*) healthy; clean.

sanitation (*n.*) cleanliness; hygiene.

sanity (*n.*) soundness of mind.

sap (*n.*) 1. juice flowing in plants. 2. tunnel dug secretly; a trap. SAP (*v.*) 1. to drain off the sap; to exhaust. 2. to tunnel secretly; to undermine.

sapience (*n.*) wisdom; knowledge.

sapient (*n.*) sensible; shrewd.

sapling (*n.*) a young tree.

sapper (*n.*) soldier trained in digging and engineering.

sapphire (*n.*) a blue gem. SAPPHIRE (*adj.*) deep blue.

sappy (*adj.*) juicy.

sarcasm (*n.*) hurtful mockery; taunting.

sarcastic (*adj.*) mocking; sneering. SARCASTICALLY (*adv.*).

sarcophagus (*n.*) a stone coffin. (*pl.* SARCOPHAGI).

sardine (*n.*) a small Mediterranean fish of herring family, often preserved in olive oil.

sardonic (*adj.*) mocking; scornful. SARDONICALLY (*adv.*).

sash (*n.*) 1. scarf for waist or shoulder. 2. window-frame.

Satan (*n.*) the chief of all evil spirits tempting mankind to sin; the Devil. SATANIC (*adj.*).

satchel (*n.*) flat bag hung from the shoulder; schoolbag.

satellite (*n.*) 1. planet revolving round a larger one; a moon. 2. a follower; hanger-on.

satin (*n.*) silk cloth, glossy on one side.

satire (*n.*) a taunting speech or writing; ridicule.

satirical (*adj.*) bitter; sneering. SATIRICALLY (*adv.*).

satirist (*n.*) writer of satire.

satirize (*v.*) to scoff at; to ridicule.

satisfaction (*n.*) contentment; gratification.

satisfactory (*adj.*) adequate; suitable. SATISFACTORILY (*adv.*).

satisfied (*adj.*) pleased; contented.

satisfy (*v.*) to content; to gratify.

saturate (*v.*) to soak; to drench.

saturated (*adj.*) fully soaked.

saturation (*n.*) a complete soaking.

Saturday (*n.*) seventh and last day of week. See appendix.

Saturn (*n.*) ringed planet lying between Jupiter and Neptune. See appendix.

saturnine (*adj.*) frowning; gloomy.

satyr (*n.*) fabled creature, half man, half goat.

sauce (*n.*) 1. a liquid seasoning; relish. 2. impudence.

saucepan (*n.*) small, metal cooking-utensil.

saucer (*n.*) flat dish to support a cup.

saucy (*adj.*) 1. disdainful. 2. cheeky. SAUCILY (*adv.*).

saunter (*v.*) to stroll lazily; to dawdle. SAUNTER (*n.*) a leisurely ramble.

sausage (*n.*) minced meat enclosed in a skin.

savage (*adj.*) 1. untamed, fierce. 2. barbarian; uncivilized. 3. angry; enraged.

SAVAGE (*n.*) a barbarian; uncivilized person. SAVAGELY (*adv.*).

savagery (*n.*) living in the wilds; barbarian life.

save (*v.*) 1. to rescue; to liberate. 2. to keep; to put by. 3. to be sparing; economical. SAVE (*prep.*) leaving out; except.

saving (*adj.*) frugal; economical.

savings (*n. pl.*) money put by in the bank; a reserve.

saviour (*n.*) a rescuer; liberator. THE SAVIOUR, Jesus Christ.

savour (*n.*) the taste or smell; flavour.

savoury (*adj.*) appetizing, delicious.

savoy (*n.*) a curly-leaved cabbage.

saw (*n.*) 1. a toothed blade for cutting through wood or metal. 2. a proverb. SAW (*v.*) to cut with a saw.

sawdust (*n.*) wood dust made by sawing.

sawyer (*n.*) one who saws timber into planks.

Saxon (*n.*) 1. one of the North-West German race which invaded and conquered Britain in the fifth and sixth centuries; a Teuton. 2. native of modern Saxony. 3. language of the Saxons.

saxophone (*n.*) powerful wind-instrument.

say (*v.*) to speak; to state.

saying (*n.*) 1. an utterance. 2. a proverb; household word.

scabbard (*n.*) sheath for sword or bayonet.

scaffold (*n.*) 1. framework supporting platforms on which men can work at heights. 2. a place of execution.

scald (*v.*) 1. to injure with hot liquid. 2. to cook in steam. SCALD (*n.*) injury from hot liquid or steam. SCALDED (*adj.*).

scale (*n.*) 1. a balance; weighing machine. 2. a thin flake. 3. a measuring instrument. 4. a succession of musical notes. SCALE (*v.*) 1. to weigh. 2. to climb up and over.

scalp (*n.*) skin and hair of the head.

scaly (*adj.*) scale-covered.

scamp (*n.*) a rascal; scapegrace. SCAMP (*v.*) to do slipshod or imperfect work.

scamper (*v.*) to run in a flurry. SCAMPER (*n.*) a headlong flight.

scan (*v.*) to examine closely.

scandal (*n.*) shameful conduct causing offence to others.

scandalize (*v.*) to offend by shameful conduct.

scandalous (*adj.*) disgraceful; offensive. SCANDALOUSLY (*adv.*).

scant (*adj.*) slight; skimpy. SCANT (*v.*) to supply grudgingly; to stint.

scantiness (*n.*) the littleness; lack.

scanty (*adj.*) barely sufficient.

scapegoat (*n.*) one blamed for another's fault.

scapegrace (*n.*) mischievous, harebrained person.

scar (*n.*) 1. mark left by a healed wound. 2. a cliff. SCAR (*v.*) to leave or cause a scar; to sear.

scarce (*adj.*) hard to obtain; rare. SCARCELY (*adv.*) hardly; barely.

scarcity (*n.*) dearth; shortage.

scare (*v.*) to frighten; to alarm. SCARE (*n.*) a fright.

scarecrow (*n.*) guy placed to frighten birds from crops.

scaremonger (*n.*) spreader of alarming news.

scarf (*n.*) light neck-wrap.

scarlet (*n.*) a bright red colour. SCARLET (*adj.*).

scarp (*n.*) very steep slope. SCARPED (*adj.*).

scarred (*adj.*) marked by scars.

scathe (*v.*) to injure; to bruise. SCATHE (*n.*) the harm suffered. SCATHING (*adj.*). SCATHELESS (*adj.*).

scatter (*v.*) 1. to strew about; to sprinkle. 2. to separate; to disperse. SCATTERED (*adj.*).

scatter-brain (*n.*) a giddy, thoughtless person.

scattering (*n.*) a spreading here and there; dispersal.

scene (*n.*) 1. the view. 2. place where an event happens. 3. part of a stage play. 4. a dispute; noisy argument.

scenery (*n.*) 1. the landscape; view. 2. painted scenes used on a stage.

scent (*v.*) 1. to smell. 2. to perfume. 3. to find the trail of. 4. to suspect. SCENT (*n.*) 1. a smell; odour. 2. a perfume; fragrance. 3. a trail; track.

scented (*adj.*) perfumed; fragrant.

sceptic (*n.*) a doubter; scoffer.

sceptical (*adj.*) doubtful; unbelieving. SCEPTICALLY (*adv.*).

scepticism (*n.*) doubt; disbelief.

sceptre (*n.*) sovereign's staff which symbolizes authority.

schedule (*n.*) a list of details; a plan. SCHEDULE (*v.*) 1. to put on a list. 2. to plan a future programme.

scheme (*n.*) 1. a plan; design. 2. a plot. SCHEME (*v.*) 1. to plan. 2. to conspire. SCHEMER (*n.*).

scheming (*n.*) the details of planning. SCHEMING (*adj.*) planning; conspiring.

scholar (*n.*) 1. a pupil; student. 2. a learned person.

scholarly (*adj.*) eager to learn; studious.

scholarship (*n.*) 1. learning; knowledge. 2. an award gained by a student.

scholastic (*adj.*) concerning schools and learning.

school (*n.*) 1. place of instruction. 2. a shoal of fish. SCHOOL (*v.*) to teach; to train.

schooling (*n.*) instruction in school; tuition.

schoolmaster (*n.*) a teacher; tutor. (*fem.* SCHOOLMISTRESS).

schooner (*n.*) two or more masted sailing ship with masts rigged fore and aft (front and rear of ship).

science (*n.*) knowledge of natural laws and truths.

scientific (*adj.*) true; factual.

scientifically (*adv.*) by giving proof; by demonstrating.

scientist (*n.*) one learned in a science; a savant.

scintillate (*v.*) to sparkle; to twinkle.

scissors (*n. pl.*) two cutting-blades moving on a central pin.

scoff (*v.*) to mock; to jeer. SCOFF (*n.*) a jibe; taunt. SCOFFER (*n.*).

scoffing (*n.*) mockery; ridicule.

scold (*v.*) 1. to find fault with; to rebuke. 2. a noisy, complaining woman.

scolding (*n.*) a good talking to; a chiding.

scone (*n.*) small, flat cake.

scoop (*n.*) 1. a bowl-like shovel. 2. special or exclusive news. SCOOP (*v.*) 1. to dig out with the hands. 2. to ladle from one container to another. 3. to discover special news.

scope (*n.*) 1. extent of room or space. 2. range of one's plans, aims, etc.

scorch (*v.*) 1. to blacken by burning; to singe. 2. to drive too quickly; to speed. SCORCHED (*adj.*).

scorching (*adj.*) hot; parching. SCORCHING (*n.*) speeding.

score (*v.*) 1. to mark with scratches. 2. to make another feel small; to humble. 3. to gain wins or points in games. SCORE (*n.*) 1. a scratch. 2. a total; sum. 3. a win; an advantage. 4. a set of twenty. SCORER (*n.*).

scorn (*n.*) contempt; disdain. SCORN (*v.*) to despise; to spurn.

scornful (*adj.*) disdainful; contemptuous. SCORNFULLY (*adv.*).

scorpion (*n.*) lobster-like creature with poisonous sting.

Scot (*n.*) 1. member of the Gaelic tribe which migrated from Ireland to Scotland in the sixth century. 2. a native of Scotland. SCOTTISH (*adj.*).

scot-free (*adj.*) unharmed; untouched.

scoundrel (*n.*) a rascal; rogue.

scoundrelly (*adj.*) villainous; base.

scour (*v.*) 1. to cleanse by rubbing; to brighten. 2. to range in pursuit.

scourge (*v.*) 1. to whip; to oppress. 2. to afflict by plague. 3. to annoy; to bother. SCOURGE (*n.*) 1. a whip; lash. 2. a plague; pestilence. 3. a nuisance.

scourging (*n.*) a flogging; punishment.

scouring (*n.*) a cleansing; polishing.

scout (*v.*) 1. to reject with scorn; to ridicule. 2. to explore; to survey. 3. to spy. SCOUT (*n.*) 1. an explorer. 2. a spy. 3. member of the Boy Scouts' movement.

scowl (*v.*) to frown; to glower. SCOWL (*n.*) an angry, sullen look.

scowling (*adj.*) sullen; frowning. SCOWLINGLY (*adv.*).

scramble (*v.*) 1. to climb on all-fours; to crawl. 2. to mix; to jumble. 3. to jostle; to push. SCRAMBLE (*n.*) 1. a rush to be first; a struggle. 2. a clambering; a climbing.

scrap (*n.*) 1. a piece; fragment. SCRAP (*v.*) to break up or throw away.

scrape (*v.*) 1. to rub with an edged tool. 2. to save; to hoard. SCRAPE (*n.*) 1. a rub. 2. a difficulty; plight.

scraper (*n.*) a tool for scraping.

scrap-heap (*n.*) a waste-heap; junk-heap.
scrappy (*adj.*) made up of bits and pieces.
scratch (*v.*) 1. to tear with a point; to claw. 2. to withdraw from a contest. SCRATCH (*n.*) mark torn on the surface. SCRATCH (*adj.*) taken at random.
scrawl (*v.*) to write hastily; to scribble. SCRAWL (*n.*) unreadable writing; scribble.
scream (*v.*) to utter shrill cries; to shriek. SCREAM (*n.*) a yell; shriek.
screamingly (*adj.*) very; immensely.
screech (*v.*) to scream shrilly. SCREECH (*n.*) a shrill cry as of an owl.
screen (*v.*) 1. to pass through a test. 2. to cover; to protect. SCREEN (*n.*) 1. a sieve. 2. a partition. 3. cinema picture-sheet.
screw (*n.*) 1. pin with a spiral groove cut round it. 2. a ship's propeller. SCREW (*v.*) to twist; to squeeze.
screw-driver (*n.*) tool for turning screws.
scribble (*v.*) to scrawl. SCRIBBLE (*n.*) unreadable writing. SCRIBBLER (*n.*).
scribe (*n.*) a writer; clerk.
script (*n.*) 1. handwriting. 2. text of a broadcast talk. 3. film scenario.
scriptural (*adj.*) according to the Bible.
Scriptures (*n. pl.*) the Books of the Bible.
scroll (*n.*) roll of parchment or paper.
scrub (*v.*) to rub; to cleanse. SCRUB (*n.*) 1. a cleansing. 2. brushwood; shrubs.
scruff (*n.*) loose skin at back of neck.
scruple (*v.*) to doubt; to hesitate. SCRUPLE (*n.*) 1. a feeling of doubt. 2. a small weight (20 grains).
scrupulous (*adj.*) careful; exact. SCRUPULOUSLY (*adv.*).
scrutinize (*v.*) to examine with great care.
scrutiny (*n.*) a searching examination.
scuffle (*v.*) to brawl; to fight. SCUFFLE (*n.*) a brawl.
scull (*n.*) light, single-handed oar. SCULL (*v.*) to propel with sculls. SCULLER (*n.*).
scullery (*n.*) place where dishes are washed; a back-kitchen.
sculptor (*n.*) a carver of statues. (*fem.* SCULPTRESS).
sculpture (*n.*) art of carving in wood or stone. SCULPTURED (*adj.*).
scum (*n.*) froth or dirt on the surface of a liquid; dross.
scurry (*v.*) to scamper off in affright.

scurviness (*n.*) meanness; nastiness.
scurvy (*n.*) disease due to lack of fresh vegetables. SCURVY (*adj.*) mean; nasty. SCURVILY (*adv.*).
scuttle (*v.*) 1. to scamper off quickly. 2. to sink a ship purposely. SCUTTLE (*n.*) 1. a ship's hatchway. 2. a coal-bucket.
scythe (*n.*) long, curved blade for mowing.
sea (*n.*) large extent of salt water.
seaboard (*n.*) the coast.
seafarer (*n.*) a sailor; mariner.
seafaring (*adj.*) sailing; nautical.
seal (*n.*) 1. fur-bearing sea mammal. 2. wax impressed with a personal design. SEAL (*v.*) 1. to hunt seals. 2. to affix a seal to a document.
sealskin (*n.*) skin of the seal prepared as fur.
seam (*n.*) 1. line where edges are sewn together. 2. layer of coal in rock.
seaman (*n.*) a sailor; mariner.
seamanship (*n.*) skill in navigating a ship.
seamless (*adj.*) without a seam; whole.
seamstress (*n.*) a sewing-woman.
seamy (*adj.*) showing the inside; least attractive.
seaport (*n.*) a harbour-town.
sear (*v.*) to scorch; to wither. SEAR (*adj.*) dry; scorched.
search (*v.*) to look for. SEARCH (*n.*) 1. a seeking. 2. an inquiry. 3. an investigation. SEARCHER (*n.*).
searching (*adj.*) keen; penetrating. SEARCHINGLY (*adv.*).
searchlight (*n.*) apparatus casting a powerful light on distant objects.
seascape (*n.*) scene at sea, or painting of such.
seaside (*n.*) a place by the sea.
season (*n.*) 1. one of year's four divisions. 2. the suitable time. SEASON (*v.*) 1. to get used to; to inure. 2. to flavour.
seasonable (*adj.*) 1. suitable to the season. 2. fit; convenient.
seasonal (*adj.*) according to the season.
seasoning (*n.*) a flavouring; relish.
seat (*n.*) 1. something to sit on. 2. place in which anything is situated; site. 3. a family mansion. SEAT (*v.*) 1. to sit down. 2. to provide seats for. 3. to place on a site.

seaweed (*n.*) plant that grows in the sea.

seaworthiness (*n.*) fitness of a ship for its voyage.

seaworthy (*adj.*) fit to put to sea.

secede (*v.*) to leave; to withdraw.

secession (*n.*) a leaving; withdrawal.

seclude (*v.*) to keep away from others; to isolate.

secluded (*adj.*) lonely; unfrequented.

seclusion (*n.*) isolation; privacy.

second (*n.*) 1. next after the first. 2. a helper; supporter. 3. measure of time and angle (1/60 minute). SECOND (*v.*) to aid; to support.

secondary (*adj.*) 1. coming second. 2. less important.

seconder (*n.*) a supporter.

second-hand (*adj.*) already used; not new.

secondly (*adv.*) in the second place.

secrecy (*n.*) silence; concealment.

secret (*adj.*) hidden; known only to one or a few. SECRETLY (*adv.*).

secretarial (*adj.*) work proper to a secretary.

secretary (*n.*) business man's assistant with correspondence. (*pl.* SECRETARIES).

secrete (*v.*) to hide away; to conceal.

secretion (*n.*) a concealment.

secretive (*adj.*) reserved; unconfiding.

sect (*n.*) body of people holding the same beliefs.

section (*n.*) a part; portion.

sectional (*adj.*) in parts. SECTIONALLY (*adv.*).

sector (*n.*) 1. part of a circle between two radii. 2. a district.

secular (*adj.*) worldly, not sacred or religious matters.

secure (*adj.*) safe; carefree. SECURE (*v.*) 1. to get; to procure. 2. to keep safely; to fasten firmly. SECURELY (*adv.*).

security (*n.*) a pledge; guarantee; safety.

sedate (*adj.*) grave; dignified. SEDATELY (*adv.*).

sedateness (*n.*) calmness; placidity.

sedative (*n.*) remedy that soothes.

sedentary (*adj.*) used to sitting; done in a chair.

sedge (*n.*) grassy plant growing in wet ground.

sediment (*n.*) solids that settle at the bottom of a liquid; dregs.

sedimentary (*adj.*) made of a sediment.

sedition (*n.*) disloyal talk.

seditious (*adj.*) disloyal; unpatriotic. SEDITIOUSLY (*adv.*).

seduce (*v.*) to tempt to do wrong; to lead astray.

seduction (*n.*) a temptation; enticement.

sedulous (*adj.*) diligent; tireless. SEDULOUSLY (*adv.*).

see (*v.*) 1. to look at with the eye; to perceive. 2. to know; to understand. SEE (*n.*) district under a bishop; diocese.

seed (*n.*) grain from which a plant grows. SEEDLESS (*adj.*).

seediness (*n.*) 1. an abundance of seeds. 2. a feeling of sickness.

seedling (*n.*) very young plant.

seedsman (*n.*) a dealer in seeds; a grower.

seedy (*adj.*) 1. unwell; out of sorts. 2. shabby.

seek (*v.*) 1. to look for; to try to find. 2. to inquire. SEEKER (*n.*).

seem (*v.*) 1. to look like; to appear to be. 2. to pretend; to sham.

seeming (*adj.*) like; resembling. SEEMINGLY (*adv.*).

seemliness (*n.*) rightness; suitability.

seemly (*adj.*) fitting; proper.

seep (*v.*) to leak drop by drop; to ooze.

seepage (*n.*) a slow leakage; trickle.

seer (*n.*) one who foresees; a prophet. (*fem.* SEERESS).

seethe (*v.*) 1. to bubble; to boil. 2. to hold back anger or annoyance.

seething (*adj.*) 1. boiling. 2. annoyed; angry.

segment (*n.*) a part that breaks off naturally.

segmented (*adj.*) divided into distinct parts.

seize (*v.*) 1. to grip. 2. to capture; to arrest.

seizing (*n.*) the grasping; capturing.

seizure (*n.*) 1. a capture; arrest. 2. sudden attack of illness.

seldom (*adv.*) not often; rarely.

select (*v.*) to pick; to choose. SELECT (*adj.*) choice; exclusive.

selected (*adj.*) chosen; picked.

selection (*n.*) 1. a choice. 2. a set, from which to choose the best.

selective (*adj.*) able to separate one from another, like a sieve.

self (*n.*) one's own person. (*pl.* SELVES).

NOTE: SELF- is joined to many words which you will understand if you refer to the JOINED WORD, e.g., SELF-DEFENCE. Others in common use are:

self-centred (*adj.*) selfish.

self-conceit (*n.*) pride in oneself; vanity.

self-conscious (*adj.*) uncomfortable among people.

self-denial (*n.*) ready to put others first; forbearance.

self-esteem (*n.*) holding a good opinion of oneself; conceit.

self-evident (*adj.*) true; obvious.

self-importance (*n.*) overrating one's own merit; conceit.

self-indulgence (*n.*) placing one's own desires first.

self-interest (*n.*) selfishness.

selfish (*adj.*) caring only for oneself; having one's own way. SELFISHLY (*adv.*).

selfishness (*n.*) disregard for others.

self-made (*adj.*) successful by one's own efforts.

self-possessed (*adj.*) calm; cool.

self-possession (*n.*) reliability in emergency.

self-reliant (*adj.*) trusting to one's own powers. SELF-RELIANCE (*n.*).

self-respect (*n.*) regard for one's character and reputation.

selfsame (*adj.*) the same; identical.

self-seeking (*adj.*) selfish; greedy.

sell (*v.*) to exchange for money. SELLER (*n.*).

semaphore (*n.*) signalling by arm-movements.

semblance (*n.*) a likeness; similarity.

semi- prefix meaning half; partly, to some extent.

seminary (*n.*) a school; college.

Semitic (*adj.*) pertaining to the Semites, or people of any race descended from Shem, son of Noah, but especially the Hebrews and Arabs.

semolina (*n.*) hard grains left after the grinding of flour; used in puddings.

senate (*n.*) a law-making council.

senator (*n.*) a member of a senate. SENATORIAL (*adj.*).

send (*v.*) 1. to dispatch; to transmit. 2. to hurl; to fling.

sender (*n.*) 1. one who dispatches. 2. a telegraphic transmitter.

senile (*adj.*) 1. old; aged. 2. weak; childish.

senility (*n.*) old age and its infirmities.

senior (*adj.*) 1. older than another. 2. higher in rank or authority. SENIOR (*n.*) 1. elder of two. 2. a superior in age or experience.

seniority (*n.*) first in age or experience.

sensation (*n.*) 1. a feeling; an excitement. 2. a stirring event.

sensational (*adj.*) exciting; thrilling. SENSATIONALLY (*adv.*).

sense (*n.*) 1. ability to see, hear, smell, taste and feel. 2. understanding. 3. the meaning. SENSE (*v.*) to understand; to know.

senseless (*adj.*) 1. having little sense; stupid. 2. unable to use one's senses; unconscious. SENSELESSLY (*adv.*).

sensibility (*n.*) 1. intelligence. 2. ability to have one's feelings easily moved.

sensible (*adj.*) 1. aware; conscious. 2. intelligent; sharp. SENSIBLY (*adv.*).

sensitive (*adj.*) nervous; highly-strung.

sentence (*n.*) 1. a decision; judgment. 2. a sensible arrangement of words. SENTENCE (*v.*) to impose punishment; to condemn.

sentiment (*n.*) 1. a tender or kindly feeling. 2. a thought; idea.

sentimental (*adj.*) tender by nature; kind.

sentinel or **sentry** (*n.*) soldier on guard duty. (*pl.* SENTRIES).

separate (*v.*) to divide; to disconnect. SEPARATE (*adj.*) disconnected; distinct.

separately (*adv.*) one at a time.

separation (*n.*) a parting; division.

sepia (*n.*) a brown dye.

September (*n.*) year's ninth month. (Roman ninth month).

septennial (*adj.*) happening once in seven years.

septic (*adj.*) poisoned; infected.

septuagenarian (*n.*) person aged seventy years.

sepulchre (*n.*) a tomb; grave. SEPULCHRAL (*adj.*).

sequel (*n.*) a result; consequence.

sequence (*n.*) arrangement in which things follow one after another.

sequester (*v.*) to remove to a quiet place: to take away. SEQUESTERED (*adj.*).

seraph (*n.*) archangel. (*pl.* SERAPHIM, or SERAPHS).

seraphic (*adj.*) pure; holy.

serenade (*n.*) evening music. SERENADE (*v.*) to play or sing to a loved one. SERENADER (*n.*).

serene (*adj.*) calm; untroubled.

serenity (*n.*) peacefulness; content.

serf (*n.*) a slave-worker.

serfdom (*n.*) slavery.

serge (*n.*) strong woollen cloth.

sergeant (*n.*) 1. non-commissioned military officer. 2. a police officer.

serial (*adj.*) in successive parts or numbers.

series (*n.*) a number of things arranged in order.

serious (*adj.*) 1. solemn; important. 2. grave. SERIOUSLY (*adv.*).

seriousness (*n.*) 1. the solemnity; importance. 2. the urgency; gravity.

sermon (*n.*) address by a clergyman or minister.

serpent (*n.*) a snake. SERPENTINE (*adj.*).

serrate (*v.*) to notch. SERRATED (*adj.*).

serration (*n.*) a notch; indentation.

serried (*adj.*) arranged in rows or ranks.

serum (*n.*) the watery part of the blood.

servant (*n.*) paid household worker.

serve (*v.*) to work for or attend upon another.

service (*n.*) 1. work; duty. 2. a religious ceremony. 3. a set of table-ware. 4. a help or aid given to another.

serviceable (*adj.*) useful; hard-wearing.

servile (*adj.*) slavish; abject.

servility (*n.*) base submission or obedience.

servitude (*n.*) slavery; bondage.

session (*n.*) a sitting of a meeting or assembly.

set (*v.*) 1. to place. 2. to plant. 3. to become solid. 4. to sink as the sun. SET (*n.*) 1. body of people with the same interests. 2. group of things of the same kind. SET (*adj.*) fixed; regular.

set-back (*n.*) a check; disappointment.

settee (*n.*) long seat with a back and arms.

setter (*n.*) a game-dog.

setting (*n.*) 1. a background. 2. the hardening of cement, etc.

settle (*v.*) 1. to rest. 2. to sink to the bottom. 3. to pay in full. 4. to colonize. SETTLE (*n.*) a bench with a high back.

settled (*adj.*) 1. decided. 2. paid in full. 3. colonized.

settlement (*n.*) 1. a full repayment. 2. a fixed arrangement. 3. a colony.

settler (*n.*) one who makes a home in a new country; a colonist.

sever (*v.*) to cut; to separate.

several (*adj.*) 1. separate; distinct. 2. few; some. 3. various; different.

severally (*adv.*) apart from others; separately.

severance (*n.*) a separation; parting.

severe (*adj.*) 1. stern; strict. 2. plain; unadorned. SEVERELY (*adv.*).

severity (*n.*) 1. harshness. 2. simplicity.

sew (*v.*) to fasten with needle and thread; to stitch.

sewage (*n.*) refuse draining to a sewer.

sewer (*n.*) 1. one who sews. 2. an underground drain.

sewerage (*n.*) the system of drainage.

sewing (*n.*) work done by sewing.

sex (*n.*) being male or female.

sextant (*n.*) instrument for finding position at sea.

sexton (*n.*) a church caretaker; a grave-digger.

shabbiness (*n.*) 1. untidiness; raggedness. 2. meanness.

shabby (*adj.*) 1. worn out; threadbare. 2. paltry; mean. SHABBILY (*adv.*).

shack (*n.*) a shed; hut.

shackle (*n.*) a chain; fetter. SHACKLE (*v.*) to bind the limbs; to fetter.

shade (*v.*) 1. to screen from strong light. 2. to colour; to tint. SHADE (*n.*) 1. anything that screens light from the eyes. 2. a blend of colours.

shadiness (*n.*) amount of shade or shadow.

shadow (*n.*) a patch of shade. SHADOW (*v.*) 1. to darken. 2. to watch; to follow.

shadowy (*adj.*) gloomy; faint.

shaft (*n.*) 1. an arrow. 2. a pole; a long handle. 3. a deep mine. 4. a column; pillar.

shagginess (*n.*) roughness; coarseness.

shaggy (*adj.*) coarse; tousled. SHAGGILY (*adv.*).

shake (*v.*) 1. to tremble; to shiver. 2. to

wave; to brandish. SHAKE (*n.*) 1. a shudder. 2. a shock; jolt.

shakiness (*n.*) weakness; insecurity.

shaky (*adj.*) weak; tottering. SHAKILY (*adv.*).

shale (*n.*) a hard, slaty rock.

shall verb and auxiliary verb expressing determination, compulsion and future time.

shallow (*adj.*) 1. having little depth. 2. slight; empty-headed.

shallowness (*n.*) 1. lack of depth. 2. unreliability.

sham (*v.*) to pretend; to feign. SHAM (*n.*) a pretence, counterfeit. SHAM (*adj.*) false; imitation.

shamble (*v.*) to walk clumsily and unsteadily; to shuffle. SHAMBLE (*n.*) a shuffling walk or gait. SHAMBLES (*n. pl. used as sing.*) a slaughter-house; a scene of bloodshed.

shame (*n.*) feeling of disgrace or guilt. SHAME (*v.*) to disgrace; to dishonour.

shamefaced (*adj.*) confused; bashful.

shameful (*adj.*) disgraceful; shocking. SHAMEFULLY (*adv.*).

shameless (*adj.*) bold; brazen. SHAMELESSLY (*adv.*).

shamelessness (*n.*) boldness; audacity.

shampoo (*v.*) to lather and wash the hair.

shamrock (*n.*) three-leaved clover; national emblem of Ireland.

shank (*n.*) 1. leg from knee to ankle. 2. long, thin handle of any instrument.

shanty (*n.*) 1. a hut. 2. an old-time sailor-song.

shape (*n.*) the outward form; the figure. SHAPE (*v.*) to form; to fashion.

shapeless (*adj.*) 1. ill-formed; ugly. 2. irregular; disorganized.

shapelessness (*n.*) irregularity; ugliness.

shapeliness (*n.*) gracefulness; comeliness.

shapely (*adj.*) well-formed; neat.

share (*n.*) 1. a fixed portion; ration. 2. blade of a plough. SHARE (*v.*) to divide among; to allot.

shareholder (*n.*) one who owns a share in a business or company.

shark (*n.*) large, savage fish.

sharp (*adj.*) 1. keen-edged or pointed. 2. quick-witted. 3. painful; stinging. 4. piercing; biting. SHARPLY (*adv.*).

sharpen (*v.*) 1. to make sharp. 2. to make brisker.

sharper (*n.*) a trickster; cheat.

sharpness (*n.*) 1. keenness. 2. bitterness. 3. briskness.

sharpshooter (*n.*) a good marksman.

shatter (*v.*) 1. to smash in bits. 2. to end hopes.

shattering (*adj.*) 1. smashing; destructive. 2. heart-breaking.

shave (*v.*) 1. to remove hair with a razor. 2. to graze; to skim. SHAVE (*n.*) 1. a removal of hair. 2. a narrow escape.

shaving (*n.*) a thin slice; a flake.

shawl (*n.*) loose covering for neck and shoulders.

sheaf (*n.*) quantity of grain or flowers bound together; a bunch. (*pl.* SHEAVES).

shear (*v.*) to cut with shears; to clip.

shearing (*n.*) the clipping of sheep; fleecing.

shears (*n. pl.*) large, scissor-like clippers.

sheath (*n.*) a close-fitting case; scabbard.

sheathe (*v.*) to place in a sheath.

shed (*v.*) 1. to make flow. 2. to throw off. 3. to spread; to scatter. SHED (*n.*) a hut; cabin.

sheen (*n.*) a shine; gloss.

sheep (*n.*) a wool-bearing animal. (*pl.* SHEEP).

sheepish (*adj.*) timid; bashful. SHEEPISHLY (*adv.*).

sheepishness (*n.*) shyness; bashfulness.

sheer (*adj.*) 1. steep. 2. thorough.

sheet (*n.*) any plain, flat surface, especially of water, paper, glass and cloth.

shelf (*n.*) 1. board or ledge on which to place things. 2. ridge of rocks in the sea; a reef. (*pl.* SHELVES).

shell (*n.*) 1. hard outer case; husk. 2. case filled with explosive. SHELL (*v.*) 1. to remove the shell. 2. to bombard with shells.

shellac (*n.*) a varnish made from resin.

shelter (*n.*) 1. a shield; protection. 2. a harbour; refuge. SHELTER (*v.*) to protect; to screen.

shelve (*v.*) 1. to place on a shelf. 2. to set aside; to postpone. 3. to slope; to incline.

shepherd (*n.*) one who tends sheep. SHEPHERD (*v.*) to tend; to guide.

sheriff (*n.*) chief law-officer of a county.

sherry (*n.*) light Spanish wine.

shew (*v.*) see SHOW.

shield (*v.*) to protect; to shelter. SHIELD (*n.*) 1. plate of armour to protect the body. 2. any safeguard.

shift (*v.*) 1. to alter position. 2. to manage. SHIFT (*n.*) 1. a change; alteration. 2. a plan; trick.

shiftiness (*n.*) changeableness; unreliability.

shiftless (*adj.*) lazy; incompetent.

shiftlessness (*n.*) inefficiency; incompetence.

shifty (*adj.*) changeable; deceitful.

shilling (*n.*) to 1971 a silver coin worth twelve pence.

shimmer (*v.*) to shine faintly; to gleam. SHIMMER (*n.*).

shin (*n.*) front of leg between ankle and knee. SHIN (*v.*) to climb, using the shins.

shine (*v.*) 1. to give light. 2. to be bright and gay. SHINE (*n.*) 1. brightness; lustre. 2. gloss; polish.

shingle (*n.*) sea-shore gravel and pebbles.

shingles (*n.*) acute skin inflammation.

shininess (*n.*) glossiness; lustre.

shining (*adj.*) 1. bright; light-giving. 2. distinguished.

shiny (*adj.*) clear; luminous.

ship (*n.*) sea-going vessel or craft. SHIP (*v.*) to put on a ship.

shipmate (*n.*) a fellow-sailor; a chum.

shipment (*n.*) a dispatch of goods by ship; consignment.

shipper (*n.*) one who sends goods by ship.

shipping (*n.*) the commerce of a port, country, etc.

shipshape (*adj.*) tidy; trim.

shipwreck (*n.*) destruction of a ship at sea by breakers or storm.

shipwright (*n.*) a shipbuilder.

shire (*n.*) a county.

shirk (*v.*) to avoid work or duty.

shirker (*n.*) a lazy man; an idler.

shirt (*n.*) man's undergarment, usually of cotton or linen.

shiver (*v.*) 1. to tremble from cold or fear; to quiver. 2. to shatter; to splinter. SHIVER (*n.*) a shock; tremor.

shivered (*adj.*) smashed to pieces.

shivering (*n.*) the trembling; shuddering.

shivery (*adj.*) cold; chilly.

shoal (*n.*) 1. a swarm; school. 2. shallow water marking a sandbank. SHOAL (*v.*) 1. to swarm. 2. to become shallow.

shock (*n.*) 1. a fright. 2. a blow; collision. 3. a collapse. SHOCK (*v.*) 1. to upset severely. 2. to horrify; to disgust.

shocking (*adj.*) 1. dreadful; terrible. 2. horrible; hateful. SHOCKINGLY (*adv.*).

shod (*v.*) fitted with shoes; past tense of verb to shoe.

shoddy (*n.*) cloth made from waste wool or rags. SHODDY (*adj.*) cheap; inferior. SHODDILY (*adv.*).

shoe (*n.*) 1. covering for foot below the ankle. 2. iron plate nailed to a horse's hoof. SHOE (*v.*) to fit a horse with shoes. SHOEMAKER (*n.*).

shoeing (*n.*) the fitting of a horse with shoes.

shoot (*v.*) 1. to dart off. 2. to discharge a firearm. 3. to sprout; to bud. SHOOT (*n.*) 1. a sprout; bud. 2. a shooting match.

shop (*n.*) place where goods are sold. SHOPKEEPER (*n.*).

shoplifter (*n.*) a stealer of goods from a shop.

shopper (*n.*) a purchaser from shops.

shopping (*n.*) the visiting of shops to purchase.

shore (*n.*) 1. the beach; coast. 2. a prop; support. SHORE (*v.*) to prop; to strengthen.

short (*adj.*) 1. under normal height or length. 2. brief; concise. 3. scanty; insufficient. 4. curt; uncivil.

shortage (*n.*) a lack; an insufficiency.

shortcoming (*n.*) a fault; defect.

shorten (*v.*) to make shorter; to curtail.

shortening (*n.*) material that makes pastry short or crumbly.

shorthand (*n.*) method of writing words as quickly as they are spoken.

short-handed (*adj.*) having too few helpers.

shortly (*adv.*) 1. soon. 2. snappishly.

shortness (*n.*) 1. the conciseness; brevity. 2. a scarcity. 3. nearness.

shorts (*n. pl.*) trousers cut off above knee.

short-sighted (*adj.*) 1. unable to see far. 2. without foresight.

shot (*n.*) 1. a gun's discharge. 2. lead pellets. 3. a marksman.

shoulder (*n.*) joint joining arm to body. SHOULDER (*v.*) 1. to thrust with the shoulder. 2. to carry on the shoulder. 3. to accept responsibility.

shout (*v.*) to call loudly. SHOUT (*n.*) a loud call; an outcry. SHOUTER (*n.*).

shouting (*n.*) noise of shouts.

shove (*v.*) to push; to thrust. SHOVE (*n.*) a push; thrust.

shovel (*n.*) broad-bladed spade for lifting loose materials. SHOVEL (*v.*) to use a shovel. SHOVELLER (*n.*).

shovelful (*n.*) contents of a shovel (*pl* SHOVELFULS).

show (*v.*) 1. to display. 2. to explain. 3. to guide. 4. to reveal. SHOW (*n.*) 1. a display; an entertainment. 2. a pretence.

shower (*n.*) 1. fall of rain. 2. a large supply. SHOWER (*v.*) 1. to fall as rain, snow, etc. 2. to give liberally.

shower-bath (*n.*) bath in which water falls like rain.

showery (*adj.*) rainy.

showily (*adv.*) with much display.

showy (*adj.*) 1. attractive; bright. 2. flashy; gaudy.

shrapnel (*n.*) a shell filled with bullets and explosives.

shred (*v.*) to cut into thin flakes. SHRED (*n.*) a flake; shaving.

shrew (*n.*) 1. mouselike field-animal. 2. a quarrelsome woman; scold.

shrewd (*adj.*) 1. wise; discerning. 2. cunning; astute. SHREWDLY (*adv.*).

shrewdness (*n.*) 1. cleverness. 2. artfulness.

shrewish (*adj.*) quarrelsome; scolding. SHREWISHNESS (*n.*).

shriek (*v.*) to scream; to screech. SHRIEK (*n.*) a scream; yell.

shrill (*adj.*) keen; piercing. SHRILLY (*adv.*).

shrillness (*n.*) sharpness of a shriek or whistle.

shrimp (*n.*) 1. small, sand-loving shellfish. 2. an undersized person.

shrimping (*n.*) business of shrimpcatching. SHRIMPER (*n.*).

shrine (*n.*) a sacred place; saint's tomb.

shrink (*v.*) 1. to grow smaller; to dwindle. 2. to wince; to recoil.

shrinkage (*n.*) a decrease; contraction.

shrivel (*v.*) 1. to wither; to parch. 2. to wrinkle; to contract.

shroud (*v.*) to cover; to cloak. SHROUD (*n.*) 1. covering for a dead body. 2. a dark cloak.

shrouded (*adj.*) covered; cloaked.

Shrovetide (*n.*) Shrove Tuesday (day before Ash Wednesday), on which day people were shriven, or forgiven sins confessed, and on which merrymaking was general, as during the fasting season of Lent amusements and festivities were forbidden.

shrub (*n.*) a bush.

shrubbery (*n.*) plantation of bushes.

shrug (*n.*) a quick rise and fall of the shoulders. SHRUG (*v.*) to make a shrug.

shrunken (*adj.*) shrivelled; wrinkled.

shudder (*v.*) to shiver; to tremble. SHUDDER (*n.*) a quiver; tremble.

shuffle (*v.*) 1. to drag the feet. 2. to mix; to confuse. 3. to mislead. SHUFFLE (*n.*) 1. a scrape of the feet. 2. a jumble. 3. a dodge.

shuffler (*n.*) 1. a clumsy walker. 2. a mixer of cards. 3. a dodger.

shun (*v.*) to keep away from; to avoid.

shunt (*v.*) 1. to turn aside; to divert. 2. to switch a train to another track. 3. to turn thoughts elsewhere.

shut (*v.*) to close. SHUT (*adj.*) closed.

shutter (*n.*) protecting cover over a window or aperture.

shuttle (*n.*) weaving implement carrying threads across a loom. SHUTTLE (*v.*) to move to and fro.

shuttlecock (*n.*) 1. feathered cork struck to and fro in badminton. 2. person easily influenced.

shy (*adj.*) 1. timid; reserved. 2. modest; bashful. SHY (*v.*) 1. to hurl; to toss. 2. to hang back; to take fright. SHYLY (*adv.*).

shyness (*n.*) 1. timidity; reserve. 2. bashfulness; coyness.

sick (*adj.*) 1. ill. 2. tired; wearied.

sicken (*v.*) 1. to fall ill. 2. to disgust; to nauseate.

sickening (*adj.*) 1. making sick. 2. causing disgust.

sickle (*n.*) curved reaping-hook.

sickly (*adj.*) ailing; delicate.

sickness (*n.*) an illness; a disease.

side (*n.*) 1. part between front and back. 2. the edge between top and bottom. 3. a team; party.

side-glance (*n.*) quick look to one side.

side-light (*n.*) 1. light coming from one side. 2. indirect information.

side-line (*n.*) work additional to one's business.

sidelong (*adj.*) not directly in front; oblique.

side-show (*n.*) a minor show; exhibition.

sidesman (*n.*) a churchwarden's deputy.

sidewalk (*n.*) footway at side of the road.

sideways (*adv.*) moving side foremost; sidewise.

siding (*n.*) short length of railway leading off the main line.

sidle (*v.*) to move sideways slowly.

siege (*n.*) a surrounding army's attempt to starve a town into surrender.

siesta (*n.*) a short sleep taken in the afternoon, especially in hot countries.

sieve (*n.*) mesh-bottomed container for separating fine from coarse; a sifter. SIEVE (*v.*) to pass through a sieve.

sift (*v.*) 1. to sieve. 2. to examine closely.

sifter (*n.*) a sieve; strainer.

sigh (*v.*) 1. to moan. 2. to grieve; to lament. SIGH (*n.*) a moan.

sighing (*n.*) the utterance of moans or laments.

sight (*n.*) 1. ability to see; vision. 2. a spectacle; exhibition. SIGHT (*v.*) to see; to behold.

sightless (*adj.*) blind; unseeing.

sightlessness (*n.*) blindness.

sightliness (*n.*) comeliness; beauty.

sightly (*adj.*) pleasing to the eyes; comely.

sightseeing (*n.*) touring to see notable views, buildings, etc.

sightseer (*n.*) a tourist.

sign (*n.*) a token; signal. SIGN (*v.*) 1. to signal. 2. to write one's name in one's own hand.

signal (*v.*) 1. to beckon. 2. to send a message by means of signs. SIGNAL (*n.*) 1. message given by signs. 2. a gesture; an indication. SIGNAL (*adj.*) noteworthy; memorable.

signalize (*v.*) to make important or memorable.

signaller (*n.*) one who signals.

signature (*n.*) person's name written in his own hand.

signet (*n.*) small seal representing a signature.

significance (*n.*) true meaning; importance.

significant (*adj.*) important; noteworthy. SIGNIFICANTLY (*adv.*).

signify (*v.*) to mean; to indicate.

silence (*n.*) entire absence of sound; quietness. SILENCE (*v.*) to make soundless; to quieten.

silent (*adj.*) soundless; quiet. SILENTLY (*adv.*).

silk (*n.*) 1. fine thread spun by the silkworm. 2. cloth woven from silk thread.

silken (*adj.*) made of silk; delicate.

silkiness (*n.*) softness; smoothness.

silkworm (*n.*) caterpillar that spins silk.

silky (*adj.*) soft; smooth.

sill (*n.*) wooden or stone slab at bottom of window or door.

silliness (*n.*) foolish talk and behaviour; imbecility.

silly (*adj.*) foolish; simple-minded.

silt (*n.*) sand deposited by rivers; sediment. SILT (*v.*) to block with silt; to choke.

silver (*n.*) a white precious metal. SILVERY (*adj.*).

silver-plated (*adj.*) having a thin coat of silver.

silverware (*n.*) articles made of silver. SILVERSMITH (*n.*).

simian (*adj.*) like a monkey or ape.

similar (*adj.*) like; resembling. SIMILARLY (*adv.*).

similarity (*n.*) a likeness; resemblance.

simile (*n.*) a reference to a thing to explain another like it; a comparison.

simmer (*v.*) 1. to boil gently; to stew. 2. to suppress temper or anger.

simper (*v.*) to smile out of politeness. SIMPER (*n.*) a polite smile.

simple (*adj.*) 1. easy. 2. open; frank. 3. true; trusting.

simpleton (*n.*) a silly person.

simplicity (*n.*) 1. easiness. 2. frankness; sincerity.

simplification (*n.*) a making easy and understandable.

simplify (*v.*) 1. to make easy. 2. to find an easier way.

simply (*adv.*) 1. easily. 2. frankly. 3. barely; merely.

simulate (*v.*) to sham; to pretend. SIMULATED (*adj.*).

simulation (*n.*) a sham; pretence.

simultaneous (*adj.*) happening at the same time; being all in step.

simultaneously (*adv.*) all together; as one.

sin (*n.*) wrongdoing; wickedness. SIN (*v.*) to do wrong or evil.

since (*adv.*) ago; from then until now. SINCE (*conj.*) as; because. SINCE (*prep.*) after.

sincere (*adj.*) true; genuine. SINCERELY (*adv.*).

sincerity (*n.*) honesty; frankness.

sinew (*n.*) tendon, or tough substance joining muscle to bone.

sinewy (*adj.*) fit; wiry.

sinful (*adj.*) wicked; evil. SINFULLY (*adv.*).

sinfulness (*n.*) wickedness; wrongdoing.

sing (*v.*) to utter or voice music.

singe (*v.*) to burn on the surface; to scorch. SINGE (*n.*) a slight burn; a scorch. SINGED (*adj.*). SINGEING (*n.*).

singer (*n.*) 1. one who sings. 2. one trained to sing in public.

singing (*n.*) music made by the voice; melody.

single (*adj.*) 1. one only. 2. unmarried. SINGLE (*v.*) to pick one at a time. SINGLY (*adv.*).

singleness (*n.*) 1. a separation from all others; lonesomeness. 2. sincerity.

singular (*adj.*) 1. one only; by itself. 2. unusual; remarkable.

singularity (*n.*) the rarity; curiosity.

singularly (*adv.*) oddly; curiously.

sinister (*adj.*) 1. on the left hand. 2. harmful; threatening.

sink (*v.*) 1. to go under water; to submerge. 2. to dig; to excavate. 3. to lose strength; to droop. 4. to enter; to soak in. SINK (*n.*) shallow earthenware or metal tank connected to a drain.

sinking (*n.*) 1. a falling deeper in water. 2. a growing weaker.

sinner (*n.*) an evil doer; offender.

sip (*v.*) to drink in small quantities; to taste. SIP (*n.*) a small testing drink; a taste.

siphon (*n.*) bent tube for drawing liquid from a container. SIPHON (*v.*) to drain off with a siphon.

sir (*n.*) 1. title of knight and baronet. 2. title of respect given to men.

sire (*n.*) a father.

siren (*n.*) 1. a warning whistle; a foghorn. 2. fabled woman who trapped men by her singing. See appendix.

sirloin (*n.*) loin of beef.

sister (*n.*) 1. daughter of the same parents as another person. 2. rank given to a hospital nurse. 3. a nun.

sisterly (*adj.*) kind; affectionate.

sit (*v.*) 1. to be seated upon; to settle upon. 2. to cover and warm eggs.

site (*n.*) ground on which a building, town, etc., is fixed. SITED (*adj.*).

sitting (*n.*) 1. a placing oneself on a seat. 2. a single meeting of a council. 3. a clutch of eggs.

situate (*v.*) 1. to find a place for. 2. to place upon a site.

situation (*n.*) 1. a site; location. 2. a position in employment; a job.

sixpence (*n.*) to 1971 a silver coin worth six pennies.

sixpenny (*adj.*) worth sixpence.

size (*n.*) 1. the bigness; bulk. 2. a weak glue.

sizzle (*v.*) to hiss; to splutter. SIZZLING (*n.*).

skate (*n.*) 1. boot fitted with (i) a metal blade to glide on ice, or (ii) small wheels to glide on a floor. 2. kind of flat fish. SKATE (*v.*) to glide on skates. SKATER (*n.*).

skein (*n.*) bundle, or coil, of silk or yarn thread.

skeleton (*n.*) 1. bony framework of the body. 2. outline of a book or plan.

sketch (*n.*) 1. short one-act play. 2 a rough drawing.

sketchiness (*n.*) roughness of drawing or design.

sketchy (*adj.*) rough; unfinished. SKETCHILY (*adv.*).

skewer (*n.*) a meat-pin.

ski (*n.*) long, narrow, wooden snowshoe. SKI (*v.*) to travel on skis. SKIER (*n.*).

skid (*v.*) to slip suddenly to one side. SKID (*n.*) a sideslip.

skiff (*n.*) small, light open boat.

skiing (*n.*) sport of travelling on skis.

skilful (*adj.*) able; expert. SKILFULLY (*adv.*).

skill (*n.*) ability; efficiency.

skim (*v.*) 1. to glide, barely brushing the surface; to graze. 2. to spoon the scum off a liquid.

skimp (*v.*) to give short measure or use inferior materials; to be sparing. SKIMPING (*n.*). SKIMPY (*adj.*).

skin (*n.*) a thin outer covering; a hide. SKIN (*v.*) to remove the skin; to peel.

skinflint (*n.*) a mean person; miser.

skinner (*n.*) dealer in hides and skins.

skinniness (*n.*) leanness; thinness.

skinny (*adj.*) lean; thin.

skip (*v.*) 1. to leap; to spring. 2. to jump over a turning rope. 3. to leave out pieces here and there in reading.

skipper (*n.*) a ship's captain. SKIPPER (*v.*) to command; to direct.

skirmish (*n.*) fight between small forces. SKIRMISH (*v.*) to seek the enemy.

skirt (*n.*) part of a garment hanging below the waist. SKIRT (*v.*) to move round the edge.

skittles (*n. pl.*) game of ninepins; indoor bowls.

skulk (*v.*) to sneak away; to shirk. SKULKER (*n.*). SKULKING (*n. & adj.*).

skull (*n.*) bony case forming the head.

skunk (*n.*) small animal which gives off a vile smell.

sky (*n.*) cloud region surrounding the earth. (*pl.* SKIES).

skylark (*n.*) 1. high-flying songbird. 2. teasing fun.

skylarking (*n.*) rough-and-tumble play.

skylight (*n.*) window in a roof.

skyline (*n.*) where sea and sky seem to meet; the horizon.

skyscraper (*n.*) very high building.

slab (*n.*) thin, broad piece of timber or stone.

slack (*adj.*) 1. loose. 2. slow; lazy.

slacken (*v.*) 1. to loosen. 2. to slow down; to ease.

slackness (*n.*) 1. looseness. 2. negligence; laziness.

slag (*n.*) the waste dross or clinkers from a smelting-furnace.

slake (*v.*) to put out with water; to quench.

slam (*v.*) to shut, or put down with a bang. SLAM (*n.*) a bang.

slander (*v.*) to harm a person's good name; to defame. SLANDER (*n.*) a false statement intended to harm someone. SLANDERER (*n.*).

slanderous (*adj.*) harmful to the reputation.

slang (*n.*) popular words regarded as vulgar.

slangy (*adj.*) vulgar.

slant (*n.*) a slope; tilt. SLANT (*v.*) to slope; to lean.

slanting (*adj.*) sloping; oblique.

slantwise (*adv.*) obliquely.

slap (*v.*) to strike with the palm; to smack. SLAP (*n.*) a smack; a hard pat.

slash (*v.*) to cut with a sweeping blow; to gash. SLASH (*n.*) a sword-cut.

slat (*n.*) thin, narrow length of wood; a lath.

slate (*n.*) 1. a hard rock that splits into thin sheets. 2. a roof-tile of slate.

slattern (*n.*) untidy woman. SLATTERNLY (*adj.*).

slaughter (*v.*) to kill many persons or animals; to massacre. SLAUGHTER (*n.*) a great destruction of life.

slave (*n.*) a person held in bondage; a serf. SLAVE (*v.*) to be forced to labour.

slavery (*n.*) bondage; servitude.

slavish (*adj.*) slave-like; cowed; dispirited.

slay (*v.*) to kill.

sledge (*n.*) 1. a hand or dog-drawn carriage set on runners to slide over snow; a toboggan. 2. smith's heavy hammer.

sleek (*adj.*) smooth and glossy; velvety, like cats' fur.

sleekness (*n.*) smoothness.

sleep (*v.*) to rest in natural unconsciousness; to repose. SLEEP (*n.*) slumber; repose.

sleeper (*n.*) 1. one who sleeps. 2. log on which railway lines rest. 3. railway-coach fitted with sleeping accommodation.

sleepiness (*n.*) a readiness to sleep; drowsiness.

sleeplessness (*n.*) inability to sleep; wakefulness.

sleepy (*adj.*) drowsy; somnolent. SLEEPILY (*adv.*).

sleet (*n.*) hail or snow mixed with rain.

sleeve (*n.*) part of garment covering the arm.

sleigh (*n.*) a horse-drawn sledge.

sleighing (*n.*) riding in a sleigh.

sleight-of-hand (*n.*) a conjuring trick.

slender (*adj.*) 1. slim. 2. slight; scanty. SLENDERLY (*adv.*).

slenderness (*n.*) 1. slimness. 2. slightness; insufficiency.

sleuth (*n.*) a tracker; detective. (orig. SLEUTH-HOUND).

slice (*n.*) a thin, flat piece. SLICE (*v.*) to cut in slices.

slide (*v.*) to glide or move over a smooth or slippery surface, especially over snow or ice. SLIDE (*n.*) 1. any smooth surface upon, within, or down which, persons or objects may glide or slip. 2. a slip of glass on which a microscope specimen is mounted. 3. a glass plate bearing a picture to be projected upon a screen by a lantern.

slight (*adj.*) 1. small; unimportant. 2. slim; slender. SLIGHT (*n.*) an insult; a discourtesy. SLIGHT (*v.*) to ignore; to disregard.

slim (*adj.*) 1. slender; thin. 2. weak; fragile.

slime (*n.*) slippery mud; sludge. SLIMINESS (*n.*).

slimness (*n.*) slenderness.

slimy (*adj.*) muddy; covered with slime.

sling (*v.*) to fling; to hurl. SLING (*n.*) 1. strap for hurling pebbles. 2. support for an injured limb.

slink (*v.*) to creep about secretly; to skulk.

slip (*v.*) 1. to lose one's footing; to stumble. 2. to make a mistake. SLIP (*n.*) 1. a stumble; fall. 2. a mistake; fault. 3. a piece of paper. 4. a loose cover.

slipper (*n.*) a loose, indoor shoe.

slipperiness (*n.*) glassiness; greasiness.

slippery (*adj.*) 1. glassy; greasy. 2. crafty; cunning.

slipshod (*adj.*) untidy; slovenly.

slit (*n.*) 1. a long tear; rent. 2. a narrow opening. SLIT (*v.*) to cut open; to slash.

slither (*v.*) to slide; to slip. SLITHER (*n.*).

sliver (*n.*) a long, thin splinter.

sloe (*n.*) small, bitter wild plum.

slogan (*n.*) 1. Highland war-cry. 2. short saying used by advertisers to draw attention to their goods.

sloop (*n.*) one-masted sailing ship.

slop (*v.*) to spill or splash carelessly.

slope (*n.*) an incline; a slant. SLOPING (*adj.*).

sloppiness (*n.*) 1. muddiness. 2. untidiness.

sloppy (*adj.*) 1. wet; muddy. 2. tearful; silly. 3. untidy. SLOPPILY (*adv.*).

slot (*n.*) a narrow opening; slit.

sloth (*n.*) 1. slow, lazy, ape-like animal. 2. laziness. SLOTHFUL (*adj.*). SLOTHFULLY (*adv.*).

slothfulness (*n.*) laziness; inactivity.

slouch (*n.*) a lazy attitude or walk. SLOUCH (*v.*) to walk loosely or sloppily. SLOUCHING (*n. & adj.*).

slough (*n.*) a bog; swamp.

sloven (*n.*) an untidy, slipshod person. SLOVENLY (*adj.*).

slovenliness (*n.*) untidiness; slackness.

slow (*adj.*) 1. late; behind. 2. sluggish; tardy. SLOWLY (*adv.*).

slowness (*n.*) tardiness; sluggishness.

slug (*n.*) 1. shell-less garden snail. 2. an air-gun bullet.

sluggard (*n.*) an idler; a slacker.

sluggishness (*n.*) slowness; tardiness.

sluice (*n.*) sliding door regulating a flow of water. SLUICE (*v.*) to flood with water; to swill.

slum (*n.*) dirty, overcrowded street or district.

slumber (*v.*) to sleep; to repose. SLUMBER (*n.*) sleep. SLUMBERER (*n.*).

slump (*v.*) 1. to collapse. 2. to decrease suddenly. SLUMP (*n.*) 1. a collapse. 2. sudden fall in prices.

slur (*v.*) 1. to speak indistinctly. 2. to soil; to sully. SLUR (*n.*) a bad mark; slander.

slurred (*adj.*) passed over; carelessly done.

slush (*n.*) thawing snow. SLUSHY (*adj.*).

slut (*n.*) a slovenly woman; a slattern.

sly (*adj.*) artful; underhand. SLYLY (*adv.*).

slyness (*n.*) craftiness; cunning.

smack (*n.*) 1. a sharp slap. 2. a slight flavour. 3. a small fishing-boat. SMACK (*v.*) to beat with the hand; to slap.

smacking (*n.*) a beating; slapping.

small (*adj.*) 1. little; tiny. 2. unimportant.

smallness (*n.*) 1. littleness. 2. unimportance; paltriness.

smallpox (*n.*) an infectious fever.

smart (*v.*) to pain; to sting. SMART (*adj.*) 1. neat; up-to-date. 2. quick; clever.

smarten (*v.*) to enliven; to make brisk.

smartness (*n.*) 1. neatness. 2. alertness.

smash (*v.*) to break in pieces; to shatter. SMASH (*n.*) breakage; a collision.

smattering (*n.*) a slight knowledge of.

smear (*v.*) to make dirty marks. SMEAR (*n.*) a daub; blotch.

smell (*v.*) to be aware of an odour; to scent. SMELL (*n.*) 1. an odour; fragrance. 2. a stench.

smelly (*adj.*) giving off an unpleasant odour.

smelt (*n.*) fish of salmon family. SMELT (*v.*) to melt metals from their ores.

smile (*v.*) to move the lips to show joy, pleasure, etc. SMILE (*n.*) a lip-movement expressing welcome.

smiling (*adj.*) 1. showing a smile. 2. prosperous; well-governed. SMILINGLY (*adv.*).

smirch (*v.*) to soil; to stain. SMIRCH (*n.*) a stain.

smirk (*v.*) to smile in an affected or conceited manner; to simper. SMIRK (*n.*) a conceited smile; a simper.

smite (*v.*) 1. to hit with the fist. 2. to overthrow in battle. 3. to afflict with pestilence.

smith (*n.*) a forger of metal. SMITHY (*n.*).

smitten (*adj.*) 1. struck; killed. 2. excited; captivated.

smock (*n.*) loose overall.

smoke (*n.*) sooty vapour rising from a fire. SMOKE (*v.*) 1. to give off smoke. 2. to cure or preserve in smoke. 3. to draw tobacco smoke into the mouth.

smoker (*n.*) person who smokes tobacco. SMOKING (*n.*).

smokeless (*adj.*) free from smoke.

smokiness (*n.*) the amount of smoke; the reek.

smoky (*adj.*) full of smoke.

smooth (*adj.*) 1. even; polished. 2. pleasing; persuasive.

smoothly (*adv.*) calmly; evenly.

smoothness (*n.*) 1. the ease; evenness. 2. the blandness.

smother (*v.*) to suffocate; to choke.

smoulder (*v.*) to burn without flame.

smudge (*v.*) to make a dirty mark; to smear. SMUDGE (*n.*) a smear. SMUDGY (*adj.*).

smug (*adj.*) pleased with oneself; self-satisfied. SMUGLY (*adv.*).

smuggle (*v.*) to bring goods into a country secretly or unlawfully.

smuggler (*n.*) one who smuggles. SMUGGLING (*n.*).

smut (*n.*) speck of soot or dirt.

snack (*n.*) a quick, light meal.

snaffle (*n.*) a bridle with a single rein for holding and managing an unmounted horse. SNAFFLE (*v.*) to lead or control with a snaffle.

snag (*n.*) 1. a jagged point. 2. a difficulty; hindrance.

snail (*n.*) small, slimy garden pest which lives in a shell.

snake (*n.*) long, legless reptile which squirms; a serpent.

snap (*v.*) 1. to bite at quickly. 2. to break or crack. 3. to speak crossly to. SNAP (*n.*) sound of a crack.

snappy (*adj.*) bad-tempered; touchy.

snapshot (*n.*) an instantaneous photograph.

snare (*n.*) 1. a trap; net. 2. a temptation.

snarl (*v.*) 1. to growl and show teeth. 2. to speak in a surly manner. SNARLING (*adj.*).

snatch (*v.*) to grab at or from quickly. SNATCH (*n.*) a quick grab.

sneak (*v.*) to creep about secretly; to spy. SNEAK (*n.*) one who tries to injure; a trouble-maker.

sneer (*v.*) to curl the lips in scorn. SNEER (*n.*) a taunt; jeer.

sneeze (*n.*) noisy rush of air from the nose. SNEEZE (*v.*) to eject air through the nose noisily.

sniff (*v.*) to draw a short breath up the nose; to smell. SNIFF (*n.*) a noise made when smelling.

snigger (*n.*) a nervous laugh; a giggle. SNIGGER (*v.*) to giggle.

snip (*v.*) to make small, quick cuts with scissors. SNIP (*n.*) a single cut; a snippet.

snipe (*n.*) marsh-dwelling game bird.

snippet (*n.*) fragment cut off; a clipping.

snivel (*v.*) 1. to run at the nose. 2. to whine; to whimper.

snob (*n.*) person who ignores those less prosperous; an upstart.

snobbery (*n.*) patronizing conduct; self-importance.

snobbish (*adj.*) self-proud; self-important. SNOBBISHLY (*adv.*).

snooze (*n.*) a short sleep; a nap. SNOOZE (*v.*) to doze.

snore (*v.*) to breathe noisily while asleep. SNORE (*n.*).

snort (*v.*) to blow down the nostrils noisily; to show impatience. SNORT (*n.*).

snout (*n.*) 1. an animal's long nose; muzzle. 2. the nozzle of a pipe.

snow (*n.*) white flakes of frozen vapour. SNOW (*v.*) to fall as snow.

snowball (*n.*) ball of tightly-pressed snow. SNOWBALL (*v.*) to bombard with snow-balls.

snowbound (*adj.*) shut in by snow.

snowcap (*n.*) cap of snow on a mountain-top. SNOWCAPPED (*adj.*).

snowdrift (*n.*) bank of snow heaped by the wind.

snowdrop (*n.*) early spring plant with nodding white flower.

snowflake (*n.*) flake or crystal of snow.

snowplough (*n.*) machine for clearing snow from roads and railways.

snowshoes (*n. pl.*) shoes like rackets for walking on snow.

snowy (*adj.*) white; spotless.

snub (*v.*) to show a person he is not wanted; to reprimand. SNUB (*n.*) a slight; rebuke. SNUB (*adj.*) short and stumpy, or turned up.

snub-nosed (*adj.*) having a short, stumpy nose.

snuff (*v.*) 1. to trim a candle wick. 2. to take snuff. SNUFF (*n.*) finely powdered tobacco.

snuffle (*n.*) to speak when the nose is stopped with a cold.

snug (*adj.*) cosy; comfortable. SNUGLY (*adv.*).

snuggery (*n.*) small, cosy room; a den. (*pl.* SNUGGERIES).

snuggle (*v.*) to press close to; to nestle. SNUGGLE (*n.*) a cuddle.

so (*adv.*) 1. in this or that manner. 2. very, or very much. SO (*conj.*) on condition that; therefore.

soak (*v.*) to wet through; to drench.

soap (*n.*) cleansing material made from fats. SOAP (*v.*) 1. to rub or wash with soap. 2. to flatter; to wheedle.

soapstone (*n.*) soft stone with a soapy feel.

soapsuds (*n.*) lather or froth made by soap in warm water.

soapy (*adj.*) 1. containing soap. 2. flattering; persuasive.

soar (*v.*) 1. to fly upwards. 2. to be ambitious; to aspire.

sob (*v.*) to gulp while crying. SOB (*n.*) sound of crying.

sobbing (*adj.*) weeping bitterly. SOBBING (*n.*) the crying; weeping.

sober (*adj.*) 1. not drunk; temperate. 2. grave; calm.

sober-minded (*adj.*) grave; sensible.

sobriety (*n.*) temperance; moderation.

sociability (*n.*) friendliness; good-fellow-ship.

sociable (*adj.*) fond of company; friendly. SOCIABLY (*adv.*).

social (*n.*) party in which all join. SOCIAL (*adj.*) friendly; companionable.

society (*n.*) 1. all those one knows and mixes with. 2. a body of people with the same interests. 3. the community generally. 4. the wealthy or noble classes. (*pl.* SOCIETIES).

sock (*n.*) a short-legged stocking.

socket (*n.*) hole into which something fits; a support.

sod (*n.*) slab of turf. SOD (*v.*) to cover with turf.

soda (*n.*) material used in making glass.

soda-water (*n.*) bubbly beverage containing a gas.

sodden (*adj.*) 1. soaked through; drenched. 2. not well cooked; heavy.

sodium (*n.*) white, waxy metal.

sofa (*n.*) a couch.

soft (*adj.*) 1. not hard; yielding. 2. gentle; tender. 3. weak-minded.

soften (*v.*) to make less hard; to quieten.

soft goods (*n. pl.*) woven materials; fabrics.

softhearted (*adj.*) sympathetic; kind.

softly (*adv.*) quietly; gently.

softness (*n.*) 1. the yielding; easiness. 2. mildness; quietness.

soggy (*adj.*) soaked; sodden.

soil (*v.*) to make dirty; to stain. SOIL (*n.*) earth; mould.

soiled (*adj.*) dirty; grimy.

sojourn (*v.*) to live in for a short time; to stay awhile. SOJOURN (*n.*) a short visit.

sojourner (*n.*) a visitor; traveller.

solace (*n.*) comfort; consolation. SOLACE (*v.*) to comfort; to cheer.

solar (*adj.*) concerning the sun; measured by the sun.

solar system (*n.*) sun, with planets that revolve round it.

solder (*n.*) a metal alloy which joins metals together. SOLDER (*v.*) to join; to unite.

soldier (*n.*) man who serves in an army; a military man.

soldierly (*adj.*) disciplined; military.

sole (*n.*) 1. under-part of a foot and of footwear. 2. a flat sea-fish. SOLE (*v.*) to fix a sole on a shoe. SOLE (*adj.*) one and only; single.

solely (*adv.*) 1. entirely; wholly. 2. without another; singly.

solemn (*adj.*) 1. religious; sacred. 2. serious; grave. SOLEMNLY (*adv.*).

solemnity (*n.*) 1. reverence; awe. 2. seriousness; impressiveness.

sol-fa (*v.*) to sing the musical scale, the seven notes of which are named, do, re, mi, fa, so, la, te.

solemnize (*v.*) 1. to do reverently. 2. to perform a religious ceremony.

solicit (*v.*) to ask for repeatedly; to try to gain.

solicitation (*n.*) an asking or pleading.

solicitor (*n.*) a lawyer; legal adviser.

solicitous (*adj.*) 1. eager to obtain. 2. anxious; troubled.

solicitude (*n.*) anxiety; concern.

solid (*n.*) 1. substance that does not flow. 2. object that is not hollow. SOLID (*adj.*) 1. hard; firm. 2. not hollow. 3. sound; reliable.

solidarity (*n.*) a sticking together; unity.

solidification (*n.*) a making solid; a hardening.

solidify (*v.*) to make solid; to harden.

solidity (*n.*) hardness; firmness.

solitary (*adj.*) 1. alone; single. 2. lonely; desolate.

solitude (*n.*) loneliness; isolation.

solo (*n.*) music performed by one person.

soloist (*n.*) one who plays or sings a solo.

solubility (*n.*) quickness or slowness in dissolving.

soluble (*adj.*) can be dissolved or solved.

solution (*n.*) 1. liquid having something dissolved in it. 2. the answer to a problem.

solvable (*adj.*) has an explanation or solution.

solve (*v.*) to find an answer or explanation.

solvent (*n.*) liquid which will dissolve a substance. SOLVENT (*adj.*) able to pay one's debts; sound. SOLVENCY (*n.*).

sombre (*adj.*) gloomy; cheerless. SOMBRELY (*adv.*).

sombreness (*n.*) gloom; dullness.

some (*adj.*) more or less; uncertain in number; about. SOME (*pron.*) a certain number of persons, or quantity of things.

somebody (*n.*) 1. an unknown person. 2. an important person.

somersault (*v.*) to spring and turn heels over head. SOMERSAULT (*n.*) a heels-over-head turn.

somnambulist (*n.*) a sleep-walker.

somnolence (*n.*) sleepiness; drowsiness.

somnolent (*adj.*) sleepy; tired. SOMNOLENTLY (*adv.*).

son (*n.*) a male child.

sonata (*n.*) a type of musical composition.

song (*n.*) music made by the human voice.

songster (*n.*) a song-bird; poet. (*fem.* SONGSTRESS).

son-in-law (*n.*) husband of one's daughter. (*pl.* SONS-IN-LAW).

sonnet (*n.*) poem containing fourteen lines.

sonorous (*adj.*) sounding when struck; loud. SONOROUSLY (*adv.*).

soon (*adv.*) shortly; before long.

soot (*n.*) specks of black substance in smoke. SOOTY (*adj.*).

soothe (*v.*) to comfort; to soften.

soothing (*adj.*) comforting; quietening. SOOTHINGLY (*adv.*).

soothsayer (*n.*) one who foretells the future; a seer.

soporific (*n.*) drug that causes sleep.

soprano (*n.*) 1. highest part in music; treble. 2. woman able to sing high notes.

sorcerer (*n.*) a magician; conjurer. (*fem.* SORCERESS).

sorcery (*n.*) magic; witchcraft. (*pl.* SORCERIES).

sordid (*adj.*) 1. dirty; degraded. 2. mean; miserly. SORDIDLY (*adv.*).

sordidness (*n.*) baseness; meanness.

sore (*n.*) painful skin injury. SORE (*adj.*) painful; hurtful.

sorely (*adv.*) 1. painfully. 2. severely; violently.

sorrel (*n.*) 1. plant having sour juice. 2. reddish-brown colour.

sorrow (*n.*) sadness; grief.

sorrowful (*adj.*) unhappy; mournful. SORROWFULLY (*adv.*).

sorry (*adj.*) 1. grieved. 2. poor; miserable.

sort (*v.*) to separate into kinds; to arrange. SORT (*n.*) a kind; class. SORTER (*n.*).

sortie (*n.*) sudden attack on an enemy.

sough (*v.*) to sigh like the wind. SOUGH (*n.*) a moan; sigh.

soul (*n.*) spiritual or immortal part of a person.

soulful (*adj.*) full of feeling or life.

soulless (*adj.*) unfeeling; lifeless.

sound (*adj.*) 1. whole; complete. 2. strong; healthy. 3. sensible. SOUND (*v.*) 1. to examine; to test. 2. to measure the depth. SOUND (*n.*) 1. anything heard. 2. a strait; channel. SOUNDLY (*adv.*).

soundless (*adj.*) 1. noiseless; silent. 2. bottomless.

soundness (*n.*) 1. the firmness; rightness. 2. health; strength.

soup (*n.*) liquid food made of meat and vegetables.

sour (*adj.*) 1. sharp in taste; bitter. 2. bad-tempered; surly.

source (*n.*) 1. the origin; beginning. 2. a spring.

sourly (*adv.*) crossly; unpleasantly.

sourness (*n.*) 1. bitterness. 2. surliness.

souse (*v.*) to soak in water; to plunge.

sousing (*n.*) a drenching.

south (*n.*) cardinal point opposite north.

southerly (*adj.*) to or from the south.

southern (*adj.*) belonging to the south.

souvenir (*n.*) a keepsake; memento.

sovereign (*n.*) 1. a monarch; ruler. 2. gold coin that was equal to a £. SOVEREIGN (*adj.*) chief; supreme.

sovereignty (*n.*) supreme power to rule.

sow (*n.*) a female pig.

sow (*v.* pron. SO) to scatter seed; to plant.

sower (*n.*) one who sets seed.

spa (*n.*) health resort having a mineral spring.

space (*n.*) 1. room. 2. boundlessness. 3. a period of time.

spaced (*adj.*) 1. spread apart. 2. placed at regular intervals.

spacious (*adj.*) vast; extensive. SPACIOUSLY (*adv.*).

spaciousness (*n.*) roominess; vastness.

spade (*n.*) flat-bladed digging-tool.

spaghetti (*n.*) macaroni made in thin cords.

span (*n.*) 1. measure of length (eight inches). 2. short period of time. 3. distance across an arch. 4. yoke or team of oxen. SPAN (*v.*) to measure the width.

spangle (*n.*) tiny sparkling piece of material.

spaniel (*n.*) dog with long, silky hair and hanging ears.

spank (*v.*) to smack; to slap.

spanking (*n.*) a smacking. SPANKING (*adj.*) lively; brisk.

spanner (*n.*) tool for screwing nuts on bolts.

spar (*n.*) a strong pole; ship's mast. SPAR (*v.*) 1. to fight with the fists; to box. 2. to argue.

spare (*adj.*) scanty; poor. SPARE (*v.*) 1. to do without; to use frugally. 2. to stop; to desist.

sparing (*adj.*) careful; frugal. SPARINGLY (*adv.*).

spark (*n.*) 1. a fiery particle. 2. small, quick flash of light. SPARK (*v.*) to throw off sparks.

sparkle (*v.*) to flash; to glitter. SPARKLE (*n.*) a twinkle; gleam.

sparkling (*adj.*) 1. glittering. 2. lively; witty.

sparrow (*n.*) small, brownish bird which nests in hedges or houses.

sparse (*adj.*) scanty; thin. SPARSELY (*adv.*).

spartan (*adj.*) hardy; enduring. See appendix.

spasm (*n.*) a sudden pain; a seizure.

spasmodic (*adj.*) having spasms; fitful. SPASMODICALLY (*adv.*).

spate (*n.*) a river overflow; a flood.
spatter (*v.*) to scatter in drops; to sprinkle. SPATTERING (*n.*).
spawn (*n.*) eggs of fishes and frogs.
speak (*v.*) 1. to talk; to discourse. 2. to make an address.
speaker (*n.*) 1. a talker. 2. an orator. THE SPEAKER (*n.*) Chairman of the House of Commons.
speaking (*adj.*) true; expressive.
spear (*n.*) long-handled, sharp-pointed, piercing weapon. SPEAR (*v.*) to pierce with a spear.
spearhead (*n.*) 1. the point of a spear. 2. point where an attack is strongest.
special (*adj.*) particular; distinctive.
specialist (*n.*) one who studies a particular subject; an expert.
speciality (*n.*) 1. something distinctive. 2. work one does best or knows most about.
specialize (*v.*) to study one particular subject.
specie (*n.*) coined money (not paper money).
species (*n.*) a plant or animal family; a sort.
specific (*adj.*) exact; precise. SPECIFICALLY (*adv.*).
specification (*n.*) a full description: a list.
specify (*v.*) to give all details; to name.
specimen (*n.*) a sample; pattern.
specious (*adj.*) seemingly right; plausible.
speck (*n.*) a tiny spot; a grain.
speckle (*n.*) a tiny mark; stain. SPECKLE (*v.*) to spot; to stain.
speckled (*adj.*) spotted.
spectacle (*n.*) a splendid display; a parade.
spectacles (*n. pl.*) glasses or lenses which assist sight.
spectacular (*adj.*) brilliant; magnificent.
spectator (*n.*) one who looks on or watches.
spectral (*adj.*) ghostly; visionary.
spectre (*n.*) a phantom; vision.
spectrum (*n.*) band of colour seen in a rainbow or through a glass prism.
speculate (*v.*) 1. to ponder; to meditate. 2. to buy hoping to sell later at a profit.
speculation (*n.*) 1. an idea; a hope. 2. an attempt to profit.
speculative (*adj.*) uncertain; risky.

speculator (*n.*) one who speculates or hopes.
speech (*n.*) 1. ability to speak. 2. an address; oration.
speechless (*adj.*) silent; dumb.
speed (*n.*) rapid movement; haste. SPEED (*v.*) 1. to hasten. 2. to prosper: to help.
speedily (*adv.*) quickly; rapidly.
speediness (*n.*) the quickness; rapidity.
speedometer (*n.*) a speed indicator.
speedway (*n.*) a motor-racing track.
speedy (*adj.*) 1. prompt; rapid. 2. early; near.
spell (*v.*) to say the letters forming a word. SPELL (*n.*) 1. a charm. 2. a short length of time; a while.
spellbound (*adj.*) 1. immovable. 2. held by wonder: fascinated.
spend (*v.*) 1. to pay out money. 2. to use up time, energy, etc.
spendthrift (*n.*) wasteful or unwise spender.
spent (*adj.*) exhausted; used up.
sphere (*n.*) a ball; globe.
spherical (*adj.*) perfectly round; like a ball.
sphinx (*n.*) 1. fabled monster, lion with a woman's head. 2. a silent, secretive person.
spice (*n.*) 1. a flavour; relish. 2. a fragrance.
spick (*adj.*) smart; faultless.
spicy (*adj.*) tasty; fragrant. SPICILY (*adv.*).
spider (*n.*) tiny creature that spins threads.
spidery (*adj.*) web-like; delicate.
spike (*n.*) 1. long, pointed nail. 2. many flowers on a stalk.
spiked (*adj.*) pointed.
spiky (*adj.*) full of spikes.
spill (*v.*) to let liquid run over or be upset. SPILL (*n.*) 1. a fall; tumble. 2. slip of paper or wood used as a lighter.
spin (*v.*) 1. to make thread from fibre. 2. to whirl like a top. SPIN (*n.*) 1. a rotation: revolution. 2. a cycle-ride.
spinach (*n.*) garden vegetable with thick leaves.
spinal (*adj.*) concerning the backbone.
spindle (*n.*) pin on which spun thread is wound.

spine (*n.*) 1. a thorn. 2. the backbone.

spinner (*n.*) one who spins.

spinney (*n.*) a small wood; a grove.

spinster (*n.*) 1. an unmarried woman. 2. woman who spins thread.

spiny (*adj.*) covered with spines; prickly.

spiral (*adj.*) coiling like a screw.

spire (*n.*) tall cone built on top of a tower; a steeple.

spirit (*n.*) 1. the soul. 2. a phantom; vision. 3. a liquid containing alcohol. 4. courage; zeal.

spirited (*adj.*) full of life; energetic.

spiritless (*adj.*) lifeless; discouraged.

spiritual (*adj.*) coming from God; holy. SPIRITUALLY (*adv.*).

spit (*n.*) 1. rod on which meat is roasted. 2. a low cape; headland. SPIT (*v.*) 1. to thrust through; to pierce. 2. to eject saliva.

spite (*n.*) ill-will; malice. SPITE (*v.*) to hurt or vex someone disliked.

spiteful (*adj.*) eager to annoy; malicious. SPITEFULLY (*adj.*).

spitfire (*n.*) a sharp-tongued, hot-tempered person.

splash (*v.*) to scatter water; to bespatter. SPLASH (*n.*) sound of something falling in water.

spleen (*n.*) bad temper; glumness.

splendid (*adj.*) grand; magnificent. SPLEN-DIDLY (*adv.*).

splendour (*n.*) magnificence; grandeur.

splice (*v.*) to join; to unite. SPLICE (*n.*) a join; connection.

splint (*n.*) flat piece of wood used to support a broken bone.

splinter (*n.*) small, sharp piece of broken wood.

split (*v.*) to cleave into parts. SPLIT (*n.*) 1. a division; separation. 2. a rent; tear. SPLIT (*adj.*) cleft; fractured.

spoil (*v.*) 1. to make useless. 2. to plunder. 3. to decay. SPOIL (*n.*) plunder; loot.

spoke (*n.*) bar or rod joining rim of wheel to hub.

spokesman (*n.*) one who speaks for others; a representative.

spoliation (*n.*) a plundering; robbing.

sponge (*n.*) 1. a sea-creature. 2. the wash-cloth made from its soft skeleton. SPONGE (*v.*) to wash with a sponge.

spongy (*adj.*) soft; porous.

sponsor (*n.*) person who becomes responsible for another.

spontaneous (*adj.*) 1. done naturally and freely. 2. produced without human labour.

spook (*n.*) a ghost; spectre.

spooky (*adj.*) weird; frightening.

spool (*n.*) reel on which thread is wound.

spoon (*n.*) long-handled shallow bowl.

spoonful (*n.*) quantity a spoon holds. (*pl.* SPOONFULS).

spoor (*n.*) track or scent of an animal. SPOOR (*v.*) to track; to follow.

sporadic (*adj.*) happening here and there, or at odd times

sporran (*n.*) pouch worn in front of the kilt by Highlanders in full dress.

sport (*n.*) 1. fun; amusement. 2. game or pastime requiring skill and training.

sports (*n. pl.*) competitive games.

sportsman (*n.*) one fond of sports and fair play.

spot (*n.*) 1. a small mark; blot. 2. a place. SPOT (*v.*) 1. to make a spot. 2. to catch sight of; to notice.

spotless (*adj.*) stainless; blameless.

spotlessness (*n.*) perfection; purity.

spotlight (*n.*) powerful light thrown upon a particular spot. SPOTLIGHT (*v.*) 1. to throw light upon. 2. to draw attention to.

spotted (*adj.*) marked with spots.

spotty (*adj.*) covered with spots.

spouse (*n.*) a husband or wife.

spout (*v.*) to rush or gush out. SPOUT (*n.*) pipe from which a liquid flows.

sprain (*v.*) 1. to overstrain. 2. to twist or wrench a joint. SPRAIN (*n.*) injury caused by spraining.

sprat (*n.*) small fish of herring family.

sprawl (*v.*) to spread out the limbs; to loll about. SPRAWL (*n.*) a lolling posture.

sprawling (*adj.*) outspread; ungainly.

spray (*n.*) 1. a bunch of flowers. 2. windblown drops of water. 3. instrument for spreading liquid in fine drops. SPRAY (*v.*) to spread with a spray; to sprinkle.

spread (*v.*) 1. to extend; to scatter. 2. to distribute; to broadcast. SPREAD (*n.*) a covering; a scattering.

spree (*n.*) a lively frolic; merry party.

sprig (*n.*) a twig; shoot.

sprightliness (n.) cheerfulness; briskness.
sprightly (adj.) lively; active.
spring (n.) 1. flow of water from the ground. 2. a leap; jump. 3. year's first season. 4. metal coil that jumps back after being stretched. SPRING (v.) 1. to flow from. 2. to jump; to leap. 3. to recoil; to rebound. 4. to sprout; to bud.
springbok (n.) the African antelope.
springiness (n.) ability to recoil; elasticity.
springtime (n.) season of Spring; budding time.
sprinkle (v.) to scatter in drops; to shower.
sprinkling (n.) a scattering of drops.
sprint (v.) to run a short distance at full speed. SPRINT (n.) a short run or race.
sprinter (n.) runner of short-distance races.
sprite (n.) a fairy; brownie. SPRITELY (adj.).
sprout (v.) to begin to grow; to shoot. SPROUT (n.) 1. a shoot; sprig. 2. vegetable of cabbage family.
spruce (adj.) trim; tidy. SPRUCE (n.) kind of fir tree.
spry (adj.) active; nimble.
spume (n.) froth; foam.
spur (n.) 1. prickly wheel fastened to a horseman's heel. 2. anything that urges into action. SPUR (v.) to urge; to goad.
spurious (adj.) false; sham.
spurn (v.) to thrust back; to refuse with scorn.
spurt (v.) 1. to gush or spout out. 2. to make a short, utmost effort in running, etc. SPURT (n.) a sudden outflow; an utmost effort.
spy (n.) secret watcher in an enemy's country. SPY (v.) 1. to explore secretly; to scout. 2. to catch sight of; to notice.
spyglass (n.) a small telescope.
squabble (v.) to quarrel noisily; to bicker. SQUABBLE (n.) a noisy quarrel.
squad (n.) small party of soldiers or workmen.
squadron (n.) section of a fleet, cavalry or air force.
squalid (adj.) dirty; disgusting.

squall (n.) 1. sudden, heavy gust of wind. 2. a loud yell. SQUALL (v.) to yell; to scream.
squally (adj.) gusty.
squalor (n.) filthiness; wretchedness.
squander (v.) to waste time or money needlessly.
square (n.) 1. figure having four equal sides and four right angles. 2. four-sided area with buildings round. 3. product of a number multiplied by itself. SQUARE (adj.) straightforward.
squared (adj.) 1. made square. 2. settled; adjusted.
squash (v.) 1. to crush; to squeeze flat. 2. to silence. SQUASH (n.) a crush; crowd.
squat (v.) 1. to sit on the heels. 2. to settle on another's land without leave. SQUAT (adj.) short; dumpy.
squatter (n.) one who occupies without leave.
squaw (n.) an American Indian woman.
squawk (v.) to cry out in pain or fear. SQUAWK (n.) a startled cry.
squeak (v.) to utter a short, shrill cry. SQUEAK (n.) 1. a mouse-like cry. 2. a narrow escape.
squeaky (adj.) shrill, like rusty hinges.
squeal (v.) to utter a loud, shrill cry; to yell. SQUEAL (n.) a loud cry of pain or fear.
squeamish (adj.) easily disgusted; shocked.
squeeze (v.) to press tightly; to crush. SQUEEZE (n.) 1. a firm grip. 2. an embrace. 3. a tight fit.
squib (n.) small, explosive firework.
squid (n.) a cuttlefish; an octopus.
squint (n.) 1. an eye defect. 2. a quick look at. SQUINT (v.) to look at with eyes differently directed.
squire (n.) a country landowner.
squirm (v.) to wriggle; to writhe.
squirrel (n.) small, bushy-tailed animal.
squirt (v.) to throw a jet of liquid from a nozzle. SQUIRT (n.) a syringe.
stab (v.) to pierce with a short, pointed weapon. STAB (n.) a wound caused by a thrust.
stability (n.) solidity; firmness.
stabilize (v.) to make firm or lasting.
stable (n.) building with separate stalls for horses. STABLE (v.) to put or keep

a horse in a stable. STABLE (adj.)
1. firm; steadfast. 2. reliable.

stack (n.) a pile; heap. STACK (v.) to
heap; to pile.

stadium (n.) a sports or games arena.

staff (n.) 1. a supporting pole or rod.
2. persons employed in a business,
school, etc. STAFF (v.) to provide
workers; employees.

stag (n.) a male deer.

stage (n.) 1. a platform. 2. part of a
journey between two rests. STAGE (v.)
to produce on a stage.

stagger (v.) 1, to totter; to reel. 2. to
amaze. 3. to distribute evenly over a
period.

stagnant (adj.) 1. inactive; dull. 2. foul;
bad.

stagnate (v.) 1. to cease flowing. 2. to
become foul.

stagnation (n.) inactivity; dullness.

staid (adj.) solemn; grave.

stain (v.) 1. to discolour. 2. to disgrace.
STAIN (n.) 1. a dirty mark. 2. a disgrace. 3. a paint or dye.

stained (adj.) 1. discoloured. 2. disgraced. 3. dyed.

stainless (adj.) spotless; faultless.

stair (n.) a step in a flight.

staircase (n.) a flight or series of stairs.

stake (n.) 1. a strong, pointed post.
2. money risked on a bet. STAKE (v.)
1. to mark a boundary with stakes.
2. to risk; to hazard.

stalactite (n.) limy deposit growing down
from a cave roof.

stalagmite (n.) limy deposit growing up
from a cave floor.

stale (adj.) 1. not fresh; musty. 2. uninteresting; dull.

staleness (n.) a loss of freshness; over-
training.

stalk (v.) 1. to walk proudly. 2. to
follow game; to hunt. STALK (n.) stem
of a plant.

stalker (n.) a tracker; hunter.

stall (n.) 1. stand for displaying goods.
2. compartment in a stable. 3. seat in
a theatre. STALL (v.) 1. to stop; to
halt. 2. to lose airspeed and fall to
earth.

stallion (n.) a male horse.

stalwart (adj.) strong; resolute. STALWART
(n.) a reliable person.

stamen (n.) part of a flower which contains
pollen.

stamina (n.) strength; endurance.

stammer (v.) to falter in speech; to
stutter.

stamp (v.) 1. to put the foot down
forcibly. 2. to impress with a mark
or design. 3. to affix a postage stamp.
STAMP (n.) 1. a heavy tread. 2. an
instrument for impressing. 3. a
postage stamp.

stampede (v.) to flee in fear. STAMPEDE
(n.) a sudden flight caused by fear;
panic.

staunch (v.) to stop the flow of blood.

stand (v.) 1. to be upright on the feet.
2. to hold a position or an opinion
firmly; to maintain. 3. to be an
election candidate. 4. to put up with;
to endure. STAND (n.) 1. a stall;
booth. 2. a support for an object.
3. a witness-box. 4. firmness in holding
an opinion.

standard (n.) 1. the fixed measure of
length, weight, etc. 2. a banner.
STANDARD (adj.) fixed; legal.

standardize (v.) to make from the same
model or pattern.

standing (n.) 1. rank; position. 2. reputation.

standpoint (n.) one's own way of regarding
something.

standstill (n.) a stop.

stanza (n.) a division of a song or poem.

staple (n.) 1. a U-shaped wire with
pointed ends. 2. the chief production
or industry. STAPLE (adj.) chief;
main.

star (n.) 1. a shining heavenly body.
2. a notable actor. STAR (v.) 1. to
play the leading part. 2. to mark with
an asterisk.

starboard (n.) the right-hand side of a
ship, when one is facing forward.

starch (n.) 1. the chief substance in all
grains. 2. substance used for stiffening
linen.

starchy (adj.) 1. containing starch.
2. stiff; dignified.

stare (n.) a fixed gaze. STARE (v.) to
look at fixedly; to gape.

starfish (n.) sea-animal with radiating
limbs.

stargazer (n.) an astronomer.

starlight (*adj.*) lighted by stars.
starling (*n.*) small bird of crow family.
starry (*adj.*) twinkling; sparkling.
start (*v.*) 1. to begin. 2. to make a sharp, sudden movement. START (*n.*) 1. a beginning. 2. a sudden movement.
startle (*v.*) 1. to frighten. 2. to surprise; to astonish.
startling (*adj.*) 1. sudden; alarming. 2. unexpected.
starvation (*n.*) hunger; famine.
starve (*v.*) to suffer or die from hunger or cold; to famish.
starveling (*n.*) an ill-nourished person or animal.
state (*n.*) 1. a thing's condition. 2. a nation. STATE (*v.*) to say; to relate.
stateliness (*n.*) dignity; nobility.
stately (*adj.*) dignified; imposing.
statement (*n.*) an account; a declaration.
statesman (*n.*) one skilled in managing state affairs.
statesmanship (*n.*) ability and authority of a statesman.
static (*adj.*) at rest; still.
station (*n.*) 1. place where a thing stands. 2. a position; rank. 3. stopping place for trains. 4. a headquarters for troops, police, etc. STATION (*v.*) to place in position.
stationary (*adj.*) still; unmoving.
stationer (*n.*) one who sells writing-materials.
stationery (*n.*) writing-materials.
statistician (*n.*) one skilled in collecting statistics.
statistics (*n.*) facts and figures collected and arranged to give information.
statuary (*n.*) 1. a group of statues. 2. art of carving statues.
statue (*n.*) carved figure of person or animal. Beware STATUTE.
statuesque (*adj.*) having the beauty of a statue.
statuette (*n.*) a small statue.
stature (*n.*) a person's height; tallness.
status (*n.*) rank; position.
statute (*n.*) a law; an enactment. Beware STATUE.
statutory (*adj.*) 1. enacted; ordered. 2. compulsory.
staunch (*adj.*) steadfast; loyal.
staunchness (*n.*) reliability; loyalty.
stave (*n.*) 1. strip of wood forming side of a cask. 2. a pole. 3. a fragment of a song. STAVE (*v.*) to break a hole in.
stay (*v.*) 1. to remain. 2. to prop. STAY (*n.*) a prop; support.
steadfast (*adj.*) firm; unmoving.
steadfastness (*n.*) reliability; constancy.
steadiness (*n.*) firmness; dependability.
steady (*adj.*) regular; dependable. STEADILY (*adv.*).
steak (*n.*) a slice of meat.
steal (*v.*) 1. to take another's property; to thieve. 2. to walk unnoticed or secretly.
stealing (*n.*) 1. theft. 2. moving silently.
stealth (*n.*) secrecy; slyness.
stealthy (*adj.*) sly; sneaking. STEALTHILY (*adv.*).
steam (*n.*) vapour into which water is changed by boiling. STEAM (*v.*) 1. to cook in steam. 2. to use steam power.
steamer (*n.*) ship driven by steam-engines. STEAMY (*adj.*).
steel (*n.*) hard, tough metal made from iron. STEEL (*v.*) to brace oneself to meet danger; to strengthen.
steely (*adj.*) 1. made of steel. 2. strong; hard.
steelyard (*n.*) a balance in which a weight moves along a rod.
steep (*adj.*) sloping; precipitous. STEEP (*n.*) a precipice. STEEP (*v.*) to dip; to soak.
steeple (*n.*) spire built on a tower.
steeple-chase (*n.*) a cross-country race by horsemen or runners.
steeplejack (*n.*) a builder or repairer of steeples and tall chimneys.
steepness (*n.*) the precipitousness; sheerness.
steer (*v.*) to pilot; to guide. STEER (*n.*) a young ox.
steersman (*n.*) a man at the wheel; helmsman.
stellar (*adj.*) concerning the stars.
stem (*n.*) 1. main part or stalk of a plant. 2. forepart of a ship. STEM (*v.*) to dam or block; to struggle against.
stench (*n.*) a disagreeable smell.
stencil (*n.*) thin sheet having a cut-out design through which paint is dabbed. STENCIL (*v.*) to use a stencil.

stenographer (*n.*) a shorthand writer.

stenographic (*adj.*) written in shorthand.

stentor (*n.*) instrument for broadcasting loudly. See appendix.

stentorian (*adj.*) loud-voiced; roaring.

stereoscope (*n.*) instrument that makes two pictures appear as one image which seems to stand out from the background.

stereotyped (*adj.*) 1. fixed; unchanging. 2. monotonous.

sterile (*adj.*) 1. unfruitful; barren. 2. free from germs.

sterility (*n.*) unfruitfulness.

sterilize (*v.*) to free from germs.

sterilizer (*n.*) a germ-killer.

sterling (*n.*) the standard of British coinage. STERLING (*adj.*) true; of solid worth.

stern (*adj.*) strict; severe. STERN (*n.*) hinder part of a ship, etc.

sternly (*adv.*) severely; harshly.

sternwise (*adv.*) backwards.

stethoscope (*n.*) instrument which enables movements of the heart to be heard.

stevedore (*n.*) man employed in loading and unloading ships.

stew (*v.*) to cook by simmering. STEW (*n.*) 1. dish of stewed meat and vegetables. 2. a difficulty; scrape.

steward (*n.*) 1. one who manages another's property. 2. a waiter on a ship. (*fem.* STEWARDESS).

stick (*n.*) a rod; staff. STICK (*v.*) 1. to pierce; to thrust into. 2. to fix on; to stay.

stickleback (*n.*) small, spiny, freshwater fish.

sticky (*adj.*) like gum or glue; adhesive. STICKILY (*adv.*).

stiff (*adj.*) 1. hard to bend; rigid. 2. hard to be friendly with; standoffish.

stiffen (*v.*) 1. to strengthen. 2. to become more obstinate.

stiffening (*n.*) a strengthening; support.

stiff-necked (*adj.*) obstinate; stubborn.

stiffness (*n.*) 1. rigidity. 2. obstinacy. 3. coldness; reserve.

stifle (*v.*) 1. to smother; to suffocate. 2. to suppress; to stop.

stifling (*adj.*) airless; oppressive.

stigma (*n.*) a stain on one's reputation; a slur.

stigmatize (*v.*) to reproach; to slur.

stile (*n.*) fixed steps carrying a footpath over a fence.

stiletto (*n.*) a short dagger.

still (*adj.*) 1. calm; motionless. 2. silent; quiet. STILL (*n.*) apparatus for making spirits. STILL (*adv.*) however; nevertheless.

stillness (*n.*) 1. calmness. 2. silence; hush.

stilly (*adj.*) peaceful; tranquil.

stilt (*n.*) one of a pair of poles having raised footrests for walking above ground-level.

stilted (*adj.*) stiff and pompous in speaking.

stimulant (*n.*) anything that arouses or excites.

stimulate (*v.*) to arouse to action; to stir up energy.

stimulus (*n.*) a spur; an urge.

sting (*n.*) the needle-like weapon of many insects and plants. STING (*v.*) to pierce or wound with a sting.

stinginess (*n.*) meanness; miserliness.

stingy (*adj.*) mean; niggardly. STINGILY (*adv.*).

stink (*n.*) an unpleasant smell. STINK (*v.*) to give off an unpleasant smell.

stint (*v.*) to be sparing; to pinch.

stipend (*n.*) a fixed salary.

stipendiary (*n.*) a salaried magistrate.

stipulate (*v.*) to insist upon; to make a condition.

stipulation (*n.*) a condition; necessity.

stir (*v.*) 1. to move; to arouse. 2. to upset; to excite. STIR (*n.*) 1. movement; activity. 2. excitement; fuss.

stirring (*adj.*) exciting; thrilling.

stirrups (*n. pl.*) rests, hanging from a saddle, for a rider's feet.

stitch (*v.*) to sew with needle and thread; to fasten. STITCH (*n.*) 1. a single fastening with thread. 2. a sudden pain in the side.

stoat (*n.*) the ermine, a kind of weasel.

stock (*n.*) 1. a store of anything. 2. a farmer's cattle. 3. a handle. 4. family. STOCK (*v.*) to put by; to store.

stockade (*n.*) defensive fence built round a camp.

stocking (*n.*) close-fitting, woven or knitted covering for the foot and leg.

stocks (*n. pl.*) 1. framework on which a ship is built. 2. ancient instrument of punishment consisting of two boards having holes for the legs. 3. shares in a company.

stock-still (*adj.*) perfectly still.

stoke (*v.*) to feed a fire or furnace.

stoker (*n.*) one who keeps furnaces fired or fuelled.

stole (*n.*) narrow band of silk worn round the neck by a clergyman.

stolid (*adj.*) slow; dull.

stolidity (*n.*) dullness; stupidity.

stomach (*n.*) bodily organ that receives and digests food.

stone (*n.*) 1. piece of rock. 2. large, hard fruit-seed. 3. an Imperial weight of 14 pounds. 4. a gem; jewel. STONE (*v.*) 1. to throw stones. 2. to extract stones from fruit.

stonework (*n.*) masonry.

stony (*adj.*) 1. full of stones. 2. unfeeling; pitiless. STONILY (*adv.*).

stooge (*n.*) a person ridiculed in comedy.

stool (*n.*) low, backless seat for one.

stoop (*v.*) 1. to bend the body forward. 2. to lower one's dignity by unseemly conduct. 3. to submit; to yield. STOOP (*n.*) a forward bending of the body.

stop (*v.*) 1. to cease; to bring to a standstill. 2. to plug; to block. 3. to stay with a short time. 4. to fill a tooth. STOP (*n.*) 1. a check; cessation. 2. a short stay. 3. a punctuation mark. 4. hole or mechanism in a musical instrument which regulates its sounds.

stopper (*n.*) a cork or plug which prevents the inflow or outflow of a fluid.

storage (*n.*) 1. the placing of goods in a store or warehouse for safe-keeping. 2. the price for keeping in store.

store (*n.*) 1. a supply for future use. 2. a keeping-place for supplies; warehouse. 3. a shop supplying a great variety of goods; an emporium. STORE (*v.*) 1. to collect a stock for future use; to accumulate. 2. to place in a keeping-place.

storey or **story** (*n.*) a set of rooms on the same level or floor of a building.

stork (*n.*) long-legged wading-bird of heron family, having a long, straight bill.

storm (*n.*) 1. a violent disturbance of the air; a tempest. 2. an attack on a fortified place; an assault. 3. a public commotion. 4. a noisy display of anger. STORM (*v.*) 1. to blow as a gale or tempest. 2. to assault a citadel. 3. to display great anger. STORMY (*adj.*).

story (*n.*) an account of real or imaginary happenings. (*pl.* STORIES).

stout (*adj.*) 1. strongly made. 2. fat; corpulent. 3. resolute; staunch. STOUT (*n.*) a strong kind of porter.

stove (*n.*) 1. a closed metal fireplace for cooking or heating. 2. a gas, oil or electric cooker. STOVE (*v.*) to keep warm with cloths heated in boiling water.

stow (*v.*) 1. to pack closely in a room, ship, etc. 2. to roll up, as a sail; to furl. STOW AWAY (*v.*) to hide in an outward-bound ship to obtain a free passage. STOWAWAY (*n.*).

straggle (*v.*) 1. to wander away from or behind the main company. 2. to stretch beyond proper limits, as overhanging branches. STRAGGLER (*n.*).

straight (*adj.*) 1. uncurved; unbent. 2. honest; upright.

straighten (*v.*) 1. to remove bends or defects. 2. to set in good order; to clear up.

straightforward (*adj.*) 1. direct; simple. 2. trustworthy.

straightforwardness (*n.*) honesty; frankness.

straightness (*n.*) freedom from bends; directness.

straightway (*adv.*) at once.

strain (*v.*) 1. to overdo; to overwork. 2. to wrench; to sprain. 3. to filter; to sift. STRAIN (*n.*) 1. an over-exertion. 2. a sprain. 3. a style of speaking. 4. an air of music.

strained (*adj.*) 1. stretched. 2. filtered. 3. unfriendly.

strainer (*n.*) a filter; sifter.

strait (*n.*) 1. a narrow channel. 2. a difficulty; plight. STRAIT (*adj.*) narrow; strict.

straitened (*adj.*) 1. difficult. 2. impoverished.

straitlaced (*adj.*) narrow-minded; strict.

strand (n.) 1. a shore; border. 2. single thread of wire or rope. 3. a thread of hair. STRAND (v.) 1. to become lost. 2. to run aground.

stranded (adj.) 1. lost; shipwrecked. 2. divided into strands.

strange (adj.) 1. unusual. 2. foreign. 3. odd; peculiar. 4. wonderful.

strangely (adv.) curiously; oddly.

strangeness (n.) oddness; unfamiliarity.

stranger (n.) an unknown person; a foreigner.

strap (n.) band of leather having a buckle. STRAP (v.) to beat or fasten with a strap.

strapping (n.) a beating. STRAPPING (adj.) well-built; robust.

stratagem (n.) a plan to surprise an enemy; a deception.

strategist (n.) a clever planner. STRATEGIC (adj.).

strategy (n.) skilful planning; generalship.

stratify (v.) to arrange in layers.

stratum (n.) a layer of rock. (pl. STRATA).

straw (n.) 1. stem of a grain-plant. 2. a trifle.

strawberry (n.) plant and its sweet, pulpy fruit. (pl. STRAWBERRIES).

stray (v.) to lose the way; to wander. STRAY (n.) a lost person or animal.

streak (n.) 1. a stripe. 2. a narrow band; a flash of light. STREAK (v.) 1. to mark with stripes. 2. to shine. 3. to run quickly.

streaky (adj.) striped. STREAKILY (adv.).

stream (n.) 1. small river. 2. current of air. 3. crowd of moving people. STREAM (v.) to flow; to pour from.

streamer (n.) a long ribbon blowing in the wind.

streamlet (n.) a little stream.

streamline (v.) to give an aeroplane the best shape possible for flying, or a ship for sailing.

street (n.) road bordered by buildings.

strength (n.) power; might.

strengthen (v.) to make stronger.

strenuous (adj.) energetic; requiring much exertion.

strenuousness (n.) activity; eagerness.

stress (n.) 1. strain; pressure. 2. an accent or emphasis. STRESS (v.) to emphasize; to accent.

stretch (v.) 1. to draw out; to lengthen. 2. to exaggerate. STRETCH (n.) a length; an extension.

stretcher (n.) a litter for carrying an injured person.

strew (v.) to spread about; to scatter.

stricken (adj.) afflicted; smitten.

strict (adj.) 1. exact; precise. 2. stern; severe. STRICTLY (adv.).

strictness (n.) 1. accuracy. 2. severity.

stricture (n.) blame; criticism.

stride (v.) to walk with long steps; to make rapid progress. STRIDE (n.) a long step.

strident (adj.) loud; harsh

strife (n.) 1. conflict. 2. trouble.

strike (v.) 1. to hit. 2. to refuse to work because of a dispute. 3. to enter the mind.

striking (adj.) extraordinary; impressive. STRIKINGLY (adv.).

string (n.) 1. cord; twine. 2. fine cord or wire of musical instrument. 3. series of things or persons connected, or following one after another. STRING (v.) 1. to put on a string. 2. to provide with a string. STRINGED (adj.).

stringency (n.) urgency; necessity.

stringent (adj.) strict; binding.

strings (n. pl.) stringed instruments in an orchestra.

stringy (adj.) like string; threadlike.

strip (v.) 1. to undress; to peel. 2. to empty. STRIP (n.) a narrow length; a ribbon-like piece.

stripe (n.) 1. a stroke of colour. 2. mark made by a lash. 3. rank-mark on a uniform sleeve. STRIPE (v.) to mark with stripes. STRIPED (adj.).

stripling (n.) a youth; lad.

strive (v.) to try; to attempt.

stroke (n.) 1. a blow. 2. sudden attack of illness; shock. 3. sweep of an oar when rowing. 4. leading oarsman in a boat. 5. a pen or pencil mark. STROKE (v.) to smooth gently with the hand.

stroll (v.) to walk slowly; to saunter.

stroller (n.) a rambler.

strong (adj.) 1. powerful. 2. glaring; dazzling.

stronghold (n.) a fortress.

strong-minded (adj.) determined; resolute.

structural (*adj.*) concerned with structure. STRUCTURALLY (*adv.*).

structure (*n.*) 1. a way of building. 2. a building; edifice.

struggle (*v.*) 1. to fight to escape. 2. to strive. STRUGGLE (*n.*) a fight; contest.

strut (*v.*) to walk in a proud, pompous manner. STRUT (*n.*) 1. a pompous walk. 2. a prop; support.

stub (*n.*) a stump; a tag-end. STUB (*v.*) to extinguish.

stubble (*n.*) corn-stumps left after reaping.

stubbly (*adj.*) short and stiff.

stubborn (*adj.*) obstinate; unbending.

stubbornness (*n.*) obstinacy; perverseness.

stubby (*adj.*) short and thick.

stucco (*n.*) plaster.

stud (*n.*) 1. a large-headed nail. 2. a collar-fastener. 3. a knob; button. STUD (*v.*) to adorn with studs.

studded (*adj.*) adorned with button-like ornaments.

student (*n.*) one who studies; a pupil.

studied (*adj.*) planned; deliberate.

studio (*n.*) an artist's workroom.

studious (*adj.*) fond of study; scholarly.

study (*v.*) 1. to learn; to examine. 2. to think; to reflect. STUDY (*n.*) 1. learning; scholarship. 2. room set apart for study.

stuff (*n.*) materials of any kind. STUFF (*v.*) 1. to fill by overcrowding. 2. to eat gluttonously.

stuffed (*adj.*) filled with material or seasoning.

stuffiness (*n.*) airlessness; oppressiveness.

stuffing (*n.*) 1. filling-material. 2. seasoning.

stuffy (*adj.*) ill-ventilated; airless.

stumble (*v.*) to trip; to blunder. STUMBLE (*n.*) a trip; fall.

stumbling-block (*n.*) an obstacle; a nuisance.

stump (*n.*) 1. the small piece of post, pencil, etc., remaining after the larger portion has been cut off, or used. 2. one of the three rods making up a wicket and supporting the bails. STUMP (*v.*) 1. to cut down to a stump. 2. to walk clumsily and heavily. 3. to travel about making speeches. 4. to break down the wicket with a ball when the batsman is out of his ground.

5. to present or be presented with too difficult a question or problem.

stumpy (*adj.*) short and thick.

stun (*v.*) 1. to make senseless; to stupefy. 2. to amaze; to bewilder.

stunt (*v.*) to check or stop the growth. STUNT (*n.*) 1. a check in growth. 2. a display of daring; bravado.

stunted (*adj.*) undersized; dwarf-like.

stupefaction (*n.*) 1. insensibility. 2. bewilderment; muddle.

stupefy (*v.*) to make senseless; to stun.

stupendous (*adj.*) immense; vast. STUPENDOUSLY (*adv.*).

stupid (*adj.*) foolish; silly. STUPIDLY (*adv.*).

stupidity (*n.*) folly; senselessness.

stupor (*n.*) insensibility; coma.

sturdiness (*n.*) robustness; vigour.

sturdy (*adj.*) stalwart; athletic. STURDILY (*adv.*).

sturgeon (*n.*) large, shark-like fish covered with bony plates, whose roe is made into the delicacy caviare.

stutter (*v.*) to falter in speaking; to stammer. STUTTER (*n.*) a stammer. STUTTERER (*n.*).

sty (*n.*) 1. a place for pigs. 2. an inflamed boil on the eyelid. (*pl.* STIES).

style (*n.*) 1. way in which something is done. 2. the fashion in dress, furnishing, etc.

stylish (*adj.*) fashionable. STYLISHLY (*adv.*).

suave (*adj.*) agreeable; persuasive. SUAVELY (*adv.*).

suavity (*n.*) gentleness; persuasiveness.

subconscious (*adj.*) not fully conscious; not fully perceived.

subdivide (*v.*) to divide into smaller parts.

subdivision (*n.*) a smaller part; part of the whole.

subdue (*v.*) to overcome; to conquer.

subject (*adj.*) under the power of another; dependent upon. SUBJECT (*v.*) to subdue; to have authority over. SUBJECT (*n.*) 1. a citizen. 2. a dependant. 3. a topic of conversation; a theme.

subjection (*n.*) defeat; dependence.

subjugate (*v.*) to conquer; to master.

subjugation (*n.*) conquest; defeat.

sublime (*adj.*) glorious; majestic. SUBLIMELY (*adv.*).

sublimity (*n.*) perfection; glory.

submarine (*n.*) an underseas warship. SUBMARINE (*adj.*) living or growing under the sea.

submerge (*v.*) to go under water; to sink.

submergence (*n.*) a plunge; dive.

submersion (*n.*) a placing under water; an immersion.

submission (*n.*) a surrender; yielding.

submissive (*adj.*) obedient; tame. SUBMISSIVELY (*adv.*).

submit (*v.*) 1. to give in; to yield. 2. to suggest; to propose.

subordinate (*adj.*) 1. of less importance. 2. under another's authority. SUBORDINATE (*n.*) one who ranks below another. SUBORDINATE (*v.*) 1. to regard as less important. 2. to place under control.

subscribe (*v.*) to give a contribution; to help. SUBSCRIBER (*n.*).

subscription (*n.*) a contribution; donation.

subsequent (*adj.*) coming after; happening later.

subservience (*n.*) slavishness.

subservient (*adj.*) useful; helpful.

subside (*v.*) to sink or fall lower; to die down.

subsidence (*n.*) a falling in; a landslide.

subsidy (*n.*) a grant; aid.

subsist (*v.*) to live; to endure.

subsistence (*n.*) a livelihood; maintenance.

substance (*n.*) 1. anything that is real—not imaginary. 2. the meaning; importance. 3. wealth; possessions.

substantial (*adj.*) real; solid.

substitute (*v.*) to exchange; to use instead of something else. SUBSTITUTE (*n.*) one who acts instead of another, or takes his place.

substitution (*n.*) the putting of a person or thing in the place of another.

subterfuge (*n.*) a trick; dodge.

subterranean (*adj.*) underground.

subtle (*adj.* pron. SUTTLE) cunning; ingenious. SUBTLY (*adv.*).

subtlety (*n.*) craftiness; artfulness.

subtract (*v.*) to take one quantity from another.

subtraction (*n.*) a taking from; a reduction.

suburb (*n.*) district on the outskirts of a town. SUBURBAN (*adj.*).

subvert (*v.*) to upset; to make disloyal. SUBVERSIVE (*adj.*).

subway (*n.*) an underground passage.

succeed (*v.*) 1. to prosper; to thrive. 2. to follow after; to inherit.

success (*n.*) prosperity; achievement.

successful (*adj.*) prosperous; happy. SUCCESSFULLY (*adv.*).

successive (*adj.*) coming one after another; in turn.

successor (*n.*) one who follows in another's place.

succinct (*adj.*) brief; concise. SUCCINCTLY (*adv.*).

succour (*v.*) to help; to aid. SUCCOUR (*n.*) help; relief.

succulent (*adj.*) juicy; tasty. SUCCULENTLY (*adv.*).

succumb (*v.*) to give way; to yield.

such (*adj.*) 1. the same as referred to; as that. 2. denoting a particular person or thing. 3. certain; very great.

suck (*v.*) to draw into the mouth. SUCK (*n.*) a sip.

suction (*n.*) a drawing or sucking of air or liquid from something.

sudden (*adj.*) without warning; quick. SUDDENLY (*adv.*).

suddenness (*n.*) the quickness; unexpectedness.

suds (*n. pl.*) a froth of soap and water.

sue (*v.*) to entreat; to plead.

suede (*n.* pron. SWADE) a soft leather made from undressed kidskin.

suet (*n.*) fat of certain parts of animals.

suffer (*v.*) 1. to undergo pain; to bear. 2. to permit; to allow.

sufferance (*n.*) something one is allowed to do though permission is not given in words; silent consent.

sufferer (*n.*) one who suffers.

suffering (*n.*) agony; distress.

suffice (*v.*) to be enough; to satisfy.

sufficient (*adj.*) enough; plenty. SUFFICIENTLY (*adv.*).

suffix (*n.*) letter or syllable added to the end of a word.

suffocate (*v.*) to smother; to choke.

suffocation (*n.*) death from lack of air.

suffrage (*n.*) the right to vote.

suffuse (*v.*) to spread over or throughout; to blush.

sugar (*n.*) sweet substance obtained from the sugar-cane and beetroot. SUGARY (*adj.*).

suggest (*v.*) to propose; to advise.

suggestion (*n.*) a proposal; plan.

suggestive (*adj.*) containing suggestions.

suicide (*n.*) the act of deliberately killing oneself.

suit (*v.*) to please; to satisfy. SUIT (*n.*) 1. a request; prayer. 2. an action in a law court. 3. an outfit of clothing.

suitable (*adj.*) fitting; convenient. SUITABLY (*adv.*).

suite (*n.*) 1. a set of rooms. 2. a body of attendants.

suitor (*n.*) 1. one who sues in a law court. 2. a lover; wooer.

sulk (*v.*) to be sullen or dull.

sulkiness (*n.*) sullenness; resentment.

sulky (*adj.*) sullen; morose. SULKILY (*adv.*).

sullen (*adj.*) sulky; unforgiving. SULLENLY (*adv.*).

sullenness (*n.*) sulkiness; resentment.

sully (*v.*) to soil; to stain.

sulphur (*n.*) a yellow mineral substance used in medicine and chemistry; brimstone.

sulphurous (*adj.*) smelling of burning sulphur; evil-smelling.

sultan (*n.*) a Muslim ruler.

sultana (*n.*) 1. a sultan's wife. 2. a small raisin.

sultriness (*n.*) closeness; oppressiveness. SULTRY (*adj.*).

sum (*n.*) the total; entire amount. SUM (*v.*) to find the total; to add.

summarize (*v.*) 1. to state the main points. 2. to note what is important.

summary (*n.*) an outline; brief account. SUMMARY (*adj.*) short; quick.

summer (*n.*) second or hot season of the year.

summit (*n.*) the highest point; the top.

summon (*v.*) 1. to command; to call. 2. to charge before a magistrate.

summons (*n.*) an order to appear in court. (*pl.* SUMMONSES).

sumptuous (*adj.*) rich; luxurious. SUMPTUOUSLY (*adv.*).

sumptuousness (*n.*) luxury; splendour.

sun (*n.*) heavenly body giving light and heat to the earth. SUN (*v.*) to sit in the sunshine.

sunbeam (*n.*) a ray of sunlight.

Sunday (*n.*) first day of the week; the Christian Sabbath.

sunder (*v.*) to divide; to separate.

sundial (*n.*) dial that indicates time by the shadow cast by the sun.

sundries (*n. pl.*) odds and ends of different things.

sundry (*adj.*) different; various.

sunken (*adj.*) 1. under water; sunk. 2. lower than ground-level.

sunlight (*n.*) light given by the sun. SUNLIT (*adj.*).

sunshine (*n.*) the sun's light and heat.

sunstroke (*n.*) illness due to over-exposure to sun's rays.

sup (*v.*) 1. to take into the mouth; to sip. 2. to eat the evening meal.

super (*prefix*) above; extra.

super-abundance (*n.*) excess; superfluity.

super-abundant (*adj.*) excessive; teeming.

superb (*adj.*) splendid; excellent.

supercilious (*adj.*) scornful; disdainful. SUPERCILIOUSLY (*adv.*).

superciliousness (*n.*) disdain; contempt.

superficial (*adj.*) showing on the surface; shallow.

superfluity (*n.*) over-abundance; excess.

superfluous (*adj.*) needless; unwanted.

superhuman (*adj.*) more than human; divine.

superintend (*v.*) to control; to manage.

superintendence (*n.*) control; supervision.

superintendent (*n.*) 1. a person in charge. 2. a high-ranking police officer.

superior (*adj.*) higher or better than others. SUPERIOR (*n.*) person higher in authority than another.

superiority (*n.*) the advantage; pre-eminence.

superlative (*adj.*) excellent; unequalled. SUPERLATIVELY (*adv.*).

superman (*n.*) a human being supposedly gifted with more-than-human mental or physical powers.

supermarket (*n.*) self-service store.

supernatural (*adj.*) not natural; miraculous.

supersede (*v.*) to take the place of another; to displace.

superstition (*n.*) a belief in omens and magic; credulity.

superstitious (*adj.*) believing in magic. SUPERSTITIOUSLY (*adv.*).

supervise (v.) to see work properly done; to check.

supervision (n.) inspection; control.

supervisor (n.) a manager; superintendent.

supine (adj.) 1. sluggish; slothful. 2. lying on one's back; prostrate.

supper (n.) an evening meal.

supplant (v.) to take another's place; to overthrow.

supple (adj.) easily bent; pliable.

supplement (v.) to add to; to continue. SUPPLEMENT (n.) an addition; postscript.

suppleness (n.) flexibility; pliability.

suppliant (n.) one who begs or entreats. SUPPLIANT (adj.) imploring; entreating.

supplicate (v.) to beg; to implore.

supplication (n.) a prayer; petition.

supplies (n. pl.) money granted by Parliament.

supply (v.) to provide; to furnish. SUPPLY (n.) a stock; provision. (pl. SUPPLIES).

support (v.) 1. to uphold; to prop. 2. to provide for; to befriend. 3. to encourage; to defend. SUPPORT (n.) 1. a prop; buttress. 2. a help; aid.

suppose (v.) to fancy; to imagine. SUPPOSED (adj.).

supposedly (adv.) as may be assumed.

supposition (n.) a hope; an assumption.

suppress (v.) 1. to stop; to crush. 2. to hold back; to keep secret.

suppression (n.) 1. a conquest. 2. secrecy.

supremacy (n.) mastery; sovereignty.

supreme (adj.) greatest; utmost. SUPREMELY (adv.).

sure (adj.) 1. certain. 2. safe; reliable.

sureness (n.) certainty; conviction.

surety (n.) a pledge; guarantee.

surf (n.) foam of breaking waves.

surface (n.) the outside; exterior. SURFACE (v.) to rise to the surface of water.

surfeit (v.) to overfeed; to glut. SURFEIT (n.) an excess; a glut.

surge (v.) to heave; to swell. SURGE (v.) the rise and fall of waves.

surgeon (n.) person who cures by operations.

surgery (n.) 1. work of curing by operation on the body. 2. a doctor's consulting room.

surliness (n.) sullenness; churlishness.

surly (adj.) sullen; sulky. SURLILY (adv.).

surmise (v.) to suppose; to imagine. SURMISE (n.) a belief; guess.

surmount (v.) to overcome; to climb.

surname (n.) a family name.

surpass (v.) to outdo; to beat.

surplice (n.) white gown or vestment worn by clergyman and choir.

surplus (n.) an amount more than is needed; excess. SURPLUS (adj.) needless; unnecessary.

surprise (n.) an unexpected happening; wonder. SURPRISE (v.) 1. to startle. 2. to astonish.

surprising (adj.) remarkable; astonishing SURPRISINGLY (adv.).

surrender (v.) to give in; to yield. SURRENDER (n.) a yielding; submission.

surreptitious (adj.) underhand; sly. SURREPTITIOUSLY (adv.).

surround (v.) to hem in; to encircle.

surroundings (n. pl.) the country round about; the scenery.

survey (v.) 1. to look about; to view. 2. to measure the land. SURVEY (n.) 1. a view; inspection. 2. the measuring and mapping of an area or district.

surveyor (n.) skilled examiner and measurer of land.

survival (n.) a living on after illness or disaster.

survive (v.) to continue living; to outlive.

survivor (n.) one saved from a disaster.

susceptibility (n.) tenderness; sensitiveness.

susceptible (adj.) tender-hearted; sympathetic.

suspect (v.) 1. to doubt; to mistrust. 2. to suppose; to imagine. SUSPECT (n.) a suspected person. SUSPECT (adj.) under suspicion; doubtful about.

suspend (v.) 1. to hang from. 2. to delay; to postpone.

suspense (n.) doubt; uncertainty.

suspension (n.) 1. a hanging from something. 2. a keeping in doubt or uncertainty.

suspicion (n.) doubt; distrust.

suspicious (adj.) doubtful; distrustful. SUSPICIOUSLY (adv.).

sustain (v.) 1. to support; to assist. 2. to suffer; to endure. 3. to approve; to confirm.

sustenance (*n.*) food and supplies; nourishment.

swab (*v.*) to wash with a mop; to cleanse. SWAB (*n.*) mop or pad for cleaning.

swagger (*v.*) to strut about; to boast. SWAGGER (*n.*) boastfulness; brag.

swain (*n.*) 1. a young peasant; a rustic. 2. a peasant lover. 3. an admirer or lover.

swallow (*n.*) 1. a small, swift, migratory bird. 2. a gulp. SWALLOW (*v.*) 1. to take into the throat; to consume. 2. to believe readily.

swamp (*v.*) to flood; to overwhelm. SWAMP (*n.*) a marsh; quagmire.

swan (*n.*) large, long-necked and web-footed bird.

swannery (*n.*) a rearing-place for swans.

sward (*n.*) a grassy place; lawn.

swarm (*n.*) 1. a cloud of insects. 2. a crowd; multitude. SWARM (*v.*) 1. to move in a crowd. 2. to climb.

swarming (*n.*) a moving in a swarm; emigration.

swarthiness (*n.*) brownness; sunburn.

swarthy (*adj.*) dark; sunburnt.

swathe (*v.*) to wrap round with clothing; to bandage.

sway (*v.*) 1. to move from side to side; to swing. 2. to rule; to control. SWAY (*n.*) rule; authority.

swear (*v.*) 1. to take an oath; to testify. 2. to use bad language.

sweat (*v.*) to perspire. SWEAT (*n.*) perspiration.

sweater (*n.*) a heavy, woollen jersey.

Swede (*n.*) a native of Sweden.

swede (*n.*) a yellow Swedish turnip.

sweep (*v.*) 1. to brush. 2. to glide swiftly. 3. to make a curving movement. SWEEP (*n.*) 1. a long, swift glide. 2. one who sweeps chimneys.

sweeping (*adj.*) wide; extensive.

sweet (*adj.*) 1. tasting like sugar. 2. pleasant; fragrant. SWEET (*n.*) a sweetmeat; confection.

sweeten (*v.*) to make sweeter or more pleasant.

sweetheart (*n.*) a lover.

sweetmeat (*n.*) a toffee; confection.

sweetness (*n.*) 1. a sweet taste; flavour. 2. pleasantness; tenderness. 3. fragrance; melody.

swell (*v.*) 1. to grow bigger or louder; to enlarge. 2. to rise and fall like waves.

swelling (*n.*) 1. a bulge. 2. an increase; enlargement.

swelter (*v.*) to feel too hot; to perspire. SWELTERING (*adj.*).

swerve (*v.*) to turn or move to one side suddenly. SWERVE (*n.*) a sudden turning aside.

swift (*adj.*) quick; rapid. SWIFT (*n.*) speedy bird of swallow family.

swill (*v.*) 1. to drink greedily or to excess. 2. to cleanse by flooding with water. SWILL (*n.*) liquid food given to pigs.

swim (*v.*) 1. to move through water by motions of the limbs or of fins. 2. to cross water by swimming. SWIM (*n.*) a bathe.

swimmingly (*adv.*) smoothly; successfully.

swindle (*v.*) to cheat; to defraud. SWINDLE (*n.*) a trick; fraud.

swindler (*n.*) a trickster; knave.

swine (*n.*) a pig; pigs.

swing (*v.*) 1. to sway to and fro. 2. to brandish. SWING (*n.*) a contrivance for swinging on.

swirl (*v.*) to rotate rapidly; to spin. SWIRL (*n.*) an eddy.

switch (*v.*) 1. to change direction. 2. to shunt. 3. to hit sharply. SWITCH (*n.*) 1. a whip; lash. 2. device for turning electricity on or off.

swivel (*n.*) a pin or pivot on which a loosely-connected ring revolves freely. SWIVEL (*v.*) to revolve on a pin or pivot.

swoon (*v.*) to faint. SWOON (*n.*) a faint.

swoop (*v.*) to sweep down upon and seize; to prey upon. SWOOP (*n.*) a downward rush.

sword (*n.*) long, narrow-bladed weapon used for cutting and thrusting.

sycamore (*n.*) a maple or plane-tree.

syllable (*n.*) a single sound in a word.

syllabus (*n.*) a programme of work; a plan.

sylvan (*adj.*) wooded; rural.

symbol (*n.*) a sign; an emblem.

symbolic (*adj.*) represented by a symbol or sign.

symmetrical (*adj.*) even; balanced.

symmetry (*n.*) regularity; balance.

sympathetic (*adj.*) kind; loving. SYM-PATHETICALLY (*adv.*).

sympathy (*n.*) fellow-feeling; understanding.

symphony (*n.*) a harmony of sounds; an elaborate musical composition.

symptom (*n.*) a sign indicating the kind of illness.

synagogue (*n.*) a Jewish place of worship.

syndicate (*n.*) an association of people or firms.

synonym (*n.*) a word that has the same meaning as another word.

synonymous (*adj.*) similar.

synopsis (*n.*) a summary, an outline.

syntax (*n.*) the rules necessary for forming sentences.

syringe (*n.*) a squirt; spray. SYRINGE (*v.*) to squirt; to spray.

syrup (*n.*) 1. the thick fluid obtained in the refining of sugar. 2. any thick, sugary liquid.

system (*n.*) 1. a regular method or way. 2. the whole universe. 3. the human body.

systematic (*adj.*) working by a method; orderly. SYSTEMATICALLY (*adv.*).

T

tab (*n.*) a small flap or tongue of cloth or leather.

tabard (*n.*) a herald's coat.

tabby (*n.*) a female cat.

tabernacle (*n.*) a place of worship.

table (*n.*) 1. flat-topped piece of furniture supported on legs. 2. an arranged list of facts or figures.

tableau (*n.*) picture formed by living people.

tableland (*n.*) a plateau.

tablespoon (*n.*) large serving-spoon.

tablespoonful (*n.*) contents of a tablespoon. (*pl.* TABLESPOONFULS).

tablet (*n.*) 1. small memorial plate. 2. a writing-block. 3. small pill. 4. portion of soap.

taboo (*v.*) to forbid; to prohibit. TABOO (*n.*) a ban; prohibition. TABOO (*adj.*) forbidden.

tabulate (*v.*) to arrange as a table or index. TABULATION (*n.*).

tacit (*adj.*) permitted but unspoken; implied. TACITLY (*adv.*).

taciturn (*adj.*) silent; moody.

taciturnity (*n.*) silence; reticence.

tack (*n.*) 1. short, broad-headed nail. 2. a long stitch. 3. ship's course in a side wind. TACK (*v.*) 1. to fasten with tacks. 2. to sail with a side wind.

tackle (*n.*) 1. instruments needed for fishing. 2. ropes and pulleys for lifting weights. 3. the holding of an opponent in football. TACKLE (*v.*) 1. to begin a task. 2. to grasp; to hold.

tact (*n.*) ability to speak and act without causing offence.

tactful (*adj.*) prudent; discreet. TACTFULLY (*adv.*).

tactical (*adj.*) according to plan.

tactician (*n.*) person skilled in planning.

tactics (*n. pl.*) 1. skill in managing troops in battle. 2. the method used to gain success.

tadpole (*n.*) a very young frog with tail and gills.

tag (*n.*) 1. a tie-on label. 2. the end or tail.

tail (*n.*) 1. long, hanging end of an animal's backbone. 2. the hinder part of anything.

tailor (*n.*) maker of men's clothing. (*fem.* TAILORESS).

tailoring (*n.*) work of a tailor.

taint (*v.*) to soil; to infect. TAINT (*n.*) a stain; blemish.

tainted (*adj.*) spoiled; decaying.

take (*v.*) 1. to receive; to grasp. 2. to photograph. 3. to lead.

taking (*adj.*) pleasing; attractive.

takings (*n. pl.*) money received for goods, entertainment, etc.

talcum (*n.*) a smooth, soft skin-powder.

tale (*n.*) a story; narrative.

talebearer (*n.*) one eager to spread scandal.

talent (*n.*) natural skill or ability. TALENTED (*adj.*).

talisman (*n.*) a lucky charm or magical word.

talk (*v.*) to speak. TALK (*n.*) 1. a conversation. 2. an address; a lecture. 3. gossip. TALKER (*n.*).

talkative (*adj.*) fond of talking; garrulous

tall (*adj.*) 1. above the usual height. 2. high; lofty.

tallow (*n.*) fat melted down for use in candles, soap, etc.

tally (*v.*) to fit exactly; to match. TALLY (*n.*) the score or bill.

talon (*n.*) claw of a bird of prey.

tamable (*adj.*) can be tamed.

tambour (*n.*) 1. small bass drum. 2. frame for embroidering.

tambourine (*n.*) small hand-drum with bells round the side.

tame (*adj.*) gentle and obedient. TAME (*v.*) to make gentle; to domesticate. TAMELY (*adv.*).

tameness (*n.*) 1. quietness; submission. 2. dullness; inactivity.

tamer (*n.*) trainer of wild animals.

tamper (*v.*) to meddle; to interfere.

tan (*n.*) 1. oak-bark used for tanning. 2. sunburn. 3. a yellowish-brown.

tandem (*n.*) 1. carriage drawn by two horses, one in front of the other. 2. bicycle for two riders.

tang (*n.*) 1. prong as of a fork or buckle. 2. sharp or biting taste.

tangent (*n.*) straight line which touches a curve, but does not cut it.

tangerine (*n.*) small, orange-like fruit.

tangible (*adj.*) real; solid. TANGIBLY (*adv.*).

tangle (*v.*) to muddle; to complicate. TANGLE (*n.*) a jumbled mass or knot.

tank (*n.*) 1. large water-container; a cistern. 2. armoured war-vehicle moving on caterpillar tracks.

tankard (*n.*) large beer-mug.

tanker (*n.*) ship or road vehicle with tank for carrying liquids, oil etc.

tanned (*adj.*) 1. made into leather. 2. sunburned.

tanner (*n.*) one who tans hides into leather.

tannery (*n.*) factory where hides are tanned.

tanning (*n.*) 1. leather-making. 2. a beating. 3. sunburn.

tantalize (*v.*) to tease; to torment. See appendix.

tantalizing (*adj.*) annoying; provoking.

tantalum (*n.*) rare metal used in electric bulbs.

tantamount (*adj.*) equal to; the same as.

tantrum (*n.*) a fit of temper.

tap (*n.*) 1. short outlet pipe, which can be opened or stopped. 2. light pat or touch. TAP (*v.*) 1. to cause to flow. 2. to touch; to pat.

tape (*n.*) a long ribbon of cloth.

taper (*v.*) to become narrower towards one end. TAPER (*n.*) 1. a narrowing. 2. a long, narrow candle.

tapestry (*n.*) large cloth ornamented with woven designs. TAPESTRIED (*adj.*).

tapioca (*n.*) starchy food prepared from cassava-root.

tapir (*n.*) a pig-like wild animal with a short, flexible nose found in America.

tar (*n.*) thick, black liquid obtained from coal. TAR (*v.*) to coat with tar.

tarantula (*n.*) a large poisonous spider.

tardy (*adj.*) slow; late. TARDILY (*adv.*). TARDINESS (*n.*).

tare (*n.*) 1. a weed. 2. allowance made for weight of case or vehicle weighed with goods.

target (*n.*) object or point aimed at.

tariff (*n.*) 1. a charge or duty paid on imported or exported goods. 2. list of charges at hotel or restaurant.

tarmac (*n.*) 1. runway for aircraft. 2. material for road-making.

tarn (*n.*) small, mountain lake.

tarnish (*v.*) to discolour; to dim. TARNISHED (*adj.*).

tarpaulin (*n.*) canvas sheet tarred to make it waterproof.

tart (*adj.*) sharp or sour in flavour. TART (*n.*) 1. a fruit pie. 2. a pastry containing jam.

tartan (*n.*) woollen cloth woven in the colours of a Highland clan.

tartar (*n.*) 1. one who is more than one's match, like the fierce warriors of Tartary, Asia. 2. a hard substance which forms on the teeth.

task (*n.*) 1. work set to be done. 2. drudgery; toil.

taskmaster (*n.*) a hard master.

tassel (*n.*) ornamental tuft of loosely hanging threads.

taste (*n.*) 1. sense enabling one to test food or drink. 2. one's judgment in liking anything. 3. a small, trial portion of food. TASTE (*v.*) 1. to savour. 2. to test.

tasteful (*adj.*) good; pleasing. TASTEFULLY (*adv.*).

tasteless (*adj.*) 1. without flavour; insipid. 2. lacking in good judgment.

tasty (*adj.*) pleasant-tasting; savoury.

tatter (*v.*) to tear to rags. TATTER (*n.*) a rag. TATTERED (*adj.*).

tattle (*n.*) gossip. TATTLE (*v.*) to gossip; to chatter. TATTLER (*n.*).

tattoo (*n.*) 1. a drumbeat. 2. a military display at night. TATTOO (*v.*) to prick a design into the skin.

taught (*v.*) past tense of TEACH.

taunt (*v.*) to sneer at; to ridicule. TAUNT (*n.*) ridicule; mockery.

taut (*adj.*) stretched; very tight. TAUTLY (*adv.*).

tavern (*n.*) a public-house; an inn.

tawdry (*adj.*) showy, but worthless. See appendix.

tawny (*adj.*) tan colour; orange-brown.

tax (*n.*) money lawfully demanded from a citizen for the payment of national expenses. TAX (*v.*) 1. to demand or impose a tax. 2. to accuse; to charge.

taxable (*adj.*) liable to be taxed.

taxation (*n.*) the total tax levied.

taxi (*n.*) a motor-car fitted with a taximeter employed for hire. (*pl.* TAXIS).

taximeter (*n.*) apparatus which indicates the fare for the distance travelled.

tea (*n.*) beverage brewed from the dried leaves of the tea plant.

teach (*v.*) to instruct; to inform.

teacher (*n.*) one who instructs; a tutor.

teaching (*n.*) the instruction given.

teak (*n.*) a hard, durable timber.

teal (*n.*) kind of small, wild duck.

team (*n.*) 1. set of persons playing or working together. 2. a group of animals harnessed together.

teamster (*n.*) driver of a team of animals.

tear (*v.*) 1. to pull apart; to rip. 2. to rush along. TEAR (*n.*) a rent; rip.

tear (*n.*) a drop of water from the eye.

tearful (*adj.*) shedding tears; weeping. TEARFULLY (*adv.*).

tearing (*adj.*) violent; rushing.

tearless (*adj.*) without tears; unmoved.

tease (*v.*) 1. to annoy; to torment. 2. to untangle. TEASE (*n.*) a tormentor.

teaser (*n.*) a hard question.

technical (*adj.*) concerning some particular art, craft or science.

technicality (*n.*) anything that must be done to manufacture or produce.

technique (*n.*) the method of doing something; the mechanical skill.

technology (*n.*) the science or study of manufacturing processes.

tedious (*adj.*) wearisome; tiresome. TEDIOUSLY (*adv.*).

tedium (*n.*) boredom; weariness.

teem (*v.*) to overflow; to swarm. TEEMING (*adj.*).

teens (*n.*) the years of youth, between twelve and twenty.

teethe (*v.*) to grow or cut teeth. TEETHING (*n.*).

teetotal (*adj.*) believing in not drinking beer, wine or spirits. TEETOTALLER (*n.*) one who drinks no beer, etc.

telecamera (*n.*) a television camera.

telecast (*n.*) a televised programme. TELECAST (*v.*) to send a televised programme.

telegram (*n.*) message sent by telegraph.

telegraph (*n.*) apparatus for sending messages by electricity. TELEGRAPHIC (*adj.*).

telegraphy (*n.*) system of communicating by telegraph.

telephone (*n.*) electrical apparatus enabling a person to speak to another at a distance. TELEPHONIC (*adj.*).

telephony (*n.*) system of constructing and using telephones.

telephoto (*n.*) photograph or image transmitted by wireless.

telescope (*n.*) instrument that makes distant objects seem near and large.

telescopic (*adj.*) visible only through a telescope.

teleview (*v.*) to watch a televised programme.

televise (*v.*) to transmit by television.

television (*n.*) the wireless transmission of visual images.

televisor (*n.*) a television receiver.

tell (*v.*) 1. to give an account; to relate. 2. to count. 3. to produce an effect.

teller (*n.*) 1. one who relates. 2. one who counts votes. 3. bank official who pays and receives money.

telling (*adj.*) striking; impressive.

tell-tale (*n.*) 1. one who cannot keep a secret. 2. a device which gives warning. TELL-TALE (*adj.*) revealing a secret.

telotype (*n.*) apparatus that prints telegraphic messages.

temerity (*n.*) rashness; foolhardiness.

temper (*v.*) 1. to mix in right quantities. 2. to give metals their right hardness. 3. to calm; to check. TEMPER (*n.*) 1. a right mixing or hardening. 2. one's state of mind; mood. 3. anger; annoyance.

temperament (*n.*) one's natural state of mind; disposition.

temperance (*n.*) moderation; soberness.

temperate (*adj.*) moderate; restrained.

temperature (*n.*) 1. the hotness or coldness of a thing. 2. degree of heat as shown by a thermometer.

tempest (*n.*) a violent storm; a gale.

tempestuous (*adj.*) stormy. TEMPESTUOUSLY (*adv.*).

temple (*n.*) 1. part of the head between forehead and ear. 2. a place of religious worship.

temporal (*adj.*) concerned with earthly affairs.

temporarily (*adv.*) for a short time; the present.

temporary (*adj.*) lasting only for a time; brief.

temporize (*v.*) to hold back; to delay; to gain time.

tempt (*v.*) 1. to test; to try. 2. to persuade; to lead astray.

temptation (*n.*) an attraction; enticement.

tempter (*n.*) one who tempts. (*fem.* TEMPTRESS).

tempting (*adj.*) attractive; alluring. TEMPTINGLY (*adv.*).

ten (*adj.*) twice five; nine and one. TEN (*n.*) 1. the sum of five and five; the number, one more than nine. 2. the symbol for 10 units, as 10 or X.

tenacious (*adj.*) 1. gripping tightly; sticking. 2. stubborn.

tenacity (*n.*) 1. grip; firmness. 2. obstinacy.

tenancy (*n.*) property for which rent is paid.

tenant (*n.*) one who rents property.

tenantry (*n.*) all the tenants of one landlord.

tench (*n.*) freshwater fish of carp family.

tend (*v.*) 1. to lean towards; to incline. 2. to care for.

tendency (*n.*) an inclination; a trend.

tender (*n.*) 1. an offer to do something for an agreed payment. 2. small vessel attending on a large one. 3. the supply vehicle behind a locomotive. TENDER (*adj.*) 1. soft; easily cut. 2. gentle; mild. 3. sore; painful. TENDER (*v.*) to offer; to volunteer. TENDERLY (*adv.*).

tenderness (*n.*) 1. softness. 2. gentleness. 3. soreness.

tendon (*n.*) a strong cord joining bone and muscle.

tendril (*n.*) the shoot by which a climbing plant grips a support.

tenement (*n.*) 1. a tenanted house. 2. a building divided into several dwellings.

tenet (*n.*) a firm belief; a creed.

tennis (*n.*) game played with rackets and balls on a lawn or hard court.

tenor (*n.*) 1. singer with the highest adult male voice. 2. one's ordinary way of living. 3. general meaning of a speech or document.

tense (*adj.*) tight; stretched. TENSE (*n.*) form taken by a verb to indicate time.

tension (*n.*) 1. strain. 2. the mental effort.

tent (*n.*) a portable canvas dwelling or shelter.

tentacle (*n.*) long, slender feeler of an insect.

tentative (*adj.*) done as a trial; experimental. TENTATIVELY (*adv.*).

tenuous (*adj.*) thin; slim.

tenure (*n.*) the right by which land is held.

tepid (*adj.*) 1. slightly warm; lukewarm. 2. half-hearted.

tepidity (*n.*) 1. lukewarmness. 2. mildness.

tercentenary (*n.*) the 300th anniversary.

term (*v.*) to name; to call. TERM (*n.*) 1. a word; an expression. 2. a period of time; season. 3. a boundary; limit.

termed (*adj.*) called; named.

terminal (*n.*) a connecting point for electrical apparatus. TERMINAL (*adj.*) concerned with the end.

terminate (*v.*) to end; to stop.

termination (*n.*) an end; a conclusion.

terminus (*n.*) 1. end of a journey. 2. a boundary; border.

termite (*n.*) the white ant.

tern (*n.*) seabird like a gull, but smaller.

terrace (*n.*) 1. a raised, level bank of earth. 2. a row of houses on a slope.

terrapin (*n.*) a freshwater tortoise.

terrestrial (*adj.*) concerned with the earth; earthly.

terrible (*adj.*) causing terror; dreadful.

terribly (*adv.*) extremely.

terrier (*n.*) small, active dog, good at hunting.

terrific (*adj.*) terrible; awful. TERRIFICALLY (*adv.*).

terrify (*v.*) to frighten; to horrify.

territorial (*adj.*) relating to territory. TERRITORIAL (*n.*) a member of the Territorial Army.

territory (*n.*) large area of land; a country.

terror (*n.*) great fear or dread.

terrorize (*v.*) to fill with fear; to threaten.

terse (*adj.*) short; brief. TERSELY (*adv.*).

terseness (*n.*) brevity; conciseness.

test (*v.*) to try the quality or worth; to examine. TEST (*n.*) a trial; an examination. TESTED (*adj.*).

testament (*n.*) 1. a will. 2. a declaration or witness. 3. one of two divisions of the Bible.

testator (*n.*) one who makes a will. (*fem.* TESTATRIX).

testify (*n.*) to declare; to give evidence.

testimonial (*n.*) 1. a statement about a person's character or abilities. 2. gift presented as a mark of esteem.

testimony (*n.*) a statement of fact; evidence.

tether (*v.*) to fasten an animal so that it cannot stray. TETHER (*n.*) a rope; halter.

text (*n.*) 1. actual words spoken or written by someone. 2. a passage from Scripture. 3. a subject; topic.

textbook (*n.*) a pupil's study-book.

textile (*n.*) a material; fabric. TEXTILE (*adj.*) concerned with fabrics.

texture (*n.*) the structure or quality of a fabric.

than (*conj.*) compared with.

thank (*v.*) to express gratitude.

thankful (*adj.*) grateful; obliged. THANK-FULLY (*adv.*).

thankfulness (*n.*) gratitude.

thankless (*adj.*) ungrateful.

thanks (*n. pl.*) one's expression of gratitude.

thanksgiving (*n.*) gratitude given to God.

that (*pron.* or *adj.*) person or thing farther away. (*pl.* THOSE).

thatch (*v.*) to cover a roof with straw. THATCH (*n.*) straw for a roof-covering.

thaw (*v.*) 1. to change from ice to water; to melt. 2. to become more pleasant; to unbend.

theatre (*n.*) 1. building in which plays are acted, 2. room in which surgical operations are performed.

theatrical (*adj.*) done for effect; dramatic. THEATRICALLY (*adv.*).

theft (*n.*) stealing; robbery.

their (*pron. pl.*) belonging to them.

them (*pron. pl.*) those persons or things; those.

theme (*n.*) 1. a subject; topic. 2. a repeated melody in music.

then (*adv.*) 1. at that time. 2. hereafter; afterward. 3. for this reason. THEN (*conj.*) in that case; therefore.

thence (*adv.*) from that place or time.

theodolite (*n.*) surveying instrument for measuring angles.

theologian (*n.*) one learned in theology.

theological (*adj.*) concerned with religion.

theology (*n.*) study of God and religion.

theorem (*n.*) an idea which needs to be proved or tried.

theorize (*v.*) to have ideas; to think about things.

theory (*n.*) an idea; a supposition. (*pl.* THEORIES).

there (*adv.*) at, or in, that place.

therm (*n.*) the unit measure of the quantity of heat.

thermometer (*n.*) an instrument for measuring temperature.

thermos (*n.*) a flask for keeping liquids hot.

these. See THIS.

thesis (*n.*) the subject of an essay; a theme.

thews (*n. pl.*) sinews; muscles.

thick (*adj.*) 1. deep between opposite surfaces. 2. crowded; packed. 3. misty; dense. 4. stiff or slow-flowing. 5. slow-thinking; stupid. THICKLY (*adv.*).

thicken (*v.*) to make thicker, denser or stiffer.

thicket (*n.*) group of closely-planted trees or shrubs.

thickness (*n.*) the measure of depth.

thief (*n.*) one who steals; a robber.

thieve (*v.*) to steal; to pilfer.

thievish (*adj.*) inclined to steal. THIEVISHLY (*adv.*).

thigh (*n.*) leg, between hip and knee.

thimble (*n.*) metal cap protecting the finger when sewing.

thin (*adj.*) 1. having opposite surfaces near. together. 2. not fat; lean. 3. slim; slender. THIN (*v.*) to make less thick or more fluid. 2. to reduce in bulk or number.

thing (*n.*) an object; article.

think (*v.*) to reason; to have an opinion.

thinker (*n.*) one able to reason.

thinking (*n.*) thought; reason. THINKING (*adj.*) reasoning.

thinness (*n.*) slimness; slenderness.

thin-skinned (*adj.*) very sensitive; easily upset.

third (*adj.*) the next after the second. THIRD (*n.*) one of three equal parts into which anything is divided.

thirst (*n.*) want of drink. THIRST (*v.*) to desire a drink.

thirstily (*adv.*) eagerly.

thirsty (*adj.*) 1. dry; parched. 2. eager. THIRSTINESS (*n.*).

this (*pron.* or *adj.*) person or thing last mentioned. (*pl.* THESE).

thistle (*n.*) prickly plant with purple flowers; national emblem of Scotland.

thistly (*adj.*) prickly.

thither (*adv.*) to that place; yonder.

thong (*n.*) narrow strip of leather; a whiplash.

thorax (*n.*) the chest.

thorium (*n.*) metal that shoots out electrons when heated.

thorn (*n.*) spiky growth on a plant; a prickle.

thorny (*adj.*) 1. prickly. 2. rough; difficult.

thorough (*adj.*) complete; entire.

thoroughbred (*adj.*) pure-blooded.

thoroughfare (*n.*) a through road.

thoroughly (*adv.*) completely; fully.

thoroughness (*n.*) whole-heartedness; completeness.

those (*pron.*). See THAT.

though (*adv.*) admitting; however.

thought (*n.*) process of thinking or reasoning.

thoughtful (*adj.*) 1. thinking deeply. 2. considerate; regardful.

thoughtless (*adj.*) inconsiderate; careless. THOUGHTLESSNESS (*n.*).

thousand (*n.*) ten hundred.

thraldom (*n.*) slavery.

thrall (*n.*) a slave.

thrash (*v.*) 1. to beat; to chastise. 2. to beat the grain from ears of corn.

thrashing (*n.*) 1. a beating. 2. the separation of ears from the grain.

thread (*n.*) 1. spun fibres of cotton, linen or silk. 2. the spiral ridge on a screw. 3. the trend or gist of a talk. THREAD (*v.*) 1. to pass thread through a needle's eye. 2. to string beads on a thread. 3. to pick a way through a crowd.

threadbare (*adj.*) worn out; shabby.

threat (*n.*) a warning of evil; menace.

threaten (*v.*) to warn; to menace.

threatening (*adj.*) warning; menacing. THREATENINGLY (*adv.*).

three (*adj.*) two and one. THREE (*n.*) 1. the sum of two and one. 2. the figure or symbol 3 or III.

thresh (*v.*) to separate grain from the husk by beating; to thrash.

threshold (*n.*) 1. plank or stone at bottom of entrance-door. 2. the beginning; start.

thrift (*n.*) care in saving or economizing.

thriftiness (*n.*) frugality; economy.

thriftless (*adj.*) wasteful; extravagant.

thrifty (*adj.*) frugal; economical. THRIFTILY (*adv.*).

thrill (*n.*) a feeling of excitement. THRILL (*v.*) to excite; to stir.

thrive (*v.*) to succeed; to prosper. THRIVING (*adj.*).

throat (*n.*) the front of the neck; the gullet.

throb (*v.*) to beat steadily, as does the heart; to palpitate. THROB (*n.*) a heartbeat.

throe (*n.*) a severe spasm of pain; a pang.

throne (*n.*) a sovereign's or bishop's chair of state.

throng (*n.*) a crowd; multitude. THRONG (*v.*) to crowd or flock.

throstle (*n.*) the song-thrush.

throttle (*v.*) to choke; to strangle. THROTTLE (*n.*) 1. the throat; windpipe.

2. valve for regulating the flow of steam or air into an engine.

through (*prep.* and *adv.*) from one end or side to the other.

throughout (*prep.* and *adv.*) in every part of.

throw (*v.*) to cast; to hurl. THROW (*n.*) a fling; toss.

thrush (*n.*) 1. a song-bird. 2. a disease of the mouth and throat.

thrust (*v.*) to push into; to pierce. THRUST (*n.*) a push; a stab.

thud (*n.*) a dull, low sound; thump. THUD (*v.*) to fall with a thump.

thug (*n.*) 1. one of a brotherhood of stranglers and robbers which once infested India. 2. a brutal robber; ruffian.

thumb (*n.*) the short, thick finger of the hand. THUMB (*v.*) to handle or soil with the thumb; to handle clumsily.

thump (*v.*) to beat; to strike with the fist. THUMP (*n.*) a heavy blow; stroke.

thunder (*n.*) sound following a lightning-flash. THUNDER (*v.*) 1. to roll; to peal. 2. to rumble.

thunderbolt (*n.*) a lightning-flash.

thunderstruck (*adj.*) astounded; amazed.

thundery (*adj.*) threatening a thunder-storm.

Thursday (*n.*) fifth day of week. See appendix.

thus (*adv.*) in this way, or manner.

thwart (*v.*) to upset someone's plans; to frustrate. THWART (*n.*) an oarsman's seat across a boat.

thwarted (*adj.*) hindered; outdone.

thy (*adj.*) belonging to thee; thine.

thyme (*n.*) a fragrant herb.

tiara (*n.*) a jewelled head-dress.

tick (*n.*) 1. sound of a clock or watch. 2. a mark made when checking a list.

ticket (*n.*) small card used as a pass or receipt.

tickle (*v.*) 1. to touch lightly. 2. to compel laughter; to amuse. TICKLE (*n.*) 1. a touch which compels laughter. 2. a throat irritation.

ticklish (*adj.*) 1. easily tickled. 2. difficult; requiring care.

tidal (*adj.*) concerned with the tides; rising and falling.

tide (*n.*) 1. the regular rise and fall, or flow and ebb, of the sea. 2. a time or season.

tidings (*n. pl.*) news; information.

tidy (*adj.*) neat; orderly. TIDILY (*adv.*). TIDINESS (*n.*).

tie (*v.*) 1. to bind; to knot. 2. to score equally. TIE (*n.*) 1. a link; connection. 2. an equal score. 3. a neck-cloth. 4. a hindrance.

tied (*adj.*) fastened; knotted.

tier (*n.*) one of a number of rows of seats which rise above and behind each other.

tiff (*n.*) a slight quarrel.

tiger (*n.*) striped jungle-animal of cat family. (*fem.* TIGRESS).

tigerish (*adj.*) tiger-like; fierce.

tight (*adj.*) 1. closely and firmly put together. 2. stretched; taut. TIGHTLY (*adv.*).

tighten (*v.*) to make tight; or tighter.

tile (*n.*) thin slab of baked clay used for roofing or paving.

tiler (*n.*) one who makes or lays tiles.

till (*v.*) to cultivate; to plough. TILL (*n.*) shopkeeper's money-drawer.

tillage (*n.*) 1. land prepared for crops. 2. agriculture.

tilled (*adj.*) cultivated.

tiller (*n.*) 1. a ploughman; cultivator. 2. handle of a ship's rudder; the helm.

tilt (*v.*) to slope to one side; to lean over. TILT (*n.*) a slope; slant.

timber (*n.*) 1. wood prepared for carpentry, etc. 2. trees providing such wood. TIMBERED (*adj.*).

time (*n.*) 1. the measure or duration of the past, present and future. 2. the moment of the day as shown by the clock. TIME (*v.*) to measure the duration of an action, event, etc.

timeliness (*n.*) promptness; punctuality.

timely (*adj.*) early; suitable.

timepiece (*n.*) a clock.

timetable (*n.*) list of train times, lesson hours, etc.

timid (*adj.*) easily frightened. TIMIDLY (*adv.*).

timidity (*n.*) faint-heartedness; fear.

timorous (*adj.*) full of fear. TIMOROUSLY (*adv.*).

tin (*n.*) a soft white metal. TIN (*v.*) 1. to coat with tin. 2. to preserve in a tin.

tincture (*n.*) 1. a drug dissolved in alcohol. 2. a tinge or shade of colour.

tinder (*n.*) a very dry substance which a spark will set on fire.

ting (*n.*) sharp sound of a bell.

tinge (*v.*) to colour slightly. TINGE (*n.*) a touch or shade of colour. TINGED (*adj.*).

tingle (*v.*) to have a prickly feeling like pins and needles.

tinker (*n.*) one who mends kettles and pans. TINKER (*v.*) to mend roughly.

tinkle (*n.*) sound of a small bell.

tinsel (*n.*) glittering material; cheap finery.

tint (*n.*) a shade of colour; hue. TINT (*v.*) to colour; to dye.

tiny (*adj.*) very small; little.

tip (*v.*) 1. to tilt or upset. 2. to reward. 3. to touch lightly. TIP (*n.*) 1. a small money present. 2. the point or end. 3. a useful hint.

tipple (*v.*) to drink alcoholic liquors habitually and to excess. TIPPLE (*n.*) strong drink.

tirade (*n.*) a noisy scolding or speech.

tire (*v.*) to become weary; to exhaust. TIRED (*adj.*).

tiredness (*n.*) weariness; fatigue.

tireless (*adj.*) unwearied. TIRELESSLY (*adv.*).

tiresome (*adj.*) troublesome; annoying.

tissue (*n.*) 1. a fine-woven fabric. 2. the material of which living things are made.

titanic (*adj.*) huge; gigantic. See appendix.

titbit (*n.*) a tasty morsel of food or news.

tithe (*n.*) a tax on farm produce and stock allotted to support the clergy; the one-tenth part.

titivate (*v.*) to smarten or adorn oneself.

title (*n.*) 1. special name denoting rank, profession, etc. 2. the name of a book, play, etc.

titled (*adj.*) bearing a title of nobility.

titter (*v.*) to laugh quietly, as to oneself. TITTER (*n.*) a restrained laugh.

tittle-tattle (*n.*) gossip; prattle.

tit-mouse (*n.*) small, active bird of the tit family, which nests in a hole in a tree.

toad (*n.*) warty, frog-like amphibian.

toadstool (*n.*) a mushroom-like, poisonous fungus.

toast (*v.*) 1. to heat bread before a fire and make crisp. 2. to drink a person's health. TOAST (*n.*) 1. fire-browned bread. 2. a drinking a health.

tobacco (*n.*) dried leaves of tobacco plant prepared for smoking.

tobacconist (*n.*) seller of tobacco.

toboggan (*n.*) long, narrow sled for use on snow. TOBOGGAN (*v.*) to slide on a toboggan.

to-day (*n.*) this day.

toddle (*v.*) to walk with short, uncertain steps like a baby. TODDLER (*n.*).

toe (*n.*) 1. a digit of the foot. 2. part of shoe or boot; toe-cap.

toffee (*n.*) any sweet made of butter and sugar.

together (*adv.*) 1. in company. 2. unitedly.

toil (*v.*) to work hard; to strive. TOIL (*n.*) work; labour. TOILER (*n.*).

toilet (*n.*) act of dressing.

toilsome (*adj.*) laborious; wearisome.

token (*n.*) a sign; symbol.

tolerable (*adj.*) 1. endurable. 2. fairly good.

tolerance (*n.*) patience; forbearance.

tolerant (*adj.*) not bigoted; liberal.

tolerate (*v.*) to put up with; to allow.

toleration (*n.*) recognition of the rights of others.

toll (*n.*) 1. a payment to use a bridge, road, etc. 2. a single stroke of a heavy bell; knell. TOLL (*v.*) to sound a knell.

tomahawk (*n.*) Red-Indian war-axe.

tomato (*n.*) pulpy, red, edible fruit. (*pl.* TOMATOES).

tomb (*n.*) a grave; burial-vault.

tome (*n.*) large, heavy volume or book.

to-morrow (*n.*) day after to-day.

tom-tit (*n.*) small bird of the tit family.

tomtom (*n.*) African native drum.

ton (*n.*) an Imperial measure of weight (2240 lbs.).

tone (*n.*) 1. a musical sound. 2. the tint of a colour. 3. a state of health. TONE (*v.*) to blend colours pleasingly.

tongs (*n. pl.*) hinged nippers for picking up coal, etc.

tongue (*n.*) 1. organ of speech and taste. 2. a language. 3. a long, low promontory.

tonic (*n.*) medicine that strengthens.

to-night (*n.*) this night.

tonne (*n.*) metric unit of mass; 1000 kilogrammes.

tonsil (*n.*) one of the two glands at the back of the throat.

tonsillitis (*n.*) inflammation of the tonsils.

too (*adv.*) 1. overmuch; more than enough. 2. besides; likewise.

tool (*n.*) any implement required in doing work.

toot (*n.*) sound of a horn or trumpet. TOOT (*v.*) to sound a horn.

tooth (*n.*) 1. one of the small bones in the jaws used for chewing. 2. a tooth-like projection on a saw, comb, etc. (*pl.* TEETH). TOOTHED; TOOTHLESS (*adjs.*).

toothache (*n.*) pain in a tooth, or the teeth.

toothpick (*n.*) implement for removing food from the teeth.

toothsome (*adj.*) pleasant to eat; tasty.

top (*n.*) 1. the highest part; the summit. 2. a toy that spins. 3. the head; chief.

topaz (*n.*) a precious stone.

toper (*n.*) one who drinks strong liquors to excess frequently; a drunkard.

topic (*n.*) a subject for discussion; a theme. TOPICAL (*adj.*).

topography (*n.*) the features of a landscape or district; the lie of the land.

topple (*v.*) to totter and fall down.

topsy-turvy (*adv.*) upside down.

tor (*n.*) small hill, or rocky peak.

torch (*n.*) 1. piece of blazing material carried to give light. 2. an electric hand-lamp.

torment (*v.* pron. tor-MENT) to inflict pain; to torture. TORMENT (*n.* pron. TOR-ment) severe bodily or mental suffering; agony. TORMENTOR (*n.*).

tornado (*n.*) a destructive whirlwind; a cyclone.

torpedo (*n.*) explosive shell that travels underwater. (*pl.* TORPEDOES). TORPEDO (*v.*) to strike with a torpedo.

torrent (*n.*) 1. a swiftly-rushing stream. 2. heavy downpour of rain. 3. string of quickly-spoken words.

torrential (*adj.*) flooding; overwhelming.

torrid (*adj.*) extremely hot; tropical.

tortoise (*n.*) reptile quite enclosed in a scaly shell; a land-turtle.

tortuous (*adj.*) winding; twisting.

torture (*v.*) to cause bodily or mental agony. TORTURE (*n.*) unbearable suffering; torment.

toss (*v.*) to throw up or across. TOSS (*n.*) an upward throw, or a jerk of the head; a fall from a horse.

tot (*n.*) a small child. TOT (*v.*) to add.

total (*n.*) the full amount; the whole. TOTAL (*v.*) to add; to complete. TOTAL (*adj.*) whole; complete.

totally (*adv.*) wholly; completely.

totter (*v.*) to stand or walk unsteadily; to stagger.

tottery (*adj.*) ready to fall; shaky.

touch (*v.*) 1. to make contact with; to feel. 2. to win sympathy. TOUCH (*n.*) 1. light stroke with the hand, pencil, etc. 2. anything felt lightly.

touching (*adj.*) pitiful; pathetic.

touchstone (*n.*) a test; standard.

touchy (*adj.*) apt to take offence; irritable.

tough (*adj.*) 1. hard to bite or cut. 2. hardy; enduring.

toughen (*v.*) to make hardy; to give strength to.

toughness (*n.*) 1. the resistance to cutting. 2. the endurance; hardihood.

tour (*v.*) to travel from place to place. TOUR (*n.*) a journey for pleasure or health.

tourist (*n.*) a traveller; sightseer.

tournament (*n.*) a contest; combat.

tow (*v.*) 1. to pull a boat, vehicle, etc., with a rope. TOW (*n.*) 1. anything towed. 2. coarse flax or hemp.

toward, towards (*prep.*) in the direction of.

towel (*n.*) a cloth for wiping or drying.

towelling (*n.*) 1. towel-making material. 2. a brisk rubbing with a towel.

tower (*n.*) narrow, lofty building rising high above others. TOWER (*v.*) to rise above or over others.

towering (*adj.*) 1. high; lofty. 2. violent.

town (*n.*) 1. settlement larger than a village, but smaller than a borough. 2. the inhabitants of a town.

townsfolk (*n.*) inhabitants of a town.

toxin (*n.*) poison produced by germs. TOXIC (*adj.*).

toy (*n.*) a plaything. TOY (*v.*) to play with.

trace (*v.*) 1. to seek and find. 2. to copy a drawing on paper placed over it. TRACE (*n.*) 1. a mark left by something. 2. strap by which a horse draws a vehicle.

traceable (*adj.*) can be traced.

tracery (*n.*) ornamental stonework forming a window.

track (*n.*) 1. a pathway; trail. 2. a railroad. 3. traces left by a person. TRACK (*v.*) to follow tracks.

tracker (*n.*) one trained to follow a trail.

trackless (*adj.*) wild; untrodden.

tract (*n.*) 1. large land area; a region. 2. a short pamphlet or booklet.

tractable (*adj.*) easily managed; docile.

traction (*n.*) the propulsion of vehicles; haulage.

tractor (*n.*) vehicle able to move itself and pull another.

trade (*n.*) 1. business of buying and selling. 2. commerce. 3. one's work or craft. TRADE (*v.*) to buy and sell.

trader (*n.*) 1. a merchant. 2. a cargo ship.

tradesman (*n.*) 1. a shopkeeper. 2. a craftsman.

tradition (*n.*) an old-time custom or belief handed down.

traditional (*adj.*) as ordered by tradition; customary. TRADITIONALLY (*adv.*).

traduce (*v.*) to slander; to defame. TRADUCER (*n.*).

traffic (*n.*) 1. the moving from place to place of people, vehicles and ships. 2. trade and commerce. TRAFFIC (*v.*) to trade.

tragedian (*n.*) writer of, or actor in, tragedies.

tragedy (*n.*) 1. an accident or crime causing death; a serious disaster. 2. a play depicting crime and punishment. (*pl.* TRAGEDIES).

tragic (*adj.*) disastrous; shocking. TRAGICALLY (*adv.*).

trail (*v.*) 1. to pull along. 2. to walk wearily behind. TRAIL (*n.*) track followed by a hunter.

trailer (*n.*) 1. vehicle pulled by a car or lorry. 2. extracts from a film shown to advertise it.

train (*v.*) 1. to teach how to live rightly or work efficiently. 2. exercise oneself in games, sports, etc. TRAIN (*n.*) 1. a line of railway-coaches with engine attached. 2. the trailing part of a dress.

trained (*adj.*) skilled; efficient.

trainer (*n.*) 1. an instructor. 2. a tamer of wild animals.

training (*n.*) teaching; instruction.

trait (*n.*) a feature of one's character; a personal habit or mannerism.

traitor (*n.*) one disloyal to country or sovereign. (*fem.* TRAITRESS).

traitorous (*adj.*) disloyal. TRAITOROUSLY (*adv.*).

tram (*n.*) passenger-car running on rails laid in a public road or street.

trammel (*v.*) to hinder; to obstruct.

tramp (*v.*) 1. to tread heavily. 2. to travel on foot. TRAMP (*n.*) 1. a heavy tread. 2. a ramble. 3. a homeless beggar. 4. a ship without a regular run.

trample (*v.*) to tread underfoot.

trance (*n.*) a state of insensibility; a coma.

tranquil (*adj.*) peaceful; untroubled. TRANQUILLY (*adv.*).

tranquillity (*n.*) calmness; peacefulness.

transact (*v.*) 1. to do; to perform. 2. to carry on business.

transaction (*n.*) 1. a deed. 2. business action.

transcend (*v.*) 1. to rise above; to surpass. 2. to be beyond belief or understanding.

transcendent (*adj.*) supreme; marvellous.

transcribe (*v.*) to copy out in writing. TRANSCRIBER; TRANSCRIPT (*nn.*).

transcription (*n.*) the writing of a copy; the copying.

transfer (*v.*) 1. to remove elsewhere. 2. to give a possession to another. TRANSFERRED (*v.*). TRANSFER (*n.*) 1. a removal. 2. a change of ownership. 3. small picture which can be moved from one sheet of paper to another.

transfigure (*v.*) to change the form or appearance of a person or thing; to make more beautiful and glorious. TRANSFIGURATION (*n.*).

transfix (v.) 1. to pierce through. 2. to look at steadily; to stare at.

transform (v.) to make different; to change completely.

transformation (n.) a complete change.

transformer (n.) apparatus for changing one kind of electric current into another.

transfuse (v.) to transfer blood from one person to another.

transfusion (n.) a transfer of blood.

transgress (v.) to break the law; to sin. TRANSGRESSION (n.). TRANSGRESSOR (n.) 1. a lawbreaker. 2. sinner.

transient (adj.) short-lived; quickly passing.

transistor (n.) an electronic device replacing valves in radios.

transit (n.) a passing across or over.

transition (n.) a change from one condition to another.

translate (v.) to turn from one language into another.

translation (n.) the changing of one language into another; an interpretation. TRANSLATOR (n.).

translucent (adj.) letting light pass through, but not vision.

transmission (n.) the act of sending messages, etc.

transmit (v.) to send a message; to communicate.

transmitter (n.) wireless set which sends out messages or broadcasts.

transparency (n.) 1. clearness; uncloudedness. 2. colour photograph on film viewed when lit from behind.

transparent (adj.) 1. easy to see through; clear. 2. frank; obvious.

transpire (v.) to become known; to leak out.

transplant (v.) to plant in another place; to settle in a new country.

transport (v.) 1. to convey people or goods elsewhere. 2. to delight; to enrapture. TRANSPORT (n.) 1. a conveyance. 2. a troopship. 3. delight; rapture.

transportation (n.) 1. carriage; conveyance. 2. banishment from the country.

transpose (v.) 1. to put a thing in the place of another; to substitute. 2. to change music into another key.

trap (n.) 1. contrivance for catching and holding wild animals. 2. an ambush;

a pitfall. 3. a two-wheeled carriage. TRAP (v.) to catch in a trap.

trapeze (n.) a short wooden bar suspended by ropes at each end, at a great height above ground, on which acrobatic feats are performed.

trapper (n.) one who traps wild animals.

trappings (n. pl.) ornaments; adornments.

trash (n.) anything worthless. TRASHY (adj.).

travail (n.) hard work; toil.

travel (v.) to journey; to voyage. TRAVEL (n.) a journey; tour.

travelled (adj.) informed; experienced.

traveller (n.) one who travels.

travelling (n.) the moving; journeying.

traverse (v.) to go across, from side to side.

traversing (adj.) crossing.

travesty (n.) a silly imitation; a burlesque.

trawl (n.) large fishing-net which is dragged along the sea-bed. TRAWL (v.) to catch fish with a trailing net.

trawler (n.) a ship that trawls.

tray (n.) plate with raised edges for carrying things.

treacherous (adj.) disloyal; traitorous. TREACHEROUSLY (adv.).

treachery (n.) disloyalty; betrayal.

treacle (n.) a thick, sweet syrup obtained from sugar.

tread (v.) to walk heavily; to trample. TREAD (n.) 1. a single, heavy step. 2. flat part of a step or stair.

treadle (n.) part of a machine moved by the foot.

treason (n.) an attempt to injure one's country or sovereign.

treasonable (adj.) taking part in treason.

treasure (n.) a store of valuables; great riches. TREASURE (v.) to prize; to idolize.

treasurer (n.) one who has charge of money and accounts.

treasury (n.) 1. storage place for valuables. 2. government department which conducts the nation's money affairs.

treat (v.) 1. to handle; to deal with. 2. to entertain. TREAT (n.) something which gives pleasure; a party.

treatise (n.) essay or article giving special information.

treatment (*n.*) method used to gain a purpose or cure.

treaty (*n.*) an agreement between nations; a compact.

treble (*n.*) the highest part in music. TREBLE (*v.*) to multiply by three. TREBLE (*adj.*) threefold; thrice.

tree (*n.*) any tall, long-lived plant having a single woody stem from which leaf-bearing branches spread. TREE (*v.*) to drive into, or compel to climb, a tree.

trellis (*n.*) light frame criss-crossed with laths or wires.

tremble (*v.*) to shake; to shiver. TREMBLE (*n.*) a shudder.

trembling (*n.*) a shivering fit.

tremendous (*adj.*) 1. immense; huge. 2. dreadful; alarming.

tremor (*n.*) a shudder; vibration.

tremulous (*adj.*) 1. trembling. 2. timid. TREMULOUSLY (*adv.*).

trench (*n.*) long, narrow channel cut in the earth; a ditch.

trenchant (*adj.*) severe; unsparing. TRENCHANTLY (*adv.*).

trencher (*n.*) wooden plate on which food was served.

trend (*v.*) to lean towards a certain direction; to incline. TREND (*n.*) an inclination towards; a tendency.

trepidation (*n.*) trembling caused by fear.

trespass (*v.*) 1. to go on another's property without permission; to invade. 2. to disturb another's privacy; to intrude. 3. to sin. TRESPASS (*n.*) 1. an invasion. 2. an intrusion. 3. a sin.

trespasser (*n.*) 1. an intruder. 2. a sinner.

tress (*n.*) a curl of hair; ringlet.

trestle (*n.*) a movable frame supporting a table-top.

trial (*n.*) 1. a test; an experiment. 2. a hardship; distress. 3. an action in a law-court. 4. a try; an attempt.

triangle (*n.*) a three-sided figure. TRIANGULAR (*adj.*).

tribal (*adj.*) belonging to a tribe.

tribe (*n.*) family or race of people under a chief.

tribulation (*n.*) suffering; distress.

tribunal (*n.*) a court of justice.

tributary (*n.*) stream that flows into a larger one; a feeder. TRIBUTARY (*adj.*) inferior; submissive.

tribute (*n.*) 1. a tax paid by one country to another. 2. praise given in recognition of worth or service.

trice (*n.*) a short time; an instant.

trick (*n.*) 1. a piece of conjuring; puzzle. 2. a dishonest action; swindle. 3. the cards played in one round. TRICK (*v.*) 1. to deceive with puzzles. 2. to cheat; to swindle.

trickery (*n.*) cheating; swindling.

trickish (*adj.*) fraudulent; knavish.

trickle (*v.*) to flow in a small stream; to dribble. TRICKLE (*n.*) a rill; dribble.

trickling (*adj.*) dripping; dribbling.

trickster (*n.*) a cheat; knave.

tricky (*adj.*) artful; cunning. TRICKILY (*adv.*).

tricycle (*n.*) a three-wheeled cycle.

trident (*n.*) a three-pronged spear.

tried (*adj.*) tested; proved.

triennial (*adj.*) happening once every three years. TRIENNIALLY (*adv.*).

trifle (*n.*) 1. an unimportant thing or matter. 2. dish of cake soaked in cream, etc. TRIFLE (*v.*) to treat a matter lightly.

trifling (*adj.*) unimportant; valueless. TRIFLINGLY (*adv.*).

trigger (*n.*) a catch which, when pulled, fires a gun.

trilby (*n.*) man's soft, felt hat.

trill (*n.*) a tremor in singing or whistling. TRILL (*v.*) to make the voice tremble.

trim (*adj.*) tidy; neat. TRIM (*v.*) 1. to make neat. 2. to adorn; to decorate. TRIM (*n.*) the condition a thing is in.

trimly (*adv.*) in good order; neatly.

trimming (*n.*) ornaments added to a hat, etc.

trimness (*n.*) neatness; orderliness.

trinket (*n.*) small or cheap piece of jewellery.

trio (*n.*) group of three persons or musicians.

trip (*v.*) 1. to stumble. 2. to run lightly on the toes. TRIP (*n.*) 1. a stumble. 2. an excursion; outing.

tripe (*n.*) the large stomach of cattle prepared for food.

triple (*adj.*) 1. consisting of three parts. 2. threefold. TRIPLE (*v.*) to multiply by three.

triplet (*n.*) one of three children born together.

triplex (*adj.*) threefold.

tripod (*n.*) three-legged table or stand.

tripper (*n.*) a tourist; an excursionist.

trite (*adj.*) worn out; stale. TRITELY (*adv.*).

triumph (*n.*) a great success; victory.

triumphal (*adj.*) honouring a success. TRIUMPHALLY (*adv.*).

triumphant (*adj.*) successful; victorious. TRIUMPHANTLY (*adv.*).

trivial (*adj.*) small; paltry.

triviality (*n.*) a small matter; trifle.

trojan (*n.*) a hero; champion

trolley (*n.*) 1. a hand-cart; truck. 2. arm connecting an electric car with a wire overhead.

trombone (*n.*) trumpet having a sliding tube.

troop (*n.*) 1. a party; band. 2. a number of soldiers. TROOP (*v.*) to gather; to flock.

trophy (*n.*) something kept in memory of a victory.

tropic (*n.*) one of the two circles on either side of the equator between which lie the earth's hottest regions or zones.

tropical (*adj.*) 1. within the tropics. 2. extremely hot. TROPICALLY (*adv.*).

trot (*v.*) to run slowly. TROT (*n.*) a slow run.

troth (*n.*) 1. truth; fidelity. 2. the promise to marry given to each other by a man and a woman; betrothal.

trouble (*n.*) 1. worry; vexation. 2. disaster; distress. TROUBLE (*v.*) 1. to disturb; to inconvenience. 2. to distress; to molest.

troubled (*adj.*) worried; bothered.

troublesome (*adj.*) causing trouble.

trough (*n.*) 1. long, shallow vessel from which animals feed. 2. a shallow water-channel.

trounce (*v.*) to beat; to punish.

trouncing (*n.*) a beating.

troupe (*n.*) company of performers.

trousers (*n. pl.*) two-legged outer garment reaching from waist to ankles.

trousseau (*n.*) a bride's outfit. (*pl.* TROUSSEAUX).

trout (*n.*) a freshwater fish.

trowel (*n.*) steel tool for spreading mortar or lifting plants.

troy (*n.*) measure by which gold, silver and jewels are weighed.

truant (*n.*) one absent from duty without permission; a shirker.

truce (*n.*) agreement to stop fighting for a time; a lull.

truck (*n.*) a low waggon for carrying heavy goods.

trudge (*v.*) to walk wearily; to plod. TRUDGE (*n.*) a walk over heavy ground; a wearisome tramp.

true (*adj.*) 1. real; genuine; in accordance with fact. 2. faithful; loyal. 3. trustworthy; reliable.

truly (*adv.*) justly; sincerely.

trump (*n.*) a card of the suit which, when a hand is played, takes a card of any other suit. TRUMP (*v.*) to take with a trump-card.

trumpery (*n.*) rubbish. TRUMPERY (*adj.*) worthless.

trumpet (*n.*) 1. a metal wind instrument. 2. an elephant's cry. TRUMPET (*v.*) 1. to blow a trumpet. 2. to proclaim. 3. to spread good news.

truncheon (*n.*) a short cudgel or club.

trundle (*v.*) to roll, bowl or push along.

trunk (*n.*) 1. stem of a tree. 2. body of an animal apart from its limbs. 3. large chest or packing-case. 4. elephant's long nose. 5. telephone line between two exchanges.

truss (*n.*) 1. bundle of hay or straw. 2. a bandage or support. TRUSS (*v.*) to tie up in a bundle.

trust (*v.*) 1. to believe in; to rely upon. 2. to give credit to. 3. to confide in. TRUST (*n.*) 1. belief; faith. 2. confidence; reliance. 3. property given into the care of trustworthy persons for a special purpose.

trustee (*n.*) one to whom property is entrusted.

trustful (*adj.*) ready to trust. TRUSTFULLY (*adv.*).

trustworthy (*adj.*) upright; reliable.

trusty (*adj.*) dependable; loyal.

truth (*n.*) whatever is true or factual.

truthful (*adj.*) truly spoken; reliable. TRUTHFULLY (*adv.*).

truthless (*adj.*) untrue; false.

try (*v.*) 1. to attempt. 2. to test; to examine.

trying (*adj.*) 1. difficult; severe. 2. annoying; provoking.

tryst (*n.*) an appointment; a meeting.

tub (*n.*) a shallow, open-topped cask.

tube (*n.*) a long pipe for conveying water, gas, etc. THE TUBE. The London Underground Railway.

tuberculosis (*n.*) a lung disease.

tuck (*v.*) to fold. TUCK (*n.*) a fold in a garment.

Tuesday (*n.*) third day in the week. See appendix.

tuft (*n.*) bunch of hair or feathers.

tug (*v.*) 1. to pull along; to tow. 2. to give a sharp pull. TUG (*n.*) 1. boat which tows another. 2. a sharp pull.

tuition (*n.*) teaching; instruction.

tulip (*n.*) bell-shaped flower grown from a bulb.

tulle (*n.*) a fine silk fabric.

tumble (*v.*) to fall; to topple. TUMBLE (*n.*) a fall; sprawl.

tumble-down (*adj.*) decayed; ruinous.

tumbler (*n.*) 1. an acrobat. 2. a drinking-glass. 3. a breed of pigeon.

tumult (*n.*) great disorder; uproar.

tumultuous (*adj.*) noisy; violent. TUMUL-TUOUSLY (*adv.*).

tumulus (*n.*) a Stone Age mound-tomb.

tunable (*adj.*) musical; melodious.

tune (*n.*) musical melody or air. TUNE (*v.*) to prepare an instrument for playing.

tuneful (*adj.*) pleasing to the ear; melodious. TUNEFULLY (*adv.*).

tunic (*n.*) a short coat.

tunnel (*n.*) an underground passage. TUNNEL (*v.*) to dig or bore a passage underground; to burrow.

tunnelling (*n.*) work of tunnel-making.

tunny (*n.*) great ocean-fish of mackerel family. (*pl.* TUNNIES).

turban (*n.*) headdress worn by men in the East, consisting of a long strip of silk or cotton wound round and round the head.

turbid (*adj.*) muddy; clouded.

turbine (*n.*) an engine driven by jets of steam or water.

turbot (*n.*) a large, flat sea-fish.

turbulence (*n.*) great disorder; riot. TUR-BULENT (*adj.*).

tureen (*n.*) large, deep vessel for holding soup.

turf (*n.*) earth on which grass is rooted.

turgid (*adj.*) 1. swollen; bloated. 2. pompous; bombastic. TURGIDLY (*adv.*).

turkey (*n.*) large, domestic fowl, liked as food.

turmoil (*n.*) tumult; uproar.

turn (*v.*) 1. to face in another direction. 2. to revolve. 3. to alter; to convert. TURN (*n.*) 1. a change of direction. 2. a revolution; rotation. 3. a change of opinion.

turncoat (*n.*) one who leaves his friends to join their opponents; a renegade.

turner (*n.*) one who shapes articles on a lathe.

turning (*n.*) a bend in a road, lane, etc.

turnip (*n.*) large, ball-shaped root-vegetable.

turnover (*n.*) total money or trade taken in a business.

turnpike (*n.*) a private road for the use of which travellers pay a toll.

turnstile (*n.*) a revolving barrier allowing one person to pass at a time.

turpentine (*n.*) spirit made from pine-tree resin.

turpitude (*n.*) baseness; wickedness.

turquoise (*n.*) a blue gem.

turret (*n.*) small tower often built on a wall.

turtle (*n.*) a sea-tortoise.

tusk (*n.*) a long, curving tooth or fang.

tussle (*n.*) a struggle; wrestle.

tussock (*n.*) clump of turf or grass.

tutor (*n.*) a teacher; instructor.

tutorial (*adj.*) concerned with teachers and teaching. TUTORIALLY (*adv.*).

twaddle (*n.*) silly talk; nonsense. TWADDLE (*v.*) to talk nonsense.

twain (*adj.*) two. TWAIN (*n.*) a pair.

twang (*n.*) sound of a plucked string. TWANG (*v.*) to pluck a string.

tweak (*v.*) to pinch with a sudden twist. TWEAK (*n.*) a sudden jerk and twist.

tweed (*n.*) a heavy woollen cloth.

tweezers (*n. pl.*) small pincers for pulling out splinters, etc.

twelve (*adj.*) one more than eleven; a dozen. TWELVE (*n.*) 1. the sum of eleven and one. 2. the symbol 12 or XII.

twenty (*adj.*) twice ten. TWENTY (*n.*) 1. the sum of nineteen and one. 2. the symbol 20 or XX. (*pl.* TWENTIES).

twice (*adv.*) two times; once and again.

twig (*n.*) a small shoot or branch.

twilight (*n.*) faint daylight before sunrise and after sunset.

twill (*n.*) cloth so woven that diagonal lines or ribs appear on its surface. TWILL (*v.*) to weave such cloth.

twin (*n.*) one of two children born together.

twine (*v.*) to twist together; to wind round one another. TWINE (*n.*) strong string made of threads twisted together.

twinge (*n.*) a sharp, shooting pain.

twinkle (*v.*) to sparkle. TWINKLE (*n.*) a gleam from the eye.

twirl (*v.*) to whirl or spin round. TWIRL (*n.*) a spinning twist with the fingers

twist (*v.*) to wind or turn out of the true shape. TWIST (*n.*) a turning out of shape.

twitch (*v.*) to jerk; to pluck. TWITCH (*n.*) a sudden jerk.

twitching (*n.*) the jerking of a muscle.

twitter (*n.*) chirping notes of a bird. TWITTER (*v.*) to chirp.

tying (*n.*) the fastening with a knot. See TIE.

type (*n.*) 1. letters and symbols from which books are printed. 2. a specimen; sample. 3. a kind of species. TYPE (*v.*) to use a typewriter.

typewriter (*n.*) a hand-machine for printing letters and figures.

typhoid (*n.*) an infectious fever.

typhoon (*n.*) a violent hurricane; a whirlwind.

typhus (*n.*) a dangerous fever.

typical (*adj.*) serving as an example or model of a type or species.

typist (*n.*) one who uses a typewriter.

typography (*n.*) the art of printing.

tyrannical (*adj.*) cruel; oppressive. TYRANNICALLY (*adv.*).

tyrannize (*v.*) to rule or direct with extreme severity.

tyrannous (*adj.*) severe; rigorous. TYRANNOUSLY (*adv.*).

tyranny (*n.*) cruelty; oppression.

tyrant (*n.*) an overbearing master.

tyre (*n.*) metal band or rubber tube round the rim of a wheel.

tyro (*n.*) a beginner; novice.

U

ubiquitous (*adj.*) existing everywhere. UBIQUITOUSLY (*adv.*).

ubiquity (*n.*) being everywhere at once.

udder (*n.*) bag from which a cow gives milk.

ugliness (*n.*) a lack of beauty; unpleasantness.

ugly (*adj.*) 1. unpleasant to see. 2. ill-natured; dangerous.

ulcer (*n.*) an open sore; a boil.

ulster (*n.*) long, loose overcoat.

ultimate (*adj.*) furthest away; last. ULTIMATELY (*adv.*).

ultimatum (*n.*) the last offer or demand.

ultimo (*n.*) last month.

umber (*n.*) a dark-brown colour.

umbrage (*n.*) displeasure; resentment.

umbrella (*n.*) a folding, cloth-covered frame to hold over the head.

umpire (*n.*) one chosen to act as judge in games and disputes; a referee. UMPIRE (*v.*) to judge; to referee.

unabashed (*adj.*) undaunted; bold,

unable (*adj.*) not able; powerless.

unabridged (*adj.*) not shortened; complete.

unacceptable (*adj.*) unwelcome; disagreeable.

unaccepted (*adj.*) refused; rejected.

unaccompanied (*adj.*) alone; solitary.

unaccountable (*adj.*) not responsible; cannot be explained.

unaccustomed (*adj.*) not used to; strange.

unaided (*adj.*) single-handed; without help.

unaltered (*adj.*) unchanged; steady.

unamiable (*adj.*) unfriendly. UNAMIABLY (*adv.*).

unanimity (*n.*) agreement; unity.

unanimous (*adj.*) with the agreement of all. UNANIMOUSLY (*adv.*).

unanswerable (*adj.*) conclusive; incontestable.

unarmed (*adj.*) defenceless.

unassuming (*adj.*) modest; humble. UNASSUMINGLY (*adv.*).

unattached (*adj.*) free; at liberty.

---

*NOTE.—Some words beginning with UN are omitted. UN is a prefix and is used in front of a word when it usually means *not* or *the opposite of.* For instance, *unashamed* means *not ashamed.* You would therefore look up the word *ashamed.*

Q

unattainable (*adj.*) cannot be gained; inaccessible.

unavailing (*adj.*) useless; ineffectual. UNAVAILINGLY (*adv.*).

unavoidable (*adj.*) certain; inevitable. UNAVOIDABLY (*adv.*).

unaware (*adj.*) without knowledge; ignorant.

unawares (*adv.*) suddenly; unexpectedly.

unbearable (*adj.*) cannot be borne. UNBEARABLY (*adv.*).

unbecoming (*adj.*) unsuitable; unseemly. UNBECOMINGLY (*adv.*).

unbelief (*n.*) doubt; disbelief.

unbelievable (*adj.*) cannot be believed; incredible.

unbending (*adj.*) stubborn; unyielding.

unblemished (*adj.*) pure; faultless.

unblushing (*adj.*) impudent; shameless. UNBLUSHINGLY (*adv.*).

unbounded (*adj.*) vast; immense.

unbroken (*adj.*) whole; entire.

unburden (*v.*) 1. to release from a burden. 2. to ease a troubled mind.

uncanny (*adj.*) mysterious; weird. UNCANNILY (*adv.*).

unceasing (*adj.*) endless; continual. UNCEASINGLY (*adv.*).

uncertain (*adj.*) doubtful; insecure. UNCERTAINLY (*adv.*).

uncertainty (*n.*) doubtfulness; unsettlement.

unchanging (*adj.*) steadfast; fixed.

uncivil (*adj.*) impolite; discourteous.

uncivilized (*adj.*) ill-mannered; boorish.

uncle (*n.*) 1. one's father's or mother's brother. 2. one's aunt's husband.

unclean (*adj.*) dirty; sullied. UNCLEANLY (*adv.*).

uncleanliness (*n.*) dirtiness; filthiness.

uncomfortable (*adj.*) uneasy; disagreeable. UNCOMFORTABLY (*adv.*).

uncommon (*adj.*) rare; remarkable. UNCOMMONLY (*adv.*).

uncompromising (*adj.*) unyielding; firm. UNCOMPROMISINGLY (*adv.*).

unconcern (*n.*) lack of anxiety; indifference.

unconcerned (*adj.*) indifferent; unmoved. UNCONCERNEDLY (*adv.*).

unconditional (*adj.*) without conditions. UNCONDITIONALLY (*adv.*).

uncongenial (*adj.*) unpleasant; disagreeable.

unconscious (*adj.*) 1. insensible; senseless. 2. unaware. UNCONSCIOUSLY (*adv.*).

unconstitutional (*adj.*) unlawful; illegal. UNCONSTITUTIONALLY (*adv.*).

uncontrollable (*adj.*) unmanageable; unruly. UNCONTROLLABLY (*adv.*).

unconvincing (*adj.*) uncertain; indecisive. UNCONVINCINGLY (*adv.*).

uncouth (*adj.*) clumsy; awkward.

uncouthness (*n.*) clumsiness; boorishness.

uncover (*v.*) to disclose; to reveal.

undaunted (*adj.*) brave; fearless. UNDAUNTEDLY (*adv.*).

undecayed (*adj.*) unweakened; strong.

undeceive (*v.*) to free from error; to correct.

undecided (*adj.*) 1. hesitating; doubtful. 2. irresolute; wavering.

undeniable (*adj.*) certain; evident. UNDENIABLY (*adv.*).

under (*prep.*) beneath; below. UNDER (*adv.*) in a lower condition. UNDER (*adj.*) lower in rank.

underbid (*v.*) to offer less than another.

undercarriage (*n.*) landing gear of an aircraft.

undercharge (*v.*) to charge less than the worth.

undercurrent (*n.*) current below the surface of the water.

undercut (*v.*) 1. to strike upwards from under. 2. to charge less than the proper price. UNDERCUT (*n.*) 1. piece of meat called tenderloin. 2. pugilist's blow struck upwards.

underdo (*v.*) to cook insufficiently.

underdone (*adj.*) not cooked enough.

underestimate (*v.*) to undervalue; to belittle.

undergo (*v.*) to bear; to suffer.

undergraduate (*n.*) university student who has not taken his first degree.

underground (*adj.*) below the ground; subterranean.

undergrown (*adj.*) not fully grown; undersized.

undergrowth (*n.*) shrubs growing among larger trees.

underhand (*adj.*) sly; secret. UNDERHAND (*adv.*) by deceit; by fraud.

underhanded (*adj.*) secret; sly.

underlie (*v.*) to form the foundation; to support.

underline (v.) to draw a line under; to underscore.

underlying (adj.) lying under; basic.

undermine (v.) 1. to dig beneath and cause to fall. 2. to weaken or impair health.

underneath (adv. & prep.) beneath; below.

underrate (v.) to rate too low; to undervalue.

understand (v.) to know the meaning of; to comprehend.

understandable (adj.) excusable; forgivable.

understanding (adj.) sensible; intelligent. UNDERSTANDING (n.) 1. intelligence. 2. judgment.

understate (v.) to describe insufficiently.

understatement (n.) an insufficient description.

understudy (n.) an actor ready to play another's part in emergency.

undertake (v.) 1. to try; to attempt. 2. to promise; to guarantee.

undertaker (n.) one who makes funeral arrangements.

undertaking (n.) 1. a venture; an enterprise. 2. a business; work.

undertone (n.) a low or subdued utterance or colour.

undervalue (v.) 1. to value below true worth. 2. to esteem lightly; to despise.

underwear (n.) undergarments.

underwrite (v.) to sign the conditions of insurance.

underwriter (n.) an insurer of ships and cargoes.

underwriting (n.) the business of insuring ships; marine insurance.

undeserved (adj.) not deserved; unmerited. UNDESERVEDLY (adv.).

undesirable (adj.) not wanted; unwelcome. UNDESIRABLY (adv.).

undesirous (adj.) unwilling; reluctant.

undischarged (adj.) 1. not freed from duty or responsibility. 2. not unloaded or emptied. 3. not fired or exploded.

undisciplined (adj.) unruly; untrained.

undiscovered (adj.) not found out; hidden.

undisguised (adj.) open; sincere.

undisputed (adj.) not denied; unquestioned. UNDISPUTABLY (adv.).

undistinguishable (adj.) 1. not clearly seen. 2. cannot be picked out.

undisturbed (adj.) 1. not troubled. 2. cool; calm.

undivided (adj.) whole; complete.

undo (v.) 1. to untie; to unfasten. 2. to reverse; to ruin.

undoing (n.) 1. a reversal. 2. ruin; destruction.

undoubted (adj.) certain; undeniable. UNDOUBTEDLY (adv.).

undulating (adj.) 1. wave-like; wavy. 2. hilly.

undulation (n.) a wave motion; a vibration.

unduly (adv.) excessively; improperly.

undutiful (adj.) disobedient; rebellious. UNDUTIFULLY (adv.).

undying (adj.) permanent; immortal.

unearned (adj.) not earned; not gained by service or work.

unearth (v.) 1. to discover; to disclose. 2. to dig up.

unearthly (adj.) weird; uncanny.

uneasiness (n.) 1. discomfort. 2. disquiet.

uneasy (adj.) restless; anxious. UNEASILY (adv.).

uneducated (adj.) untaught; ignorant.

unemployed (adj.) out of work; idle.

unequalled (adj.) matchless; peerless.

unerring (adj.) straight; true. UNERRINGLY (adv.).

unessential (adj.) not necessary.

uneven (adj.) 1. not level. 2. not of equal length. 3. not of uniform quality throughout.

uneventful (adj.) unexciting; dull. UNEVENTFULLY (adv.).

unexpected (adj.) not foreseen; surprising. UNEXPECTEDLY (adv.).

unfair (adj.) unjust; wrong. UNFAIRLY (adv.).

unfaithful (adj.) deceitful; disloyal.

unfaltering (adj.) steady; determined. UNFALTERINGLY (adv.).

unfamiliar (adj.) strange; uncommon.

unfamiliarity (n.) oddness; unusualness.

unfashionable (adj.) out-of-date; outmoded. UNFASHIONABLY (adv.).

unfathomable (adj.) 1. deep; bottomless. 2. mysterious.

unfavourable (adj.) discouraging; adverse. UNFAVOURABLY (adv.).

unfeeling (adj.) unsympathetic; unkind.

unfeigned (*adj.*) true; sincere.

unfit (*adj.*) 1. unsuitable; unqualified. 2. unwell; sick.

unflinching (*adj.*) bold; brave. UNFLINCH-INGLY (*adv.*).

unfold (*v.*) 1. to open; to display. 2. to disclose; to reveal.

unforgettable (*adj.*) memorable; exceptional.

unforgiving (*adj.*) hard; merciless.

unfortunate (*adj.*) 1. unlucky; ill-fated. 2. unsuccessful. UNFORTUNATELY (*adv.*).

unfounded (*adj.*) 1. groundless; baseless. 2. untrue.

unfriendly (*adj.*) antagonistic; hostile.

unfriendliness (*n.*) unkindness; disfavour.

ungainly (*adj.*) clumsy; awkward. UNGAINLINESS (*n.*).

ungenerous (*adj.*) mean; selfish. UNGENEROUSLY (*adv.*).

ungracious (*adj.*) unfriendly; discourteous. UNGRACIOUSLY (*adv.*).

ungrateful (*adj.*) thankless; unthankful. UNGRATEFULLY (*adv.*).

unguarded (*adj.*) 1. unprotected. 2. careless; heedless. UNGUARDEDLY (*adv.*).

unhandy (*adj.*) clumsy; unskilled. UNHANDILY (*adv.*).

unhappy (*adj.*) 1. sad; miserable. 2. unfortunate; disastrous. UNHAPPILY (*adv.*).

unhealthy (*adj.*) 1. unwholesome. 2. sickly; ill. UNHEALTHILY (*adv.*).

unheeded (*adj.*) neglected; ignored.

unheeding (*adj.*) careless; inattentive. UNHEEDINGLY (*adv.*).

unhesitating (*adj.*) prompt; ready. UNHESITATINGLY (*adv.*).

unicorn (*n.*) fabled animal with a single straight horn.

uniform (*adj.*) always the same; unchanging. UNIFORM (*n.*) special dress of a soldier, policeman, etc.

unify (*v.*) to make as or into one; to consider as one.

unimaginable (*adj.*) cannot be imagined.

unimaginative (*adj.*) having no imagination; dull.

unimportance (*n.*) littleness; triviality.

unimportant (*adj.*) small; slight.

uninhabitable (*adj.*) unfit to live in.

uninhabited (*adj.*) empty; deserted.

unintelligent (*adj.*) simple; foolish. UNINTELLIGENTLY (*adv.*).

unintelligible (*adj.*) cannot be understood. UNINTELLIGIBLY (*adv.*).

unintentional (*adj.*) not intended; accidental. UNINTENTIONALLY (*adv.*).

uninteresting (*adj.*) boring; tedious.

uninviting (*adj.*) unpleasant; unattractive.

union (*n.*) 1. a joining as one; a combining. 2. an association of workers for trade purposes. 3. a joining of countries under one government or sovereign.

unique (*adj.*) having no like or equal. UNIQUELY (*adv.*).

unison (*n.*) 1. harmony. 2. agreement; accord.

unit (*n.*) 1. a single thing or person; one. 2. a standard of measurement.

unite (*v.*) 1. to join together. 2. to combine; to amalgamate.

united (*adj.*) joined; combined. UNITEDLY (*adv.*).

unity (*n.*) 1. the digit, one. 2. agreement; concord.

universal (*adj.*) belonging to all; known everywhere. UNIVERSALLY (*adv.*).

universe (*n.*) the whole of Creation.

university (*n.*) institution where instruction is given in all branches of learning. (*pl.* UNIVERSITIES).

unjust (*adj.*) not just; not fair. UNJUSTLY (*adv.*).

unkempt (*adj.*) uncombed; untidy.

unkind (*adj.*) harsh; cruel. UNKINDLY (*adv.*).

unkindness (*n.*) an unfriendly action.

unknown (*adj.*) 1. undiscovered; unexplored. 2. that can never be known.

unlawful (*adj.*) against the law; illegal. UNLAWFULLY (*adv.*).

unlearned (*adj.*) ignorant; illiterate.

unless (*conj.*) except; if not.

unlike (*adj.*) different; dissimilar.

unlikelihood (*n.*) the improbability.

unlikely (*adj.*) improbable.

unlimited (*adj.*) boundless; infinite.

unlooked for (*adj.*) unexpected; unforeseen.

unloosen (*v.*) to untie; to set free.

unlucky (*adj.*) unfortunate; unsuccessful. UNLUCKILY (*adv.*).

unmanageable (*adj.*) impossible to control or direct.

unmanly (*adj.*) weak; timid.

unmannerly (*adj.*) uncivil; rude.

unmentionable (*adj.*) not to be spoken of. UNMENTIONABLY (*adv.*).

unmerciful (*adj.*) cruel; inhuman. UN-MERCIFULLY (*adv.*).

unmerited (*adj.*) undeserved.

unmethodical (*adj.*) slipshod; haphazard. UNMETHODICALLY (*adv.*).

unmindful (*adj.*) forgetful; heedless. UN-MINDFULLY (*adv.*).

unmindfulness (*n.*) carelessness; negligence.

unmistakable (*adj.*) plain; undoubted. UNMISTAKABLY (*adv.*).

unmoved (*adj.*) unshaken; steadfast.

unnatural (*adj.*) not normal.

unnecessary (*adj.*) needless; useless. UN-NECESSARILY (*adv.*).

unnerve (*v.*) to weaken; to enfeeble.

unnoticed (*adj.*) overlooked; ignored.

unobservant (*adj.*) inattentive; unnoticing.

unobtrusive (*adj.*) modest; reserved. UNOBTRUSIVELY (*adv.*).

unparalleled (*adj.*) unequalled; matchless.

unpardonable (*adj.*) inexcusable; unforgivable. UNPARDONABLY (*adv.*).

unpatriotic (*adj.*) undutiful; disloyal. UNPATRIOTICALLY (*adv.*).

unperceived (*adj.*) unseen; unnoticed.

unperturbed (*adj.*) calm; unexcited.

unpleasant (*adj.*) displeasing; disagreeable. UNPLEASANTLY (*adv.*).

unpleasantness (*n.*) annoyance; offensiveness.

unpopular (*adj.*) disliked; detested.

unpopularity (*n.*) dislike; disfavour.

unprejudiced (*adj.*) fair; just.

unpretentious (*adj.*) modest; reserved. UNPRETENTIOUSLY (*adv.*).

unprincipled (*adj.*) dishonest; wicked.

unproductive (*adj.*) fruitless; unprofitable. UNPRODUCTIVELY (*adv.*).

unprofitable (*adj.*) serving no useful purpose. UNPROFITABLY (*adv.*).

unpromising (*adj.*) unfavourable; unsatisfactory.

unpunctual (*adj.*) careless about time. UNPUNCTUALITY (*n.*).

unquestionable (*adj.*) certain; evident. UNQUESTIONABLY (*adv.*).

unravel (*v.*) to disentangle; to solve.

unreasonable (*adj.*) absurd; foolish. UN-REASONABLY (*adv.*).

unreliability (*n.*) untrustworthiness; fickleness.

unreliable (*adj.*) untrustworthy; uncertain. UNRELIABLY (*adv.*).

unrest (*n.*) 1. disquiet; uneasiness. 2. rebellion.

unrivalled (*adj.*) unequalled; matchless.

unruffled (*adj.*) calm; quiet.

unruly (*adj.*) misbehaved; disobedient.

unsatisfactory (*adj.*) displeasing; poor. UNSATISFACTORILY (*adv.*).

unsatisfied (*adj.*) 1. discontented. 2. not paid.

unsavoury (*adj.*) disagreeable; tasteless.

unscathed (*adj.*) untouched; unhurt.

unscrupulous (*adj.*) without regard for honesty and right. UNSCRUPULOUSLY (*adv.*).

unseeing (*adj.*) 1. blind. 2. not understanding. UNSEEINGLY (*adv.*).

unseen (*adj.*) 1. not seen; unnoticed. 2. invisible.

unselfish (*adj.*) generous; liberal.

unsettle (*v.*) to upset; to disturb.

unshaken (*adj.*) firm; resolute. UN-SHAKENLY (*adv.*).

unsightliness (*n.*) ugliness.

unsightly (*adj.*) displeasing to see; ugly.

unskilful (*adj.*) clumsy; awkward. UN-SKILFULLY (*adv.*).

unskilfulness (*n.*) clumsiness; inefficiency.

unskilled (*adj.*) untrained; inexpert.

unsociable (*adj.*) unfriendly; reserved. UNSOCIABLY (*adv.*).

unsophisticated (*adj.*) simple; innocent.

unsparing (*adj.*) 1. generous; bountiful. 2. severe; merciless. UNSPARINGLY (*adv.*).

unstable (*adj.*) unsteady; insecure.

unsuccessful (*adj.*) unprosperous; unfortunate. UNSUCCESSFULLY (*adv.*).

unsuspecting (*adj.*) having no suspicion; trusting.

unsympathetic (*adj.*) unkind; heartless. UNSYMPATHETICALLY (*adv.*).

unsystematic (*adj.*) without method. UN-SYSTEMATICALLY (*adv.*).

untidiness (*n.*) a lack of neatness; slovenliness.

untidy (*adj.*) careless; slovenly. UNTIDILY (*adv.*).

until (*prep. & conj.*) till; to the time when.

untiring (*adj.*) ceaseless; tireless. UN-
TIRINGLY (*adv.*).

unto (*prep.*) to.

untold (*adj.*) vast; uncountable.

untrue (*adj.*) 1. false; inaccurate.
2. faithless; disloyal. UNTRULY (*adv.*).

untruth (*n.*) a falsehood; lie.

untruthful (*adj.*) given to telling lies.
UNTRUTHFULLY (*adv.*).

unusual (*adj.*) uncommon; strange. UN-
USUALLY (*adv.*).

unusualness (*n.*) uncommonness; rarity.

unvarying (*adj.*) steady; reliable.

unwarily (*adv.*) carelessly; heedlessly.

unwariness (*n.*) rashness; incautiousness.

unwary (*adj.*) rash; incautious.

unwell (*adj.*) ill; indisposed.

unwholesome (*adj.*) not good for health.
UNWHOLESOMENESS (*n.*).

unwieldy (*adj.*) bulky; awkward.

unwind (*v.*) 1. to wind off; to loosen.
2. to disentangle.

unwise (*adj.*) foolish; rash. UNWISELY
(*adv.*).

unwonted (*adj.*) rare; extraordinary.

unworthiness (*n.*) shame; dishonour.

unworthy (*adj.*) bad; dishonourable.
UNWORTHILY (*adv.*).

unwrap (*v.*) to undo; to open.

unyielding (*adj.*) determined; firm. UN-
YIELDINGLY (*adv.*).

up (*adv.*) 1. to a higher place; on high.
2. out of bed. 3. over; finished.

upbraid (*v.*) to blame; to find fault with.

upbraiding (*n.*) a scolding; rebuke.

uphill (*adj.*) hard; toilsome.

uphold (*v.*) to defend; to support. UP-
HOLDER (*n.*).

upholster (*v.*) to stuff and cover chairs,
etc.

upholstery (*n.*) curtains, carpets, bedding,
etc.; furnishings.

upkeep (*n.*) cost of keeping anything in
good order; maintenance.

upland (*n.*) high ground; hilly country.
UPLAND (*adj.*) high; hilly.

upon (*prep.*) on.

upper (*adj.*) higher in place. UPPER (*n.*)
upper part of a shoe.

uppermost (*adj.*) highest in place or
authority; topmost.

uppishness (*n.*) arrogance; high-handed-
ness.

upright (*adj.*) 1. vertical; erect. 2.

honest; straightforward. UPRIGHT (*n.*)
a vertical post or support. UPRIGHTLY
(*adv.*).

uprightness (*n.*) 1. erectness. 2. honesty.

uprise (*v.*) 1. to rise up; to ascend.
2. to revolt.

uprising (*n.*) 1. rising of the sun.
2. getting out of bed. 3. a revolt.

uproar (*n.*) a noisy disturbance; tumult.

uproarious (*adj.*) noisy; clamorous. UP-
ROARIOUSLY (*adv.*).

uproot (*v.*) 1. to pull up by the roots.
2. to move from an old home and
friends.

upset (*v.*) 1. to overturn. 2. to disarrange; to confuse. 3. to cause
discomfort. UPSET (*n.*) disorder; confusion.

upshot (*n.*) the result; consequence.

upstairs (*adj.*) on an upper floor.

upstart (*n.*) one who rises suddenly to
wealth or authority and behaves arrogantly.

upward (*adj.*) towards something higher;
overhead.

upwards (*adv.*) towards a height; more.

uranium (*n.*) hard, white, radio-active
metal.

Uranus (*n.*) planet next beyond Saturn.
See appendix.

urban (*adj.*) belonging to a town.

urbane (*adj.*) polite; well-mannered.

urbanity (*n.*) courtesy; civility.

urchin (*n.*) 1. a child. 2. a hedgehog.
3. a sea-hedgehog.

urge (*v.*) to push; to press. URGE (*n.*) a
longing; yearning.

urgency (*n.*) the need to act at once.

urgent (*adj.*) needing immediate attention;
pressing. URGENTLY (*adv.*).

urn (*n.*) 1. a large vase. 2. container for
a large supply of brewed tea.

usable (*adj.*) can be used.

usage (*n.*) 1. the method of using. 2. the
custom; habit.

use (*v.*) 1. to do something with; to
employ. 2. to consume; to exhaust.
USE (*n.*) 1. the work done; employment. 2. the benefit; gain.

useful (*adj.*) helpful; profitable. USEFULLY
(*adv.*).

usefulness (*n.*) helpfulness; advantage.

useless (*adj.*) ineffectual; doing no good.
USELESSLY (*adv.*).

uselessness (*n.*) worthlessness; futility.

usher (*n.*) person who takes people to their seats. USHER (*v.*) to bring in; to introduce.

usual (*adj.*) common; normal.

usually (*adv.*) ordinarily; regularly.

usurp (*v.*) to seize and hold another's place or property.

usurpation (*n.*) forcible seizing of another's position.

usurper (*n.*) one who takes forcibly.

utensil (*n.*) household tool or vessel in everyday use.

utilitarian (*n.*) one who considers only a thing's usefulness.

utility (*n.*) 1. usefulness. 2. the profit; benefit.

utilization (*n.*) 1. the work; service. 2. the benefit; advantage.

utilize (*v.*) to make useful or beneficial.

utmost (*adj.*) 1. the farthest; most distant. 2. the greatest; strongest.

Utopia (*n.*) imaginary land where everything is perfect.

Utopian (*adj.*) imaginary; ideal.

utter (*v.*) 1. to speak; to pronounce. 2. to circulate false coins. UTTER (*adj.*) 1. outer; extreme. 2. total; complete.

utterance (*n.*) 1. anything said or spoken. 2. an issue of false coins.

utterly (*adv.*) completely; fully.

uttermost (*adj.*) farthest out. UTTERMOST (*n.*) 1. the farthest; extreme. 2. the greatest; strongest.

V

vacancy (*n.*) 1. emptiness. 2. an unfilled situation.

vacant (*adj.*) 1. empty; unfilled. 2. dreamy; stupid.

vacate (*v.*) to leave; to quit.

vacation (*n.*) holiday-time.

vaccinate (*v.*) to safeguard against small-pox.

vaccination (*n.*) protection against small-pox.

vacillate (*v.*) to hesitate; to waver.

vacillating (*adj.*) uncertain; unsteady.

vacillation (*n.*) hesitation; uncertainty.

vacuum (*n.*) space from which all air has been taken.

vagabond (*n.*) an idle wanderer; a rascal.

vagary (*n.*) a whim; fancy.

vagrancy (*n.*) homelessness.

vagrant (*n.*) wanderer without a settled home; a nomad.

vague (*adj.*) not clear in meaning; uncertain. VAGUELY (*adv.*).

vagueness (*n.*) uncertainty; indistinctness.

vain (*adj.*) 1. useless. 2. proud of oneself; conceited. VAINLY (*adv.*).

vale (*n.*) a small valley; a dale.

valediction (*n.*) a farewell; good-bye.

valentine (*n.*) a love-token sent on St. Valentine's Day (14th February). See appendix.

valet (*n.*) a man's personal attendant.

valiant (*adj.*) brave; fearless. VALIANTLY (*adv.*).

valid (*adj.*) lawful; true. VALIDLY (*adv.*).

validity (*n.*) the lawfulness; genuineness.

valise (*n.*) small travelling-bag or suitcase.

valley (*n.*) low land lying between hills; a vale.

valorous (*adj.*) brave; gallant. VALOR-OUSLY (*adv.*).

valour (*n.*) courage; gallantry.

valuable (*adj.*) 1. prized; precious. 2. costly; expensive.

valuation (*n.*) an estimate of the money-value of anything.

value (*n.*) 1. the money-worth of an article; price. 2. the utility; importance.

valued (*adj.*) much thought of; prized.

valueless (*adj.*) 1. worthless. 2. useless.

valuer (*n.*) person skilled in valuation.

valve (*n.*) device allowing a liquid or gas to flow in one direction only.

vamp (*v.*) to play made-up or improvised music. VAMP (*n.*) a shoe's upper leather.

vamping (*n*) an improvised accompaniment to a song.

vampire (*n.*) 1. species of large bat. 2. a person who preys upon others.

van (*n.*) 1. a large delivery-cart. 2. front part of an army or fleet. 3. railway guard's and luggage coach.

vandal (*n.*) 1. a destroyer of beautiful things. 2. a hooligan.

vandalism (*n.*) wilful and wanton destruction.

vane (*n.*) 1. a weathercock. 2. blade of a windmill, propeller, etc.

vanilla (*n.*) tropical plant and the flavouring obtained from its pod.

vanish (*v.*) to pass out of sight; to disappear.

vanity (*n.*) 1. self-pride; conceit. 2. idle or empty show.

vanquish (*v.*) to overcome; to conquer. VANQUISHER (*n.*).

vantage (*n.*) 1. the advantage; benefit. 2. score in lawn-tennis.

vaporize (*v.*) to turn into vapour; to boil.

vapour (*n.*) 1. anything in the form of a gas. 2. steam; mist.

variable (*adj.*) changeable; fickle.

variation (*n.*) change; alteration.

varied (*adj.*) different; unlike one another.

variegate (*v.*) to decorate with different colours.

variegated (*adj.*) marked with different colours; mottled.

variegation (*n.*) a variety of different colours; a medley.

variety (*n.*) 1. a difference; an unlikeness. 2. anything a little different from others of its kind or species.

various (*adj.*) 1. different. 2. several; sundry. VARIOUSLY (*adv.*).

varnish (*n.*) clear liquid which glosses painted work. VARNISH (*v.*) to coat with varnish; to gloss.

vary (*v.*) 1. to change; to alter. 2. to differ; to disagree.

vase (*n.*) ornamental jar or vessel of various forms.

vaseline (*n.*) petroleum jelly.

vassal (*n.*) 1. one who gave loyalty, work and military service to a master in return for the land he used. 2. a humble dependant; slave.

vast (*adj.*) boundless; immense. VASTLY (*adv.*).

vastness (*n.*) the greatness; immensity.

vat (*n.*) large barrel for storing oil, wine, etc.

vault (*n.*) 1. an arched roof. 2. cellar with an arched roof. 3. a leap over something; bound. VAULT (*v.*) 1. to arch. 2. to leap over.

vaulted (*adj.*) arched.

vaunt (*v.*) to boast; to swagger. VAUNT (*n.*) a boast; brag.

vaunting (*adj.*) boasting; showing-off.

veal (*n.*) calf-flesh.

veer (*v.*) to turn aside. VEERING (*adj.*).

vegetable (*n.*) 1. any living thing not animal. 2. plant used as food.

vegetarian (*n.*) person who eats no flesh-food.

vegetate (*v.*) to live a dull, useless life.

vegetation (*n.*) plant life.

vehemence (*n.*) violence; force.

vehement (*adj.*) passionate; violent. VEHEMENTLY (*adv.*).

vehicle (*n.*) 1. any conveyance used for land travel. 2. the means by which something is done.

veil (*n.*) any covering hiding something; a curtain. VEIL (*v.*) to cover; to conceal.

vein (*n.*) 1. blood-vessel carrying blood to the heart. 2. a rib of a leaf. 3. a layer or seam of mineral.

veined (*adj.*) 1. having veins. 2. streaked; branching.

vellum (*n.*) a fine parchment.

velocipede (*n.*) name given to first bicycle.

velocity (*n.*) swiftness; speed.

velvet (*n.*) soft, thick silk cloth.

velveteen (*n.*) cotton imitation of velvet.

velvety (*adj.*) soft; silky.

vend (*v.*) to sell; to trade.

vender or **vendor** (*nn.*) a seller.

vendetta (*n.*) a lasting feud in which the family of a slain or injured man seek vengeance against the offender and his family; a blood-feud.

veneer (*v.*) to overlay a common wood with a thin layer of finer wood. VENEER (*n.*) a superficial beauty; a gloss.

venerable (*adj.*) 1. old, and worthy of esteem. 2. an archdeacon's title.

venerate (*v.*) to respect highly; to regard as sacred.

veneration (*n.*) great regard; reverence.

vengeance (*n.*) injury inflicted in return for injury; revenge.

vengeful (*adj.*) determined to revenge. VENGEFULLY (*adv.*).

venison (*n.*) deer-flesh.

venom (*n.*) 1. poison. 2. ill-feelings such as spite; hatred.

venomous (*adj.*) 1. poisonous; virulent. 2. spiteful; malicious. VENOMOUSLY (*adv.*).

vent (*n.*) an outlet; a way of escape. VENT (*v.*) 1. to let out. 2. to pour out one's anger or complaint.

ventilate (*v.*) 1. to replace foul air with fresh. 2. to discuss a matter.

ventilation (*n.*) the process of purifying the air in a room.

ventilator (*n.*) any contrivance that admits fresh air.

ventriloquism (*n.*) ability to make one's voice appear to come from some other person, or from a distant place.

ventriloquist (*n.*) person skilled in ventriloquism.

venture (*n.*) a dangerous undertaking; a risk. VENTURE (*v.*) to run a risk; to dare. VENTURER (*n.*).

venturesome (*adj.*) 1. reckless; foolhardy. 2. fearless; brave.

Venus (*n.*) bright planet between Mercury and the earth. See appendix.

veracious (*adj.*) truthful; reliable. VERACIOUSLY (*adv.*).

veracity (*n.*) the truth; truthfulness.

veranda (*n.*) a covered balcony.

verb (*n.*) chief word in any sentence; word which gives a sentence its meaning.

verbal (*adj.*) spoken, not written. VERBALLY (*adv.*).

verbatim (*adv.*) exactly as said; word for word.

verbiage (*n.*) use of unnecessary words; too many words.

verbose (*adj.*) having too much to say; long-winded.

verbosity (*n.*) wordiness; talkativeness.

verdant (*adj.*) 1. green; grassy. 2. flourishing. 3. simple; ignorant.

verdict (*n.*) 1. answer of a jury. 2. a decision; judgment.

verdigris (*n.*) the green rust of copper or brass.

verdure (*n.*) greenness of vegetation.

verge (*n.*) the edge; border. VERGE (*v.*) 1. to incline towards; to slope. 2. to border upon.

verger (*n.*) a church attendant or clerk.

verifiable (*adj.*) can be proved true.

verification (*n.*) proof that a thing is true; a confirmation.

verify (*v.*) to prove the truth or accuracy of; to confirm.

verily (*adv.*) in truth; beyond all doubt.

veritable (*adj.*) 1. real; actual. 2. genuine; authentic.

verity (*n.*) truth; fact. (*pl.* VERITIES).

vermicelli (*n.*) flour paste made into small threads.

vermilion (*n.*) a bright-red colour.

vermin (*n.*) small creatures destructive of foodstuffs and crops; pests.

verminous (*adj.*) overrun or infested with vermin.

vernacular (*n.*) one's native or mother tongue; the ordinary speech of a country.

versatile (*adj.*) good or clever in many ways; adaptable.

versatility (*n.*) ability to do many things well.

verse (*n.*) 1. poetry. 2. a line of poetry.

versify (*v.*) to write in verse.

version (*n.*) 1. a description; an account. 2. a translation.

versus (*prep.*) against.

vertebra (*n.*) one of the separate bones forming the backbone. (*pl.* VERTEBRÆ).

vertebrate (*adj.*) backboned. VERTEBRATE (*n.*) an animal having a backbone or spine.

vertex (*n.*) the highest point; summit. (*pl.* VERTICES).

vertical (*adj.*) upright; perpendicular. VERTICALLY (*adv.*).

vertigo (*n.*) giddiness; dizziness.

verve (*n.*) energy; enthusiasm.

very (*adj.*) real; true. VERY (*adv.*) in a high degree.

vesper (*n.*) the evening; evening star.

vespers (*n. pl.*) evening religious service.

vessel (*n.*) 1. container for holding liquids. 2. a ship.

vest (*n.*) 1. undergarment worn next to the skin. 2. a waistcoat. VEST (*v.*) 1. to clothe. 2. to put in possession of.

vested (*adj.*) given possession of; possessed.

vestibule (*n.*) a porch or entrance to a house.

vestige (*n.*) the faintest mark; a trace.

vestment (*n.*) an official or ceremonial garment.

vestry (*n.*) room in a church where vestments, registers, etc., are kept.

vet (*n. abbrev.*) a veterinary surgeon; an animal doctor.

veteran (*adj.*) long experienced; old in service. VETERAN (*n.*) an old and experienced man.

veterinary (*adj.*) concerned with the diseases of domestic animals.

veto (*v.*) to forbid. VETO (*n.*) power or right to forbid.

vex (*v.*) to annoy; to anger.

vexation (*n.*) anger; irritation.

vexatious (*adj.*) troublesome; provoking. VEXATIOUSLY (*adv.*).

vexed (*adj.*) 1. annoyed; irritated. 2. disputed; unsettled.

via (*prep.*) by way of; passing through.

viaduct (*n.*) a long, arched road or railway bridge.

viands (*n. pl.*) foodstuffs; eatables.

vibrant (*adj.*) trembling; throbbing.

vibrate (*v.*) to tremble; to quiver.

vibration (*n.*) a tremble; quiver.

vicar (*n.*) 1. a parish priest. 2. a deputy.

vicarage (*n.*) residence of a vicar.

vice (*n.*) 1. a sin; fault. 2. instrument with two jaws which screw together and grip tightly. VICE- (*prefix*) in the place of; second to.

vice-admiral (*n.*) one next in command to an admiral.

viceroy (*n.*) governor of a country which he rules for his king or queen.

vicinity (*n.*) all places near by; the neighbourhood.

vicious (*adj.*) evil; malign. VICIOUSLY (*adv.*).

viciousness (*n.*) evil; malice.

victim (*n.*) 1. a killed or injured living creature. 2. a sufferer. 3. a cheated person; a dupe.

victimization (*n.*) the act of making a victim.

victimize (*v.*) to make a victim of; to prey upon.

victor (*n.*) a conqueror; master.

victorious (*adj.*) 1. successful. 2. conquering; triumphant. VICTORIOUSLY (*adv.*).

victory (*n.*) 1. success; mastery. 2. conquest; triumph.

victual (*v.*) to supply with food.

victualler (*n.*) a supplier of provisions.

victuals (*n. pl.*) food; provisions.

vie (*v.*) to strive against one another; to contend.

view (*n.*) 1. all that can be seen; the scene. 2. an opinion. VIEW (*v.*) 1. to look at; to observe. 2. to inspect; to survey.

vigil (*n.*) 1. a watch; night-sitting with the sick. 2. the eve before a religious feast.

vigilance (*n.*) watchfulness; alertness.

vigilant (*adj.*) 1. watchful; wakeful. 2. cautious; wary. VIGILANTLY (*adv.*).

vigorous (*adj.*) 1. active; energetic. 2. manly; robust. VIGOROUSLY (*adv.*).

vigour (*n.*) 1. strength; force. 2. intelligence.

Viking (*n.*) a Scandinavian sea-rover; Northman.

vile (*adj.*) 1. evil; shameful. 2. unpleasant; loathsome. VILELY (*adv.*).

vileness (*n.*) 1. badness; wickedness. 2. baseness.

vilify (*v.*) 1. to speak against; to slander. 2. to abuse; to revile.

villa (*n.*) a country residence.

village (*n.*) a small group of houses in the country; a hamlet. VILLAGER (*n.*).

villain (*n.*) a scoundrel; rascal.

villainous (*adj.*) vile; dishonourable. VILLAINOUSLY (*adv.*).

villainy (*n.*) rascality; crime.

vim (*n.*) energy; vigour.

vindicate (*v.*) to prove to be just or true; to defend.

vindication (*n.*) a proof of innocence; rightness.

vindicator (*n.*) a defender; an upholder.

vindictive (*adj.*) revengeful; spiteful. VINDICTIVELY (*adv.*).

vindictiveness (*n.*) spitefulness; malevolence.

vine (*n.*) climbing plant that bears grapes.

vinegar (*n.*) a sour liquid obtained from wine. VINEGARY (*adj.*).

vinery (*n.*) a glass-house for vines.

vineyard (*n.*) plantation of vines.

vintage (*n.*) vineyard's produce in grapes or wine.

viola (*n.*) 1. pansy-like plant of violet family. 2. stringed instrument like the violin.

violate (*v.*) 1. to treat roughly. 2. to profane; to pollute.

violation (*n.*) 1. an outrage; attack. 2. a desecration.

violator (*n.*) one who attacks or injures.

violence (*n.*) 1. force; brutality. 2. outrage; attack.

violent (*adj.*) 1. forceful; fierce. 2. wild; turbulent. VIOLENTLY (*adv.*).

violet (*n.*) tiny wild flower and its colour.

violin (*n.*) stringed musical instrument played with a bow; a fiddle.

violinist (*n.*) a violin player.

violoncellist (*n.*) a violoncello player. (*abbrev.* 'CELLIST).

violoncello (*n.*) a bass-violin; a 'cello.

viper (*n.*) 1. a venomous snake; an adder. 2. a treacherous person.

virago (*n.*) a scolding woman.

virgin (*n.*) an unmarried woman; a maiden. VIRGIN (*adj.*) 1. maidenly. 2. untilled; uncultivated.

virility (*n.*) manliness; strength. VIRILE (*adj.*).

virtue (*n.*) one's natural goodness or excellence; morality.

virtuous (*adj.*) morally good or worthy. VIRTUOUSLY (*adv.*).

virulence (*n.*) hatred; evil. VIRULENT (*adj.*).

virus (*n.*) the cause of various diseases.

visage (*n.*) the face; countenance.

viscid (*adj.*) like glue; sticky.

viscount (*n.*) nobleman next in rank above a baron.

viscous (*adj.*) sticky; syrupy.

visibility (*n.*) 1. the plainness of an object. 2. the distance an object can be seen distinctly.

visible (*adj.*) can be seen; discernible. VISIBLY (*adv.*).

vision (*n.*) 1. power of seeing; sight. 2. something imagined; a phantom.

visionary (*adj.*) 1. unreal; imaginary. 2. dreamy; imaginative. VISIONARY (*n.*) an imaginative or romantic person.

visit (*v.*) 1. to go to see or to stay with. 2. to reward or punish.

visitation (*n.*) 1. an official inspection of a hospital, school, etc. 2. a punishment; an infliction.

visitor (*n.*) a caller; guest.

vista (*n.*) the distant view; prospect.

visual (*adj.*) 1. relating to sight. 2. visible; seeable.

visualization (*n.*) ability to make a picture in the mind; a mental image.

visualize (*v.*) to make a mind-picture of something described.

visually (*adv.*) by sight.

vital (*adj.*) 1. necessary to life. 2. very important.

vitality (*n.*) life; vigour.

vitally (*adv.*) essentially.

vitals (*n. pl.*) parts of the body essential to life.

vitamins (*n. pl.*) substances the body needs to keep it healthy.

vitiate (*v.*) to make faulty; to spoil.

vitriol (*n.*) a very strong acid.

vitriolic (*adj.*) 1. bitter; burning. 2. fierce; savage.

vituperate (*v.*) to find fault with; to scold

vituperation (*n.*) abuse; scolding.

vivacious (*adj.*) lively; bright. VIVACIOUSLY (*adv.*).

vivacity (*n.*) liveliness; animation.

vivid (*adj.*) 1. true to life; striking. 2. unforgettable. VIVIDLY (*adv.*).

vividness (*n.*) trueness; clearness.

vivify (*v.*) to vitalize; to animate.

vixen (*n.*) 1. a female fox. 2. a bad-tempered woman.

viz. (*adv.*) that is; namely.

vocabulary (*n.*) a dictionary; a stock of words.

vocal (*adj.*) 1. having a voice. 2. sung or spoken.

vocalist (*n.*) a singer.

vocation (*n.*) an occupation; a business.

vocational (*adj.*) concerned with one's occupation.

vociferate (*v.*) to exclaim; to shout.

vociferous (*adj.*) loud; noisy. VOCIFEROUSLY (*adv.*).

vogue (*n.*) the popular fashion; the mode.

voice (*n.*) 1. sound made by the vocal organs; utterance. 2. a wish; an opinion. VOICE (*v.*) 1. to speak; to utter. 2. to express a wish or opinion.

voiceless (*adj.*) 1. speechless; dumb. 2. silent; voteless.

void (*adj.*) 1. empty; vacant. 2. null; invalid. VOID (*n.*) 1. an empty space. 2. a deep chasm.

volatile (*adj.*) 1. changing to vapour quickly. 2. flighty; fickle.

volcanic (*adj.*) concerned with volcanoes.

volcano (*n.*) hill which throws out smoke and ashes through an opening. (*pl.* VOLCANOES). See appendix.

vole (*n.*) a field-mouse.

volley (*n.*) 1. the discharge of many firearms at once, and the missiles so fired. 2. rapid, continuous, noisy uttering of words. 3. the return of a tennis ball in play before it touches the ground.

volt (*n.*) measure of electric power or energy. See appendix.

voltage (*n.*) power of an electric current.

volubility (*n.*) talkativeness.

voluble (*adj.*) talkative. VOLUBLY (*adv.*).

volume (*n.*) 1. a book. 2. the bulk; capacity.

voluminous (*adj.*) 1. consisting of many volumes. 2. bulky; capacious.

voluntary (*adj.*) of one's own will; without compulsion. VOLUNTARILY (*adv.*).

volunteer (*v.*) to do of one's own will; to offer. VOLUNTEER (*n.*) one who serves from desire, not compulsion.

voluptuous (*adj.*) fond of pleasure and luxury. VOLUPTUOUSLY (*adv.*).

vomit (*v.*) to throw up from the stomach; to cast out.

voracious (*adj.*) greedy; gluttonous. VORACIOUSLY (*adv.*).

voracity (*n.*) greed; rapacity.

vortex (*n.*) 1. a whirlpool; whirlwind. 2. vapour trail of an aeroplane. (*pl.* VORTICES).

votary (*n.*) an enthusiastic supporter of a cause. (*fem.* VOTARESS).

vote (*v.*) to express a wish or decision. VOTE (*n.*) 1. one's decision. 2. decision of the majority of voters.

voter (*n.*) person having a legal right to vote.

vouch (*v.*) to bear witness; to confirm.

voucher (*n.*) a paper which is evidence; a receipt.

vow (*n.*) a solemn promise or oath. VOW (*v.*) to promise solemnly.

vowel (*n.*) a simple voice-sound, a, e, i, o, u, or the letter denoting it.

voyage (*n.*) a journey by sea; cruise. VOYAGE (*v.*) to travel by sea. VOYAGER (*n.*).

vulcanite (*n.*) a hardened form of india-rubber.

vulcanize (*v.*) to make indiarubber into vulcanite. See appendix.

vulgar (*adj.*) 1. common; general. 2. rude; boorish. VULGARLY (*adv.*).

vulgarity (*n.*) rudeness; coarseness.

vulgarize (*v.*) to make common or general; to popularize.

vulnerable (*adj.*) weak; defenceless.

vulture (*n.*) large, greedy, scavenger-bird.

vying (*adj.*) competing; rivalling. See VIE.

W

wad (*n.*) soft fibre tightly pressed.

wadding (*n.*) soft material for padding.

waddle (*v.*) to rock in walking. WADDLE (*n.*) clumsy, rocking walk.

waddling (*adj.*) walking unsteadily.

wade (*v.*) to walk through water; to read without interest.

wader (*n.*) long-legged bird that wades.

waders (*n. pl.*) high, waterproof boots for wading.

wafer (*n.*) 1. thin cake or biscuit. 2. thin disc of paste or paper for sealing.

waft (*v.*) to float along through air or on water.

wag (*v.*) to shake to and fro. WAG (*n.*) a joker; humorist.

wage (*n.*) agreed payment for work done. WAGE (*v.*) to carry on war.

wager (*n.*) a bet. WAGER (*v.*) to bet.

waggish (*adj.*) witty; joking. WAGGISHLY (*adv.*).

waggon (*n.*) 1. large four-wheeled cart. 2. a railway truck.

waggoner (*n.*) a waggon-driver.

wagtail (*n.*) small, long-tailed bird.

waif (*n.*) a homeless person.

wail (*v.*) to weep loudly; to lament. WAIL (*n.*) long, loud cry; a lament.

wailing (*n.*) grief; lamentation.

wainscot (*n.*) wooden panels covering lower part of a room wall.

wainwright (*n.*) a waggon-maker.

waist (*n.*) 1. narrow part of body between hips and ribs. 2. middle of a ship.

waistcoat (*n.*) sleeveless garment worn under the coat.

wait (*v.*) 1. to tarry; to stay. 2. to serve food. WAIT (*n.*) a tarrying.

waiter (*n.*) one who serves food; a steward. (*fem.* WAITRESS).

waiting (*n.*) 1. a tarrying; staying. 2. attendance.

waits (*n. pl.*) Christmas carol-singers.

waive (*v.*) to give up; to refuse.

wake (*v.*) 1. to rouse from sleep. 2. to enliven; to excite.

wakeful (*adj.*) 1. not sleepy. 2. watchful; alert. WAKEFULLY (*adv.*).

wakefulness (*n.*) 1. inability to sleep. 2. vigilance; alertness.

waken (*v.*) 1. to cease sleeping. 2. to stir into action.

wakening (*n.*) an arousing.

walk (*v.*) to move on one's feet without running. WALK (*n.*) 1. a stroll. 2. a pathway. 3. one's manner of walking. 4. one's part in life; career.

walker (*n.*) person fond of walking.

walking-stick (*n.*) stick giving support when walking.

wall (*n.*) 1. side of a building. 2. stone or brick fence.

wallflower (*n.*) fragrant flower growing wild on walls.

wall-paper (*n.*) paper for covering walls of room.

wallaby (*n.*) small kangaroo.

wallet (*n.*) pocket-case for carrying paper-money, etc.

wallop (*v.*) to beat; to thrash. WALLOP (*n.*) a blow; stroke.

wallow (*v.*) to roll in mud; to welter.

walnut (*n.*) tree yielding valuable timber and its nut.

walrus (*n.*) large, tusked sea-mammal of seal family.

waltz (*n.*) dance for two persons and its music. WALTZ (*v.*) to dance a waltz.

wan (*adj.*) pale; ashen. WANLY (*adv.*).

wand (*n.*) 1. a rod denoting authority. 2. a conjurer's rod.

wander (*v.*) 1. to roam; to go astray. 2. to ramble in one's talk; to digress. WANDERER (*n.*).

wandering (*n.*) 1. roaming. 2. digressing.

wane (*v.*) 1. to weaken; to fail. 2. to sink; to ebb.

waning (*n.*) a decrease; an ebb.

want (*v.*) 1. to lack; to need. 2. to wish for; to desire. 3. to neglect; to omit. WANT (*n.*) 1. shortage; scarcity. 2. need; poverty. 3. desire; craving.

wanting (*adj.*) 1. lacking; short. 2. absent. 3. backward. WANTING (*prep.*) without; minus.

wanton (*adj.*) 1. frolicsome; playful. 2. irresponsible; reckless. WANTONLY (*adv.*).

wantonness (*n.*) 1. playfulness. 2. recklessness.

war (*n.*) struggle between nations and their armed forces. WAR (*v.*) to fight with armed forces.

warble (*v.*) to sing softly; to trill. WARBLE (*n.*) 1. a bird's song; a trill. 2. a song; melody.

warbler (*n.*) 1. a song-bird. 2. a singer.

warbling (*adj.*) singing; trilling.

war-cry (*n.*) defiant shout of men in battle.

ward (*v.*) 1. to defend; to protect. 2. to turn aside; to fend. WARD (*n.*) 1. a watchman; protector. 2. person under a guardian's care. 3. a town district. 4. a room in a hospital.

warden (*n.*) 1. a guardian. 2. head of a school or college. 3. an officer in charge.

warder (*n.*) a prison-guard.

wardrobe (*n.*) 1. tall chest for storing clothes. 2. clothes.

ware (*adj.*) cautious; watchful. WARE (*n.*) goods; merchandise.

warehouse (*n.*) building for storage of goods.

warfare (*n.*) the waging of war; hostilities.

warily (*adv.*) carefully; cautiously.

wariness (*n.*) watchfulness; caution.

warlike (*adj.*) threatening war; hostile.

warm (*adj.*) 1. containing heat; fairly hot. 2. friendly; affectionate.

warm-hearted (*adj.*) 1. affectionate; loving. 2. generous; sympathetic.

warmly (*adv.*) with warmth; affectionately.

warmth (*n.*) 1. moderately high temperature. 2. enthusiasm; vigour.

warn (*v.*) 1. to caution; to admonish. 2. to give notice beforehand.

warning (*n.*) 1. a caution; admonition. 2. a notification. WARNING (*adj.*) cautioning; advising. WARNINGLY (*adv.*).

warp (*v.*) 1. to twist; to distort. 2. to spoil a person's character or nature. 3. to haul a ship with a cable; to tow.

WARP (*n.*) 1. a twist; distortion. 2. lengthwise threads in woven material. 3. a towing-rope.

warped (*adj.*) distorted; crooked.

warrant (*v.*) 1. to certify; to guarantee. 2. to authorize; to license. 3. to permit; to justify. WARRANT (*n.*) 1. an official and legal order; a commission. 2. an order to arrest or summons; a writ.

warrantable (*adj.*) 1. authorized; empowered. 2. rightful.

warranted (*adj.*) certified; guaranteed.

warren (*n.*) a rabbit colony.

warrior (*n.*) 1. a soldier; brave fighter. 2. a champion.

wart (*n.*) small, hard growth on the skin. WARTY (*adj.*).

wart-hog (*n.*) African warty-faced wild animal of pig family.

wary (*adj.*) careful; cautious.

wash (*v.*) 1. to cleanse with water. 2. to overflow. 3. to sweep away. 4. to paint. WASH (*n.*) 1. a cleansing with water. 2. a thin coat of colour.

washable (*adj.*) can be washed.

washer (*n.*) rubber or metal ring which keeps joints tight.

washing (*n.*) collection of material washed at one time.

washy (*adj.*) watery; lacking force.

wasp (*n.*) slender, winged insect with sharp sting. WASPISH (*adj.*).

wastage (*n.*) loss by use or decay.

waste (*v.*) 1. to spend unprofitably; to squander. 2. to use unnecessarily. 3. to wither; to decay. WASTE (*n.*) 1. refuse; rubbish. 2. a desert; wilderness. 3. extravagance.

wasteful (*adj.*) 1. causing waste; destructive. 2. extravagant; thriftless. WASTE-FULLY (*adv.*).

waster (*n.*) idle, useless person.

wastrel (*n.*) an idler; a scamp.

watch (*v.*) 1. to observe; to note. 2. to guard. 3. to be wakeful or vigilant. WATCH (*n.*) 1. a guard; sentry. 2. a pocket-timepiece. 3. one of the seven periods into which a ship's day (noon to noon) is divided at sea. 4. the portion of a ship's crew allotted to a watch.

watch-dog (*n.*) dog trained to guard property.

watchful (*adj.*) alert; vigilant. WATCH-FULLY (*adv.*).

watchfulness (*n.*) heedfulness; vigilance.

watchmaker (*n.*) maker and repairer of watches. WATCHMAKING (*n.*).

watchman (*n.*) man employed to guard premises.

watchword (*n.*) a password; countersign.

water (*n.*) 1. clear liquid without taste or smell. 2. large body of water; lake. 3. colour or lustre of a diamond. WATER (*v.*) 1. to supply with water. 2. to place in water. 3. to add water to.

water-colour (*n.*) pigment that mixes with water.

watercress (*n.*) edible plant growing in watery places.

waterfall (*n.*) flow of a stream over a precipice; a cascade.

waterfowl (*n.*) birds nesting in or by water; aquatic birds.

water-lily (*n.*) water-plant with large floating leaves and flowers.

waterlogged (*adj.*) saturated with water.

water-main (*n.*) chief pipe conveying water to houses.

watermark (*n.*) 1. line marking rise and fall of water. 2. trade-mark worked into paper.

water-mill (*n.*) mill whose machinery is water-driven.

water-polo (*n.*) ball game played by swimmers.

water-power (*n.*) power of water to turn a wheel which drives machinery.

watershed (*n.*) high land dividing two river basins.

waterspout (*n.*) pillar of water drawn from the sea by a whirlwind.

watery (*adj.*) 1. containing too much water. 2. tasteless; insipid.

watt (*n.*) electrical unit of power or work done. See appendix.

wattle (*n.*) 1. twig or rod. 2. a hurdle. 3. fleshy growth under a fowl's throat.

wave (*n.*) 1. a vibration. 2. ridge of water on the sea. 3. a signalling motion of the hand. WAVE (*v.*) 1. to shake to and fro. 2. to signal.

wave-length (*n.*) distance between the crests of two successive waves.

wavelet (*n.*) a little wave; a ripple.

waver (*v.*) to hesitate; to totter. WAVERER (*n.*).

wavering (*adj.*) hesitating; uncertain. WAVERINGLY (*adv.*).

wavy (*adj.*) blowing to and fro, or up and down.

wax (*n.*) 1. fatty substance made by bees. 2. substance that gathers in the ears. WAX (*v.*) 1. to smear with wax. 2. to increase in size or strength.

waxen (*adj.*) made of wax.

waxwork (*n.*) figure or object made of wax.

way (*n.*) 1. a road; route. 2. a method; plan. 3. a style; habit.

wayfarer (*n.*) a traveller WAYFARING (*adj.*).

waylay (*v.*) to lie in wait for; to ambush.

wayside (*n.*) the roadside.

wayward (*adj.*) contrary; perverse. WAYWARDLY (*adv.*).

waywardness (*n.*) contrariness; unruliness.

weak (*adj.*) 1. having little strength; frail. 2. having little will power; easily influenced. 3. delicate; sickly. 4. watery; thin.

weaken (*v.*) to make weak or weaker.

weakling (*n.*) a delicate, feeble person.

weakly (*adv.*) in a feeble manner. WEAKLY (*adj.*) infirm.

weak-minded (*adj.*) simple; foolish.

weakness (*n.*) 1. feebleness; frailty. 2. something one has a fondness or taste for.

weal (*n.*) 1. welfare; prosperity. 2. public well-being. 3. mark made on the skin by a lash.

wealth (*n.*) riches; abundance.

wealthiness (*n.*) the amount of wealth; the prosperity.

wealthy (*adj.*) rich; prosperous. WEALTHILY (*adv.*).

wean (*v.*) 1. to teach a baby to do without mother's milk. 2. to teach oneself or another to give up a habit or desire.

weapon (*n.*) an instrument with which to fight; arm.

wear (*v.*) 1. to have on one's body; to be clothed in. 2. to use up; to rub away. 3. to show; to display. WEAR (*n.*) 1. slow exhaustion due to use. 2. clothing; fashion.

wearable (*adj.*) fit to be worn.

wearied (*adj.*) tired; exhausted.

weariness (*n.*) tiredness; exhaustion.

wearisome (*adj.*) dull; tedious. WEARISOMELY (*adv.*).

weary (*adj.*) exhausted; fatigued. WEARY (*n. pl.*) all who suffer and are distressed. WEARY (*v.*) to tire; to bore. WEARILY (*adv.*).

weasel (*n.*) slender, stoat-like animal.

weather (*n.*) the mildness or storminess of the air. WEATHER (*v.*) 1. to endure unpleasant weather. 2. to win through a period of hardship or distress.

weather-beaten (*adj.*) hardened by rough weather; well-seasoned.

weathercock (*n.*) indicator showing the wind's direction; a vane.

weather-glass (*n.*) a barometer.

weave (*v.*) 1. to plait; to interlace. 2. to make on a loom. WEAVER (*n.*).

web (*n.*) 1. anything woven; cloth. 2. spider's trap. 3. thin skin between toes of waterbirds.

webbed or **web-footed** (*adj.*) having toes joined by a web.

webbing (*n.*) strong, wide, hempen ribbon.

wed (*v.*) to marry.

wedded (*adj.*) married.

wedding (*n.*) a marriage; marriage ceremony.

wedge (*n.*) a V-shaped piece of wood or metal used for splitting, forcing open or fastening. WEDGE (*v.*) to jam or fasten with a wedge.

wedged (*adj.*) jammed; shut tightly.

wedlock (*n.*) marriage; matrimony.

Wednesday (*n.*) fourth day of the week. See appendix.

wee (*adj.*) very small; tiny.

weed (*n.*) 1. wild plant that grows where it is not wanted. 2. tobacco. WEED (*v.*) to uproot weeds.

weediness (*n.*) 1. uselessness. 2. lankiness.

weeding (*n.*) work of uprooting weeds.

weedy (*adj.*) 1. full of weeds. 2. badly grown.

week (*n.*) a period of seven days.

week-day (*n.*) any day except Sunday; a working day.

weekly (*adj.*) 1. happening once a week. 2. published each week. WEEKLY (*n.*) publication issued weekly.

weep (*v.*) to cry; to sob.

weeping (*adj.*) shedding tears; lamenting. WEEPING (*n.*) a lamentation; mourning.

weevil (*n.*) a plant-eating beetle.

weft (*n.*) threads crossing a fabric from edge to edge; the woof.

weigh (*v.*) 1. to find how heavy something is. 2. to estimate. 3. to haul in an anchor.

weighing (*n.*) 1. the act of finding the weight. 2. judging; estimating.

weight (*n.*) 1. the heaviness; pressure. 2. the load; burden. 3. the importance; seriousness.

weightiness (*n.*) 1. the heaviness. 2. the importance.

weighty (*adj.*) 1. heavy; burdensome. 2. important; serious. WEIGHTILY (*adv.*).

weir (*n.*) barrier or dam across a stream.

weird (*adj.*) mysterious; uncanny. WEIRDLY (*adv.*).

weirdness (*n.*) uncanniness; unearthliness.

welcome (*v.*) to receive with joy; to greet. WELCOME (*n.*) a joyful greeting. WELCOME (*adj.*) pleasant; agreeable.

weld (*v.*) to hammer together when white hot; to unite firmly. WELD (*n.*) a metal joint made by welding.

welfare (*n.*) prosperity; happiness.

welkin (*n.*) the sky.

well (*n.*) 1. a spring of water. 2. a hole sunk to reach water or oil. 3. a space containing a staircase or lift. WELL (*v.*) to flow out; to gush. WELL (*adj.*) 1. healthy. 2. right; satisfactory. WELL (*adv.*) 1. rightly. 2. thoroughly.

well-behaved (*adj.*) good-mannered.

well-being (*n.*) welfare; happiness.

well-bred (*adj.*) polite; courteous.

well-doing (*n.*) good conduct.

well-informed (*adj.*) having much knowledge.

well-nigh (*adv.*) almost; nearly.

well-to-do (*adj.*) rich; prosperous.

Welsh (*n. pl.*) 1. the natives or inhabitants of Wales. 2. (*n. sing.*) the language of the Welsh. WELSH (*adj.*) relating to Wales or its inhabitants.

welt (*n.*) leather strip between sole and upper of a shoe. WELT (*v.*) to provide with a welt.

welter (*v.*) to roll; to wallow. WELTER (*n.*) 1. a tossing. 2. a mixture; confusion. 3. boxer between middleweight and heavyweight.

wench (*n.*) a young woman; a maid.

wend (*v.*) to walk along; to make one's way.

Wesleyan (*n.*) member of the religious denomination or Church founded by John Wesley. WESLEYAN (*adj.*) relating to John Wesley or the Wesleyan Church. See appendix.

west (*n.*) the direction of sunset.

westerly (*adj. & adv.*) from the west.

western (*adj.*) in the west.

westward (*adv.*) towards the west.

wet (*adj.*) 1. containing water. 2. rainy; showery. WET (*n.*) water; moisture. WET (*v.*) to moisten; to drench with water.

wetness (*n.*) moisture; dampness.

whack (*v.*) to thump; to strike. WHACK (*n.*) a blow; thump.

whale (*n.*) the largest sea-mammal.

whalebone (*n.*) an elastic substance from the whale's jaws; baleen.

whale oil (*n.*) fat obtained from blubber.

whaler (*n.*) a whale-fishing ship.

whaling (*n.*) whale-fishing.

wharf (*n.*) quay at which ships load and unload; a mole. (*pl.* WHARVES).

what (*pron.*) that which; whatever. WHAT (*adj.*) asking the kind, quality or amount; that, those, which; as much as; how great.

wheat (*n.*) plant yielding bread-flour. WHEATEN (*adj.*).

wheedle (*v.*) to coax; to cajole. WHEEDLING (*n.*).

wheel (*n.*) a circular frame joined by bars or spokes to an axle on which it turns. WHEEL (*v.*) 1. to move on wheels. 2. to revolve.

wheelbarrow (*n.*) a light, one-wheeled conveyance.

wheeled (*adj.*) having wheels; vehicular.

wheelwright (*n.*) a maker of wheels.

wheeze (*v.*) to breathe hoarsely. WHEEZE (*n.*) a hoarse breath.

wheeziness (*n.*) hoarseness; chestiness.

whelk (*n.*) large periwinkle-like shellfish.

whelp (*n.*) a pup; a cub.

when (*adv.*) at or after the time that; at what time. WHEN (*conj.*) although.

where (*adv.*) in or to what place; whither.

wherry (*n.*) a light, shallow boat; a heavy barge used in Norfolk.

whet (*v.*) 1. to sharpen by rubbing. 2. to sharpen one's appetite; to excite.

whether (*pron.*) which of the two. WHETHER, a conjunction requiring the answer yes or no to two alternatives, e.g., Tell me whether you will come or not.

whetstone (*n.*) oiled stone for sharpening implements by rubbing; a hone.

whey (*n.*) watery part of milk.

which (*pron.*) who, of a number of persons; what one of a number of things.

whiff (*n.*) 1. a puff of air; gust. 2. a smoke. WHIFF (*v.*) to puff; to smoke.

while (*n.*) a time; period. WHILE (*conj.*) at the time that. WHILE (*v.*) to make pass by; to spend time without being wearied.

whim (*n.*) a fancy; a notion.

whimper (*v.*) to whine; to moan. WHIMPER (*n.*) a whining cry.

whimpering (*n.*) sobbing. WHIMPERING (*adj.*) whining.

whimsical (*adj.*) odd; capricious. WHIMSICALLY (*adv.*).

whin (*n.*) gorse; furze.

whine (*v.*) to speak in a crying voice. WHINE (*n.*) a peevish tone.

whining (*adj.*) peevish; spoiled. WHININGLY (*adv.*).

whinny (*n.*) a horse's cry; a neigh. WHINNY (*v.*) to neigh.

whip (*v.*) to lash; to scourge. WHIP (*n.*) 1. lash for driving animals. 2. Member of Parliament who summons Members to attend and vote. 3. a Whip's summons to vote.

whiphand (*n.*) 1. hand grasping the whip. 2. an advantage.

whipper-snapper (*n.*) an unimportant person; a nonentity.

whipping (*n.*) a beating; thrashing.

whir (*v.*) to fly or spin with a buzzing sound. WHIR (*n.*) a buzz.

whirl (*v.*) to rotate rapidly; to spin. WHIRL (*n.*) a spin; rotation.

whirligig (*n.*) 1. a spinning toy. 2. constant change.

whirling (*n.*) the spinning; rotating.

whirlpool (*n.*) a spinning water-current; an eddy.

whirlwind (*n.*) a spinning wind; a cyclone.

whirring (*n.*) a buzzing sound.

whisk (*n.*) 1. a quick sweeping movement. 2. a snatch; jerk. 3. a contrivance for beating eggs. 4. a small, feathery brush. WHISK (*v.*) 1. to sweep lightly away. 2. to snatch; to jerk away.

whisker (*n.*) 1. the hair on a man's cheeks. 2. stiff hairs round an animal's mouth.

whisking (*adj.*) moving along rapidly.

whisky (*n.*) strong spirit distilled from grain.

whisper (*v.*) to speak with breath only, not voice. WHISPER (*n.*) 1. words breathed or hissed. 2. a hint; rumour. WHISPERER (*n.*).

whispering (*adj.*) hissing softly; murmuring.

whist (*n.*) card-game for four players. WHIST (*interj.*) hush; be silent.

whistle (*v.*) to make a high, shrill sound; to pipe. WHISTLE (*n.*) a shrill, piercing sound made by (1) the lips, or (2) a tube or pipe, or (3) the wind.

whistling (*n.*) shrill sound of a whistle or the wind.

whit (*n.*) a particle or jot.

white (*adj.*) 1. sunlight-coloured. 2. pale; snowy. 3. clean; spotless. WHITE (*n.*) 1. the colour of sunlight, 2. albumen in an egg. 3. the eye-ball round the iris. 4. a member of the white race.

whitebait (*n.*) a small fish.

white elephant (*n.*) 1. a pale-skinned elephant. 2. a rarity. 3. an unwanted article; junk.

white-hot (*adj.*) made hotter than red-hot.

whiten (*v.*) to make white or whiter.

whiteness (*n.*) 1. the paleness; wanness. 2. the purity; innocence.

whitethroat (*n.*) small singing-bird.

whitewash (*n.*) preparation of lime and water for liming walls. WHITEWASH (*v.*) 1. to coat with whitewash. 2. to clear a person's reputation.

whither (*adv.*) to which or what place.

whithersoever (*adv.*) to whatever place.

whiting (*n.*) small sea-fish of cod family.

Whit Sunday (*n.*) the seventh Sunday after Easter.

Whitsuntide (*n.*) week beginning with Whit Sunday.

whittle (*v.*) to cut away with a knife; to slice off wastefully. WHITTLE (*n.*) a pocket-knife.

whiz (*n.*) a hissing or humming sound. WHIZ (*v.*) to hiss; to hum.

whole (*adj.*) 1. entire; complete. 2. sound; perfect. WHOLE (*n.*) the total; entirety.

whole-hearted (*adj.*) generous; zealous.

wholesale (*n.*) the buying and selling of goods in large quantities. WHOLESALE (*adj.*) in quantity; extensive.

wholesome (*adj.*) beneficial; nourishing.

wholly (*adv.*) completely; perfectly.

whoop (*n.*) a loud cry: a yell. WHOOP (*v.*) to yell; to hoot.

whooping-cough (*n.*) ailment in which breath is drawn in with a whooping noise.

why (*adv.*) for what reason or purpose.

wick (*n.*) cotton thread or tape for burning in a candle or lamp.

wicked (*adj.*) 1. evil; sinful. 2. naughty; mischievous. WICKEDLY (*adv.*).

wickedness (*n.*) 1. sinfulness. 2. naughtiness.

wicker (*adj.*) made of willow-twigs or branches.

wickerwork (*n.*) basket-work of osiers.

wicket (*n.*) 1. a small door made in a large one. 2. three upright rods bowled at in cricket.

wide (*adj.*) broad; extensive. WIDE (*adv.*) far away; astray. WIDE (*n.*) a ball bowled out of the batsman's reach.

wide-awake (*adj.*) alert; shrewd.

widely (*adv.*) extensively; very much.

widen (*v.*) to make wider or broader.

wideness (*n.*) the width; breadth.

widespread (*adj.*) extensive; far-reaching.

widow (*n.*) a woman whose husband is dead.

widower (*n.*) a man whose wife is dead.

width (*n.*) distance from side to side; breadth.

wield (*v.*) 1. to use powerfully; to control. 2. to flourish; to brandish.

wieldy (*adj.*) manageable; controllable.

wife (*n.*) a married woman. (*pl.* WIVES).

wig (*n.*) an artificial covering of hair for the head. WIGMAKER (*n.*).

wigged (*adj.*) wearing a wig.

wigwam (*n.*) a Red Indian tent.

wild (*adj.*) 1. untamed; undomesticated.

2. uninhabited; uncultivated. 3. disorderly; savage.

wilderness (*n.*) the desert; a waste.

wildly (*adv.*) rashly; recklessly.

wildness (*n.*) 1. savagery; ferocity. 2. disorder; violence.

wilds (*n. pl.*) the uncivilized places.

wile (*n.*) a trick; deception.

wilful (*adj.*) intentional; deliberate. WILFULLY (*adv.*).

wilfulness (*n.*) unruliness; perverseness.

wilily (*adv.*) fraudulently; trickily.

wiliness (*n.*) artfulness; guile.

will (*n.*) 1. one's power to decide and to control one's actions. 2. determination; resolution. 3. desire; intention. 4. a written document disposing of one's property after death. WILL (*v.*) 1. to decide; to determine. 2. to wish; to intend. 3. to leave; to bequeath.

willing (*adj.*) ready; eager. WILLINGLY (*adv.*).

willingness (*n.*) wishfulness; readiness.

will-o'-the-wisp (*n.*) 1. a false light; deception. 2. an elusive person.

willow (*n.*) 1. tree with slender, flexible branches, and its wood. 2. a cricket-bat.

willowy (*adj.*) slender; flexible.

willy-nilly (*adv.*) willingly or unwillingly.

wilt (*v.*) to fade; to droop.

wily (*adj.*) crafty; tricky.

win (*v.*) 1. to gain; to earn. 2. to accomplish; to achieve. WIN (*n.*) a victory; a success.

wince (*v.*) to start back from; to flinch. WINCE (*n.*) a shrinking away; flinch.

winch (*n.*) a handle for turning a wheel; a windlass.

wind (*n.*) 1. a current of air; breeze. 2. breath. WIND (*v.*) 1. to turn or coil round something; to reel. 2. to twist; to curve.

wind-bag (*n.*) a bombastic speaker.

winded (*adj.*) out of breath.

windfall (*n.*) 1. fruit blown down by the wind. 2. an unexpected gain.

winding (*adj.*) twisting; curving.

windjammer (*n.*) a sailing ship.

windlass (*n.*) roller turned with a winch and used for hoisting.

windmill (*n.*) mill worked by sails or vanes turned by the wind.

window (*n.*) a glazed opening in the wall of a building to let in light. WINDOWED (*adj.*).

window-frame (*n.*) wooden frame fitted into a wall to hold the glass.

window-pane (*n.*) piece of glass set in a window-frame.

window-sill (*n.*) flat slab of wood or stone on which the frame rests.

windpipe (*n.*) passage from the mouth and nose admitting air into the lungs.

windward (*n.*) point from which the wind blows.

windy (*adj.*) breezy; stormy.

wine (*n.*) liquor produced from the juice of grapes or other fruit.

wine-glass (*n.*) small glass from which wine is drunk.

wine-press (*n.*) place in which grapes are pressed.

wing (*n.*) 1. organ of flight of birds. 2. building added to a side of another. 3. supporting part or plane of an aeroplane. 4. the side of a stage. WING (*v.*) 1. to fly. 2. to shoot in the wing.

winged (*adj.*) provided with wings.

wink (*v.*) 1. to open and close the eyelid quickly. 2. to pretend not to see. 3. to flicker. WINK (*n.*) 1. a quick flutter of an eyelid. 2. a flicker of light. 3. short period of sleep.

winking (*n.*) the act of blinking; flickering.

winkle (*n.*) see PERIWINKLE.

winner (*n.*) a victor.

winning (*adj.*) charming; attractive. WINNING (*n.*) the gaining of a prize or victory. WINNINGLY (*adv.*).

winnow (*v.*) to blow chaff away from grain; to fan.

winsome (*adj.*) attractive; agreeable. WINSOMELY (*adv.*).

winter (*n.*) the fourth, or cold season of the year. WINTER (*v.*) to spend the winter in a warm or sheltered district.

wintry (*adj.*) cold; cheerless.

wipe (*v.*) to rub; to clean. WIPE (*n.*) a rub.

wire (*n.*) 1. metal thread or string. 2. a telegram. WIRE (*v.*) 1. to bind or fence with wire. 2. to telegraph.

wired (*adj.*) fitted with electric light and power.

wireless (*n.*) systems of telegraphing and telephoning without wires; radio.

wire-puller (*n.*) person who uses influence; a schemer.

wireworm (*n.*) thin, hard grub of a destructive beetle.

wiriness (*n.*) strength; toughness.

wiry (*adj.*) tough; hardened. WIRILY (*adv.*).

wisdom (*n.*) ability to use knowledge; sense.

wise (*adj.*) sensible; intelligent. WISE (*n.*) 1. a way; manner. 2. sensible people. WISELY (*adv.*).

wiseacre (*n.*) one who knows everything.

wish (*v.*) to long for; to desire. WISH (*n.*) a longing; desire.

wishful (*adj.*) expectant; desirous. WISHFULLY (*adv.*).

wishfulness (*n.*) expectation; hopefulness.

wisp (*n.*) small tuft of hair, wool, etc.

wispy (*adj.*) light; feathery.

wistful (*adj.*) thoughtful; pensive. WISTFULLY (*adv.*).

wistfulness (*n.*) loneliness; vague longing.

wit (*n.*) understanding; intelligence.

witch (*n.*) an enchantress; a sorceress.

witchcraft (*n.*) magic; sorcery.

witchery (*n.*) enchantment; spellbinding.

with (*prep.*) in the company of; by the aid of.

withdraw (*v.*) 1. to go away from; to retire. 2. to take back one's words or accusation; to recall.

withdrawal (*n.*) 1. a departure; retreat. 2. a removal; recall.

withe (*n.*) a flexible twig.

wither (*v.*) 1. to fade; to perish. 2. to shrivel; to blight.

withered (*adj.*) shrunken; faded.

withering (*adj.*) 1. cold; bitter. 2. biting; sarcastic. WITHERINGLY (*adv.*).

withers (*n. pl.*) ridge where horse's neck joins the shoulder-bones.

withershins (*adv.*) the wrong way; left-handed.

withhold (*v.*) to keep back; to restrain. WITHHOLDER (*n.*).

within (*prep.*) inside the limits. WITHIN (*adv.*) inwardly; indoors.

without (*prep.*) beyond the limits. WITHOUT (*adv.*) outwardly; externally.

withstand (*v.*) to resist; to oppose.

withy (*n.*) a willow-tree or twig. See WITHE.

witless (*adj.*) simple-minded; stupid. WITLESSLY (*adv.*).

witlessness (*n.*) foolishness; stupidity.

witness (*n.*) 1. a watcher; an observer. 2. evidence; testimony. WITNESS (*v.*) 1. to see; to observe. 2. to give evidence; to testify.

witness-box (*n.*) place wherein a witness stands when examined before a court.

witticism (*n.*) a witty remark.

wittingly (*adv.*) knowingly; consciously.

witty (*adj.*) 1. sensible; shrewd. 2. funny; humorous. WITTILY (*adv.*).

wizard (*n.*) 1. an enchanter; sorcerer. 2. a conjurer; magician.

wizardry (*n.*) sorcery; enchantment.

wizened (*adj.*) dry; shrivelled.

woad (*n.*) a herb and its blue dye.

wobble (*v.*) to sway from side to side; to stagger. WOBBLE (*n.*) a stagger; totter. WOBBLER (*n.*).

wobbling (*adj.*) unsteady. WOBBLING (*n.*) unsteadiness.

woe (*n.*) misery; anguish.

woebegone (*adj.*) overcome with sorrow; greatly troubled.

woeful (*adj.*) distressing; tragic. WOEFULLY (*adv.*).

wold (*n.*) open hill-country.

wolf (*n.*) 1. wild, fierce animal of dog family. 2. a cruel, rapacious person. (*pl.* WOLVES). WOLF (*v.*) to eat ravenously.

wolf-hound (*n.*) hound trained to hunt wolves.

wolfish (*adj.*) savage; ravenous. WOLF-ISHLY (*adv.*).

wolverine (*n.*) a small, gluttonous animal.

woman (*n.*) a female human adult. (*pl.* WOMEN).

womanhood (*n.*) women collectively; womankind; female maturity.

womanish (*adj.*) suitable to a woman.

womankind (*n.*) the female sex.

womanliness (*n.*) femininity.

womanly (*adj.*) befitting a woman; feminine.

wombat (*n.*) Australian pouched mammal.

wonder (*v.*) 1. to marvel; to be amazed. 2. to ponder; to doubt. WONDER (*n.*) 1. a marvel; rarity. 2. astonishment; amazement. WONDERER (*n.*).

wonderful (*adj.*) amazing; remarkable. WONDERFULLY (*adv.*).

wondering (*adj.*) 1. marvelling. 2. pondering.

wonderland (*n.*) a place of marvels; a dreamland.

wonderment (*n.*) astonishment; bewilderment.

wondrous (*adj.*) remarkable; curious. WONDROUSLY (*adv.*).

wont (*adj.*) used to; accustomed to. WONT (*n.*) custom; habit.

won't (*abbrev.*) will not.

wonted (*adj.*) usual; ordinary.

woo (*v.*) to make love to; to court.

wood (*n.*) 1. a plantation of trees; a small forest. 2. timber. 3. musical instruments of wood.

woodbine (*n.*) the honeysuckle.

woodcock (*n.*) wild bird of snipe family.

wood-cut (*n.*) an engraving on wood, and a print from such.

wooded (*adj.*) tree-covered.

wooden (*adj.*) 1. made of wood. 2. stiff; awkward. WOODENLY (*adv.*).

woodenness (*n.*) stiffness; awkwardness.

woodland (*n.*) tree-covered country; forest.

woodman (*n.*) man who works in the woods; a tree-feller.

woodpecker (*n.*) bird that pecks holes in the bark of trees.

wood pulp (*n.*) wood chopped to pulp for paper-making.

woodworm (*n.*) destructive grub that bores into wood.

woody (*adj.*) consisting of wood; wooded.

woof (*n.*) the threads running across, or from side to side in weaving; the weft.

wooing (*n.*) courtship.

wooingly (*adv.*) persuasively.

wool (*n.*) 1. soft, curled hair growing on sheep. 2. hairy covering of plants.

wool-gathering (*adj.*) day-dreaming.

woollen (*adj.*) made of wool.

woolliness (*n.*) 1. the softness or fleeciness of wool. 2. absent-mindedness.

woolly (*adj.*) like wool; soft; warm.

woolsack (*n.*) large bag filled with wool on which the Lord Chancellor sits in the House of Lords.

word (*n.*) 1. a single part of speech; a term. 2. news; information. 3. a talk; conversation. 4. a promise; pledge. WORD (v.) to express in suitable words; to phrase.

worded (adj.) expressed in spoken or written words.

wordiness (n.) a fulness of words; verbosity.

words (n. pl.) argument; anger.

wordy (adj.) containing too many words; verbose.

work (n.) 1. something done or to be done; labour. 2. business; employment. 3. a literary or musical composition. 4. production. WORK (v.) 1. to toil; to labour. 2. to produce; to perform.

workable (adj.) can be done; practicable.

worker (n.) one who works; an employee.

working (adj.) 1. employed; busy. 2. operating; producing.

workmanlike (adj.) well-made; skilful.

workmanship (n.) 1. the quality and style of work; craftsmanship. 2. skill.

works (n. pl.) a factory; mill.

workshop (n.) place where simple work or repairing is done.

world (n.) 1. the earth and all it contains. 2. the universe and all creation. 3. the present existence. 4. this life and its affairs.

worldliness (n.) love of wealth and pleasure.

worldly (adj.) eager for enjoyment, pleasure, etc.

world-wide (adj.) known over the world; extensive.

worm (n.) 1. soft-bodied, limbless creature that bores underground. 2. the thread of a screw.

wormeaten (adj.) bored by worms; worthless.

wormwood (n.) plant with a bitter taste; a tonic.

worn (adj.) 1. used. 2. tired; wearied. WORN, past participle of verb to wear.

worried (adj.) anxious; troubled. WORRIEDLY (adv.).

worry (n.) care; anxiety. WORRY (v.) 1. to disturb; to make anxious. 2. to tease; to annoy.

worse (adj.) more bad; more ill. WORSE (adv.) more badly.

worship (n.) 1. reverence; adoration. 2. title given to a mayor or magistrate.

WORSHIP (v.) to reverence; to adore.

worshipful (adj.) worthy of respect; estimable. WORSHIPFULLY (adv.).

worshipper (n.) one who worships; a churchgoer.

worshipping (adj.) giving worship; praising.

worst (v.) to defeat; to conquer.

worsted (adj.) defeated. WORSTED (n.) woollen yarn.

worth (n.) 1. the value; cost. 2. the merit; excellence. WORTH (adj.) 1. having value. 2. meriting; possessing.

worthily (adv.) rightly; justly.

worthiness (n.) merit; excellence.

worthless (adj.) without merit; useless.

worthlessness (n.) uselessness; baseness.

worthy (adj.) 1. admirable; excellent. 2. upright; honest.

wound (n.) a hurt; injury. WOUND (v.) 1. to injure. 2. to grieve; to upset.

wounded (adj.) 1. injured. 2. grieved; stricken.

wrack (n.) 1. seaweed cast ashore. 2. shipwreck; ruin.

wraith (n.) a spectre; an apparition.

wrangle (v.) to dispute angrily; to brawl. WRANGLE (n.) a noisy quarrel; a brawl.

wrangler (n.) 1. one who wrangles; a brawler. 2. candidate who gains high honours in mathematics at Cambridge University.

wrangling (n.) a dispute; altercation.

wrap (v.) to fold up or round; to enclose. WRAP (n.) a shawl; scarf.

wrapper (n.) 1. anything in which an article can be wrapped. 2. a loose, warm outer garment.

wrapping (n.) a covering; an envelope.

wrath (n.) anger; rage.

wrathful (adj.) angry; furious. WRATHFULLY (adv.).

wreak (v.) to inflict punishment or vengeance.

wreath (n.) a garland or circlet of flowers.

wreathe (v.) to entwine; to encircle.

wreck (v.) 1. to ruin; to blight. 2. to be shipwrecked. WRECK (n.) 1. destruction; ruin. 2. a shipwreck. 3. a person ruined in health.

wreckage (n.) the remains of a wrecked vessel or cargo.

wren (n.) small, insect-eating bird.

wrench (v.) to twist round; to sprain.

WRENCH (*n.*) 1. a strain; sprain. 2. a tool to turn a nut or bolt.

wrest (*v.*) 1. to pull from by force. 2. to fail to tell the whole truth; to distort.

wrestle (*v.*) 1. to struggle; to strive. 2. to grapple in sport and try to throw.

wrestler (*n.*) one skilled in wrestling.

wrestling (*n.*) hand-to-hand grappling contest.

wretch (*n.*) 1. a miserable, unhappy person. 2. a base, worthless person.

wretched (*adj.*) 1. sad; pitiable. 2. contemptible; mean. WRETCHEDLY (*adv.*).

wretchedness (*n.*) misery; distress.

wriggle (*v.*) to twist like a snake or worm. WRIGGLE (*n.*) a worm-like twist. WRIGGLER (*n.*).

wriggling (*n.*) a writhing; squirming.

wring (*v.*) 1. to twist and squeeze; to squeeze out. 2. to shake the hands in sorrow.

wringer (*n.*) machine for squeezing water out of fabrics; a mangle.

wrinkle (*n.*) fold or crease in the skin due to age. 2. a helpful hint. WRINKLE (*v.*) to make creases in the brow.

wrist (*n.*) joint uniting hand and arm.

wristlet (*n.*) band with watch worn round the wrist.

writ (*n.*) a legal document conveying an order; summons.

write (*v.*) 1. to use pen or pencil in setting down words. 2. to do literary work. 3. to communicate by letter; to correspond.

writer (*n.*) 1. a clerk; scribe. 2. an author.

writhe (*v.*) to twist about in pain; to wriggle.

writing (*n.*) 1. the written words. 2. the letter; document.

written (*adj.*) given or done in writing.

wrong (*adj.*) 1. incorrect; inaccurate. 2. bad; wicked. 3. unjust; unfair. WRONG (*v.*) to treat unjustly; to injure. WRONG (*n.*) 1. an injustice; unfairness. 2. a misdeed; sin.

wrongdoer (*n.*) an offender; a sinner.

wrongdoing (*n.*) evil; sin.

wrongful (*adj.*) 1. injurious; unfair. 2. unlawful.

wrongly (*adv.*) unjustly; illegally.

wroth (*adj.*) angry; enraged.

wry (*adj.*) turned to one side; twisted.

wryly (*adv.*) in a twisted, crooked way.

wryneck (*n.*) small bird of woodpecker family.

X

Xmas (*n. abbrev.*) Christmas.

X-rays (*n. pl.*) rays which enable photographs to be taken of broken bones and other unseen objects.

xylonite (*n.*) a kind of celluloid; imitation ivory.

xylophone (*n.*) musical instrument made of wooden bars which sound when struck with wooden hammers.

Y

yacht (*n.*) a ship built for pleasure-sailing or racing. YACHT (*v.*) to cruise in a yacht.

yachting (*n.*) cruising in a yacht. YACHTSMAN (*n.*).

yak (*n.*) wild and domesticated ox of Central Asia.

yam (*n.*) a tropical plant and its edible, potato-like root.

yank (*v.*) to jerk; to pull sharply. YANK (*n.*) a jerk.

Yankee (*n.*) an inhabitant of the United States; an American.

yap (*v.*) to bark; to yelp. YAP (*n.*) a bark; yelp.

yard (*n.*) 1. an Imperial measure of length (3 feet). 2. a beam slung across a mast to support a sail. 3. a court or enclosure near a building.

yarn (*n.*) 1. spun thread. 2. a story; tale. YARN (*v.*) to tell a tale.

yarrow (*n.*) wild plant with a strong smell.

yawl (*n.*) a small fishing-boat.

yawn (*v.*) to open the mouth widely when tired; to gape. YAWN (*n.*) a gape caused by fatigue.

yawning (*adj.*) wide-open; gaping.

yea (*adv.*) yes; ay.

year (*n.*) the time taken by the earth to revolve once round the sun (365 days).

yearling (*n.*) an animal one year old.

yearly (*adj.*) happening once a year; annual.

yearn (*v.*) to long for; to desire.

yearning (*n.*) a longing; craving. YEARNING (*adj.*) longing for; desiring. YEARNINGLY (*adv.*).

yeast (*n.*) the froth of beer when fermented. YEASTY (*adj.*).

yell (*v.*) to shout out suddenly; to bawl. YELL (*n.*) a loud shout; bawl.

yellow (*n.*) a bright golden colour. YELLOW (*adj.*) 1. golden. 2. suspicious; envious.

yellow fever (*n.*) a serious tropical fever.

yellow-hammer (*n.*) a yellow-headed bunting.

yelp (*n.*) 1. a dog's cry in pain. 2. a sharp, sudden cry. YELP (*v.*) to cry out suddenly.

yeoman (*n.*) 1. a farmer. 2. a member of the Yeoman of the Guard; beefeater. 3. one of the yeomanry.

yeomanry (*n. pl.*) a body of volunteer cavalry once composed of farmers.

yeoman service (*n.*) hard work well done.

yes (*adv.*) word expressing agreement or consent; ay.

yesterday (*n.*) the day before to-day.

yet (*adv.*) still; further. YET (*conj.*) however; nevertheless.

yew (*n.*) evergreen tree with spreading branches.

yield (*v.*) 1. to submit; to surrender. 2. to produce; to supply. YIELD (*n.*) the product; crop.

yielding (*adj.*) 1. giving way; bending. 2. submissive; docile.

yoke (*n.*) a beam or chain forcing two or more things to work together; bond. YOKE (*v.*) 1. to couple; to link together. 2. to enslave.

yokel (*n.*) a countryman; farm worker.

yolk (*n.*) the yellow part of an egg.

yon; yonder (*adjs.*) over there; in that direction.

yore (*adv.*) a long time ago; in olden days.

you (*pron.*) the person or persons spoken to.

young (*adj.*) 1. under twenty-one years of age; not adult. 2. childish.

youngster (*n.*) a child.

youth (*n.*) 1. a lad in his 'teens; a young man. 2. the early part of life.

youthful (*adj.*) young; juvenile.

yowl (*v.*) to howl like a dog. YOWL (*n.*) a howl.

yule (*n.*) Christmas.

yule-log (*n.*) a log kept for the Christmas fire.

yule-tide (*n.*) the Christmas season.

Z

zany (*n.*) a clown; buffoon.

zeal (*n.*) enthusiasm; keenness.

zealot (*n.*) a person filled with zeal; fanatic.

zealous (*adj.*) eager; enthusiastic. ZEALOUSLY (*adv.*).

zebra (*n.*) African horse-like animal with striped body.

zenith (*n.*) 1. point in the sky exactly overhead. 2. the height of success or prosperity.

zephyr (*n.*) 1. a warm, gentle breeze. 2. an athlete's thin jersey for running, rowing, etc., in.

zero (*n.*) the symbol or cipher 0, meaning nothing.

zero hour (*n.*) 1. the moment fixed to begin. 2. twelve o'clock midday.

zest (*n.*) 1. zeal; eagerness. 2. enjoyment; gusto.

zigzag (*n.*) a series of sharp bends, like those in the letter Z. ZIGZAG (*v.*) to make Z-like bends. ZIGZAG (*adj.*) bending or turning Z-like.

zinc (*n.*) a blue-white metal.

zip (*n.*) a bag or clothes fastener worked by a sliding catch.

zither (*n.*) a harp-like instrument laid flat to play.

zodiac (*n.*) the sun's apparent circular path in the sky.

zone (*n.*) 1. a belt; girdle. 2. one of the belts into which the earth is divided according to climate.

zoo (*n.*) place where wild animals are exhibited.

zoological (*adj.*) concerned with animals.

zoologist (*n.*) one versed in zoology.

zoology (*n.*) the study of animals and animal life.

Zulu (*n.*) one of a South African native warrior race.

APPENDIX A

WORDS WITH AN ORIGIN IN FABLE, LEGEND OR HISTORY

Amazons. A race of warrior women, who lived in Asia Minor. They fought against the Greeks in the Trojan War.

Amp or **Ampère.** So named to honour André Ampère (1775–1836), a French scientist, who made important discoveries in electricity.

Apollo. Greek sungod, also name given to American series of space missions to the moon.

Atlas. A Titan or giant, who, according to Greek legend, upheld the heavens upon his shoulders. The figure of Atlas supporting the globe was often put upon the front page of an atlas.

Augustus. The first Roman Emperor, whose reign (27 B.C.–A.D. 14) is called the Golden Age. In his honour the Roman Calendar was altered, days being taken from some months to form a new month, August.

Braille. From the name of Louis Braille (1809–52) who invented this method of teaching the blind.

Cardigan. Named after the 7th Earl of Cardigan (1797–1868), who led the charge of the Light Brigade at Balaclava (1854) in the Crimean War.

Celsius. From Anders Celsius, a Swedish scientist, who invented the Celsius thermometer. (1701–44).

Cicerone. Cicero (106–43 B.C.) was a notable Roman orator and statesman. A guide is so named because he is the chief speaker to sightseers.

Colossus. The name of a gigantic statue of Apollo, the sun god, 100 ft. high, the work of the sculptor, Charos. It stood astride the harbour-mouth of Rhodes. It was a landmark and a Wonder of the World.

Dahlia. So named to honour Anders Dahl, a Swedish botanist.

Dunce. Though John Duns Scotus (1265–1308) was the greatest British philosopher in his day, his Dunsmen or followers became so narrow-minded that they were treated with contempt.

Echo. A mountain nymph. Her chatter annoyed Hera, who caused her to fade into a voice able only to repeat the last words of another.

Epicurean. A follower of the Greek philosopher, Epicurus (341–270 B.C.). He taught that happiness was the greatest blessing men could gain, but many misunderstood him and sought happiness in pleasure and luxury.

Europe. From the name of Europa, a maiden carried across the sea to Europe by Jupiter in the shape of a bull.

Farad. So named to honour Michael Faraday, a great English scientist (1791–1867).

Fate. The early Greeks believed that each human life was directed by three Fates or Destinies named Clotho, Lachesis and Atropos. The first spun the thread of life; the second wove it into its pattern until the third cut it.

Fauna. A Roman nymph of fields and woodlands, who, with her brother, Faunus, became the protector of animals.

Filbert. So named from St. Philibert, whose day (August 22) fell in the nutting season.

Flora. The Roman goddess of flowers.

Fortuna. A fickle Roman goddess, who scattered good and evil gifts at random from her Horn of Plenty.

Friday. The day of Frigga or Freya, wife of the Norse god, Woden or Odin, and goddess of youth.

Fuchsia. So named to honour Leonard Fuchs (1501–66), a German botanist.

Fury. The Furies were Alecto, Megaera and Tisiphone, dreaded Greek goddesses of vengeance, who relentlessly sought and punished the guilty.

Galvanism. So named to honour Luigi Galvani (1737–98), an Italian scientist, who discovered some important effects of an electric current.

Gamboge. The gum resin which gives the colour gamboge originally came from Cambodia, in Eastern Asia.

Gamp. Mrs. Sarah Gamp was a character portrayed by Charles Dickens in *Martin Chuzzlewit*. She was an old nurse, a busybody who liked strong tea, and whose bulky, badly-rolled umbrella was as well known as she herself.

Gaunt. Like John of Gaunt (1340–99), that is, of Ghent, his birthplace in Flanders. He was the 4th son of Edward III, and brother of the Black Prince. In appearance he was haggard, lean and grim.

Gauss. So named to honour Karl Gauss (1777–1855), a German mathematician, and early investigator of magnetism.

Gorgon. One of three snake-haired hags of Greek fable. Medusa, the most dreaded, turned those upon whom she looked into stone. Perseus slew her, then used her head to save Andromeda from a dragon.

Guillotine. Named after Joseph Guillotin (1738–1814), a French physician who invented this machine.

Guy. The effigy of a man burned on November 5th represents Guy Fawkes, a conspirator who, in 1605, planned to blow up the House of Lords where James I and both Houses of Parliament were about to assemble.

Harpy. One of three loathsome monsters who, the Greeks believed, caused the storms and floods which destroyed their crops and cattle.

Hector. The brave son of Priam, King of Troy. He defended Troy against the Greeks for ten years, when he was slain by Achilles in single combat. He was not a bully. His name was misused when, in the 17th century, London was disturbed by gangs of hooligans who called themselves Hectors.

Herculean. Hercules was the mightiest and most celebrated of all fabled heroes. He wrought twelve labours, each thought to be impossible to any man, and on his death was carried by the gods to Mt. Olympus.

Hermetic. Hermes, whom the Romans named Mercury, was the son of Jupiter, and the god of Science, the secrets of which he kept sealed in his head. See MERCURY.

Hesperus. Belonging to Hesperia, in ancient Italy.

Hyacinth. Hyacinthus was a Spartan youth, befriended by the god Apollo, who slew him accidentally with his quoit. The hyacinth flower sprang from his blood.

Hygiene. Hygieia was the Greek goddess of health and healing.

Iris. The Greek goddess of the rainbow, which the gods built as a bridge from heaven to earth to enable her to carry their messages.

January. The month of Janus, a Roman god protecting doorways and entrances. He opened the Door of the Year, and had two faces, one looking into the past; the other into the future.

Joule. So named to honour James Joule (1818–89), an English scientist famous for his study of electrical currents.

Joviality. Jupiter, when in a friendly mood, was worshipped as Jove. Children born at such times were gifted by him with a merry and happy disposition. See JUPITER.

July. Julius Cæsar (100–46 B.C.), Roman general and consul, reformed the Roman Calendar in 46 B.C., giving the year 365¼ days. To honour him the seventh month was given his name.

Jupiter. The ruler of the Roman gods, and protector of the Earth. His great statue, carved by Phidias, became a Wonder of the World. His name was given to the largest planet.

Lambert. Named to honour Johann Lambert (1728–1777), the German scientist.

Lynx. The sharp-eyed Linceus was Jason's look-out on the *Argo* when he sought the Golden Fleece. His keen sight distinguished small objects at immense distances.

Macadamize. From the name of John McAdam (1756–1836), a Scottish civil engineer, and inventor of the method of surfacing a road with small, broken stones.

Mackintosh. From the name of Charles Mackintosh, who invented the waterproof coat in 1823.

Mammon. Milton, in *Paradise Lost*, gave this name to the devil of greed for gold.

March. The month sacred to Mars, during which his festivals were celebrated in Rome.

Marconigram. From the name of Guglielmo (William) Marconi (1874–1937), a great Italian engineer and the inventor of wireless telegraphy.

Mars. The Roman god of war, and father of Romulus, founder of the Roman people. Mars, known as the "red planet", reminded the Romans of warfare and strife.

Martial. Like Mars, or warlike.

Mausoleum. Mausolus, King of Caria (377–53 B.C.), was laid in a tomb named the Mausoleum after him. It was so magnificent that it became a Wonder of the World.

Mentor. The name taken by the goddess Athene, who disguised herself as a wise old man to advise the warrior Ulysses and his son Telemachus.

Mercury. A Roman god whom the Greeks called Hermes, and the fleet messenger of the gods. The planet Mercury, being nearest to the sun, revolves round it rapidly. The liquid metal mercury, or quicksilver, flows very swiftly. See HERMES.

Mesmerize. So named after Mesmer, an Austrian physician who practised hypnotism and died in 1815.

Morphia. Named after Morpheus, Greek god of dreams, who sent sleep to ease pain.

Morse. The name of Samuel Morse (1791–1872), a Scottish-American electrician, who invented the electric telegraph (1843) and the "dot-and-dash" alphabet or code used to send telegraphic messages.

Mosaic. Called after Moses, the great leader and law-giver of the Israelites during the Exodus from Egypt.

Museum. Named from the Mouseion, the Greek temple of the Muses, the nine daughters of Zeus, or Jupiter, each of whom was a goddess representing an art, namely, music, drama, poetry, etc.

Narcissus. A beautiful Greek youth whose reflection in a pool so filled him with self-love that he pined and died, whereupon he was changed into the flower.

Nemesis. The Greek goddess of vengeance, who punished evildoers.

Neptune. The Roman god of the sea, over which he rode with his mermaids, on a dolphin, or on a white-maned horse.

Newton. So named to honour Sir Isaac Newton (1642–1727), the great scientist who discovered the laws of gravitation.

Oersted. So named to honour Hans Christian Oersted, the Danish scientist who discovered electro-magnestism. Born 1777, died 1851.

Ohm. Named to honour Georg Ohm (1787–1854), a German scientist who investigated electricity.

Orion. A fabled Greek hero and hunter. He offended the god Apollo, who brought about his death. To make his name immortal he was placed among the stars.

Panic. The Greek god Pan protected fields and flocks, but he was dreaded as he had power to fill all living creatures with fear.

Peony. Named from Paionios, a Greek god of medicine, the physician of the gods.

Petrel. The Bird of St. Peter, who walked upon the Lake of Gennesareth.

Pluto. The son of Saturn, and god of the underground world and its wealth. He was a brother of Jupiter and Neptune, whose names are also given to planets.

Pyramid. The shape is that of the great Pyramids of Egypt, built by the Pharaohs.

Python. The great serpent which rose from the mud left by the Flood which nearly destroyed the world. It dwelt in a deep cave, but was slain by Apollo.

Sandwich. A picnic favourite so named because it was invented by the 4th Earl of Sandwich.

Saturday. The day sacred to Saturn.

Saturn. The god of civilization and culture, and father of Jupiter, Neptune and Pluto. He was regarded as an evil god or power bringing gloom or woe, hence SATURNINE.

Siren. Sirens were fabled sea-nymphs who lured mariners to death by the sweetness of their songs. Ulysses, sailing near them, heard their song, but escaped destruction by stopping the ears of his sailors with wax.

Spartan. The men of Sparta, during the 6th to 4th centuries B.C., were brought up from babyhood strictly as soldiers. Their training was so rigorous that weaklings died. Those who lived became celebrated as brave soldiers unequalled in the ancient world.

Stentor. A Grecian herald who fought in the Trojan War. His voice was louder than the voices of fifty men together.

Tantalize. Tantalus was a son of Jupiter, who punished him with terrible torment for revealing his secrets. He was inflicted with intense hunger and thirst, and placed in a pool of water while luscious fruits dangled before his eyes. When he tried to drink or eat the water sank away and the fruits swung beyond his reach.

Tawdry. At the Fair of St. Audrey (October 17th) cheap, showy necklets and lace were sold.

Thursday. The day of Thor, the strong, brave Norse god of thunder, which was the sound of his hammer-blow.

Titanic. The Titans, the twelve children of Uranus, were powerful giants. They warred against Jupiter, who defeated them, and imprisoned all

except Oceanus in the Underworld where they represent the power of the earthquake and volcano.

Tuesday. Tiw was the name of the old Germanic God of War, and Tuesday is named after him.

Uranus. The ancient god of the heavens. He and his son, Saturn, were dethroned by Jupiter, who became the chief of the gods.

Valentine. St. Valentine was a Roman priest who became a Christian martyr. His day (14th February) happened to be that on which, by ancient custom, English people drew lots for lovers, who gave each other presents. When the old custom died, the day became one on which young people sent one another humorous love-tokens or greeting-cards.

Venus. The goddess of love and beauty whom the Greeks called Aphrodite, because she sprang from the sea foam. Cupid, who shot his arrows into the hearts of people to cause them to fall in love, was her son. The light from her planet is extremely brilliant and beautiful.

Volcano. So named after Vulcan, god of fire, and maker of all things wrought by the aid of fire. His workshop lay beneath Mt. Etna, Sicily, where he forged thunder-bolts for Jupiter. His workmen were the powerful giants called Cyclops.

Volt. So named to honour Alessandro Volta (1745–1827), an Italian scientist who invented many electrical instruments, and who is notable especially for his voltaic pile.

Vulcanize. From Vulcan, god of fire. See VOLCANO.

Watt. So named to honour James Watt (1736–1819), a celebrated Scottish engineer, and the first to make practical use of steam-power.

Wednesday. The Day of Woden or Odin, Norse god of wisdom, agriculture and war. In Valhalla he feasted with those slain in battle.

Wesleyan. So called after John Wesley (1703–1791), who founded the Methodist Church.

APPENDIX B

ABBREVIATIONS

A.A. Automobile Association
A.A.A. Amateur Athletic Association.
A.B. Able-bodied Seaman.
a.c. alternating current.
A.D. In the year of our Lord. (L. *anno Domini*).
A.D.C. Aide-de-camp.
ad lib. at pleasure; as desired. (L. *ad libitum*).
advt. advertisement.
A.F.C. Air Force Cross.
A.F.M. Air Force Medal.
A.d. Alderman.
a.m. before noon. (L. *ante meridiem*).
amp. ampére.
anon. anonymous or unknown.
appro. approval.
asst. assistant.
Aug. August.

B. or **b.** Born; Battle; bowled.
B.A. Bachelor of Arts.
Bart. Baronet.
Battn. Battalion.
B.B.C. British Broadcasting Corporation.
B.C. Before Christ.
B.E.A. British European Airways.
Beds. Bedfordshire.
B.E.M. British Empire Medal.
Berks. Berkshire.
B.M.A. British Medical Association.
B.O.A.C. British Overseas Airways Corporation.
Brit. Britain; British.
B.R. British Rail.
Bro. Brother.
B.R.S. British Road Services.
B.Sc. Bachelor of Science.
B.S.T. British Summer Time.
Bucks. Buckinghamshire.

C Celsius (Thermometer); Century; Roman numeral 100.

c. about (L. *circa*); chapter; cent.
c. or **cub.** cubic.
Cambs. Cambridgeshire.
Cantab. of Cambridge University.
Cantuar. of Canterbury.
Capt. Captain.
Cath. Catholic; Cathedral.
C.B. Companion of the Bath.
C.B.E. Commander, Order of the British Empire.
c.c. or **cm³** cubic centimetre(s).
C.C.F. Combined Cadet Force.
C.E. Church of England; Civil Engineer.
C.E.G.B. Central Electricity Generating Board.
C.H. Companion of Honour.
ch. chapter.
chem. chemistry; chemical.
Ches. Cheshire.
C.I.D. Criminal Investigation Department.
C.I.G.S. Chief of Imperial General Staff.
C.-in-C. Commander-in-Chief.
cm centimetre(s)
C.M.G. Companion of St. Michael and St. George.
C.M.S. Church Missionary Society.
c/o. care of.
C.O. Commanding Officer.
Co. County; Company.
C.O.D. Cash on Delivery.
Col. Colonel.
conj. conjunction.
Co-op. Co-operative (stores).
Cpl. Corporal.
C.P.R. Canadian Pacific Railway.
Cr. Credit.
C.T.C. Cyclists' Touring Club.
C.V.O. Companion of the (Royal) Victorian Order.
cwt hundredweight(s).

D. Roman numeral 500.

d penny; pence (L. *debarius*); daughter; died.

D.B.E. Dame Commander of the British Empire.

d.c. direct current.

D.C.M. Distinguished Conduct Medal.

D.D. Doctor of Divinity.

Dec. December.

deg. degree(s).

Dept. Department.

Derby. Derbyshire.

Devon. Devonshire.

D.F.C. Distinguished Flying Cross.

D.F.M. Distinguished Flying Medal.

D.G. by the grace of God (L. *Dei gratia*).

D.Lit. Doctor of Literature or Letters.

do. ditto; the same.

doz. dozen.

Dr. Doctor (physician); debtor; debit.

D.S.C. Distinguished Service Cross.

D.Sc. Doctor of Science.

D.S.M. Distinguished Service Medal.

D.S.O. Distinguished Service Order.

D.V. God willing (L. *Deo volente*).

dwt. pennyweight(s).

E. East.

Ebor. of York.

ed. editor or edited by.

E.E.C. European Economic Community.

E.F.T.A. European Free Trade Association.

e.g. for example (L. *exempli gratia*).

Eng. England; English.

E.R. Elizabeth Regina (Queen).

Esq. Esquire.

etc. and the rest. (L. *et cetera*).

exor. executor.

F. or Fahr. Fahrenheit (Thermometer).

F.A. Football Association.

F.D. Defender of the Faith. (L. *Fidei Defensor*).

Feb. February.

fem. feminine.

F.H. Fire hydrant.

F.M. Field Marshal.

F.O. Foreign Office; Flying Officer.

f.o.b. free on board.

Fri. Friday.

F.R.S. Fellow of the Royal Society.

ft foot or feet; fort.

fur furlong(s).

g gramme.

G.B. Great Britain.

G.C. George Cross.

G.H.Q. General Headquarters.

G.L.C. Greater London Council.

Glos. Gloucestershire.

G.M. George Medal.

G.M.T. Greenwich Mean Time.

G.O.C. General Officer Commanding.

Govt. Government.

G.P. General Practitioner.

G.P.O. General Post Office.

G.T. Gran Turismo.

h hour.

Hants. Hampshire.

H.C.F. Highest Common Factor.

H.E. His Excellency; His Eminence.

h.e. high explosive.

Herts. Hertfordshire.

H.H. His (Her) Highness; His Holiness (the Pope).

H.M. His (Her) Majesty.

H.M.I. His (Her) Majesty's Inspector of Schools.

H.M.S. His (Her) Majesty's Ship.

Hon. Honourable; Honorary.

Hon. Sec. Honorary Secretary.

Hon. Treas. Honorary Treasurer.

H.P. High Pressure; Half-pay; Hire Purchase.

h.p. horse-power.

H.Q. Headquarters.

H.R.H. His (Her) Royal Highness.

ht. height; heat.

h.t. high tension.

Hunts. Huntingdonshire.

I.C.I. Imperial Chemical Industries.

i.e. that is. (L. *id est*).

I.L.O. International Labour Office (Geneva).

in inch(es).

incog. incognito, or unknown.

infra dig. undignified. (L. *infra dignitatem*).

inst. of this month (instant).

Inst.C.E. Institution of Civil Engineers.

I.O.M. Isle of Man.

I.O.W. Isle of Wight.

I.Q. Intelligence Quotient.

I.T.A. Independent Television Authority.

i.t.a. Initial Teaching Alphabet.

ital. italic.

Jan. January.
J.P. Justice of the Peace.
jr. or jun. junior.

K. King.
K.C. King's Counsel.
k.c. kilocycle.
kg kilogram(me).
km kilometre(s).
Kt. Knight.
kw kilowatt(s).

l litre.
L. Roman numeral 50; Learner.
L.A.C. Leading Aircraftman.
Lancs, Lancashire.
Lat. Latitude.
lb pound(s) weight.
l.b.w. leg before wicket.
l.c.m. lowest common multiple.
Leics. Leicestershire.
Lincs. Lincolnshire.
Litt.D. Doctor of Letters or Literature.
LL.B. Bachelor of Laws.
LL.D. Doctor of Laws.
Long. Longitude.
Lsd Pounds (*Librae*), shillings (*solidi*) pence (*denarii*). Also £.s.d.
Lt. or Lieut. Lieutenant.
L.T.A. Lawn Tennis Association.
Ltd. Limited.

M. Majesty; Roman numeral 1,000; Monsieur.
m metre(s); mile(s); minute(s); married.
M.A. Master of Arts.
Maj. Major. MAJ-GEN. Major-General.
Mar. March.
masc. masculine.
maths. mathematics.
max. maximum.
M.B. Bachelor of Medicine.
M.B.E. Member, Order of the British Empire.
M.C. Military Cross.
M.C.C. Marylebone Cricket Club.
M.D. Doctor of Medicine.
memo. memorandum.
Messrs. Sirs. (Used as a plural of Mr.).
Meth. Methodist.
M.F.H. Master of Fox Hounds.
min. minute(s); minimum.
misc. miscellaneous.
ml millilitre.

Mlle. Mademoiselle.
M.M. Military Medal.
Mme. Madame (French).
M.O. Medical Officer.
Mon. Monday.
M.P. Member of Parliament.
m.p.h. miles per hour.
M.P.S. Member of the Pharmaceutical Society.
Mr. Mister; Master. MRS. Mistress.
M.R.C.P. Member of the Royal College of Physicians.
M.R.C.S. Member of the Royal College of Surgeons.
M.R.C.V.S. Member of the Royal College of Veterinary Surgeons.
M.S. Manuscript. (*pl.* MSS.).
M.Sc. Master of Science.
Mt. Mount; mountain.
Mt. Rev. Most Reverend.
MTB. Motor torpedo-boat.
Mus.B, Bachelor of Music.
Mus.Doc. Doctor of Music.
Mus.M. Master of Music.
M.V.O. Member of the (Royal) Victorian Order.
myth. mythological.

N. North.
N.A.A.F.I. Navy, Army and Air Force Institutes.
Nat. National.
N.A.T.O. North Atlantic Treaty Organization.
N.B. Note well; take notice. (L. *nota bene*).
N.C.B. National Coal Board.
N.C.L. National Carriers Limited.
N.C.O. Non-commissioned officer.
nem. con. unanimously. (L. *nemine contradicente*).
neut. neuter.
N.F.S. National Fire Service.
N.H.I. National Health Insurance.
No. Number. (L. *numero*).
nom. nominative.
Northants. Northamptonshire.
Northumb. Northumberland.
Notts. Nottinghamshire.
Nov. November.
N.S.P.C.C. National Society for the Prevention of Cruelty to Children.
N.S.W. New South Wales, Australia.
N.T. New Testament.

num. numeral; number.

N.Z. New Zealand.

Ob. died. (L. *obit*).

O.B.E. Officer of the British Empire.

O.C. Officer Commanding.

Oct. October.

O.E.E.C. Organization for European Economic Co-operation.

O.H.M.S. On His (Her) Majesty's Service.

O.M. (Member of the) Order of Merit.

opp. opposite.

O.S. Ordinary Seaman; Old Style (Calendar); Ordnance Survey.

O.T. Old Testament.

Oxon. Oxfordshire.

oz ounce(s).

p. after. (L. *post*); page; pressure perch(es).

p.a. yearly. (L. *per annum*).

par. paragraph; parish.

P.A.Y.E. Pay As You Earn. (Income Tax).

P.C. Privy Councillor; Police Constable.

p.c. post card.

pd. paid.

P.E. Physical Education.

per cent. by the hundred. (L. *per centum*).

Ph.D. Doctor of Philosophy.

P.M. Prime Minister.

p.m. after noon. (L. *post meridiem*).

P.M.G. Postmaster-General; Paymaster-General.

P.O. Post Office; Postal Order; Petty Officer.

P.O.W. Prisoner of War.

P.R.A. President of the Royal Academy.

prep. preposition.

pro. professional.

Prof. Professor.

pron. pronoun; pronunciation.

pro tem. for the time being. (L. *pro tempore*).

Prov. Provost; Province. PROV. provisional.

prox. in or of the next month. (L. *proximo*).

P.S. Postscript. (L. *post scriptum*). (*pl.* PSS).

ps. psalm.

P.T. Physical Training.

Pt. Point; Port (geog.).

pt pint(s); part; participle.

Pte. Private solider.

P.T.O. Please turn over.

Q.C. Queen's Counsel.

Q.E.D. which was to be proved. (L. *quod erat demonstrandum*).

Q.M. Quartermaster. Q.M.G. Quartermaster-general. Q.M.S. Quartermaster-Sergeant.

qr quarter(s); quire(s).

qt quart(s).

quad. quadrangle; quadrilateral.

q.v. which see. (L. *quod vide*). (*pl.* qqv.)

R. King, Queen. (L. *Rex, Regina*).

R.A. Royal Academician; Royal Artillery.

R.A.C. Royal Automobile Club; Royal Armoured Corps.

R.A.F. Royal Air Force.

R.A.M. Royal Academy of Music.

R.A.M.C. Royal Army Medical Corps.

R.A.O.C. Royal Army Ordnance Corps.

R.A.S.C. Royal Army Service Corps.

R.C. Roman Catholic; Red Cross.

R.C.M. Royal College of Music. R.C.O., of Organists. R.C.P., of Physicians. R.C.S., of Surgeons.

Rd. Road.

R.D.C. Rural District Council.

R.E. Royal Engineers.

recd. received.

ref. referee; reference.

Regt. Regiment.

Rev. Reverend.

R.G.S. Royal Geographical Society.

R.I.P. May he rest in peace. (L. *Requiescat in pace*).

R.M.S. Royal Mail Steamer.

R.N. Royal Navy. R.N.R., Royal Naval Reserve. R.N.V.R., Royal Naval Volunteer Reserve.

R.O.C. Royal Observer Corps.

r.p.m. or **rev/min** revolutions per minute.

R.S.M. Regimental Sergeant-Major.

R.S.P.C.A. Royal Society for Prevention of Cruelty to Animals.

R.S.V.P. Please reply. (Fr. *répondéz s'il vous plaît*).

Rt. Hon. Right Honourable.

Rt. Rev. Right Reverend.

R.U. Rugby Union (Football).

Ry. Railway.

R.Y.S. Royal Yacht Squadron.

S. South.

s second(s); shilling(s).

S.A. Salvation Army; South Africa.

S.A.Y.E. Save As You Earn.

Salop. Shropshire.

Sat. Saturday.

Scot. Scotland.

Sec. Secretary.

Sept. September.

Sergt. Sergeant.

S.H.A.E.F. Supreme Headquarters of the Allied Expeditionary Force.

S.H.A.P.E. Supreme Headquarters of the Allied Powers, Europe.

SI Système International d'Unités, a form of metric system.

S.M. Sergeant-Major.

Soc. Society.

S.P.C.K. Society for the Promotion of Christian Knowledge.

S.P.G. Society for the Propogation of the Gospel.

sp. gr. specific gravity.

Sqd. Ldr. Squadron Leader (R.A.F.).

S.S. Steamship.

St. Saint; Street; Strait.

st stone (weight).

Staffs. Staffordshire.

Sun. Sunday.

Supt. Superintendent.

Th. Thursday.

Toc H Talbot House.

Treas. Treasurer.

T.U. Trades Union.

T.U.C. Trades Union Congress.

Tues. Tuesday.

TV. Television.

U.D.C. Urban District Council.

U.K. United Kingdom (England, Scotland, Wales and Northern Ireland.)

ult. last month. (L. *ultimo*).

U.N.E.S.C.O. United Nations Educational, Scientific and Cultural Organization.

Univ. University.

U.N.O. United Nations Organization.

U.N.R.R.A. United Nations Relief and Rehabilitation Administration.

U.S.A. United States of America.

U.S.S.R. Union of Soviet Socialist Republics.

U.H.F. Ultra High Frequency.

V Volt; Roman numeral 5.

v. against (L. *versus*); velocity.

V.A.D. Voluntary Aid Detachment.

vb. verb.

V.C. Victoria Cross.

V.H.F. Very high frequency (wireless).

V.T.O.L. Vertical take-off and landing.

W. West.

W.D. War Department.

W.E.A. Workers' Educational Association.

Wed. Wednesday.

wkt. wicket.

Wilts. Wiltshire.

W/L wave-length.

W.O. War Office; Warrant Officer; Wireless Operator.

Worcs. Worcestershire.

W.R.A.C. Women's Royal Army Corps.

W.R.A.F. Women's Royal Air Force.

W.R.N.S. Women's Royal Naval Service.

W/T Wireless Telegraphy.

wt. weight.

W.V.S. Women's Voluntary Service.

X. Roman numeral 10.

yd yard(s).

Y.H.A. Youth Hostel Association.

Y.M.C.A. Young Men's Christian Association.

Yorks. Yorkshire.

Y.W.C.A. Young Women's Christian Association.

EXERCISES

for use

in connection with

A SIMPLIFIED DICTIONARY

SCHOFIELD & SIMS LTD

HUDDERSFIELD

FOREWORD

A DICTIONARY is always a useful book to have—in school, at home, and elsewhere.

This dictionary is particularly useful, because it is a simplified edition. That means it has been made easier for you to use by omitting words you are not likely to require, but including those you ought to know.

To obtain the utmost value from the dictionary, you must learn to use it quickly and well. The exercises which follow this foreword should help you to do both.

The words in a dictionary are arranged in alphabetical order, so that the first thing is to learn exactly where the letters come—near the beginning, in the middle, or towards the end. You will then not waste time searching in the wrong place, but will go straight to the word you wish to find.

Words frequently have more than one meaning and also more than one use, so be sure to look at the complete explanation *carefully*.

It may be necessary to take more than one step in order to discover the meaning of a word, so that you can fully understand its meaning.

e.g., a vision (p. 251) means a 'phantom'; but (p. 162) a 'phantom' simply means 'a ghost'.

You will find the Appendices A and B and also the list of Abbreviations at the end of the book extremely useful, and if you work the exercises and the word-puzzles correctly or almost correctly, you will have learnt how to use A Simplified Dictionary.

© 1959

SCHOFIELD & SIMS LTD

7217 0122 1

Reprinted 1961	Reprinted 1970
Reprinted 1962	Reprinted 1971
Reprinted 1963	Reprinted 1972
Reprinted 1964	Reprinted (twice) 1973
Reprinted 1965	Reprinted 1974
Reprinted 1967	Reprinted 1975
Reprinted 1968	Reprinted 1976
Reprinted 1969	Reprinted 1977
	Reprinted 1978

EXERCISE 1

Place the pairs of letters in the circle in front of the letters on the right to form the names of animals. (The first has been done.)

ze
we ha
do le an
sq fe ja
be ot
ho

*ja*ckal, - - rse, - - re,

- - asel, - - ter, - - aver,

- - bra, - - opard, - - nkey,

- - rret, - - telope, - - uirrel.

EXERCISE 2

pot - - -, mut - - -, tof - - -, qui - - -, pas - - -, wal - - -, muf - - -, pla - - -, mar - - -, che - - -.

These six-letter words when completed are the names of things to eat. Choose any three letters from the row below to complete the words.

a c c e e e e e f f i i n n n n o o o r r s t t t t u w y

(It is a good plan to write the list on a piece of paper, and to cross out the letters as they are used. Do not cross them out in this book.)

EXERCISE 3

The words below all contain a long e sound like the e in be. Complete the words, filling the spaces with ei, ie, ee or ea.

rec - - ve, gr - - f, gr - - dy, rep - - t, bes - - ge, dec - - ve, w - - ve, br - - f, s - - thing, th - - ve, f - - rce, sm - - r.

EXERCISE 4

Write in the missing letters in these words which are connected with books of all kinds:

ch - p - er, ti - le, poe - - y, p - - - e, fict - - -, ve - s -, char - - - er, no - - l, pr - nt, aut - - -, pr - f - - e, cont - - - s.

EXERCISE 5

Some articles belonging to a gardener, a sailor, a builder, a policeman and a draughtsman have got mixed up. Can you sort them out?

ruler, rake, sextant, hoe, baton, whistle, compass, plumb, compasses, hammer.

3

EXERCISE 6

per	end	rig	iol
aci	ani	hl	na
ov	ns	ch	ow

Use the groups of letters above to complete these names of flowers:

ger - - - um, or - - id, cl - - er, lav - - - er, pim - - - nel,
ma - - - old, da - - ia, car - - tion, sn - - drop, hy - - - nth,
pa - - y, v - - - et.

EXERCISE 7

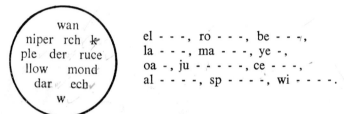

el - - -, ro - - -, be - - -,
la - - - -, ma - - - -, ye - -,
oa - -, ju - - - - - -, ce - - -,
al - - - - -, sp - - - - -, wi - - - - -.

Use the groups of letters in the circle to finish the names of trees alongside.

EXERCISE 8
What would you expect to see in the following?

granary, rectory, aviary, swannery, vinery, apiary, rookery, cannery, colliery, dairy.

EXERCISE 9
From Appendix A (p. 264) find with whom these words are connected:

atlas, mackintosh, filbert, siren, watt.

EXERCISE 10
These words end either with -le or with -el. Write them in two columns accordingly.

mirac - -, assemb - -, dishev - -, probab - -, shrapn - -,
mors - -, spectac - -, shriv - -, mobi - -, muss - -.

EXERCISE 11

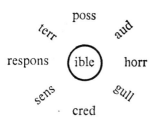

poss
terr
aud
respons (ible) horr
sens
gull
cred

The words above all end in -ible. Write them out and find what each word means.

EXERCISE 12
Did you enjoy working out Exercise 2? Here is a *similar* exercise with words of seven letters.

let - - - -, rhu - - - -, spi - - - -, her - - - -, tre - - - -, sau - - - -, par - - - -, apr - - - -, bis - - - -, cur - - - -.

a a a a a b b c c c c c e e e e g g h i i i l l n n n o r r r s s t t t t u u y

EXERCISE 13
Here are the clues to help you to find four words. They are all connected with the number two, and they all begin with tw.

two times, tw - - -; a pair, tw - - -; faint daylight, tw - - - - - -; two children born at the same time, tw - - -.

EXERCISE 14
Find words which have the same meaning as those in italics:

flickering light, *legible* handwriting, *rancid* butter, *variable* weather, *reliable* friend, *shivering* child, *trifling* incident, *accurate* figures, *vertical* line, *noisy* crowd.

5

EXERCISE 15
Look up the meaning of the adjectives on the left, then write a suitable noun alongside.

mouldy	,	official	,
glorious	,	stately	,
oriental	,	portable	,
meagre	,	protective	,
glowing	,	ordinary	,

EXERCISE 16
The first letter of the Greek alphabet is alpha; the last letter is om - - -.

EXERCISE 17
Pair (*a*) these goods:

sweetmeats, spectacles, hat, nectarines, goose, pliers, flex, sulphur, dahlias, elastic

with (*b*) the kind of shopkeeper who sells them:

electrician, fruiterer, milliner, optician, chemist, ironmonger, confectioner, florist, poulterer, haberdasher.

EXERCISE 18

(*a*) pedal, pebble, peer, peck, peculiar, peg.
(*b*) grain, grand, gown, graceful, grammar, granary.
(*c*) snarl, snake, snip, sneak, smug, snare.

How quickly can you arrange the above words in alphabetical order?

EXERCISE 19
Complete these names of precious stones:

tur - - - - - -, op - -, pe - - -, aga - -, top - -, ja - -, dia - - - -, gar - - -, r - - -, sap - - - - -, on - -, co - - -, em - - - - -.

Try to find the colour of each stone.

EXERCISE 20

With the help of the clues finish these names of different kinds of cloth:

i. woven from flax (li - - -); *ii.* rich silk or fine linen (dam - - -); *iii.* cloth glossy on one side (sa - - -); *iv.* made from plastic material (ny - - -); *v.* heavy woollen cloth (tw - - -); *vi.* thick silky cloth (ve - - - - -); *vii.* cotton cloth printed with coloured patterns (cr - - - - - -); *viii.* thin, gauzy cotton cloth (mu - - - -); *ix.* strong, coarse cloth (can - - -); *x.* soft woollen cloth (fl - - - - -).

EXERCISE 21

Write these words in a list, and alongside write a word with a similar meaning:

academy, talon, ode, flurry, infirmary, odious, flake, diadem, bundle, pleat.

EXERCISE 22

All these words are names connected with a bicycle:

(*a*) the part one presses with one's foot (p——); (*b*) the rider's seat (s——); (*c*) the tiny hole which sometimes occurs in the rubber part of the wheel (p——); (*d*) the steering part (h——); (*e*) the part used for slowing or stopping the machine (b——); (*f*) the centre of the wheel (h——); (*g*) cogged wheels (g——); (*h*) the object used for blowing air into the inner tube (p——).

EXERCISE 23

These words are the names of stringed or wind musical instruments. Make two lists accordingly.

violin, flute, trumpet, guitar, trombone, banjo, saxophone, mandolin, cello.

EXERCISE 24

Which of these words are connected with the study of music?

treble, bassoon, sonnet, cord, baton, festoon, crochet, sonata, chord, crotchet.

EXERCISE 25

The central part of a church is the (knave, nave).
Choose the correct word from the bracket.

EXERCISE 26

telegram, telescope, telephone, telegraphy, television, telephoto.

From the words above find the answers to:

(*a*) the wireless transmission of images which can be seen.
(*b*) message sent by telegraph.
(*c*) photograph transmitted by wireless.
(*d*) electrical apparatus which enables a person to speak to another at a distance.
(*e*) system of communicating by telegraph.
(*f*) instrument which makes distant objects seem near.

EXERCISE 27

(*a*) Pair the words which are similar in meaning:

project, rebel, rebuke, detest, protrude, scold, serious, revolt, loathe, momentous.

(*b*) Three of these words have a similar meaning; write the one which is different:

scarcity, abundance, dearth, famine.

EXERCISE 28

What would you expect to find in

(*a*) a scuttle, (*b*) a tank, (*c*) a caddy, (*d*) a sty, (*e*) a vat?

EXERCISE 29

In each line find the word which is different in meaning:

(*a*) traditional, customary, unusual.
(*b*) inscribe, describe, engrave.
(*c*) gratuity, gratefulness, gratitude.
(*d*) fictitious, vicious, invented.
(*e*) neglectful, remiss, amiss.
(*f*) oppose, resist, desist.
(*g*) reasonable, seasonable, sensible.
(*h*) actual, factual, compact.
(*i*) durable, pliable, flexible.
(*j*) wasteful, economical, thrifty.

8

EXERCISE 30

barrister, vestry, reredos, summons, plaintiff, mitre, felony, lectern, cloister, larceny, verdict, chancel, pew, writ.

Write the words connected with the Law in one column, and those connected with the Church in another.

EXERCISE 31

(*a*) Snow covered the trees like a (mantle, mantel).

(*b*) The stately (galleon, gallon) sailed into the Spanish port.

Choose the correct words from the brackets.

EXERCISE 32

medal, site, steal, grown, meddle, feat, sight, vein, steel, vain, way, feet, weigh, groan, stile, style.

These clues will help you to find the answers in the list above:

(*a*) to interfere; (*b*) a fashion in dress; (*c*) a moaning sound; (*d*) a notable deed; (*e*) a blood-vessel carrying blood to the heart; (*f*) a plot of ground on which to build; (*g*) to rob; (*h*) to find how heavy something is.

EXERCISE 33

Thomas Cook, Hon. Sec., F.O. John Ellis, Mary Dales, B.Sc., Frederick Ames, V.C., Hon. Percy Mann, Sergt. David Foster, Roland Avery, Mus.D., Hector Noble, Q.C., Mme. Averil Deslangue, Robert Neill, M.P.

From the list above write the name of:

(*a*) the soldier; (*b*) the person who had studied science; (*c*) the French lady; (*d*) the person who had studied music; (*e*) the soldier who had shown exceptional bravery; (*f*) the man who did secretarial work; (*g*) the man who would be most likely to appear in court; (*h*) the son of a peer; (*i*) the man who is interested in the governing of the country; (*j*) the officer in the Royal Air Force.

EXERCISE 34

Find the meanings of the words VICE and VIRTUE.

Make two columns and write these words accordingly:

sloth, reliance, punctuality, greed, contentment, sarcasm, loyalty, obstinacy, avarice, friendliness, laziness, peevishness, steadfastness, meekness.

9

EXERCISE 35
Alongside each word on the left write two words of similar meaning:

                          1.   2.

honourable
laborious
stubborn
weary
credible

EXERCISE 36
Plants are often referred to as annuals, biennials, triennials, perennials.

Annual means   •
Biennial means   •
Triennial means   •
Perennial means   •

EXERCISE 37
Mono means one; bi means two; tri means three; quad means four.

(*a*) Write these syllables (prefixes) to complete these words:
- - - - gram, - - ped, - - - - rangle, - - - - plane, - - - o,
- - - - ruped, - - - pod, - - cycle.
(*b*) Find the meanings of the words

EXERCISE 38

pianist, chiropodist, philatelist, realist, manicurist, harpist, pugilist, geologist, psychologist, ventriloquist.

Choose words from the list above.

(*a*) A player on the harp is a ——.
(*b*) One who attends to one's hands is a ——, whilst a —— attends to one's feet.
(*c*) A man who boxes is a ——.
(*d*) A —— is a person who plays the piano.
(*e*) A collector of postage-stamps is a ——.
(*f*) The earth's structure is studied by a ——.
(*g*) A —— is a person who is able to make his voice appear to come from another direction.
(*h*) A —— is a person interested in actual things, not ideas.
(*i*) One who studies the mind is a ——.

EXERCISE 39

Rev., H.M.I., M.P.S., J.P., Mlle., Corp., M.P., M.R.C.V.S., Dr., P.C., Col.

These titles and abbreviations belong to the names below. Write out the names with the suitable abbreviations. Remember to write the title before the name.

e.g., Col. John Hope.

John Rogers (minister of the Church), Henry Sawyer (chemist), John Hope (officer in the Army), Eric Allen (physician), Vincent Taylor (veterinary surgeon), David Hardcastle (Inspector of Schools), Lucille Banon (an unmarried French lady), Richard James (a member of Parliament), Albert Webb (a magistrate), Brian Scott (a policeman), Peter Ford (a non-commissioned soldier).

EXERCISE 40

In this dictionary, after the words in heavy type, you will find letters in italics in brackets which tell you what part of speech the word is. Quite often a word does the work of more than one part. Make a list of the words below, and alongside write what part of speech they are.

e.g., light   noun, verb, adjective.

square, pay, smoke, thin, pearl, thread, when, necessary, little, limp.

EXERCISE 41

Fill in the spaces below with the corresponding parts of speech.

(a) Noun	Adjective	Verb
falsehood	false	falsify
purity	——	purify
intensity	——	intensify
——	safe	save
description	——	——
——	performing	——
——	——	originate
offence	——	——

11

(b)

Noun	Adjective	Verb
instruction	instructive	instruct
——	imaginary	——
——	——	neglect
pleasure	——	——
——	nourishing	——
——	——	enjoy
economy	——	——
——	——	protect
satisfaction	——	——
advice	——	——

EXERCISE 42
Choose the correct word from each bracket:

(a) The rich freely gave (arms, alms) to the poor.

(b) The rent was promptly paid when it fell (due, dew).

(c) The partners crossed the (lynx, links) after their game of golf.

(d) Both men prepared for the (dual, duel).

(e) The children found a (creek, creak) among the rocks.

(f) The (draft, draught) caused the papers to be blown off the desk.

(g) A (hoard, horde) of savages came towards us.

EXERCISE 43
What is meant by the following?

gamp, gym., pram., duck (sport), vet., perm., maths., T.V., lab., Toc H.

EXERCISE 44
These words are interesting because they read the same both ways:

civic, sexes, minim, sees, deed, level.

Try to find as many other words which follow this rule as you can.

EXERCISE 45
Fill in the spaces below with suitable words:

Mr. Read was what one might call a pru - - - - man. He had worked hard throughout his life, and as a result of his th - - - -, had amas - - - quite a large am - - - - of money.

12

He had no family of his own, being a bach - - - -, so he intended to beq - - - - - his money to his nieces and nephews. His sol - - - - - - was given explicit instructions, and Mr. Read felt happy in the hope that those who would benefit would use their le - - - - wisely.

EXERCISE 46

Here are some advertisements. Try to complete them suitably.

(a) For sa - -, s - - - -detached house, rur - - area, fo - - bedrooms, two enter - - - - - - - rooms, kit - - - -, etc. Gar - - -. Large garden at r - - -. On bus ro - - -. Box 123.

(b) Dou - - - -fronted bun - - - - - for sale. Bu - - t 1950. In ex - - - - - - - condition. Overlooking riv - - -. Easy acc - - - to station. Owner going abr - - - -. Box 999.

(c) Wanted to h - - - or pur - - - - - -. Cara - - -, 4 be - - -, well-equi - - - -, stove, kit - - - - -. State pr - - - and dct - - - - -. Box 456.

EXERCISE 47

1. A stingy person is a - - - - person.
2. Is an artichoke a flower or a vegetable?
3. Lowing is the cry of - - - - - - -.
4. A vein carries blood - - the heart, and an artery carries blood - - - - the heart.
5. The words NO and NOT are called neg - - - - - -.
6. Nicotine is a - - - - - - - - - substance found in tobacco.
7. What does one do to tether an animal?
8. A fathom measures —— feet.
9. Wine is sometimes put into a fl - - - -.
10. A kipper is a ——, which has been cured by smoke.

EXERCISE 48

1. A bright red colour is sometimes v - - - - - - - - -.
2. If you sat on a verandah would you be under cover?
3. A small, white heron is called an e - - - - -.
4. Can you eat an edible fruit?
5. Is teak strong wood?
6. A t - - - - - is a bicycle for two riders.
7. An enigma is a - - - - - - or a - - - - - -.

8. Can indelible writing be rubbed out?
9. Which of these words can be used to describe a very active person?
   feeble, vigorous, energetic, slothful.
10. Is amber a glowing coal, or the colour yellow?

EXERCISE 49
1. To what family does a dolphin belong?
2. What colour does a female glow-worm's tail shine at night?
3. Rats, mice, squirrels and rabbits are called ro - - - - - because they g - - -.
4. Is a madrigal played or sung?
5. Which of these are trees?
   magnolia, mandrill, acacia, mahogany.
6. Write the missing letter in each word:
   choc - late, sno - drop, ex - ept, r - ubarb, g - arl.
7. The distant line where the earth and sky seem to meet is called the h - - - - - -.
8. Are oats, rice, barley 'serials' or 'cereals'?
9. Would a sombre room be a pleasant room?
10. In what country are marmosets found?

EXERCISE 50
1. How many people take part in a duel?
2. Nutriment is another word for n - - - - - - - - - - -.
3. What animal does Reynard represent?
4. When was the coin known as a guinea last minted?
5. The moon and the earth are - - - - - - - -.
6. Where would you find a dungeon?
7. Which of these are tools and which are machines?
   awl, drill, bit, lathe, loom, gimlet.
8. When horses stampede do they stand quite still?
9. Is an escapade the story of an escape or of a naughty prank?
10. Would John's mother be pleased if John went home minus his new cap?

EXERCISE 51
1. Where is a pillion-seat on a motor-cycle?
2. Pewter is a mixture of —— and ——; brass is a mixture of —— and ——.

14

3. Lions are car - - - - - - - - or flesh-eating animals, but dogs eat all kinds of food. They are om - - - - - - - - creatures.
4. Have fictitious characters in books really lived?
5. Where would you fish for roach, trout, mackerel, pike?
6. How many pints does it take to make one gallon?
7. How much wine does a hogshead hold when full?
8. On a Fahrenheit thermometer what numbers would be seen at (a) freezing point (b) boiling point?
9. To what country would you go to find a banyan tree?
10. In what part of the ship would the helmsman stand?

EXERCISE 52

1. Is a tapir a long, narrow candle or an animal?
2. Would your father be pleased if the suit he had bought turned out to be shoddy?
3. Would you be more likely to swelter on a hot or on a cold day?
4. Does placid mean sour or calm?
5. Is the deep ditch round a castle a ' moat ' or a ' mote '?
6. If your friend told you that he had had a molar extracted, would it be a front or a back tooth?
7. Which is your index finger?
8. Mr. Peters is an octogenarian, Mr. Roland is a septuagenarian. Who is the older? How many years older?
9. If your sister had an olive-green dress, would it be greeny-blue, yellowish-green or bluish-green?
10. What was there unusual about Stentor's voice?

EXERCISE 53

1. After a name there appeared the letters D.B.E. Was the name that of a man or a woman?
2. After whom is the dahlia flower so named?
3. Brian admired the flowers on a furze bush; Keith preferred those on a myrtle shrub. Which boy liked the white flowers?
4. Eric asked his brother to help him sail his y - - - - on the pond, but Alan said that he was going to the canal-bridge to watch a b - - - - go by.

15

5. Who was the wise old man Mentor really?
6. When is Valentine's Day?
7. Did a Fahrenheit thermometer exist in the 17 C?
8. Mr. Taylor was unable to attend an important meeting; instead he sent his de - - - -.
9. A poster advertised
    St. Judes *v* St. John's.
    Write the word *v* stands for.
10. Wolves, foxes, jackals are can - - - animals.

EXERCISE 54

Here are some amusing but helpful puzzles. The first has been started for you.

```
1.  1.              5.            9.
    C     4. D I S C   8. O - - N       N
    H        N         -       -        -
    I        E         -       -        -
2. P O S T   6. L - - E  10. K - - H
             3.          7.            11.
```

Clues
1. A tiny piece
2. A heavy beam
3. to care for
4. flat circular object
5. a monk's hood
6. lemon-like fruit
7. to resound
8. opposite of 'shut'
9. secluded corner
10. relatives
11. song of praise

```
2.  1.              5.            9.
    G     4. L I M P   8. D - - H       R
    O        I         -       -        -
    A        V         -       -        -
2. T R U E   6. K - - W  10. Y - - N
             3.          7.            11.
```

Clues
1. a horned animal
2. genuine
3. sin
4. to walk lamely
5. colour
6. to understand
7. a breeze
8. shallow plate
9. sacred
10. spun thread
11. not far away